Monetary Policy Strategy

Monetary Policy Strategy

Frederic S. Mishkin

The MIT Press
Cambridge, Massachusetts
London, England

MIT Press books may be purchased at special quantity discounts for business or sales promotional use. For information, please e-mail special_sales@mitpress.mit.edu or write to Special Sales Department, The MIT Press, 55 Hayward Street, Cambridge, MA 02142.

This book was set in Times New Roman and Syntax on 3B2 by Asco Typesetters, Hong Kong and was printed and bound in the United States of America.

Library of Congress Cataloging-in-Publication Data

Mishkin, Frederic S.
Monetary policy strategy / by Frederic S. Mishkin.
   p.   cm.
Includes bibliographical references and index.
ISBN 978-0-262-13482-8 (hardcover : alk. paper)
1. Monetary policy. I. Title.
HG230.3M57   2007
339.5′3—dc22   2006033821

10 9 8 7 6 5 4 3 2

To Laura and Matthew

Contents

Preface

Although my father fought in Europe in World War II, the central event in his life was the Great Depression. When I expected (and hoped) that he would regale us with stories about his war experience, he instead told us about life in the 1930s and how devastating the collapse in the economy had been to him and his family. This experience is what set me on the path to becoming an economist. My father's stories made me realize how large an impact the state of the economy could have on people's lives, and I wanted to understand how better policies could lead to improved outcomes for the aggregate economy.

When I started taking graduate courses at MIT in 1972 (I actually started my PhD program while still an undergraduate in my senior year at MIT, and then continued officially in 1973), I was exposed to two wonderful teachers in monetary economics, Stanley Fischer and Franco Modigliani. Both made me see that monetary policy played a key role in the health of the macro economy and I was hooked: I knew that I was going to become a monetary economist. A major intellectual influence on my thinking was Milton Friedman and Anna Schwartz's *A Monetary History of the United States*, which Stan encouraged his students to read telling us that if we were serious about being monetary economists, then we had to read Friedman and Schwartz before going to bed. Being a dutiful student, I took Stan's advice and was enthralled by the book. Friedman and Schwartz made it abundantly clear that bad monetary policies could lead to disaster. In addition, their use of historical episodes to demonstrate the importance of monetary policy to the economy led me to value the use of case studies as a research tool, which features prominently in a lot of the economics discussed in this book.

Given this intellectual background, my research in academia has focused on issues that are central to monetary policymaking. However, after I was the director of research and executive vice president of the Federal Reserve Bank of New York from 1994 to 1997, my research took on a more practical bent and I began to write far more extensively on strategies for the conduct of monetary policy. This book is a collection of my work on this subject, particularly over the past decade.

The book's introduction outlines the intellectual environment and history of economic ideas that influenced my writings, which should help put each chapter in perspective. Each main part of the book—part I, "Fundamental Issues in the Conduct of Monetary Policy"; part II, "Monetary Policy Strategy in Advanced Economies"; part III, "Monetary Policy Strategy in Emerging Market and Transition Economies"; and part IV, "What Have We Learned?"—opens with a short introduction that provides a brief summary of each chapter in that part, describing how these came to be written and how they fit together. The final part of the book contains a concluding chapter that tries to put it all together by summarizing what we have learned about monetary policy during the past twenty-five to thirty years.

I have many people to thank for stimulating my thinking on monetary policy issues over the years. Not only do these include my coauthors on several chapters in this book, Ben Bernanke, Guillermo Calvo, Arturo Estrella, Jiri Jonas, Miguel Savastano, and Klaus Schmidt-Hebbel, but also those who commented on presentations of this material, who are thanked individually in each chapter. I also benefited from my interactions with Peter Fisher and William McDonough when I was at the Federal Reserve Bank of New York, as well as with Michael Woodford and Lars Svensson, with whom I have had numerous, extremely productive conversations over the years about issues in monetary policy strategy. I have learned a lot from all of them. Note that any views expressed in this book are mine and not those of Columbia University, the National Bureau of Economic Research, or the individuals thanked in each chapter.

I also thank my editor at The MIT Press, Elizabeth Murry, who provided much valuable input on how this book should be structured. And finally, I want to thank my wonderful family: my wife, Sally, who makes sure our marriage is never boring, and my two children, Laura and Matthew, who always make me laugh and help make life an adventure.

1 How Did We Get Here?

Frederic S. Mishkin

The past three decades have seen an extraordinary transformation in the conduct of monetary policy. In the 1970s, inflation had risen to very high levels, with most countries, including the United States, experiencing inflation rates in the double digits. Today, almost all nations in the world are in a low inflation environment. Of 223 countries, 193 currently have annual inflation rates less than or equal to 10 percent, while 149 have annual inflation rates less than or equal to 5 percent.[1] Why and how has the strategy of the conduct of monetary policy changed such that it has become so successful in taming inflation?

The answer provided in the following chapters is that monetary authorities and governments in almost all countries of the world have come to accept the following ideas: 1) there is no long-run trade-off between output (employment) and inflation; 2) expectations are critical to monetary policy outcomes; 3) inflation has high costs; 4) monetary policy is subject to the time-inconsistency problem; 5) central bank independence is needed to produce successful monetary policy; and 6) a strong nominal anchor is the key to producing good monetary policy outcomes. But this list, which central bankers now subscribe to, is not where monetary policymakers started. In the 1960s, central bankers had a very different world view, which produced very bad monetary policy outcomes.

1.1 Central Banking in the 1960s

The 1960s began with a relatively benign inflation environment, particularly in the United States where inflation was running at an annual rate of just over 1 percent. (Inflation rates were at higher rates in countries such as Germany, France, Japan, and the United Kingdom but were still below 4 percent in 1960.) At the Federal Reserve and at many other central banks, the focus was on "money market conditions": on variables such as nominal interest rates, bank borrowings from the central bank, and free reserves (excess reserves minus borrowings).[2] In addition, in the wake of the Great Depression of the 1930s, the economics professions became dominated by

Keynesians, the followers of John Maynard Keynes, who viewed the Depression as directly resulting from policy inaction when adverse shocks hit the economy. This led to an era of policy activism in which economists armed with Keynesian macroeconometric models argued that they could fine-tune the economy to produce maximum employment with only slight inflationary consequences. This was the intellectual environment that I was exposed to when I first started my study of economics as an undergraduate in 1969.

Particularly influential at the time was a famous paper published in 1960 by Paul Samuelson and Robert Solow, both MIT professors, which argued that work by A. W. Phillips, which became known as the Phillips curve, suggested that there was a long-run trade-off between unemployment and inflation and that this trade-off should be exploited.[3] Indeed, Samuelson and Solow even mentioned that a nonperfectionist goal of a 3 percent unemployment rate could be attained at what they considered to be a low inflation rate of 4 to 5 percent per year. This thinking, not only by Samuelson and Solow, but also by the then-dominant Keynesian economists, led to increased monetary and fiscal policy activism to get the economy to full employment. However, the subsequent economic record was not a happy one: inflation accelerated, with the inflation rate in the United States and other industrialized countries eventually climbing above 10 percent in the 1970s, leading to what has been dubbed "The Great Inflation," while the unemployment rate deteriorated from the performance in the 1950s.

1.1.1   No Long-Run Trade-Off between Output (Employment) and Inflation

The Monetarists, led by Milton Friedman, first mounted the counterattack to policy activism. Milton Friedman, in a series of famous publications in 1963, established that fluctuations in the growth rate of the money supply were far more capable of explaining economic fluctuations and inflation than nominal interest rates.[4] In Congressional testimony, Karl Brunner and Allan Meltzer criticized the use of "money market conditions" to guide monetary policy and suggested that targeting monetary aggregates would produce better policy outcomes.[5] In his famous 1968 presidential address to the American Economic Association, Milton Friedman along with Edmund Phelps argued that there was no long-run trade-off between unemployment and inflation rate: rather, the economy would gravitate to some natural rate of unemployment in the long run no matter what the rate of inflation was.[6] In other words, the long-run Phillips curve would be vertical, and attempts to lower unemployment below the natural rate would result only in higher inflation. The monetarist counterattack implied that monetary policy should be focused on controlling inflation and the best way to do this would be pursuing steady growth in the money supply.

1.2 Central Banking in the 1970s

At first, the monetarist counterattack was not successful in getting central banks to increase their focus on controlling inflation and money supply growth. In the early 1970s, estimates of the parameters of the Phillips curve did not yet suggest that in the long run the Phillips curve was vertical. Economists and policymakers also were not as fully aware of how important expectations are to monetary policy's effect on the economy, a realization that would have led them to accept the Friedman-Phelps natural rate hypothesis more quickly. Also, estimates of the natural rate of unemployment were far too low, thus suggesting that increases in inflation that were occurring at then-prevalent unemployment rates were the result of special factors and not overly expansionary monetary policy.[7]

1.2.1 The Rational Expectations Revolution

Starting in the early 1970s, in a series of papers Robert Lucas launched the rational expectations revolution, which demonstrated that the public's and the markets' expectations of policy actions have important effects on almost every sector of the economy.[8] The theory of rational expectations made it immediately clear why there could be no long-run trade-off between unemployment and inflation, so that attempting to lower unemployment below the natural rate would lead only to higher inflation and no improvement in performance in output or employment. Indeed, one implication of rational expectations in a world of flexible wages and prices was the *policy ineffectiveness proposition*, which indicated that if monetary policy were anticipated, it would have no real effect on output; only unanticipated monetary policy could have a significant impact. An implication of the policy ineffectiveness proposition was that a constant-money-growth-rate rule along the lines suggested by Milton Friedman would do as well as any other deterministic policy rule with feedback.[9] The only result of all the policy activism advocated by Keynesian economists would be higher and more variable rates of inflation. Although evidence for the policy ineffectiveness proposition is weak,[10] the rational expectation revolution's point that monetary policy's impact on the economy is substantially influenced by expectations about monetary policy has become widely accepted.

1.2.2 Recognition of the High Costs of Inflation and the Benefits of Price Stability

Events on the ground were also leading to a rejection of policy activism. Inflation began a steady rise in the 1960s and then in the aftermath of the 1973 oil price shock, inflation climbed to double-digit levels in many countries. Economists, but also the public and politicians, began to discuss the high costs of inflation.[11] A high inflationary environment leads to overinvestment in the financial sector, which expands to profitably act as a middleman to help individuals and businesses escape some of the costs of inflation.[12] Inflation leads to uncertainty about relative prices and the future price level, making it harder for firms and individuals to make appropriate decisions, thereby decreasing economic efficiency.[13] The interaction of the tax system and inflation also increases distortions that adversely affect economic activity.[14]

The recognition of the high costs of inflation led to the view that low and stable inflation can increase the level of resources productively employed in the economy, and might even help increase the rate of economic growth. While time-series studies of individual countries and cross-national comparisons of growth rates were not in total agreement, the consensus grew that inflation is detrimental to economic growth, particularly when inflation rates are high.[15]

1.2.3 The Role of a Nominal Anchor

The groundbreaking developments in economic theory coincided with the growing recognition among economists, politicians, and the public of the high costs of inflation. It also made clear why a *nominal anchor*—a nominal variable that monetary policymakers use to tie down the price level, such as the inflation rate, an exchange rate, or the money supply—is such a crucial element in achieving price stability. Adhering to a nominal anchor that keeps the nominal variable in a narrow range supports price stability by directly promoting low and stable inflation expectations. With stable inflation expectations, markets do much of the work for monetary policymakers: low and stable inflation expectations result in stabilizing price and wage setting behavior that lowers both the level and volatility of inflation.[16]

1.2.4 The Advent of Monetary Targeting

The three related ideas that expansionary monetary policy cannot produce higher output (employment) in the long run, that inflation is costly, and that there are advantages of a strong nominal anchor, all combined to help generate support for the idea espoused by Monetarists that central banks needed to control the growth rate of monetary aggregates. This idea led to the adoption of monetary targeting by a number of industrialized countries in the mid-1970s (see chapter 8).

Monetary targeting involves three elements: 1) the reliance on information conveyed by a monetary aggregate to conduct monetary policy, 2) the announcement of medium-term targets for monetary aggregates, and 3) some accountability mechanism to preclude large, systematic deviations from the monetary targets. The Federal Reserve started to follow weekly tracking paths for the monetary aggregate measures M1 and M2, while indicating its preferred behavior for M2. Then in response to a congressional resolution in 1975, the Fed began to announce publicly its targets for money growth. In late 1973, the United Kingdom began informal targeting of a broad monetary aggregate, sterling M3, and began formal publication of targets in

1976. The Bank of Canada instituted monetary targeting in 1975 under a program of "monetary gradualism" in which M1 growth was to be controlled with a gradually falling target range. In late 1974, both the Deutsche Bundesbank and the Swiss National Bank began to announce money stock targets: the Bundesbank chose to target central bank money, a narrow aggregate that was the sum of currency in circulation and bank deposits weighted by the 1974 required reserve ratios, and the Swiss National Bank targeted M1. In 1978, the Bank of Japan announced "forecasts" of growth rates of M2 (and after 1979, M2 plus certificate of deposits).

1.3   Central Banking in the late 1970s and the 1980s: The Failure of Monetary Targeting?

Monetary targeting had several potential advantages over previous approaches to the conduct of monetary policy. Announced figures for monetary aggregates are typically reported within a couple of weeks, and so monetary targets can send almost immediate signals to both the public and markets about the stance of monetary policy and the intentions of the policymakers to keep inflation in check. These signals can help fix inflation expectations and produce less inflation. Another advantage of monetary targets is promoting almost immediate accountability for monetary policy in order to keep inflation low.

These advantages of monetary aggregate targeting depend on one key assumption: there must be a strong and reliable relationship between the goal variable (inflation or nominal income) and the targeted aggregate. If there are large swings in velocity, so that the relationship between the monetary aggregate and the goal variable is weak, as is found in chapter 6, then monetary aggregate targeting will not work. The weak relationship implies that hitting the target will not produce the desired outcome on the goal variable and thus the monetary aggregate will no longer provide an adequate signal about the central bank's policy stance. The breakdown of the relationship between monetary aggregates and goal variables such as inflation and nominal income was common, not only in the United States, but also even in Germany, which pursued monetary targeting for a much longer period (chapter 6).[17] A similar instability problem in the money–inflation relationship has been found in emerging market countries, such as those in Latin America (chapter 14).

Why did monetary targeting in the United States, Canada, and the United Kingdom during the late 1970s and the 1980s not prove successful in controlling inflation? There are two interpretations. One is that monetary targeting was not pursued seriously, so it never had a chance to succeed (chapters 8 and 10). The Federal Reserve, Bank of Canada, and particularly the Bank of England engaged in substantial game playing in which they targeted multiple aggregates, allowed base drift (the initial starting point for the monetary target was allowed to shift up and down with realizations of the monetary aggregate), did not announce targets on a regular schedule, used artificial means to bring down the growth of a targeted aggregate, often over-shoot their targets without reversing the overshoot later, and often obscured the reasons why deviations from the monetary targets occurred.

The second reason for monetary targeting's lack of success in the late 1970s was the increasing instability of the relationship between monetary aggregates and goal variables such as inflation or nominal income, which meant that this strategy was doomed to failure. Indeed, monetary targeting was not pursued seriously because doing so would have been a mistake; the relationship between monetary aggregates and inflation and nominal income was breaking down. Once it became clear by the early 1980s that the money–income relationship was no longer strong, the United States, Canada, and the United Kingdom formally abandoned monetary targeting. Or as Gerald Bouey, a former governor, of the Bank of Canada, put it: "We didn't abandon monetary aggregates, they abandoned us."

The problems that an unstable relationship between the money supply and inflation create for monetary targeting is further illustrated by Switzerland's unhappy 1989–1992 experience described in chapter 8, during which the Swiss National Bank failed to maintain price stability after it had successfully reduced inflation.[18] The substantial overshoot of inflation from 1989 to 1992, reaching levels above 5 percent, was due to two factors. The first was that the Swiss franc's strength from 1985 to 1987 caused the Swiss National Bank to allow the monetary base (now its targeted aggregate) to grow at a rate greater than the 2 percent target in 1987, and then caused it to raise the monetary base growth target to 3 percent for 1988. The second reason arose from the introduction of a new interbank payment system, Swiss Interbank Clearing (SIC), and a wide-ranging revision of the commercial banks' liquidity requirements in 1988. The resulting shocks to the exchange rate and the shift in the demand for the monetary base arising from the above institutional changes created a serious problem for its targeted aggregate. As 1988 unfolded, it became clear that the Swiss National Bank had guessed wrong in predicting the effects of these shocks so that monetary policy was too easy even though the monetary base target was undershot. The result was a subsequent rise in inflation to above the 5 percent level. As a result of this experience, the Swiss National Bank moved away from monetary targeting first by not specifying a horizon for its monetary base target announced at the end of 1990 and then in effect moving to a five-year horizon for the target afterward, until it abandoned monetary targeting altogether in 1999.

The German experience with monetary targeting was generally successful, and coupled with the success of the initial Swiss experience, help us understand why monetary policy practice evolved toward inflation targeting. As argued by Jürgen von Hagen, the Bundesbank's adoption of monetary targeting in late 1974 arose from the decision-making and strategic problems that it faced at the time.[19] Under the Bretton Woods regime, the Bundesbank had lost the ability to control monetary policy, and focusing on a monetary aggregate was a way for the Bundesbank to reassert control over the conduct of monetary policy. German inflation was also very high (at least by German standards), having reached 7 percent in 1974, and yet the economy was weakening. Adopting a monetary target was a way of resisting political pressure and signaling to the public that the Bundesbank would keep a check on monetary expansion. The Bundesbank also was concerned that pursuing price stability and aiming at full employment and high output growth would lead to policy activism that in turn would lead to inflationary monetary policy. Monetary targeting had the additional advantage of indicating that the Bundesbank was responsible for controlling inflation in a longer run context, but was not trying to fight temporary bursts of inflation, particularly if these came from nonmonetary sources.

The circumstances influencing the adoption of monetary targeting in Germany led to several prominent design features that were key to its success. The first is that the monetary-targeting regimes were not bound by monetarist orthodoxy and were very far from a Friedman-type monetary targeting rule in which a monetary aggregate was kept on a constant-growth-rate path and is the primary focus of monetary policy.[20] The Bundesbank allowed growth outside its target ranges for periods of two to three years, and overshoots of its targets were subsequently reversed. Monetary targeting in Germany and in Switzerland was instead primarily a method of communicating the strategy of monetary policy that focused on long-run considerations and the control of inflation.

The calculation of monetary target ranges put great stress on making policy transparent (clear, simple, and understandable) and on regular communication with the public. First and foremost, a numerical inflation goal was prominently featured in a very public exercise of setting target ranges. The Bundesbank set targets using a quantity theory equation to back out the monetary-target-growth rate using the numerical inflation goal, estimated potential output growth, and expected velocity trends. The use of estimated potential output growth, and not a desired path of actual output growth, in setting the monetary targets was an important feature of the strategy because it signaled that the Bundesbank would not be focusing on short-run output objectives. Second, monetary targeting, far from being a rigid policy rule, was quite flexible in practice. As we see in chapter 8, the target ranges for money growth were missed about 50 percent of the time in Germany, often because the Bundesbank did not completely ignore other objectives including output and exchange rates.[21] Furthermore, the Bundesbank demonstrated flexibility by allowing its inflation goal to vary over time and to converge with the long-run inflation goal quite gradually.

When the Bundesbank first set its monetary targets at the end of 1974, it announced a medium-term inflation goal of 4 percent, well above what it considered to be an appropriate long-run goal for inflation. It clarified that this medium-term inflation goal differed from the long-run goal by labeling it the "unavoidable rate of price increase." Its gradualist approach to reducing inflation led to a nine-year period before the medium-term inflation goal was considered to be consistent with price stability. When this convergence occurred at the end of 1984, the medium-term inflation goal was renamed the "normative rate of price increases" and set at 2 percent, continuing at this level until it was changed to 1.5 or 2 percent in 1997. The Bundesbank also responded to restrictions in the supply of energy or raw materials, which increased the price level by raising its medium-term inflation goal; specifically, it raised the unavoidable rate of price increase from 3.5 percent to 4 percent in the aftermath of the second oil price shock in 1980.

The monetary-targeting regimes in Germany and Switzerland demonstrated a strong commitment to communicating the strategy to the general public. The money-growth targets were continually used as a framework for explaining the monetary policy strategy: the Bundesbank and the Swiss National Bank expended tremendous effort, both in their publications and in frequent speeches by central bank officials, to communicate to the public what the central bank was trying to achieve. Indeed, given that both central banks frequently missed their money-growth targets by significant amounts, their monetary-targeting frameworks are best viewed as a mechanism for transparently communicating how monetary policy was being directed to achieve inflation goals and as a means for increasing the central bank's accountability.

Many other countries envied the success of Germany's monetary policy regime in producing low inflation, which explains why it was chosen as the anchor country for the Exchange Rate Mechanism. One clear indication of Germany's success occurred in the aftermath of German reunification in 1990. Despite a temporary surge in inflation stemming from the terms of reunification, high wage demands, and the fiscal expansion, the Bundesbank was able to keep these temporary effects from becoming embedded in the inflation process, and by 1995 inflation had fallen below the Bundesbank's normative inflation goal of 2 percent.

The experience of Germany and Switzerland illustrate that much of the success of their monetary policy regime's success stemmed from their active use of the monetary-targeting strategy to clearly communicate a long-run strategy of inflation control. Both central banks in these two countries used monetary targeting to clearly state the objectives of monetary policy and to explain that policy actions remained focused on long-run price stability when targets were missed. The active communication with the public by the Bundesbank and the Swiss National Bank increased the transparency and accountability of these central banks. In contrast, the game playing that was a feature of monetary targeting in the United States, the United Kingdom, and Canada hindered the communication process so that transparency and accountability of the central banks in these countries was not enhanced.

The German and Swiss maintained flexibility in their monetary targeting approach and did not come even close to following a rigid rule. Despite a flexible approach to monetary targeting that included tolerating target misses and gradual disinflation, Germany and Switzerland demonstrated that flexibility is consistent with successful inflation control. The key to success was seriousness about pursuing the long-run goal of price stability and actively engaging public support for this task.

Despite the successes of monetary targeting in Switzerland and particularly Germany, monetary targeting does have some serious drawbacks. The weak relationship between the money supply and nominal income discussed in chapter 6 implies that hitting a particular monetary target will not produce the desired outcome for a goal variable such as inflation. Furthermore, the monetary aggregate will no longer provide an adequate signal about the stance of monetary policy. Thus, except under very unusual circumstances, monetary targeting will not provide a good nominal anchor and help fix inflation expectations. In addition, an unreliable relationship between monetary aggregates and goal variables makes it more difficult for monetary targeting to serve as a communications device that increases the transparency of monetary policy and makes the central bank accountable to the public.

1.4   The Search for a Better Nominal Anchor: The Birth of Inflation Targeting in the 1990s

The rational expectations revolution also led to a big breakthrough in our understanding of monetary policy strategy and the importance of a nominal anchor with the recognition of the time-inconsistency problem.

1.4.1   The Time-Inconsistency Problem

Papers by Finn Kydland and Edward Prescott, Guillermo Calvo, and Robert Barro and David Gordon all dealt with the time-inconsistency problem, in which monetary policy conducted on a discretionary, day-by-day basis leads to poor long-run outcomes.[22] Optimal monetary policy should not try to exploit the short-run trade-off between unemployment and inflation by pursuing overly expansionary policy because decisions about wages and prices reflect expectations about policy made by workers and firms; when they see a central bank pursuing expansionary policy, workers and firms will raise their expectations about inflation, and push wages and prices up. The rise in wages and prices will lead to higher inflation, but will not result in higher output on average. Monetary policymakers, however, are tempted to pursue a discretionary monetary policy that is more expansionary than firms or people expect because such a policy would boost economic output (or lower unemployment) in the short run. In other words, the monetary policymakers will find themselves unable to *consistently* follow an optimal plan over *time*; the optimal plan is *time-inconsistent* and so will soon be abandoned.

Putting in place a strong nominal anchor can also help prevent the time-inconsistency problem in monetary policy by providing an expected constraint on discretionary policy. A strong nominal anchor can help ensure that the central bank will focus on the long run and resist the temptation or the political pressures to pursue short-run expansionary policies that are inconsistent with the long-run price stability goal.

1.4.2 Central Bank Independence

One undesirable feature of the time-inconsistency literature first addressed by Bennett McCallum and elaborated upon in chapter 2, is that the time-inconsistency problem by itself does not imply that a central bank will pursue expansionary monetary policy that leads to inflation.[23] Simply by recognizing the problem that forward-looking expectations in the wage- and price-setting process creates for a strategy of pursuing expansionary monetary policy, monetary policymakers can decide to just *not* do it and avoid the time-inconsistency problem altogether. To avoid the time-inconsistency problem, the central bank will need to make it clear to the public that it does not have an objective of raising output or employment above what is consistent with stable inflation and will not try to surprise people with an unexpected, discretionary, expansionary policy.[24] Instead, it will commit to keeping inflation under control.

Although central bankers are fully aware of the time-inconsistency problem, the problem remains nonetheless because politicians are able to put pressure on central banks to pursue overly expansionary monetary policy.[25] Making central banks independent, however, can help insulate them from political pressures to exploit short-run trade-offs between employment and inflation. Independence insulates the central bank from the myopia that is frequently a feature of the political process arising from politicians' concerns about getting elected in the near future and should thus lead to better policy outcomes. Evidence supports the conjecture that macroeconomic performance is improved when central banks are more independent. When central banks in industrialized countries are ranked from least legally independent to most legally independent, the inflation performance is found to be the best for countries with the most independent central banks.[26]

Both economic theory and the better outcomes for countries that have more independent central banks have led to a remarkable trend toward increasing central bank independence. Before the 1990s, very few central banks were highly independent, most notably the Bundesbank, the Swiss National Bank, and, to a somewhat lesser extent, the Federal Reserve. Now almost all central banks in advanced countries and many in emerging market countries have central banks with a level of independence on par with or exceeding that of the Federal Reserve. In the 1990s, greater independence was granted to central banks in such diverse countries as Japan, New Zealand, South Korea, Sweden, the United Kingdom, and those in the Eurozone.

1.4.3   The Birth of Inflation Targeting

Putting in place a strong nominal anchor can help prevent the time-inconsistency problem in monetary policy by providing an expected constraint on discretionary policy. A strong nominal anchor can help ensure that the central bank will focus on the long run and resist the temptation or the political pressures to pursue short-run expansionary policies that are inconsistent with the long-run price stability goal. However, as we have seen, a monetary target will have trouble serving as a strong nominal anchor when the relationship between money and inflation is unstable. The disappointments with monetary targeting led to a search for a better nominal anchor and resulted in the development of inflation targeting in the 1990s, which is discussed in chapters 9 to 16.

Inflation targeting evolved from monetary targeting by adopting its most successful elements: an institutional commitment to price stability as the primary long-run goal of monetary policy and to achieving the inflation rate goal; increased transparency through communication with the public about the objectives of monetary policy and the plans for policy actions to achieve these objectives; and increased accountability for the central bank to achieve its inflation objectives. Inflation targeting, however, differs from monetary targeting in two key dimensions: 1) rather than announce a monetary aggregates target, this strategy publicly announces a medium-term numerical target for inflation, and 2) it makes use of an information-inclusive strategy, with a reduced role for intermediate targets such as money growth.

New Zealand was the first country to adopt inflation targeting. After bringing inflation down from almost 17 percent in 1985 to the vicinity of 5 percent by 1989, the New Zealand parliament passed a new Reserve Bank of New Zealand Act in 1989 that became effective on February 1, 1990. Besides moving the central bank from being one of the least independent to one of the most independent among the industrialized countries, the act also committed the Reserve Bank to a sole objective of price stability. The act stipulated that the minister of finance and the governor of the Reserve Bank should negotiate and make public a Policy Targets Agreement that sets the criteria by which monetary policy performance would be evaluated. These agreements have specified numerical target ranges for inflation and the dates by which they were to be reached.

The first Policy Targets Agreement, signed by the minister of finance and the governor of the Reserve Bank on March 2, 1990, directed the Reserve Bank to achieve an annual inflation rate of 3 to 5 percent by the end of 1990 with a gradual reduction in subsequent years to a 0 to 2 percent range by 1992 (changed to 1993), which was kept until the end of 1996 when the range was changed to 0 to 3 percent and then to 1 to 3 percent in 2002.

New Zealand's action was followed by Canada in February 1991, Israel in January 1992, the United Kingdom in October 1992, Sweden in January 1993, and Finland in February 1993. (Chile adopted a softer form of inflation targeting in January 1991).[27] Since its inception, more than twenty countries have adopted inflation targeting, and new ones are added to the inflation-targeting club every year.

Inflation targeting has superseded monetary targeting because of several advantages. First, inflation targeting does not rely on a stable money-inflation relationship and so large velocity shocks of the type discussed in chapter 6, which distort this relationship, are largely irrelevant to monetary policy performance.[28] Second, the use of more information, and not primarily one variable, to determine the best settings for policy, has the potential to produce better policy settings. Third, an inflation target is readily understood by the public because changes in prices are of immediate and direct concern, while monetary aggregates are farther removed from peoples' direct experience. Inflation targets are therefore better at increasing the transparency of monetary policy because these make the central bank's objectives clearer. This does not mean that monetary targets could not serve as a useful communication device and increase accountability to control inflation as they did in Germany and Switzerland, but once the relationship between monetary aggregates and inflation breaks down, as it has repeatedly (and especially in Switzerland), monetary targets lose a substantial degree of transparency because the central bank now has to provide complicated discussions of why it is appropriate to deviate from the monetary target. Fourth, inflation targets increase central bank accountability because its performance can now be measured against a clearly defined target. Monetary targets work less well in this regard because the unstable money-inflation relationship means that the central bank will necessarily miss its monetary targets frequently and thus makes it harder to impose accountability on the central bank. The Bundesbank, for example, missed its target ranges more than half the time and it was the most successful practitioner of this policy regime. Inflation targeting has much better odds of successful execution.

A key feature of all inflation-targeting regimes is the enormous stress put upon transparency and communication. Inflation-targeting central banks have frequent communications with the government, some mandated by law and some in response to informal inquiries, and their officials take every opportunity to make public speeches on their monetary policy strategy. Communication of this type also has been prominent among central banks that have not adopted inflation targeting, including monetary targeters such as the Bundesbank and Switzerland, as well as nontargeters such as the Federal Reserve. Yet inflation-targeting central banks have taken public outreach a number of steps further: not only have they engaged in extended public information campaigns, even engaging in the distribution of glossy brochures, but they have engaged in publishing a type of document known by its generic name *Inflation Reports* after the original document published by the Bank of England.

The publication of *Inflation Reports* is particularly noteworthy because these documents depart from the usual, dull-looking, formal central bank reports and incorporate the best elements of college textbook writing (using fancy graphics and boxes) to better communicate with the public. *Inflation Reports* are far more user-friendly than previous central bank documents and clearly explain the goals and limitations of monetary policy, including the rationale for inflation targets: the numerical values of the inflation targets and how these were determined; how the inflation targets are to be achieved, given current economic conditions; and the reasons for any deviations from targets. Almost all *Inflation Reports* also provide inflation forecasts, while the majority provide output forecasts, and some provide a projection of the policy path for interest rates (see table 5.1 in chapter 5). These communication efforts have improved private-sector planning by reducing uncertainty about monetary policy, interest rates, and inflation; these reports have promoted public debate of monetary policy, in part by educating the public about what a central bank can and cannot achieve; and these have helped clarify the responsibilities of the central bank and of politicians in the conduct of monetary policy.

Because an explicit numerical inflation target increases the central bank's accountability in controlling inflation, inflation targeting also helps reduce the likelihood that a central bank will suffer from the time-inconsistency problem in which it reneges on the optimal plan and instead tries to expand output and employment by pursuing overly expansionary monetary policy. But since time-inconsistency is more likely to come from political pressures on the central bank to engage in overly expansionary monetary policy, a key advantage of inflation targeting is that it is better able to focus the political debate on what a central bank can do best in the long-run—control inflation—rather than what it cannot do: raise economic growth and the number of jobs permanently through expansionary monetary policy. (A remarkable example of raising the level of public discussion, as recounted in chapter 10, occurred in Canada in 1996 when a public debate ensued over a speech by the president of the Canadian Economic Association criticizing the Bank of Canada.)[29] Thus, inflation targeting appears to reduce political pressures on the central bank to pursue inflationary monetary policy and thereby reduces the likelihood of time-inconsistent policymaking.

Although inflation targeting has the ability to limit the time-inconsistency problem, it does not do this by adopting a rigid rule, and thus has much in common with the flexibility of earlier monetary-targeting regimes. Inflation targeting has rule-like features in that it involves forward-looking behavior that limits policymakers from systematically engaging in policies with undesirable long-run consequences. But rather than using a rigid rule, it employs what Ben Bernanke (now chairman of the Board of Governors of the Federal Reserve) and I dubbed "constrained discretion" in chapter 9. Inflation targeting allows for some flexibility but constrains policy-makers from pursuing overly expansionary (or contractionary) monetary policy.

Inflation targeting also does not ignore traditional output stabilization, but instead puts it into a longer-run context, placing it outside the shorter-run business cycle concerns that characterized monetary policy throughout the 1960s and 1970s. Inflation-targeting regimes allow for the flexibility to deal with supply shocks and have allowed the target to be reduced gradually to the long-run inflation goal when inflation is initially far from this goal (also a feature of monetary targeters such as Germany). As Lars Svensson had shown, a gradual movement of the inflation target toward the long-run, price-stability goal indicates that output fluctuations are a concern (in the objective function) of monetary policy.[30] In addition, inflation targeters have emphasized that the floor of the range should be as binding a commitment as the ceiling, indicating that they care about output fluctuations as well as inflation. Inflation targeting is therefore better described as "flexible inflation targeting."

The above discussion suggests that although inflation targeting has evolved from earlier monetary policy strategies, it does represent true progress. But how has inflation targeting fared? Has it actually led to better economic performance?

1.4.4   Has Inflation Targeting Made a Difference?

The simple answer to this question is generally yes, with some qualifications.[31] This conclusion is derived from the following four results:[32]

• Inflation levels (and volatility), as well as interest rates, have declined after countries adopted inflation targeting.

• Output volatility has not worsened, and, if anything, improved after adoption of inflation targeting.

• Exchange rate pass-through seems to be attenuated by adoption of inflation targeting.[33]

• The fall in inflation levels and volatility, interest rates, and output volatility was part of a worldwide trend in the 1990s, and inflation targeters have not done better in terms of these variables or in terms of exchange rate pass-through than noninflation-targeting industrialized countries such as the United States or Germany.[34]

The fact that inflation-targeting countries see improvement in inflation and output performance but do not do better than countries like the United States and Germany also suggests that what is really important to successful monetary policy is the establishment of a strong nominal anchor.[35] As is pointed out in chapters 8 and 10,[36] Germany was able to create a strong nominal anchor with its monetary-targeting procedure. In the United States, the strong nominal anchor has been in the person of Alan Greenspan (chapter 2). Although inflation targeting is one way to establish a strong nominal anchor, it is not the only way. It is not at all clear that inflation targeting would have improved performance in the United States during the Greenspan era, although it well might do so after Greenspan is gone (chapter 11). Furthermore, as is emphasized in chapters 13 and 18, by itself, an inflation target is not capable of establishing a strong nominal anchor if the government pursues irresponsible fiscal policy or inadequate prudential supervision of the financial system, which might then be prone to financial blow-ups.[37]

There is, however, empirical evidence on inflation expectations that is more telling about the possible benefits of inflation targeting. Recent research has found the following additional results:

- Evidence is not strong that the adoption of inflation targeting leads to an immediate fall in inflation expectations.[38]
- Inflation persistence, however, is lower for countries that have adopted inflation targeting than for countries that have not.
- Inflation expectations appear to be more anchored for inflation targeters than nontargeters: that is, inflation expectations react less to shocks to actual inflation for targeters than nontargeters, particularly at longer horizons.[39]

These results suggest that once inflation targeting has been in place for a while, it does make a difference because it better anchors medium- and longer-term inflation expectations and thus strengthens the nominal anchor. Since, as argued earlier, establishing a strong nominal anchor is a crucial element in successful monetary policy,[40] the evidence on inflation expectations provides a stronger case that inflation targeting has represented real progress.

The benefits of inflation targeting have led me to advocate inflation targeting for the Federal Reserve and this topic is taken up in chapter 11.

1.5 An Alternative Nominal Anchor: Exchange-Rate Pegging

Pegging the value of the domestic currency to that of a large, low-inflation country is another potential nominal anchor for monetary policy. This monetary policy regime has a long history. Exchange-rate pegging has several advantages. It directly contributes to keeping inflation under control by tying the inflation rate for internationally traded goods to that found in the anchor country. It anchors inflation expectations to the inflation rate in the anchor country as long as the exchange-rate peg is credible. With a strong commitment mechanism, it provides an automatic rule for the conduct of monetary policy that mitigates the time-inconsistency problem: it forces a tightening of monetary policy when there is a tendency for the currency to depreciate, or a loosening of policy when there is a tendency to appreciate.

Given its advantages, it is not surprising that exchange-rate pegging has been used to lower inflation both in advanced economies (chapter 10) and in emerging market countries (chapters 13 and 14). There are, however, several serious problems with this strategy, as pointed out in these chapters. With capital mobility the targeting country can no longer pursue its own independent monetary policy and use it to respond to domestic shocks that are independent of those hitting the anchor country. Furthermore, an exchange-rate peg means that shocks to the anchor country are directly transmitted to the targeting country, because changes in interest rates in the anchor country lead to a corresponding change in interest rates in the targeting country.

A second disadvantage of an exchange-rate peg is that it can weaken the accountability of policymakers, particularly in emerging market countries. Because exchange-rate pegging fixes the exchange rate, it eliminates an important signal that can help limit the time-inconsistency problem by constraining monetary policy from becoming too expansionary. In industrialized countries, particularly in the United States, the bond market provides an important signal about the stance of monetary policy. Overly expansionary monetary policy or strong political pressure to engage in overly expansionary monetary policy produces an inflation scare in which inflation expectations surge, interest rates rise, and long-term bond prices sharply decline. Because both central banks and politicians want to avoid this kind of scenario, overly expansionary policy will be less likely.

In many countries, particularly emerging market countries, the long-term bond market is essentially nonexistent. Under a floating exchange-rate regime, however, if monetary policy is too expansionary, the exchange rate will depreciate. In these countries the daily fluctuations of the exchange rate can, like the bond market in the United States, provide an early warning signal that monetary policy is too expansionary. Just as the fear of a visible inflation scare in the bond market constrains central bankers from pursuing overly expansionary monetary policy and constrains politicians from putting pressure on the central bank to engage in overly expansionary monetary policy, fear of exchange-rate depreciations can make overly expansionary monetary policy less likely.

The need for signals from the foreign exchange market may be even more acute in emerging market countries because the balance sheet and actions of their central banks are not as transparent as they are in industrialized countries. Pegging the exchange rate to another currency can make it even harder to ascertain the central bank's policy actions. The public is less able to keep watch on the central bank and the politicians pressuring it, which makes it easier for monetary policy to become too expansionary.

A third, and probably the most severe, problem is that an exchange-rate peg leaves countries open to speculative attacks on their currencies, and if these attacks are successful, the collapse of the domestic currency is usually much larger, more rapid, and more unanticipated than when a depreciation occurs under a floating exchange-rate regime. A pegged regime is especially dangerous for an emerging market economy because they have so much of their debt denominated in foreign currencies, a phenomenon called *liability dollarization*. Emerging market countries with pegged exchange rates are thus especially vulnerable to twin crises, in which the currency collapse destroys firms' and households' balance sheets, which in turn provokes a financial crisis and a sharp economic contraction. Emerging market countries exiting from pegged exchange-rate regimes are more prone to higher-cost financial crises and large declines in output the longer the exchange-rate peg has been in place.[41]

As chapter 17 points out, the dangers of pegged exchange-rate regimes for emerging market countries are so clear that most of them would be far better off avoiding exchange-rate pegs as their monetary policy strategy, and instead have a flexible exchange rate with inflation targeting. However, in emerging market countries whose political and monetary institutions are particularly weak and who therefore have a history of continual bouts of very high inflation, fixing the exchange rate relative to a sound currency may be the only way to break inflationary psychology and stabilize the economy. In addition, a pegged exchange rate may encourage integration of the domestic economy with its neighbors, which may be an important goal in its own right. These considerations have led some economists to suggest that there are times when a strong commitment to a fixed exchange rate (either through a currency board or through full dollarization in which the country abandons its currency and adopts a foreign currency like the dollar as its money) might be necessary.[42]

However, as argued in chapter 18, the choice of exchange-rate regime, whether a fixed or flexible one, is likely to be of secondary importance to the development of good financial, fiscal, and monetary institutions in producing successful monetary policy in emerging market countries.

1.6   Where Is Monetary Policy Strategy Heading?

Just as inflation targeting evolved from earlier monetary policy strategies, monetary policy strategy will continue to evolve over time. There are four major issues under active debate regarding where monetary policy strategy should be headed in the future.

1.6.1   Inflation versus Price-Level Targeting?

Currently all inflation-targeting countries target an inflation rate rather than the price level. The traditional view, forcefully articulated by Stanley Fischer, argues that a price-level target might produce more output variability than an inflation target because unanticipated shocks to the price level are not treated as bygones and must be offset.[43] Specifically, a price-level target requires that an overshoot of the target must be reversed, and this might require quite contractionary monetary policy, which, with sticky prices, could lead to a sharp downturn in the real economy in the short run. Indeed, if the overshoot is large enough, returning to the target might require a deflation, which could promote financial instability and be quite harmful.

On the other hand, in theoretical models with a high degree of forward-looking behavior, a price-level target produces less output variance than an inflation target.[44] (A price-level target was used successfully in Sweden in the 1930s.)[45] Empirical evidence, however, does not clearly support forward-looking expectations formation, and models with forward-looking behavior have counter-intuitive properties that seem to be inconsistent with inflation dynamics.[46] Thus, the jury is still out on whether the monetary policy regime should move from inflation targeting to price-level targeting. Indeed, in the future central banks might experiment with hybrid policies that combine features of an inflation and a price-level target by announcing a commitment to some error correction in which target misses will be offset to some extent in the future.[47] Evaluating these hybrid policies should be a major focus of future research, but the reasoning here indicates that monetary policy should respond to persistent undershoots or overshoots of the inflation target as is discussed in chapter 19.

1.6.2 How Far Should Central Bank Transparency Go?

Inflation-targeting central banks have also been moving to greater and greater transparency over time by publishing their forecasts. The central banks in New Zealand, Colombia, and, most recently, Norway have been announcing projections of their policy path for future interest rates. Publication of forecasts and policy projections can help the public and the markets understand central bank actions, thus decreasing uncertainty and making it easier for the public and markets to assess whether the central bank is serious about achieving its inflation goal.

Lars Svensson argues that not only should central banks announce their projections of the future policy path, but also announce their objective function (the relative weights they put on output versus inflation fluctuations in their loss function).[48] I, however, argue in chapter 5 that central bank transparency can go too far if it complicates communication with the public. Announcing a policy path may confuse the public if it does not sufficiently convey that the path is conditional on events in the economy. The public may then see a deviation from this path as a central bank failure, and the central bank would then be vulnerable to attacks that it is flip-flopping, which could undermine the support for its independence and focus on price stability. This objection does not mean that providing information about the future policy path in some form has no value. It does mean that there are nuances as to how this could be done. Providing information about the future policy path in more general terms or in terms of fan charts that emphasize the uncertainty about the future policy path might achieve most of the benefits of increased disclosure and still make clear how conditional the policy path is on future events.[49] Central banks pursuing inflation targeting are likely to experiment further with different approaches to providing more information about future policy, and I discuss possible alternatives in chapter 19.

Central banks should not only care about reducing the volatility of inflation, but should also want to lower output (employment) fluctuations. In chapter 4, I argue that monetary policy that targets inflation, but does it in a flexible manner, is the best way to produce better outcomes for both output and inflation fluctuations. Indeed, central bankers do care about stabilizing output and employment, as evidenced by their actions; they are, however, very reluctant to talk about it because they are worried that it will lead to political pressure for them to pursue overly expansionary policy that will lead to inflation. The reluctance to discuss stabilization goals is what I refer to in chapter 5 as the "dirty little secret" of central banking. I argue there that central banks do need to be more transparent about the fact that they want to stabilize output and employment fluctuations, but that they should not publish an output (potential GDP) or unemployment target. As is illustrated by chapter 7, the appropriate level of output or unemployment targets is very hard to measure, and shooting for these targets is likely to lead to poor policy outcomes. How central banks should communicate their concerns about output fluctuations is discussed further in chapter 19.

1.6.3   How Should Monetary Policy Authorities Respond to Asset Prices?

A final issue confronting central banks is how they should respond to movements in asset prices and I discuss this issue in chapters 3 and 19. It is generally agreed that monetary policy should react to asset prices when changes in these prices provide useful information about future inflation and the path of the economy. The tougher issue is whether central banks should react to asset prices over and above their effects on future inflation. Bubbles in asset prices, when they collapse, can lead to financial instability; as a result some researchers have argued that monetary policy should act to limit asset price bubbles to preserve financial stability.[50] To do this successfully, the monetary authorities would need to know when a bubble exists, yet it is unlikely that government officials, even central bankers, know better what are appropriate asset prices than do private markets.[51] Ben Bernanke and Mark Gertler find that an inflation-targeting approach that does not focus on asset prices over and above their effect on the economy but does make use of an information-inclusive strategy in setting policy instruments has the ability to make asset price bubbles less likely, thereby promoting financial stability.[52] With the recent sharp run-up of housing prices in many countries and the possibility of bubbles, central banks' concerns about asset price movements and what to do about them are unlikely to abate.

1.6.4 How Should the Monetary Policy React to Exchange Rates in an Inflation-Targeting Regime?

Even if a central bank is targeting inflation, fluctuations in the exchange rate, which of course is another important asset price, are also a major concern to inflation-targeting central banks, particularly in emerging market countries because, as we have seen, sharp depreciations can trigger a financial crisis.[53] Inflation-targeting central banks therefore cannot afford to pursue a policy of benign neglect to exchange rates, as emphasized in chapter 13.[54] They may have to smooth "excessive" exchange rate fluctuations, but how they should do this is still an open question. Indeed, there is a danger that focusing on exchange rate movements might transform the exchange rate into a nominal anchor that interferes with achieving the inflation rate target. (This indeed happened in Hungary, as pointed out in chapter 15.)[55] In addition, when inflation targeters have focused on exchange rate movements, they have often made serious errors.[56] Dealing with exchange rate fluctuations is one of the most serious challenges for inflation-targeting regimes in emerging market countries.

1.7 Conclusion

The practice of central banking has made tremendous strides in recent years. We are currently in a highly desirable environment that few would have predicted fifteen years ago: not only is inflation low, but its variability and the volatility of output fluctuations are also low. This book argues that new thinking about monetary policy strategy is one of the key reasons for this success. If we learn from experience, perhaps we can replicate and refine what does work, and not repeat past mistakes.

Notes

1. See Central Intelligence Agency (2006).
2. See Mayer (1998) and Romer and Romer (2002) for a description of economic thinking and monetary policy practice in the 1960s.
3. Samuelson and Solow (1960) and Phillips (1958).
4. Friedman and Schwartz (1963a,b) and Friedman and Meiselman (1963).
5. Brunner and Meltzer (1964a,b,c).
6. Phelps (1967) and Friedman (1968).
7. Mayer (1998) and Romer and Romer (2002).

8. Lucas (1972, 1973, and 1976). The Lucas (1976) paper was already very influential in 1973, when it was first presented in 1973 at the first Carnegie-Rochester Conference. Note that although Muth (1960, 1961) introduced the idea of rational expectations more than ten years earlier, his work went largely unnoticed until resurrected by Lucas.

9. Sargent and Wallace (1975).

10. See Mishkin (1982a,b, 1983).

11. For example, see the surveys in Fischer (1993) and Anderson and Gruen (1995).

12. English (1996).

13. Briault (1995).

14. Fischer (1994) and Feldstein (1997).

15. For example, see the survey in Anderson and Gruen (1995).

16. The importance of a strong nominal anchor to successful monetary policy is also a key feature of recent theory on optimal monetary policy, referred to as the new neoclassical synthesis (Woodford, 2003, and Goodfriend and King, 1997).

17. For evidence in the United States, see Stock and Watson (1989), Friedman and Kuttner (1993), and chapter 6.

18. Also see Rich (1997).

19. von Hagen (1999).

20. Issing (1996).

21. Also see von Hagen (1995), Neumann and von Hagen (1993), Clarinda and Gertler (1997), Mishkin and Posen (1997), and Bernanke and Mihov (1997).

22. Kydland and Prescott (1977), Calvo (1978), and Barro and Gordon (1983).

23. McCallum (1995).

24. When a central bank does not pursue an objective of raising output or employment above what is consistent with stable inflation, there will be no *inflation bias* (average inflation above the optimal long-run level). In a model with a forward-looking, New Keynesian, Phillips curve, however, there will still be a problem of *stabilization bias* (too much focus on reducing output fluctuations relative to inflation fluctuations) and a lack of *history dependence* (response to initial conditions that would produce better outcomes). See Woodford (2003).

25. For an example of how the time-inconsistency problem can be modeled as resulting from political pressure, see Mishkin and Westelius (2005).

26. For example, Alesina and Summers (1993), Cukierman (1992), and Fischer (1994), and the recent surveys in Forder (2000), and Cukierman (2006).

27. The dating of adoption of inflation targeting is not always clear-cut. The dates used here are from chapter 16.

28. An unstable relationship between money and inflation could make inflation targeting more difficult because there is less information in the monetary aggregates to help forecast inflation. However, successful inflation targeting is not dependent on having a stable money-inflation relationship as long as other information enables the monetary authorities to forecast future inflation and the impact of the current monetary policy stance on the economy.

29. Also see Mishkin and Posen (1997) or Bernanke et al. (1999).

30. Svensson (1997).

31. This is the conclusion in a recent paper presented to the Executive Board of the IMF. Roger and Stone (2005).

32. There is also some mildly favorable evidence on the impact of inflation targeting on sacrifice ratios. Bernanke et al. (1999) did not find that sacrifice ratios in industrialized countries fell with adoption of inflation targeting, while Corbo, Landerretche, and Schmidt-Hebbel (2002) with a larger sample of inflation targeters have concluded that inflation targeting did lead to an improvement in sacrifice ratios. However,

defining sacrifice ratios is extremely tricky, so I would put less weight on this evidence. Sabbán, Rozada, and Powell (2003) also find that inflation targeting leads to nominal exchange rate movements that are more responsive to real shocks rather than nominal shocks. This might indicate that inflation targeting can help the nominal exchange rate to act as a shock absorber for the real economy.

33. Lower exchange rate pass-through might be seen as a drawback because it weakens this channel of the monetary policy transmission mechanism. As long as other channels of monetary policy transmission are still strong, however, the monetary authorities still have the ability to keep inflation under control.

34. For evidence supporting the first three results, see Bernanke et al. (1999), Corbo, Landerretche, and Schmidt-Hebbel (2002), Neumann and von Hagen (2002), Hu (2003), Truman (2003), and Ball and Sheridan (2005).

35. Ball and Sheridan (2005) is one of the few empirical papers that is critical of inflation targeting: it argues that the apparent success of inflation-targeting countries is just a reflection of regression toward the mean; that is, countries that start with higher inflation are more likely to find that inflation will fall faster than countries that start with an initially low inflation rate. Since countries that adopted inflation targeting generally had higher initial inflation rates, their larger decline in inflation just reflects a general tendency of all countries, both targeters and nontargeters, to achieve better inflation and output performance in the 1990s when inflation targeting was adopted. This paper has been criticized on several grounds and its conclusion that inflation targeting had nothing to do with improved economic performance is unwarranted; see Hyvonen (2004), Gertler (2005), and Mishkin and Schmidt-Hebbel (2005). However, Ball and Sheridan's paper does raise a serious question because inflation targeting is an endogenous choice and finding that better performance is associated with inflation targeting may not imply that inflation targeting causes this better performance. Mishkin and Schmidt-Hebbel (2005) does attempt to explicitly deal with potential endogeneity of adoption of inflation targeting through use of instrumental variables and continues to find favorable results on inflation targeting performance.

36. Also see Mishkin and Posen (1997), Bernanke et al. (1999), and Neumann and von Hagen (2002).

37. Also see Sims (2005).

38. For example, Bernanke et al. (1999) and Levin, Natalucci, and Piger (2004) do not find that inflation targeting leads to an immediate fall in expected inflation, but Johnson (2002, 2003) does find some evidence that expected inflation falls after announcement of inflation targets.

39. Levin, Natalucci, and Piger (2004) and Castelnuovo, Nicoletti-Altimari, and Palenzuela (2003).

40. The importance of a strong nominal anchor to successful monetary policy is also a key feature of recent theory on optimal monetary policy, referred to as the new neoclassical synthesis (Woodford, 2003, and Goodfriend and King, 1997).

41. Eichengreen and Masson (1998), Eichengreen (1999), and Aizenman and Glick (2005).

42. See chapter 13, Calvo and Reinhart (2000), and McKinnon and Schnabl (2004).

43. Fischer (1994).

44. For example, Clarida, Gali, and Gertler (1999), Dittmar, Gavin, and Kydland (1999), Dittmar and Gavin (2000), Eggertson and Woodford (2003), Svensson (1999), Svensson and Woodford (2003), Vestin (2000), Woodford (1999, 2003).

45. Berg and Jonung (1999).

46. Fuhrer (1997) and Estrella and Fuhrer (1998).

47. Research at the Bank of Canada and the Bank of England (Black, Macklem, and Rose, 1998; Battini and Yates, 2003; and King, 1999) suggests that an inflation target with a small amount of error correction can substantially reduce the uncertainty about the price level in the long run, but still generate very few episodes of deflation.

48. Svensson (2002).

49. However, announcing a specific policy path as has recently occurred in the United States when it announced that it would remove accommodation at a measured pace, and then having seventeen straight FOMC meetings starting in June of 2004 in which it raised the policy rate by twenty-five basis points each time, did not sufficiently convey the degree of uncertainty about the future path.

50. For example, Cecchetti, Genberg, Lipsky, and Wadhwani (2000), and Borio and Lowe (2002).

51. Bernanke and Gertler (2001) point out that Cecchetti et al. (2000) only find that asset prices should be included in the central bank's policy rule because they assume that the central bank knows with certainty that the asset price rise is a bubble and knows exactly when the bubble will burst.

52. Bernanke and Gertler (1999, 2001).

53. Mishkin (1996, 1999).

54. Also see Mishkin (2000).

55. It also happened in Israel (Bernanke et al. 1999).

56. For example, New Zealand and Chile in 1997 and 1998 (Mishkin, 2001).

References

Aizenman, Joshua, and Reuven Glick. 2005. "Pegged Exchange Rate Regimes—A Trap?" National Bureau of Economic Research Working Paper 11652, September 2005.

Alesina, Alberto, and Lawrence H. Summers. 1993. "Central Bank Independence and Macroeconomic Performance: Some Comparative Evidence." *Journal of Money, Credit, and Banking* 25, no. 2 (May): 151–162.

Andersen, Palle, and David Gruen. 1995. "Macroeconomic Policies and Growth." In Palle Andersen, Jacqueline Dwyer, and David Gruen, eds., *Productivity and Growth.* Sydney: Reserve Bank of Australia. 279–319.

Ball, Laurence, and Naihm Sheridan. 2005. "Does Inflation Targeting Matter?" In Ben S. Bernanke and Michael Woodford, eds., *The Inflation Targeting Debate.* University of Chicago Press for the National Bureau of Economic Research: Chicago, 2005. 249–276.

Barro, Robert J., and David Gordon. 1983. "A Positive Theory of Monetary Policy in a Natural Rate Model." *Journal of Political Economy* 91, no. 4 (August): 589–610.

Batini, Nicoletta, and Anthony Yates. 2003. "Hybrid Inflation and Price-Level Targeting," *Journal of Money, Credit and Banking* 35 (3) (June): 283–300.

Berg, Claes, and Lars Jonung. 1999. "Pioneering Price Level Targeting: The Swedish Experience 1931–37." *Journal of Monetary Economics* 43 (3) (June): 525–551.

Bernanke, Ben S., and Mark Gertler. 1999. "Monetary Policy and Asset Volatility." Federal Reserve Bank of Kansas City, *Economic Review* Fourth Quarter 84 (4): 17–52.

Bernanke, Ben S., and Mark Gertler. 2001. "Should Central Banks Respond to Movements in Asset Prices?" *American Economic Review* 91 (2) (May): 253–257.

Bernanke, Ben S., Thomas Laubach, Frederic S. Mishkin, and Adam S. Posen. 1999. *Inflation Targeting: Lessons from the International Experience.* Princeton, N.J.: Princeton University Press.

Bernanke, Ben S., and Ilian Mihov. 1997. "What Does the Bundesbank Target?" *European Economic Review* 41, no. 6 (June): 1025–1053.

Black, Richard, Tiff Macklem, and David Rose. 1998. "On Policy Rules for Price Stability." *Price Stability, Inflation Targets and Monetary Policy.* Proceedings of a conference held by Bank of Canada, May 1997. Ottawa, Canada: 411–461.

Borio, Claudio E. V., and Philip W. Lowe. 2002. "Asset Prices, Financial and Monetary Stability: Exploring the Nexus." BIS Working Paper No. 114 (July).

Briault, Clive. 1995. "The Costs of Inflation." *Bank of England Quarterly Bulletin* 35, February: 33–45.

Brunner, Karl, and Alan Meltzer. 1964a. "Some General Features of the Federal Reserve's Approach to Policy." U.S. Congress, Committee on Banking and Currency, Subcommittee on Domestic Finance, 88th Congress, 2nd session.

Brunner, Karl, and Alan Meltzer. 1964b. "An Alternative Approach to the Monetary Mechanism." U.S. Congress, Committee on Banking and Currency, Subcommittee on Domestic Finance, 88th Congress, 2nd session.

Brunner, Karl, and Alan Meltzer. 1964c. "The Federal Reserve's Attachment to Free Reserves." U.S. Congress, Committee on Banking and Currency, Subcommittee on Domestic Finance, 88th Congress, 2nd session.

Calvo, Guillermo. 1978. "On the Time Consistency of Optimal Policy in the Monetary Economy." *Econometrica* 46, no. 6 (November): 1411–1428.

Calvo, Guillermo, and Frederic S. Mishkin. 2003. "The Mirage of Exchange Rate Regimes for Emerging Market Countries." *Journal of Economic Perspectives*, vol. 17, no. 4 (Fall 2003): 99–118.

Calvo, Guillermo, and Carmen Reinhart. 2000. "Fixing for Your Life," National Bureau of Economic Research Working Paper 8006 (2000).

Castelnuovo, Efrem, Sergio Nicoletti-Altimari, and Diego Rodriguez Palenzuela. 2003. "Definition of Price Stability, Range and Point Targets: The Anchoring of Long-Term Inflation Expectations." In Otmar Issing, ed., *Background Studies for the ECB's Evaluation of Its Monetary Policy Strategy*. European Central Bank: Frankfurt-am-Main, Germany, 2003. 43–90.

Cecchetti, Stephen, Hans Genberg, John Lipsky, and Sushil Wadhwani. 2000. *Asset Prices and Central Bank Policy*. Geneva: International Center for Monetary and Banking Studies.

Central Intelligence Agency. 2006. *The World Factbook*, https://www.cia.gov/cia/publications/factook/index.html

Clarida, Richard, Jordi Gali, and Mark Gertler. 1999. "The Science of Monetary Policy—A New Keynesian Perspective." *Journal of Economic Literature* 37 (December): 1661–1707.

Clarida, Richard, and Mark Gertler. 1997. "How the Bundesbank Conducts Monetary Policy." In Christina D. Romer and David H. Romer, eds., *Reducing Inflation: Motivation and Strategy*. Chicago: University of Chicago Press. 363–406.

Corbo, Vittorio, Oscar Landerretche, and Klaus Schmidt-Hebbel. 2002. "Does Inflation Targeting Make a Difference?" In Norman Loayza and Raimundo Soto, eds., *Inflation Targeting: Design, Performance, Challenges*. Central Bank of Chile: Santiago. 221–269.

Cukierman, Alex. 1992. *Central Bank Strategy, Credibility, and Independence: Theory and Evidence*. Cambridge: MIT Press.

Cukierman, Alex. 2006. "Central Bank Independence and Monetary Policymaking Institutions: Past, Present, and Future." Central Bank of Chile Working Papers No. 360 (April).

Dittmar, Robert, and William Gavin. 2000. "What Do New-Keynesian Phillips Curves Imply for Price-Level Targeting?" Federal Reserve Bank of St. Louis *Review* 82 (2) (March–April): 21–30.

Ditmar, Robert, William T. Gavin, and Finn E. Kydland. 1999. "The Inflation-Output Variability Trade-off and Price Level Targets," Federal Reserve Bank of St. Louis *Review*: 23–31.

Eggertsson, G. B., and M. Woodford. 2003. "The Zero Bound on Interest Rates and Optimal Monetary Policy." *Brookings Papers on Economic Activity* 1: 139–211.

Eichengreen, Barry. 1999. "Kicking the Habit: Moving from Pegged Exchange Rates to Greater Exchange Rate Flexibility." *Economic Journal* (March): C1–C14.

Eichengreen, Barry, and Paul Masson. 1998. "Exit Strategies: Policy Options for Countries Seeking Greater Exchange Rate Flexibility." Occasional Paper No. 98/168. International Monetary Fund: Washington DC.

English, William B. 1996. "Inflation and Financial Sector Size." Board of Governors of the Federal Reserve System Finance and Economics Discussion Series, no. 96-16, April.

Estrella, Arturo, and Jeffrey Fuhrer. 1998. "Dynamic Inconsistencies: Counterfactual Implications of a Class of Rational Expectations Models." Federal Reserve Bank of Boston Working Paper: 98/05, July 1998.

Estrella, A., and F. S. Mishkin. 1997. "Is There a Role for Monetary Aggregates in the Conduct of Monetary Policy?" *Journal of Monetary Economics* 40, no. 2 (October): 279–304.

Feldstein, Martin. 1997. "Price Stability." In *Achieving Price Stability*. Kansas City: Federal Reserve Bank of Kansas City.

Fischer, Stanley. 1993. "The Role of Macroeconomic Factors in Growth." *Journal of Monetary Economics* 32: 485–512.

Fischer, Stanley. 1994. "Modern Central Banking." In Forest Capie, Charles Goodhart, Stanley Fischer, and Norbert Schnadt, eds., *The Future of Central Banking*. Cambridge, U.K.: Cambridge University Press. 262–308.

Forder, James. 2000. "Central Bank Independence and Credibility: Is There a Shred of Evidence?: Review." *International Finance*, vol. 3, no. 1, April: 167–185.

Friedman, Benjamin M., and Kenneth N. Kuttner. 1993. "Another Look at the Evidence on Money-Income Causality." *Journal of Econometrics* 57: 189–203.

Friedman, Milton. 1968. "The Role of Monetary Policy." *American Economic Review* 58 (March): 1–17.

Friedman, Milton, and David Meiselman. 1963. "The Relative Stability of Monetary Velocity and the Investment Multiplier." In Commission on Money and Credit, ed., *Stabilization Policies*. Upper Saddle River, N.J.: Prentice Hall: 165–268.

Friedman, Milton, and Anna J. Schwartz. 1963a. *A Monetary History of the United States, 1867–1960*. Princeton N.J.: Princeton University Press.

Friedman, Milton, and Anna J. Schwartz. 1963b. "Money and Business Cycles." *Review of Economics and Statistics*. 45, Supplement: 32–64.

Fuhrer, Jeffrey C. 1997. "The (Un)Importance of Forward-Looking Behavior in Price Specifications." *Journal of Money, Credit, and Banking*, vol. 29, no. 3, August 1997: 338–350.

Gertler, Mark. 2005. "Comment on Ball, Laurence and Niamh Sheridan, 'Does Inflation Targeting Matter?'" In Ben S. Bernanke and Michael Woodford, eds., *The Inflation Targeting Debate*. University of Chicago Press for the National Bureau of Economic Research: Chicago, 2005. 276–281.

Goodfriend, Marvin, and Robert G. King. 1997. "The New Neoclassical Synthesis and the Role of Monetary Policy." NBER *Macroeconomics Annual*: 231–283.

Hu, Yifan. 2003. "Empirical Investigations of Inflation Targeting." Institute for International Economics, Working Paper No. 03-6 (July).

Hyvonen, M. 2004. "Inflation Convergence Across Countries." Reserve Bank of Australia Discussion Paper 2004-04.

Issing, Otmar. 1996. "Is Monetary Targeting in Germany Still Adequate?" In Horst Siebert, ed., *Monetary Policy in an Integrated World Economy: Symposium 1995*. Tübingen: Mohr.

Johnson, David R. 2002. "The Effect of Inflation Targeting on the Behavior of Expected Inflation: Evidence from an 11 Country Panel." *Journal of Monetary Economics*, vol. 49, no. 8 (November): 1493–1519.

Johnson, David R. 2003. "The Effect of Inflation Targets on the Level of Expected Inflation in Five Countries." *Review of Economics and Statistics*, vol. 55, no. 4 (November): 1076–1081.

Jonas, Jiri, and Frederic S. Mishkin. "Inflation Targeting in Transition Countries: Experience and Prospects." In Michael Woodford, ed., *Inflation Targeting*. University of Chicago Press: Chicago, 2005. 353–413.

King, Mervyn. 1999. "Challenges for Monetary Policy: New and Old." In *New Challenges for Monetary Policy*. Kansas City, Mo.: Federal Reserve Bank of Kansas City: 11–57.

Kydland, Finn, and Edward Prescott. 1977. "Rules Rather than Discretion: The Inconsistency of Optimal Plans." *Journal of Political Economy* 85, no. 3 (June): 473–492.

Levin, Andrew, Fabio M. Natalucci, and Jeremy M. Piger. 2004. "The Macroeconomic Effects of Inflation Targeting." Federal Reserve Bank of St. Louis *Review*, forthcoming.

Lucas, Robert E., Jr. 1972. "Expectations and the Neutrality of Money." *Journal of Economic Theory* 4: 103–124.

Lucas, Robert E., Jr. 1973. "Some International Evidence on Output-Inflation Tradeoffs." *American Economic Review* 63: 326–334.

Lucas, Robert E., Jr. 1976. "Econometric Policy Evaluation: A Critique." In *The Phillips Curve and Labor Markets*. K. Brunner and A. Meltzer, eds. Carnegie-Rochester Conference Series on Public Policy 1: 19–46.

Mayer, Thomas. 1998. *Monetary Policy and the Great Inflation in the United States: The Federal Reserve and the Failure of Macroeconomic Policy, 1965–1979*. Cheltenham, U.K.: Edward Elgar.

McCallum, Bennett T. 1995. "Two Fallacies Concerning Central-Bank Independence." *American Economic Review* 85, no. 2 (May): 207–211.

McKinnon, Ronald, and Gunther Schnabl. 2004. "The East Asian Dollar Standard, Fear of Floating and Original Sin." *Review of Development Economics*, vol. 8, no. 3 (2004): 331–360.

Mishkin, Frederic S. 1982a. "Does Anticipated Monetary Policy Matter? An Econometric Investigation." *Journal of Political Economy* 90 (February 1982): 21–51.

Mishkin, Frederic S. 1982b. "Does Anticipated Aggregate Demand Policy Matter? Further Econometric Results." *American Economic Review* 72 (September 1982): 788–802.

Mishkin, Frederic S. 1983. *A Rational Expectations Approach to Macroeconometrics: Testing Policy Ineffectiveness and Efficient Markets Models*. University of Chicago Press for The National Bureau of Economic Research: Chicago.

Mishkin, Frederic S. 1996. "Understanding Financial Crises: A Developing Country Perspective." In Michael Bruno and Boris Pleskovic, eds., *Annual World Bank Conference on Development Economics*, World Bank, Washington DC: 29–62.

Mishkin, Frederic S. 1999. "Lessons from the Asian Crisis." *Journal of International Money and Finance* 18, 4: 709–723.

Mishkin, Frederic S. 2000. "Inflation Targeting in Emerging Market Countries." *American Economic Review*, vol. 90, no. 2: 105–109.

Mishkin, Frederic S. 2001. "Issues in Inflation Targeting." In *Price Stability and the Long-Run Target for Monetary Policy*. Bank of Canada: Ottawa, Canada: 203–222.

Mishkin, Frederic S., and Adam Posen. 1997. "Inflation Targeting: Lessons from Four Countries." Federal Reserve Bank of New York, *Economic Policy Review* 3 (August): 9–110.

Mishkin, Frederic S., and Klaus Schmidt-Hebbel. 2005. "Does Inflation Targeting Make a Difference?" In Frederic S. Mishkin and Klaus Schmidt-Hebbel, eds., *Monetary Policy Under Inflation Targeting*. Santiago, Chile: Central Bank of Chile, forthcoming.

Mishkin, Frederic S., and Niklas Westelius. 2005. "Inflation Band Targeting and Optimal Inflation Contracts." Columbia University mimeo (November).

Muth, John F. 1960. "Optimal Properties of Exponentially Weighted Forecasts." *Journal of the American Statistical Association* 55: 299–306.

Muth, John F. 1961. "Rational Expectations and the Theory of Price Movements." *Econometrica* 29: 315–335.

Neumann, Manfred J. M., and Jürgen von Hagen. 1993. "Germany." In M. Fratianni and D. Salvatore, eds., *Handbook of Monetary Policy in Industrialized Countries*. Westport, Conn.: Greenwood.

Neumann, Manfred J. M., and Jürgen von Hagen. 2002. "Does Inflation Targeting Matter?" Federal Reserve Bank of St. Louis *Review* (July/August): 127–148.

Phelps, Edmund. 1967. "Phillips Curves, Expectations and Optimal Unemployment Over Time." *Economica* 34 (August): 254–281.

Phillips, A. W. 1958. "The Relationship Between Unemployment and the Rate of Change of Money Wages in the United Kingdom, 1861–1957." *Economica* vol. 25 (1958): 283–299.

Rich, Georg. 1997. "Monetary Targets as a Policy Rule: Lessons from the Swiss Experience." *Journal of Monetary Economics* 39, no. 1 (June): 113–141.

Roger, Scott, and Mark Stone. 2005. "On Target? Inflation Performance in Inflation Targeting Countries," IMF Working Paper No. 5 (February): 163.

Romer, Christina D., and David H. Romer. 2002. "The Evolution of Economic Understanding and Postwar Stabilization Policy." In *Rethinking Stabilization Policy*. Kansas City, Mo.: Federal Reserve Bank of Kansas City: 11–78.

Samuelson, Paul, and Robert M. Solow. 1960. "Analytic Aspects of Anti-Inflation Policy." *American Economic Review* 50 (May): 368–379.

Sargent, Thomas J., and Neil Wallace. 1975. "Rational Expectations, the Optimal Monetary Instrument and the Optimal Money Supply Rule." *Journal of Political Economy* 83: 241–254.

Sabbán, Verónica Cohen, Martín Gonzalez Rozada, and Andrew Powell. 2003. "A New Test for the Success of Inflation Targeting." Universidad Torcuato Di Tella mimeo., January 2003.

Sims, Christopher. 2005. "Limits to Inflation Targeting." In Ben S. Bernanke and Michael Woodford, eds., *The Inflation Targeting Debate*. University of Chicago Press for the National Bureau of Economic Research: Chicago, 2005. 283–308.

Stock, James H., and Mark W. Watson. 1989. "Interpreting the Evidence on Money-Income Causality." *Journal of Econometrics* 40: 161–182.

Svensson, Lars E. O. 1997. "Inflation Forecast Targeting: Implementing and Monitoring Inflation Targets." *European Economic Review* 41: 1111–1146.

Svensson, Lars E. O. 1999. "Price-Level Targeting Versus Inflation Targeting: A Free Lunch." *Journal of Money, Credit and Banking* 31: 277–295.

Svensson, Lars E. O. 2002. "Monetary Policy and Real Stabilization." In Federal Reserve Bank of Kansas City, *Rethinking Stabilization Policy*: 261–312.

Svensson, Lars E. O., and Michael Woodford. 2003. "Optimal Policy with Partial Information in a Forward-Looking Model: Certainty-Equivalence Redux." NBER Working Paper 9430.

Truman, Edward M. 2003. *Inflation Targeting in the World Economy*. Institute for International Economics: Washington DC.

Vestin, David. 2000. "Price Level Targeting Versus Inflation Targeting in a Forward Looking Model." Mimeo., IIES, Stockholm University, May.

von Hagen, Jürgen. 1995. "Inflation and Monetary Targeting in Germany." In Leonardo Leiderman and Lars E. O. Svensson, eds., *Inflation Targets*. London: Centre for Economic Policy Research. 107–121.

von Hagen, Jürgen. 1999. "Money Growth Targeting by the Bundesbank." *Journal of Monetary Economics* 43: 681–701.

Woodford, Michael. 1999. "Optimal Monetary Policy Inertia." NBER Working Paper No. 7261.

Woodford, Michael. 2003. *Interest and Prices: Foundations of a Theory of Monetary Policy*. Princeton University Press: Princeton.

Fundamental Issues in the Conduct of Monetary Policy

Introduction to Part I

I open the book with a series of chapters that examine some of the most basic questions in the conduct of monetary policy: what should be the institutional setup for central banks and how should they operate; how far should central bank transparency go; how does monetary policy affect the economy; and what should the role be of asset prices, output stabilization, monetary aggregates, and NAIRU (Non-Accelerating Inflation Rate of Unemployment) in the conduct of monetary policy?

The first chapter in part I, "What Should Central Banks Do?," was written for the Homer Jones Lecture given at the Federal Reserve Bank of St. Louis in 2000. I outline what economic theory and experience tells us about how central banks, as institutions, should best be set up to conduct monetary policy effectively, and then I apply the resulting lessons to see if there is room for institutional improvement in the way the Federal Reserve operates. The lecture begins by discussing seven guiding principles for central banks: 1) price stability provides substantial benefits, 2) fiscal policy should be aligned with monetary policy, 3) time-inconsistency is a serious problem to avoid, 4) monetary policy should be forward-looking, 5) accountability is a basic principle of democracy, 6) monetary policy should be concerned with output as well as price fluctuations, and 7) the most serious economic downturns are associated with financial instability. These seven principles are then used to derive seven criteria for how central banks should operate: 1) price stability should be the overriding, long-run goal of monetary policy, 2) an explicit nominal anchor should be adopted, 3) a central bank should be goal-dependent, 4) a central bank should be instrument-independent, 5) a central bank should be accountable, 6) a central bank should stress transparency and communication, and 7) a central bank should also have the goal of financial stability. This framework is then used to assess how the institutional features of the Federal Reserve measure up. As a professor, I can't resist giving grades and I evaluate the Fed by giving it a grade on each of the seven criteria. The point I want to emphasize is that despite the Fed's extraordinarily successful performance in recent years, we should not be complacent. Changes in the way the

Federal Reserve is set up to conduct its business are needed to help ensure that the Fed continues to be successful in the future.

When I started studying economics in 1969 there was a raging debate on how important monetary policy was to the economy. Prior to the mid-1960s, the Keynesian thinking that dominated the economics profession suggested that monetary policy does not matter at all to movements in aggregate output and hence to the business cycle. The view that the money supply was unimportant was primarily based on the view that monetary policy was easy during the Great Depression in the United States because interest rates on Treasury securities were at such low levels. Since the only way that monetary policy affected the economy in the early Keynesian (ISLM) model was through interest rates, and the model did not distinguish between real and nominal interest rates, the conclusion was that monetary policy could not explain the greatest contraction in American history and so could not be important to economic fluctuations. In addition, early Keynesian evidence did not find a strong link between interest rates and investment, and since this mechanism was viewed as the primary way monetary policy impacted the economy, the conclusion was that money didn't matter. The Monetarists, led by Milton Friedman, led a counterattack against the early Keynesian view that money didn't matter with a series of remarkable works all published in 1963: Friedman and Schwartz (1963a), *A Monetary History of the United States, 1867–1960*; Friedman and Schwartz (1963b), "Money and Business Cycles"; and Friedman and Meiselman (1963), "The Relative Stability of Monetary Velocity and the Investment Multiplier." This revisionist monetarist research, which challenged the early Keynesian view that money was easy during the Great Depression and that money doesn't matter, led to an explosion of research on the monetary transmission mechanism led by economists such as Franco Modigliani.

When I began graduate work in economics at MIT in 1972, I was greatly influenced by Franco and became intensely interested in the transmission mechanism of monetary policy because I was convinced that monetary policy was indeed highly important, but that there had to be important ways that monetary policy affected the economy that did not operate through the traditional interest rate channels. My interest in the monetary transmission mechanisms led to my PhD thesis, which was completed in 1976, and to a series of publications early in my career (Mishkin, 1976a,b,c, 1977a,b,c, 1978a,b; and Kearl and Mishkin, 1977), which posited that an important element of the monetary transmission mechanism operated through asset price effects on household balance sheets. My early interest in the role of asset prices in the monetary transmission mechanism naturally led to thinking about what role asset prices should play in monetary policy and led to the survey written for a conference at the Austrian National Bank in 2001 that constitutes chapter 3. This chapter outlines the literature on the transmission mechanisms of monetary policy beyond the standard interest rate channel by focusing on how monetary policy affects firms' and households' investment and consumption decisions through asset prices: stock prices, real estate prices, and exchange rates. Given the role that asset prices play in transmission mechanisms, central banks often have been tempted to use these as monetary policy targets. Chapter 3 shows that despite the significance of asset prices in the conduct of monetary policy, targeting asset prices—whether they are exchange rates, real estate, or stock prices—is likely to worsen the performance of monetary policy. Targeting asset prices worsens economic performance because the response of monetary policy to asset price fluctuations depends on the nature of shocks to asset prices and the degree of the shock's permanence. Furthermore, targeting asset prices is likely to erode support for central banks' independence because controlling these asset prices is beyond central bank capabilities.

As will be emphasized throughout this book, much of the recent success of central banks has resulted from their increased focus on price stability as the overriding long-run objective of monetary policy. However, it is clear that central banks should care not only about promoting low and stable inflation, but should also want to promote maximum sustainable output and employment. Indeed, the goals of both price stability and maximum sustainable employment, referred to as the *dual mandate*, are embedded in central bank legislation in many countries, most prominently in the United States. Does the dual mandate suggest that central banks should have an employment or output target? What role does the dual mandate suggest that output stabilization should have in the conduct of monetary policy? Chapter 4, written in 2002, addresses these questions and provides the following answers. Activist monetary policy—in which the monetary authorities focus on output fluctuations in the setting of their policy instrument and in policy statements—is likely to produce worse outcomes not only for inflation but also for output fluctuations. Activist policy of this type not only will lead to inappropriate monetary policy, but will also complicate the monetary authority's communication strategy and can weaken the support for the independence of the central bank. The analysis in chapter 4 suggests that a flexible inflation-targeting approach to monetary policymaking, which is discussed extensively in parts II and III of this book, enables the central bank to communicate effectively to the public that it cares about output fluctuations, but makes it less likely that the central bank will fall into the time-inconsistency trap and try to exploit the short-run trade-off between output and inflation.

In recent years, there has been a major sea change in the way central banks communicate with the markets and the public. Now central bank communication is seen as a central issue in monetary policy strategy. A key issue in chapter 4 is how central banks should communicate their concerns about output fluctuations. Chapter 5, which was written for a conference at the Reserve Bank of Australia in 2004, pursues the issue of central bank communication strategy in more depth. The trend in central banking has been to move to ever greater transparency, but should there be a limit? Can central bank transparency go too far?

Chapter 5 argues that although recent increases in transparency have been very beneficial and in some ways need to go further, transparency can indeed go too far. The lens with which I view whether transparency is beneficial is the question, Does increased transparency help the central bank do its job—that is, does it enable the central bank to conduct monetary policy optimally, with an appropriate focus on long-run objectives? The answer could well be no if the increase in transparency violates the KISS (Keep It Simple Stupid) principle and thereby makes the central bank's communication strategy too complicated. With this perspective, I argue that there are substantial dangers from a central bank announcing its projections of the future path of policy rates; I am therefore quite critical of the Federal Reserve's language in its post-FOMC statements from 2003 to 2006, when in effect it announced exactly what the policy action would be for the next several FOMC meetings. I also argue that central banks should not announce their objective functions, in disagreement with the view Lars Svensson has strongly advocated, and that central banks should be wary about publishing too prominently their estimates of current and future output gaps (the difference between output and its potential).

On the other hand, there is one area in which central bank transparency, even at central banks that announce an explicit, numerical, inflation target, does not go far enough: many monetary policymakers are unwilling to honestly discuss that they do care about output fluctuations, a concern that I refer to as central banking's "dirty little secret." By describing procedures for how the path and horizon of inflation targets would be modified in the face of large shocks, by emphasizing that monetary policy will be just as vigilant in preventing inflation from falling too low as it is in preventing it from becoming too high, and by indicating that expansionary policies will be pursued when output falls very far below potential, central banks can increase support for their policies and independence.

The final two chapters in part I, both written with Arturo Estrella, my colleague at the Federal Reserve Bank of New York when I was the director of research from 1994 to 1997, are quite a bit more technical than the other chapters in part I and in the rest of the book. Ever since the monetarist counterrevolution, monetary aggregates often have been seen as having a potentially valuable role in guiding monetary policy. Experiments with monetary targeting, which are discussed later in chapters 8 and 10, put monetary aggregates at the center of the conduct of monetary policy, while some central banks give a particularly prominent role to monetary aggregates, most notably the European Central Bank. Other central banks virtually ignore monetary aggregates.

In chapter 6, written in 1996, Arturo and I examine whether monetary aggregates contain useful information to guide monetary policy. We look at proposals for use of these aggregates in monetary policy rules and perform empirical tests on the strength and stability of the empirical relationships that those rules presuppose. More generally, we ask what role the aggregates can play if the approach to policy is more eclectic. Our empirical results show that in the United States since 1979, the monetary aggregates do not provide reliable information on the economy's future course that would be helpful in guiding monetary policy. Somewhat surprisingly, our results with the German monetary aggregate M3 are hardly more favorable. Although these results do not rule out that monetary aggregates cannot be used in some complicated way as an information variable, the straightforward use of these aggregates for monetary policy is not supported in countries that have reasonably low inflation. Monetary aggregates thus are not usable as part of a strategy in these countries to increase the transparency of monetary policy to the public and the markets. This is why I am skeptical of the prominence given to monetary aggregates in the European Central Bank's monetary policy strategy.

Another piece of information that has been used widely by central banks to guide the stance of monetary policy is the gap between realized unemployment and NAIRU, the nonaccelerating inflation rate of unemployment. In simpler words, NAIRU is the unemployment rate at which inflation is expected neither to increase nor decrease. The NAIRU concept has come under serious attack in recent years, particularly since 1995 when unemployment fell below 6 percent, which is what many economists thought was a reasonable value for NAIRU, and yet inflation subsequently did not accelerate, but instead actually fell. In chapter 7, which was written for a conference on monetary policy rules organized by John Taylor in 1996, Arturo Estrella and I rethink the NAIRU concept to examine whether it might have a useful role in monetary policy. We show that trying to drive the unemployment rate toward NAIRU would lead to poor policy outcomes and, therefore, having any kind of NAIRU target for monetary policy is inappropriate. On the other hand, NAIRU can be useful in the conduct of monetary policy if it is defined as a short-run, rather than a long-run, construct, and we show how this can be done.

References

Friedman, Milton, and David Meiselman. 1963. "The Relative Stability of Monetary Velocity and the Investment Multiplier." In *Stabilization Policies*. Commission on Money and Credit, ed. (Upper Saddle River, N.J.: Prentice Hall): 165–268.

Friedman, Milton, and Anna Jacobson Schwartz. 1963a. *A Monetary History of the United States, 1867–1960*. Princeton, N.J.: Princeton University Press.

Friedman, Milton, and Anna Jacobson Schwartz. 1963b. "Money and Business Cycles." *Review of Economics and Statistics*, vol. 45, Supplement: 32–64.

Kearl, James R., and Frederic S. Mishkin. 1977. "Illiquidity, the Demand for Residential Housing, and Monetary Policy." *Journal of Finance* 37, no. 5 (December): 1571–1586.

Mishkin, Frederic S. 1976a. "Illiquidity, Consumer Durable Expenditure, and Monetary Policy." *American Economic Review* 66, no. 4 (September): 642–654.

Mishkin, Frederic S. 1976b. "Household Liabilities and the Generalized Stock-Adjustment Model." *Review of Economics and Statistics* LVIII, no. 4, (November): 481–485.

Mishkin, Frederic S. 1976c. "Liquidity and the Role of Monetary Policy in Consumer Durable Demand." *New England Economic Review* (November/December): 31–42.

Mishkin, Frederic S. 1977a. *Illiquidity, the Demand for Consumer Durables, and Monetary Policy*. Federal Reserve Bank of Boston, Report 61. 1976 PhD thesis, MIT.

Mishkin, Frederic S. 1977b. "A Note on Short-Run Asset Effects on Household Saving and Consumption." *American Economic Review* no. 2 (March): 246–248.

Mishkin, Frederic S. 1977c. "What Depressed the Consumer? The Household Balance-Sheet and the 1973–75 Recession." *Brookings Paper on Economic Activity* (1): 123–164.

Mishkin, Frederic S. 1978a. "Monetary Policy and Liquidity: Simulation Results." *Economic Inquiry* 16, no. 1 (January): 16–36.

Mishkin, Frederic S. 1978b. "The Household Balance-Sheet and the Great Depression." *Journal of Economic History* 38 (December): 918–937.

2 What Should Central Banks Do?

Frederic S. Mishkin

2.1 Introduction

In the last twenty years, there has been substantial rethinking about how central banks should do their job. This rethinking has led to major changes in how central banks operate, and we are now in an era in which central banks in many countries throughout the world have had notable success—keeping inflation low, while their economies experience rapid economic growth. In this chapter, I outline what we think we have learned about how central banks should be set up to conduct monetary policy and then apply these lessons to see if there is room for institutional improvement in the way the Federal Reserve operates.

The chapter begins by discussing seven guiding principles for central banks and then uses these principles to outline what the role of central banks should be. This framework is then used to see how the institutional features of the Fed measure up. I will take the view that despite the Fed's extraordinarily successful performance in recent years, we should not be complacent. Changes in the way the Fed is set up to conduct its business may be needed to help ensure that the Fed continues to be as successful in the future.

2.2 Guiding Principles for Central Banks

Recent theorizing in monetary economics suggests seven basic principles that can serve as useful guides for central banks to help them achieve successful outcomes in their conduct of monetary policy. These are:

- Price stability provides substantial benefits;
- Fiscal policy should be aligned with monetary policy;
- Time inconsistency is a serious problem to be avoided;
- Monetary policy should be forward looking;

• Accountability is a basic principle of democracy;

• Monetary policy should be concerned about output as well as price fluctuations; and

• The most serious economic downturns are associated with financial instability.

We will look at each of these principles in turn.

2.2.1   Price Stability Provides Substantial Benefits to the Economy

In recent years a growing consensus has emerged that price stability—a low and stable inflation rate—provides substantial benefits to the economy. Price stability prevents overinvestment in the financial sector, which in a high-inflation environment expands to profitably act as a middleman to help individuals and businesses escape some of the costs of inflation.[1] Price stability lowers the uncertainty about relative prices and the future price level, making it easier for firms and individuals to make appropriate decisions, thereby increasing economic efficiency.[2] Price stability also lowers the distortions from the interaction of the tax system and inflation.[3]

All of these benefits of price stability suggest that low and stable inflation can increase the level of resources productively employed in the economy, and might even help increase the rate of economic growth. While time-series studies of individual countries and cross-national comparisons of growth rates are not in total agreement, there is a consensus that inflation is detrimental to economic growth, particularly when inflation is at high levels.[4] Therefore, both theory and evidence suggest that monetary policy should focus on promoting price stability.

2.2.2   Align Fiscal Policy with Monetary Policy

One lesson from the "unpleasant monetarist arithmetic" discussed in Sargent and Wallace (1981) and the recent literature on fiscal theories of the price level (Woodford, 1994 and 1995) is that irresponsible fiscal policy may make it more difficult for the monetary authorities to pursue price stability. Large government deficits may put pressure on the monetary authorities to monetize the debt, thereby producing rapid money growth and inflation. Restaining the fiscal authorities from engaging in excessive deficit financing thus aligns fiscal policy with monetary policy and makes it easier for the monetary authorities to keep inflation under control.

2.2.3   Time Inconsistency Is a Serious Problem to Be Avoided

One of the key problems facing monetary policymakers is the time-inconsistency problem described by Calvo (1978), Kydland and Prescott (1977), and Barro and Gordon (1983). The time-inconsistency problem arises because there are incentives for a policymaker to try to exploit the short-run tradeoff between employment and inflation to pursue short-run employment objectives, even though the result is poor long-run outcomes. Expansionary monetary policy will produce higher growth and employment in the short-run. Therefore, policymakers will be tempted to pursue this policy even though it will not produce higher growth and employment in the long-run because economic agents adjust their wage and price expectations upward to reflect the expansionary policy. Unfortunately, however, expansionary monetary policy will lead to higher inflation in the long-run, with its negative consequences for the economy.

McCallum (1995) points out that the time-inconsistency problem by itself does not imply that a central bank will pursue expansionary monetary policy that leads to inflation. Simply by recognizing the problem that forward-looking expectations in the wage- and price-setting process promotes a strategy of pursuing expansionary monetary policy, central banks can decide not to play that game. From my first-hand experience as a central banker, I can testify that central bankers are very aware of the time-inconsistency problem and are, indeed, extremely averse to falling into a time-inconsistency trap. However, even if central bankers recognize the problem, there still will be pressures on the central bank to pursue overly expansionary monetary policy by politicians. Thus, overly expansionary monetary policy and inflation may result, so that the time-inconsistency problem remains. The time-inconsistency problem is just shifted back one step; its source is not in the central bank, but rather, resides in the political process.

The time-inconsistency literature points out both why there will be pressures on central banks to pursue overly expansionary monetary policy and why central banks whose commitment to price stability is in doubt are more likely to experience higher inflation. In order to prevent high inflation and the pursuit of a suboptimal monetary policy, monetary policy institutions need to be designed in order to avoid the time-inconsistency trap.

2.2.4 Monetary Policy Should Be Forward Looking
The existence of long lags from monetary policy actions to their intended effects on output and inflation suggests that monetary policy should be forward looking. If policymakers wait until undesirable outcomes on inflation and output fluctuations actually arise, their policy actions are likely to be counterproductive. For example, by waiting until inflation has already appeared before tightening monetary policy, the monetary authorities will be too late; inflation expectations will already be embedded into the wage- and price-setting process, creating an inflation momentum that will be hard to contain. Once the inflation process has gotten rolling, the process of stopping it will be slower and costlier. Similarly, by waiting until the economy is already in recession, expansionary policy may kick in well after the economy has recovered, thus promoting unnecessary output fluctuations and possible inflation.

To avoid these problems, monetary authorities must behave in a forward-looking fashion and act preemptively. For example, assume that it takes two years for monetary policy to have a significant effect on inflation. Under these circumstances, even if inflation is quiescent currently (with an unchanged stance of monetary policy) and policymakers forecast inflation to rise in two years time, they must act immediately to head off the inflationary surge.

2.2.5   Policymakers Should Be Accountable

A basic principle of democracy is that the public should have the right to control the actions of the government: In other and more famous words, "The government should be of the people, by the people and for the people." Thus, the public in a democracy must have the capability to "throw the bums out" or punish incompetent policymakers through other methods in order to control their actions. If policymakers cannot be removed from office or punished in some other way, this basic principle of democracy is violated. In a democracy, government policymakers need to be held accountable to the public.

A second reason why accountability of policymakers is important is that it helps to promote efficiency in government. Making policymakers subject to punishment makes it more likely that incompetent policymakers will be replaced by competent ones and creates better incentives for policymakers to do their jobs well. Knowing that they are subject to punishment when performance is poor, policymakers will strive to get policy right. If policymakers are able to avoid accountability, then their incentives to do a good job drop appreciably, making poor policy outcomes more likely.

2.2.6   Monetary Policy Should Be Concerned with Output as well as Price Fluctuations

Price stability is a means to an end—a healthy economy—and should not be treated as an end in itself. Thus, central bankers should not be obsessed with inflation control and become what Mervyn King (1997) has characterized as "inflation nutters." Clearly, the public cares about output as well as inflation fluctuations, and so the objectives for a central bank in the context of a long-run strategy should not only include minimizing inflation fluctuations, but should also include minimizing output fluctuations. Objective functions with these characteristics have now become standard in the monetary economics literature, which focuses on the conduct of monetary policy (e.g., see the papers in Taylor, 1999).

2.2.7   The Most Serious Economic Downturns Are Associated with Financial Instability

A reading of U.S. monetary history (Friedman and Schwartz, 1963, Bernanke, 1983, and Mishkin, 1991) indicates that the most serious economic contractions in U.S. history, including the Great Depression, have all been associated with financial instability. Indeed, this literature suggests that financial instability is a key reason for the depth of these economic contractions. The recent financial crises and depressions in Mexico and East Asia also support this view (Mishkin, 1996, 1999a and Corsetti, Pesenti, and Roubini, 1998). Preventing financial instability is, therefore, crucial to promoting a healthy economy and reducing output fluctuations, an important objective for central banks, as we have seen above.

2.3   Implications for the Role of a Central Bank

Armed with these seven guiding principles, we can now look at what institutional features a central bank should have in conducting its operations. We derive the following implications/criteria for the role of a central bank:

• Price stability should be the overriding, long-run goal of monetary policy;
• An explicit nominal anchor should be adopted;
• A central bank should be goal dependent;
• A central bank should be instrument independent;
• A central bank should be accountable;
• A central bank should stress transparency and communication;
• A central bank should also have the goal of financial stability.

2.3.1   Price Stability Should Be the Overriding, Long-Run Goal of Monetary Policy

Together, the first three principles for monetary policy outlined above suggest that the overriding, long-run goal of monetary policy should be price stability. A goal of price stability immediately follows from the benefits of low and stable inflation, which promote higher economic output. Furthermore, an institutional commitment to price stability is one way to make time-inconsistency of monetary policy less likely. An institutional commitment to the price stability goal provides a counter to time-inconsistency because it makes it clear that the central bank must focus on the long-run and thus resist the temptation to pursue short-run expansionary policies that are inconsistent with the long-run, price stability goal.

The third principle, that fiscal policy should be aligned with monetary policy, provides another reason why price stability should be the overriding, long-run goal of monetary policy. As McCallum (1990) has pointed out, "unpleasant monetarist arithmetic" only arises if the fiscal authorities are the first mover. In other words, if the fiscal authorities are the dominant player and can move first—thus setting fiscal policy exogenously, knowing that the monetary authorities will be forced to accommodate their policies to maintain the long-run government budget constraint—then fiscal policy will determine the inflation rate. Indeed, this is the essence of the fiscal theory of the price level. On the other hand, as McCallum (1990) points out, if the monetary authorities are the dominant player and move first, then it will be fiscal policy that will accommodate in order to satisfy the long-run government budget constraint and monetary policy will determine the inflation rate. An institutional commitment to price stability as the overriding, long-run goal, is just one way to ensure that monetary policy moves first and dominates, forcing fiscal policy to align with monetary policy.

The sixth guiding principle, that output fluctuations should also be a concern of monetary policy, suggests that a fanatic pursuit of price stability could be problematic because policymakers should see not only price fluctuations, but also output fluctuations as undesirable. This is why the price stability goal should be seen as overriding in the long-run but not in the short-run. As Lars Svensson (1999) states, central banks should pursue what he calls "flexible inflation targeting," in which the speed at which a central bank tries to get to price stability reflects their concerns about output fluctuations. The more heavily a central bank cares about output fluctuations, the more time it should take to return to price stability when it is not already there. However, because a "flexible inflation targeter" always sets a long-term price stability goal for inflation, the fact that a central bank cares about output fluctuations is entirely consistent with price stability as the long-run, overriding goal.

2.3.2 An Explicit Nominal Anchor Should Be Adopted

Although an institutional commitment to price stability helps solve time-inconsistency and fiscal alignment problems, it does not go far enough because price stability is not a clearly defined concept. Typical definitions of price stability have many elements in common with the commonly used legal definition of pornography in the United States—you know it when you see it. Thus, constraints on fiscal policy and discretionary monetary policy to avoid inflation might end up being quite weak because not everyone will agree on what price stability means in practice, providing both monetary policymakers and politicians a loophole to avoid making tough decisions to keep inflation under control. A solution to this problem, which supports the first three guiding principles, is to adopt an explicit nominal anchor that ties down exactly what the commitment to price stability means.

There are several forms that an explicit nominal anchor can take. One is a commitment to a fixed exchange rate. For example, in 1991, Argentina established a currency board that required the central bank to exchange U.S. dollars for new pesos at a fixed exchange rate of one to one. A second nominal anchor is for the central bank to have a money-growth target, as was the case in Germany. A third nominal anchor is for there to be an explicit numerical inflation goal as in inflation-targeting countries such as New Zealand, Canada, the United Kingdom, Australia, and Brazil, among others. All these forms of explicit nominal anchors can help reduce the time-inconsistency problem, as the success of countries using them in lowering and controlling inflation demonstrates (Mishkin, 1999b). These nominal anchors also help restrain fiscal policy and also are seen as an important benefit of inflation targeting in countries such as New Zealand and Canada (Mishkin and Posen, 1997, and Bernanke, Laubach, Mishkin, and Posen, 1999).

One criticism of adopting an explicit nominal anchor, such as an inflation target, is that it will necessarily result in too little emphasis on reducing output fluctuations, which is inconsistent with the guiding principle that monetary policy should be concerned with output as well as price fluctuations. However, this view is mistaken. Inflation targeting, as it has actually been practiced (Mishkin and Posen, 1997, and Bernanke, Laubach, Mishkin, and Posen, 1999), has been quite flexible and has not led to larger output fluctuations. Indeed, adoption of an inflation target can actually make it easier for central banks to deal with negative shocks to the aggregate economy. Because a decline in aggregate demand also leads to lower-than-expected inflation, a central bank is able to respond with a monetary easing, without causing the public to question its anti-inflationary resolve. Furthermore, inflation targeting can make it less likely that deflation, a fall in the price level, would occur. There are particularly valid reasons for fearing deflation in today's world, including the possibility that it might promote financial instability and precipitate a severe economic contraction. Indeed, deflation has been associated with deep recessions or even depressions, as in the 1930s, and the recent deflation in Japan has been one factor that has weakened the financial system and the economy. Targeting inflation rates of above zero, as all inflation targeters have done, makes periods of deflation less likely. The evidence on inflation expectations from surveys and interest rate levels suggests that maintaining a target for inflation above zero (but not too far above) for an extended period does not lead to instability in inflation expectations or to a decline in the central bank's credibility.

2.3.3 Central Banks Should Be Goal Dependent

Although there is a strong rationale for the price stability goal and an explicit nominal anchor, who should make the institutional commitment? Should the central bank independently announce its commitment to the price stability goal or would it be better to have this commitment be mandated by the government?

Here the distinction between goal independence and instrument independence made by Debelle and Fischer (1994) and Fischer (1994) is quite useful. Goal independence is the ability of the central bank to set its own goals for monetary policy, while instrument independence is the ability of the central bank to independently set the instruments of monetary policy to achieve the goals. The fifth guiding principle, that the public must be able to exercise control over government actions and that policymakers must be accountable, so basic to democracy, strongly suggests that the goals of monetary policy should be set by the elected government. In other words, a central bank should not be goal independent. The corollary of this view is that the institutional commitment to price stability should come from the government in the form of an explicit, legislated mandate for the central bank to pursue price stability as its overriding, long-run goal.

Not only is the principle of a legislated mandate and goal dependence of the central bank consistent with basic principles of democracy, but it has the further advantage that it is consistent with the second and third guiding principles—it makes time-inconsistency less likely, while making alignment of fiscal policy with monetary policy more likely. As we discussed above, the source of the time-inconsistency problem is more likely to be embedded in the political process than it is in the central bank. Once politicians commit to the price stability goal by passing central bank legislation with a price stability mandate, it becomes harder for them to put pressure on the central bank to pursue short-run expansionary policies that are inconsistent with the price stability goal. Furthermore, a government commitment to price stability also is a commitment to making monetary policy dominant over fiscal policy, ensuring a better alignment of fiscal policy with monetary policy.

An alternative way to solve time-inconsistency problems has been suggested by Rogoff (1985): Grant both goal and instrument independence to a central bank and then appoint conservative central bankers to run it, who put more weight on controlling inflation (relative to output) than does the general public. The result will be low inflation, but at the cost of higher output variability than the public desires.

There are two problems with this solution. First, having "conservative" central bankers impose different preferences from those of the public on the conduct of monetary policy is inherently undemocratic. Basic democratic principles indicate that the preferences of policymaking should be aligned with those of the society at large. Second, in the long run, a central bank cannot operate without the support of the public. If the central bank is seen to be pursuing goals that are not what the public wants, support for central bank independence is likely to erode. Thus appointment of "conservative" central bankers may not be stable in the long run and will not provide a permanent solution to the time-inconsistency problem.

The same principles that suggest that the central bank should be goal dependent, with the commitment to the price stability goal mandated by the government, also suggest that the commitment to an explicit nominal anchor should be made by the government. In the case of an exchange-rate target, the government should set the target, as in Argentina, or in the case of an inflation target, the government should set the numerical inflation goal. The fact that the government sets these targets so that the central bank is goal dependent does not mean that the central bank should be cut out of the decision-making process. Because the central bank has both prestige and expertise in the conduct of monetary policy, governments will almost always be better served by setting these targets in consultation with the central bank.

Although it is clear that the government should set the goal for the explicit nominal anchor in the long-run, it is more controversial whether it should set it in the short-run or intermediate-run. If a government, for example, set a short-run inflation or exchange rate target that was changed every month or every quarter, this could easily lead to time-inconsistency in which short-run objectives would dominate. In many countries that target inflation, the Ministry of Finance, as the representative of the government, does set an annual inflation target; however, as documented in Bernanke, Laubach, Mishkin, and Posen (1999), the target rarely is changed once price stability is achieved. Thus, even though (in theory) governments could manipulate an annual inflation target to pursue short-run objectives, the transparency of goal-setting leads to a long-run approach to setting inflation targets even when it is done on an annual basis. The situation for the United States is even more complicated. Because of our congressional system, the Treasury Secretary is not the representative of Congress, in contrast to the Minister of Finance who does represent parliament in a parliamentary system. Instead the Treasury Secretary represents the executive branch. Thus, who represents the American government in setting a short- or intermediate-term target for monetary policy is not clear-cut. This problem is not as severe for setting the long-run goal of monetary policy, which could be done by a congressional commission with representatives from both the executive and legislative branches, as well as from the public and the central bank. However, the difficulties of delegating the setting of shorter run targets for monetary policy in a congressional system may require that the central bank keep this responsibility.[5]

2.3.4 Central Banks Should Be Instrument Independent

Although the arguments above suggest that central banks should be goal dependent, the guiding principles in the previous section provide a strong case that central banks should be instrument independent. Allowing central banks to control the setting of monetary policy instruments provides additional insulation from political pressures to exploit short-run tradeoffs between employment and inflation. Instrument independence means that the central bank is better able to avoid the pursuit of time-inconsistent policies in line with the third guiding principle.

The fourth guiding principle, that monetary policy needs to be forward looking in order to take account of the long lags in the effect of monetary policy on inflation, provides another rationale for instrument independence. Instrument independence insulates the central bank from the myopia that is frequently a feature of the political process arising from politicians' concerns about getting elected in the near future.

Thus, instrument independence makes it more likely that the central bank will be forward looking and adequately allow for the long lags from monetary policy actions to inflation in setting their policy instruments.

Recent evidence seems to support the conjecture that macroeconomic performance is improved when central banks are more independent. When central banks in industrialized countries are ranked from least legally independent to most legally independent, the inflation performance is found to be the best for countries with the most independent central banks (see Alesina and Summers, 1993, Cukierman, 1992, and Fischer, 1994, among others). However, there is some question whether causality runs from central bank independence to low inflation or, rather, whether a third factor is involved, such as the general public's preferences for low inflation that create both central bank independence and low inflation (Posen, 1995).

The bottom line is that basic principles for monetary policy and democracy suggest that central banks should have instrument but not goal independence. This degree of independence for central banks is analogous to the relationship between the U.S. military and the government during the successfully prosecuted Gulf War in 1991. The military had instrument independence: It had complete control over the prosecution of the war with little interference from the government (in contrast to the less successfully waged Vietnam War). On the other hand, the military did not have goal independence: It was the Commander in Chief, George Bush, who made the decisions as to what the objectives and goals of the war would be.

2.3.5 Central Banks Should Be Accountable

The fifth guiding principle, that policymakers should be accountable, indicates that the central bank should be subject to government and public scrutiny. One way of ensuring accountability is to make the independence of the central bank subject to legislative change by allowing the act that created the central bank to be modified by legislation at any time. Another way is to mandate periodic reporting requirements to the government, for example, as was done in the Humphrey-Hawkins legislation which requires the Chairman of the Federal Reserve to testify to Congress twice a year.

The need for central banks to be accountable provides an additional reason why central banks should have an explicit nominal anchor. If there is no explicit nominal anchor, it is far less clear upon what criterion the central bank should be judged, and thus it is harder to hold it accountable. On the other hand, with an explicit nominal anchor, like a target for inflation or the exchange rate, the public and the politicians have a clear-cut benchmark to assess the performance of the central bank. Thus, an explicit nominal anchor enhances the accountability of the central bank. Indeed, with an explicit nominal anchor, accountability can be enforced by making the central bank governor subject to dismissal if he or she breaches the goals set by the government, as is the case in New Zealand.

2.3.6   Central Banks Should Stress Transparency and Communication

Increased transparency of monetary policymaking is another important way to increase central bank accountability in line with the fifth guiding principle. Central banks need to communicate clearly their monetary policy strategy in order to explain their objectives and how they plan to achieve them. Each time they change their policy instruments, such as the interbank interest rate, they also need to clearly state the decision and then explain the rationale for it. Transparency can be further increased by publication of the central bank's forecast and the minutes of the discussion of monetary policy.

In addition, central banks need to pursue many outreach vehicles to communicate with the public. These include the continual making of speeches to all elements of society, more openness with the press and media, and the development of brochures and reports that are accessible to the public. Particularly noteworthy in this regard are the "Inflation Report" type documents initially developed by the Bank of England and now emulated by many other central banks. These documents depart from the usual dull-looking, formal reports of central banks to take on the best elements of textbook writing (fancy graphics, use of boxes) in order to better communicate with the public.

Increasing transparency and accountability not only helps to align central banks with democratic principles, and is thus worthy in its own right, but it also has benefits for the ability of central banks to conduct monetary policy successfully. Transparency reduces the uncertainty about monetary policy, interest rates, and inflation, thus making private-sector planning easier. Transparency and communication also promote a better public understanding of what central banks can do—promote price stability which, as suggested by the first guiding principle, has the potential to enhance economic growth in the long run—and what central banks cannot do—create permanent increases in output and employment through expansionary policy. Better public understanding of what central banks can and cannot do is then likely to help generate more public support for monetary policy, which is focused on price stability becoming the long-run, overriding goal.

Although central bankers find their life to be a more comfortable one when they are not accountable and can avoid intense public scrutiny, increased transparency and accountability have important benefits for central bankers, helping them to adhere to the first five guiding principles outlined in the previous section. Because transparency and accountability can increase the public support for the price stability goal and longer-term thinking on the part of the central bank, they can reduce political pressures on the central bank to pursue inflationary monetary policy and, thus, limit the time-inconsistency problem, while generating more support for forward-looking policy by the central bank. Also, greater transparency and communication can help the central bank convince the public that fiscal policy needs to be aligned with monetary policy.

In addition, transparency and accountability can increase support for independence of the central bank.[6] An instructive example is provided by the granting of instrument independence to the Bank of England in May 1997. Prior to this date, monetary-policy decisions in the United Kingdom were made by the government (the Chancellor of the Exchequer) rather than by the Bank of England. When, on May 6, 1997, the Chancellor of the Exchequer, Gordon Brown, announced the granting of instrument independence to the Bank of England, giving it the power to set the overnight interest rate, he made it particularly clear at the press conference that, in his view, the action had been made possible by the increased transparency and accountability of policy under the recently adopted inflation-targeting regime.

2.3.7 Central Banks Should Also Have a Financial Stability Goal

Because central banks should care about output fluctuations (Principle 6) and the most serious economic contractions arise when there is financial instability (Principle 7), central banks also need to focus on preventing financial instability. The primary way that central banks prevent financial instability is by acting as a lender of last resort, that is, by supplying liquidity to the financial system to keep a financial crisis from spinning out of control. Because acting as a lender of last resort, in effect, provides a safety net for financial institutions to whom the funds will be channeled, it creates a moral hazard problem in which these institutions who are potential borrowers have incentives to take on excessive risk, which can make financial instability more likely. Thus, central banks need to consider the tradeoff between the moral hazard cost of the role as lender of last resort and the benefit of preventing financial crises. Keeping moral hazard from getting out of hand indicates that central banks should not perform the role of lender of last resort unless it is absolutely necessary; and, therefore, this role should occur very infrequently.

Because lender-of-last-resort lending should be directed at providing funds to solvent, but illiquid, financial institutions and not to insolvent institutions, in order to reduce incentives to take on too much risk by these institutions, the central bank needs to have information regarding to whom it might have to extend loans when it performs this role. One way for the central bank to get this information is for it to have a supervisory role over these institutions. This is an argument for giving central banks a role in prudential supervision (see, e.g., Mishkin, 1992, and Bernanke, 2000). In addition, a supervisory role for the central bank can help it obtain information about whether a situation really is likely to lead to a financial crisis and, thus, requires a lender-of-last-resort intervention. Without this information, the central bank may either intervene too frequently or fail to do so when it is really needed, thus making financial instability more likely. It is possible that central banks can acquire the information they need from supervisory agencies which are separate from the central bank, but some central bank officials doubt this (see Peek, Rosengren, and Tootell, 2000). Thus, there is an argument for the central bank to have a role in prudential supervision, but it is by no means clear-cut. Furthermore, there are arguments against central bank involvement in prudential supervision because it may cause a central bank to lose its focus on the price-stability objective.

2.4   A Federal Reserve Scorecard

Now that we have outlined what the role of a central bank should be, we can assess how the institutional features of the Federal Reserve measure up. We provide an assessment of whether the way the Fed is set up to conduct its operations is consistent with each of the seven criteria discussed in the previous section.

2.4.1   Price Stability Should Be the Overriding, Long-Run Goal of Monetary Policy

Through their testimony and speeches, high officials in the Federal Reserve System, and especially Alan Greenspan, have made it quite clear that the overriding, long-run goal for Fed monetary policy is price stability. However, there is no clear mandate from the U.S. government that price stability should be a long-run, overriding goal. The Humphrey-Hawkins Act passed in 1978, with the revealing title, "Full Employment and Balanced Growth Act," stipulates that monetary policy should have goals of full employment and economic growth, as well as price stability. It is true that the Humphrey-Hawkins Act could be interpreted as allowing for price stability to be the overriding, long-run goal because, as was indicated previously, price stability is a means of promoting high economic growth and full employment in the long-run. However, it is even easier to interpret the legislation as supporting an emphasis on pursuit of full employment and economic growth in the short-run, which is inconsistent with the pursuit of price stability. The lack of a clear mandate for price stability can lead to the time-inconsistency problem in which political pressure is put on the Fed to engage in expansionary policy to pursue short-run goals.

In contrast to the United States, many other countries now have legislation which mandates price stability as the overriding, long-run goal of monetary policy, and this is a growing trend. For example, a mandate for price stability as the overriding, long-run goal for monetary policy was a requirement for entry into the European Monetary Union, and the Maastricht Treaty gives this mandate to the central banking system for the European Monetary Union, which is most accurately referred to as the Eurosystem.[7] This trend also has been evident even in emerging market countries, where many central banks have had their mandate revised to focus on price stability.

On the first criterion of the need for an institutional commitment to price stability, as the overriding long-run goal, the United States does not score well.

2.4.2   An Explicit Nominal Anchor Should Be Adopted

Not only has the U.S. government not committed to price stability as the overriding, long-run goal, but also neither it nor the Fed has adopted an explicit nominal anchor. The actions and rhetoric of the Greenspan Fed have made it clear that it will fight to keep inflation from rising from the current level of around 2 percent, and it is fair to characterize the Fed as having an implicit nominal anchor. Nonetheless, the Federal Reserve has not come out and articulated an explicit goal for inflation and has, instead, stated its commitment to price stability. This has been loosely defined by Alan Greenspan as a situation in which changes in the price level are not a major consideration for businesses and households. At the present time, the public (and maybe even members of the FOMC) have no idea of whether the Fed's goal for inflation is 1 percent, 2 percent, or possibly higher. I think it is fair to say that right now the nominal anchor in the United States is Alan Greenspan. The problem is that this leaves some ambiguity as to what the Fed's target is. Even more importantly, the existence of this implicit nominal anchor depends on personalities. Alan Greenspan, despite his recent reappointment, will not be around forever. When he steps down, will the public believe that there is sufficient commitment to a nominal anchor to keep inflation from appearing again?

On the criterion of having an explicit nominal anchor, the institutional set up of the Fed also does not score well.

2.4.3   Central Banks Should Be Instrument Independent

The Federal Reserve has been set up to be far more independent than other government agencies in the United States. Members of the Board of Governors are appointed by the government for 14-year terms, insulating them from political pressure, while Reserve Bank presidents, who also sit on the FOMC, are appointed by the boards of directors at each Reserve Bank and are not subject to Congressional review. Even more important is that the Federal Reserve generates substantial profits, on the order of $20 billion per year, most of which it returns to the U.S. Treasury, so that it has its own revenue base and is not dependent on funds from the government. Indeed, by law the Federal Reserve is exempt from General Accounting Office (GAO) audits of deliberations, decisions, or actions on monetary policy matters.

Given its insulation from the political process and its financial independence, it should be no surprise that the Fed has complete control over setting its monetary policy instruments. This has the benefits of enabling the Fed to resist political pressure to engage in time-inconsistent expansionary policy and to be forward-looking in the setting of its policy instruments.

On the criteria of instrument independence the Fed scores well.

2.4.4   Central Banks Should Be Goal Dependent

We have already seen that independence can go too far. Instrument independence is desirable but goal independence is problematic. The independence of the Fed—described above—and the lack of a clear mandate from the government allows the Fed to make the decisions on what the goals of its policies should be. Thus the Fed has a high degree of goal independence. In some ways goal independence makes the Fed's job easier because it insulates it from political pressure, but it does have a downside. The substantial goal independence of the Federal Reserve creates a fair amount of tension in a democratic society because it allows an elite group to set the goals of monetary policy. Indeed, recent criticism of the Federal Reserve may have been prompted by the impression that the Federal Reserve, and particularly its Chairman, has become too powerful.

The goal independence of the Federal Reserve should not be seen as total, however. Politicians do have the ability to influence the goals of the Fed because the Congress can modify the Federal Reserve Act at any time. Also, the Fed has a great interest in other legislation that affects its operations. A case in point is the recent Gramm-Bliley-Leach Financial Services Modernization Act, passed in 1999, which had major implications for whether the Federal Reserve would continue to have supervisory responsibilities over large banking organizations (which it continued to keep). Furthermore, Congress can criticize the budget of the Fed for items that are unrelated to monetary policy or foreign-exchange operations. As an example, in 1996 Senators Dorgan and Reid called for Congress to exercise budgetary authority over the nonmonetary activities of the Federal Reserve because they were concerned that the Fed was too focused on fighting inflation and not enough on reducing unemployment.

As a comparison, the Eurosystem should be seen in some ways as more goal independent than the Federal Reserve System and in other ways less. The Maastricht Treaty specifies that the overriding, long-run goal of the ECB is price stability, so that the goal for the Eurosystem is more clearly specified than it is for the Federal Reserve System. However, Maastricht did not specify exactly what this price stability means so the Eurosystem has defined the quantitative goal for monetary policy, an inflation rate between 0 and 2 percent. From this perspective, the Federal Reserve System is slightly less goal dependent than the Eurosystem. On the other hand, the Eurosystem's statutes cannot be changed by legislation, but only by alterations to the Maastricht Treaty. From this perspective, the Eurosystem is much less goal dependent than the Federal Reserve System because its statutes are specified in a treaty and thus are far harder to change than statutes that are embedded in legislation.

As the examples above indicate, the Federal Reserve is not goal dependent, but we should not take this view too far. Thus, on the goal dependence criteria, the Fed's score is mixed.

2.4.5 Central Banks Should Be Accountable

Closely related to goal dependence is the accountability of the central bank to meet its goals. There are formal accountability mechanisms for the Fed. For example, the Chairman of the Board of Governors has been required to testify twice a year to Congress about the conduct of monetary policy under the Humphrey-Hawkins legislation. Also, as we have seen, the Fed is subject to punitive actions by the Congress if it so chooses, either by amending the Federal Reserve Act or through passage of other legislation that affects the Fed.

On these grounds the Federal Reserve System is more accountable than the Eurosystem. As we have seen, the Eurosystem's statutes cannot be modified by legislation but, rather, requires amendment to a treaty, a far more difficult process. Moreover, although the President of the European Central Bank is required to testify once a year to the European Parliament, this requirement may not guarantee sufficient oversight of the Eurosystem's policies. Since the European Parliament is currently significantly less powerful than the national parliaments of the countries that make up the Monetary Union, scrutiny by that organization would not influence the Eurosystem's behavior as strongly as would oversight by a more powerful body, such as a consortium of national parliaments or the individual parliaments themselves. It is not clear to whom the Eurosystem would be accountable.

However, the absence of an explicit nominal anchor means that there is no benchmark against which the public or Congress can measure the performance of the Federal Reserve System. In contrast, the Eurosystem has outlined its price-stability goal of inflation between 0 and 2 percent, so there is a predetermined criterion to judge its performance. Thus, despite the requirement that the Fed testify to Congress, the accountability of the Fed is not very strong. The Federal Reserve is able to obscure what its strategy and goals are and has indeed done this in the past. This leaves open the possibility that there could be a political backlash against a "high-handed" Federal Reserve that could have adverse consequences on its independence and ability to successfully conduct monetary policy in the future.

On the accountability criteria, the Fed also does not score very well.

2.4.6 Central Banks Should Stress Transparency and Communication

In recent years, the Fed has come a long way on the transparency and communication front. In the past, the Fed had a reputation for not only being unclear about its goals and strategy, but for keeping markets in the dark about its setting of policy instruments. This has changed dramatically in recent years. Starting in 1994, the Fed began to announce its policy actions after every FOMC meeting. It then moved in 1999 to announcing the bias in the direction of future moves in the federal funds rate, which caused some confusion, and so replaced this announcement at the beginning of this year with one that indicates the balance of risks for the future—whether toward higher inflation or toward a weaker economy. Fed officials also have been more active in articulating the strategy of monetary policy, its need to be preemptive, and the importance of the pursuit of price stability.

Despite improved transparency and communication, the lack of explicit goals has meant that Fed transparency is still much less than at many other central banks. In contrast to central banks that have adopted inflation targeting, the Fed produces nothing like an "Inflation Report" in which it clearly lays out in plain English the strategy for monetary policy and how well the central bank has been doing. One consequence of the weakness of Fed transparency and communication is that the public debate on monetary policy in the United States still has a tendency to focus on short-run considerations, as reflected in politicians' focus on "jobs, jobs, jobs" when discussing monetary policy. This focus on short-run considerations is substantially less in countries where central banks use communication vehicles such as "Inflation Reports" to refocus the public debate on longer-run considerations such as price stability.

It is interesting to contrast the way public debate is conducted with what has occurred in Canada, which has adopted an inflation-targeting regime with high transparency and accountability. In 1996, the president of the Canadian Economic Association made a speech criticizing the Bank of Canada for pursuing monetary policy that (he claimed) was too contractionary. His speech sparked off a widespread public debate. Instead of degenerating into calls for the immediate expansion of monetary policy with little reference to the long-run consequences of such a policy change, the debate was channeled into a substantive discussion over what should be the appropriate target for inflation, with both the Bank and its critics obliged to make explicit their assumptions and estimates of the costs and benefits of different levels of inflation. Indeed, the debate and the Bank of Canada's record and responsiveness led to increased support for the Bank of Canada, with the result that criticism of the Bank and its conduct of monetary policy was not a major issue in the 1997 elections as it had been during the 1993 elections.

On the transparency and communication criteria, the Fed's score is mixed, although it has been improving over time.

2.4.7 Central Banks Should Also Have a Financial Stability Goal

Here the Fed's performance has been very strong. The Greenspan Fed has made it very clear that it will act decisively to prevent financial crises and has done so not only with words but with actions. The Fed's actions immediately after the October

19, 1987, stock market crash are a textbook case of how a lender-of-last-resort role can be performed brilliantly.[8] The Fed's action was immediate, with Greenspan announcing right before the market opened on October 20 of the Federal Reserve System's "readiness to serve as a source of liquidity to support the economic and financial system," which operated to decrease uncertainty in the marketplace. Reserves were injected into the system, but once the crisis was over, they were withdrawn. Not only was a crisis averted so that the business cycle expansion continued, but also the inflationary consequences of this exercise of the lender-of-last-resort role were small. The 75 basis point decrease in the federal funds rate in the Fall of 1998 immediately after the Russian financial crisis and the near-failure of Long-Term Capital Management, which roiled U.S. capital markets, also illustrated the Fed's commitment to act decisively to prevent financial instability. The aftermath was an economy that continued to expand, with inflation staying at the 2 percent level.

On the criteria of the commitment to the financial stability goal, the Fed's score is excellent.

2.5   Conclusion: What Should the Fed Do?

Our scorecard for the Fed indicates that although the institutional set up of the Fed scores well on some criteria, there is room for improvement in others. But, is there a need for the Fed as an institution to change? The Fed's performance in recent years has been extraordinary. It has been able to bring down inflation in the United States to the 2 percent level, which can reasonably be characterized as being consistent with price stability, while the economy has been experiencing the longest business cycle expansion in U.S. history, with very high rates of economic growth. As my son likes to say, "It don't get no better than this." The natural question then arises: If it ain't broke, why fix it?

However, our Fed scorecard suggests that we do need to consider institutional improvements in the way the central bank operates. The absence of an institutional commitment to price stability, along with weak Fed transparency, which stems from the absence of an explicit nominal anchor, leaves the Fed open to political pressure to pursue short-run objectives (i.e., job creation). This might lead to time-inconsistent expansionary policy and would produce inflation. In the past, after a successful period of low inflation, the Federal Reserve has "fallen off the wagon" and reverted to inflationary monetary policy—the 1970s are one example—and, without an explicit nominal anchor, this could certainly happen again in the future.

Indeed, the most serious problem with the Fed's institutional framework and the way it currently operates is the strong dependence on the preferences, skills, and trustworthiness of the individuals in charge of the central bank. Yes, the Fed under Alan Greenspan has been doing a great job, and so the Fed's prestige and credibility with the public have risen accordingly. But the Fed's leadership will eventually change, and there is no guarantee that the new leadership will be committed to the same approach. Nor is there any guarantee that the relatively good working relationship that now exists between the Fed and the executive branch will continue. In a different economic or political environment—and considering the possibility for a backlash against the Fed's lack of accountability—the Fed might face far stronger attacks on its independence and increased pressure to engage in over-expansionary policies, further raising the possibility that inflation will shoot up again.

So what should the Fed do? The answer is that the Fed should continue in the direction that it has already begun to increase its transparency and accountability. First, it should advocate a change in its mandate to put price stability as the overriding, long-run goal of monetary policy. Second, it should advocate that the price-stability goal should be made explicit, with a numerical long-run inflation goal. Government involvement in setting this explicit goal would be highly desirable, making the Fed goal independent, which should help retain public support for the Fed's instrument independence. Third, the Fed should produce an "Inflation Report" type of document that clearly explains its strategy for monetary policy and how well it has been doing in achieving its announced inflation goal.

The outcome of these changes is that the Fed would be moving to an inflation-targeting regime of the type described in our book, which has been recently published by the Princeton University Press (Bernanke, Laubach, Mishkin, and Posen, 1999). Clearly, the U.S. Congress and executive branch need to play an important role in encouraging the Fed to move toward inflation targeting. A detailed outline of a proposal for how this might be done can be found in our book. I leave you to read it on your own. Otherwise, you will be subjected to another full lecture.

Notes

This chapter was prepared for the Homer Jones Lecture, Federal Reserve Bank of St. Louis, March 30, 2000. I thank Dan Thornton, Bill Poole, Lars Svensson, and the participants in the Macro Lunch at Columbia University for their helpful comments. Any views expressed in this chapter are those of the author only and not those of Columbia University or the National Bureau of Economic Research.

1. E.g., see English (1996).

2. E.g., see Briault (1995).

3. E.g., see Fischer (1994) and Feldstein (1997).

4. See the survey in Andersen and Gruen (1995).

5. For further discussion of who should set an inflation target in the United States, see Bernanke, Laubach, Mishkin, and Posen (1999).

6. Blinder (1998) also makes a strong case for increased transparency and accountability of central banks.

7. The Eurosystem currently is made up of the eleven national central banks of the countries that have joined EMU, with the European Central Bank (ECB) at the center having a role similar to that of the Board of Governors in the Federal Reserve System.

8. Indeed, this example appears in my textbook (Mishkin, 1998).

References

Alesina, Alberto, and Lawrence H. Summers. "Central Bank Independence and Macroeconomic Performance: Some Comparative Evidence," *Journal of Money, Credit, and Banking* (May 1993), pp. 151–62.

Andersen, Palle, and David Gruen. "Macroeconomic Policies and Growth," in *Productivity and Growth*, Palle Andersen, Jacqueline Dwyer, and David Gruen, eds., Reserve Bank of Australia, 1995, pp. 279–319.

Barro, Robert J., and David Gordon. "A Positive Theory of Monetary Policy in a Natural Rate Model," *Journal of Political Economy* (August 1983), pp. 589–610.

Bernanke, Ben S. "Non-Monetary Effects of the Financial Crisis in the Propagation of the Great Depression," *American Economic Review* (March 1983), pp. 257–76.

———, "Comment on 'The Synergies Between Bank Supervision and Monetary Policy: Implications for the Design of Bank Regulatory Structure,'" in *Prudential Supervision: What Works and What Doesn't*, Frederic S. Mishkin, ed., University of Chicago Press, 2000.

———, Thomas Laubach, Frederic S. Mishkin, and Adam S. Posen. *Inflation Targeting: Lessons from the International Experience*, Princeton University Press, 1999.

Blinder, Alan S. *Central Banking in Theory and Practice*, MIT Press, 1998.

Briault, Clive. "The Costs of Inflation," *Bank of England Quarterly Bulletin* (February 1995), pp. 33–45.

Calvo, Guillermo. "On the Time Consistency of Optimal Policy in the Monetary Economy," *Econometrica* (November 1978), pp. 1411–28.

Corsetti, Giorgio, Paolo Pesenti, and Noriel Roubini. "What Caused the Asian Currency and Financial Crisis? Part I and II," NBER Working Papers, nos. 6833 and 6834, 1998.

Cukierman, Alex. *Central Bank Strategy, Credibility, and Independence: Theory and Evidence*, MIT Press, 1992.

Debelle, Guy, and Stanley Fischer. "How Independent Should a Central Bank Be?" in *Goals, Guidelines, and Constraints Facing Monetary Policymakers*, Jeffrey C. Fuhrer, ed., Federal Reserve Bank of Boston, 1994, pp. 195–221.

English, William B. "Inflation and Financial Sector Size," Finance and Economics Discussion Series No. 96-16, Board of Governors of the Federal Reserve System, April 1996.

Feldstein, Martin. "Capital Income Taxes and the Benefits of Price Stabilization," NBER Working Paper 6200, September 1997.

Fischer, Stanley. "Modern Central Banking," in *The Future of Central Banking*, Forrest Capie, Charles A. E. Goodhart, Stanley Fischer, and Norbert Schnadt, eds., Cambridge University Press, 1994, pp. 262–308.

Friedman, Milton, and Anna J. Schwartz. *A Monetary History of the United States, 1867–1960*, Princeton University Press, 1963.

King, Mervyn, "Changes in UK Monetary Policy: Rules and Discretion in Practice," *Journal of Monetary Economics*, (June 1997), pp. 81–97.

Kydland, Finn, and Edward Prescott. "Rules Rather than Discretion: The Inconsistency of Optimal Plans," *Journal of Political Economy* (June 1977), pp. 473–91.

McCallum, Bennett T. "Inflation: Theory and Evidence," in *Handbook of Monetary Economics*, Ben M. Friedman and Frank H. Hahn, eds., Elsevier Press, 1990, pp. 963–1012.

———. "Two Fallacies Concerning Central-Bank Independence," *American Economic Review* (May 1995), pp. 207–11.

Mishkin, Frederic S. "Asymmetric Information and Financial Crises: A Historical Perspective," in *Financial Markets and Financial Crises*, R. Glenn Hubbard, ed., University of Chicago Press, 1991, pp. 69–108.

———. "An Evaluation of the Treasury Plan for Banking Reform," *Journal of Economic Perspectives* (Winter 1992), pp. 133–53.

———. "Understanding Financial Crises: A Developing Country Perspective," in *Annual World Bank Conference on Development Economics*, 1996, pp. 29–62.

———. *The Economics of Money, Banking, and Financial Markets*, 5th ed., Addison-Wesley Publishing Co., 1998.

———. "Lessons from the Asian Crisis," *Journal of International Money and Finance* (August 1999a), pp. 709–23.

———. "International Experiences with Different Monetary Policy Regimes," *Journal of Monetary Economics* (June 1999b), pp. 579–605.

———, and Adam S. Posen. "Inflation Targeting: Lessons from Four Countries," *Economic Policy Review*, Federal Reserve Bank of New York (August 1997), pp. 9–110.

Peek, Joe, Eric Rosengren, and Geoffrey Tootell, "The Synergies Between Bank Supervision and Monetary Policy: Implications for the Design of Bank Regulatory Structure," in *Prudential Supervision: What Works and What Doesn't*, Frederic S. Mishkin, ed., University of Chicago Press, 2000.

Posen, Adam S. "Declarations Are Not Enough: Financial Sector Sources of Central Bank Independence," in *NBER Macroeconomics Annual*, Ben S. Bernanke and Julio J. Rotemberg, eds., MIT Press, 1995, pp. 253–74.

Rogoff, Kenneth. "The Optimal Degree of Commitment to an Intermediate Monetary Target," *Quarterly Journal of Economics* (November 1985), pp. 1169–89.

Sargent, Thomas, and Neil Wallace. "Some Unpleasant Monetarist Arithmetic," *Quarterly Review*, Federal Reserve Bank of Minneapolis (Fall 1981), pp. 1–17.

Svensson, Lars. "Inflation Targeting as Monetary Policy Rule," *Journal of Monetary Economics* (June 1999), pp. 607–54.

Taylor, John, ed. *Monetary Policy Rules*, University of Chicago Press, Chicago, 1999.

Woodford, Michael. "Monetary Policy and Price Level Determinacy in a Cash-in-Advance Economy," *Economic Theory*, vol. 4, no. 3 (1994), pp. 345–80.

———. "Price-Level Determinacy with Control of a Monetary Aggregate," *Carnegie-Rochester Conference Series on Public Policy* (December 1995), pp. 1–46.

3 The Transmission Mechanism and the Role of Asset Prices in Monetary Policy

Frederic S. Mishkin

Although the instrument set by monetary policymakers is typically an interest rate, monetary policy affects the economy through other asset prices besides those on debt instruments. Thus, movements in these other asset prices are likely to play an important role in how monetary policy is conducted. But what is the appropriate role for them to play? This chapter answers this question by first surveying the monetary transmission mechanism through these other asset prices and then discussing their role in the conduct of monetary policy.

3.1 Asset Prices in the Monetary Transmission Mechanism

In the literature on the monetary transmission mechanism, there are three categories of asset prices besides those on debt instruments that are viewed as providing important channels through which monetary policy affects the economy: 1) stock market prices, 2) real estate prices, and 3) exchange rates.

3.1.1 Stock Market Prices

Fluctuations of the stock market, which are influenced by monetary policy, have important impacts on the aggregate economy. Transmission mechanisms involving the stock market are of three types: 1) stock market effects on investment, 2) firm balance-sheet effects, 3) household liquidity effects and 4) household wealth effects.

Stock Market Effects on Investment Tobin's q-theory (Tobin, 1969) provides an important mechanism for how movements in stock prices can affect the economy. Tobin's q is defined as the market value of firms divided by the replacement cost of capital. If q is high, the market price of firms is high relative to the replacement cost of capital, and new plant and equipment capital is cheap relative to the market value of firms. Companies can then issue stock and get a high price for it relative to the cost of the facilities and equipment they are buying. Investment spending will rise because firms can now buy a lot of new investment goods with only a small issue of stock.

The crux of the Tobin q-model is that a link exists between stock prices and investment spending. But how might monetary policy affect stock prices? Expansionary monetary policy which lowers interest rates makes bonds less attractive relative to stocks and results in increased demand for stocks that bids up their price. Combining this with the fact that higher stock prices will lead to higher investment spending, leads to the following transmission mechanism of monetary policy which can be described by the following schematic:

$$M \uparrow \Rightarrow P_s \uparrow \Rightarrow q \uparrow \Rightarrow I \uparrow \Rightarrow Y \uparrow \qquad\qquad (3.1)$$

where $M \uparrow$ indicates expansionary monetary policy, leading to a rise in stock prices $(P_s \uparrow)$, which raises q $(q \uparrow)$, which raises investment $(I \uparrow)$, thereby leading to an increase in aggregate demand and a rise in output $(Y \uparrow)$.

Another way of getting to this same mechanism is by recognizing that firms not only finance investment through bonds but also by issuing equities (common stock). When stock prices rise, it now becomes cheaper for firms to finance their investment because each share that is issued produces more funds. Thus a rise in stock prices leads to increased investment spending. Therefore, an alternative description of this mechanism is that expansionary monetary policy $(M \uparrow)$ which raises stock prices $(P_s \uparrow)$ lowers the cost of capital $(c \downarrow)$ and so causes investment and output to rise $(I \uparrow, Y \uparrow)$.[1] In other words:

$$M \uparrow \Rightarrow P_s \uparrow \Rightarrow c \downarrow \Rightarrow I \uparrow \Rightarrow Y \uparrow \qquad\qquad (3.1')$$

Firm Balance-Sheet Effects   The presence of asymmetric information problems in credit markets provides another transmission mechanism for monetary policy that operates through stock prices. This mechanism is often referred to as the "credit view," and it works through the effect of stock prices on firms's balance sheets so it is also referred to as the balance-sheet channel.[2]

The lower the net worth of business firms, the more severe is the adverse selection and moral hazard problems in lending to these firms. Lower net worth means that there is effectively less collateral for the loans made to a firm and so potential losses from adverse selection are higher. A decline in net worth, which increases the severity of the adverse selection problem, thus leads to decreased lending to finance investment spending. The lower net worth of business firms also increases the moral hazard problem because it means that owners of firms have a lower equity stake, giving them greater incentives to engage in risky investment projects. Since taking on riskier investment projects makes it more likely that lenders will not be paid back, a decrease in net worth leads to a decrease in lending and hence in investment spending.

Monetary policy can affect firms' balance sheets and aggregate spending through the following mechanism. Expansionary monetary policy (M ↑), which causes a rise in stock prices (P_s ↑) along lines described earlier, raises the new worth of firms (NW ↑), which reduces adverse selection and moral hazard problems, and so leads to higher lending (L ↑). Higher lending then leads to higher investment spending (I ↑) and aggregate spending (Y ↑). This leads to the following schematic for this balance-sheet channel of monetary transmission.

$$M \uparrow \Rightarrow P_s \uparrow \Rightarrow NW \uparrow \Rightarrow L \uparrow \Rightarrow I \uparrow \Rightarrow Y \uparrow \tag{3.2}$$

Household Liquidity Effects   Another way of looking at balance-sheet channels of monetary transmission is to look at household balance sheets, particularly liquidity effects on consumer durable and housing expenditures.[3] In the liquidity effects view, balance sheet effects work through their impact on consumer's desire to spend rather than on lender's desire to lend. Because of asymmetric information about their quality, consumer durables and housing are very illiquid assets. If, as a result of a bad income shock, consumers needed to sell their consumer durables or housing to raise money, they would expect a big loss because they could not get the full value of these assets in a distress sale. In contrast, if consumers held financial assets (such as money in the bank, stocks, or bonds), they could easily sell them quickly for their full market value and raise the cash. Hence if consumers expect a higher likelihood of finding themselves in financial distress, they would rather be holding fewer illiquid consumer durable or housing assets and more liquid financial assets.

A consumer's balance sheet should be an important influence on his or her estimate of the likelihood of suffering financial distress. Specifically, when consumers have a large amount of financial assets relative to their debts, their estimate of the probability of financial distress is low, and they will be more willing to purchase consumer durables or housing. When stock prices rise, the value of financial assets rises as well; consumer durable expenditure will also rise because consumers have a more secure financial position and a lower estimate of the likelihood of suffering financial distress. This leads to another transmission mechanism for monetary policy, operating through the link between money and stock prices:

$$M \uparrow \Rightarrow P_s \uparrow \Rightarrow \text{Financial Assets} \uparrow \Rightarrow$$

$$\text{Likelihood of Financial Distress} \downarrow \Rightarrow C_d \uparrow, H \uparrow \Rightarrow Y \uparrow \tag{3.3}$$

where C_d ↑ indicates a rise in consumer durable expenditure and H ↑ a rise in residential housing spending.

Household Wealth Effects   Another balance-sheet channel operating through the consumer involves household wealth effects. Modigliani's life cycle model states that consumption is determined by the lifetime resources of consumers. An important component of consumers' lifetime resources is their financial wealth, a major component of which is common stocks. Thus expansionary monetary policy which raises stock prices, raises the value of household wealth, thereby increasing the lifetime resources of consumers, which causes consumption to rise. This produces the following transmission mechanism:

$$M \uparrow \Rightarrow P_s \uparrow \Rightarrow W \uparrow \Rightarrow C \uparrow \Rightarrow Y \uparrow \tag{3.4}$$

where $W \uparrow$ and $C \uparrow$ indicate household wealth and consumption rises. Research has found this transmission mechanism to be quite strong in the United States, but the size of the wealth effect is still controversial.[4]

3.1.2 Real Estate Prices

Another set of asset prices that play an important role in the monetary transmission mechanism are real estate prices. Real estate prices can affect aggregate demand through three routes: 1) direct effects on housing expenditure, 2) household wealth, and 3) bank balance sheets.

Direct Effects on Housing Expenditure   Monetary expansion ($M \uparrow$), which lowers interest rates, lowers the cost of financing housing and so increases their price ($P_h \uparrow$). With a higher price of housing relative to its construction cost, construction firms find it more profitable to build housing, and thus housing expenditure will rise ($H \uparrow$) and so aggregate demand will rise ($Y \uparrow$).[5] This transmission mechanism is then described by the following schematic.

$$M \uparrow \Rightarrow P_h \uparrow \Rightarrow H \uparrow \Rightarrow Y \uparrow \tag{3.5}$$

Household Wealth Effects   Housing prices are an important component of household wealth, which as we have seen, affects consumption spending. Hence, expansionary monetary policy ($M \uparrow$), which raises housing prices ($P_h \uparrow$), also raises household wealth ($W \uparrow$), which raises consumption spending ($C \uparrow$) and aggregate demand ($Y \uparrow$): i.e.,

$$M \uparrow \Rightarrow P_h \uparrow \Rightarrow W \uparrow \Rightarrow C \uparrow \Rightarrow Y \uparrow \tag{3.6}$$

Bank Balance Sheets   The credit view of the monetary transmission mechanism suggests that banks play a special role in the financial system because they are especially well suited to solve asymmetric information problems in credit markets. Certain borrowers will then not have access to the credit markets unless they borrow from banks.[6] Banks engage in a substantial amount of real estate lending, in which the value of the real estate acts as collateral. If real estate prices rise as a result of monetary expansion, then banks' loan losses will decrease, which increases their bank capital. Higher bank capital then allows banks to engage in more lending, and because banks are special, with many customers dependent on them, investment and aggregate demand will rise. The bank balance-sheet channel thus can be described as follows:

$$M \uparrow \Rightarrow P_r \uparrow \Rightarrow NW_b \uparrow \Rightarrow L \uparrow \Rightarrow I \uparrow \Rightarrow Y \uparrow \tag{3.7}$$

where expansionary monetary policy ($M \uparrow$), which raises real estate prices ($P_r \uparrow$), raises bank capital ($NW_b \uparrow$) and causes bank lending to rise ($L \uparrow$), thereby causing investment and output to rise ($I \uparrow$ and $Y \uparrow$).

When the opposite happens and real estate prices fall, this transmission mechanism has often been described as a "capital crunch" and was operational in the United States in the early 1990s (Bernanke and Lown, 1991) and has been an important source of stagnation in Japan in recent years.

3.1.3 Exchange Rates

There are two primary mechanisms that operate through exchange rates: 1) exchange rate effects on net exports and 2) exchange rate effects on balance sheets.

Exchange Rate Effects on Net Exports   With the growing internationalization of economies throughout the world and the advent of flexible exchange rates, more attention has been paid to how monetary policy affects exchange rates, which in turn affect net exports and aggregate output. Clearly this channel does not operate if a country has a fixed exchange rate, and the more open an economy is, the stronger is this channel.

Expansionary monetary policy affects exchange rates because when it leads to a fall in domestic interest rates, deposits denominated in domestic currency become less attractive relative to deposits denominated in foreign currencies. As a result, the value of domestic deposits relative to other currency deposits falls, and the exchange rate depreciates (denoted by $E \downarrow$).[7] The lower value of the domestic currency makes domestic goods cheaper than foreign goods, thereby causing a rise in net exports ($NX \uparrow$) and hence in aggregate spending ($Y \uparrow$). The schematic for the monetary transmission mechanism that operates through the exchange rate is:

$$M \uparrow \Rightarrow E \downarrow \Rightarrow NX \uparrow \Rightarrow Y \uparrow \tag{3.8}$$

Exchange Rate Effects on Balance Sheets   Fluctuations in exchange rates also can have important effects on aggregate demand by affecting the balance sheets of both financial and nonfinancial firms when a substantial amount of domestic debt is denominated in foreign currency, which is the case for most emerging market countries. In these countries, monetary expansion often can have a negative impact on aggregate demand if it leads to a depreciation of the exchange rate through the following mechanism.

With debt contracts denominated in foreign currency, expansionary monetary policy (M ↑) which leads to a depreciation or devaluation of the domestic currency (E ↓) results in the debt burden of domestic nonfinancial firms to increase. Since assets are typically denominated in domestic currency and so do not increase in value, there is a resulting decline in net worth (NW ↓). This deterioration in balance sheets then increases adverse selection and moral hazard problems, which as discussed above, leads to a decline in lending (L ↓), a decline in investment (I ↓) and hence in economic activity (Y ↓). The schematic for this transmission mechanism is as follows:

$$M \uparrow \Rightarrow E \downarrow \Rightarrow NW \downarrow \Rightarrow L \downarrow \Rightarrow I \downarrow \Rightarrow Y \downarrow \tag{3.9}$$

This mechanism was very important in the recent financial crises in Mexico and East Asia.[8] For example, this mechanism was particularly strong in Indonesia, the worst hit of all the crisis countries, which saw the value of its currency decline by over 75 percent, thus increasing the rupiah value of foreign-denominated debt by a factor of four. Even a healthy firm is likely to be driven into insolvency by such a shock if it had a significant amount of foreign-denominated debt, and then no one will lend to it even if it has productive investment opportunities.

A second mechanism through which an exchange rate depreciation can lead to a decline in aggregate demand in emerging markets operates through deterioration of bank balance sheets. For example, in Mexico and the East Asian countries, banks and many other financial institutions had many liabilities denominated in foreign currency, which increased sharply in value when a depreciation occurred. On the other hand, the problems of firms and households meant that they were unable to pay off their debt, also resulting in loan losses on the asset side of financial institutions' balance sheets. The result was that banks' and other financial institutions' balance sheets were squeezed from both the assets and liabilities side. Moreover, many of these institutions' foreign-currency denominated debt was very short term, so that the sharp increase in the value of this debt led to liquidity problems because this debt needed to be paid back quickly. The result of the further deterioration in banks' and other financial institutions' balance sheets and their weakened capital base is that they cut back lending. In the case of Indonesia, these forces were severe enough to cause a banking panic in which numerous banks were forced to go out of business.

The effect of depreciations on bank balance sheets implies that expansionary monetary policy (M ↑) may actually be contractionary in emerging market countries by causing bank balance sheets to deteriorate (NW_b ↓), and bank lending to fall (L ↓), which then causes investment and aggregate output to fall (I ↓ and Y ↓): i.e.,

$$M \uparrow \Rightarrow E \downarrow \Rightarrow NW_b \downarrow \Rightarrow L \downarrow \Rightarrow I \downarrow \Rightarrow Y \downarrow \qquad (3.10)$$

It is important to note that the possible contractionary effects from expansionary monetary policy operating through exchange rate effects on balance sheets only operate if the economy has a substantial amount of debt denominated in foreign currency. These mechanisms are thus rarely important in industrialized countries whose debt is typically denominated in domestic currency, but they can be very important in emerging market countries whose debt structure may be entirely different, with much of the debt denominated in foreign currency.

3.2   The Role of Asset Prices in Monetary Policy

The survey in the previous section suggests that monetary policy works not just through its direct effects on interest rates, but also through its effects on other asset prices. Since other asset prices are an important element of the monetary transmission mechanism, how can monetary policymakers incorporate movements of these asset prices into their decisions about the conduct of monetary policy?

In looking at the role of asset prices in monetary policy, it is worth separating the discussion into how central banks might respond to exchange rates and how they might respond to fluctuations in stock market and real estate prices.

3.2.1   Exchange Rates

The asset price that typically receives the most attention in discussions of monetary policy is the exchange rate. Central banks clearly care about the value of the domestic currency for several reasons. Changes in the exchange rate can have a major impact on inflation, particularly in small, open economies. For example, depreciations lead to a rise in inflation as a result of the pass-through from higher import prices and greater demand for net exports, as discussed in the previous section. In addition, the public and politicians pay attention to the exchange rate and this puts pressure on the central bank to alter monetary policy. An appreciation of the domestic currency can make domestic businesses uncompetitive, while a depreciation is often seen as a failure of the central bank, as has recently been the case for the European Central Bank, which has been blamed, I think unfairly, for the euro's decline.

Emerging market countries, quite correctly, have an even greater concern about exchange rate movements. Not only can a real appreciation make domestic industries less competitive, but it can lead to large current account deficits which might make the country more vulnerable to currency crisis if capital inflows turn to outflows. Depreciations in emerging market countries are particularly dangerous because they can be contractionary, as described in the previous section, and can trigger a financial crisis along the lines suggested in Mishkin (1996, 1999a).

Concern about exchange rate fluctuations might lead countries to choose to peg their exchange rates to that of another country. In other work, I have discussed the pros and cons of pegging exchange rates as a monetary policy strategy and I will not discuss this issue further.[9] However, if a country decides that it wants to have its own independent monetary policy, then with open capital markets it has to allow the exchange rate to fluctuate. However, the fact that exchange rate fluctuations are a major concern in so many countries raises the danger that monetary policy may put too much focus on limiting exchange rate movements. This indeed was a problem for Israel in the early stages of its inflation targeting regime. As part of this regime, Israel had an intermediate target of an exchange rate band around a crawling peg, whose rate of crawl was set in a forward-looking manner by deriving it from the inflation target for the coming year. Even though the Bank of Israel downplayed the exchange rate target relative to the inflation target over time, it did slow the Bank's effort to win support for disinflation and lowering of the inflation targets (e.g., see Bernanke, Laubach, Mishkin and Posen, 1999).

The second problem from a focus on limiting exchange rate fluctuations is that it can induce the wrong policy response when a country is faced with real shocks such as a terms of trade shock. Two graphic examples occurred in New Zealand and Chile in the late 1990s.

Because of the direct impact of exchange rates on inflation, the Reserve Bank of New Zealand tended to focus on the exchange rate as an indicator of the monetary policy stance. By early 1997, the Reserve Bank institutionalized this focus by adopting as its primary indicator of monetary policy a Monetary Conditions Index (MCI) similar to that developed by the Bank of Canada. The idea behind the MCI, which is a weighted average of the exchange rate and a short-term interest rate, is that both interest rates and exchange rates on average have offsetting impacts on inflation. When the exchange rate falls, this usually leads to higher inflation in the future, and so interest rates need to rise to offset the upward pressure on inflation. However, the offsetting effects of interest rates and exchange rates on inflation depend on the nature of the shocks to the exchange rates. If the exchange rate depreciation comes from portfolio considerations, then it does lead to higher inflation and the optimal response is an interest rate rise. However, if the reason for the exchange rate depreciation is a real shock such as a negative terms of trade shock which decreases the demand for a country's exports, then the situation is entirely different. The negative terms of trade shock reduces aggregate demand and is thus likely to be deflationary. The correct interest rate response is then a decline in interest rates, not a rise as the MCI suggests.

With the negative terms of trade shock in 1997, the adoption of the MCI in 1997 led to exactly the wrong monetary policy response to the East Asian crisis. With depreciation setting in after the crisis began in July 1997 after the devaluation of the

Thai baht, the MCI began a sharp decline, indicating that the Reserve Bank needed to raise interest rates, which it did by over 200 basis points. The result was very tight monetary policy, with the overnight cash rate exceeding 9% by June of 1998. Because the depreciation was due to a substantial, negative terms of trade shock which decreased aggregate demand, the tightening of monetary policy, not surprisingly, led to a severe recession and an undershoot of the inflation target range with actual deflation occurring in 1999.[10] The Reserve Bank of New Zealand did eventually re-alize its mistake and reversed course, sharply lowering interest rates beginning in July 1998 after the economy had entered a recession, but by then it was too late. It also recognized the problems with using an MCI as an indicator of monetary policy and abandoned it in 1999. Now the Reserve Bank operates monetary policy in a more conventional way, using the overnight cash rate as its policy instrument, with far less emphasis on the exchange rate in its monetary policy decisions.

Chile, which also adopted inflation targeting in the early 1990s, also included a focus on limiting exchange rate fluctuations by having an exchange rate band with a crawling peg which was (loosely) tied to lagged domestic inflation.[11] This focus on the exchange rate induced a serious policy mistake in 1998 because the central bank was afraid it might lose credibility in the face of the financial turmoil if it allowed the exchange rate to depreciate after what had taken place in financial markets after the East Asian crisis and the Russian meltdown. Thus instead of easing monetary policy in the face of the negative terms of trade shock, the central bank raised interest rates sharply and even narrowed its exchange rate band. In hindsight, these decisions ap-pear to have been a mistake: the inflation target was undershot and the economy entered a recession for the first time in the 1990s. With this outcome, the central bank came under strong criticism for the first time since it had adopted its inflation targeting regime in 1990, weakening support for the independence of the central bank and its inflation targeting regime. During 1999, the central bank did reverse course, easing monetary policy by lowering interest rates and allowing the peso to decline.

The contrast of the experience of New Zealand and Chile during this period with that of Australia, another small open economy with an inflation targeting regime, is striking. Prior to adoption of their inflation targeting regime in 1994, the Reserve Bank of Australia had adopted a policy of allowing the exchange rate to fluctuate without interference, particularly if the source of the exchange rate change was a real shock, like a terms of trade shock. Thus when faced with the devaluation in Thailand in July 1997, the Reserve Bank recognized that it would face a substantial negative terms of trade shock because of the large component of its foreign trade conducted with the Asian region and thus decided that it would not fight the depre-ciation of the Australian dollar that would inevitably result.[12] Thus in contrast to New Zealand, it immediately lowered the overnight cash rate by 50 basis points to

5% and kept it near this level until the end of 1998, when it was lowered again by another 25 basis points.

Indeed, the adoption of the inflation targeting regime probably helped the Reserve Bank of Australia to be even more aggressive in its easing in response to the East Asian crisis and helps explain why their response was so rapid. The Reserve Bank was able to make clear that easing was exactly what inflation targeting called for in order to prevent an undershooting of the target, so that the easing was unlikely to have an adverse effect on inflation expectations. The outcome of the Reserve Bank's policy actions was extremely favorable. In contrast to New Zealand and Chile, real output growth remained strong throughout this period. Furthermore, there were no negative consequences for inflation despite the substantial depreciation of the Australian dollar against the U.S. dollar by close to 20%: inflation remained under control, actually falling during this period to end up slightly under the target range of 2 to 3%.

The analysis above and the recent experiences of countries like New Zealand, Chile and Australia strongly suggest that central banks' concerns about the exchange rate is not a reason for them to stop keeping their eyes on the inflation ball.

Is a focus on achieving the inflation goal inconsistent with central banks paying some attention to the exchange rate? Of course not. As we have seen in the previous section, an important transmission mechanism for monetary policy is the exchange rate and its level has important effects on inflation and aggregate demand depending on the nature of the shocks, particularly in small, open economies. Therefore, central banks will closely monitor exchange rate developments and factor them into its decisions on setting monetary policy instruments. A depreciation of the exchange rate due to portfolio shocks like terms of trade shocks requires a tightening of monetary policy in order to keep inflation from rising. On the other hand, a depreciation when there is a negative terms of trade shock requires a different response, an easing of monetary policy as Australia did in 1997.

Does the avoidance of a target for the exchange rate imply a policy of benign neglect of exchange rates? This issue is particularly relevant for emerging market countries as is emphasized in Mishkin (2000) and Mishkin and Savastano (2001). For the reasons discussed earlier, emerging market countries with a lot of foreign-denominated debt may not be able to afford sharp depreciations of their currencies, which can destroy balance sheets and trigger a sharp fall in aggregate demand. Central banks in these countries may thus have to smooth "excessive" exchange rate fluctuations, while making it clear to the public that they will not preclude the exchange rate from reaching its market-determined level over longer horizons. The stated rationale for exchange rate smoothing is similar to that of interest-rate smoothing, which is practiced by most central banks, even those engaged in inflation targeting: the policy is not aimed at resisting market-determined movements in an asset price, but at mitigating potentially destabilizing effects of abrupt changes in that price.

3.2.2 Stock and Real Estate Prices

With the bursting of the stock market and real estate bubble in Japan at the beginning of the 1990s and the recent stock market boom (and partial reversal) in the United States, there has been a growing debate about how the monetary authorities might best react to stock market and real estate fluctuations.[13] This section will argue that the reaction to these asset prices raises similar issues to the reaction to exchange rate fluctuations. Improved economic performance will result if the policy response depends on the nature of the shocks, while the central bank is not perceived as having a target for any asset price, whether it is an exchange rate, or stock market or real estate prices.

The discussion of the monetary transmission mechanism in the previous section indicates that real estate and stock price movement do have an important impact on aggregate demand and thus must be followed closely to evaluate the stance of monetary policy. Indeed, with a standard loss function in which the central bank minimizes a weighted average of squared deviations of inflation from its target level and output from potential output, optimal monetary policy will react to changes in real estate and stock market prices. However, depending on the nature of the shock to these prices, and depending on whether the shock is considered to be temporary or permanent, the optimal response of monetary policy would differ. Thus, just as targets for exchange rates would be problematic, so too would targets for real estate and stock prices.

But this still begs the question of whether monetary authorities can improve their performance by trying to prick asset price bubbles, because subsequent collapses of these asset prices might be highly damaging to the economy, as they were in Japan in the 1990s. Cecchetti, Genburg, Lipsky and Wadhwani (1999), for example, argue that central banks should at times target asset prices in order to stop bubbles from getting too far out of hand. However, there are serious flaws in their argument. First is that it is very hard for monetary authorities to identify that a bubble has actually developed. To assume that they can is to assume that the monetary authorities have better information and predictive ability than the private sector. If the central bank has no informational advantage, and if it knows that a bubble has developed that will eventually crash, then the market knows this too and then the bubble would unravel and thus would be unlikely to develop. Without an informational advantage, the central bank is as likely to mispredict the presence of a bubble as the private market and thus will frequently be mistaken, thus frequently pursuing the wrong monetary policy. Cecchetti, Genburg, Lipski and Wadhwani (1999) find favorable results in their simulations when the central bank conducts policy to prick an asset price bubble because they assume that the central bank knows the bubble is in progress. This assumption is highly dubious because it is hard to believe that the central bank has this kind of informational advantage over private markets. Indeed, the view that government officials know better than the markets has been proved wrong over and over again.

A second problem with the central bank targeting stock prices is that it is likely to make the central bank look foolish. The linkage between monetary policy and stock prices, although an important part of the transmission mechanism, is still neverthe-less a weak one. Most fluctuations in stock prices occur for reasons unrelated to monetary policy, either reflecting real fundamentals or animal spirits. The loose link between monetary policy and stock prices therefore means that the ability of the cen-tral bank to control stock prices is very limited. Thus, if the central bank indicates that it wants stock prices to change in a particular direction, it is likely to find that stock prices may move in the opposite direction, thus making the central bank look inept. Recall that when Alan Greenspan made his speech in 1997 suggesting that the stock market might be exhibiting "irrational exuberance," the Dow Jones average was around 6,500. This didn't stop the market from rising, with the Dow subse-quently climbing to above 11,000.

An additional problem with targeting asset prices is that it may weaken support for a central bank because it looks like it is trying to control too many elements of the economy. Part of the recent successes of central banks throughout the world has been that they have narrowed their focus and have more actively communicated what they can and cannot do. Specifically, central banks have argued that they are less capable of managing short-run business cycle fluctuation and should therefore focus more on price stability as their primary goal. A key element of the success of the Bundesbank's monetary targeting regime was that it did not focus on short-run output fluctuation in setting its monetary policy instruments.[14] This communication strategy for the Bundesbank has been very successful, as pointed out in Bernanke, Laubach, Mishkin and Posen (1999), and has been adopted as a key element in infla-tion targeting, a monetary regime that has been gaining in popularity in recent years. By narrowing their focus, central banks in recent years have been able to increase public support for their independence.[15] Extending their focus to asset prices has the potential to weaken public support for central banks and may even cause the public to worry that the central bank is too powerful, having undue influence over all aspects of the economy.

3.3   Conclusions

The discussion in this chapter shows that other asset prices, and not just interest rates, are important elements of the monetary transmission mechanism. This provides a rationale for why monetary authorities pay a lot of attention to these other asset prices in the conduct of monetary policy. However, this chapter has also argued that targeting other asset prices, whether they are exchange rates, real estate or stock market prices, is likely to worsen the performance of monetary policy. This is because the response of monetary policy to asset price fluctuations depends on the nature of the shocks to asset prices and the degree of permanence of the shocks. Furthermore, targeting asset prices is likely to erode support for the independence of central banks because control of these asset prices is beyond central banks' capabilities.

Notes

Prepared for the Oesterrische Nationalbank conference on "The Monetary Transmission Mechanism," November 9, 2001. The views expressed herein are those of the authors and not necessarily those of the National Bureau of Economic Research.

1. See Bosworth (1975) and Hayashi (1982) for a demonstration that this alternative description of the link between stock prices and investment is equivalent to the Tobin's q-approach.

2. For surveys on the credit view, see Bernanke and Gertler (1995), Cecchetti (1995), Hubbard (1995, 2001) and Bernake, Gertler and Gilchrist (1999).

3. See Mishkin (1976, 1977).

4. See Modigliani (1971) and Lettau, Ludvigson and Steindel (2002).

5. This model of housing expenditure is really a variant of Tobin's q-theory in which q for housing investment is the price of housing relative to its replacement cost. For a recent empirical analysis of a model of this type, see McCarthy and Peach (2002).

6. See Kashyap and Stein (1994) and Gertler and Gilchrist (1994).

7. In the literature, a depreciation of the currency is typically denoted as $e \uparrow$, but I have used the notation $E \downarrow$ because I think it is more intuitive.

8. For example, see Mishkin (1996, 1999a).

9. See Mishkin (1999b) and Mishkin and Savastano (2001).

10. The terms of trade shock, however, was not the only negative shock the New Zealand economy faced during that period. Its farm sector experienced a severe drought which also hurt the economy. Thus, a mistake in monetary policy was not the only source of the recession. Bad luck played a role too. See Drew and Orr (1999) and Brash (2000).

11. See Landerretche, Morandé and Schmidt-Hebbel (1999), and Mishkin and Savastano (2001).

12. See MacFarlane (1999) and Stevens (1999).

13. For example, see Cecchetti, Genburg, Lipsky and Wadwani (1999) and Bernanke and Gertler (1999).

14. See Bernanke, Laubach, Mishkin and Posen (1999).

15. See Mishkin (1999b) and Bernanke, Laubach, Mishkin and Posen (1999).

References

Bernanke, Ben S., Thomas Laubach, Frederic S. Mishkin and Adam S. Posen. 1999. *Inflation Targeting: Lessons from the International Experience*, Princeton, NJ: Princeton University Press.

Bernanke, Ben S., and Mark Gertler. 1995. "Inside the Black Box: The Credit Channel of Monetary Policy Transmission," *Journal of Economic Perspectives*, Fall, 9, 27–48.

Bernanke, Ben S., and Mark Gertler. 1999. "Monetary Policy and Asset Price Volatility," in *New Challenges for Monetary Policy*, Federal Reserve Bank of Kansas City: Kansas City.

Bernanke, Ben S., Mark Gertler and Simon Gilchrist. 1999. "The Financial Accelerator in a Quantitative Business Cycle Framework," in John Taylor and Michael Woodford, eds., *Handbook of Macroeconomics*, vol. 10 (Elsevier: Amsterdam): 1341–1393.

Bernanke, B. S., and C. Lown. 1991. "The Credit Crunch," *Brookings Papers on Economic Activity*, 2, pp. 205–39.

Bosworth, Barry. 1975. "The Stock Market and the Economy," *Brookings Papers on Economic Activity* 2, 257–90.

Brash, Donald T. 2000. "Inflation Targeting in New Zealand, 1988–2000," Speech to the Trans-Tasman Business Cycle, Melbourne, February 9.

Cecchetti, Stephen G. 1995. "Distinguishing Theories of the Monetary Transmission Mechanism," Federal Reserve Bank of St. Louis *Review*, May/June, 77, 83–97.

Cecchetti, Stephen G., Hans Genburg, John Lipski and Sushil Wadhwani. 2000. *Asset Prices and Central Bank Policy*, Geneva Reports on the World Economy (International Center for Monetary and Banking Studies and Centre for Economic Policy Research, London).

Drew, Aaron, and Adrian Orr. 1999. "The Reserve Bank's Role in the Recent Business Cycle: Actions and Evolution," *Reserve Bank of New Zealand Bulletin*, 62, No. 1.

Gertler, Mark, and Simon Gilchrist. 1994. "Monetary Policy, Business Cycles and the Behavior of Small Manufacturing Firms," *Quarterly Journal of Economics* 109, 309–340.

Hayashi, Fumio. 1982. "Tobin's Marginal q and Average q: A Neoclassical Interpretation," *Econometrica*, vol. 50, #1: 213–24.

Hubbard, R. Glenn. 1995. "Is There a 'Credit Channel' for Monetary Policy?" Federal Reserve Bank of St. Louis *Review*, May/June, 77, 63–74.

Hubbard, R. Glenn. 2001. "Capital Market Imperfections, Investment, and the Monetary Transmission Mechanism," in Deutsche Bundesbank, ed., *Investing Today for the World of Tomorrow* (Springer-Verlag: New York): 165–194.

Kashyap, Anil K., and Jeremy C. Stein. 1994. "Monetary Policy and Bank Lending," in N. G. Mankiw, ed., *Monetary Policy* (University of Chicago Press; Chicago).

Landerretche, O., F. Morandé and K. Schmidt-Hebbel. 1999. "Inflation Targets and Stabilization in Chile," Central Bank of Chile, Working Paper 55, December.

Lettau, Martin, Sydney Ludvigson and Charles Steindel. 2002. "Monetary Policy Transmission Through the Consumption-Wealth Channel," in Federal Reserve Bank of New York, *Economic Policy Review* (May): 117–133.

Macfarlane, Ian J. 1999. "Statement to Parliamentary Committee," in *Reserve Bank of Australia Bulletin*, January: 16–20.

McCarthy, Jonathan, and Richard W. Peach. 2002. "Monetary Policy Transmission to Residential Investment," in Federal Reserve Bank of New York, *Economic Policy Review* (May): 139–158.

Mishkin, Frederic S. 1976. "Illiquidity, Consumer Durable Expenditure, and Monetary Policy," *American Economic Review*, 66 No. 4 (September): 642–654.

Mishkin, Frederic S. 1977. "What Depressed the Consumer? The Household Balance-Sheet and the 1973–75 Recession," *Brookings Paper on Economic Activity* 1: 123–164.

Mishkin, Frederic S. 1996. "Understanding Financial Crises: A Developing Country Perspective," in Michael Bruno and Boris Pleskovic, eds., *Annual World Bank Conference on Development Economics*, World Bank, Washington D.C.: 29–62.

Mishkin, Frederic S. 1999a. "Lessons from the Asian Crisis," *Journal of International Money and Finance*, 18, 4: 709–723.

Mishkin, Frederic S. 1999b. "International Experiences with Different Monetary Policy Regimes," *Journal of Monetary Economics*, Vol. 43, #3: 579–606.

Mishkin, Frederic S. 2000. "Inflation Targeting in Emerging Market Countries," *American Economic Review* (May), Vol. 90, #2.

Mishkin, F., and M. Savastano. 2001. "Monetary Policy Strategies for Latin America," *Journal of Development Economics*, October.

Modigliani, Franco. 1971. "Monetary Policy and Consumption," in *Consumer Spending and Monetary Policy: The Linkages*, Boston: Federal Reserve Bank of Boston, 9–84.

Stevens, Glenn R. 1999. "Six Years of Inflation Targeting," *Reserve Bank of Australia Bulletin*, May: 46–61.

Tobin, James. 1969. "A General Equilibrium Approach to Monetary Theory," *Journal of Money, Credit, and Banking*, February, 1, 15–29.

4   The Role of Output Stabilization in the Conduct of Monetary Policy

Frederic S. Mishkin

4.1   Introduction

In recent years, central banks have increased their focus on price stability, so much so that price stability could be characterized as the central bank mantra. However, the public, politicians and central banks also care about the business cycle. What role does this suggest output stabilization should have in the conduct of monetary policy?

Because standard formulations of the objectives of monetary policy indicate that monetary policy aim at minimizing inflation and output fluctuations, the seemingly obvious answer is that monetary policy which is optimal focuses on output as well as inflation fluctuations. Indeed, the famous Taylor rule suggests exactly this, indicating that the monetary policy authorities should set their interest-rate instrument so that it reacts to deviations of output from its potential as well as to deviations of inflation from its target. However, this chapter will argue that this answer is unlikely to be the correct one.

The chapter makes the following arguments:

1. Too great a focus on output fluctuations may produce undesirable outcomes: greater fluctuations of output and inflation around their targets.

2. On the other hand, monetary policy that targets inflation is likely to produce better outcomes for both output and inflation fluctuations.

3. In addition, language which stresses output goals can make a central bank's communication strategy less effective and can, thereby, weaken monetary policy credibility.

4. A communication strategy that, instead, focuses on the control of inflation, is likely to make it easier for the monetary policy authorities to focus on the long run, thereby enhancing monetary policy credibility.

The fact that, in practice, it may be extremely difficult to obtain accurate measures of the output gap, the difference of actual from potential output, provides one rationale for the first two arguments. However, the first two and the remaining arguments are valid even if accurate measures of the output gap could be obtained. This analysis then leads to the following conclusion: despite monetary policy makers' concerns about the business cycle, they will be far more successful in reducing output and inflation fluctuations if they focus less directly on output stabilization and more on inflation stabilization. However, the fact that monetary policy makers downplay the importance of output in their operating procedure does not mean that they are unconcerned about output fluctuations, and there are ways for them to communicate this effectively.

4.2 Output Fluctuations and the Setting of Monetary Policy Instruments in a Simple Canonical Model

To clarify the discussion of the role of output fluctuations in the setting of monetary policy instruments, I will make use of a simple, canonical model outlined in Svensson (1997). Despite this model's simplicity, it does capture the basic framework that is often used in monetary policy analysis. Furthermore, more complicated models and those with more forward-looking behaviour such as the dynamic new Keynesian model in Clarida et al. (1999) yield similar conclusions to those outlined here.[1] The canonical model comprises an aggregate supply curve in which the change in inflation is affected by the output gap with a 1-period (1-year) lag:

$$\pi_t = \pi_{t-1} + \gamma y_{t-1} + \varepsilon_t \tag{4.1}$$

and an aggregate demand curve in which the output gap is a function of the past output gap to reflect persistence and to the real interest rate, again with a 1-period (1-year) lag:

$$y_t = \rho y_{t-1} - \phi(i_{t-1} - \pi_{t-1}) + \eta_t \tag{4.2}$$

where $\pi_t = p_t - p_{t-1}$ is the inflation rate at time t (with p_t the log of the price level), y_t is the output gap (the log of the actual to potential output), i_t is the nominal interest rate, and ε_t and η_t are i.i.d. (independent and identically distributed) aggregate supply and demand shocks, respectively.

Optimal monetary policy involves setting the interest rate for each period to minimize the intertemporal loss function:

$$E_t \sum_{\tau=t}^{\infty} \delta^{\tau-t} L_\tau \tag{4.3}$$

where $\delta < 1$ is the authorities' discount rate and where the period-by-period loss function is

$$L_\tau = \frac{(\pi_\tau - \pi^\star)^2}{2} + \frac{\lambda y_\tau^2}{2} \tag{4.4}$$

The optimal setting of the interest rate is then a "Taylor rule,"

$$i_t = \pi_t + b_1(\pi_t - \pi^\star) + b_2 y_t \tag{4.5}$$

in which the interest rate responds to both the inflation gap, $\pi_t - \pi^\star$, and the output gap, y_t.

This simple model illustrates several important points. First, this model indicates that monetary policy should focus on output fluctuations for two reasons. Even if $\lambda = 0$ so that the monetary authority does not care about output fluctuations and so can be characterized as an "inflation nutter" (King 1996), the b_2 coefficient on the output gap in the Taylor rule will still be positive. This is because the output gap enters the aggregate supply curve in (4.1) and, therefore, helps to forecast future inflation. Thus, optimal monetary policy, even if the focus is solely on hitting an inflation target and not at all on output fluctuations, still reacts to the state of the business cycle, as reflected in the output gap y_t. Another reason for monetary policy focusing on output fluctuations arises when minimizing output fluctuations is important to the monetary authority so that $\lambda > 0$. Then, the b_2 coefficient will be even larger. Indeed, case studies of the behaviour of monetary authorities who pursue inflation targeting described in Bernanke et al. (1999) do suggest that they care about output fluctuations which, of course, makes sense because the general public surely cares about the trade-off between output and inflation fluctuations.

Instead of characterizing optimal monetary policy with what Svensson (1999) has called an "instrument rule" like the Taylor rule in (4.5) above, optimal monetary policy can be described by a "target rule" in which the setting of forecasted variables relative to a target is specified. In the case of $\lambda = 0$ in the simple model here, Svensson (1997) has shown that setting the optimal setting of the interest rate according to (4.5) is equivalent to setting the interest rate so that the following target rule is followed:

$$E_t \pi_{t+2} = \pi^\star \tag{4.6}$$

In other words, the monetary policy instrument is set so as to attain the inflation target over the policy horizon, which, in this model, is two periods (years) ahead. If $\lambda > 0$, so that monetary policy makers are also concerned abut output fluctuations, then the interest rate instrument is also set according to (4.5), which is equivalent to following a target rule in which the approach to the inflation target is more gradual, i.e.,

$$E_t \pi_{t+2} - \pi^\star = c(E_t \pi_{t+1} - \pi^\star) \tag{4.7}$$

Svensson (1997) calls this type of policy reaction "flexible inflation targeting," and the evidence discussed in Bernanke et al. (1999) suggests that it is a realistic approximation of what inflation-targeting countries do in practice.

In the simple model outlined here, the instrument rule in (4.5) is equivalent to the target rules in (4.6) if $\lambda = 0$, or in (7) if $\lambda > 0$. Output fluctuations influence the setting of the monetary policy instrument for either of two reasons. First, output fluctuations matter because they affect the forecast of future inflation, even if policy makers do not care about minimizing output fluctuations in their objectives ($\lambda = 0$). Indeed, in this canonical model, the only way that policy makers can control inflation is by manipulating the output gap. Second, output fluctuations affect the setting of the monetary policy instrument because policy makers do care about minimizing output fluctuations ($\lambda > 0$), and so it is optimal to approach the inflation target more slowly. Hence either the instrument rule or the target rule leads to the obvious conclusion that monetary policy should be "activist," i.e., it should respond actively to deviations of output from its potential.

4.3   Criticisms of the Canonical Model and Its Elements

Although the canonical model produces important insights, it can be criticized on the grounds that the world is not as simple as it suggests. If other variables affect the aggregate demand or supply equations, then the Taylor rule in (4.5) will no longer be optimal, while the target rules in (4.6) or (4.7) will. This is a key reason why Svensson and others take the position that target rules have inherent advantages over instrument rules. As argued by Bernanke et al. (1999) and Mishkin (1999), target rules also have important advantages in communicating with the public, an issue we will return to in section 4.4.

The world is also complicated by the fact that it may be quite difficult to measure the output gap, y_t. There are two reasons why measuring the output gap is so difficult. The first is that it is hard to measure potential output and the second is that it is not at all clear what is the proper theoretical concept of the output gap.

4.3.1   Measuring Potential Output Is Hard to Do

One measurement problem occurs because monetary policy authorities have to estimate the output gap with real-time data, i.e., data that is available at the time they set the policy instrument. GDP data is frequently revised substantially and this is one reason why output gaps are mismeasured in real time. Even more important: it is notoriously hard to know what potential GDP actually is without hindsight. For example, it was not until the 1980s that policy makers recognized that potential GDP growth had slowed markedly after 1973. Orphanides (2001) shows that the errors in measures of output gaps have been very large in the postwar period, while Orpha-nides (1998) shows that the use of real-time data might lead to such inaccurate esti-mates that active monetary policy which reacts strongly to output fluctuations actually increases economic instability. Indeed, Orphanides (2002) argues that the reason for the Federal Reserve's poor performance during the 1970s was *not* that it was unconcerned with inflation, but rather that it was too activist, i.e., it had a large weight on output gaps in its Taylor-rule reaction function. Orphanides' work thus indicates that even though monetary policy that is set optimally should react actively to the output gap if it were correctly estimated, too large a focus on the output fluc-tuations actually leads to worse economic outcomes.

4.3.2 What Is the Proper Concept of the Output Gap?

A second measurement problem occurs because conceptually the y_t that belongs in the aggregate supply curve in (4.1) is not at all clear and may be quite different from conventionally measured output gaps. Clarida et al. (1999) point out that new Keynesian aggregate supply curves should have y_t specified as a marginal cost mea-sure rather than an output gap and they find that the marginal cost measure has sub-stantially different movements and timing than the conventionally measured output gap. McCallum and Nelson (2000) and McCallum (2001) argue that conventionally measured output gaps which estimate the gap as deviations from a trend differ sub-stantially from more theoretically grounded measures based on the output level that would prevail in the absence of nominal price stickiness. They find that monetary policy rules that react to conventional output gap measures produce excessive vola-tility of output and inflation.

Empirical evidence also questions the usefulness of relying on the output gap to forecast inflation (Atkenson and Ohanian 2001). Estrella and Mishkin (1999) also find that Taylor rules which are based on conventional output gaps do not take suf-ficient account of other factors affecting the inflation process and would have led to monetary policy which was far too tight in the last half of the 1990s. Conventional views of the output gap suggested that the Federal Reserve should have tightened monetary policy considerably in the late 1990s as the unemployment rate fell well be-low 6%, the level below which most economists at the time thought would lead to accelerating inflation. Alan Greenspan, the chairman of the Federal Reserve, resisted this view because his reading of the data did not suggest inflationary pressures in the economy. The result was that the Federal Reserve kept interest rates low, thus help-ing to promote the longest business cycle expansion in US history, along with a de-cline in inflation to levels that are consistent with price stability.

One way of characterizing the success of the Greenspan Federal Reserve in the 1990s is that it operated more from the perspective of the target rule in (4.7) rather than from the instrument rule in (4.5). The Greenspan Federal Reserve recognized that standard measures of potential output gap were possibly inaccurate and that measures of the output gap were probably overestimated. The Federal Reserve was thus more cautious in relying on output gap models and, instead, concentrated on developments on the inflation front in its conduct of policy. As a result, it was unwilling to reign in a rapidly growing economy if it was not leading to a rise in inflation. In other words, instead of focusing on output gaps, the Federal Reserve kept its focus on the inflation ball, and this was a key factor in its success in the late 1990s.

4.4   Communicating the Policy Process

The analysis above suggests that, because output gaps are hard to measure, too great a focus on output fluctuations in the setting of monetary policy instruments is undesirable because it is likely to lead to greater inflation and output variability. Focusing on output fluctuations can be undesirable for another reason: it can make the communication process of the monetary authorities less effective, which can also lead to worse economic outcomes. Indeed, even if output gaps could be measured accurately, it still might be undesirable for the monetary authorities to focus on output fluctuations in setting monetary policy because of the harm it would do to the communication process. The argument for a de-emphasis on the discussion of output stabilization in communicating monetary policy rests on the benefits it provides in terms of a focus on the long run, enhancing monetary policy credibility and simplifying communication and transparency. This does not mean that central banks will not indicate to the public that they care about output fluctuations, but they can do so in the context of outlining how they will pursue inflation stabilization.

4.4.1   Long-Run Focus
The optimizing framework in section 4.3 assumes that the monetary authorities are able to avoid the time-inconsistency problem and can commit either to target rules or to instrument rules. This framework does involve the monetary authorities taking account of both output and inflation fluctuations in their objective function, but rules out exploitation of short-run trade-offs between output growth and inflation, which is the crux of the time-inconsistency problem. As emphasized in Mishkin (1999, 2000), the source of the time-inconsistency problem is rarely inside the central bank because central bankers understand that trying to exploit short-run trade-offs will only produce worse long-run outcomes. However, the time-inconsistency problem is highly relevant to the conduct of central banking because politicians have incentives to pursue short-run interests and put political pressure on central banks to exploit the short-run trade-off between output and inflation, thereby resulting in overly expansionary monetary policy.

Thus an important issue is how can monetary authorities minimize the time-inconsistency problem? A successful communication strategy is a key part of the answer. To avoid political pressures to pursue short-run trade-offs, central banks need to focus the debate on what a central bank can do in the long run—control inflation—rather than what it cannot do on a sustainable basis—raise economic growth through expansionary monetary policy. A focus on output fluctuations in discussing the conduct of monetary policy is likely to make it harder to achieve this objective. When monetary authorities explain their monetary policy actions by referring to the need to moderate swings in output growth, the political debate about monetary policy is likely to focus on short-run issues, such as whether the central bank is doing enough to create jobs and lower unemployment, or whether its policies are anti-growth. Indeed, in the past, the political debate has frequently taken on these features in the USA.

To focus the political debate on longer-run issues, central banks have used several communication strategies. The Bundesbank before the creation of the EMU (when it had its own independent monetary policy) couched the discussion of monetary policy in terms of monetary aggregate targets, and it was considered to be one of the most successful central banks in the world. A key feature of the German monetary targeting regime was that the calculation of the monetary target ranges was a very public exercise that focused on long-run issues (Bernanke and Mishkin 1992; Laubach and Posen 1997; Mishkin and Posen 1997). First, a numerical inflation goal was prominently featured in the setting of the target ranges. Then, with estimates of potential output growth and velocity trends, a quantity-equation framework was used to back out target growth rates for the monetary aggregates. An important feature of this calculation was that potential GDP trends were used rather than actual GDP, thus reflecting the Bundesbank's articulated position that it should focus on long-run considerations, particularly price stability, rather than on short-run output fluctuations.

Central banks in countries that have adopted inflation targeting also put a lot of effort into focusing the public on long-run goals of monetary policy, as documented by Bernanke et al. (1999). Instead of articulating monetary policy in terms of an instrument rule and potential reactions to output fluctuations, monetary policy is discussed in the context of a target rule like (4.7) in which achievement of the inflation goal is emphasized. Particularly noteworthy in this regard are the publication of *Inflation Reports*. These documents explain to the general public the long-run goals and limitations of monetary policy, the rationale for inflation targets and how monetary policy has to be forward looking to achieve these targets. They and other communications of the central bank, including speeches, testimony to the legislature and even glossy brochures, have been able to shift the debate on monetary policy away from a focus on short-run job creation to longer-run considerations.

A remarkable episode in Canada in the aftermath of a speech in 1996 by the president of the Canadian Economic Association, Fortin (1996), discussed in Mishkin (1999) and Bernanke et al. (1999), illustrates how successful such a strategy can be in shifting the public debate away from a short-run focus. The speech criticized the Bank of Canada for pursuing overly contractionary monetary policy and it sparked off a widespread public debate. What was remarkable was that the communication strategy embodied in the inflation-targeting regime was able to channel the debate into a substantive discussion over what should be the appropriate target of inflation, with the Bank defending its 1–3% target range, while Fortin ended up advocating a 2–4% range. This debate, which involved discussion of the costs and benefits of different levels of inflation, thus became focused on the long-run goals of monetary policy, which is exactly where such a debate should be focused for the time-inconsistency problem to be avoided.

4.4.2 Credibility

A second problem with discussing monetary policy in terms of its reaction to output fluctuations is that it can have undesirable consequences for central bank credibility. A focus on output fluctuations may lead economic agents to believe that the monetary authorities will try to eliminate any decline in output below potential. As a result, it is more likely that workers and firms will raise wages and prices because they know that the monetary authorities are likely to accommodate these rises by pursuing expansionary policy to prevent unemployment from developing. The result is that a self-fulfilling equilibrium can occur in which wages and prices rise, then monetary policy accommodates this rise, and this leads to further rises in wages and prices, and so on, thus leading to a new equilibrium with higher inflation without a reduction in output fluctuations. Chari et al. (1998) have described this bad equilibrium as an "expectation trap."[2] Discussing monetary policy objectives in terms of output fluctuations can thus lead to a loss of inflation-fighting credibility for the central bank, with the result that the inflation-output fluctuations trade-off worsens.

4.4.3 Simplifying Communication and Transparency

A third problem with monetary authorities discussing output fluctuations in the conduct of monetary policy is that it complicates their communication strategy. The KISS (keep it simple stupid) principle suggests that monetary policy should be articulated in as simple a way as possible. The beauty of inflation target regimes is that, by focusing on one objective—inflation—communication is fairly straightforward. On the other hand, when there are two objectives, the public is likely to become confused. Discussion of output as well as inflation objectives is thus likely to obscure the transparency of monetary policy and make it less likely that the public will support a monetary policy that focuses on long-run considerations, which is so necessary to successful monetary policy performance.[3]

4.4.4 How Can Central Banks Communicate that They Care about Output Fluctuations?

The conclusion from the above analysis is that too much focus on output fluctuations in discussions of monetary policy is likely to worsen economic performance. We have already seen, though, that central banks do care about output fluctuations in their objective function, which was described in (4.3) and (4.4). How can monetary authorities convince the public that they are not "inflation nutters," which may be very important to retaining support for the central bank and its policies? The answer is that the central bank can discuss the setting of its policy instruments in terms of the target rule in (4.7). It would do this by indicating that it will not try to hit its inflation target over too short a horizon because this would result in unacceptably high output losses. Indeed, inflation-targeting central banks have been moving in exactly this direction: for example, the Reserve Bank of New Zealand has modified its inflation-targeting regime to lengthen the horizon over which it tries to achieve its inflation target (Sherwin 1999; Drew and Orr 1999; Reserve Bank of New Zealand 2000).

Monetary authorities can further the public's understanding that they care about reducing output fluctuations in the long run by emphasizing that monetary policy needs to be just as vigilant in preventing inflation from falling too low as it is from preventing it from being too high. Indeed, an explicit inflation target may help the monetary authorities to stabilize the economy because they can be more aggressive in easing monetary policy in the face of negative demand shocks to the economy without being concerned that this will cause a blowout in inflation expectations. However, to keep the communication strategy clear, the explanation of a monetary policy easing in the face of negative demand shocks needs to indicate that it is consistent with the preservation of price stability.

4.5 Implications for the Federal Reserve

Although the Federal Reserve has not adopted inflation targeting and has no explicitly announced inflation goal, it nonetheless has emphasized the price stability goal for monetary policy. Indeed, a fair characterization of the Federal Reserve, under Alan Greenspan, is that it has been acting in accordance with the optimizing framework described in section 4.1 and that it has not put too much emphasis on output fluctuations in the conduct of monetary policy. Starting in February 1994, the Greenspan Federal Reserve began raising the federal funds rate, its policy instrument, so as to pre-emptively head off a rise in inflation. These actions were completely consistent with the inflation target rule that the central bank set the interest rate instrument to keep inflation near its target several years down the road. Then, as was mentioned earlier, in the late 1990s, the Federal Reserve refrained from raising interest rates even when output appeared to be rising above potential output because it was focusing on inflation control and yet it was unclear that inflation pressures were building up. This is exactly what following an inflation target rule would have prescribed for Federal Reserve behaviour.

It is also not clear that the Federal Reserve has any less inflation-fighting credibility than other central banks that have adopted inflation targeting. Thus, we seem to be in a situation of "if it ain't broke, why fix it?" However, one concern that I have raised elsewhere (Mishkin 2000) is that the Federal Reserve's credibility is very much based on individual personalities. Alan Greenspan is a highly effective nominal anchor in the USA currently but, unfortunately, he will not be around forever. In addition, the Greenspan Federal Reserve has been operating in a particularly favourable political environment in recent years. There has been tremendous cooperation between the US Treasury and the Federal Reserve, while both President Bush and Clinton have refrained from criticizing the Federal Reserve, in contrast to some earlier presidents. Furthermore, government fiscal policy has been favourable for monetary policy making (at least until recently), with budget surpluses or small deficits. When Greenspan steps down from the chairmanship of the Federal Reserve and if the political environment for monetary policy deteriorates, the credibility of the Federal Reserve and its ability to pursue its price stability goal might be severely compromised.

The argument above suggests that developing an institutional basis for the way the Greenspan Federal Reserve has been conducting monetary policy would help to promote better outcomes for inflation and output fluctuations in the future. This is indeed the rationale for the Federal Reserve to move in the direction of more explicit inflation targeting. However, it also raises concerns about the Federal Reserve's current communication strategy, specifically in the way it announces its policy stance at the conclusion of every FOMC meeting. Currently, with the announcement of the federal funds rate target, the Federal Reserve provides the so-called "bias" or "balance of risks" statement in which it states that the balance of risks are balanced, or are "mainly toward conditions that may generate inflation pressures in the foreseeable future," or are "mainly toward conditions that may generate economic weakness in the foreseeable future." When there is a long period of time in which the statements have a balance of risks toward economic weakness in the economy, it may encourage the public to believe that the Federal Reserve has shifted to a short-run focus on preventing economic downturns.

Since its FOMC meeting in January 2001, when the Federal Reserve indicated that the balance of risks was toward economic weakness, most of its statements have continued to indicate that the risks are to economic weakness. Indeed, for nearly two years (as of this writing), none of the Federal Reserve's statements have indicated that there are concerns about inflationary pressures. The absence in the balance of risk statements of concerns about inflation have the potential to weaken the Federal Reserve's credibility as an inflation fighter in the future and it might lead to less concern in political circles about inflation control. This could lead in the future to increased political pressure on the Federal Reserve to pursue short-term rather than long-term policies. Neither of these problems might be severe while Alan Greenspan remains at the Federal Reserve, but when he departs, they could lead to a worsening of the trade-off between output and inflation fluctuations, thereby worsening economic performance.

One solution to the above problem might be to eliminate the balance-of-risks statement, but this statement does have value in enhancing the transparency of Federal Reserve policy making. In addition, it also allows members of the FOMC to reach consensus when there is some disagreement about whether to change the federal funds rate: possible dissenters may be willing to vote with the majority if the FOMC adopts a balance-of-risks statement which suggests a future change in interest rates in the direction that they would like to see. Another solution is to modify the balance-of-risks statement to put more focus on the price stability goal of the Federal Reserve. For example, the balance-of-risks when the risk is of higher inflation in the future could still remain as "mainly toward conditions that may generate inflation pressures in the foreseeable future." However, if the risk is to weakness in the economy, the statement could be modified to be "mainly toward conditions that may generate economic weakness and deflationary pressures in the foreseeable future." This is quite a small change in the communication strategy of the Federal Reserve but, when it is ready to reverse course and raise interest rates to head off future inflation, having the balance-of-risks statement always focus on inflationary pressures might enhance Federal Reserve credibility and political support for inflation control.

4.6 Conclusions

An important issue for monetary policy makers is how activist they should be, i.e., to what extent should they focus on output fluctuations in the conduct of monetary policy? The debate on this question is an old one, and the answer that Milton Friedman (1968) gave many years ago was that activisim would worsen monetary policy performance. Developments in the monetary economics field in recent years lead to the same answer. This paper argues that an activist monetary policy is likely to worsen the trade-off between output and inflation fluctuations, because it will lead to suboptimal monetary policy, but also because it complicates monetary authorities' communication strategy and can weaken the credibility of central banks. The bottom line is that for the monetary authorities to be successful in minimizing output and inflation fluctuations, they must never take their eye of the inflation ball. This is why continual repeating of the central bank mantra of price stability will not only be good for the soul, but for the economy as well.

Notes

I thank two anonymous referees for their helpful comments. Any views expressed in this chapter are those of the author only and not those of Columbia University or the National Bureau of Economic Research.

1. The model in Clarida et al. (1999) modifies (4.1) and (4.2) as follows:

$$\pi_t = \beta E_t \pi_{t-1} + \gamma y_{t-1} + \varepsilon_t \tag{4.1'}$$

$$y_t = E_t y_{t+1} - \phi(i_t - E_t \pi_{t+1}) + \eta_t \tag{4.2'}$$

Given the same loss function in (4.3) and (4.4), optimal policy still results in the Taylor rule in (4.5) because inflation and the output gap are sufficient statistics for the model, i.e., no other variables enter the aggregate supply and demand functions. Note, however, that the coefficients in the Taylor rule equation will differ depending on the degree of forward-looking behaviour.

2. I made a similar argument in the first and later editions of my textbook, Mishkin (1986), but it was not until Chari et al. (1998) that the argument was formalized.

3. A similar argument has been made by many critics, myself included, against the two-pillar strategy of the European central bank: that it is confusing to the public.

References

Atkenson, Andrew, and Lee E. Ohanian (2001), "Are Phillips Curves Useful for Forecasting Inflation?" *Federal Reserve Bank of Minneapolis Quarterly Review* 25(1), (Winter), 2–11.

Bernanke, Ben S., and Frederic S. Mishkin (1992), "Central Bank Behavior and the Strategy of Monetary Policy: Observations from Six Industrialized Countries," in Olivier Blanchard and Stanley Fischer (eds), *NBER Macroeconomics Annual*, Cambridge, MA: MIT Press, 183–238.

Bernanke, Ben S., Thomas Laubach, Frederic S. Mishkin and Adam S. Posen (1999), *Inflation Targeting: Lessons from the International Experience*. Princeton, NJ: Princeton University Press.

Chari, V. V., Lawrence J. Christiano and Martin Eichenbaum (1998), "Expectation Traps and Discretion," *Journal of Economic Theory*, 81(2), 462–92.

Clarida, Richard, Jordi Gali and Mark Gertler (1999), "The Science of Monetary Policy," *Journal of Economic Literature*, 34(4), (December), 1661–707.

Drew, Aaron, and Adrian Orr (1999), "The Reserve Bank's Role in the Recent Business Cycle: Actions and Evolution," *Reserve Bank of New Zealand Bulletin*, 62, No. 1.

Estrella, Arturo, and Frederic S. Mishkin (1999), "The Role of NAIRU in Monetary Policy: Implications of Uncertainty and Model Selection," in John Taylor (ed.), *Monetary Policy Rules*, Chicago: University of Chicago Press for the NBER, 405–30.

Fortin, Pierre (1996), "The Great Canadian Slump," *Canadian Journal of Economics*, 29, 761–87.

Friedman, Milton (1968), "The Role of Monetary Policy," *American Economic Review*, 58, 1–17.

King, Mervyn (1996), "How Should Central Banks Reduce Inflation? Conceptual Issues," in *Achieving Price Stability*, Federal Reserve Bank of Kansas City, Kansas City, MO: 53–91.

Laubach, Thomas, and Adam S. Posen (1997), "Disciplined Discretion: Monetary Targeting in Germany and Switzerland," Essays in International Finance No 206, Department of Economics, International Finance Section, Princeton University.

McCallum, Bennett T. (2001), "Should Monetary Policy Respond Strongly to Output Gaps?," *American Economic Review*, 91, (May), 258–62.

McCallum, Bennett T., and Edward Nelson (2000), "Timeless Perspective vs Discretionary Monetary Policy in Forward-Looking Models," NBER Working Paper No. 7915, September.

Mishkin, Frederic S. (1986), *The Economics of Money, Banking, and Financial Markets.* Boston, MA: Little Brown and Co.

Mishkin, Frederic S. (1999), "International Experiences with Different Monetary Policy Regimes," *Journal of Monetary Economics*, 43(3), (June), 579–606.

Mishkin, Frederic S. (2000), "What Should Central Banks Do?," *Federal Reserve Bank of St. Louis Review*, 82(6), (November/December), 1–13.

Mishkin, Frederic S., and Adam S. Posen (1997), "Inflation Targeting: Lessons from Four Countries," *Federal Reserve Bank of New York Economic Policy Review*, 3(3), (August), 9–110.

Orphanides, Athanasios (1998), "Monetary Policy Evaluation with Noisy Information," Federal Reserve Board FEDS Paper No. 98-50, October.

Orphanides, Athanasios (2001), "Monetary Policy Rules Based on Real-Time Data," *American Economic Review*, 91(4), (September), 964–85.

Orphanides, Athanasios (2002), "Monetary Policy Rules and the Great Inflation," *American Economic Review*, 92(2), (May), 115–20.

Reserve Bank of New Zealand (2000), *Monetary Policy Statement, March 2000.* Wellington, NZ: Reserve Bank of New Zealand.

Sherwin, Murray (1999), "Inflation Targeting: 10 Years On," speech to New Zealand Association of Economists Conference, Rotorua, New Zealand, July 1.

Svensson, Lars E. O. (1997), "Inflation Forecast Targeting: Implementing and Monitoring Inflation Targets," *European Economic Review*, 41, 1111–46.

Svensson, Lars E. O. (1999), "Inflation Targeting as a Monetary Policy Rule," *Journal of Monetary Economics*, 43(3), (June), 607–54.

5 Can Central Bank Transparency Go Too Far?

Frederic S. Mishkin

5.1 What Are the Issues?

Since the beginning of the 1990s we have seen a revolution in the way central banks communicate with the markets and the public. In the old days, central banks were generally very secretive institutions. Not only did they not clarify what their objectives and strategies were, but they even kept the markets guessing about what the actual settings of policy instruments were. Central banks were perfectly happy to cultivate a mystique as wise but mysterious institutions, prompting popular books about central banks to have titles like *The Secrets of the Temple* (Greider 1987).

The rationale for the secretive behaviour of central banks was that, as one former Fed official put it bluntly, "secrecy is designed to shield the Fed from political oversight."[1] Although central bank secrecy reflects the natural desire of a bureaucracy to maximise power and prestige by avoiding accountability, the theory of time-inconsistency of optimal policies articulated by Kydland and Prescott (1977) and Calvo (1978) suggests that there might be a rationale for central bank secrecy because, as this same Fed official stated, "most politicians have a shorter time horizon than is optimal for monetary policy." In order to avoid the pressures from politicians on central banks to pursue overly expansionary monetary policy to exploit the short-run trade-off between employment and inflation, central banks might want to obscure their actions and avoid the time-inconsistency problem by focusing on the long run and "just doing it" as McCallum (1995) has proposed.[2] Another way to deal with the time-inconsistency problem is to appoint conservative central bankers, as suggested by Rogoff (1985), who put more weight on controlling inflation relative to output than does the general public and thus will resist inflationary policies. However, for this to work, conservative central bankers need to be independent of the political process, which is facilitated by central bank secrecy.

There are several problems with this secrecy approach to dealing with the time-inconsistency problem. First, having secretive central banks is inherently undemocratic. Although it makes sense to insulate central banks from short-run pressures to pursue overly expansionary monetary policy, basic democratic principles require that the central bank be accountable for its actions: this requires that the public understands what the central bank is doing. In addition, democratic principles indicate that the preferences of policy-makers need to be aligned with those of the society at large. Furthermore, in the long run a central bank cannot operate without the support of the public. A secretive central bank may heighten suspicions that it is not acting in the public interest and so can eventually lead to curbs on its independence.

With the advent of inflation targeting in the early 1990s, central banks have been taking a different route to solving the time-inconsistency problem. They now recognise that transparency and improved communication with the public and the markets is the key to having a successful monetary policy. Inflation targeting has promoted a huge increase in transparency about inflation objectives and stresses regular communication with the public.[3] Inflation-targeting central banks now have frequent, periodic communications with the government, and central bank officials take every opportunity to make public speeches on their monetary policy strategy. These channels are also commonly now used by central banks that have not adopted inflation targeting, such as the Federal Reserve, but inflation-targeting central banks have taken public outreach a step further: not only have they engaged in extended public information campaigns, even engaging in the distribution of glossy brochures as in New Zealand, but they have engaged in the publication of inflation report-type documents. Inflation reports are far more user-friendly than previous central bank documents and explain the goals and limitations of monetary policy, including the rationale for inflation targets, the numerical values of the inflation targets and how they were determined, how the inflation targets are to be achieved, given current economic conditions, and reasons for any deviations from targets.

This emphasis on transparency and communication has produced several benefits for central banks. By explicitly announcing their objectives on the inflation front, central banks have been able to increase their credibility and anchor inflation expectations (Levin, Natalucci and Piger 2004). Not only has this helped them achieve low and stable inflation, but output volatility has, if anything, fallen. The strengthening of the nominal anchor apparently helps move the economy toward the efficient frontier of the trade-off between inflation and output gap variability, generating better performance on both the inflation and output fronts.[4]

Transparency and communication, especially when it has demonstrated the success in achieving a pre-announced and well-defined inflation target, has also helped build public support for a central bank's independence and for its policies. As documented in Mishkin and Posen (1997) and Bernanke et al. (1999), the increased transparency of its inflation-targeting regime led to increased support for the Bank of Canada's policies, while it led to the granting of operational independence to the Bank of England in May 1997. Indeed, when announcing the decision, Gordon Brown, the

Chancellor of the Exchequer, indicated that a key factor behind granting the Bank of England greater independence was that the increased transparency of the inflation-targeting regime enhanced political oversight. An important benefit of the transparency of an inflation-targeting regime, therefore, is that it makes it more palatable to have an independent central bank which focuses on long-run objectives, but which is consistent with a democratic society because it is accountable.

Although inflation targeting has increased transparency with substantial benefits, transparency is far from complete. As seen in table 5.1, although almost all inflation-targeting central banks publish their inflation forecasts in their *Inflation Reports* (the Bank of Israel and Central Bank of the Republic of Turkey being the only exceptions),[5] a larger number do not publish output forecasts (the central banks of Australia, the Philippines, Poland, Romania, South Africa, South Korea and Turkey).[6] Furthermore, except for the Reserve Bank of New Zealand and most recently the central bank of Colombia, inflation-targeting central banks do not formally announce their forecasts of the future path for the interest-rate policy instrument.[7] No central bank describes their objective function for monetary policy, while almost all central banks are reluctant to discuss publicly their concerns about output fluctuations. This raises the question of whether central banks should increase transparency much further. Some monetary economists, with the most prominent example being Lars Svensson (2002), suggest that the answer is yes. Indeed, he advocates not only publication of output and inflation forecasts, but also announcement of projections of the future policy path and the central bank objective function. But can transparency go too far?

To answer this question, we need to keep the following basic question in mind: Does increased transparency help the central bank to do its job—that is, enable it to conduct monetary policy optimally with an appropriate focus on long-run objectives? The answer might well be no, particularly if the increase in transparency violates the KISS (Keep It Simple Stupid) principle. This chapter uses this basic question as the lens through which it evaluates how far transparency should go. In the next three sections I look at the following three questions: (i) Should the central bank publish its forecasts, including projections of the future path of policy rates? (ii) Should the central bank announce its objective function? (iii) How should the central bank talk about output fluctuations? The final section contains some concluding remarks.

5.2   Should the Central Bank Publish Its Forecasts, Including Projections of the Future Path of Policy Rates?

Inflation-targeting theory, as illustrated in the simple model of Svensson (1997), shows that inflation forecasts are central to the conduct of monetary policy. His

Table 5.1
Do Inflation-Targeting Central Banks Publish Their Forecasts?

Central bank	Policy rate projections?	Inflation forecasts?	Output growth forecasts?	Output gap forecasts?
Australia	No	Yes	No[a]	No
Brazil	No[†]	Yes	Yes	No
Canada	No	Yes	Yes	No[‡]
Chile	No	Yes	Yes	No
Colombia	Yes	Yes	Yes	Yes
Czech Republic	No[†]	Yes	Yes	Yes
Hungary	No[†]	Yes	Yes	Yes
Iceland	No[†]	Yes	Yes	Yes
Israel	No	No	No	No
Mexico	No	Yes	Yes	No
New Zealand	Yes	Yes	Yes	Yes
Norway	No[†]	Yes	Yes	Yes
Peru	No	Yes	Yes	No
Philippines	No	Yes	No	No
Poland	No[†]	Yes[b]	No	No
Romania	No	Yes	No	No
Slovakia[c]	No	Yes	Yes	No
South Africa	No	Yes	No	No
South Korea	No	Yes	Yes[d]	No
Sweden	No	Yes	Yes	No[‡]
Switzerland	No	Yes	Yes	No
Thailand	No	Yes	Yes	No
Turkey[e]	No	No	No	No
UK	No[†]	Yes	Yes	No

Notes: [†] Indicates central banks which publish the market expectations of future policy rates even though there is no official policy-rate forecast. The central banks of Hungary, Iceland and Poland publish macro forecasts based on a constant policy-rate path, the Czech Republic and Norway based on market expectations of the policy-rate path, and Brazil and the UK based on both a constant policy-rate path and market expectations of the policy-rate path.
[‡] The central banks of Canada and Sweden publish estimates of the current output gap.
[a] The Reserve Bank of Australia does not publish output growth forecasts in the *Statement on Monetary Policy*. However, GDP forecasts are given twice a year in the Governor's Opening Statement to the House of Representatives Standing Committee on Economics, Finance and Public Administration.
[b] The National Bank of Poland publishes extensive survey-based inflation expectations by market participants, but refrains from making an exact inflation forecast of its own. Instead, a commentary on the likelihood of fulfilling the inflation target is included in the *Inflation Report*.
[c] The National Bank of Slovakia does not refer to itself as an inflation targeter. However, the ECB defines it as an "implicit inflation targeter." (Source: "The acceding countries' strategies towards ERM II and the adoption of the euro: an analytical review," ECB Occasional Paper No 10, February 2004)
[d] The Bank of Korea does not publish output growth forecasts in the *Inflation Report*. However, GDP forecasts for the year ahead are given twice a year in their publication *Economic Prospects*.
[e] The Central Bank of the Republic of Turkey does not call its framework "inflation targeting" but rather "implicit inflation targeting." However, it follows an end-of-year inflation target, which is negotiated by the government and the IMF.
Sources: Central bank websites as of August 2004.

model comprises an aggregate supply curve in which the change in inflation is affected by the output gap with a one-period (one year) lag:

$$\pi_t = \pi_{t-1} + \gamma y_{t-1} + \varepsilon_t \tag{5.1}$$

and an aggregate demand curve in which the output gap is a function of the past output gap to reflect persistence, and of the real interest rate, again with a one-period (one year) lag:

$$y_t = \rho y_{t-1} - \varphi(i_{t-1} - \pi_{t-1}) + \eta_t \tag{5.2}$$

where $\pi_t = p_t - p_{t-1}$ is the inflation rate at time t (with p_t the log of the price level), y_t is the output gap (the log of the ratio of actual to potential output), i_t is the nominal interest rate, and ε_t and η_t are independently and identically distributed aggregate supply and demand shocks, respectively.

Optimal monetary policy involves setting the interest rate each period to minimise the intertemporal loss function:

$$E_t \sum_{\tau=t}^{\infty} \delta^{\tau-t} L_\tau \tag{5.3}$$

where $\delta < 1$ is the authorities' discount rate and where the period-by-period loss function is:

$$L_\tau = (\pi_\tau - \pi^*)^2/2 + \lambda y_\tau^2/2 \tag{5.4}$$

given the inflation target π^*. In the case of $\lambda = 0$, where the central bank only cares about inflation fluctuations, Svensson (1997) has shown that the optimal setting of the interest rate is one in which the following target rule is followed:

$$E_t \pi_{t+2} = \pi^* \tag{5.5}$$

In other words, the monetary policy instrument is set so as to attain the inflation target over the horizon at which policy changes take effect, which in this model is two periods (years) ahead. If $\lambda > 0$, so that monetary policy-makers are also concerned about output fluctuations, then the interest rate instrument is set according to a target rule in which the approach to the inflation target is more gradual, that is:[8]

$$E_t \pi_{t+2} - \pi^* = c(E_t \pi_{t+1} - \pi^*) \tag{5.6}$$

Svensson (1997) calls this type of policy reaction "flexible inflation targeting," and the evidence discussed in Bernanke et al. (1999) suggests that it is a more realistic approximation of what inflation-targeting countries do in practice.

Equations (5.5) and (5.6) illustrate that central bank decisions about monetary policy necessarily focus on the inflation forecast, and so inflation targeting is more

precisely described as being "inflation forecast targeting." Clearly, if inflation forecasts are the key to the conduct of monetary policy in an inflation-targeting regime,
then full transparency requires that the inflation forecasts of the central bank
be revealed to the public. Because inflation forecasts are generated with forecasts
of other variables, especially output, full transparency also requires that forecasts of
these variables are published.[9] There are a number of advantages from publication
of forecasts. First, publication of forecasts can help the public and the markets understand central bank actions, thus making it easier for them to assess whether the
central bank is serious about achieving its inflation goal. Second, publication of forecasts enables the public to evaluate the quality of central bank forecasts which will
enhance central bank credibility if these forecasts are viewed as constructed using
best practice. Third, publication of forecasts increases the incentives for the central
bank to produce good forecasts because a poor forecasting record would be
embarrassing.

The three advantages above together point to the more general advantage from
publication of forecasts, that it increases central bank accountability. Because of the
long lags in the effects of monetary policy, which in the simple Svensson model is two
periods (years), inflation outcomes are revealed only after a substantial lag. Thus
without additional information, the inflation target by itself does not provide an immediate signal to both the public and the markets as to whether the current stance of
monetary policy is appropriate. Because, as Equations (5.5) and (5.6) illustrate, optimal monetary policy involves "inflation forecast targeting," publication of forecasts
provides immediate information that helps the public to assess whether the central
bank is taking the appropriate steps to meet its objectives. If the public and the markets think that the central bank's forecasts are not honest, or that the current policy
stance is inconsistent with the inflation forecast, or that the inflation forecast differs
too markedly from the stated target, they can immediately voice their criticisms of
the central bank. Increased accountability of the central bank is then the result.

However, despite the obvious advantages of publishing forecasts, there are some
thorny problems. The first is the tricky issue: What path of the policy interest rate
should the forecast be conditioned on? There are three choices: (i) a constant interest
rate path; (ii) market forecasts of future policy rates; or (iii) a central bank projection
of the policy interest rate path. A constant interest path would almost surely never be
optimal because future projected changes in interest rates will be necessary to keep
inflation on the appropriate target path.[10] The second choice is also problematic because, as Bernanke and Woodford (1997) have shown, there is a circularity problem
if the central bank sets its policy rate on the basis of market forecasts. The markets'
forecasts are just guesses of what the central bank will be doing, so if the central
bank just does what the market expects, there is nothing that pins down the system
and inflation outcomes will be indeterminate. Theory therefore tells us that the only

appropriate and logically consistent choice is the third one, the central bank projection of the policy path. Clearly, an inflation forecast is meaningless without specifying what policy it is conditioned on, and this is why Svensson (2002) argues that in publishing its forecasts the central bank also needs to announce its projection of the policy-rate path used in producing its forecast, which will almost surely be time-varying.

Although Svensson's argument for announcing the projection of the policy path is theoretically sound, announcing the policy path is highly problematic. One objection to a central bank announcing its policy projection, raised by Charles Goodhart (2001), a former member of the Monetary Policy Committee of the Bank of England, is that it would complicate the decision-making process of the committee that makes monetary policy decisions. The current procedure of most central banks is to make decisions only about the current setting of the policy rate. Goodhart argues that "a great advantage of restricting the choice of what to do now, this month, is that it makes the decision relatively simple, even stark."[11] If a policy projection with time-varying rates is announced, this clearly requires that the monetary policy committee come to an agreement on this policy path. Svensson (2002) argues that this could be done by a "simple" voting procedure, but this procedure is far from simple and I agree with Goodhart that this is unlikely to work. Forcing committee members to make a decision about the future path of rates and not just the rate today may complicate matters so much that the decision-making process could be impaired. Although committee members might have some idea of a future direction for policy rates, they are likely to have trouble thinking about a precise policy-rate path rather than just the setting of the rate today. Furthermore, getting committee members to agree on a future path of the policy rate might be very difficult and could end up being very contentious.[12]

I had a glimpse of the problems with projections of the policy-rate path when I sat in on Federal Open Market Committee (FOMC) meetings while I was the director of research at the Federal Reserve Bank of New York from 1994 to 1997. Upon my arrival at the Fed, the Green Book forecasts (prepared by the Board staff) were conditioned on a non-constant interest rate path. Several of the FOMC members objected to this procedure and this was probably for two reasons. First, having a staff projection of future interest rates might lead to some prejudgement of the committee's decision. Second, it is far easier to make a decision just on the rate today and not have to discuss the path for future policy rates at the same time. The objections eventually won the day: the procedure for generating the Green Book forecasts was changed so that they are now conditioned on a constant policy-rate path, at least in the short term. Thus, I side with Goodhart. Announcing a projection for the policy-rate path which would require agreement on this path by the committee deciding on monetary policy would be counterproductive.

The second problem with announcing a projection of the policy-rate path is that it might complicate communication with the public. Although economists understand that any policy path projected by the central bank is inherently conditional because changes in the state of the economy will require a change in the policy path, the public is far less likely to understand this. When new information comes in and the central bank changes the policy rate from its projected path, the public may see this as a reneging on its announced policy or an indication that the central bank's previous policy settings were a mistake. Thus even when the central bank is conducting its policy in an optimal manner, deviations from its projected policy path may be viewed as a central bank failure and could hurt the central bank's credibility. In addition, the deviations of the policy rate from its projected path might be seen as flip flops on the part of the central bank. As we often see in political campaigns, when a candidate changes his position, even if it reflects changes in circumstances and thus reflects sound judgement, the candidate is vulnerable to attacks by his or her opponents that he or she does not have leadership qualities. Wouldn't central banks be subject to the same criticism when changing circumstances would force them to change the policy rate from its previously projected path? The result might be a weakening of support for the central bank and its independence.

The recent Federal Reserve experience with the language of their post-FOMC statement illustrates the problem of the public not understanding that projected policy paths are conditional on the evolution of the data. In order to underscore its commitment to preventing a deflationary spiral from getting underway in the United States, the FOMC announced in August 2003 that it would maintain policy accommodation for a "considerable period." As Eggertsson and Woodford (2003) have shown, a commitment to keeping the policy rate unusually low beyond the time when the economy begins to recover is an important policy tool to deal with deflationary shocks. However, as is clear from Eggertsson and Woodford (2003), the length of the "considerable period" is dependent on the actual evolution of the economy. The public may not fully understand this and so if the economy comes back far stronger than is anticipated, monetary policy may need to be tightened even when there has been a commitment to easy monetary policy for a "considerable period." We would then have the problems described above where the central bank's credibility might be tarnished. Thus the commitment to a policy path, even when it is needed, is not without its problems. As is indicated in Ito and Mishkin (2004), I still believe that deflationary environments, like the one we see in Japan, are sufficiently damaging that a commitment to the zero interest rate for an extended period is needed to reflate the economy. However, the cost of a commitment to a projected policy-rate path is trickier when the deflation risks are not as serious. This problem has been recognised by officials at the Fed, and explains why they have been seeking an exit strategy from their commitment to a policy-rate path by first changing the language, in January 2004, to say that the FOMC can be "patient" in removing policy accommodation and then, in May 2004, to say that policy accommodation can be removed at a pace that is likely to be "measured."

The bottom line is that except in exceptional deflationary circumstances like the one Japan has experienced, announcement of a policy-rate path does not have much to recommend it. It is likely to complicate policy discussion within central banks which might impair the quality of monetary policy decisions, and it also may lead to a loss of credibility of the central bank and a weakening of the support for central bank policies. Thus announcement of its projection of the policy-rate path may make it harder for the central bank to conduct monetary policy optimally with an appropriate focus on long-run objectives.

The problem with announcing the projection of the future policy path creates a problem for publishing forecasts. Clearly, in order for a forecast to be evaluated, the central bank must reveal the policy path on which it is conditioned. But if it does not make sense for central banks to announce their projection of a time-varying, policy-rate path, then the forecasts that they publish cannot be based on such a projection. The alternative is for the central bank to publish forecasts that are either conditioned on the policy rate remaining unchanged or on market expectations of future policy rates. Indeed this is what almost all central banks that publish forecasts do. Only the central banks of New Zealand and Colombia publish their forecasts based on a projected policy-rate path which they intend to set in the future.[13]

If publishing forecasts based on a projected policy-rate path may do more harm than good, and yet this is the only logically consistent approach for producing these forecasts, then is publishing forecasts based on a constant policy rate or on market expectations of the policy rate truly transparent? After all, the central bank knows that neither of these interest rate paths is what it plans to do and the public and markets know this as well.[14] Publishing these logically inconsistent forecasts might even be viewed as non-transparent and so could potentially damage the central bank's credibility.[15] The case for publishing forecasts is thus no longer clear cut: there are costs and benefits. However, for central banks that have lower credibility, particularly those in emerging market economies, there may be a greater need for them to publish forecasts in order to provide more information to the public, even if the forecasts are not based on the central bank's projection of future policy rates.

5.3   Should the Central Bank Reveal Its Objective Function?

In order for the public and the markets to fully understand what a central bank is doing they need to understand the central bank's objectives. As argued in the introduction, the announcement of an explicit, numerical objective for inflation is an important step in the right direction and has clear-cut benefits. However, central banks are not "inflation nutters" (King 1997): they do care about output fluctuations as well as inflation fluctuations, and so λ is greater than 0 in the central bank objective function in Equation (5.4). Thus announcing an inflation target is not enough: full transparency requires that the central bank reveal its objective function (Svensson 2002).

Again, we need to ask the question whether revealing its objective function will help the central bank to do its job. I will argue that the answer is no because pushing transparency further in this direction violates the KISS (Keep It Simple Stupid) principle and is likely to hinder the communication process.

The first problem with announcing an objective function is that it might be quite hard for members of a monetary policy committee to specify an objective function. Having watched how members of a monetary policy committee operate, I can attest that members of monetary policy boards don't think in terms of objective functions and would have a very hard time in describing what theirs is. Indeed, I would suggest that most monetary economists, even brilliant ones, would have trouble specifying what their λ would be. A counter to this argument is that the λ could be backed out by revealed preference. Monetary policy committee members could be confronted with hypothetical choices about acceptable paths of inflation and output gaps and then their choices would reveal their λs. Although committee members would be able to do this when confronted with a real world situation, and this is effectively what was done in Brazil in early 2003, I think they would find this difficult to do when the choices are hypothetical—I know I would.

A second problem, raised by Goodhart (2001), is that it would be difficult for a committee to agree on its objective function. As mentioned above, committee members might have trouble defining their own objective function, but because the composition of the committee changes frequently and existing members may change their views on objectives depending on circumstances, they would also have to revisit the decision on the committee's objective function frequently. Deciding on the committee's objective function would thus substantially increase the complexity of the decision process and might also be quite contentious. This violation of the KISS principle would then have the potential to weaken the quality of monetary policy decisions.

A third problem is that it is far from clear who should decide on the objective function. If the members of the monetary policy board do so, isn't this a violation of the democratic principle that the objectives of bureaucracies should be set by the political process? An alternative would be for the government to do so. But if we think that it would be hard enough for a monetary policy committee to do this, it would clearly be even more difficult for politicians to decide on the objective function.

Even if it were easy for the monetary policy committee or the government to come to a decision on the objective function, would it be easy to communicate it to the public? If economists and members of a monetary policy committee have trouble quantifying their objective function, is it likely that the public would understand what the central bank was talking about when it announced its objective function? Announcement of the objective function would only be likely to complicate the communication process with the public and is another violation of the KISS principle.

The announcement of the central bank's objective function can add a further complication to the communication process that might have even more severe consequences for the ability of the central bank to do its job well. The KISS principle argues for articulation of monetary policy in as simple a way as possible. The beauty of inflation-target regimes is that by focusing on one objective—inflation—communication is fairly straightforward. On the other hand, with the announcement of the objective function, the central bank will be announcing that it has two objectives, minimising both output and inflation fluctuations. Discussion of output as well as inflation objectives can confuse the public and make it more likely that the public will see the mission of the central bank as elimination of short-run output fluctuations, thus worsening the time-inconsistency problem.

One outcome is that it may make it more likely that workers and firms will raise wages and prices because they know that the monetary authorities are likely to accommodate these rises by pursuing expansionary policy to prevent output gaps from developing. The result is that a self-fulfilling equilibrium can occur in which wages and prices rise, then monetary policy accommodates this rise, and this leads to further rises in wages and prices, and so on, thus leading to a new equilibrium with higher inflation but without a reduction in output fluctuations. Chari, Christiano and Eichenbaum (1998) have described this bad equilibrium as an "expectation trap." Discussing monetary policy objectives in terms of output fluctuations can thus lead to a loss of inflation-fighting credibility for the central bank, with the result that the trade-off between inflation and output fluctuations worsens.

Announcement of the objective function not only requires the announcement of λ and the inflation target, but it also requires the central bank to announce its estimates of the current and future output gaps and hence its estimate of potential output and its growth rate. The announcement of estimates of potential output, and particularly its growth rate, may increase the probability that the public sees them as a target for monetary policy and thus may increase political pressures on the central bank to eliminate output gaps and pursue high growth in the short run, with the resulting negative consequences mentioned above. This problem is likely to be even more damaging because potential output is very hard to measure.

One measurement problem for potential output occurs because the monetary policy authorities have to estimate it with real-time data, that is, data that are available at the time they set the policy instrument. GDP data are frequently revised substantially and this is one reason why output gaps are mismeasured in real time. Even more important: it is notoriously hard to know what potential GDP and its growth rate actually are without hindsight. For example, in the United States it was not until the 1980s that policy-makers recognised that potential GDP growth had slowed markedly after 1973: Orphanides (2001) has shown that the errors in measures of output gaps have been very large in the post-war period.

An even more severe measurement problem occurs because conceptually the y_t that belongs in the aggregate supply curve in Equation (5.1) is not at all clear and may be quite different from conventionally measured output gaps. Clarida et al. (1999) point out that new Keynesian aggregate supply curves should have y_t specified as a marginal cost measure rather than an output gap and they find that the marginal cost measure has substantially different movements and timing than the conventionally measured output gap. McCallum and Nelson (2000) and McCallum (2001) argue that conventionally measured output gaps, which estimate the gap as deviations from a trend, differ substantially from more theoretically grounded measures based on the output level that would prevail in the absence of nominal price stickiness. It is true that there are measurement problems with inflation as well as output gaps, but both the conceptual and real-time measurement problems for inflation are of a far smaller magnitude.

The severe measurement problems for the output gap could interact with an increased focus on eliminating output gaps to produce serious policy mistakes as occurred in the United States in the 1970s. Orphanides (1998) shows that the use of real-time data on output gaps might lead to such inaccurate estimates that active monetary policy which reacts strongly to output gaps increases economic instability. Indeed, Orphanides (2002) argues that the reason for the Federal Reserve's poor performance during the 1970s was *not* that it was unconcerned with inflation, but rather that it focused too much on eliminating output gaps.

Given the objections raised here, it is not surprising that no central bank has revealed its objective function to the public. Furthermore, the discussion here suggests that even if the central bank does not announce its objective function, announcement of current and future potential output and output gap estimates still has the potential to worsen monetary policy performance. Thus the discussion also argues against the publication of central bank estimates and forecasts of potential output and the output gap even if publication of inflation and output forecasts is felt to be beneficial. Indeed, although the majority of inflation-targeting central banks publish output and inflation forecasts, only the central banks of Colombia, the Czech Republic, Hungary, Iceland, New Zealand and Norway publish their forecasts of potential output or output gaps, while the central banks of Canada and Sweden publish only current estimates of the output gap (table 5.1).

5.4   How Should Central Banks Talk about Output Fluctuations?

One advantage of a central bank announcing its objective function is that it would make clear the central bank's views on how it will deal with output fluctuations. But since central banks do not announce their objective functions, and arguments against doing this are strong, they still have the problem of how to talk about output fluctuations. The reality is that central bankers, whether they target inflation or not, are extremely reluctant to discuss concerns about output fluctuations even though their actions show that they do care about them. This lack of transparency is the "dirty little secret of central banking." One remarkable manifestation of this occurred in August 1994 at the Federal Reserve Bank of Kansas City's Jackson Hole Conference, when Alan Blinder, then the vice-chairman of the FOMC, had the temerity to mention that a short-run trade-off between output and inflation exists and that, therefore, monetary policy should be concerned about minimising output as well as inflation fluctuations. Blinder was then pilloried by many central bankers and in the press, with a *Newsweek* columnist declaring that he was not qualified to be a central banker (Samuelson 1994). From an academic economist's perspective, this was quite amazing since Alan Blinder didn't say anything that was inconsistent with what our models tell us or what central bankers deep down believe. However, it does indicate the discomfort that central bankers as a group have with discussing the role of output fluctuations in the conduct of monetary policy.

The problems with revealing the objective function discussed in the previous section explain why central bankers have difficulty with being transparent about their concerns about output fluctuations. Central bankers fear that if they are explicit about the need to minimise output fluctuations as well as inflation fluctuations, politicians will use this to pressure the central bank to pursue a short-run strategy of overly expansionary policy that will lead to poor long-run outcomes. Furthermore, a focus on output gaps could lead to policy mistakes similar to those that occurred in the United States in the 1970s. The response to these problems is that central bankers engage in a "don't ask, don't tell" strategy.

However, the unwillingness of central banks to talk about their concerns regarding reducing output fluctuations creates two very serious problems. First, a don't-ask-don't-tell strategy is just plain dishonest. Doing one thing but saying another is the height of non-transparency, and central banks not admitting that they care about output fluctuations can erode confidence in other elements of their transparency that are clearly beneficial. Second, if central bankers do not discuss their concerns about output fluctuations, they may end up being characterised as "inflation nutters," and this can cause an erosion of support for a central bank's policies and independence because this set of preferences is clearly inconsistent with the public's.

The case for increasing transparency with regard to central banks' concerns about output fluctuations is quite strong. But how can central banks do this?

One answer is that a central bank can discuss the setting of its policy instruments in terms of the target rule in Equation (5.6). It can announce that it will not try to hit its inflation target over too short a horizon because this would result in unacceptably high output losses, especially when the economy gets hit by shocks that knock it substantially away from its long-run inflation goal. Inflation-targeting central banks have been moving in this direction: for example, the Reserve Bank of New Zealand has modified its inflation-targeting regime to lengthen the horizon over which it tries to achieve its inflation target.[16]

Although inflation-targeting central banks have lengthened the horizon for their targets to two years or so, with the Bank of England being a prominent example, this still does not solve the problem because it gives the impression that the horizon for inflation targets is fixed, which is not flexible enough.[17] Up to now, the use of a specific horizon like two years has not been a problem for inflation targeting in advanced countries like the United Kingdom; because inflation has not been subject to large shocks, it has remained close to the target level. In this case, having the horizon for the target equal to the two-year horizon at which policy changes take effect, as in Equation (5.5), is consistent with optimal policy. However, as we have seen in Equation (5.6), when there is a concern about output fluctuations and the inflation rate is shocked sufficiently away from its long-run target, the path for the medium-term inflation-target horizon needs to be modified.

A striking example of how large shocks to inflation can be handled occurred in Brazil recently (Fraga, Goldfajn and Minella 2003). Brazil experienced a major exchange rate shock in 2002 because of concerns that the likely winner in the presidential election would pursue populist policies that would lead to currency depreciation. The resulting depreciation then led to a substantial overshoot of the Brazilian inflation target. In January 2003, the Banco Central do Brasil announced a procedure for how it would modify its inflation targets. First, the central bank estimated the regulated-price shock to be 1.7 percent. Then taking into account the nature and persistence of the shocks, it estimated the inertia from past shocks to be 4.2 percent of which two-thirds was to be accepted, resulting in a further adjustment of 2.8 percent. Then the central bank added these two numbers to the previously announced target of 4 percent to get an adjusted target for 2003 of 8.5 percent ($= 4\% + 1.7\% + 2.8\%$). The central bank then announced the adjusted target in an open letter sent to the Minister of Finance in January 2003, which explained that getting to the non-adjusted target of 4 percent too quickly would entail far too high a loss of output. Specifically, the announcement indicated that an attempt to achieve an inflation rate of 6.5 percent in 2003 would be expected to entail a decline of 1.6 percent of GDP, while trying to achieve the previous target of 4 percent would be expected to lead to an even larger decline of GDP of 7.3 percent.

The procedure followed by the Banco Central do Brasil had tremendous transparency, both in articulating why the inflation target was missed and also in explaining why the new target path for inflation was chosen. The discussion of alternative target paths, with the explanation that lower inflation paths would lead to large output losses, showed that the central bank did indeed care about output fluctuations, thus demonstrating that it was not an "inflation nutter" and that its concern about output losses was aligned with similar concerns by the public.

Even though advanced economies have not yet had inflation shocks of the magnitude that Brazil has recently experienced, outlining the procedures that they will use to respond to future adverse shocks provides a vehicle for them to explain that they do indeed care about output fluctuations.[18] By announcing that they would do what the Brazilians did if a situation arose in which inflation shifted substantially away from the long-run goal, central bankers can get the dirty little secret out of the closet that they do have an appropriate concern about output fluctuations. Yet, they will still be able to assure the public that they continue to worry about the long run and the importance of achieving price stability. A procedure like the one followed by Brazil conveys the idea that the central bank cares about output fluctuations in a forward-looking context because it highlights decisions that the central bank will make about the future path of inflation and the horizon over which inflation will return to the target. It therefore continues to make clear that the central bank is focused on output fluctuations in a longer-run and not a short-run context, which is necessary for minimising the time-inconsistency problem.

Monetary authorities can further the public's understanding that they care about reducing output fluctuations in the long run by emphasising that monetary policy needs to be just as vigilant in preventing inflation from falling too low as it is in preventing it from being too high. They can do this (and some central banks have) by explaining that an explicit inflation target may help the monetary authorities stabilise the economy because they can be more aggressive in easing monetary policy in the face of negative demand shocks to the economy without being concerned that this will cause a blowout in inflation expectations. However, in order to keep the communication strategy clear, the explanation of a monetary policy easing in the face of negative demand shocks needs to indicate that it is consistent with the preservation of price stability.

In addition, central banks can also clarify that they care about reducing output fluctuations by indicating that when the economy is very far below any reasonable measure of potential output, they will take expansionary actions to stimulate economic recovery. In this case, measurement error of potential output is likely to be swamped by the size of the output gap. Thus, it is far clearer that expansionary policy is appropriate and that inflation is unlikely to rise from such actions. In this situation, the case for taking actions to close the output gap is much stronger and does not threaten the credibility of the central bank in its pursuit of price stability.

5.5 Concluding Remarks

Transparency is a virtue, but like all virtues it can go too far. The famous fashion designer Chanel came up with the marvelous dictum that "You can never be too rich or too thin." But you can be too thin—either anorexia or starvation is a killer. Similarly central banks can be too transparent. Central bank transparency must always be thought of as a means to an end. Transparency is beneficial when it serves to simplify communication with the public and helps generate support for central banks to conduct monetary policy optimally with an appropriate focus on long-run objectives. Some types of transparency may not do this.

This chapter has argued that some suggestions for increased transparency, particularly a central bank announcement of its objective function or projections of the path of the policy interest rate, will complicate the communication process and weaken support for a central bank focus on long-run objectives. Transparency can indeed go too far.

However, there is one area in which the lack of central bank transparency does create problems: the unwillingness of many central banks to honestly discuss that they do care about reducing output fluctuations. Here transparency could be substantially improved. By describing procedures for how the path and horizon of inflation targets would be modified in the face of large shocks, by emphasising that monetary policy will be just as vigilant in preventing inflation from falling too low as it is in preventing it from being too high, and by indicating that expansionary policies will be pursued when output falls very far below potential, central banks can get the dirty little secret out of the closet that they do care about output fluctuations. These steps to improve transparency will increase support for the central bank's policies and independence, but avoid a focus on the short run that could interfere with the ability of the central bank to do its job effectively.

Notes

I thank Emilia Simeonova for her excellent research assistance. I also thank Don Kohn, Ken Kuttner, my discussant Warwick McKibbin, and participants at the conference. Any views expressed in this chapter are those of the author only and not those of Columbia University or the National Bureau of Economic Research.

1. As quoted in "Monetary zeal: how Federal Reserve under Volcker finally slowed down inflation," *Wall Street Journal*, 7 December, 1984, p 23.

2. The model of Barro and Gordon (1983) has the time-inconsistency problem residing inside the central bank. But as I have argued elsewhere in Mishkin (2000), the source of the time-inconsistency problem is in the political process because central bankers are very aware of the time-inconsistency problem and are indeed extremely averse to falling into a time-inconsistency trap.

3. For example, see Bernanke et al. (1999) and Mishkin (1999).

4. The so-called Taylor curve first outlined in Taylor (1979).

5. The Bank of Israel publishes an inflation forecast based on a survey of private sector expectations, but not its own inflation forecast. The Central Bank of the Republic of Turkey (CBRT) does not officially call its framework inflation targeting but instead refers to it as "implicit inflation targeting." However, the end-of-year inflation target is agreed on by the government and the IMF. Like Israel, the CBRT does not publish its own forecasts, but does publish inflation forecasts based on a private sector survey. Note that although the European Central Bank (ECB) does not call itself an inflation targeter, it does have an explicit inflation objective and so has some elements of an inflation-targeting regime. The ECB does publish its inflation and output forecasts.

6. The central banks of Australia and South Korea do announce output forecasts in other settings, but the frequency of these forecasts is not as high as in *Inflation Reports*.

7. The central banks of Brazil, the Czech Republic, Hungary, Iceland, Norway, Poland and the United Kingdom do publish projections of the future policy-rate path, but it is based on market expectations and not their assessment of the expected policy-rate path. The central bank of Norway does have an extensive discussion of future monetary policy in their *Inflation Report*, but it is still quite qualitative. Other inflation-targeting central banks, such as the central banks of the Czech Republic, Iceland and Romania, have provided less formal discussions of their assessment of the future policy-rate path.

8. Models with more forward-looking behaviour such as the dynamic new Keynesian model in Clarida, Galí and Gertler (1999) would yield similar conclusions.

9. However, for reasons outlined in the next section, there are arguments against the publication of forecasts of output gaps.

10. See Svensson (2003a, 2003b) and Woodford (2003).

11. Goodhart (2001, p 173).

12. Kohn (2000) comes to a similar conclusion. He reports that members of the Bank of England's Monetary Policy Committee stressed the difficulty of getting agreement on a future path of interest rates.

13. The central banks of Brazil, the Czech Republic, Norway and the United Kingdom publish forecasts based on projections of the future policy-rate path that are *based on market expectations*. Norway does have an extensive section in its *Inflation Report* on the setting of future policy rates which is qualitative.

14. This criticism of the Bank of England's published forecasts has been raised by Martijn and Samiei (1999).

15. Although a forecast based on a constant-interest-rate path is logically inconsistent, it is internally consistent: that is, a forecast can be conditioned on any assumption about an interest-rate path. Indeed, Edey and Stone (this volume) argue that if a monetary policy committee makes decisions based on unchanged future policy then the publication of these forecasts is consistent with transparency.

16. See Sherwin (1999), Drew and Orr (1999) and Reserve Bank of New Zealand (2000).

17. The fixed horizon is also problematic because it is inconsistent with optimal monetary policy: for example, see Woodford (2004). Indeed, critics of inflation targeting, most notably Don Kohn (2004), who is a member of the Board of Governors of the Federal Reserve, have also worried that inflation targeting may be too rigid because inflation-targeting central banks in advanced economies have often adopted a fixed horizon for their inflation targets.

18. Central banks in advanced countries do have an awareness of the need to modify the inflation path if the economy is subjected to large shocks. For example, in the United Kingdom, the inflation-targeting regime stipulates that if inflation is knocked more than 1 percentage point away from the target (now 2 percent), then the Bank of England will need to specify the path of inflation and the length of time that it will take to get back to the target.

References

Barro R. J. and D. B. Gordon (1983), "A positive theory of monetary policy in a natural rate mode," *Journal of Political Economy*, 91(4), pp 589–610.

Bernanke B. S., T. Laubach, F. S. Mishkin and A. S. Posen (1999), *Inflation targeting: lessons from the international experience*, Princeton University Press, Princeton.

Bernanke B. S. and M. Woodford (1997), "Inflation forecasts and monetary policy," *Journal of Money, Credit and Banking*, 29(4), pp 653–684.

Calvo G. (1978), "On the time consistency of optimal policy in the monetary economy," *Econometrica*, 46(6), pp 1411–1428.

Chari V. V., L. J. Christiano and M. Eichenbaum (1998), "Expectation traps and discretion," *Journal of Economic Theory*, 81(2), pp 462–492.

Clarida R., J. Galí and M. Gertler (1999), "The science of monetary policy: a new Keynesian perspective," *Journal of Economic Literature*, 37(4), pp 1661–1707.

Drew A. and A. Orr (1999), "The Reserve Bank's role in the recent business cycle: actions and evolution," Reserve Bank of New Zealand *Bulletin*, 62(1), pp 5–24.

Eggertsson G. B. and M. Woodford (2003), "The zero bound on interest rates and optimal monetary policy," *Brookings Papers on Economic Activity*, 1, pp 139–211.

Fraga A., I. Goldfajn and A. Minella (2003), "Inflation targeting in emerging market economies," in M. Gertler and K. Rogoff (eds), *NBER Macroeconomics Annual 2003*, MIT Press, Cambridge, pp 365–400.

Goodhart C. A. E. (2001), "Monetary transmission lags and the formulation of the policy decision on interest rates," Federal Reserve Bank of St. Louis *Review*, 83(4), pp 165–181.

Greider W. (1987), *Secrets of the temple: how the Federal Reserve runs the country*, Simon and Schuster, New York.

Ito T. and F. S. Mishkin (2004), "Monetary policy in Japan: problems and solutions," Columbia University, mimeo.

King M. (1997), "Changes in UK monetary policy: rules and discretion in practice," *Journal of Monetary Economics*, 39(1), pp 81–97.

Kohn D. L. (2000), "Report to the non-executive directors of the Court of the Bank of England on monetary processes and the work of monetary analysis," 18 October, available at http://www.bankofengland.co.uk/kohn/pdf.

Kohn D. L. (2004), "Inflation targeting," in Panel Discussion on "Inflation Targeting: Prospects and Problems," Federal Reserve Bank of St. Louis *Review*, 86(4), pp 179–183.

Kydland F. E. and E. C. Prescott (1977), "Rules rather than discretion: the inconsistency of optimal plans," *Journal of Political Economy*, 85(3), pp 473–491.

Levin A., F. M. Natalucci and J. M. Piger (2004), "The macroeconomic effects of inflation targeting," Federal Reserve Bank of St. Louis *Review*, 86(4), pp 51–80.

Martijn J. K. and H. Samiei (1999), "Central bank independence and the conduct of monetary policy in the United Kingdom," IMF WP 99/170.

McCallum B. T. (1995), "Two fallacies concerning central-bank independence," *American Economic Review*, 85(2), pp 207–211.

McCallum B. T. (2001), "Should monetary policy respond strongly to output gaps?" *American Economic Review*, 91(2), pp 258–262.

McCallum B. T. and E. Nelson (2000), "Timeless perspective vs. discretionary monetary policy in forward-looking models," NBER Working Paper No 7915.

Mishkin F. S. (1999), "International experiences with different monetary policy regimes," *Journal of Monetary Economics*, 43(3), pp 579–605.

Mishkin F. S. (2000), "What should central banks do?" Federal Reserve Bank of St. Louis *Review*, 82(6), pp 1–13.

Mishkin F. S. and A. S. Posen (1997), "Inflation targeting: lessons from four countries," *Federal Reserve Bank of New York Economic Policy Review*, 3(3), pp 9–110.

Orphanides A. (1998), "Monetary policy evaluation with noisy information," Board of Governors of the Federal Reserve System, Finance and Economics Discussion Series No 1998-50.

Orphanides A. (2001), "Monetary policy rules based on real-time data," *American Economic Review*, 91(4), pp 964–985.

Orphanides A. (2002), "Monetary-policy rules and the great inflation," *American Economic Review*, 92(2), pp 115–120.

Reserve Bank of New Zealand (2000), *Monetary policy statement*, March.

Rogoff K. (1985), "The optimal degree of commitment to an intermediate target," *Quarterly Journal of Economics*, 100(4), pp 1169–1189.

Samuelson R. (1994), "Economic amnesia," *Newsweek*, 12 September, p 52.

Sherwin M. (1999), "Inflation targeting: 10 years on," speech to the New Zealand Association of Economists Conference, Rotorua, 1 July.

Svensson L. E. O. (1997), "Inflation forecast targeting: implementing and monitoring inflation targets," *European Economic Review*, 41(6), pp 1111–1146.

Svensson L. E. O. (2002), "Monetary policy and real stabilization," in *Rethinking stabilization policy*, a symposium sponsored by the Federal Reserve Bank of Kansas City, Jackson Hole, pp 261–312.

Svensson L. E. O. (2003a), "The inflation forecast and the loss function," in P. Mizen (ed), *Central banking, monetary theory and practice: essays in honour of Charles Goodhart, volume one*, Edward Elgar, Cheltenham, pp 135–152.

Svensson L. E. O. (2003b), "What is wrong with Taylor rules? Using judgement in monetary policy through targeting rules," *Journal of Economic Literature*, 41(2), pp 426–477.

Taylor J. B. (1979), "Estimation and control of a macroeconomic model with rational expectations," *Econometrica*, 47(5), pp 1267–1286.

Woodford M. (2003), *Interest and prices: foundations of a theory of monetary policy*, Princeton University Press, Princeton.

Woodford M. (2004), "Inflation targeting and optimal monetary policy," *Federal Reserve Bank of St. Louis Review* (July–August): 15–41.

6 Is There a Role for Monetary Aggregates in the Conduct of Monetary Policy?

Arturo Estrella and Frederic S. Mishkin

6.1 Introduction

The economics literature contains prescriptions for the use of monetary aggregates in macroeconomic policy that range from exclusive focus on the aggregates to their almost complete disregard. In principle, there are various potential uses for monetary aggregates. For instance, the aggregates may be used as information variables to provide a guide for the conduct of monetary policy. Such an informal role places only minimal demands on the aggregates, concerning mainly their informational content. More ambitious uses of the aggregates are also possible. For example, they could be used to signal the intentions of the central bank so as to make it accountable for carrying out policies that are consistent with its basic mandates and to enhance its credibility and the public's expectations of the attainment of its goals. Alternatively, the aggregates could be used in the context of a policy rule, such as the McCallum (1988) proposal for using the monetary base to target nominal income growth.[1] Such rules pose the greatest demands on the performance of the aggregates, presupposing stable causal relationships with the ultimate policy goals.

In all of these potential applications, however, it is necessary first and foremost that the aggregates have some value as information variables. It is therefore on this question that we focus in this chapter. We look at some recent proposals for the use of monetary aggregates in formal rules and perform empirical tests of the strength and stability of the empirical relationships that those rules presuppose. More generally, we ask what role the aggregates can have even if the approach to policy is more eclectic than that implied in these recent proposals.

Section 6.2 of the chapter presents preliminary empirical analysis of the relationships between money and nominal income and between money and inflation that need to hold if the aggregates are to be successfully used in any of the ways mentioned above. We focus on the monetary base, which is McCallum's (McCallum, 1988) preference, and on M2, which was advocated by Feldstein and Stock (1994). Some results for M1 are also included in the appendix. This chapter differs from most previous work in this literature in that we rely primarily on monthly data, which provide a richer sample than quarterly data although, as the appendix shows, the results are largely consistent with those obtained with quarterly data.

In section 6.3 of the chapter, we formulate a theoretical model that establishes conditions under which a rule such as McCallum's is optimal. The analysis suggests ways to improve on the rule while retaining its general form. With these results in hand, we return in section 6.4 to the performance of the base and of M2 in multivariate analysis of their relationships with money and nominal income or inflation, in both cases incorporating adjustments based on the improvements suggested by the analysis of section 6.3. Section 6.5 presents results from incorporating additional adjustments to these aggregates based on decomposing velocity into spectral components corresponding to low, medium (business cycle) and high frequency cycles.

Since economists and policymakers in Germany are more likely supporters of monetary aggregates than those in the United States, we repeat in section 6.6 some of the analysis of sections 6.2, 6.4 and 6.5 with German data. We focus on the informational content of M3 for growth and inflation in western Germany.

Our analysis, summarized in the final section, concludes that the empirical relationships involving monetary aggregates, nominal income, and inflation are not sufficiently strong and stable in the United States and Germany to support a straightforward role for monetary aggregates in the conduct of monetary policy.

6.2   Preliminary Multivariate Analysis

The use of monetary aggregates in policy is feasible only if the relationships between money and income or prices are both strong and stable over time. In this section, we examine these empirical relationships in a multivariate vector autoregression (VAR) context that includes nominal income, inflation and either the monetary base or M2.

The analysis in this section is similar to that of Feldstein and Stock (1994), who focus on what may be interpreted as alternative formulations of the nominal income equation from a series of VARs with different sets of variables. There are two main differences, however. First, we use monthly rather than quarterly data. Although the concept of nominal income is most directly captured by nominal GDP, as used by Feldstein and Stock, our proxy based on the Commerce Department/Conference Board index of coincident indicators and the consumer price index is very similar and allows for the use of the available monthly money series. Specifically, nominal growth is defined as the sum of the log changes in the coincident index and the consumer price index.

The results using monthly data do not differ appreciably from those using quarterly data, as evidenced by the similarity between the monthly results in the text and the quarterly results provided for reference in the appendix. Testing for the appropriate lag length in our VAR led to the use of nine monthly lags. This is consistent with the Feldstein–Stock specification, which uses three quarterly lags.

A second key difference between this and the Feldstein–Stock paper is related to a break in the data that is frequently identified as having occurred in 1979–1980. We focus on the period since October 1979 as one in which the performance of the monetary aggregates is poor, rather than on identifying the exact timing of the break, which seems to be a higher priority for Feldstein and Stock. A detailed discussion of the timing of the break is also found in Huizinga and Mishkin (1986).

Table 6.1 contains summary Granger–Sims causality statistics for a VAR containing nominal growth, inflation and growth in the monetary base. Specifically, the table reports the significance probability (p-value) of each of the F tests that corresponds to the joint hypothesis that the coefficients of all the lags of a given variable are equal to zero. The full sample results in the upper panel of the table suggest an orderly pattern in which, at a 5% level of significance, the monetary aggregate helps predict both income and inflation, but is itself not predicted by income and inflation. However, this apparent order is called into question by the analysis of subperiods.

The upper panel, which contains the p-value for a Chow test of a break in October 1979, presents strong evidence that the model is not stable. Furthermore, the results for the post-October 1979 sample, presented in the lower panel, give a totally different picture of the relationships. In this panel, only a variable's own lags are significant at the 5% level. Specifically, the monetary base is very insignificant in both the nominal income and inflation equations.[2] Although we will look at various refinements of this analysis, these results do not bode well for the use of the monetary base in a policy rule, or even for its use as an information variable. Table 6.1 (like some subsequent tables) also contains t statistics for the sums of the lag coefficients of the key regressors. In addition to the significance of these sums, the t statistics indicate whether the relationships have the appropriate signs.

Table 6.2 contains analogous results for a VAR containing M2. The results differ from those of table 6.1 in several important respects. First, the pattern of the full sample results is different: lags of M2 do not help explain inflation, but lags of both inflation and nominal growth help explain money growth. Second, the evidence of a break in October 1979 is much weaker in the first two equations, especially in the nominal income equation. This is consistent with the Feldstein–Stock results, and it is a point that they emphasize in their reading of the results.

Nevertheless, if we turn to the results in the lower panel for the latter part of the sample, the significance levels of M2 growth are not encouraging in either the nominal income or the inflation equations. In this sense, the post-October 1979 results are very similar to those obtained with the monetary base. One difference encountered here is that lags of inflation are significant in the equation for M2. This could be potentially important if M2 had been used over this period in countercyclical policy to

Table 6.1
Joint Significance Tests in VAR with Nominal Growth, Inflation, and Monetary Base (Monthly, 9 Lags)

Period	Dependent variable	p-values for			R^2	p-values for break (Oct. 79)	Coeff. sum on	t Statistic	p-value
		Nominal growth	Inflation	Money					
Mar. 60–Dec. 95	Nominal growth	0.000	0.002	0.021	0.289	0.019	Money	2.70	0.007
	Inflation	0.001	0.000	0.001	0.608	0.006	Money	1.44	0.150
	Money	0.162	0.384	0.000	0.366	0.020	Growth	-0.10	0.918
							Inflation	0.49	0.627
Oct. 79–Dec. 95	Nominal growth	0.000	0.078	0.673	0.310		Money	1.68	0.096
	Inflation	0.092	0.000	0.384	0.631		Money	0.34	0.731
	Money	0.693	0.852	0.000	0.353		Growth	-1.58	0.115
							Inflation	0.10	0.919

Nominal growth = $\Delta \log(\text{COIN}) + \Delta \log(\text{CPI}) = \Delta x_t$.
Inflation = $\Delta \log(\text{CPI}) = \Delta p_t$.
Money = $\Delta \log(\text{BASE}) = \Delta m_t$.

Table 6.2
Joint Significance Tests in VAR with Nominal Growth, Inflation, and M2 (Monthly, 9 Lags)

Period	Dependent variable	p-values for			R^2	p-values for break (Oct. 79)	Coeff. sum on	t Statistic	p-value
		Nominal growth	Inflation	Money					
Mar. 60–Dec. 95	Nominal growth	0.000	0.036	0.009	0.293	0.449	Money	3.74	0.000
	Inflation	0.002	0.000	0.484	0.590	0.080	Money	0.03	0.977
	Money	0.004	0.007	0.000	0.625	0.036	Growth	−1.87	0.063
							Inflation	1.50	0.134
Oct. 79–Dec. 95	Nominal growth	0.000	0.130	0.456	0.319		Money	1.55	0.122
	Inflation	0.253	0.000	0.482	0.628		Money	0.71	0.477
	Money	0.122	0.014	0.000	0.643		Growth	−0.45	0.656
							Inflation	0.35	0.730

Nominal growth $= \Delta \log(\text{COIN}) + \Delta \log(\text{CPI}) = \Delta y_t$.
Inflation $= \Delta \log(\text{CPI}) = \Delta p_t$.
Money $= \Delta \log(\text{M2}) = \Delta m_t$.

control the variability of inflation because, in that case, successful monetary policy might make it impossible to detect a predictive relationship running from money to inflation. This possibility is explored further in section 6.4.

Feldstein and Stock also estimate what amounts practically to the nominal growth equation in our VAR using an error correction specification, which allows for cointegration of M2 velocity and short-term interest rates.[3] We performed a similar exercise by estimating a cointegrating equation with the level of M2 velocity and the three-month Treasury bill rate and inserting the first lag of the residual from this equation into the nominal growth equation in the VAR. For the full 1959–1995 sample, the results were consistent with those of Feldstein and Stock in that the joint significance of the M2 lags and the error correction term was somewhat stronger, with the latter term in itself significant at the 1% level (joint p-value of 0.005 compared with 0.009 for M2 in table 6.2). In the post-1979 sample, however, the error correction term was not significant and there was no improvement in the joint significance level with its introduction (joint p-value of 0.547 compared with 0.456 for M2 in table 6.2).

6.3   Optimal Policy and the McCallum Rule

Proponents of the monetary aggregates have generally recognized that the lack of stability in the relationships identified in the previous section exist. McCallum (1988), for example, saw the need for adjusting for the fact that the relationship between the monetary base and nominal output changes over time, albeit in his view slowly and systematically. Thus, he proposed a policy rule that incorporates a time-varying adjustment.

The potential usefulness of McCallum's (McCallum, 1988) rule may be justified and interpreted in various ways. Although McCallum (1988) was not an attempt to come up with an optimal rule, we use his general reasoning in this section to develop a parsimonious framework in which a monetary policy rule of the McCallum type is optimal. This approach is then used to suggest possible improvements in the rule. This also has the advantage that it suggests how a monetary aggregate can be adjusted to provide empirical testing of the rule, which is conducted in section 6.4.

Previous research has been largely silent on the issue of the theoretical justification of money-based rules. The arguments given are generally informal, for example, in McCallum (1988) and Judd and Motley (1991), and the justification provided is typically based on artificial simulation results. Feldstein and Stock (1994) do calculate the optimal policy rule in a general vector autoregression context, but they too rely on simulations as the primary basis for their policy conclusions. Here, we connect these two approaches by deriving a policy rule which is formally similar—under some conditions identical—to that of McCallum.

Our model is based on the following assumptions. First, we use the identity associated with the quantity theory: nominal income equals money times velocity. Since this relationship may be viewed as the definition of velocity, it presupposes very little structure. Second, we assume that money is exogenous in the sense that its growth rate can be determined independently of current-period information. Third, we assume that velocity in the current period is unknown, but that the optimal prediction of velocity can be adequately characterized by a univariate ARIMA model. Fourth, we assume that the policy objective is to minimize the mean squared deviations of nominal income from a pre-specified target path. This objective is consistent with the analysis of all the papers cited in the previous paragraph.

The quantity theory, in log-difference form, may be expressed as:

$$\Delta x_t = \Delta m_t + \Delta v_t \tag{6.1}$$

where x is the log of nominal income, m is the log of money, and v is the log of money velocity. The process for velocity is assumed to have an ARIMA specification. For convenience, this ARIMA relationship is written in the form:

$$\Delta v_t = a(L)\Delta v_{t-1} + u_t + b(L)u_{t-1} \tag{6.2}$$

where u is white noise. The objective function is to minimize the mean squared deviation of nominal income (x_t) from its target level (x_t^*), conditional on the information available at time t.

To derive the policy rule, first write

$$\Delta v_t = E_{t-1}\Delta v_t + u_t \tag{6.3}$$

where E_t represents the expectation based on information available at time t. Combining Eqs. (6.1) and (6.3), and defining x_t^* as the target nominal income in period t, we obtain

$$\Delta x_t^* - \Delta x_t = \Delta x_t^* - \Delta m_t - E_{t-1}\Delta v_t - u_t$$

and, rearranging terms,

$$x_t^* - x_t = x_t^* - x_{t-1} - \Delta m_t - E_{t-1}\Delta v_t - u_t. \tag{6.4}$$

Since u_t is orthogonal to all the other terms in the right-hand side of Eq. (6.4), which are either policy choices or are predetermined as of time t, the conditional variance of Eq. (6.4) is given by

$$V_{t-1}(x_t^* - x_t) = V_{t-1}w_t + V_{t-1}u_t$$

where

$$w_t \equiv x_t^* - x_{t-1} - \Delta m_t - E_{t-1}\Delta v_t. \tag{6.5}$$

Thus, the conditional variance of Eq. (6.4) is minimized by setting $w_t = 0$, that is, by applying a money supply rule of the form

$$\Delta m_t^* = \Delta x_t^* - E_{t-1}\Delta v_t + x_{t-1}^* - x_{t-1}. \tag{6.6}$$

The ARIMA representation, Eq. (6.2), for Δv_t implies that

$$E_{t-1}\Delta v_t = a(L)\Delta v_{t-1} + b(L)u_{t-1}. \tag{6.7}$$

Substituting Eq. (6.7) into Eq. (6.6), and noting from Eqs. (6.4) and (6.5) that $w_t = 0$ implies that $u_t = -(x_t^* - x_t)$, produces the optimal monetary policy rule

$$\Delta m_t^* = \Delta x_t^* - a(L)\Delta v_{t-1} + (1 + b(L))(x_{t-1}^* - x_{t-1}). \tag{6.8}$$

Example 6.1 If the lag polynomials in the ARIMA expression for Δv_t are of the form

$$a(L) = \frac{1}{n}\sum_{j=0}^{n-1} L^j$$

that is, the autoregressive part consists of a simple average of lagged Δv_t, and if $b(L) = \beta$, a constant, then the optimal rule, Eq. (6.8), becomes

$$\Delta m_t^* = \Delta x_t^* - \overline{\Delta v}_{t-1} + (1 + \beta)(x_{t-1}^* - x_{t-1}) \tag{6.9}$$

where

$$\overline{\Delta v}_t = \frac{1}{n}\sum_{j=0}^{n-1} \Delta v_{t-j} = \frac{1}{n}(v_t - v_{t-n}).$$

With n corresponding to 48 months, Eq. (6.9) is the rule suggested by McCallum (1988).[4]

The resulting rule is plausible, but does not fit the data well. The first equation in table 6.3 provides an empirical estimate of β, which is the only parameter in the McCallum rule, obtained by estimating the constrained form of the ARIMA Eq. (2), over the period from March 1963 to December 1995. As noted in the introduction, we use the index of coincident indicators and the consumer price index as monthly measures of real activity and prices. McCallum (1988) does not estimate this parameter, but uses a range of values $0 \le \lambda = 1 + \beta \le 0.5$ in his simulations. Our estimate of $\lambda = 1 + \beta$ is 1.175, which is substantially larger than any of McCallum's assumed values. In fact, when inserted in the monetary rule, this estimate implies that the reaction to a gap between actual and target nominal income in the previous period is larger than the gap itself.[5]

The ARIMA formulation may be relaxed to allow the simple average of the lagged Δv_t to have a coefficient different from 1. These results appear in the second

Table 6.3
Univariate ARIMA Models of Velocity for the Monetary Base and M2 (Monthly)

Equation	Monetary aggregate	Estimation period	Coefficient estimates (standard error)			Standard error (Eq.)	R^2
			AR1 (α)	MA1 (β)	McCallum (γ)		
(1)	Base	Mar. 63–Dec. 95	0	0.175 (0.050)	1	0.00509	0.076
(2)	Base	Mar. 63–Dec. 95	0	0.173 (0.050)	0.629 (0.162)	0.00506	0.089
(3)	Base	Mar. 63–Dec. 95	0.889 (0.046)	−0.708 (0.071)	0	0.00494	0.133
(4)	Base	Mar. 63–Dec. 95	0.846 (0.073)	−0.662 (0.097)	0.062 (0.067)	0.00494	0.135
(5)	Base	Mar. 59–Dec. 95	0.846 (0.056)	−0.647 (0.081)	0	0.00502	0.127
(6)	Base	Oct. 79–Dec. 95	0.871 (0.064)	−0.613 (0.103)	0	0.00487	0.168
(7)	M2	Mar. 59–Dec. 95	0.753 (0.062)	−0.403 (0.086)	0	0.00514	0.221
(8)	M2	Oct. 79–Dec. 95	0.736 (0.092)	−0.342 (0.128)	0	0.00519	0.250

Equation is of the form:

$$\Delta v_t = \alpha \Delta v_{t-1} + \varepsilon_t + \beta \varepsilon_{t-1} + \gamma \overline{\Delta v_{t-1}}$$

where $\Delta v_t = \Delta \log(\text{COIN}) + \Delta \log(\text{CPI}) - \Delta \log(M)$

COIN = Commerce Department/Conference Board index of coincident indicators
CPI = consumer price index
M = Monetary base or M2
$\overline{\Delta v_t} = 1/48(v_t - v_{t-48})$.

equation of table 6.3. The fit is somewhat better and equality of the parameter to 1 is rejected. However, the estimate of the moving average parameter β is very close to the estimate from the previous equation and is therefore also outside the anticipated range of values. As the following example shows, a simpler ARIMA formulation produces a better fit.

Example 6.2   Consider an ARIMA$(1, 1, 1)$ model for v_t, that is, with both $a(L) = \alpha$ and $b(L) = \beta$ constant. Then the optimal monetary rule is

$$\Delta m_t^* = \Delta x_t^* - \alpha \Delta v_{t-1} + (1 + \beta)(x_{t-1}^* - x_{t-1}). \tag{6.10}$$

The empirical support for Eq. (6.10) is considerably stronger than that for Eq. (6.9). Estimates of the ARIMA$(1, 1, 1)$ model corresponding to Eq. (6.2) are shown in line 3 of table 6.3 (higher-order terms are insignificant for both the autoregressive and the moving average components). The autoregressive component implies a lagged velocity adjustment of 0.889 times the previous period's change in velocity, plus a reaction to the previous period's gap between actual and target nominal income that corresponds to 0.292 of the gap. This latter figure is well within the range assumed by McCallum in his simulations, but is used in conjunction with a velocity adjustment based on only one lag.

In order to decide which specification is better, the ARIMA$(1, 1, 1)$ model versus the model with the McCallum-type 48-month term, in Eq. (6.4) of table 6.3, we include both the one-lag velocity adjustment corresponding to the ARIMA$(1, 1, 1)$ model and the McCallum-type term. Only the one-lag term is significant; the longer moving average adjustment is insignificant with a t-statistic on its coefficient smaller than one. In the fifth equation in the table, the ARIMA$(1, 1, 1)$ form is estimated over the longer sample period starting with March 1959, since the MA(1) term only requires using up one observation at the beginning while the model with the McCallum average uses up 48 observations. The results are stable in comparison with the same model estimated over shorter periods, as in the third and sixth equations. A test for a break at October 1979 in Eq. (6.5) is insignificant, with a p-value of 0.24.

In the seventh equation of table 6.3, the ARIMA$(1, 1, 1)$ model is estimated using M2 in place of the monetary base, with very similar results. The parameter estimates are close to those obtained with the base, and higher-order autoregressive and moving average terms are again insignificant. The implication is that the monetary policy rule represented by Eq. (6.10) is also feasible with M2 as the instrument and with parameters that are similar to those that are optimal with the base. The M2 velocity equation is also stable, as illustrated by the last equation in the table. A test for a break at October 1979 is also insignificant in this case, with a p-value of 0.43.

6.4 Multivariate Analysis with Time Domain Adjustments

Although the Granger-causality tests presented in section 6.2 are not very encouraging for the use of monetary aggregates in a policy rule, the analysis in section 6.3 suggests that forecasts of velocity, explicit or implicit, might be used to help improve the performance of a money-based policy rule. For instance, the McCallum rule may be interpreted as a way of adjusting for changing trends in velocity in order to target nominal income more accurately. In this section, we adjust the money growth variable that appears in the VARs of the previous section by adding to it some measure of the expected change in velocity. Formally, the variable in the VAR is

$$\Delta m_t^A = \Delta m_t + A_t$$

where, for example,

$$A_t = \frac{1}{48}(v_{t-1} - v_{t-49}) = \frac{1}{48}(\Delta v_{t-1} + \cdots + \Delta v_{t-48})$$

the McCallum 4-year simple average of changes in velocity. Alternatively,

$$A_t = \frac{1}{48}(v_{t-1} - v_{t-49}) + \beta \varepsilon_{t-1}$$

the McCallum average adjusted for moving average errors, or

$$A_t = \alpha \Delta v_{t-1} + \beta \varepsilon_{t-1}$$

the change in velocity forecast from the ARIMA$(1, 1, 1)$ model.

Table 6.4 presents the p-values for the adjusted monetary base in the nominal growth and inflation equations from the VAR. The first row repeats results from table 6.1 for comparison, and the results of the above adjustments are shown in the next three rows. (The results in the last row are discussed in the following section.) In the nominal growth equation, none of the three adjustments do anything to improve the significance of the aggregate; in fact, the p-values are higher. Note, however, that in each case, the Chow test for the break becomes insignificant, so that the adjustments do succeed in producing more stable equations.

The effect of the adjustments on the inflation equation is in a sense the opposite. With each of the three adjustments, there is a reduction in the p-values, although clearly even the lowest figure of 0.334 (for the 48-month average with a moving average term) is unacceptably high. In this case, however, the adjustments fail to make a dent in the stability problem, with very strong signals of a break for all three adjustments.

Comparable results for M2 are found in table 6.5. As in the case of the monetary base, there is no improvement in the significance of M2 in the nominal income

Table 6.4
Significance and Stability (*p*-values) of Adjusted Monetary Base in Nominal Growth and Inflation Equations (Monthly, 9 Lags, Oct. 79 to Dec. 95)

| | Equation | | | |
| | Nominal growth | | Inflation | |
Adjustment to base	Significance	Break[a]	Significance	Break[a]
None	0.673	0.019	0.384	0.006
48-monthly average	0.796	0.105	0.351	0.006
48-monthly average with MA term	0.792	0.160	0.334	0.004
ARIMA(1,1,1)	0.772	0.127	0.373	0.002
Low frequencies excluded	0.460	0.265	0.285	0.003

Adjusted base $= \Delta m_t^A = \Delta m_t + A_t$ where

$A_t = 1/48(v_{t-1} - v_{t-49})$ (48-month average)
$= 1/48(v_{t-1} - v_{t-49}) + 1.171\varepsilon_{t-1}$ (48-month average with MA term)
$= 0.846\Delta v_{t-1} + 0.353\varepsilon_{t-1}$ (ARIMA(1, 1, 1))
$=$ components of VAR variables with cycles > 8 yrs excluded (low frequencies excluded)

[a] Break in Oct. 79 when estimated from Feb. 59 to Dec. 95.

Table 6.5
Significance and Stability (*p*-values) of Adjusted M2 in Nominal Growth and Price Equations (Monthly, 9 Lags, Oct. 79 to Dec. 95)

| | Equation | | | |
| | Nominal growth | | Inflation | |
Adjustment to M2	Significance	Break[a]	Significance	Break[a]
None	0.456	0.449	0.482	0.080
48-monthly average	0.562	0.589	0.532	0.255
48-monthly average with MA term	0.503	0.635	0.432	0.290
ARIMA(1,1,1)	0.546	0.444	0.366	0.131
Low frequencies excluded	0.294	0.395	0.255	0.019

Adjusted M2 $= \Delta m_t^A = \Delta m_t + A_t$ where

$A_t = 1/48(v_{t-1} - v_{t-49})$ (48-month average)
$= 1/48(v_{t-1} - v_{t-49}) + 1.304\varepsilon_{t-1}$ (48-month average with MA term)
$= 0.753\Delta v_{t-1} + 0.597\varepsilon_{t-1}$ (ARIMA(1, 1, 1))
$=$ components of VAR variables with cycles > 8 yrs excluded (low frequencies excluded)

[a] Break in Oct. 79 when estimated from Feb. 59 to Dec. 95.

Table 6.6
Significance (*p*-values) of Target Variables in Money and Interest Rate Equations (Monthly, 9 Lags, Oct. 79 to Dec. 95)

Dependent variable	Adjustment[a]	Target variable (lags)	Joint significance of lags	Sum of lags	Significance of sum
Base	48-month average with MA term	Nominal income	0.007	−0.098	0.311
Base	ARIMA(1,1,1)	Nominal income	0.003	0.293	0.013
M2	48-month average with MA term	Nominal income	0.000	0.036	0.710
M2	ARIMA(1,1,1)	Nominal income	0.000	0.338	0.005
M2	None	Inflation	0.014	0.036	0.730
M2	48-month average	Inflation	0.007	0.174	0.164
M2	48-month average with MA term	Inflation	0.008	0.167	0.183
M2	ARIMA(1,1,1)	Inflation	0.023	−0.022	0.841
M2	Low frequencies excluded	Inflation	0.020	−0.292	0.160

[a] Adjustments are described in Tables 6.4 and 6.5.

equation with any of the three adjustments. In the inflation equation, two of the three adjustments improve significance, but not nearly enough to make the levels acceptable.

Thus, the McCallum insight of adjusting for predictable components in the change in velocity produces some empirical gains, especially in the inflation equation, but these gains are too marginal to make the relationships useful in practice. This conclusion holds even with the weak requirements associated with the use of the aggregates as information variables, and even more strongly in the context of their employment in formal policy rules.

We must note one caveat to the foregoing interpretation of the results. The insignificance of the aggregates, adjusted or unadjusted, in the nominal income growth and inflation equations since October 1979 might be attributable to their use in smoothing fluctuations in those variables. Faster growth in the target variable would prompt a slowing down of money growth, leading to a negative relationship.[6]

Table 6.6 investigates this phenomenon. For any VAR equation described in sections 6.2, 6.4 and 6.5, estimated from October 1979 to December 1995, in which a target variable is significant in the money equation, the table shows the sum of the coefficients of the lags of the target variable and the level of significance of the sum. For example, the first line shows the significance of lags of nominal income growth in the equation for the monetary base, the latter adjusted by McCallum's four-year velocity adjustment with a moving average term. The lags of income growth are significant at the 0.007 level and the sum of the lag coefficients is negative (-0.098), as suggested by the above discussion. However, the negative sum is not significant, and the support for the explanation is not compelling.

However, in two-thirds of the cases, the coefficient sums in table 6.6 are positive, contradicting the proposed explanation. In fact, these positive sums are in some cases significant, lending very little credence to the story that the poor performance of the aggregates as information variables is due to their use to smooth out nominal income or inflation fluctuations.

6.5   Multivariate Analysis with Frequency Domain Adjustments

An alternative way to adjust monetary aggregates to improve their performance in explaining income and inflation is to remove components in the frequency domain that might be obscuring the relationship between the monetary aggregates and nominal income and inflation. An informal justification for the long (four-year) moving average of changes in velocity in the McCallum policy rule is that it would tend to capture persistent changes in the velocity process without placing too much emphasis on short-term fluctuations. McCallum (1988, note 13) states that

As the purpose of this term is to take account of possible changes in velocity growth resulting from regulatory and technological sources, the period of averaging should be long enough to avoid dependence on cyclical conditions (which are reflected in the third term).

Here "the third term" refers to the previous period's gap between target and actual nominal income, as in Eq. (6.9).

As shown in section 6.3, this interpretation is not entirely consistent with the optimization framework presented there, since the empirical estimates suggest a simpler form with only one lag. Nevertheless, we show in this section that McCallum's reasoning does have some empirical support. If the velocity series is decomposed by spectral methods into various frequency bands, the evidence suggests that only the low frequency band exhibits instability across the October 1979 break point.

Thus, as before, define the change in velocity by

$$\Delta v_t = \Delta x_t - \Delta m_t.$$

To construct the frequency band decomposition, we computed the Fourier transform of the demeaned Δv_t series using data from February 1959 to December 1995.[7] The decomposition was accomplished by retaining only the points in each of three frequency bands and applying the inverse Fourier transform.[8] The frequency bands are:

Low frequencies   cycles longer than eight years,

Medium frequencies   cycles longer than one year and no longer than eight (corresponding to the business cycle),[9] and

High frequencies   cycles up to one year.

The stability test applied to these components is very simple: each one is regressed on a constant term and a dummy that is 1 starting with October 1979 and 0 otherwise. The results are shown in table 6.7. It is fairly clear that the velocity of the monetary base is lower in the second part of the sample. When the frequency band components are examined, only the low frequencies exhibit instability, much more strongly so than the aggregate series.

The results are similar for M2 velocity, although the change in trend is positive and not as noticeable in the aggregate series, for which the break has a level of significance of 22%. However, once the frequency decomposition is applied, it is clear that there is a break and that it is exclusively concentrated in the low-frequency component, as was the case for the velocity of the monetary base. Figure 6.1 plots the low-frequency components of both base and M2 velocities over the sample period. The trends found in table 6.7 are readily apparent in the figure, although it is also clear that these low-frequency fluctuations are more complicated than a simple step function.

This evidence of instability in the low-frequency components of the base and M2 velocities suggests that the higher-frequency relationships between money and

Table 6.7
Structural Break in Velocity: Analysis by Frequency Bands (Monthly Data, Feb. 59 to Dec. 95)

Velocity of	Frequencies[a]	t Statistic for break in Oct. 79	Significance (t prob)
Base	All	−5.51	0.000
Base	Low	−23.5	0.000
Base	Medium	0.12	0.907
Base	High	0.01	0.993
M2	All	1.22	0.223
M2	Low	4.38	0.000
M2	Medium	−0.06	0.956
M2	High	0.07	0.943

Velocity $= \Delta v_t = \Delta x_t - \Delta m_t$,
$\Delta x_t =$ nominal growth $= \Delta \log(\text{COIN}) = \Delta \log(\text{CPI})$,
$\Delta m_t =$ growth in base or M2.

[a] Variables are decomposed by computing the inverse Fourier transform of 3 spectral frequency bands: low (cycles longer than 8 yrs), medium (between 1 and 8 yrs, corresponding to business cycle), and high (up to one year).

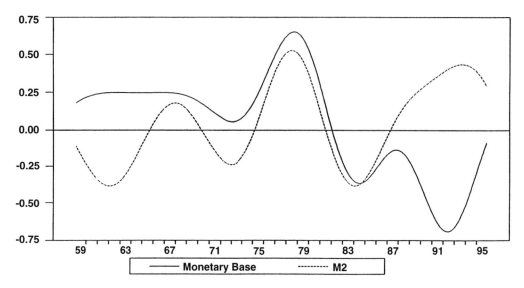

Figure 6.1
Low frequency component of change in velocity: proportion of standard deviation of change in velocity.

nominal income may be stronger and more stable than those of the aggregate series. This point is examined in the last row of tables 6.4 and 6.5, which report the results of performing the VAR exercise of the previous section on only the medium and high-frequency components of nominal income, inflation and money growth.[10] This is equivalent to running a band-spectrum VAR in the sense of the band-spectrum regressions proposed by Engle (1974).

Although there is a noticeable improvement in the significance level of the monetary variables in the band-spectrum equations, it is still insufficient to achieve standard levels of acceptability. In each case, the significance level is lower than in any of the other equations, either unadjusted or with time-domain adjustments. Nevertheless, the best performance is in the inflation equation with the monetary base, where the significance level is 28.5%. Another unattractive feature of the spectral VARs is that for both the base and M2, the inflation equation has a break in October 1979. Of course, with the low significance levels, this is of secondary importance.

6.6 Some Evidence from Germany: Output, Prices, and M3

Even though there are in the United States some notable proponents of the use of monetary aggregates in monetary policy, there are many more who would argue that the US evidence in this regard is far from compelling. It is useful, therefore, to perform some of the analysis of the foregoing sections with German data, since

Table 6.8
Joint Significance Tests in VAR for Germany with Income Growth, Inflation, and M3 (Quarterly, 3 Lags)

Period	Dependent variable	p-values for			R^2	Coeff. sum on	t Statistic	p-value
		Income growth	Inflation	Money				
Mar. 70–	Nominal growth	0.178	0.367	0.074	0.132	Money	2.65	0.009
Dec. 95	Inflation	0.043	0.247	0.096	0.253	Money	0.87	0.389
	Money	0.749	0.444	0.000	0.340	Growth	−0.43	0.668
						Inflation	1.35	0.180
	Real growth	0.315	0.058	0.046	0.135	Money	2.34	0.022
Mar. 70–	Nominal growth	0.200	0.305	0.008	0.195	Money	3.59	0.001
Sep. 90	Inflation	0.179	0.263	0.129	0.266	Money	0.89	0.379
	Money	0.880	0.658	0.001	0.342	Growth	−0.42	0.677
						Inflation	0.75	0.458
	Real growth	0.071	0.011	0.013	0.206	Money	3.21	0.002

Nominal growth = $\Delta \log(\text{nominal GDP}) = \Delta x_t$,
Inflation = $\Delta \log(\text{GDP deflator}) = \Delta p_t$,
Money = $\Delta \log(\text{M3}) = \Delta m_t$.

German economists and policymakers are more likely to be strong advocates of the monetary aggregates than their US counterparts. In this section, we apply the principal tests of sections 6.2, 6.4 and 6.5 to data for western Germany: nominal GDP growth, growth in the GDP deflator, and the broad M3 aggregate (on which the Bundesbank focuses).[11]

VAR results analogous to those presented for the United States in table 6.1 appear in table 6.8. The results are in fact very consistent with those obtained with US M2. For example, there is evidence that M3 is a strong predictor of nominal and real growth over the full sample, but not of inflation. In the German case, the joint test of the lags of M3 in the nominal growth equation for the full sample is not obviously conclusive with a p-value of 0.074. However, the sum of those coefficients is significant at the 1% level. Moreover, if the post-reunification period is excluded, recognizing the difficulty in making these data fully consistent with the past, the results are very strong. Both the joint test and the test of the sum are significant at the 1% level.

Also consistent with the US results are the consequences of focusing on data since October of 1979. For Germany, this is not as clear a break point as it is for the United States. Nevertheless, the 1980s and 1990s are associated with financial innovations that may have changed the traditional relationships among economic variables. Table 6.9 shows the German results for this latter period, both including and excluding the post-reunification period. There are essentially no significant results in either panel of table 6.9.

Other than the own lags of M3 in the top panel, the only result that is significant at the 5% level is that for the sum of the lags of inflation in the money equation, also

Table 6.9
Joint Significance Tests in VAR for Germany with Income Growth, Inflation, and M3 (Quarterly, 3 Lags)

| Period | Dependent variable | p-values for | | | R^2 | Coeff. sum on | t Statistic | p-value |
		Income growth	Inflation	Money				
Dec. 79–	Nominal growth	0.551	0.433	0.667	0.108	Money	0.20	0.840
Dec. 95	Inflation	0.741	0.156	0.335	0.168	Money	−0.65	0.517
	Money	0.378	0.160	0.001	0.390	Growth	−1.51	0.137
						Inflation	2.02	0.048
	Real growth	0.634	0.097	0.197	0.207	Money	0.51	0.613
Dec. 79–	Nominal growth	0.453	0.716	0.749	0.130	Money	−0.55	0.587
Sep. 90	Inflation	0.809	0.174	0.201	0.240	Money	−0.45	0.653
	Money	0.682	0.130	0.867	0.245	Growth	−1.13	0.265
						Inflation	1.13	0.267
	Real growth	0.443	0.091	0.288	0.243	Money	−0.43	0.669

Nominal growth $= \Delta \log(\text{nominal GDP}) = \Delta x_t$,
Inflation $= \Delta \log(\text{GDP deflator}) = \Delta p_t$,
Money $= \Delta \log(\text{M3}) = \Delta m_t$.

in the top panel. As discussed in section 6.4, the significance of this sum might be an indication that M3 was set in reaction to current observed inflation, a procedure which, if successful, could obscure the observed effects of M3 on inflation. This interpretation is not supported, however, since the positive sign would imply that M3 would grow faster in reaction to higher inflation.

When interpreting the results of table 6.9, it should be noted that the post-1979 and pre-reunification sample is not very large, which could certainly affect significance. The problem is worse in Germany than in the United States because of the possible differences in the post-reunification data.

To summarize, the results of the multivariate analysis in Germany are very similar to those obtained for the United States. For the full sample period, there is evidence in both countries that monetary aggregates are predictors of subsequent economic growth. However, for the period since October 1979, there are no clear signs that M3 is useful as an information variable. While it is possible that the estimation of a more detailed structural model could extract more information than our straightforward predictive analysis, it seems unlikely that strong relationships can be ascertained for the latter period.[12]

6.7 Conclusion

At the outset, we identified various possible roles for monetary aggregates in monetary policy, but noted that all those roles presuppose that the aggregates perform at least as information variables. Our empirical results show that in the United States since 1979, the monetary aggregates fall considerably short of those requirements. We have tried to present the aggregates in the best possible light by employing sensible adjustments suggested in the literature and by developing further adjustments to increase their precision. Some of the new adjustments proved more successful than the earlier suggestions, but not enough to make a compelling case.

The results with German M3 were hardly more favorable for the use of M3 as an information variable. In fact, the German results are very consistent with those for the United States, particularly with US M2, and do not exhibit any obvious significance in the period since 1979.

Although our results have not ruled out that monetary aggregates cannot be used in some complicated way as an information variable, they do indicate that the monetary aggregates, the monetary base and M2 in particular, currently cannot be used in a straightforward way for monetary policy purposes. Whatever their informational content may have been in earlier time periods, they do not seem to provide adequate and consistent information at present in the United States. The inability of monetary aggregates to perform well as straightforward information variables in recent periods has the implication that they cannot be used to signal the stance of monetary policy, an important requirement if money growth targets are to be used as part of a strategy to increase the transparency of monetary policy to the public and the markets.

We should note, however, that the majority of the period we focus on has been one of relative price stability in the United States and Germany. The problem with monetary aggregates as a guide to monetary policy is that there frequently are shifts in velocity that alter the relationship between money growth and nominal income. A way of describing this situation is to think of velocity shocks as the noise that obscures the signal from monetary aggregates. In a regime in which changes in nominal income, inflation and the money supply are subdued, the signal-to-noise ratio is likely to be low, making monetary aggregates a poor guide for policy. However, in other economies or in other time periods in which we experience more pronounced changes in money and inflation, the velocity shocks might become small relative to the swings in money growth, thus producing a higher signal-to-noise ratio. In these situations, the results could very well be different and monetary aggregates could usefully play a role in the conduct of monetary policy.

Acknowledgments

We thank Ben McCallum and participants at the Swiss National Bank's 1996 Gerzensee Conference, and participants at a seminar at the Federal Reserve Bank of New York for their helpful comments, and Betsy Reynolds for her research assistance.

Any views expressed in this chapter are those of the authors only and not those of Columbia University, the NBER, the Federal Reserve Bank of New York or the Federal Reserve System.

Appendix A: Quarterly Results and VARs with Both Money and Interest Rates

Previous papers examining the relationship between monetary aggregates, income growth and inflation have typically focused on GNP/GDP and have therefore used quarterly data. To facilitate comparison of the results of this paper with the earlier literature, tables 6.10 and 6.11 present quarterly results based on nominal GDP growth and the GDP deflator. In general, the results with quarterly data are less significant than the corresponding results with monthly data. The one exception is the significance of the monetary base in the equation for inflation in which low-frequency components have been excluded from all three variables. The lags of the base are jointly significant and the sum of their coefficients is positive with a p-value of 0.001. These results suggest that there is information in the monetary base with regard to future inflation, not with regard to nominal GDP as the McCallum approach would require.

In the past, M1 has also been proposed as an instrument of monetary policy, although recent experience has been less encouraging than that for M2. Table 6.12 presents results from a VAR with monthly data for M1 growth, inflation and nominal income growth. The results tend to be less significant than those for M2 (e.g., table 6.2 in the text).

Table 6.10
Joint Significance Tests in VAR with Nominal Growth, Inflation, and Monetary Base (Quarterly, 3 Lags)

Period	Dependent variable	p-Values for Nominal growth	Inflation	Money	R^2	p-Values for break (Oct. 79)
Q1 60–Q4 95	Nominal growth	0.031	0.518	0.249	0.171	0.004
	Inflation	0.955	0.000	0.164	0.672	0.006
	Money	0.337	0.508	0.000	0.560	0.069
Q4 79–Q4 95	Nominal growth	0.021	0.137	0.085	0.306	
	Inflation	0.534	0.000	0.091	0.764	
	Money	0.225	0.933	0.000	0.417	
Low frequencies excluded:						
Q4 79–Q4 95	Nominal growth	0.027	0.196	0.109	0.243	
	Inflation	0.278	0.354	0.036	0.260	
	Money	0.152	0.055	0.002	0.427	

Nominal growth $= \Delta \log(\text{nominal GDP}) = \Delta x_t$,
Inflation $= \Delta \log(\text{GDP deflator}) = \Delta p_t$,
Money $= \Delta \log(\text{BASE}) = \Delta m_t$ (quarterly average of monthly data).

Table 6.11
Joint Significance Tests in VAR with Nominal Growth, Inflation, and M2 (Quarterly, 3 Lags)

| Period | Dependent variable | p-Values for | | | R^2 | p-Values for break (Oct. 79) |
		Nominal growth	Inflation	Money		
Q1 60–Q4 95	Nominal growth	0.592	0.690	0.000	0.256	0.244
	Inflation	0.933	0.000	0.369	0.667	0.817
	Money	0.522	0.390	0.000	0.564	0.032
Q4 79–Q4 95	Nominal growth	0.073	0.235	0.172	0.286	
	Inflation	0.478	0.000	0.873	0.739	
	Money	0.130	0.694	0.000	0.527	
Low frequencies excluded:						
Q4 79–Q4 95	Nominal growth	0.051	0.160	0.557	0.186	
	Inflation	0.268	0.662	0.943	0.143	
	Money	0.196	0.284	0.424	0.226	

Nominal growth $= \Delta \log(\text{nominal GDP}) = \Delta x_t$,
Inflation $= \Delta \log(\text{GDP deflator}) = \Delta p_t$,
Money $= \Delta \log(\text{M2}) = \Delta m_t$ (quarterly average of monthly data).

Table 6.12
Joint Significance Tests in VAR with Nominal Growth, Inflation, and M1 (Monthly, 9 Lags)

| Period | Dependent variable | p-Values for | | | R^2 | p-Values for break (Oct. 79) |
		Nominal growth	Inflation	Money		
Jan. 60–Dec. 95	Nominal growth	0.000	0.016	0.227	0.275	0.016
	Inflation	0.001	0.000	0.194	0.594	0.041
	Money	0.001	0.028	0.000	0.362	0.013
Oct. 79–Dec. 95	Nominal growth	0.000	0.159	0.910	0.300	
	Inflation	0.195	0.000	0.615	0.626	
	Money	0.009	0.126	0.000	0.473	
Low frequencies excluded:						
Oct. 79–Dec. 95	Nominal growth	0.000	0.056	0.867	0.261	
	Inflation	0.117	0.007	0.418	0.347	
	Money	0.015	0.313	0.000	0.414	

Nominal growth $= \Delta \log(\text{COIN}) + \Delta \log(\text{CPI}) = \Delta x_t$,
Inflation $= \Delta \log(\text{CPI}) = \Delta p_t$,
Money $= \Delta \log(\text{M1}) = \Delta m_t$.

Notes

1. The basic structure of the McCallum rule has been analyzed and extended in the recent literature, for example, by Judd and Motley (1991), Hess et al. (1993), and Feldstein and Stock (1994).

2. These results are consistent with those obtained by Friedman and Kuttner (1992) with quarterly data for the 1970–1990 period. In this paper, however, we examine whether it is possible to improve on the Friedman–Kuttner results by using monthly data, by adding data since 1990, and by including several refinements in the measure of money. We do not include here Friedman and Kuttner's preferred measure, the commercial paper-Treasury bill spread, since it has been shown elsewhere to perform poorly in the 1990s. See, for example, Watson (1991) and Estrella and Mishkin (1998).

3. A seminal discussion of cointegration, error correction, and their relationship with VARs is found in Engle and Granger (1987).

4. McCallum uses quarterly data, in which case $n = 16$. Also, in more recent papers, e.g., McCallum (1993a, 1994), he has considered variants of this rule in which the target is defined in terms of nominal income growth, rather than its level. The available simulation evidence for these variants is not as extensive as for the levels version, but McCallum (1993b) finds that it works better in Japan with an interest rate instrument.

5. McCallum has indicated that a λ of this magnitude leads to instability when used in his simulation experiments. We should note that our estimates using monthly data may produce in principle an implicit value of λ that differs from that obtained with quarterly data, which is the frequency used by McCallum. Nevertheless, time aggregation of an MA(1) or ARIMA(1, 1, 1) process from monthly to quarterly data leads to an ARMA structure of the same order (see Harvey, 1981, p. 44), and our estimate of β with quarterly data is 0.191, which is very close to the monthly estimate of 0.175.

6. Note however that the expected signs of these relationships may depend on whether policymakers are reacting to demand shocks or to supply shocks. The presence of supply shocks in the sample could make it more difficult to observe the signs we postulate in the text. A more careful analysis of these possibilities could proceed by formulating and estimating a policy reaction function, which is beyond the scope of this chapter. Some analysis of a policy reaction function may be found in Taylor (1993) for the United States and in Clarida and Gertler (1996) for Germany.

7. We used the Fourier and inverse Fourier transforms in the RATS econometrics package with the algorithm provided for choosing the number of frequency points in the frequency domain. No smoothing was applied.

8. For a thorough discussion of Fourier transforms and spectral analysis in general, see Brillinger (1981).

9. The recent literature typically adopts frequencies of 18 months or two years as the lower bound for the business cycle. We find, however, that such representations do not coincide with the NBER turning points, particularly with regard to the two separate recessions in 1980–1982. Our convention fits the NBER dates more closely and corresponds to that of Granger and Hatanaka (1964).

10. We also estimated the VAR with either the high- or the medium-frequency component (rather than the low-frequency component) excluded from all three variables. In both cases, the significance of the key parameter estimates was reduced considerably. Thus, the only frequency domain adjustment that seems promising is the exclusion of the low frequencies, as reported in the text.

11. Data for GDP, the GDP deflator and M3 were obtained from the Bundesbank. GDP and the deflator are for western Germany only, even in the post-reunification period.

12. Clarida and Gertler (1996) have found evidence that the German repo rate reacts to deviations of both real growth and inflation from target levels. Also, Bernanke and Mihov (1996) have found evidence that expected German M3 influences the Lombard rate. Their results are not directly comparable to those of this chapter, since they test whether money is a target for the Bundesbank, not whether it influences or is influenced by output or inflation.

References

Bernanke, B. S., Mihov, I., 1996. What Does the Bundesbank Target? International Seminar on Macroeconomics, NBER and Institute for Advanced Studies.

Brillinger, D. R., 1981. *Time Series: Data Analysis and Theory*. Holden Day, San Francisco.

Clarida, R., Gertler, M., 1996. How the Bundesbank Conducts Monetary Policy. New York University Working Paper RR # 96–14.

Engle, R. F., 1974. Band spectrum regression. *International Economic Review* 15, 1–11.

Engle, R. F., Granger, C. W. J., 1987. Cointegration and error correction: representation, estimation, and testing. *Econometrica* 55, 251–276.

Estrella, A., Mishkin, F. S., 1998. Predicting U.S. recessions: financial variables as leading indicators. *Review of Economics and Statistics*, 80.

Feldstein, M., Stock, J. H., 1994. The use of a monetary aggregate to target nominal GDP. In: Gregory Mankiw, N. (Ed.), *Monetary Policy*. University of Chicago, Chicago, pp. 7–62.

Friedman, B. M., Kuttner, K. N., 1992. Money, income, prices, and interest rates. *American Economic Review* 82, 472–492.

Granger, C. W. J., Hatanaka, M., 1964. *Spectral Analysis of Economic Time Series*. Princeton University Press.

Harvey, A. C., 1981. *Time Series Models*. Philip Allan, Oxford.

Hess, G. D., Small, D. H., Brayton, F., 1993. Nominal income targeting with the monetary base as instrument: an evaluation of McCallum's rule. Federal Reserve Board Finance and Economic Discussion Series.

Huizinga, J., Mishkin, F. S., 1986. Monetary policy regime shifts and the unusual behavior of real interest rates. *Carnegie-Rochester Conference Series on Public Policy*, 231–274.

Judd, J. P., Motley, B., 1991. Nominal feedback rules for monetary policy. *Federal Reserve Bank of San Francisco Economic Review* 3–17.

McCallum, B. T., 1988. Robustness properties of a rule for monetary policy. *Carnegie-Rochester Conference Series on Public Policy* 29, 173–204.

McCallum, B. T., 1993a. Concluding observations. In: Goodfriend, M., Small, D. H. (Eds.), *Proceedings of the Conference on Operating Procedures and the Conduct of Monetary Policy*. Federal Reserve Board.

McCallum, B. T., 1993b. Specification and analysis of a monetary policy rule for Japan. *Bank of Japan Monetary and Economic Studies* 11, 1–45.

McCallum, B. T., 1994. 'Comment' on Feldstein, M., Stock, J. H., The Use of a Monetary Aggregate to Target Nominal GDP. In: Gregory Mankiw, N. (Ed.), *Monetary Policy*. University of Chicago, Chicago, 66–69.

Taylor, J. B., 1993. Discretion versus policy rules in practice. *Carnegie-Rochester Conference Series on Public Policy*, 195–214.

Watson, M., 1991. Using econometric models to predict recessions. *Federal Reserve Bank of Chicago Economic Perspectives* 15, 14–25.

7 Rethinking the Role of NAIRU in Monetary Policy: Implications of Model Formulation and Uncertainty

Arturo Estrella and Frederic S. Mishkin

7.1 Introduction

Because the effects of monetary policy on the aggregate economy have long lags, monetary policy must necessarily be preemptive; that is, it must act well before inflation starts to rise.[1] This, of course, is easier said than done. In order to act preemptively, monetary policymakers must have signals that help them forecast future changes in inflation. One such signal that has received substantial attention both in the academic literature and in the press is the gap between unemployment and NAIRU, the nonaccelerating inflation rate of unemployment.[2] In other words, NAIRU is the unemployment rate at which inflation is expected to neither increase or decrease.

The NAIRU concept has come under quite serious attack in recent years. In the early to mid-1990s, the common view in the economics profession was that NAIRU in the United States was around 6 percent. However, when the unemployment rate began to fall below 6 percent in 1995 and remained well below that level thereafter without any increase in inflation—indeed inflation actually fell—concern arose that the NAIRU concept might be seriously flawed. In addition, recent academic research has shown that there is great uncertainty in the estimates of NAIRU (e.g., Staiger et al. 1997a, 1997b), suggesting that looking at the unemployment rate relative to NAIRU might not be a very helpful guide for monetary policy.

In this chapter, we rethink the NAIRU concept and examine whether NAIRU might have a useful role in monetary policy making. We argue that the answer is yes. However, the positive answer depends critically on redefining NAIRU very carefully and distinguishing it from a long-run concept like the natural rate of unemployment, something that is not typically done in the literature. Furthermore, as we will see, the view that the NAIRU concept implies that the monetary authorities should try to move the economy toward the NAIRU, thus to some extent treating it as a target, is both incorrect and misguided.

The first step in our analysis, in section 7.2, is to think about defining NAIRU in the context of setting monetary policy instruments. We adopt a definition that focuses on NAIRU as a reference point for monetary policy and show that our definition of NAIRU is a short-run concept and is not the same as the natural rate of unemployment. Understanding that short-run NAIRU and the natural rate of unemployment differ is important, not only for the theoretical analysis to follow, but also because it suggests that short-run NAIRU is likely to be highly variable, in contrast to the natural rate of unemployment. One immediate implication is that thinking of NAIRU as a level at which the unemployment rate should settle is not very useful for policy purposes.

Our approach to the construction of short-run NAIRU is fairly general. Although we define this concept in the context of a particular model of inflation that is adapted from the current literature, the same approach can be applied to any predictive model of inflation in which unemployment plays an important role.

Once we have defined short-run NAIRU, we then go on to examine how it might be used in policy making. We do this in several steps. First, we look in section 7.3 at the certainty-equivalent case, when only inflation enters the policymakers' objective function and then when unemployment (or equivalently, output) as well as inflation are part of policymakers' objectives. Although the certainty-equivalent case is useful as a starting point for the analysis, we cannot stop here because several sources of uncertainty have important implications for how monetary policy should be conducted. In addition to uncertainty about estimates of the actual value of NAIRU, there is uncertainty about the estimated parameters of the model, especially the parameters that measure the effect of the NAIRU gap on inflation and the impact of monetary policy instruments on the NAIRU gap. We examine in section 7.4 what effect these sources of uncertainty have on how short-run NAIRU might be used in monetary policy making, again under the pure price stability objective and then when unemployment as well as inflation enter the policymakers' objective function.

Our theoretical analysis shows that uncertainty about the level of short-run NAIRU does not necessarily imply that monetary policy should react less to the NAIRU gap. However, uncertainty about the effect of the NAIRU gap on inflation does require an adjustment to the reference point for monetary tightening in terms of the level of unemployment and to the weight applied to the gap between actual and target inflation. Furthermore, as in Brainard (1967), uncertainty about the effect of the monetary policy instrument on the NAIRU gap reduces the magnitude of the policy response.

There is another sense in which uncertainty about NAIRU may have an effect on policy. There may be uncertainty not just about the level of NAIRU or its effect but about the way it is modeled: the exact form of the model specification may be unknown. Errors in model selection may result in excess uncertainty regarding both inflation forecasts and the parameters of the model. Thus model selection has the potential to increase uncertainty about the effect of the NAIRU gap and to reduce the effectiveness of policy, and the magnitude of this problem may be more difficult to determine than that of simple parameter uncertainty. In section 7.5, we focus on the losses associated with leaving out key information from the model.

Although our theoretical framework shows the qualitative effects of uncertainty on how monetary policy should be conducted, it cannot tell us whether these effects are economically important. To examine this question, we estimate in section 7.6 a simple NAIRU gap model for the United States to obtain quantitative measures of uncertainty and to assess how these measures affect our view of the optimal reaction of monetary policy to movements in unemployment relative to short-run NAIRU. Using an analogous model based on monthly data, we then examine how in practice the short-run NAIRU concept could be used in the actual conduct of monetary policy. The estimated models provide us with measures of short-run NAIRU that indicate that it is highly variable, suggesting that trying to drive the unemployment rate toward NAIRU, whether it is a short-run or a long-run concept, would be an inappropriate way to think about how monetary policy should be conducted. In particular, we use our analysis to evaluate whether the setting of monetary policy instruments in the face of rapidly falling unemployment rates in recent years makes sense.

7.2   Defining Short-Run NAIRU: Why It Differs from the Natural Rate of Unemployment

The concept of the natural rate of unemployment was first developed by Friedman (1968) and Phelps (1968) to argue that there would be no long-run trade-off between unemployment and inflation. The natural rate of unemployment is defined as the level of unemployment to which the economy would converge in the long run in the absence of structural changes to the labor market. An implication of this definition is that expansionary monetary policy that leads to higher inflation would not be able to produce lower unemployment on average. Indeed, as mentioned in Friedman (1968), higher inflation might even have the opposite effect of raising unemployment in the long run because it would interfere with efficient functioning of labor markets. The concept of a natural rate of unemployment leads to the following characterization of an expectations-augmented Phillips curve:

$$\pi_t = \pi_t^e + \beta(L)(u_t - \bar{u}_t) + \delta'z_t + \varepsilon_t,$$

where

$\pi_t = $ inflation rate from $t - 1$ to t

$\pi_t^e = $ inflation rate expected at $t - 1$

$u_t = $ unemployment rate at time t

$\bar{u}_t = $ natural rate of unemployment at time t, which could be a constant but could shift with structural changes in the economy

z_t = a vector of variables such as supply shocks, which have zero ex ante expectation

ε_t = an unspecified disturbance term

In order to estimate this expectations-augmented Phillips curve, researchers typically assume that the expected inflation can be measured as a distributed lag on past inflation and other variables, and that the inflation rate is integrated of order one, so that $\Delta\pi_t$ is stationary. The resulting Phillips curve is then

$$\Delta\pi_t = \beta(L)(u_t - \bar{u}_t) + \gamma(L)\Delta\pi_{t-1} + \delta'z_t + \varepsilon_t. \tag{7.1}$$

The NAIRU concept was first developed in a paper by Modigliani and Papademos (1975) and is defined as the rate of unemployment at which there is no tendency for inflation to increase or decrease. In empirical work such as Staiger et al. (1997a, 1997b) and Gordon (1997), NAIRU is viewed as being equivalent to the natural rate of unemployment, $\bar{u}_t$, in equation (7.1) and is typically estimated by assuming that $\bar{u}_t$ is a constant, a random walk, or a linear transformation of some step function or spline.[3]

For policy purposes, equation (7.1) indicates that it is perfectly appropriate to think about the unemployment gap, $u_t - \bar{u}_t$, as one determinant of changes in the rate of inflation, recognizing that other factors, represented by the past history of inflation and the z_t variables, also affect the inflation process. However, current unemployment is frequently compared with the estimated value of NAIRU, and the resulting NAIRU gap is taken to be an indicator of inflationary pressure. Under a strong form of this view, if policymakers wish to drive inflation down, they need to raise the unemployment level above NAIRU, whereas if inflation is at its desired level, monetary policy needs to keep unemployment from falling below NAIRU.

Policy discussions, therefore, frequently focus on the difference between the current level of unemployment and NAIRU as estimated above, in other words, on the variable that enters the first term of equation (7.1) in a distributed lag. This implicit comparison has the advantage of simplicity: it focuses the discussion on a single indicator of inflationary pressure, the unemployment gap, that we know from the model should be zero in long-run equilibrium. However, this advantage is overwhelmed by a number of serious problems associated with this procedure.

First, monetary policy does not generally focus only on long-run equilibrium, so the gap as defined above may be of limited usefulness. Second, even if equation (7.1) is viewed as a short-run forecasting equation, the dependent variable is contemporaneous monthly or quarterly inflation, which is quite unlikely to be the policy target in practice. Third, the current unemployment gap is only one of many explanatory variables in the equation, including several lags of the gap itself. Focusing on only one variable gives an incomplete picture. Fourth, the equation may not even represent the optimal forecast of inflation, since other potentially important variables may be omitted.

Finally, focusing on the unemployment gap may create the impression that the goal of policy is to drive unemployment toward NAIRU as a target level. As equation (7.1) illustrates, the current unemployment gap, $u_t - \bar{u}_t$, is only one of many explanatory variables in the Phillips curve equation. The presence of lags of $\Delta \pi$ in the equation suggests that inflation may decelerate because expected inflation is falling, even if the unemployment rate is below the natural rate of unemployment. Similarly, if there have been favorable supply shocks, inflation in the future may decelerate even though the unemployment rate is well below the natural rate. The presence of lags of the unemployment gap suggests complicated dynamics in which a current negative unemployment rate could also be associated with decelerating inflation. The presence of many other variables besides the current unemployment gap in the expectations-augmented Phillips curve equation therefore implies that the unemployment rate at which there is no tendency for inflation to rise or fall over the policy horizon can be quite different from the natural rate of unemployment, $\bar{u}_t$. In other words, it can be quite misleading to focus on NAIRU, as an estimate in equation (7.1) of the natural rate of unemployment, because it is not clear that the introduction of policy shocks designed to drive unemployment toward this characterization of NAIRU will do anything to control inflation either in the short run or in the long run.

Therefore, we propose an alternative way of thinking about NAIRU as a reference point for unemployment that reflects inflationary pressures over the short- or intermediate-run policy horizon. The key idea is that the reference point for unemployment at which inflation will neither increase nor decrease over the relevant policy horizon, which can be thought of as a short-run NAIRU, embodies not only $\bar{u}_t$, the natural rate of unemployment, but also the other variables that help predict inflation. In other words, we would like to express the change in inflation over the relevant policy horizon as a function of $u_t - n_t$, where n_t is an appropriately constructed short-run NAIRU.

Thus suppose that the policy horizon for inflation is from j to $j + k$ months ahead and define

$$\Delta \pi_t^{(j,k)} = (1200/k) \log(p_{t+j+k}/p_{t+j}) - 100 \log(p_t/p_{t-12})$$

as the difference between current annual inflation and inflation over the policy horizon, where p_t is the price level in month t. We then construct equation (7.2):

$$\Delta \pi_t^{(j,k)} = \alpha + \beta(L)\mu_t + \gamma(L)\Delta \pi_t + \delta' x_t + \varepsilon_t, \qquad (7.2)$$

which is similar to equation (7.1), save for the dependent variable and the inclusion of a vector x that contains any predetermined variables that help predict inflation at the targeted horizon.[4]

In order to express the change in inflation as a function of the difference between unemployment and a short-run NAIRU, equation (7.2) can always be rewritten as

$$\Delta\pi_t^{(j,k)} = \beta_0(\mu_t - n_t) + \varepsilon_t \tag{7.3}$$

with

$$n_t = \text{short-run NAIRU}$$
$$= -[\alpha + (\beta(L) - \beta(0))u_t + \gamma(L)\Delta\pi_t + \delta'x_t]/\beta(0), \tag{7.4}$$

where all the predictive power of the equation has been subsumed in the short-run NAIRU n_t. This short-run NAIRU is not an estimate of the long-run equilibrium natural rate, but a reference rate that represents the level of current unemployment that would correspond to a forecast of no inflation change over the policy horizon.[5] Another important point that immediately falls out of this equation is that since short-run NAIRU is related to past lags of unemployment, inflation, and any other variables that help forecast changes in inflation, short-run NAIRU may undergo substantial fluctuations even if the natural rate of unemployment is a constant.

Equation (7.3) has several important advantages over equation (7.1). In contrast to the conventional equation, the dependent variable in equation (7.3) is the change in inflation over the target horizon. Second, the current NAIRU gap, $u_t - n_t$, is the only explanatory variable in the equation and it subsumes all the predictive power of the equation. Third, the equation provides an optimal forecast of targeted inflation, given current information.

We note, however, that our approach to short-run NAIRU is fairly general and is largely independent of the particular form of equation (7.3). The definition of short-run NAIRU in equation (7.4) simply collects all the systematic terms in equation (7.3), other that the current rate of unemployment. Hence, this technique is applicable to any forecasting equation for $\Delta\pi_t^{(j,k)}$, as long as the current unemployment rate u_t enters significantly in the equation.[6]

The analysis of this chapter will focus on equations (7.2) and (7.3) and on our corresponding definition of short-run NAIRU. For the purposes of theoretical analysis, we use a simplified version of these equations with a limited lag structure. We return to the more general specification, however, when we consider empirical estimates using monthly data in section 7.6.

7.3   The Role of NAIRU in Policy Making: The Certainty-Equivalent Case

7.3.1   Objective Function with Inflation Only

For the theoretical analysis, we start with a simple joint model of unemployment and inflation that is isomorphic to the one employed by Svensson (1997) with an output gap. In addition to inflation π and an unemployment gap $\tilde{u}$, the model contains an exogenous variable x and a monetary policy control variable r. This model will be the basis for the next few sections of the chapter. However, some specific assumptions will be adjusted in subsequent sections in order to address particular issues. Assume for the purposes of this section that the parameters of the model are known with certainty.

$$\pi_t = \pi_{t-1} - a_1\tilde{u}_{t-1} + a_3 x_{t-1} + \varepsilon_t, \tag{7.5}$$

$$\tilde{u}_t = b_1\tilde{u}_{t-1} + b_2 r_{t-1} + b_3 x_{t-1} + \eta_t, \tag{7.6}$$

$$x_t = c_3 x_{t-1} + v_t, \tag{7.7}$$

where $\tilde{u}_t = u_t - \bar{u}$ and r_t is the monetary policy variable. Equation (7.5) is a dynamic Phillips curve in which both unemployment and x are predictors of inflation one period ahead, say a year. Equation (7.6) is an IS curve, and equation (7.7) defines the dynamics of the exogenous variable x. The equilibrium level of all the variables is zero. Note, therefore, that the policy variable r might be more similar to a change in the interest rate rather than the level.

The reduced-form expression for inflation two periods ahead based on current values of the variables is

$$\pi_{t+2} = \pi_t - a_1(1 + b_1)\tilde{u}_t - a_1 b_2 r_t + [a_3(1 + c_3) - a_1 b_3]x_t + \xi_{t+2}, \tag{7.8}$$

where

$$\xi_{t+2} = -a_1\eta_{t+1} + a_3 v_{t+1} + \varepsilon_{t+1} + \varepsilon_{t+2}.$$

Assume now that the policy objective is to minimize

$$E_t(\pi_{t+2} - \pi^*)^2 = (E_t\pi_{t+2} - \pi^*)^2 + V_t\pi_{t+2}.$$

Although this assumption seems simplistic, Svensson (1997) has shown that the solution obtained in this manner is equivalent to the dynamic solution of a model in which the target is a weighted sum of all future squared deviations of inflation from the target level. Note also that equation (7.8) is analogous to equation (7.2) above in that it corresponds to an optimal forecast of inflation acceleration over the policy horizon, which is given by

$$E_t\pi_{t+2} = \pi_t - a_1(1 + b_1)\tilde{u}_t - a_1 b_2 r_t + [a_3(1 + c_3) - a_1 b_3]x_t.$$

The conditional variance of inflation is

$$V_t\pi_{t+2} = \sigma_\xi^2.$$

Since the variance of inflation does not depend on the policy variable, the result is determined by certainty equivalence; that is, the optimal rule may be obtained by setting expected inflation equal to the target, π^*, and solving for the value of the policy variable. The optimal value of the policy variable is given by

$$r_t^* = -\frac{1+b_1}{b_2}\tilde{u}_t + \frac{a_3(1+c_3) - a_1b_3}{a_1b_2}x_t + \frac{1}{a_1b_2}(\pi_t - \pi^*)$$

$$= -\frac{1+b_1}{b_2}(\tilde{u}_t - n_t) + \frac{1}{a_1b_2}(\pi_t - \pi^*), \tag{7.9}$$

where the short-run NAIRU (defined as a deviation from $\bar{u}$) is

$$n_t = \frac{a_3(1+c_3) - a_1b_3}{a_1(1+b_1)}x_t. \tag{7.10}$$

Equation (7.9) is a variant of the Taylor (1993) rule, which differs in that it is expressed in terms of unemployment rather than output. In addition, it allows for the reference point for monetary tightening in terms of the level of unemployment to be a short-run NAIRU rather than a fixed natural rate. In effect what this variation on the Taylor rules does is bring in additional information that helps forecast inflation in deriving an optimal setting of the policy instruments.

Even in this relatively simple setting, short-run NAIRU n_t is not a constant but is instead a function of the exogenous variable x. If lags of inflation, unemployment, and the policy variable appear in equations (7.5) and (7.6), their role in the policy rule—and therefore in the definition of short-run NAIRU—would be like that of x in the model. Of course, if the only variable that helps predict inflation over the policy horizon, other than the unemployment rate, is a constant, then NAIRU will be constant as in a more standard formulation. Note also that, like $\tilde{u}$, the short-run NAIRU of our theoretical model is measured in relation to $\bar{u}$. In empirical applications, we would want to focus on the equivalent of $n_t + \bar{u}$ as a measure of short-run NAIRU.

Equation (7.9) also helps to clarify the proper use of NAIRU for policy purposes. The policy objective is not to drive unemployment to NAIRU, which is a temporary and variable reference point, but to use the NAIRU unemployment gap as one indicator of the direction to move the policy variable, by an amount dictated by the coefficients of the model. Also, the NAIRU gap indicator is not to be interpreted in isolation but must be weighed against the effect on the optimal setting of the policy variable suggested by the other indicator that is also included in the reaction function, the gap between actual and target inflation.

It is also important to recognize that our equation (7.9) variant of the Taylor rule is completely consistent with the result of Svensson (1997). Setting the policy instrument according to equation (7.9) is equivalent to setting expected inflation over the policy horizon equal to the inflation target π^*, which is the Svensson (1997) optimality condition if only inflation is in the objective function.

We can also draw some conclusions about the sign of the coefficient of x in the definition of NAIRU, based on whether x represents a supply or a demand effect. For example, if x is a supply effect such as an oil price shock, then a_3 and b_3 would have the same sign. Since the other parameters in equation (10) were chosen to have positive values, the two terms in the coefficient would be offsetting and the net effect of x on short-run NAIRU would be indeterminate. In contrast, if x represents a demand effect, then a_3 and b_3 would have opposite signs and the two terms would be reinforcing. The sign of the effect is positive if the demand variable x increases inflation and vice versa. In other words, a demand shock that raises inflation would lead to a higher value of short-run NAIRU, which implies more tightening given the same value of unemployment.

Supply and demand shocks also have differential effects on the overall implication about the optimal setting of the policy variable. The cumulation of supply effects would tend to drive both unemployment and inflation in the same direction, producing offsetting effects in equation (7.9). Cumulated demand effects, however, would drive inflation and unemployment in different directions, providing an unambiguous policy reaction. Therefore, demand effects that raise inflation should provoke a policy tightening.

7.3.2 Output as well as Inflation in the Objective Function

Even when inflation is the only concern of policymakers, as in subsection 7.3.1, the optimal policy assigns a significant role to the level of unemployment or to the unemployment gap, as seen in equation (7.9). In this section, we explore how policy should be conducted when policymakers include both inflation and output in their objectives. We do this by including a second term in the objective function, which now becomes

$$E_t(\pi_{t+2} - \pi^*)^2 + \lambda E_t \tilde{u}_{t+1}^2.$$

The economic significance of this change is that the policy objective assigns some weight to reducing the variability of unemployment around zero, which is the equilibrium level.[7]

The optimal value of the policy variable in this case is

$$r_t^{(\lambda)} = \frac{1}{(a_1^2 + \lambda)b_2} \{-[(1 + b_1)(a_1^2 + \lambda) - \lambda]\tilde{u}_t$$

$$+ [a_1 a_3(1 + c_3) - (a_1^2 + \lambda)b_3]x_t + a_1(\pi_t - \pi^*)\}.$$

The modification of the objective function to reflect an unemployment target changes the weights on u, x, and $\pi_t - \pi^*$ in the optimal policy rule but does not affect its general form. Specifically, the weight on $\tilde{u}_t$ relative to the weight on $\pi_t - \pi^*$ rises with λ. In the extreme, if the weight on unemployment becomes infinitely large (λ approaches infinity), the optimal rule simplifies to

$$r_t^{(\infty)} = -\frac{b_1}{b_2}\tilde{u}_t - \frac{b_3}{b_2}x_t,$$

in which the inflation gap has disappeared and only an unemployment gap remains. This result may also be obtained by certainty equivalence, setting expected unemployment equal to its equilibrium level and solving for the value of the policy variable.

7.4   NAIRU and Policy Making: Implications of Parameter Uncertainty

7.4.1   Objective Function with Inflation Only

Uncertainty about the Natural Rate of Unemployment   We begin to examine the consequences of uncertainty in the model of section 7.3 by looking at the effects of uncertainty regarding the natural rate of unemployment or, equivalently, long-run NAIRU. We start with this particular question for two reasons. First, it seems that in the policy discussion on the use of NAIRU, it is this question that is most frequently in the mind of the policymaker, although it is not always precisely formulated. Second, the examination of this narrower issue provides helpful intuition for the more general results that follow in the rest of this section.

Thus consider a more focused version of the model of section 7.3 in which traditional long-run NAIRU is the appropriate reference point for monetary policy in terms of the unemployment rate:

$$\pi_t = \pi_{t-1} - a_1(u_{t-1} - \bar{u}) + \varepsilon_t$$

$$= \pi_{t-1} - a_1 u_{t-1} + a_0 + \varepsilon_t, \tag{7.5a}$$

$$u_t - \bar{u} = b_1(u_{t-1} - \bar{u}) + b_2 r_{t-1} + \eta_t, \tag{7.6a}$$

where $a_0 = a_1\bar{u}$ and, as in section 7.3, $\bar{u}$ is the natural rate and r_t is the monetary policy variable. We write these equations explicitly in terms of $\bar{u}$ in order to focus on uncertainty with regard to this parameter. For the same reason, we assume that the parameters b_1 and b_2 in equation (7.6a) are known.

The second expression for equation (7.5a), under the natural stochastic assumptions, may be estimated using least squares. It is straightforward then to calculate the asymptotic distribution of the parameter estimates, which are consistent. In particular, we can derive that $TV(\hat{a}_1, \hat{a}_0)$, the asymptotic variance of the vector of estimates $(\hat{a}_1, \hat{a}_0)$ multiplied by the number of observations T, is

$$\left(\frac{\sigma_\varepsilon^2}{\sigma_u^2}\right)\begin{bmatrix} 1 & \bar{u} \\ \bar{u} & \bar{u}^2 + \sigma_u^2 \end{bmatrix},$$

where $\bar{u}$ and σ_u^2 are the unconditional asymptotic mean and variance of u_t and $\sigma^2\varepsilon$ is the variance of ε_t. Now, if J is the Jacobian of the transformation $(a_1, a_0) \mapsto (a_1, \bar{u}) = (a_1, a_0/a_1)$, then asymptotically $TV(\hat{a}_1, \hat{\bar{u}}) = TJV(\hat{a}_1, \hat{a}_0)J'$, which equals

$$\begin{bmatrix} \sigma_\varepsilon^2/\sigma_u^2 & 0 \\ 0 & \sigma_\varepsilon^2/a_1^2 \end{bmatrix},$$

where we have made use of the fact that the unconditional mean of equation (7.5a) is $\overline{\Delta\pi} = 0$.

The foregoing derivations may now be incorporated into the optimization problem of section 7.3, again with the objective function $E_t(\pi_{t+2} - \pi^*)^2$, but now

$$E_t\pi_{t+2} = \pi_t - a_1(1 + b_1)(u_t - \bar{u}) - a_1 b_2 r_t$$

and

$$V_t\pi_{t+2} = \sigma_{a_1}^2[(1 + b_1)(-u_t + \bar{u}) - b_2 r_t]^2 + a_1^2(1 + b_1)^2\sigma_{\bar{u}}^2 + \sigma_{a_1}^2\sigma_{\bar{u}}^2(1 + b_1)^2 + \sigma_\zeta^2.$$

In the expression for the variance, the terms that include $\sigma_{\bar{u}}^2$ do not depend on the policy variable. Since the estimators of $\bar{u}$ and a_1 are orthogonal, the optimal rule will not depend on the uncertainty with regard to $\bar{u}$, as shown in the expression

$$r_t^* = -\frac{1 + b_1}{b_2}(u_t - \bar{u}) + \frac{1}{1 + \tau_1^{-2}} \cdot \frac{\pi_t - \pi^*}{a_1 b_2},$$

where $\tau_1 = a_1/\sigma_{a_1}$.

Thus uncertainty about the natural rate, in and of itself, does not affect the solution to the policymaker's optimization problem, as defined in this section and in section 7.3. However, the uncertainty about the natural rate does increase the cost function because, as seen above, it increases the conditional variance of π_{t+2}. The uncertainty about the parameter a_1, the effect on inflation acceleration of the gap between unemployment and the natural rate, does figure in the optimal policy through the term $(1 + \tau_1^{-2})^{-1}$, which is essentially a function of the t-statistic on a_1. Its effect, however, is not on the term containing the unemployment gap, but rather on the term containing the gap between current and target inflation. The greater the uncertainty about a_1, the lower τ_1 and therefore $(1 + \tau_1^{-2})^{-1}$, so the less weight the policymaker should place on the current inflation gap. This result is very robust, as it obtains in the models of subsequent sections, in which we introduce more complex specifications with fairly general parameter uncertainty.

General Parameter Uncertainty   Consider again the model defined by equations (7.5), (7.6), and (7.7) of subsection 7.3.1, but assume now that there is uncertainty at time t about all the coefficients of the model $(a_1, a_3, b_1, b_2, b_3, b_3, c_3)$ and about the disturbance of the reduced form (ξ), but that the uncertainty in all of these variables is pairwise orthogonal. Although these uncertainty assumptions are not entirely general—on account of the assumed orthogonality—they are more extensive than those that the previous literature has examined.[8] The orthogonality assumptions are easily relaxed for coefficients belonging to the same equation, but the inclusion of the corresponding covariances does not provide greater intuition and is therefore not pursued here. Thus, at time t, the expectation and variance of inflation at time $t + 2$ are given by

$$E_t \pi_{t+2} = \pi_t - a_1(1 + b_1)\tilde{u}_t - a_1 b_2 r_t + [a_3(1 + c_3) - a_1 b_3]x_t$$

and

$$
\begin{aligned}
V_t \pi_{t+2} = & [a_1^2 \sigma_{b_1}^2 + \sigma_{a_1}^2 (1 + b_1)^2 + \sigma_{a_1}^2 \sigma_{b_1}^2]\tilde{u}_t^2 + (a_1^2 \sigma_{b_2}^2 + \sigma_{a_1}^2 b_2^2 + \sigma_{a_1}^2 \sigma_{b_2}^2)r_t^2 \\
& + [a_3^2 \sigma_{c_3}^2 + \sigma_{a_3}^2 (1 + c_3)^2 + \sigma_{a_3}^2 \sigma_{c_3}^2 + a_1^2 \sigma_{b_3}^2 + \sigma_{a_1}^2 b_3^2 + \sigma_{a_1}^2 \sigma_{b_3}^2]x_t^2 \\
& + 2\sigma_{a_1}^2 [(1 + b_1)b_2 \tilde{u}_t r_t + b_2 b_3 r_t x_t + (1 + b_1)b_3 \tilde{u}_t x_t] + \sigma_\xi^2,
\end{aligned}
$$

where the values of the coefficients denote their expected values.[9]

As in subsection 7.3.1, the policy objective is to choose r_t so as to minimize the objective function

$$E_t(\pi_{t+2} - \pi^*)^2 = (E_t \pi_{t+2} - \pi^*)^2 + V_t \pi_{t+2}.$$

In this case, the optimal value of the policy variable is given by

$$r_t^* = \frac{1}{1 + \tau_2^{-2}}\left[-\frac{1 + b_1}{b_2}\tilde{u}_t - \frac{b_3}{b_2}x_t + \frac{1}{1 + \tau_1^{-2}}\left(\frac{\pi_t - \pi^*}{a_1 b_2} + \frac{a_3(1 + c_3)}{a_1 b_2}x_t\right)\right], \tag{7.11}$$

where $\tau_1 = a_1/\sigma_{a_1}$ and $\tau_2 = b_2/\sigma_{b_2}$. Equation (7.11) can be rewritten as

$$r_t^* = \frac{1}{1 + \tau_2^{-2}}\left(-\frac{1 + b_1}{b_2}(\tilde{u}_t - (n_t + \phi_t)) + \frac{1}{1 + \tau_1^{-2}}\frac{1}{a_1 b_2}(\pi_t - \pi^*)\right), \tag{7.12}$$

where

$$\phi_t = -\frac{1}{1 + \tau_1^2} \cdot \frac{a_3(1 + c_3)}{a_1(1 + b_1)}x_t.$$

Comparison of equations (7.9) and (7.12) indicates that the presence of uncertainty introduces two multiplicative terms of the form $(1 + \tau_i^{-2})^{-1}$. These terms are essentially functions of the t-statistics corresponding to the parameters a_1 and b_2, respectively, which correspond to the one-period-ahead effects of unemployment on inflation and of the policy variable on unemployment. All other variance-related terms in the objective function drop out of the calculation. When there is no uncertainty about a_1 and b_2, the two multiplicative terms become one, reverting to the certainty-equivalent case of subsection 7.3.1.

One of the two uncertainty effects—the one related to b_2, the coefficient on the policy variable in equation (7.6)—takes a form that is predictable from the analysis by Brainard (1967). Specifically, as σ_{b_2} rises, the term $(1 + \tau_2^{-2})^{-1}$ falls so that uncertainty about the magnitude of the effect of the policy variable leads to a partial policy reaction—a reaction that is less than that in the certainty-equivalent case.

In contrast, uncertainty about a_1, the effect of unemployment on the change in inflation in equation (7.5), has an effect not on the scale of the policy reaction, but rather on the weight applied to $\pi_t - \pi^*$ and on the reference point in terms of unemployment at which that reaction occurs. Specifically, as σ_{a_1} rises, the term $(1 + \tau_1^{-2})^{-1}$ falls so that the weight on $\pi_t - \pi^*$ falls. A rise in σ_{a_1} causes the term $(1 + \tau_1^2)^{-1}$ and the absolute value of the adjustment term ϕ_t to rise. If x has a positive impact on inflation (i.e., $a_3 x_t$ is positive), then ϕ_t is negative and so the reference point for monetary tightening in terms of unemployment, $n_t + \phi_t$, falls.

The effect of uncertainty about a_1 on how the reference point responds to change in x is somewhat more complex. The net effect on the reference point $n_t + \phi_t$ depends on whether x is a supply or demand variable, as discussed in subsection 7.3.1. Consider the combined expression

$$n_t + \phi_t = \left(\frac{1}{1 + \tau_1^{-2}} \cdot \frac{a_3(1 + c_3)}{a_1(1 + b_1)} - \frac{b_3}{1 + b_1} \right) x_t.$$

If x is a supply variable, the direction of the effect of uncertainty on the magnitude of the reference point is unclear. It is clear, however, that as uncertainty about a_1 approaches infinity, the sign of the coefficient is the same as the sign of $-b_3$. If x is a demand variable, uncertainty reduces the absolute magnitude of the reference point unambiguously.

7.4.2 Output as well as Inflation in the Objective Function

We now modify the results of the previous subsection by assuming that the policy objective function includes both inflation and unemployment. As in subsection 7.3.2, the objective function becomes

$$E_t(\pi_{t+2} - \pi^*)^2 + \lambda E_t \tilde{u}_{t+1}^2.$$

The optimal value under parameter uncertainty is

$$r_t^{(\lambda)} = \frac{1}{1 + \tau_2^{-2}} \left[\left(-\frac{1 + b_1}{b_2} + \frac{\lambda}{a_1^2 + \sigma_{a_1}^2 + \lambda} \right) \tilde{u}_t \right.$$
$$\left. + \left(-\frac{b_3}{b_2} + \frac{a_1 a_3 (1 + c_3)}{a_1^2 + \sigma_{a_1}^2 + \lambda} \right) x_t + \frac{a_1 (\pi_t - \pi^*)}{a_1^2 + \sigma_{a_1}^2 + \lambda} \right].$$

The effect of including a target for unemployment, as represented by λ, is analogous to the effect of uncertainty about a_1. In the above equation, these two terms occur additively in the same expression in the terms corresponding to the exogenous variable and the inflation gap. Only in the unemployment term does λ appear separately. Intuitively, the reason for this is that uncertainty about a_1 makes the relationship expressed in equation (7.5) less reliable, so policy becomes more concerned with affecting the "intermediate target" of equilibrium unemployment.

If the weight on unemployment becomes infinitely large, the optimal rule simplifies to

$$r_t^{(\infty)} = \frac{1}{1 + \tau_2^{-2}} \left(-\frac{b_1}{b_2} \tilde{u}_t - \frac{b_3}{b_2} x_t \right)$$

in which, as in the certainty-equivalent case, the inflation gap has disappeared and only an unemployment gap remains. Here the only effect of uncertainty is of the rescaling type, as identified by Brainard (1967).

7.5   NAIRU and Policy Making: The Implications of Model Selection

In this section, we discuss another type of uncertainty that affects the definition of short-run NAIRU, its computation, and the policy rule that results from inflation targeting. Specifically, we focus on uncertainty regarding the correct form of the basic model and the associated problem of model selection. Whereas in section 7.4 we assumed that the form of the model was known but that the parameters were estimated with uncertainty, we now suppose that the policymaker ignores some key information variable in the optimization problem.[10]

In general, if inflation two periods ahead is the policy target, and if a variable helps predict inflation at that horizon, it is inefficient not to include the information in the model. For example, the models of sections 7.3 and 7.4 define the policy rule in terms of a short-run NAIRU, which in turn is a function of the exogenous variable x. What is the result of ignoring the predictive content of x? Alternatively, what is the cost of relying on a long-run equilibrium NAIRU (zero in this case) when a short-run informative NAIRU is available?

Thus suppose that the policymaker ignores the presence of x in the basic model (7.5)–(7.7). The values of a_3 and b_3 are implicitly set to zero, while the third equation is dropped altogether. Under these conditions, the constrained optimal rule for inflation targeting becomes

$$\tilde{r}_t^* = \frac{1}{1+\tau_2^{-2}} \left(-\frac{1+b_1}{b_2} \tilde{u}_t + \frac{1}{1+\tau_1^{-2}} \cdot \frac{\pi_t - \pi^*}{a_1 b_2} \right).$$

We know, of course, that the value of the objective function has to be higher (i.e., worse) when evaluated at this constrained optimum than when evaluated at the unconstrained optimum r_t^* as in subsection 7.4.1. In fact, we can calculate the difference between the constrained and unconstrained values as

$$\frac{1}{1+\tau_2^{-2}} \cdot \frac{1}{a_1^2 + \sigma_{a_1}^2} [a_1 a_3 (1 + c_3) - (a_1^2 + \sigma_{a_1}^2) b_3]^2 x_t^2.$$

Somewhat surprisingly, uncertainty about b_2 ameliorates the left-out-variable problem.[11] Uncertainty about a_1, in contrast, can make matters worse.

The left-out-variable problem can also increase uncertainty regarding the estimates of the included coefficients, with consequences for the size of the policy response or the reference point for monetary tightening in terms of unemployment. To see this, suppose the inflation equation (7.5) is estimated by ordinary least squares, leaving out the variable x, after rewriting it in the following form

$$\pi_t - \pi_{t-1} = -a_1 \tilde{u}_{t-1} + \varepsilon_t. \tag{7.5'}$$

One implication of leaving out x, well known from econometrics textbooks, is that the estimate of a_1 may be biased. This occurs unless x and u are contemporaneously uncorrelated.[12] However, even if the two regressors are indeed uncorrelated so that the estimate of a_1 is unbiased, uncertainty in the estimate is greater by the amount

$$\frac{\Sigma_t \pi_t^2}{\Sigma_t \tilde{u}_{t-1}^2} \cdot \frac{R_u^2 - R_c^2}{n},$$

where the numerator of the last term is the difference between the R^2s of the unconstrained and constrained models. Thus excluding the variable x from the model, in addition to producing a policy rule that improperly excludes x, increases uncertainty about a_1. One possible consequence is that, for the reasons provided in section 7.4, the policymaker may react to the higher level of σ_{a_1} by adjusting the weight on $\pi_t - \pi^*$ downward and by increasing the absolute size of the NAIRU adjustment ϕ_t.

7.6 Empirical Estimates of Short-Run NAIRU

7.6.1 Empirical Evidence on the Importance of Uncertainty

Although our theoretical framework shows qualitatively the effects of uncertainty on how monetary policy should be conducted, it cannot tell us whether these effects are

Table 7.1
Estimates of Annual U.S. Model, 1956–96

Coefficient	Estimate	t	$(1 + t^{-2})^{-1}$
α_0	1.67	1.49	
α_1	1.24	4.68	.956
α_2	.98	3.70	
R^2	.366		
β_0	.70	1.31	
β_1	1.00	7.06	
β_2	−.23	−2.18	
β_3	.48	6.30	.975
β_4	−.36	−3.84	
R^2	.833		

economically important. To examine this question, we estimate in this section a simple NAIRU gap model for the United States to obtain measures of uncertainty and to assess how these measures affect our view of the optimal reaction of monetary policy to movements in unemployment relative to short-run NAIRU. In order to have in the model a simple lag structure that mimics that of the theoretical model (7.5)–(7.7), we start by estimating a model with annual U.S. data over the period 1956–96. The model is

$$\pi_t - \pi_{t-1} = \alpha_0 - \alpha_1 u_{t-1} + \alpha_2 u_{t-2} + \varepsilon_t, \tag{7.13}$$

$$u_t = \beta_0 + \beta_1 u_{t-1} + \beta_2 u_{t-2} + \beta_3 r_{t-1} + \beta_4 r_{t-2} + \eta_t, \tag{7.14}$$

where π is the log change in the CPI from December of year $t - 1$ to December of year t, u is the unemployment rate in December of year t, and r is the average monthly three-month Treasury bill rate during year t. Note that α_1 and β_3 correspond to a_1 and b_2 in the theoretical model, and that the key uncertainty ratios τ_1^{-2} and τ_2^{-2} will be based on the former. The results are presented in table 7.1.

These estimates provide some guidelines regarding the importance of uncertainty for monetary policy in this context. First, the adjustments to the unemployment reference point and to the policy reaction as a result of parameter uncertainty are not large. The key parameters are estimated with some precision, and the implied multiplicative adjustment factors are both close to one. The Brainard-type adjustment—a 2.5 percent reduction—is particularly small, suggesting that the magnitude of the policy reaction should only be shaded down slightly to reflect parameter uncertainty. However, the unemployment effect adjustment is also less than 5 percent.

These results are confirmed by looking at the implicit optimal policy that corresponds to the two-year-ahead inflation target of the theoretical model in which only

Table 7.2
Implicit Interest Rate Rules

Rule	Weight on lagged interest rate	Inflation gap	Unemployment or output gap
Unadjusted			
Annual	.77	1.70	−2.56
Quarterly	.94	.47	−.70
With output gap	.94	.47	.35
Uncertainty adjusted			
Annual	.77	1.59	−2.49
Quarterly	.94	.44	−.69
With output gap	.94	.44	.34

inflation is included in the objective function. The rule that results is very similar to the simple Taylor (1993) rule when adjustments are made for the fact that Taylor's rule was defined in terms of quarterly data and an output gap. The annual and quarterly results are presented in table 7.2. If δ is the weight on the lagged interest rate in the annual model, the corresponding quarterly lag is assigned a weight of $\delta^{1/4}$ and the weights on the inflation and unemployment gaps are divided by $1 + \delta^{1/4} + \delta^{2/4} + \delta^{3/4}$. A rule based on the output gap is obtained by applying a simple Okun's law adjustment, dividing the unemployment weight by 2.

The table confirms that the practical significance of parameter uncertainty is quite small. Furthermore, the quarterly results with the output gap are remarkably similar, even numerically, to the parameters suggested by Taylor (1993). The only key difference is that the interest rate is assumed to be much more persistent here, since Taylor did not include a lagged interest rate in the form of his rule.[13]

7.6.2 Empirical Estimates of Short-Run NAIRU

In this subsection, we present estimates of short-run NAIRU. For these purposes, we return to the more general model (7.2)–(7.4) and estimate the equations with monthly data from January 1954 to November 1997, using a 12-month-ahead, 12-month horizon ($j = k = 12$) and 12 lags of both the change in inflation and unemployment.[14] Figure 7.1 shows estimated short-run NAIRU together with the contemporaneous unemployment rate, as well as the short-run NAIRU gap. This figure demonstrates the high variability of short-run NAIRU, in contrast with long-run measures designed to estimate a natural rate as in Gordon (1997) and Staiger et al. (1997a, 1997b). For example, consider a version of our equation (7.1), which may be used to estimate a constant $\bar{u}$ that is comparable to the long-run measure of those papers:

$$\Delta \pi_t = \beta(L)(u_t - \bar{u}_t) + \gamma(L)\Delta \pi_{t-1} + \varepsilon_t. \tag{7.1'}$$

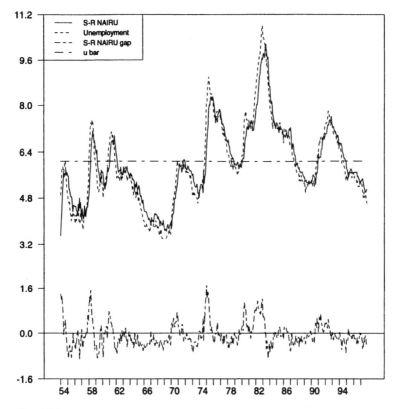

Figure 7.1
Short-run NAIRU, unemployment, and short-run NAIRU gap, January 1954 to November 1997.

When estimated over the same period as equations (7.2), (7.3), and (7.4), the estimate of $\bar{u}$ is 6.1 percent, as shown in figure 7.1.

Staiger et al. (1997a) have pointed out that such estimates of a constant long-run NAIRU tend to be quite imprecise. Using the delta method in an equation similar to (7.1'), they obtain an estimate of $\bar{u} = 6.2$ percent, with a standard error of about 0.6. Our estimate of $\bar{u} = 6.1$ has a standard error of 0.43, which is somewhat smaller—perhaps partly because of our larger sample—but is of the same order of magnitude. Estimates of short-run NAIRU n_t are more precise. The standard error of n_t is a time-varying function of the values of the variables in expression (7.4). Over the sample period, the standard errors range from 0.11 to 0.42, with a mean of 0.20, less than half of the standard error of $\bar{u}$.[15]

Thus short-run NAIRU is estimated with more than twice the precision than standard long-run NAIRU. The practical significance of this result, however, is limited, since we have shown in the theoretical sections that this type of uncertainty plays no role in the determination of the policy rule. Nevertheless, a reduction in the uncertainty may produce a reduction in the value of the cost function, as shown in section 7.5, even if the policy rule remains unaltered.

7.6.3 A Case Study: Recent Signals from a Short-Run NAIRU

Using the estimates of the NAIRU gap from subsection 7.6.2, we now examine the hypothetical results of using the methodology of this chapter in the conduct of monetary policy in the United States since June 1992, when the unemployment rate began a prolonged decline. The results will of course be somewhat simplistic, but they may provide some general support for the concepts developed in this chapter.

If we refer to one of the policy rules in the theoretical part of the chapter, say to equation (7.9), we note that the appropriate interest rate is determined essentially by two gaps: the difference between unemployment and short-run NAIRU and the difference between actual and target inflation. We present in figure 7.2a the gap between short-run NAIRU and unemployment (signed so that a positive value indicates that monetary policy should be tightened) and the level of inflation (12 previous months) since 1992.

From June 1992 to the end of 1993, declining unemployment brought the NAIRU gap from levels suggesting, if anything, the need for ease to relatively neutral levels. Meanwhile, inflation declined over the period and, in fact, continued to decline into the beginning of 1994. Beginning in 1994, however, the NAIRU gap became positive and remained so until early 1995, suggesting a need for tightening. In addition, inflation stopped declining, remaining around the 3 percent level. These two factors combined are consistent with the monetary tightening undertaken by the Federal Reserve throughout 1994 and into early 1995.

Since then, the NAIRU gap has indicated some pressure to tighten twice, in 1996 and 1997. In the first case, the pressure from the NAIRU gap was accompanied by a rise in inflation. Even though inflation subsided toward the end of the year, this episode may seem somewhat inconsistent with the absence of further tightening. Figure 7.2b suggests one reason for this result. Figure 7.2b presents the results of repeating the analysis of figure 7.2a, but using core inflation (excluding food and energy prices) instead of total inflation. Core inflation tends to be a better signal of persistent changes in inflation than total inflation.

Figure 7.2b shows both the level of core inflation as well as the gap between unemployment and short-run NAIRU computed using core inflation in equations (7.2), (7.3), and (7.4). Comparisons of the two panels of figure 7.2 suggests that the effect of using core inflation in the calculation of the NAIRU gap is very slight. But core inflation was falling in 1996, in contrast to the rising total inflation, and this fall may have offset the tightening signals from the NAIRU gap.

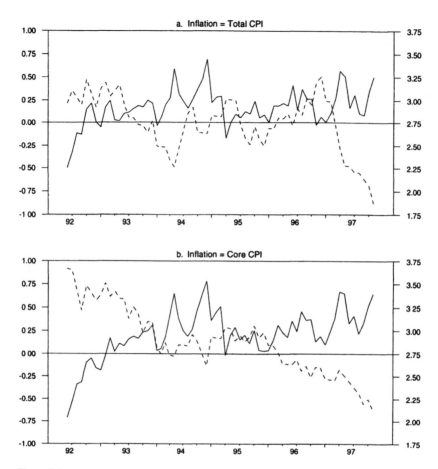

Figure 7.2
NAIRU gap (*solid line, left-hand scale*) and inflation (*dashed line, right-hand scale*), June 1992 to November 1997.

In 1997, the pressure arising from the unemployment gap seemed stronger than in the previous year. Inflation, however, both total and core, moved downward again, offsetting at least partially the signals from the NAIRU gap indicator. Arguably, only during 1994 and early 1995 were there consistent signals for tightening, and this is when the Federal Reserve engaged in most of its monetary tightening.

In order to evaluate the net effect of the unemployment and inflation indicators, it would be helpful to summarize the information in a single measure, as in the policy rules of table 7.2. We would like to do this, not to explain actual policy, but to suggest how the theoretical constructs of this chapter could be used in practice. However, this is a problem for two reasons. First, we would have to construct a full optimization model in the context of the monthly equations, which is beyond the scope of the present chapter.[16] Second, we would have to know or make an assumption about the target level of inflation. Thus we present only a limited version of a policy rule in which we deal with those problems as follows.

First, we take the weights for the NAIRU and inflation gaps from the annual results of table 7.2 allowing for uncertainty, making allowance also for the monthly frequency of our data. Since the coefficient of the lagged interest rate, $\delta^{1/12} = 0.98$, is very close to one, we further simplify by assuming that the weights are used to calculate a monthly change in the interest rate. We then divide the annual weights by $1 + \delta^{1/12} + \cdots + \delta^{11/12}$ to obtain weights of -0.23 for the NAIRU gap and 0.15 for the inflation gap with total inflation and -0.25 and 0.19, respectively, using core inflation.[17] To deal with the second problem, the fact that the inflation target is unknown, we scale the results so that the policy rule with total inflation is neutral, on average, over the period since June 1992. This assumption is equivalent to an inflation target of 3 percent.

The results are presented as the solid lines in the two panels of figure 7.3. Note that the weighted results are consistent with our earlier discussion of the individual components. In panel 7.3a, which contains the results using the total CPI, the strongest signal for tightening comes during 1994. Note also, however, that there were distinct signals for tightening in 1992–93 and 1996–97, and that there were fairly strong signals for easing at the beginning and toward the end of the sample period. In panel 7.3b, which contains results using the core CPI, there are also strong signals to tighten in 1994, but because the core inflation rate was higher than total CPI in late 1992 and early 1993, there are also strong signals to tighten in this period. In contrast to panel 7.3a, the results with the core CPI do not suggest any need to tighten in 1996.

We may contrast these results with a rule based on the standard unemployment gap—the gap between unemployment and a constant long-run NAIRU. The results are presented as the dashed lines in the two panels of figure 7.3. To obtain weights that are consistent with the assumption of a constant NAIRU, we estimated equations (7.13) and (7.14) without the second lag of unemployment, which produces an estimate of NAIRU that is constant. These new weights are -0.35 for the NAIRU gap and 0.34 for the inflation gap using total inflation and -0.36 and 0.37, respectively, using core inflation. Note, however, that if we use the same weights as before, the qualitative results are the same as with these weights.

The results for the long-run NAIRU gap, which are driven by the large steady decline in unemployment over this period, are fairly robust. The main feature of the alternative rule is that it argues for easing throughout the first part of the period, and then for tightening throughout the second part of the period. What this rule misses is that a long-run natural rate is not the best reference point for unemployment if the goal is to target inflation in the short run.

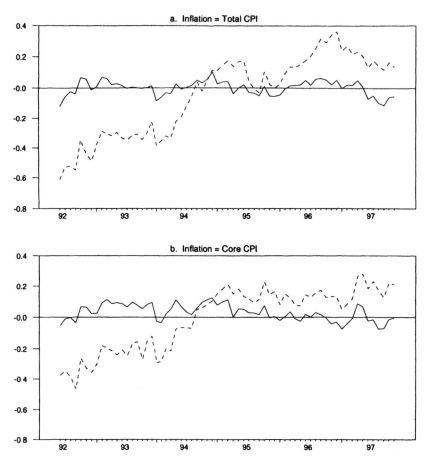

Figure 7.3
Simple policy rules based on short-run NAIRU (*solid line*) and long-run NAIRU (*dashed line*), June 1992 to November 1997.

7.7 Summary and Conclusions

In this chapter, we examine how a variant of the NAIRU concept can be usefully employed in the conduct of monetary policy. By thinking of NAIRU in this way, we obtain insights that might be quite useful to monetary policymakers. Because there are quite a few results sprinkled throughout the chapter, we list the main ones here.

• The NAIRU concept that is useful for the conduct of monetary policy differs from the estimate of the natural rate of unemployment, the long-run concept used previously by many researchers. Instead, NAIRU can be viewed as a short-run construct, which is related to past levels of unemployment and inflation as well as other economic variables, that helps forecast future accelerations or decelerations of inflation.

• Short-run NAIRU should be viewed, not as a target for policy, but as an aid in defining the reference point that policymakers can compare to the current rate of unemployment to derive a signal for the appropriate stance of policy. Furthermore, as long as inflation is an element in the policymakers' objective function, the NAIRU gap is not the only signal that should affect the setting of policy instruments: the deviation of inflation from its target level also has an important role in the determination of the appropriate stance of policy.

• The policy rule that comes out of our analysis is a variant of a Taylor rule using an unemployment gap rather than an output gap, but it has one major difference from more standard formulations. The standard Taylor rule implicitly assumes that the reference point to which unemployment should be compared in the unemployment gap term is constant, while in our formulation, the reference point is related to short-run NAIRU, which can have substantial short-run fluctuations over time.

• Uncertainty about the level of NAIRU has no influence on the setting of policy instruments, although it does affect the value of the objective function. This type of uncertainty makes the economy worse off but does not alter policy behavior.

• Uncertainty about the effect of unemployment on inflation leads to an additive adjustment to short-run NAIRU to calculate the reference point for monetary tightening in terms of the level of unemployment. In addition, uncertainty about the unemployment effect on inflation changes the weight on the inflation gap in the policy rule.

• Uncertainty about the effect of the policy variable leads to a scaling down of the reaction of the policy variable, the well-known Brainard (1967) result.

• Uncertainty about model selection can have important effects on the form of the policy rule. In particular, if a constant NAIRU is used—as occurs if NAIRU is viewed as a long-run concept—so that information about the state of the economy that could be used to forecast inflation is ignored, the performance of the policy rule can be substantially worse. In addition, leaving out relevant variables that help forecast inflation increases the uncertainty about the effect of unemployment on inflation, with the resulting implications described above.

• Although parameter uncertainty has potentially large effects on how policy should be conducted, our empirical results suggest that parameter uncertainty may not be all that important for the setting of policy. We find some evidence of changes in the policy rule resulting from the parameter uncertainty we explored in our theoretical model, but these effects are very modest. They affect the weights in the policy rule by less than 5 percent in both the case of uncertainty about the impact of unemployment and the case of uncertainty about the effect of the policy variable.

• Estimates of short-run NAIRU are highly variable over time. However, there is a fair degree of precision in these estimates.

• Substantial positive NAIRU gap estimates arose throughout 1994 and early 1995 and in parts of 1996 and 1997. However, core inflation was substantially lower in 1996 and 1997 than in 1994. Thus the one period since June 1992 during which there were consistent signals for tightening occurred during 1994 and early 1995, which is when the Fed engaged in most of its monetary tightening.

These results suggest that a short-run NAIRU is indeed a useful concept and that it can be used by policymakers, particularly in deciding how monetary policy should be conducted. However, there are some subtle issues in how the short-run NAIRU concept might be used correctly. First, because our view of NAIRU sees it as a short-run construct, it is dangerous to think of NAIRU as a potential target for unemployment that stays around a particular value, such as 6 percent, for any period of time. Second, deviation of inflation from its target is every bit as important a factor in thinking about setting policy as is the NAIRU gap. Third, uncertainty about parameter values and model selection does have effects on the optimal setting of policy instruments but does not appear to be a barrier to a useful role for the NAIRU concept in policy decisions.

We hope that this chapter helps resurrect NAIRU as a useful concept, but only if it is used properly. As we have shown, a short-run NAIRU is a useful construct because it helps tell policymakers what might happen to inflation in the future. Furthermore, the model of this chapter suggests that policymakers may want to avoid the impression that an objective of policy is to raise unemployment when it falls below NAIRU or to lower it when it is above NAIRU. To view policy in this way might lead the public to think that policymakers are against low unemployment, an outcome that can reduce support for central bank efforts to control inflation.

Notes

The authors thank participants at the conference and at seminars at the Federal Reserve Bank of New York and Columbia University for their helpful comments, and Elizabeth Reynolds for excellent research assistance. The views expressed in this chapter are those of the authors and do not necessarily represent those of the Federal Reserve Bank of New York, the Federal Reserve System, Columbia University, or the National Bureau of Economic Research.

1. If price stability has already been achieved, then inflation falling below its target is every bit as damaging as a rise in inflation above the target. Thus, in this situation, monetary policy must also be just as preemptive against declines in inflation below target levels.

2. See, e.g., Stiglitz (1997), Gordon (1997), Staiger, Stock, and Watson (1997a, 1997b), and Council of Economic Advisers (1997, 45–54). For a history of NAIRU, see Espinosa-Vega and Russell (1997). The NAIRU acronym would better be expressed as NIIRU (the nonincreasing inflation rate of unemployment) because it is the unemployment rate at which inflation is expected to neither increase or decrease.

3. See, e.g., Staiger et al. (1997a).

4. The variable x differs from z in the Gordon (1997) and Staiger et al. (1997a, 1997b) equations in that z represents primarily supply shocks that are contemporaneous with the dependent variable, whereas x is more general in that it includes any predetermined variables other than unemployment and inflation (and their lags) that help predict future inflation.

5. Eq. (7.4) is a generalization of the model of short-run NAIRU in Estrella (1997). After writing this chapter, we discovered that Layard and Bean (1988) also have a similar definition of short-run NAIRU in the context of a one-period change in inflation.

6. In eq. (7.2), we think of π as an I(1) process, which is consistent with current econometric evidence and practice. See, e.g., Stock (1991) and King and Watson (1994, sec. 4). Alternatively, one could think of π as an I(0) process and include a level of π in the x-vector in eq. (7.2).

7. Once again, this is a relatively simple objective function designed to highlight the key points of this chapter. A more complex dynamic solution of a similar model may be found in Svensson (1997), which exhibits properties that are qualitatively analogous to those of the simpler model of this chapter.

8. Other papers that look at the effect of parameter uncertainty in a similar context are Svensson (1997), Clarida, Galí, and Gertler (1999), and Wieland (1998).

9. This convention economizes on notation and is correct by definition if the coefficient estimates are unbiased.

10. The complementary problem of including too many variables in the model is in principle less serious, since consistent parameter estimates should assign zero weight to the superfluous variables.

11. The intuition is that as uncertainty about b_2 grows, the optimal response of the policy variable r is reduced so that there is less loss from using the incorrect model.

12. See, e.g., Theil (1971, sec. 11.2). This problem may be bypassed formally by thinking of x as the component of the additional variable that is uncorrelated with u.

13. Recent estimates of the Taylor rule by Rudebusch and Svensson (1999) and Rotemberg and Woodford (1999), among others, suggest that the persistence parameter is close to one. Fuhrer and Moore (1995) assume that it equals one.

14. Somewhat surprisingly, extending the horizon to $j + k = 60$ months or even longer does not materially affect the point estimates of short-run NAIRU. Of course, the fit of the equation deteriorates with longer horizons.

15. All our standard errors are estimated consistently using the Newey-West technique with a 24-lag window (Newey and West 1987).

16. A model along those lines has been developed for the United States in Clarida et al. (1999). See also the references in that paper.

17. Adjusting fully for coefficient uncertainty would require, in addition to the adjusted weights, an adjustment to short-run NAIRU corresponding to the term ϕ_t defined in subsection 7.4.1. We do not make this adjustment here because our equation for monthly NAIRU is essentially a reduced form and the components are difficult to disentangle, and also because the coefficient of the adjustment factor $(1 + \tau_1^2)^{-1} \leq 0.065$ is empirically small.

References

Brainard, William. 1967. Uncertainty and the effectiveness of policy. *American Economic Review Papers and Proceedings* 57: 411–25.

Clarida, Richard, Jordi Galí, and Mark Gertler. 1999. The science of monetary policy: A new Keynesian perspective. *Journal of Economic Literature* 37 (December): 1661–1707.

Council of Economic Advisers. 1997. *Economic report of the president*. Washington, D.C.: Government Printing Office.

Espinosa-Vega, Marco A., and Steven Russell. 1997. History and theory of the NAIRU: A critical review. *Federal Reserve Bank of Atlanta Economic Review* 82: 4–25.

Estrella, Arturo. 1997. Aggregate supply and demand shocks: A natural rate approach. Research Paper no. 9737. New York: Federal Reserve Bank of New York.

Friedman, Milton. 1968. The role of monetary policy. *American Economic Review* 58: 1–21.

Fuhrer, Jeffrey C., and George R. Moore. 1995. Monetary policy trade-offs and the correlation between nominal interest rates and real output. *American Economic Review* 85: 219–39.

Gordon, Robert J. 1997. The time-varying NAIRU and its implications for economic policy. *Journal of Economic Perspectives* 11: 11–32.

King, Robert G., and Mark W. Watson. 1994. The post-war U.S. Phillips curve: A revisionist econometric history. *Carnegie-Rochester Conference Series on Public Policy* 41: 157–219.

Layard, Richard, and Charles R. Bean. 1988. Why does unemployment persist? Discussion Paper no. 321. London: London School of Economics, Centre for Labour Economics, August.

Modigliani, Franco, and Lucas Papademos. 1975. Targets for monetary policy in the coming year. *Brookings Papers on Economic Activity*, no. 1: 141–63.

Newey, Whitney K., and Kenneth D. West. 1987. A simple-positive semi-definite, heteroskedasticity and autocorrelation consistent covariance matrix. *Econometrica* 55: 703–8.

Phelps, Edmund. 1968. Money-wage dynamics and labor-market equilibrium. *Journal of Political Economy* 76: 678–711.

Staiger, Douglas, James H. Stock, and Mark W. Watson. 1997a. How precise are estimates of the natural rate of unemployment? In *Reducing inflation: Motivation and strategy*, ed. Christina D. Romer and David H. Romer. Chicago: University of Chicago Press.

———. 1997b. The NAIRU, unemployment and monetary policy. *Journal of Economic Perspectives* 11: 33–49.

Stiglitz, Joseph. 1997. Reflections on the natural rate hypothesis. *Journal of Economic Perspectives* 11: 3–10.

Stock, James H. 1991. Confidence intervals for the largest autoregressive root in U.S. macroeconomic time series. *Journal of Monetary Economics* 28: 435–59.

Svensson, Lars E. O. 1997. Inflation forecast targeting: Implementing and monitoring inflation targets. *European Economic Review* 41: 1111–46.

Taylor, John B. 1993. Discretion versus policy in practice. *Carnegie-Rochester Conference Series on Public Policy* 39: 195–214.

Theil, Henri. 1971. *Principles of econometrics.* New York: Wiley.

Wieland, Volker. 1998. Monetary policy and uncertainty about the natural unemployment rate. Finance and Economics Discussion Paper no. 98-22. Washington, D.C.: Board of Governors of the Federal Reserve System.

II Monetary Policy Strategy in Advanced Economies

Introduction to Part II

The chapters in this part of the book examine monetary policy strategy in advanced economies with an unapologetic case-study approach. Chapters 8 to 11 approach the study of monetary policy strategy through detailed discussions of the experiences in the major advanced countries. Chapter 8 was written with Ben Bernanke, now the chairman of the Federal Reserve, for the NBER Macroeconomics Annual conference in 1992. The use of case studies in monetary economics is often highly controversial, and Ben and I experienced a contentious reception at the NBER Macro Annual conference. Many economists object to case-study research because they believe that the methodology is too ad hoc. Indeed, the discussion on our paper at the Macro Annual Conference focused almost entirely on whether a case-study approach is appropriate to study macroeconomic issues and focused very little on the content of the paper itself. The discussion of this paper was one of the most disappointing discussions of my research in my entire career.

Despite this discouragement, I continued to use (and strongly believe in) a case-study approach in my research as many of the following chapters prove. There are two strong reasons why case-study research is so valuable in monetary economics. The first is that case studies—the study of historical episodes, although some may be quite recent—can provide another way of identifying exogenous shocks to the economy, which enables the researcher to be more confident of which way causality runs in the data. (I have used this identification strategy in my monetary research in Huizinga and Mishkin [1986], as have Romer and Romer [1989].) Identification in econometric research is often more suspect because it frequently requires ad hoc assumptions. This case-study approach is the strength of Friedman and Schwartz's *Monetary History of the United States*, which argued convincingly that monetary policy matters: they first identify exogenous shocks to monetary policy, such as the one that occurred in 1936 and 1937 when the Fed raised reserve requirements and thereby lowered the money supply for purely technical reasons, and then demonstrate that the economy responded strongly afterwards. Indeed, it was the case-study approach in Friedman and Schwartz using historical episodes (what Romer and

Romer [1989] call the narrative approach), and not econometric research, that had the greatest impact on economists' views regarding whether monetary policy matters. The second reason for pursuing case-study research is that details matter, particularly when thinking about how to design successful policies. Only case studies can reveal the details that are often the difference between the success and failure of particular policies, and that can highlight the differences between theory and actual policy experience.

Chapter 8 focuses on monetary targeting by examining the monetary policy experience in six advanced economies from 1973 to 1991. Even though no countries today are pursuing monetary targeting, it is still worth studying this monetary policy regime because it has important historical lessons for other approaches currently in use, such as inflation targeting. Indeed, it was by learning what did and did not work in these countries that has resulted in the monetary policy strategies being pursued today. One pattern revealed by these case studies is that central banks adopted money-growth targets when inflation got out of control. Central banks also appeared to use money-growth targets both as guideposts for assessing the stance of monetary policy and as a means of signaling their intentions to the public; however, no central bank has adhered to monetary targets in the short run. The case studies also suggest that money-growth targets might be useful in providing a medium-term framework for monetary policy if the targeting is done in a clear and straightforward manner and if targets can be adjusted for changes in the link between target and goal variables. It appears that rigid adherence to money-growth targets in the short run is not necessary to gain some benefits of targeting, as long as there is some ultimate commitment by the central bank to reverse short-term deviations from the target. Finally, the choice of operating procedure seems to have little bearing on the success of policy.

My interest in monetary policy strategy naturally heightened when I moved from being an academic to a policymaker upon becoming the director of research at the Federal Reserve Bank of New York in September 1994. In advising the president of the bank, William McDonough, I was made increasingly aware of how important a role communication plays in the success of monetary policy. I also saw that a new policy framework, inflation targeting, seemed to be having tremendous success not only in lowering inflation in the countries that adopted it, but also in simplifying the central bank's communication strategy. As the director of research, I started a project on inflation targeting and, given my previous successful collaboration with him, I asked Ben Bernanke to participate. I also announced to my staff that I would be working on this project and one of the economists in my group, Adam Posen, immediately asked if he could come on board. Ben then brought in his student, Thomas Laubach, into the project, and thus began a highly successful collaboration among the four of us. This project not only produced chapter 9, written in 1996 with Ben Bernanke, but also led to a very long paper with Adam Posen, "Inflation Targeting:

Lessons from Four Countries" (Mishkin and Posen 1997), which took up a whole issue of the Federal Reserve Bank of New York's *Economic Policy Review* and is therefore too long to be included in this book. (It is available on the Federal Reserve Bank of New York's Web site at http://www.ny.frb.org/research/epr/1997.html.) In addition, the project led to chapter 10, and finally to our book, Bernanke, Laubach, Mishkin, and Posen (1999), *Inflation Targeting: Lessons from the International Experience.* This book, which draws heavily on the case-study approach, is one of my proudest accomplishments because I have been told it has had a substantial impact on central banking practice.

Chapter 9 describes how inflation targeting has been implemented in practice and argues that it is best understood as a broad framework for policy, which allows the central bank "constrained discretion" rather than an ironclad policy rule in the Friedman sense. The chapter discusses the potential of the inflation targeting approach for making monetary policy more coherent and transparent, and for increasing monetary policy discipline. A noteworthy feature of this work is that the term *constrained discretion*, which to the best of my knowledge Ben Bernanke and I coined, has become standard for describing inflation-targeting regimes. It clarifies that the traditional dichotomy in the academic literature between rules and discretion is misleading: useful strategies can be rule-like in that their forward-looking nature constrains policymakers from systematically engaging in policies with undesirable long-run consequences, but can also allow some discretion for dealing with unforeseen or unusual circumstances. We argue that inflation targeting should be viewed exactly in this way, rather than as a rigid policy rule.

Chapter 10, which was written for a conference at the Swedish central bank in 1998, examines the international experiences with four basic types of monetary policy regimes: 1) exchange-rate targeting, 2) monetary targeting, 3) inflation targeting, and 4) monetary policy with an implicit but not an explicit nominal anchor. The basic theme that emerges from this analysis is that transparency and accountability are crucial to constraining discretionary monetary policy so that it produces desirable long-run outcomes. Because the devil is in the details in achieving transparency and accountability, what strategy will work best in a country depends on its political, cultural, and economic institutions, as well as on its history.

Part II ends with an unabashedly polemical essay, chapter 11, which was presented at the American Economic Association meetings in 2004. I argue that despite the Federal Reserve's superb performance in recent years under Alan Greenspan, the Fed should change its monetary policy strategy and adopt a flexible form of inflation targeting. The Federal Reserve strategy under Greenspan has some serious disadvantages and continuing pursuit of this approach is likely to work less well in the future. Adoption of an inflation target would help ensure that the legacy of the Greenspan Fed of low and stable inflation is maintained.

References

Bernanke, Ben S., Thomas Laubach, Frederic S. Mishkin, and Adam S. Posen. 1999. *Inflation Targeting: Lessons from the International Experience*. Princeton University Press: Princeton.

Huizinga, John, and Frederic S. Mishkin. 1986. "Monetary Policy Regime Shifts and the Unusual Behavior of Real Interest Rates." *Carnegie-Rochester Conference Series on Public Policy* 24 (Spring): 231–274.

Mishkin, Frederic S., and Adam S. Posen. 1997. "Inflation Targeting: Lessons from Four Countries." Federal Reserve Bank of New York, *Economic Policy Review* vol. 3, no. 3 (August 1997): 9–110.

Romer, Christina, and David Romer. 1989. "Does Monetary Policy Matter? A New Test in the Spirit of Friedman and Schwartz." *NBER Macroeconomics Annual*: 121–183.

8 Central Bank Behavior and the Strategy of Monetary Policy: Observations from Six Industrialized Countries

Ben Bernanke and Frederic S. Mishkin

8.1 Introduction

In the United States, it has long been the practice of central bankers to meet periodically with outside consultants, including academic and business economists, in order to discuss the current economic situation. In the authors' experience as invited consultants, these meetings invariably end with a "go-round," in which each consultant is asked to give his or her views on current monetary policy. Often the go-round is prefaced by a question of the following sort: "The Federal Open Market Committee [the group that determines U.S. monetary policy] meets next Tuesday. What actions do you recommend that we take?"

We have each found it quite difficult to give a good answer to this type of question, not only because, as ivory-tower academics, we tend to have a less-detailed knowledge of current conditions than do the central bankers. The larger problem is that the question lacks context: Implicitly, it asks for advice on tactics without specifying the strategy. Probably the most enduring lesson of Lucas's (1976) famous critique is that the effects of any given policy action depend greatly on the expectations it engenders: Is the policy intended to be temporary or permanent? Under what circumstances will it be changed? Expectations about policy in turn depend on the public's perceptions of the authorities' policy strategy, as determined both by policymakers' explicit choices and by deeper political and institutional factors. Thus, if we hope ever to give a really satisfactory answer to the central banker's question, we must first develop some clear views about monetary policy strategy as well as tactics. These concerns motivate this chapter.

What is the optimal strategy for the monetary authorities to follow? There is a large and venerable academic literature on this question, which has tended to cast the central banker's options rather starkly as following either *rules* or *discretion*. A monetary rule specifies future monetary actions as a *simple* function of economic or monetary conditions[1]; at least in principle, monetary rules do not allow the monetary authorities to respond to unforeseen circumstances. Examples of rules are Milton

Friedman's $k\%$ money growth rule and (strict) nominal GNP targeting. Fischer (1990) describes the rationales that have been advanced for rules: The most compelling is probably Kydland and Prescott's (1977) argument that rules increase the central bank's ability to precommit to avoiding monetary surprises, which in turn permits a lower steady-state rate of inflation.

In contrast to rules, the strategy of discretion[2] puts no prior restrictions on the actions that the central bank can take at each date. The basic rationale for discretion, as discussed by Fischer (1990), is that the benefit of allowing the central bank to respond flexibly to unanticipated contingencies is greater than any advantage gained from precommitment.

The debate about rules and discretion, although motivated by real policy concerns and some (mostly U.S.) experience, has been cast largely in abstract and ahistorical terms. An alternative, and complementary, research strategy is simply to observe what central bankers at different places and times have actually done, and to see what results they have obtained. This more flatly empirical approach is taken by the present chapter. We use a simple case study methodology to analyze the conduct and performance of monetary policy in six industrialized countries for the period from the breakup of the Bretton Woods system until the present. In doing so, we hope to gain some insight into the objectives and constraints that determine central bank behavior and—at this stage, in a very tentative way—to develop some hypotheses about the attributes of successful monetary strategies.

The case study method has a poor reputation in economics, largely because of the tendency of its users to treat anecdotes as evidence. We fully agree that case studies are not a substitute either for more systematic empirical work or formal theoretical modeling. However, in our opinion, this approach can be a valuable preliminary to the more standard types of research. First, case studies can help establish the historical and institutional context, an essential first step in good applied work. Second, historical analysis of actual policy experiences is a natural way to find substantive hypotheses that subsequent work can model and test more formally. We believe that the method of developing initial hypotheses exhibited here is superior to the more typical, implicit method of developing hypotheses, which relies on introspection or on knowledge of only a few episodes.

The bulk of this chapter consists of brief narrative discussions of recent monetary policy-making in the United States, the United Kingdom, Canada, Germany, Switzerland, and Japan. From these case histories, as well as from our reading of central bank reports and the commentaries of observers, we distill a number of hypotheses— candidate empirical regularities, if you will—about central bank behavior, policy strategies, and policy outcomes. These hypotheses are of two types. *Positive hypotheses*, which receive most of our attention, are based on observations that hold for all or nearly all of the cases examined; to the extent that these observations are confirmed by additional research, they need to be explained by positive theories of central bank behavior. *Normative hypotheses*, in contrast, are about differences in the characteristics of monetary policy strategies between more and less successful economies. We call these hypotheses normative because—despite the great difficulties involved in inferring causation from correlation—we believe that these cross-sectional differences ultimately may help to provide useful lessons about the design of monetary policy. We emphasize again, though, that at this stage both the positive and normative hypotheses are to be treated not as conclusions but as suggestive propositions that are advanced for further discussion, analysis, and testing.

Of the various positive hypotheses that we extract from the case studies, three of the most important are the following:

First, in their conduct of monetary policy, central bankers appear to be pursuing multiple economic objectives; they care not only about the behavior of inflation and unemployment but sometimes also, independently, about the behavior of variables such as exchange rates and interest rates. Further, instead of giving equal weight to all objectives, a large part of the monetary policymaker's attention at any given time is devoted to the variable that is currently "in crisis," to the neglect of other concerns.

Each of the central banks we consider has employed official money growth targets over all or a substantial part of the recent period. A second positive hypothesis is that—consistent, perhaps, with their "crisis mentality"—central bankers are more likely to adopt targets for money growth, or to increase their emphasis on meeting existing targets, when inflation is perceived as the number one problem.

This tendency of central bankers to retreat to money growth targets when inflation increases is something of a puzzle. For example, as we discuss later, this behavior is not easily explained by Poole's (1970) classic analysis of target choice. We conjecture (based in part on what the central bankers themselves say) that there are two reasons why central bankers cling to money targets when inflation threatens: (1) High inflation causes policymakers to become less confident in their ability to assess the stance of policy; intermediate targets such as money growth targets are perceived to be useful as *guideposts* or compasses that aid in choosing the appropriate policy setting. (2) Perhaps more important, money growth targets may be particularly useful as *signals* of the monetary authorities' intention to get tough on inflation. As we explain later, signalling its anti-inflationary intentions may help the central bank both to manage the public's expectations and to defend its policies against political pressures for more expansionary policies.

A third positive observation is that—although banks occasionally conduct policy using a strategy approaching pure discretion—they never adhere to strict, ironclad rules. Indeed, a common strategy resembles most nearly a hybrid of rules and discretion, in which the central bank attempts (with varying degrees of success) to apply rules to its medium-term and long-term policies, while retaining "flexibility" or discretion to respond to developments in the economy in the short run. We view this observation as quite interesting because it challenges the simple view of much of the received literature that pure rules and pure discretion are the only policy strategies available.

Perhaps the most intriguing normative hypothesis suggested by our case studies is that—contrary to what might be inferred from Kydland and Prescott (1977)—hybrid monetary strategies of the type just described appear to be consistent with low and stable inflation rates. For example, as we will see, Germany and Switzerland—and to a lesser extent, Japan—have been able to pursue money growth targets as an intermediate-term objective, while at the same time maintaining considerable short-run discretion to meet objectives such as exchange rate stabilization. Several factors seem to be associated with successful use of a hybrid strategy, each of which can be construed as helping to make credible the central bank's claim that it will follow rules in the medium run, though not in the short run:

First, we observe particularly in the German and Swiss cases that the central bank's intermediate targets are explicitly linked, via a simple and public calculation, to the ultimate goals of policy (e.g., the desired inflation rate). In principle, this explicit linkage of targets to goals allows the central bank to adjust its targets when the target–goal relationship changes, without compromising its credibility.

Second, the central banks who successfully use the hybrid strategy tend to conduct policy in a more straightforward and transparent way, avoiding devices such as multiple targets, "base drift," and irregular changes in targets or target growth rates.

Finally, achieving low inflation via the hybrid strategy seems to require some commitment by the central bank to reverse short-term deviations from target over a longer period. In the case of a money growth rule, for example, periods of above-target money growth tend to be compensated for (in low-inflation countries) by subsequent money growth reductions.

The rest of the chapter is organized as follows. Section 8.2, the bulk of the chapter, presents the six case studies of monetary policy-making. Section 8.3 lists and discusses our positive hypotheses about central bank behavior. Section 8.4 both discusses our normative hypotheses and addresses important issues that remain unresolved.

8.2   The Conduct of Monetary Policy in Six Industrialized Countries, 1973–1991

To provide some empirical basis for discussing the conduct of monetary policy, this section provides brief narrative descriptions of monetary policy in six industrialized countries over the period since the breakdown of the Bretton Woods system. The countries discussed are the United States, the United Kingdom, Canada, Germany (representing the EMS bloc), Switzerland, and Japan. These six countries represent "independent" observations in the sense that, for most of the period, no two of them belonged to a common system of fixed exchange rates.[3] Other countries with independent monetary policies, such as Sweden and Australia, would be interesting to study but are excluded because of space and data limitations.

Our focus here is on general strategies and approaches used by monetary policy-makers; where possible, we abstract from the fine institutional details of monetary policy operations in the various countries, except as they impinge on the broader issues.[4] In discussing the experiences of the various countries, however, it is useful to draw the familiar distinctions among policy goals, instruments, and intermediate targets (see, e.g., McCallum, 1989, or Friedman, 1990). *Goals* are the final objectives of policy, for example, price stability and economic growth. *Instruments* are variables that the central bank controls closely on a daily or weekly basis, such as nonborrowed reserves or the interbank lending rate; the choice of instruments and the mechanisms by which they are controlled determine the central bank's *operating procedure. Intermediate targets*—monetary aggregates are the most common example—are variables that are neither under the direct day-to-day control of the central bank nor are the ultimate goals of policy, but that are used to guide policy. Values for instruments are usually set so that, given estimates of behavioral parameters such as the interest elasticity of money demand, intermediate targets for variables such as M1 growth are reached in the longer term (quarter-to-quarter or year-to-year). In turn, intermediate targets are set or reset periodically so as to be consistent with the central bank's ultimate economic objectives.

The narrative discussions that follow are supplemented by two types of more quantitative evidence. First, tables 8.1–8.6 present, for each country separately, the record of announced targets for money growth, the actual money growth outcomes, and the implied excess money growth (actual growth less the midpoint of the target range). Second, comparisons across countries of the behavior of several key monetary and macroeconomic variables are provided by figures 8.1–8.7 at the end of the chapter. The monthly data shown in the figures are as follows:[5]

(Fig. 8.1) money growth rates (from 1 year earlier) of both the narrow and the broad monetary aggregate focused on by the central bank in each country (M0, M1, M2, OR M3).

(Fig. 8.2) the variability of narrow and broad money growth (e.g., SDM1 or SDM2); measured as the standard deviation over the previous 12 months of the money growth rates in figure 8.1.[6]

(Fig. 8.3) interest rates on overnight interbank loans (RS) and on long-term government bonds (RL).

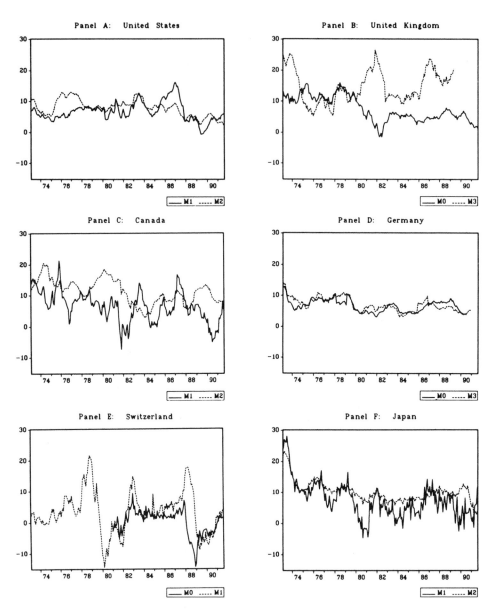

Figure 8.1
Growth rates of narrow and broad monetary aggregates. Data are the growth rates (log changes) from one year earlier of monetary aggregates. M0 refers to the monetary base for the United Kingdom and Switzerland and to central bank money for Germany. M1, M2, and M3 refer to conventional national definitions. Sources: *Federal Reserve Bulletin* and releases; *Bank of England Quarterly Bulletin* (tables 11.1 and 2); *Bank of Canada Review* (table E.1); *Bundesbank Monthly Reports* (tables I.2, I.3; supplement 4, table 33); Banque Nationale Suisse, *Bulletin mensuel* (tables 9 and 11); Bank of Japan, unpublished.

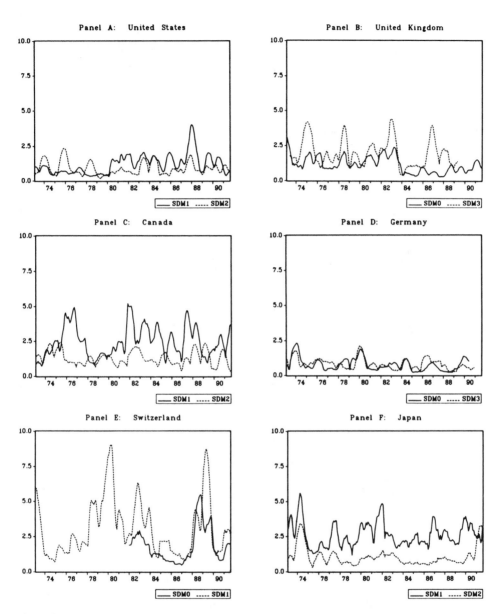

Figure 8.2
Variability of narrow and broad money growth rates. SDM0, SDM1, SDM2, and SDM3 are the standard deviations over the previous 12 months of the growth rates of the monetary aggregates M1, M1, M2, and M3, as shown in figure 8.1.
Sources: Same as figure 8.1.

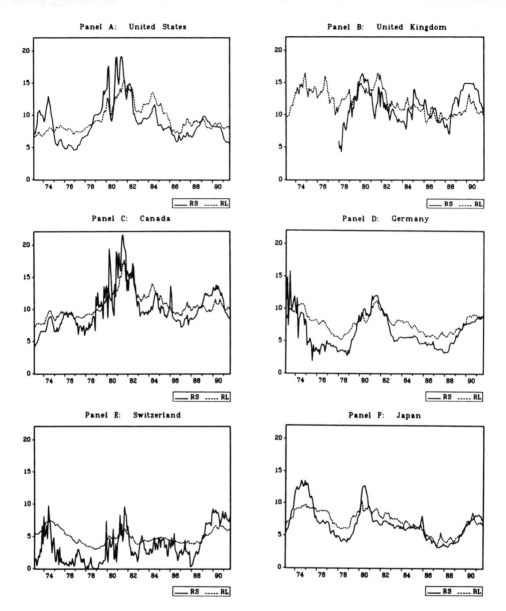

Figure 8.3
Interest rates on overnight bank loans (RS) and on long-term bonds (RL). Interest data by country are as follows: United States—federal funds rate (RS), 10-year Treasury bonds and notes (RL); United Kingdom—call money with discount market (RS), medium-dated (10-year) government bonds (RL); Canada—overnight money market financing (RS), government bonds, over 10 years (RL); Germany—day-to-day money (RS), federal government bonds, all maturities (RL); Switzerland—day-to-day money (RS), confederation bonds (RL); Japan—call money (unconditional) (RS), government bonds, interest-bearing (RL). RS for Switzerland refers to Euromarket rate, other short rates are money market rates. Long rates are secondary market rates. Rates are monthly averages, except the U.K., Canadian, Swiss, and Japanese long rates and the Canadian short rate, which are month-end.
Sources: *Federal Reserve Bulletin*; *Bank of England Quarterly Bulletin* (tables 9.2 and 9.1); *Bank of Canada Review* (figure F.1); *Bundesbank Monthly Reports* (table TV.6; supplement series 2, table 8.b); Banque Nationale Suisse, *Bulletin mensuel* (tables T.20 and T.24); Bank of Japan, *Economic Statistics Monthly* (table 63) and Tokyo Stock Exchange, *Monthly Statistics Report*.

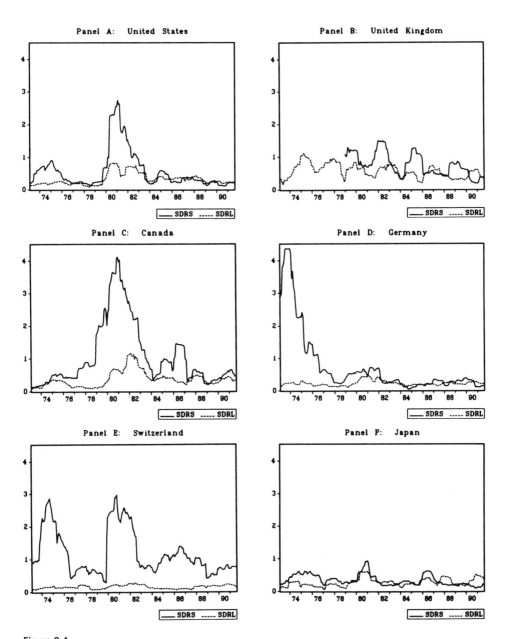

Figure 8.4
Variability of changes in short- and long-term interest rates. SDRS and SDRL are the standard deviations over the previous 12 months of RS and RL, as shown in figure 8.3.
Sources: Same as figure 8.3.

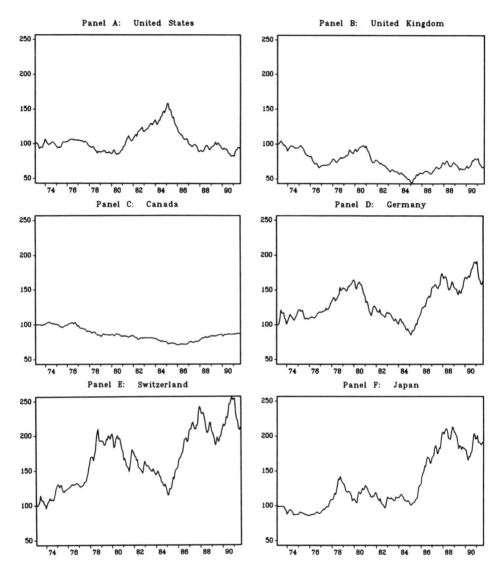

Figure 8.5
Indices of nominal exchange rates (March 1973 = 100). Shown are indices of nominal exchange rates, March 1973 = 100, with an increase indicating an appreciation. For the United States the exchange rate is the Federal Reserve's effective exchange rate index; for other countries the value of the currency in U.S. dollars is used.
Source: *Federal Reserve Bulletin.*

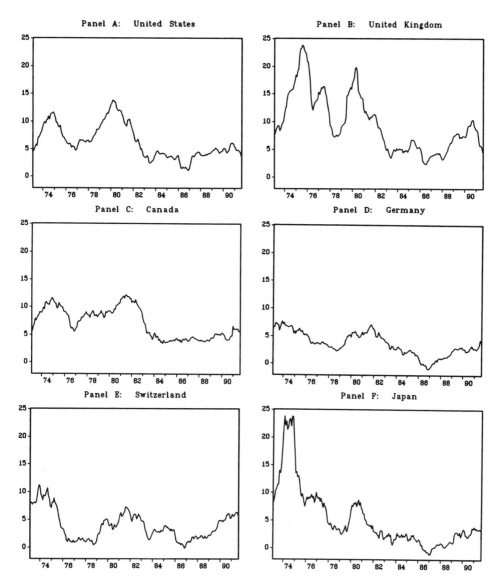

Figure 8.6
Inflation rates. Inflation rates are measured as the growth over the last 12 months of the broadest available measure of consumer prices, as follows: United States—CPI-U, all items; United Kingdom—retail price index, all items; Canada—CPI, all items; Germany—cost-of-living index, all households; Switzerland—consumer prices, all items; Japan—CPI, all households, excluding farmers, fishermen, and single persons. Sources: U.S. Bureau of Labor Statistics; U.K. Central Statistical Office, *Monthly Digest of Statistics*, table 18.1; *Bank of Canada Review*, table H.12; *Bundesbank Monthly Reports*, table V.III; (Swiss) Dept. Fed. L'Economie Publique, *La Vie Economique*, table B5.1; Bank of Japan, unpublished.

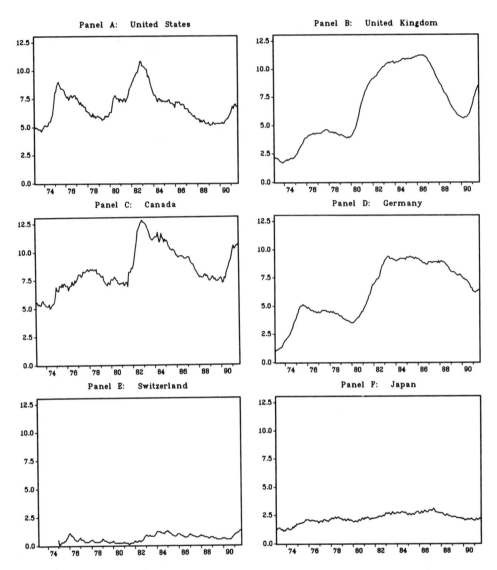

Figure 8.7
Unemployment rates. Data are civilian unemployment rates, national definitions. U.K. rate excludes school leavers.
Sources: U.S. Dept. of Labor, *The Employment Situation*, table A.1; U.K. Central Statistical Office, *Economic Trends*, table 36, col. 5; *Bank of Canada Review*, table H.7; Bundesbank, supplement to the *Monthly Reports*, series 4, table 7; (Swiss) Dept. Fed. L'Economie Publique, *La Vie Economique*, p. 3; (Japan) Labor Force Survey, Economic Planning Agency, *Japan Economic Indicators*.

(Fig. 8.4) the variability of changes in overnight interbank and long-term interest rates (SDRS or SDRL); measured using the same 12-month moving-average procedure as in figure 8.2.

(Fig. 8.5) indices of nominal exchange rates (ER); measured as the Federal Reserve's effective exchange rate index for the United States and as the value of the currency in U.S. dollars for other countries (an increase in the index always implies an appreciation).

(Fig. 8.6) inflation rates (PI); measured as the log-change of consumer prices over the last 12 months.

(Fig. 8.7) unemployment rates (UN); civilian labor force, national definitions.

The United States.[7] We begin with the United States because it is the best documented case and because the U.S. experience has played an important role in setting the agenda for previous analyses of monetary policy.

The conduct of monetary policy in the United States since the early 1970s is conventionally divided into three regimes. During the first regime (approximately 1970–1979), the federal funds rate—the interbank lending rate—was the primary instrument of monetary policy, serving in various degrees as a target of policy as well. Open market operations were used to keep the funds rate within a narrow target band (usually on the order of 50–75 basis points); over time, the band was adjusted smoothly (usually in 25 or 50 basis point increments) in response to general macroeconomic conditions.[8]

In principle, during this period, the Fed paid attention to money growth as well as to interest rates: Beginning in 1970, the FOMC selected weekly tracking paths for M1 and indicated its preferred behavior for M2 (Meulendyke, 1990), and in 1975, in response to a congressional resolution, the Fed began to announce publicly its targets for money growth (table 8.1). In practice, however, the Fed did not consider meeting money growth targets to be of high priority, placing greater weight on reducing unemployment while maintaining a relatively smooth path for interest rates. Devices employed by the Fed to avoid being overly constrained by money growth targets included the setting of targets for more than one aggregate, which usually allowed it to claim that it was hitting at least some target; and the frequent resort to "base drift," that is, the ignoring of past deviations of money growth from target when setting new targets.[9]

As can be seen from table 8.1 or figure 8.1a, M1 growth had an upward trend after 1975 despite declining target ranges. With hindsight, the money expansion of 1975–1978 appears to have been excessive: Unemployment came down steadily during the 1975–1978 period (fig. 8.7a), but the dollar fell (fig. 8.5a) and inflation heated up sharply (fig. 8.6a), even in advance of the second oil shock.

Table 8.1
Money Growth Targets and Outcomes: United States

Year	Aggregate	Target	Outcome	Outcome less target
1975	M1	5.0–7.5	5.3	−1.0
	M2	8.5–10.5	9.7	+0.2
	M3	10.0–12.0	12.3	+1.3
1976	M1	4.5–7.5	5.8	−0.2
	M2	7.5–10.5	10.9	+1.9
	M3	9.0–12.0	12.7	+2.2
1977	M1	4.5–6.5	7.9	+2.4
	M2	7.0–10.0	3.8	−4.7
	M3	8.5–11.5	11.7	+1.7
1978	M1	4.0–6.5	7.2	+2.0
	M2	6.5–9.0	8.7	+1.0
	M3	7.5–10.0	9.5	+0.8
1979	M1	3.0–6.0	5.5	+1.0
	M2	5.0–8.0	8.3	+1.8
	M3	6.0–9.0	8.1	+0.6
1980	M1	4.0–6.5	7.3	+2.1
	M2	6.0–9.0	9.6	+2.1
	M3	6.5–9.5	10.2	+2.2
1981	M1	3.5–6.0	2.3	−3.0
	M2	6.0–9.0	9.5	+2.0
	M3	6.5–9.5	11.4	+3.4
1982	M1	2.5–5.5	8.5	+4.5
	M2	6.0–9.0	9.2	+1.7
	M3	6.5–9.5	10.1	+2.1
1983	M1	4.0–8.0	10.0	+4.0
	M2	7.0–10.0	8.3	−0.2
	M3	6.5–9.5	9.7	+1.7
1984	M1	4.0–8.0	5.2	−0.8
	M2	6.0–9.0	7.7	+0.2
	M3	6.0–9.0	10.5	+3.0
1985	M1	4.0–7.0	11.9	+6.4
	M2	6.0–9.0	8.6	+1.1
	M3	6.0–9.5	7.4	−0.4
1986	M1	3.0–8.0	15.2	+9.7
	M2	6.0–9.0	8.9	+1.4
	M3	6.0–9.0	8.8	+1.3
1987	M2	5.5–8.5	4.3	−2.7
	M3	5.5–8.5	5.6	−1.4
1988	M2	4.0–8.0	5.2	−0.8
	M3	4.0–8.0	6.1	+0.1
1989	M2	3.0–7.0	4.7	−0.3
	M3	3.5–7.5	3.3	−2.2
1990	M2	3.0–7.0	3.8	−1.2
	M3	2.5–6.5	1.5	−3.0
1991	M2	2.5–6.5	2.7	−1.8
	M3	1.0–5.0	1.5	−1.5

Table 8.1
(continued)

Notes: Growth rates (%) are measured fourth quarter to fourth quarter. Outcome less target equals the outcome less the midpoint of the target range. Data reflects definitions of aggregates current at times of announcements. Target ranges are those announced at the beginning of the year (midyear changes occurred in 1979, 1983, 1985, and 1990). Target and outcome for 1981 M1 growth are adjusted for shifts into NOW accounts.
Sources: Isard and Rojas-Suarez (1986) and Fischer (1987); updates from annual "Monetary Report to Congress," March or April issues of *Federal Reserve Bulletin*.

The funds rate targeting regime—or its first act—came to an end with the dramatic news conference of Fed Chairman Paul Volcker on October 6, 1979, in which Volcker signalled a new commitment to reduce inflation by a change in Fed operating procedures. The new regime that followed the 1979 announcement was described by the Fed as targeting nonborrowed bank reserves, an operating procedure sometimes characterized (e.g., by Lombra, 1993) as intermediate between the perfectly elastic supply of reserves associated with an interest rate target and the inelastic supply of reserves associated with a strict money target. Under a system of targeted nonborrowed reserves, increases in the overall demand for reserves, arising, for example, from an increase in money demand, are reflected both by an increase in the money stock (as banks increase borrowed reserves) and by an increase in the funds rate (which must increase to make banks indifferent between borrowing more from the discount window and purchasing more federal funds on the interbank market).

Because nonborrowed reserves targets were not set far in advance and were often adjusted, however, the 1979 change in operating procedure did not in itself necessarily require a major change in the conduct of U.S. monetary policy, except perhaps at very high (daily or hourly) frequencies. For example, nonborrowed reserve targets could in principle have been set week to week to keep the funds rate from straying far from a preferred range. However, the change in operating procedures seems to have been accompanied by a decision by the Fed to place greater weight on monetary targets and to tolerate high and volatile interest rates (see figs. 8.3a and 8.4a) in order to bring down inflation.[10] The change in interest rate behavior was particularly dramatic: Instead of smoothing the funds rate in its customary way, after the October 1979 announcement, the Fed whipsawed the financial markets; the funds rose by more than 500 basis points to exceed 17% in March 1980, fell to below 10% after real GNP declined in the second quarter, and then rose to nearly 20% in 1981. M1 growth was noticeably lower during the 1979–1981 period than in previous years, but there also was a significant (and permanent) increase in the volatility of M1 growth (fig. 8.2a).[11]

What are we to make of the sharp changes in Fed operating procedures that occurred during and after 1979? The most likely explanation of these changes is political rather than technical. The Fed had decided that inflation had reached crisis levels and had to be controlled at almost any cost. As many authors have noted,[12] the new operating procedures and the greater (putative) attention to monetary targets were a useful smokescreen that obscured the link between the Fed's actions and the painful increases in interest rates. At the same time, the changes in procedure signalled to the public that they should not expect business as usual with respect to the Fed's attitude toward inflation.

Volcker's policy shift achieved its disinflationary goals but contributed to a deep recession in 1981–1982. Velocity instability associated with financial innovation and other factors also raised concerns (based on the traditional Poole, 1970, analysis) about whether monetary targets would continue to be of any value for guiding policy. In the fall of 1982, the Fed switched tactics again, this time to a borrowed reserves operating procedure. Simultaneously, it adopted a decidedly easier policy, despite the fact that money growth was above its targeted range (table 8.1). Money targets were deemphasized after 1982. In particular, M1 was allowed to deviate quite far from its targets and after 1986 was no longer targeted at all.

Because there is a close link between desired borrowed reserves and the funds rate, the borrowed reserves procedure adopted in 1982 is, in practice, quite similar to funds rate targeting.[13] Thus, the third regime of post-1973 monetary policy in the United States is a return to an emphasis on interest rate smoothing, as in the pre-1979 monetary regime (note from fig. 8.4a that after 1982, interest rate volatility returned to pre-1979 levels). During the 1990–1991 recession, the degree to which Fed policy has been guided by and expressed in terms of interest rate targets rather than money or reserve growth targets has been particularly striking. For example, the Fed's "shock treatment" of December 1991 was couched solely in terms of funds rate and discount rate reductions.[14]

While the Fed concentrated relatively more on stabilizing interest rates after 1982, it also pursued several other goals. One key objective during the latter part of the 1980s was exchange rate stabilization: The sharp appreciation of the dollar during the Volcker regime (fig. 8.5a) had contributed to a massive increase in the U.S. current account deficit. Beginning in early 1985, the Fed attempted to bring down the dollar by driving up both M1 and M2 growth rates (fig. 8.1a). By 1987, policymakers at the Fed agreed that the dollar had fallen enough, and money growth rates were brought back down. These actions by the Fed were supported by attempts at international policy coordination embodied by the Plaza Accord in September 1985 and the Louvre Accord in February 1987.

Other objectives that influenced monetary policy during the 1980s included financial market stability (particularly following the October 1987 stock market crash; see Brimmer, 1989, Mishkin, 1991) and the maintenance of Volcker's inflation gains. On the price stability front, the Fed was particularly successful, as for the first time since the early 1960s, inflation in the latter part of the 1980s remained low and stable. Whether the good inflation performance of recent years was due primarily to good luck (e.g., falling oil prices) or agile policy is controversial.

The United Kingdom.[15] As has often been discussed, there are some broad parallels between the recent histories of British and U.S. monetary policies, as there were for general economic policies under Thatcher and Reagan.

As in the United States, the British introduced money targeting in the mid-1970s in response to mounting inflation concerns. Also as in the United States, the Bank of England used interest rates as operating instruments and was committed to interest-rate smoothing during this period. Informal targeting of a broad aggregate, sterling M3 (hereafter M3), began in late 1973, and formal publication of targets began in 1976 (table 8.2), following a spike in inflation and in conjunction with an IMF support arrangement. To help ensure that M3 targets were met, the Supplementary Special Deposits Scheme—the infamous "corset"—was introduced in December 1973. The corset scheme attempted to reduce M3 growth essentially by taxing a component of M3, high-interest bank deposits.

Elementary economic analysis suggests that a scheme to reduce the growth rate of monetary aggregate artificially through tax policy would also distort the relationship between that aggregate and macroeconomic variables such as nominal income and inflation. Thus, the reliance on the corset is evidence that, during the pre-1979 period, the British monetary authorities were like their U.S. counterparts in not taking their money growth targets very seriously. It is interesting that, despite the assistance of the corset, the Bank of England had great difficulty in meeting its M3 growth targets during this period: Not only were announced targets consistently overshot, but the Bank of England frequently revised its targets midstream or abandoned them altogether (table 8.2). One result of these policies was that British monetary aggregates had greater volatility than even those in the United States (fig. 8.2b). For example, the volatility of U.S. monetary base growth (not shown in the figures) was on average well less than half that of British monetary base growth in the pre-1979 period, and the same is true for M3 growth.

Although inflation fell subsequent to the 1973 oil price shock, beginning in 1978 prices in the United Kingdom began to accelerate again, with inflation ultimately reaching nearly 20% by 1980. As in the United States, the perception of an inflationary crisis led to a change in strategy in 1979. Prime Minister Thatcher's Medium-Term Financial Strategy (MTFS, formally introduced in the government's second budget in March 1980) included three main components: a gradual deceleration in M3 growth, elimination of various controls on the economy (including the corset, exchange controls, and incomes policies), and a reduction of the PSBR (the public sector borrowing requirement, or deficit). A central goal of this program was the restoration of credibility for the government's anti-inflationary policies; it was in order

Table 8.2
Money Growth Targets and Outcomes: United Kingdom

Period	Aggregate	Target	Outcome	Outcome less target
April 1976–April 1977	M3	9–13[1]	8.0	−3.0
April 1977–April 1978	M3	9–13	15.1	+4.1
April 1978–April 1979	M3	8–12[2]	11.4	+1.4
October 1978–October 1979	M3	8–12[3]	13.7	+3.7
June 1979–October 1980	M3	7–11[4]	17.2	+8.2
February 1980–April 1981	M3	7–11[5]	19.4	+10.4
February 1981–April 1982	M3	6–10	12.8	+4.8
February 1982–April 1983	M1	8–12	12.4	+2.4
	M3	8–12	11.2	+1.2
	PSL2	8–12	11.6	+1.6
February 1983–April 1984	M1	7–11	14.0	+5.0
	M3	7–11	9.5	+0.5
	PSL2	7–11	12.6	+3.6
February 1984–April 1985	M0	4–8[6]	5.4	−0.6
	M3	6–10	11.9	+3.9
March 1985–March 1986	M0	3–7	3.4	−1.6
	M3	5–9[7]	16.7	+9.7
March 1986–March 1987	M0	2–6	4.4	+0.4
	M3	11–15[8]	19.0	+6.0
March 1987–March 1988	M0	2–6	5.6	+1.6
March 1988–March 1989	M0	1–5	6.1	+3.1
March 1989–March 1990	M0	1–5	6.3	+3.3
March 1990–March 1991	M0	1–5	2.6	−0.4
March 1991–March 1992	M0	0–4	—	—

Notes: M3 refers to sterling M3, or M3 less residents' deposits abroad. PSL2, private sector liquidity, is a broader aggregate than M3. Outcome less target equals the outcome less the midpoint of the target range.
[1] Target of 12% growth for M3 set in July 1976 superseded by 9–13% target for M3 in December 1976 'letter of intent' to IMF.
[2] New target after 6 months.
[3] New target after 8 months.
[4] Original target was to April 1980. Target was extended in October 1979 for 1 year, but then new target was set for period beginning February 1980.
[5] From 1980 to 1986, target ranges for M3 were also set for a 3–4-year horizon.
[6] Beginning in 1984, target ranges for M0 were also set for a 4-year horizon.
[7] Target suspended in October 1985.
[8] Target suspended in October 1986.
Sources: Temperton (1991), supplemented by *OECD Economic Surveys*, various issues.

to enhance the credibility of proposed reductions in money growth that the government opted for reduced government deficits instead of lower taxes, à la Reagan.[16]

Unfortunately, the British disinflationary strategy in the 1979–1982 period ran into a technical problem similar to that experienced in the United States, namely, that the relationship between the targeted aggregate and nominal income became very unstable. M3 velocity fell sharply, and M3 grew at rates well above the target ranges (table 8.2, fig. 8.1b), even as other indicators—the value of the pound, the growth rates of narrower money aggregates, and the unemployment and inflation rates—all began to signal that monetary policy was very tight (figs. 8.1b–8.7b). In retrospect, the instability of M3 is not surprising, because the removal of the corset induced banks to market high-interest deposits aggressively. Other factors, such as the phasing out of exchange controls and an increased pace of financial innovation, also affected the growth rate of M3. The monetary authorities tried several strategies in response to this instability, including the setting of multiyear target ranges (which, for the most part, were not met) and the targeting of several aggregates simultaneously.[17]

Subsequent to 1983, arguing that financial innovation was wreaking havoc with the relationship between broad money and income,[18] the Bank of England began to deemphasize M3 in favor of narrower aggregates, particularly M0 (the monetary base). The target for M3 was temporarily suspended in October 1985 and finally dropped in 1987, leaving M0 as the only money aggregate to be targeted. Generally, the attempt to target M0 was more successful than earlier attempts to target M3: Target ranges have been announced on a regular basis and have been gradually reduced over time. Also, since 1984, actual M0 growth has generally fallen within or close to the target ranges, with under- or overshootings tending to be reversed in subsequent years.

The major exception to the assertion that M0 growth has been on target occurred in the 1987–1988 period, during which the authorities became concerned about appreciation of the pound and informally "capped" sterling at 3.00 DM to the pound, resulting in more rapid money growth (see fig. 8.1b and table 8.2). Some economists, such as Belongia and Chrystal (1990), have argued that this episode was less an attempt to manage the exchange rate per se than it was an attempt to find a new nominal anchor for monetary policy, given the problems experienced with monetary aggregates. If so, in this instance the Bank of England backed the wrong horse, because following the period of the cap, inflation rose sharply, a development that was predicted by rapid growth of the monetary base during the period of the cap. Whatever interpretation one places on the "capping" episode, however, in October 1990—after much debate—the United Kingdom decided to accept the discipline of a fixed nominal exchange rate by joining the European Exchange Rate Mechanism (ERM).

Overall, a comparison with the United States and the other countries examined here does not put British monetary policy in a favorable light. As figures 8.6 and 8.7 indicate, not only has British inflation had the highest mean and the greatest volatility of any of these countries, but the unemployment rate has also been high and variable. However, in the 1980s, British inflation performance did improve considerably, remaining well below the 1970s level and becoming significantly less variable.

Canada.[19] Recent Canadian monetary experience bears some close parallels to that of the United States and Britain. This parallel experience is not purely a coincidence, of course, as Canadian monetary policy has often—although not always—been driven by the goal of maintaining a stable exchange rate with the United States (fig. 8.5c). As a result, interest rates (fig. 8.3), interest rate volatility (fig. 8.4), and inflation (fig. 8.6) have followed generally similar patterns in the two countries.

Like the other countries discussed here, Canada experienced significant inflation problems in the mid-1970s, problems that were clearly exacerbated by its attempt to contain the appreciation of its currency after the breakdown of the Bretton Woods system. Like the other countries, Canada responded by adopting money growth targets. In 1975, as part of a larger government initiative that included the imposition of wage and price controls, the Bank of Canada introduced a program of "monetary gradualism," under which M1 growth would be controlled within a gradually falling target range (table 8.3). The change in monetary strategy did not extend to a change in operating procedures, however, which continued to emphasize an interest rate instrument.

Monetary gradualism was no more successful in Canada than were initial attempts at money targeting in the United States and the United Kingdom, and arguably—as

Table 8.3
Money Growth Targets and Outcomes: Canada

Announcement date	Base period	M1 growth target	Outcome	Outcome less target
November 1975	April–June 1975	10–15	9.3	−3.2
August 1976	February–April 1976	8–12	7.7	−2.3
October 1977	June 1977	7–11	9.3	+0.3
September 1978	June 1978	6–10	5.1	−2.9
December 1979	April–June 1979	5–9	5.9	−1.1
February 1981	August–October 1980	4–8	0.4	−5.6
November 1982	M1 target withdrawn			

Notes: Outcomes are annualized growth rates (%) of seasonally adjusted M1 between the base period and the next announcement of new targets, for example, the outcome corresponding to the November 1975 announcement is the annualized growth rate of M1 between May and June 1975 and August 1976. Outcome less target equals the outcome less the midpoint of the target range.
Source: *OECD Economic Surveys* and Bank of Canada *Review*, various issues.

in the other two countries—a lack of seriousness on the part of the central bank was a contributing factor. Announcements of new money targets were made irregularly and employed base periods for the measurement of money growth that were as much as 6 months earlier than the date of the announcement (table 8.3). Although actual M1 growth was often very close to target, and the goal of reducing M1 growth was achieved during the latter part of the decade, subsequent to the adoption of gradualism Canada suffered a sharp depreciation of its currency and, like the United States and the United Kingdom, a resurgence in inflation.

In defense of the Bank of Canada, many of the same problems that plagued attempts to target money growth in other countries were present in Canada as well, including financial innovation (see Howitt, forthcoming), velocity instability of the targeted aggregate, and radically different signals of policy stance from narrow and broad money aggregates (fig. 8.1c). Overlaying these standard problems were the distortions caused by the imposition and eventual elimination of wage and price controls.

By 1978, only 3 years after money targeting had begun, the Bank of Canada began to distance itself from this strategy. A dominant factor was concern about the exchange rate, which as we have noted had been depreciating (fig. 8.5c). Exchange rate worries intensified as the U.S. dollar began its rapid appreciation of the early 1980s, threatening Canada with an inflationary shock from import prices. The Bank of Canada responded by tightening policy more than needed to meet the M1 targets; indeed, M1 growth was negative in 1981 even though the target range was for growth between 4 and 8% (fig. 8.1c and table 8.3). Because of their conflict with exchange rate goals, as well as ongoing money demand instability, the M1 targets were canceled in November 1982. Canada thus became the only country examined here to abandon formal money growth targeting completely in the early 1980s.

The period following 1982 was one of groping. In 1984 the emphasis on the exchange rate (which had been largely unchanged since 1978) was lessened, so that the Bank of Canada could attempt to assist recovery from the very deep recession that had begun in 1981. Unemployment did fall after 1984 (fig. 8.7c), and by 1988 the Canadian "misery index" (the inflation rate plus the unemployment rate) was at its lowest point in many years. Still, inflation had begun to edge up again, to some minds threatening a possible return to the 1970s pattern.

In a rather dramatic reversal of the evolving ad hoc monetary strategy, in January 1988 Governor John Crow announced that the Bank of Canada would subsequently pursue an objective of "price stability," that is literal elimination of inflation.[20] In February 1991 the Bank and the Minister of Finance jointly announced a series of declining inflation targets. Although this strategy implied that inflation itself, not money growth, would be the target of monetary policy, it was indicated that M2 would be used to guide policy. (Attention is also to be paid to an index of monetary

Table 8.4
Money Growth Targets and Outcomes: Germany

Year	Aggregate	Target	Outcome	Outcome less target
1975	CBM	8.0	9.8	+1.8
1976	CBM	8.0	9.2	+1.2
1977	CBM	8.0	9.0	+1.0
1978	CBM	8.0	11.5	+3.5
1979	CBM	6.0–9.0	6.4	−1.1
1980	CBM	5.0–8.0	4.8	−1.7
1981	CBM	4.0–7.0	3.6	−1.9
1982	CBM	4.0–7.0	6.1	+0.6
1983	CBM	4.0–7.0	7.0	+1.5
1984	CBM	4.0–6.0	4.6	−0.4
1985	CBM	3.0–5.0	4.5	+0.5
1986	CBM	3.5–5.5	7.7	+3.2
1987	CBM	3.0–6.0	8.0	+3.5
1988	M3	3.0–6.0	6.8	+2.3
1989	M3	5.0	4.7	−0.3
1990	M3	4.0–6.0[1]	5.5	+0.5
1991	M3	4.0–6.0[2]	—	—

Notes: Growth rates are measured year over year for 1975–1978 and fourth quarter to fourth quarter thereafter. Outcome less target equals the outcome less the midpoint of the target range. CBM is central bank money.
[1] The target was lowered to 3–5% in July.
[2] As of 1991, targets apply to all-German M3.
Source: Kahn and Jacobson (1989), updates for *OECD Economic Surveys*, various issues.

conditions based on interest rates and exchange rates.) It is not completely clear to what degree this new commitment to price stability implies abandonment of other objectives, but it does seem that attention to those other goals has been reduced: For example, during 1987 through 1989, the Bank of Canada permitted a much greater increase in interest rates and appreciation of the currency than would have normally been expected under previous regimes.

Germany.[21] Germany's central bank, the Bundesbank, also responded to rising inflation in the early 1970s by adopting a strategy of targeting money growth, with the first targets being announced for 1975 (see table 8.4). The monetary aggregate chosen for targeting was central bank money (denoted as M0 in figure 8.1d), the sum of currency in circulation and bank deposits held by residents, with each category of bank deposits weighted by its 1974 required reserve ratios. As Fischer (1987) points out, central bank money can be interpreted as approximating the "required monetary base," and for convenience, we label it as a narrow money aggregate in figure 8.1d.

However, the Bundesbank has noted that it views central bank money as a broad rather than narrow measure of money, arguing that the required reserve ratio weights are reasonable proxies for the relative liquidities of the various components.

Monetary targets have been announced annually and are reviewed at midyear in light of macroeconomic developments, although midyear revision of targets has been extremely unusual. (The usual function of the midyear review is to use interim information to reduce the size of the target range.) The method by which the Bundesbank's monetary targets are set is particularly interesting: The calculation of target ranges is a public rather than a clandestine exercise. The setting of targets explicitly takes into account the Bundesbank's long-term inflation goal, estimated potential output growth, and expected velocity trends, which are combined using the quantity-theory equation to determine the desired money growth rate. In theory, this explicit linkage of targets to goals has the important benefit of allowing targets to be adjusted when the target–goal relationship changes, without compromising the central bank's commitment to meeting its targets.

"Short-term" considerations such as the unemployment rate and expected transitory deviations in inflation or velocity are not formally included in the Bundesbank's target-setting exercise. Nevertheless, there is some scope for shorter-term considerations to affect monetary policy. For example, the Bundesbank freely acknowledges that one purpose of specifying target ranges[22] rather than single numbers is to give itself some scope for short-run discretionary activism. The size of the target range has varied over time—it was zero in 1989—indicating changes in the amount of short-term flexibility the Bundesbank thinks it needs.

The Bundesbank has also shown that it is willing to accept money growth outside of the target range for periods of 2–3 years. In principle, deviations of money growth from targets are supposed to be reversed subsequently, so that short-term considerations do not detract from the Bundesbank's preeminent goal of low and stable inflation in the long run. Table 8.4 shows that periods of money growth over target, such as 1975–1978, have tended to be followed by periods of slower growth, as in 1979–1981. In general, though, table 8.4 suggests that the Bundesbank has not always succeeded in fully reversing short-term deviations from the money growth targets.

Over the last two decades, the principal object of short-term discretionary policy by the Bundesbank has been the exchange rate. In particular, money growth targets were exceeded during 1975–1978 and again during 1986–1988 in order to dampen an appreciating mark. The Bundesbank's concern about the exchange rate has a number of sources: First, under international agreements including the European Exchange Rate Mechanism, the Plaza Accord, and the Louvre Accord, Germany has accepted some responsibility for stabilizing its exchange rate within agreed-upon ranges. Second, the large size of the German export sector makes the exchange rate a politically sensitive variable. Finally, maintenance of a strong and stable mark is viewed as a precondition for achieving inflation goals.

Central bank money remained the money target through 1987. In 1988, the Bundesbank adopted simple-sum M3 (the equal-weighted sum of currency in circulation, demand deposits, time deposits less than 4 years, and savings deposits). The rationale for the switch was that central bank money put too much weight on a rapidly growing currency component and thus overstated monetary ease—the so-called currency bias problem. Despite the switch in targets, Germany has not experienced nearly as much instability in the relationship between targeted aggregates and nominal income as have a number of the other major countries.

In achieving short-run money control, the Bundesbank has typically relied heavily on interest rate indicators (including the call, or overnight, rate and the repurchase rate), much in the spirit of the Federal Reserve's use of federal funds rate targeting as a mechanism for hitting monetary targets in the medium term. However, while the Bundesbank has attempted to keep interest rates stable in the short run, it has not gone so far as to set explicit targets for interest rates (Batten et al., 1990, p. 11). It is notable that the Bundesbank has consistently achieved very low variability of both interest rates (fig. 8.4d) and money growth rates (fig. 8.2d), contrary to the simple view that suggests a tradeoff between these two quantities.

German monetary policy has been quite successful in maintaining a low and stable inflation rate (fig. 8.7d), but, unlike Switzerland and Japan, Germany has not avoided a serious and persistent unemployment problem (fig. 8.7d). Fischer (1987) and others have pointed to inflexibilities in the labor market (relative to, say, Japan) as a potential cause of persistent German unemployment.

Most recently, the reunification of Germany has posed some novel problems for the Bundesbank. The exchange of West German currency for East German currency at reunification at rates favorable to the East has created nascent inflationary pressures, at the same time that the tremendous uncertainties created by the reunification have made the forecasting of prosaic items like velocity quite tricky. In addition, the political pressures to support strong real growth at the early, delicate stages of reunification are strong. It remains to be seen how well the Bundesbank's traditional policy strategy can deal with this new set of circumstances.

Switzerland.[23] The fixed-exchange-rate regime ended in Switzerland in January 1973. The Swiss National Bank began to announce money stock targets, with M1 the targeted aggregate, at the end of 1974. Like the Germans, the Swiss set money growth targets based on explicit inflation goals and forecasts of potential output and velocity growth. Announced targets were and have continued to be single-valued rather than ranges, a practice based on the interesting rationale that "from a psychological point of view, missing a target band is worse than missing a point target" (Schiltknecht, 1982, p. 73).

An unusual feature of the conduct of Swiss monetary policy has been the Swiss National Bank's consistent use of the monetary base directly as an operating instrument. Control of M1 during the early years of targeting therefore required the central bank to predict the value of the money multiplier (the ratio of M1 to the base). Perhaps because of the use of the monetary base as an instrument, Switzerland has generally had higher volatility in short-term interest rates than have other countries (fig. 8.4). However, this volatility has not carried over to long-term rates, as Switzerland has had the lowest volatility of long-term interest rates of the six countries studied here (again see fig. 8.4). Presumably, the low volatility of long-term rates reflects Switzerland's success at keeping its inflation rate low and stable in the longer term.

As in other countries, the idea underlying money targeting in Switzerland was to reduce money growth gradually in order to eradicate inflation over the longer term. However, according to the Director of the Swiss National Bank: "...the policy of well controlled, stable monetary growth was never viewed as a policy which should be adhered to rigidly year after year, or even month after month, at all costs. Rather, it was viewed as a medium- to long-term constraint, with the necessity for short-run flexibility, especially in view of exchange rate developments" (Schiltknecht, 1982, p. 72).

This approach to targets as a medium- to long-term constraint but not an impediment to short-term discretion is similar to the approach taken in Germany. Indeed, in practice the Swiss have been even more successful than the Germans in reversing deviations of money growth from target: Between 1975 and 1986, the *cumulative* excess of money growth over target in Switzerland (the sum of the "outcome less target" column in table 8.5) was only about 1.6%.

An example of short-run monetary "flexibility" occurred in 1978, when the Swiss franc began to appreciate (fig. 8.5e). In response, the Bank eased monetary policy significantly: M1 growth in 1978 was above 16% (fig. 8.1e and table 8.5), compared to a target of 5%. While rather an extreme episode, the 1978 actions illustrate the general willingness of the Swiss National Bank to subordinate money targets, at least in the short run, to exchange rate considerations. Swiss concern about the exchange rate reflects not only the extreme openness of the Swiss economy, but the fact that a stable franc is an important component of Switzerland's prominence as an international financial center.

After containment of the 1978 exchange rate emergency, the bank returned to an (unannounced) policy of money targeting in the spring of 1979. However, because of problems with forecasting the money multiplier, beginning in 1980 the monetary base rather than M1 became the targeted aggregate (as well as the policy instrument).

In 1980 and 1981 money growth was low and below target, in reaction to increased inflation and the overshooting of money targets in the previous few years.

Table 8.5
Money Growth Targets and Outcomes: Switzerland

Year	Aggregate	Target	Outcome	Outcome less target
1975	M1	6	4.4	−1.1
1976	M1	6	7.7	+1.7
1977	M1	5	5.5	+0.5
1978	M1	5	16.2	+11.2
1979	—	—	—	—
1980	M0	4[1]	−0.6[1]	−4.6
1981	M0	4	−0.5	−4.5
1982	M0	3	2.6	−0.4
1983	M0	3	3.6	+0.6
1984	M0	3	2.5	−0.5
1985	M0	3	2.2	−0.8
1986	M0	2	2.0	0.0
1987	M0	2	3.0	+1.0
1988	M0	3	−3.9	−6.9
1989	M0	2	−4.9	−6.9
1990	M0	2	−2.6	−4.6
1991	M0	1	—	—

Notes: Growth rates are measured as mean of monthly year-on-year growth rates until 1988; after 1988 growth rates are measured fourth quarter to fourth quarter. M0 is the monetary base adjusted to exclude end-of-month bulges in Swiss National Bank credit to banks.
[1] Average percentage increase over the November 1979 level.
Source: Rich (1987), with updates from *OECD Economic Surveys*, various issues.

The period from 1982 to about 1987, though, was remarkably halcyon: Money growth targets were routinely met (table 8.5). The short-term volatility of Swiss money growth remained comparatively high (fig. 8.2), however, implying that the Swiss were acting quickly to offset high-frequency deviations of money growth from target. Inflation fell to low levels (fig. 8.6e), and unemployment remained insignificant (fig. 8.7e).[24] Monetary policy was assisted considerably during the early 1980s by the fact that the link between money growth and nominal magnitudes in Switzerland appeared stable, despite transient velocity fluctuations.

In 1986 there was a significant decline in the inflation rate (from over 3% almost to zero) and in 1989 a sharp increase in inflation (from about 2% to nearly 5%), neither of which was predicted by the behavior of the monetary base (see Yue and Fluri, 1991, for a discussion). Swiss central bankers have suggested that the problem is a structural break in the demand for base money, brought about by the introduction of an electronic interbank payments system and a reduction in legal reserve requirements. In attempting to offset this fall in base money demand, the Swiss National

Table 8.6
Money Growth Targets and Outcomes: Japan

Year	Aggregate	Target[1]	Outcome	Outcome less target
1978	M2	12–13	12.6	+0.1
1979	M2 + CD	11	10.3	−0.7
1980	M2 + CD	8	7.6	−0.4
1981	M2 + CD	10	10.4	+0.4
1982	M2 + CD	8	8.3	+0.3
1983	M2 + CD	7	6.8	−0.2
1984	M2 + CD	8	7.9	−0.1
1985	M2 + CD	8	9.0	+1.0
1986	M2 + CD	8–9	8.3	−0.2
1987	M2 + CD	11–12	11.8	+0.3
1988	M2 + CD	10–11	10.6	+0.1
1989	M2 + CD	10–11	10.6	+0.1
1990	M2 + CD	ca. 11	10.0	−1.0
1991	M2 + CD	ca. 4	—	—

Notes: Growth rates are measured fourth quarter to fourth quarter. Outcome less target equals the outcome less the midpoint of the target range.
[1] Announced at the beginning of the fourth quarter and are referred to as forecasts rather than targets by the Bank of Japan.
Source: Fischer (1987) and Bank for International Settlements, *Annual Report*, various issues.

Bank permitted negative money growth for 3 years (table 8.5). The instability in the demand for base money has led the Swiss National Bank to deemphasize money base targeting and, recently, to contemplate fundamental changes in its monetary strategy.

Japan.[25] The increase in oil prices in late 1973 was a major shock for Japan, with substantial adverse effects on inflation, economic growth, and the government's budget. In response to an increase in the inflation rate to a level above 20% in 1974 (fig. 8.6f)—a surge facilitated by money growth in 1973 in excess of 20% (fig. 8.1f)—the Bank of Japan, like the other central banks we have considered, began to pay more attention to money growth rates. In 1978 the Bank began to announce "forecasts" at the beginning of each quarter for the growth rate of M2 (changed to the growth rate of M2 + CDs when CDs were introduced in 1979) from 1 year earlier to the current quarter (table 8.6).

The use of the word *forecast* rather than *target* suggests that the Bank of Japan was committed only to monitoring rather than to controlling money growth.[26] However, after 1978 there did appear to be a substantive change in policy strategy, in the direction of being more "money-focused." Particularly striking was the different response of monetary policy to the second oil price shock in 1979: Instead of allowing extremely high money growth, as occurred in 1973, the Bank of Japan quickly reduced M2 + CDs growth in 1979 and 1980 to quite a low level (fig. 8.1f). The difference in the inflation outcome in this episode was also striking, as inflation increased only moderately with no adverse effects on the unemployment situation. More generally, the Bank of Japan's forecasts and actual money growth followed a declining trend into the mid-1980s (except in 1981; see table 8.6). Thus, in contrast to the German and Swiss practice of clearly specifying central bank intentions in advance, the Japanese seemed to follow an "actions speak louder than words" approach. As we discuss further later, however, in recent years both forecasts and actual money growth in Japan have become much more variable, weakening the presumption that the Bank of Japan practices "closet monetarism."

From an institutional point of view, it was no doubt fortunate that the Bank of Japan began to focus on money at the time that it did. Traditionally, Japanese central bank policy had emphasized the control of bank credit, which proved an effective instrument in a highly regulated financial environment in which borrowers had few substitutes for bank loans. However, a slow but steady process of liberalization of financial markets began around 1975, resulting ultimately in the introduction of new financial instruments and markets and a weaker tie between bank lending and economic activity.[27]

In a financial environment that over time has become more and more similar to that of the United States, the Bank of Japan's methods of conducting monetary policy have also evolved in the direction of the U.S. example.[28] Abandoning quantitative credit controls, the Bank of Japan has moved gradually to a system emphasizing open-market operations in the interbank market,[29] more attention to money growth, and the use of interbank interest rates as the primary instruments of monetary control. However, unlike the United States, Japan has always used interest rate instruments of some type and has never experimented with the targeting of bank reserves. The outcome of these operating procedures is that the volatility of interest rates in Japan has generally been low in relation to other countries (fig. 8.4), while the volatility of the M2 + CDs aggregate focused on by the Bank of Japan has been comparable to the volatility of U.S. M2 (fig. 8.2).

Also in parallel to the United States, ultimately financial innovation and deregulation in Japan began to reduce the usefulness of the broad money target: In particular, introduction of money market certificates and large time deposits in 1985, and the repeated reductions in the minimum denominations of these assets over 1986–1989, led to increases in the demand for M2 (see, e.g., Yoshida and Rasche, 1990). In response to increased money demand, and also because of concern about appreciation of the yen, the Bank of Japan significantly increased the rate of money growth in 1987–1989 (table 8.6).

Beginning in 1989, monetary policy became oriented toward trying to arrest what many Japanese policymakers considered to be a bubble in land and stock prices, without causing a crash that might have disastrous financial consequences. Asset prices did come down as money growth slowed, but economic activity weakened also. Another factor that has recently complicated monetary policy is a slowdown in lending by Japanese banks associated with the increase in bank capital requirements mandated by the Basle Accord. In responding to these developments, as we have mentioned, the Bank of Japan has permitted a considerable increase in the variability of broad money growth since late 1990 (fig. 8.2f), and in general has engaged in a much more "discretionary" style of policy-making.

8.3   Conduct of Monetary Policy in Six Countries: Some Positive Hypotheses

What do we learn from these case studies of monetary policy-making? In this section, we discuss some positive hypotheses, so called because they seem to apply generally across the case studies. We state these hypotheses as if they were conclusions but remind the reader once again that they (as well as the more normative observations discussed in section 8.4) are intended only as propositions worthy of further examination.

(1) *Central bankers have multiple objectives and a "crisis mentality."*   It is a commonplace that central bankers care about both economic growth and inflation, which may force them to confront difficult tradeoffs. But the behavior of central bankers suggests that other variables enter their objective function as well. The leading example from the case studies is the nominal exchange rate: In all six cases examined, central bankers modified their policies in order to arrest what they considered to be undesirable exchange rate trends. Arguably, in some of these cases (when the United Kingdom "capped" the pound in 1987, e.g.) the exchange rate played the role of an intermediate target, that is, the central bank's intervention reflected concern not about the exchange rate per se but about what the exchange rate was signalling about the stance of monetary policy. However, in many of the cases, the exchange rate clearly functioned as a goal of policy, reflecting central bank concerns about the health of the traded goods sector or international commitments to meet exchange rate targets.

Interest rate stability has also in many cases been an independent objective of policy. For example, in the 1970s the Federal Reserve chose to tolerate high rates of money growth in order to avoid sharp increases in interest rates (a policy that was dramatically reversed in 1979). Japan, Germany, and to some extent Great Britain have all attempted to keep interest rate volatility low even as the economic environment and monetary policy strategies have changed (fig. 8.4). Several writers (e.g.,

Goodfriend, 1987; Howitt, 1993) have suggested that central banks view interest rate stability as important for maintaining "orderly" financial markets free from excessive speculation.

Although they have multiple objectives, over time central bankers do not devote constant proportions of their attention to each objective. Rather, at any given time, the lion's share of the central bank's attention is typically devoted to the one or two objectives that are furthest from desired levels. A possible explanation of this "crisis mentality" is that the marginal social cost of, say, high inflation really does increase sharply with the inflation rate. Alternatively, central bankers may feel that their independence and perquisites are threatened more by a public perception that some aspect of the economy is "out of control" than by a record of generally mediocre performance.

The fact that central banks have multiple objectives creates obvious tensions in the monetary policy process. For example, as Goodfriend (1987) has pointed out, the preference of the central bank for maintaining a stable nominal interest rate may lead to nonstationarity in money and prices. Multiplicity of objectives and the crisis mentality can also make even the most competent and purposeful central bank appear at best to be muddling through, or at worst to be lurching from one strategy to another. As we discuss further later, the complexity of central bank objectives and behavior may increase the value of clear communication with the public about the goals and direction of monetary policy.

(2) *The greater is the central bank's concern about inflation, the stronger will be its tendency to employ monetary aggregates as intermediate targets.* All six of the countries discussed here adopted monetary targeting in the 1970s in response to a worldwide increase in inflation and persisted with money targets until disinflation was achieved.[30] The central banks most "hawkish" on inflation, such as those of Germany and Switzerland, have been the most consistent in maintaining a money targeting strategy, while more "dovish" monetary authorities like those of the United Kingdom, Canada (before 1988), and the United States have been the least consistent.

The natural first place to look for an explanation for this aspect of central bank behavior is Poole's (1970) well-known theory of target choice, which argues essentially that the optimal intermediate target is the one with the most stable relationship with the goal variables. Unfortunately, Poole's model is of limited help in this instance, because it predicts that money targets will be preferred over interest rate targets during periods when money demand is relatively stable. What we observe is the reverse: In the halcyon pre-1974 days of stable money demand, central banks were more likely to focus on interest rate targets, while in many countries, the switch to money targets occurred and persisted during a period of severe velocity instability. Further, central bankers have typically reacted to unstable velocities not by reverting to interest rate targeting but instead by changing the particular monetary aggregate that they target—in some cases switching from a narrower to a broad aggregate (the United States, Germany) and in others from a broader aggregate to a narrower one (the United Kingdom, Switzerland).

Why then do central banks adopt money growth targets when faced with inflationary crises? The next two points discuss possible reasons.

(3) *One function of an intermediate target such as money growth, as perceived by central bankers, is to act as a guidepost or compass for monetary policy.* Central bankers face considerable uncertainty not only with regard to the state of the economy and the nature and timing of the monetary transmission mechanism, but also about the stance of policy itself. In pursuing intermediate targets, the policymakers hope to improve their measurement of their policy stance and, thus, reduce the probability of inadvertently choosing the wrong settings for their instruments. Thus, the adoption of money growth targets in the late 1970s by many central banks was intended to help avoid the overexpansionary tendencies of the earlier part of the decade. In particular, it was hoped that money growth would prove a more reliable indicator of monetary conditions than variables that had been employed earlier, such as interest rates[31] and free reserves.

The use of monetary aggregates as guideposts has been problematic in practice, however, and for some of the same reasons suggested by Poole's original analysis: The relationship between individual aggregates and macroeconomic variables has often been unstable, and different aggregates have as often as not given conflicting information, as for example in the United Kingdom in the 1979–1982 period when narrow and broad aggregates gave very different readings of the tightness of policy.

There is still a deeper question about the use of monetary aggregates as guideposts, however, which also follows from the logic of the Poole model: If the central bank is searching for a guidepost for monetary policy, why confine the search to one or two economic variables? Why not instead use a forecast that optimally weights all available information about the likely effects of policy on the economy? As we discuss further below, the answer to this question may be that there is a complementarity between using a money growth target as a guidepost and using it as a signal to the public about monetary policy intentions.

(4) *The second and probably more important reason that central bankers adopt money growth targets is to signal the central bank's goals and intentions—particularly those concerning inflation—to the public.* Both central bankers and the public consider the control of inflation to be one of the most important objectives of monetary policy. Yet of central banks' many objectives, inflation is perhaps the one related to policy actions with the longest lag. Thus, it is particularly difficult for the public to evaluate the inflationary impact of current policies. An advantage of money targeting

is that—because of the simple and widely understood quantity-theory prediction that money growth and inflation will be proportional—money growth targets may be perceived as being informative about the central bank's goals and intentions with respect to inflation.[32]

Central bankers see several potential benefits to using money growth targets to signal medium- and long-term inflation strategy. One potential benefit is that explicit targets for money growth may aid the management of inflationary expectations. If the central bank can reassure the public through a targeting procedure that it is committed to controlling inflation in the longer run, it may reduce financial market volatility and conceivably (although we have no evidence on this point) improve short-run policy tradeoffs.

Another potential benefit to the central bank of emphasizing money growth targets is that this practice keeps the central bank's inflation objectives "on the front burner" and makes the central bank more accountable to the public for keeping inflation low. Theories of bureaucratic behavior might seem to imply that a bureaucracy like a central bank will want to avoid accountability. But in fact, a central bank may want to make itself more accountable for achieving price stability because it values the price stability goal more than do politicians in the legislative and executive branches.[33] For example, if the central bank is able to point to money growth above target (with its implied inflationary consequences), it may be able to enlist public support in resisting political pressures for excessive short-run expansion. Elements of this strategy can be seen in almost all the major disinflations of the early 1980s, in which central bankers emphasized the importance of meeting money growth targets in order to deflect political demands for rapid reflation.

The notion that central banks seek to bind their own hands is of course closely related to Kydland and Prescott's (1977) seminal argument for rules, with the difference that we here emphasize an intragovernmental variant of Kydland and Prescott's precommitment game. However, as the next point emphasizes, in practice central bankers reject the notion of rigid rules in favor of looser types of precommitment.

(5) *Central banks never and nowhere adhere to strict, ironclad rules for monetary growth. Central banks' attachments to specific targets for specific monetary aggregates is at best modest and is always hostage to new developments in the economy.* As is evident from the case studies and tables 8.1–8.6, all central banks deviate significantly from their monetary targets to pursue short-term objectives, and are most explicit about their willingness to be "flexible" and "pragmatic" in the short run. Further, money growth targets and the targeted aggregates themselves may be changed fairly often.

Clearly, central banks have never taken seriously the literal "precommitment through rules" strategy implied by Kydland and Prescott's analysis of the time-inconsistency problems. If money growth rules are adopted at all, they are intended to apply only in the medium and long term. Of course, as it has been said, the long term is just a succession of short terms. Thus, for a longer-term money growth target to be meaningful, the central bank must at some point demonstrate its willingness to offset short-term deviations from the target path.[34] The feasibility and value of "hybrid" strategies, containing elements of both rules and discretion, is discussed further in the next section.

8.4   What Works? Some Normative Hypotheses and Issues for Future Research

The case studies showed that, although national experiences with monetary policy in the last two decades are diverse, a dominant theme is the adoption of money targeting strategies as a response to increased inflation. In the last section we argued that central bankers adopted money growth targets for two reasons: as guideposts, helping them to measure policy stance; and as signals, communicating to the public the medium-term goals of policy. Despite what was to some degree a common approach to monetary policy, however, some central banks have fared much better than others in meeting their ultimate policy objectives, particularly in achieving low and stable inflation.

Why have some central banks been more successful in their use of money growth targets? The case studies provide some clues that may help answer this question. We list some hypotheses suggested by the case studies that we view as being worth serious exploration in future research.

(1) *Successful use of money growth targets in conducting monetary policy seems to require that the central bank does not "play games" with its targeting procedures.* A major reason for using money growth targets, we have seen, is to communicate with the public. Hence, clarity, openness, and consistency in the targeting procedure are potentially almost as important as whether the targets are met. Central bank actions that increase the clarity of its policies include: targeting only one aggregate at a time, announcing targets on a regular schedule for a specified horizon, being as consistent as possible in the choice of aggregate to be targeted, and giving clear explanations of the reason for and expected duration of deviations of money growth from target.

A particularly interesting way in which central banks can clarify their intentions is by means of a public calculation of target ranges that makes explicit the central bank's goals and its assumptions about how the target is tied to those goals. In principle, this explicit linkage of targets to goals might have the important benefit of allowing the central bank to adjust its targets when the target–goal relationship changes, without compromising its credibility.

Generally, Germany and Switzerland did well on the above criteria over the last two decades, while the United States, the United Kingdom, and Canada did less

well. The most egregious game-player was the Bank of England, with its multiple targeted aggregates, extreme base drift, erratic changes in targets and target horizons,
and its use of artificial means (the corset) to bring down the growth of a targeted aggregate. The U.S. Fed and the Bank of Canada also did not take their targets very
seriously, at least at first, as evidenced by the Fed's multiple targets and base drift
and the Bank of Canada's practice of announcing targets irregularly for horizons
that were not clearly specified.[35] Improved inflation performance in a number of the
countries studied here coincided with the adoption of more serious and straightforward targeting procedures. The clearest example is Britain, which achieved more stable inflation after it abandoned the corset and multiple targets to focus on a regularly
announced target for a single aggregate.

Japan is an interesting intermediate case, in that it has had a very successful monetary policy despite the opacity of its targeting (or nontargeting) procedure.[36] On
the other hand, Japan is the only country to have focused on a single monetary aggregate (M2 + CDs) over the entire period; it has announced its money growth
"forecasts" on a consistent and regular basis; and it achieved a relatively steady
slowdown of money growth between the mid-1970s and mid-1980s, despite the
occurrence of a second oil shock in 1979. Thus—at least prior to its recent switch to
a more discretionary mode—the Bank of Japan created a degree of predictability
about its medium-term policies.

From the perspective of the literature on central bank credibility, it is not surprising that game-playing in targeting procedures—which leads the public to believe the
central bank is not serious—is counterproductive. A straightforward approach to
conducting monetary policy appears to be quite useful for increasing the central
bank's credibility and improving policy outcomes.

(2) *Short-run adherence to money growth targets may not be necessary for the successful use of a money targeting strategy as long as there is some commitment by the central bank to reverse deviations of money growth from target over the longer term.* As
the example of Switzerland most clearly illustrates, a money targeting strategy apparently can be used successfully even if money growth rates have large fluctuations and
are frequently outside of target ranges. However, the success of Swiss monetary
policy in keeping inflation low seems to have required a commitment by the Swiss
National Bank to compensate for high rates of money growth in one period by subsequent offsetting low rates of money growth in future periods. In other words, it
looks as if the Swiss have successfully used a hybrid strategy, in which rules are
used to guide policy in the long term but not in the short term. The German and
Japanese central banks have similarly demonstrated their willingness to make up for
periods of excessive money growth by subsequent periods of slow money growth,
although to a lesser extent than the Swiss. Again the worst record belongs to the British, who consistently missed targets in the same direction.

A cynic might ask, "What is the difference between a policy of reversing deviations from target and the highly criticized 'stop–go' policies of the 1960s and early 1970s, which also involved alternating periods of low and high money growth?" The difference, which is admittedly subtle, is that the policy of reversing deviations from target takes place in a larger framework, one that provides a basis for expecting that short-term expansions or reductions in money growth will be subsequently offset. In contrast, although the earlier regime sometimes involved reversals ex post (stop–go policies), there was no basis for people to expect ex ante that such reversals would occur. Thus—as again is consistent with the literature on credibility—it is the nature of the expectation engendered by a policy that appears to be critical to its success.

Complementary to a strategy of reversing short-term deviations from target is a policy of adjusting targets when their relationship with goal variables changes, as is practiced (in principle at least) by Germany and Switzerland. It would not be desirable to offset a deviation in money growth arising from a permanent shock to velocity, for example. Under the German–Swiss method of setting targets, a permanent shock to velocity would result in a change in the money growth target. In an unconditional money targeting scheme, by contrast, the central bank could accommodate the velocity shock only by sacrificing its commitment to the target.

(3) *The outcomes of monetary policy do not appear to be dependent on the details of the operating procedure or the choice of instruments.* A wide variety of operating procedures has been observed across the six countries studied here, but there is no evident correlation between the type of procedure and the effectiveness of monetary policy. For example, the most common procedure—using the interbank interest rate as an instrument for achieving medium-term targets for money growth—seemed to work poorly for the United States in the 1970s but has been used quite successfully by Japan and Germany.

In addition, as a comparison of operating procedures between Switzerland and Germany indicates, focus on a monetary aggregate as an operating instrument does not guarantee a more successful adherence to monetary targets. Indeed, Switzerland (which has used the monetary base as its operating instrument) has had among the most variable rates of money growth, while Germany (which employs an interbank interest rate as its instrument) has had among the lowest money growth variability (fig. 8.2). It is also interesting that, although the Swiss operating procedure has resulted in high volatility of short-term interest rates, Swiss long-term rates have shown less volatility than in any of the other countries studied here (fig. 8.4). Because it is the volatility of long-term interest rates that would seem to be the more relevant to the stability of the financial system, the Swiss example suggests that the use of the monetary base as an operating instrument need not create problems even with respect to the goal of interest rate smoothing.

This irrelevance of the operating procedure is not surprising from a theoretical viewpoint, because any of a number of procedures can be used to achieve any given set of values for the central bank's targets and goals—and it is the latter that should matter for the macroeconomy. If operating procedures are macroeconomically unimportant, why then do central banks pay so much attention to them? The "smoke-screen" argument may be relevant here. For example, by focusing on the change in operating procedure in 1979, Fed Chairman Volcker partly diverted attention from a more fundamental change in policy. Also, the Swiss example notwithstanding, the details of operating procedures may have important effects on certain segments of financial markets (banks, bond traders) which the central bank considers to be an important part of its clientele.

Although these observations about what works well in promoting successful monetary policy are suggestive, further research on several problematic points is needed.

A first troublesome issue turns on the nature of the empirical relationship between money and other economic variables. Our review of central banks' experience suggests that money growth targeting, if treated as a flexible constraint on medium-term policy, can be a useful tool. However, even the best-handled money targeting strategy requires that there be some predictable relationship between money growth and the goal variables of policy; it has been argued (most persuasively by Friedman and Kuttner, 1990) that the relationship between money and the economy is empirically so unstable that monetary aggregates are of essentially no value in guiding monetary policy. Isn't this instability fatal to the case for any type of money targeting?

This issue is of first-order importance and needs further investigation in a cross-national context. Several responses can be made at this point, however:

First, it is possible that the velocity instability that has plagued the monetary policy of countries such as the United States and the United Kingdom is itself partly endogenous, a result of erratic monetary policies that have created highly variable inflation and interest rates. Our case studies show that countries with more stable monetary policies, while not immune to velocity instability, do suffer from it to a smaller degree. In particular, Japan's ability to provide monetary stability despite major changes in its financial institutions is striking. Thus, longer-run money growth targeting might also lead to a more stable relationship of money to other variables.

Second, as we have already discussed, there are reasons to believe that the German–Swiss technique of adjusting money growth targets for expected changes in velocity is preferable to unconditional money growth targeting. If adjustments for expected velocity changes are made, then stability of velocity is not a prerequisite for successful policy, only some degree of conditional predictability of velocity. Of course, it may be that even conditional prediction is not possible; empirical work should be directed toward finding out.

A third response that can be made to the Friedman–Kuttner objection is that it does appear to be useful to central bankers to have *some* variable or variables to signal the medium-term stance of policy; for reasons of both theory and simplicity, money growth is a natural candidate. However, if velocity unpredictability disqualifies money as an appropriate target—as might have been the case in the United States and Britain during 1979–1982, for example—then one would want to consider alternative anchors for policy, such as the exchange rate, nominal GNP, or inflation forecasts. Unfortunately, as a large literature discusses, the obvious alternatives to money growth also have shortcomings, including unstable relationships with the economy and inadequate controllability and observability.

Besides the question of stability of the money-output link, another broad unresolved issue concerns the degree to which successful monetary policies are the result of a more favorable political environment, rather than superior policy techniques. To ask the question more concretely: Is the superiority of German or Swiss monetary policy over, say, British policy really due to better and more coherent policies by the Bundesbank and Swiss National Bank? Or is the better German and Swiss performance a necessary consequence of institutional factors (such as greater central bank independence) and greater political support for low inflation? If the latter is true, then the features of policy that we have observed to be associated with more successful outcomes may in fact be either endogenous or irrelevant.

Despite the obvious importance of political and institutional factors, it still seems plausible that, given their environments, central banks have considerable latitude to deliver successful or unsuccessful monetary policies. Some evidence for this proposition is that the effectiveness of monetary policy within given countries has changed substantially over time. British and U.S. monetary policies seem noticeably more successful in the 1980s than in the 1970s. Japan made the transition from high and erratic inflation in the mid-1970s to a low and stable inflation rate (despite the fact that the Bank of Japan is probably less politically independent than, say, the Bank of Canada). Political conditions (e.g., the public's aversion to inflation) can also change over time, but such changes are likely to be more gradual than the observed changes in policy outcomes. Thus, while the political dimension needs to be explored further, it remains likely that how the central bank chooses to handle monetary policy is also a major factor determining macroeconomic outcomes.

Notes

Bernanke acknowledges research support from the National Science Foundation, and Mishkin acknowledges the support of the Faculty Research Fund of the Graduate School of Business, Columbia University. We thank Mark Gertler, Bruce Kasman, and participants in seminars at NYU, Columbia, Princeton, University of Pennsylvania, Miami University, University of Kansas, University of Michigan, University of Illinois, and the NBER Macro Annual Conference for useful comments. The research is part of NBER's research programs in Monetary Economics and Economic Fluctuations. Any opinions expressed are those of the authors, not those of the NBER.

1. The requirement of simplicity is essential. Any monetary strategy at all could in principle be specified as a sufficiently complex contingent rule.

2. In what sense is discretion a strategy, rather than the absence of a strategy? If we interpret discretion as the best time-consistent (no-precommitment) policy, then it is a strategy in the formal sense, because in principle, one could calculate the policy action to be taken in every future contingency. In practice, of course, such a calculation would be difficult or impossible to carry out, so that the strategy implied by discretion is much less transparent than the strategy implied by rules.

3. On this basis we exclude France and Italy, whose exchange rates are tied to the deutschemark through the Exchange Rate Mechanism (ERM). (The U.K. did not join the ERM until 1990.) Of course, attempts to stabilize nominal exchange rates have affected monetary policy at various times in all of these countries; as we discuss later, Canada in particular has often subordinated its monetary policy to exchange rate objectives.

4. Excellent discussions of the "microstructure" of monetary institutions and policy operations can be found in Kneeshaw and Van den Bergh (1989), Batten et al. (1990), and Kasman (1991).

5. See the notes to the figures for details and sources.

6. Huizinga and Mishkin (1986) have pointed out potential problems with moving-average measures of volatility. Thus we have also calculated volatility measures using a procedure suggested by Pagan (1984), which effectively assumes an autoregressive conditional heteroscedasticity (ARCH) specification for the variability of money growth. The results using this procedure yield similar conclusions to those provided by figures 8.2 and 8.4.

7. Numerous sources discuss recent monetary policy and the policy process in the United States. See, e.g., Lombra (forthcoming), Karamouzis and Lombra (1989), Friedman (1988), Poole (1988), and Heller (1988). For a longer-term overview, see Meulendyke (1990). In this and all subsequent case studies we also made use of the OECD's *Economic Surveys*.

8. Bernanke and Blinder (forthcoming) present evidence for the veiw that, during this period, changes in the funds rate (or the spread between the funds rate and other rates) were the best signal of a changing stance of monetary policy. Cook and Hahn (1989) provide a record of funds rate target changes and show that, during the 1975–1979 period, open-market interest rates responded sensitively to changes in the Federal Reserve's target for the funds rate.

9. Walsh (1986) defends base drift as the correct response to nonstationary shocks to money demand. It seems to us that this case requires that the central bank clearly identify—and explain to the public—the source of these nonstationary shocks, otherwise base drift will be perceived as a ploy. The fact that inflation rose significantly in the late 1970s is evidence against the view that the Fed was optimally offsetting nonstationary money demand shocks.

10. Fed reaction functions estimated by McNees (1986) and by Karamouzis and Lombra (1989) show that the Fed placed a greater weight on deviations of the money supply from target during 1979–1982, relative to earlier and later periods. Cook (1989), in an excellent discussion of 1979–1982 policy, argues that high-interest rates were not an accidental byproduct of the nonborrowed reserves procedure but that non-borrowed reserves targets were intentionally adjusted so as to produce high interest rates.

11. Added complexity in the use of M1 as a policy guide was created by a redefinition of M1, to include other checkable deposits such as NOW accounts but to exclude foreign-held deposits, in 1980.

12. For example, see Greider (1987), Mussa (1993), and Mishkin (1992).

13. The demand for borrowed reserves is usually taken to be an increasing function of the spread between the federal funds rate and the discount rate, reflecting the equilibrium condition that banks must be indifferent between obtaining funds from the federal funds market and from the discount window. If this demand function is stable, then targeting borrowed reserves is equivalent to targeting the excess of the funds rate over the discount rate. See Thornton (1988). Thornton also presents evidence that, on those occasions when the demand for borrowed reserves appeared to shift, the Fed typically shifted its borrowed reserve target so as to stabilize the funds rate.

14. A principal reason for the deemphasis of money growth was the perception that the "credit crunch" in banking had interfered with the normal relationship between aggregates such as M2 and nominal GNP;

see Bernanke and Lown (1991) for a discussion of the credit crunch and its implications for monetary policy.

15. Good recent descriptions of U.K. monetary policy are to be found in Fischer (1987), Minford (1993), and Temperton (1991).

16. Another difference with the U.S. approach was that the British did not significantly reduce their commitment to interest rate smoothing with the change in strategy in 1979 (fig. 8.4b). This confirms the earlier point that there is no necessary connection between the operating procedure and the general stance of monetary policy.

17. Besides M0 and M3, the Bank of England also targeted a broad measure of private sector liquidity, PLS2; see table 8.2.

18. Leigh-Pemberton (1986).

19. Principal sources for this section are Howitt (1993), the OECD *Economic Surveys*, and various issues of the Bank of Canada *Review*.

20. As in a similar recent debate in the United States, advocates of "zero inflation" suggest that, because of difficulties in adjusting for quality change and other index number problems, zero inflation may be interpreted as a small positive rate of measured inflation.

21. This section draws on Fischer (1987), Kahn and Jacobson (1989), von Hagen (1989), and Neumann and von Hagen (1993).

22. In 1975–1978 targets were expressed as single numbers. Since 1979 targets have been set as ranges of varying size (see table 8.4).

23. Historical discussions of Swiss monetary policy may be found in Schiltknecht (1982), Beguelin and Rich (1985), Rich (1987), and Yue and Fluri (1991).

24. However, the Swiss reliance on "guest workers," who are repatriated when labor market conditions worsen, makes Swiss unemployment data more difficult to interpret.

25. Among the many useful general sources on Japanese monetary policy are Cargill and Hutchison (1987), Dotsey (1986), Hutchison (1988), Batten et al. (1990), Kasman and Rodrigues (1991), and Ueda (1991).

26. Much has been written on whether and to what degree the Bank of Japan implicitly targets money growth. See, e.g., Hutchison (1986), Ito (1989), and Ueda (1991).

27. Kasman and Rodrigues (1991) provide an excellent discussion of Japanese financial liberalization and its effects on monetary policy.

28. The similarity of Japanese and American central bank operating procedures is discussed by Dotsey (1986).

29. Open-market operations are supplemented by discount window lending, as in the United States. Unlike the United States, in Japan open-market operations are conducted in a number of other financial markets, including the CD market and (recently) the commercial paper market.

30. This statement requires that we interpret the Japanese "forecasts" as indicating a targeting strategy. It should also be noted that several central banks (notably the United States and United Kingdom) initially adopted money targets only under some external pressure; in both the U.S. and British cases, however, the seriousness with which money targets were treated increased markedly when the second oil shock worsened the inflation problem.

31. One might construct an argument on Poole-like grounds that nominal interest rates are a bad target during periods of unstable inflation, because high nominal interest rates could indicate either too tight or too easy money.

32. The empirical fact of velocity instability implies, of course, that the relationship between money growth and inflation is really not so simple. We return to this issue in section 8.4.

33. Differences in the horizons of politicians and central bankers are sufficient to create this difference in preferences. For example, as suggested by the work of Rogoff and Sibert (1988), in order to signal their economic competence, politicians may have an incentive to create an inflationary boom prior to an election. If the central banker is not up for re-election and fears that the central bank will be blamed for long-run increases in inflation, he will resist political demands for preelection increases in money growth. In a

Rogoff–Sibert-style game, all the central banker needs to do to diffuse the pressure from the politicians is to give the public full information about monetary policy—for example, announce the money growth targets consistent with noninflationary growth—thereby ensuring that the politicians receive no credit for output increases arising from excessive monetary expansion.

34. The basic Kydland–Prescott (1977) analysis suggests that central bank promises to meet money growth targets in the long run but not the short run would never be credible. However, this conclusion is dependent on the assumption that the central bank values unemployment below the natural rate. If the central bank does not view its mandate as reducing unemployment, or is content with unemployment at the natural rate, then it may be possible to make credible promises about future money growth. Further, the central bank may be able to develop a reputation for meeting its medium-term targets; see Rogoff (1987) for a comprehensive discussion of reputation and central bank credibility.

35. We should be careful of attributing the relatively less good performance of Canadian monetary policy solely to such game-playing, however; as we have noted, the degree to which Canadian monetary policy is independent from U.S. policy is problematic.

36. At least it is opaque to U.S. academics. Perhaps it is clearer to Japanese business and financial leaders.

References

Batten, Dallas S., Michael P. Blackwell, In-Su Kim, Simon E. Nocera, and Yuzuru Ozeki. (1990). The conduct of monetary policy in the major industrial countries: Instruments and operating procedures, International Monetary Fund, occasional paper no. 70, Washington, DC, July.

Beguelin, J.-P., and Georg Rich. (1985). Swiss monetary policy in the 1970's and 1980's. In *Monetary Policy and Monetary Regimes*, K. Brunner et al. (eds.). Center for Research in Government Policy and Business, University of Rochester.

Belongia, Michael, and Alec Chrystal. (1990). The pitfalls of exchange rate targeting: A case study from the United Kingdom. *Review*, September/October: 15–24. Federal Reserve Bank of St. Louis.

Bernanke, Ben, and Alan Blinder. (1992). The federal funds rate and the channels of monetary transmission. *American Economic Review* 82, no. 4 (September): 901–923.

———, and Cara Lown. (1991). The credit crunch. *Brookings Papers on Economic Activity* 2: 205–48.

Brimmer, Andrew. (1989). Central banking and systemic risks. *Journal of Economic Perspectives* Spring: 3–16.

Cargill, Thomas, and Michael Hutchison. (1987). The response of the Bank of Japan to macroeconomic and financial change. In *Monetary Policy in Pacific Basin Countries*, Hang-Sheng Cheng (ed.). Boston: Kluwer Academic Publishers.

Cook, Timothy. (1989). Determinants of the federal funds rate: 1979–1982. *Economic Review* January/February: 3–19, Federal Reserve Bank of Richmond.

———, and Thomas Hahn. (1989). The effect of changes in the federal funds rate target on market interest rates in the 1970s. *Journal of Monetary Economics* November: 331–351.

Dotsey, Michael. (1986). Japanese monetary policy, a comparative analysis, Monetary and Economic Studies, Institute of Monetary and Economic Studies, Bank of Japan, October: 105–127.

Fischer, Stanley. (n.d.). Monetary policy and performance in the U.S., Japan, and Europe, 1973–1986. In *Toward a World of Economic Stability: Optimal Monetary Framework and Policy*, Y. Suzuki and M. Okabe (eds.). University of Tokyo Press (proceedings of 1987 conference).

———. (1987). Monetary Policy. In *The Performance of the British Economy*, R. Dornbusch and R. Layard (eds.), Oxford: Clarendon Press.

———. (1990). Rules versus discretion in monetary policy. In *Handbook on Monetary Economics*, vol. 2, B. Friedman and F. Hahn (eds.). Amsterdam: North-Holland.

Friedman, Benjamin. (1988). Lessons on monetary policy from the 1980s. *Journal of Economic Perspectives* Summer: 51–72.

———. (1990). Targets and instruments of monetary policy. In *Handbook on Monetary Economics*, vol. 2, B. Friedman and F. Hahn (eds.). Amsterdam: North-Holland.

————, and Kenneth Kuttner. (1990). Money, income, and prices after the 1980s. NBER working paper no. 2852, February.

Goodfriend, Marvin. (1987). Interest rate smoothing and price level trend-stationarity. *Journal of Monetary Economics* May: 335–348.

Greider, William. (1987). *Secrets of the Temple: How the Federal Reserve Runs the Country*. New York: Simon and Schuster.

Heller, Robert. (1988). Implementing monetary policy. *Federal Reserve Bulletin* July: 419–429.

Howitt, Peter. (1993). Canada. In *Monetary Policy in Developed Economies: Handbook of Comparative Economic Policies*, M. Fratianni and D. Salvatore (eds.). Westport, Conn.: Greenwood Press, 459–508.

Huizinga, John, and Frederic S. Mishkin. (1986). Monetary policy regime shifts and the unusual behavior of real interest rates. In *Carnegie-Rochester Conference on Public Policy*, vol. 24, K. Brunner and A. Meltzer (eds.). Amsterdam: North-Holland.

Hutchison, Michael. (1986). Japan's "money-focused" monetary policy. *Economic Review* Summer: 3–45, Federal Reserve Bank of San Francisco.

————. (1988). Monetary control with an exchange rate objective: The case of Japan, 1973–1986. *Journal of International Money and Finance* 7: 261–271.

Isard, Peter, and Liliana Rojas-Suarez. (1986). Velocity of money and the practice of monetary targeting: Experience, theory, and the policy debate. Washington, DC: IMF, Staff Studies for the World Economic Outlook, July.

Ito, Takatoshi. (1989). Is the Bank of Japan a closet monetarist? Monetary targeting in Japan, 1978–1988. NBER working paper no. 2879, March.

Kahn, George, and Kristina Jacobson. (1989). Lessons from West German monetary policy. *Economic Review* April: 18–35, Federal Reserve Bank of Kansas City.

Karamouzis, Nicholas, and Raymond Lombra. (1989). Federal Reserve policymaking: An overview and analysis of the policy process. In *International Debt, Federal Reserve Operations and Other Essays, Carnegie-Rochester Conference Series on Public Policy*, vol. 30, K. Brunner and A. Meltzer (eds.). Amsterdam: North-Holland.

Kasman, Bruce. (1991). A comparison of monetary policy operating procedures in six industrial countries. Unpublished, Federal Reserve Bank of New York, December.

————, and Anthony Rodrigues. (1991). Financial reform and monetary control in Japan. Unpublished, Federal Reserve Bank of New York, November.

Kneeshaw, J. T., and P. Van den Bergh. (1989). Changes in central bank money market operating procedures in the 1980s. BIS Economic Papers, no. 23, January.

Kydland, Finn, and Edward Prescott. (1977). Rules rather than discretion: The inconsistency of optimal plans. *Journal of Political Economy* June: 473–491.

Leigh-Pemberton, R. (1986). Financial change and broad money. *Bank of England Quarterly Bulletin* December: 499–507.

Lombra, Raymond. (1993). The conduct of U.S. monetary policy: A field guide. In *Monetary Policy in Developing Economies: Handbook of Comparative Economic Policies*, M. Fratianni and D. Salvatore (eds.). Westport, Conn.: Greenwood Press.

Lucas, Robert E., Jr. (1976). Econometric policy evaluation: A critique. In *Carnegie-Rochester Series on Public Policy*, vol. 1, K. Brunner and A. Meltzer (eds.). Amsterdam: North-Holland.

McCallum, Bennett. (1989). Targets, indicators, and instruments of monetary policy. NBER working paper no. 3047, July.

McNees, Stephen. (1986). Modeling the Fed: A forward-looking monetary policy reaction function. *New England Economic Review*, November/December: 3–8, Federal Reserve Bank of Boston.

Meulendyke, Ann-Marie. (1990). A review of Federal Reserve policy targets and operating guides in recent decades. In *Intermediate Targets and Indicators for Monetary Policy: A Critical Survey*, Federal Reserve Bank of New York.

Minford, Patrick. (1993). Monetary policy in the U.K. In *Monetary Policy in Developing Economies: Handbook of Comparative Economic Policies*, M. Fratianni and D. Salvatore (eds.). Westport, Conn.: Greenwood Press, 405–432.

Mishkin, Frederic S. (1991). Asymmetric information and financial crises: A historical perspective. In *Financial Markets and Financial Crises*, R. Glenn Hubbard (ed.). Chicago: University of Chicago Press.

———. (1992). *The Economics of Money, Banking, and Financial Markets*, 3d ed. New York: HarperCollins.

Mussa, Michael. (1993). The dollar, the current account, and macroeconomic policy. In *American Economic Policy in the 1980s*. M. Feldstein (ed.). Chicago: University of Chicago Press.

Neumann, Manfred J. M., and Jurgen von Hagen. (1993). Monetary policy in Germany. In *Monetary Policy in Developing Economies: Handbook of Comparative Economic Policies*, M. Fratianni and D. Salvatore (eds.). Westport, Conn.: Greenwood Press, 299–334.

Pagan, Adrian. (1984). Econometric issues in the analysis of regressions with generated regressors. *International Economic Review* February: 221–247.

Poole, William. (1970). Optimal choice of monetary policy instruments in a simple stochastic macro model. *Quarterly Journal of Economics* May: 197–216.

———. (1986). Monetary policy and the lessons of the recent inflation and disinflation. *Journal of Economic Perspectives* Summer: 73–100.

Rich, Georg. (1987). Swiss and United States monetary policy: Has monetarism failed? *Economic Review* May/June: 3–16, Federal Reserve Bank of Richmond.

Rogoff, Kenneth. (1987). Reputational constraints on monetary policy. In *Bubbles and Other Essays, Carnegie-Rochester Conference Series on Public Policy*, vol. 26, K. Brunner and A. Meltzer (eds.). Amsterdam: North-Holland.

———, and Anne Sibert. (1988). Elections and macroeconomic policy cycles. *Review of Economic Studies* January: 1–16.

Schiltknecht, Kurt. (1983). Switzerland: The pursuit of monetary objectives. In *Central Bank Views on Monetary Targeting*, P. Meek et al. (eds.). Federal Reserve Bank of New York.

Temperton, Paul. (1991). *UK Monetary Policy: The Challenge for the 1990s*. London: MacMillan.

Thornton, Daniel. (1988). The borrowed-reserves operating procedure: Theory and evidence. *Review* January/February: 30–54, Federal Reserve Bank of St. Louis.

Ueda, Kazuo. (1991). Japanese monetary policy from 1970 to 1990: Rules or discretion? Unpublished paper, University of Tokyo, September.

von Hagen, Jurgen. (1989). Monetary targeting with exchange rate constraints: The Bundesbank in the 1980s. *Review* October: 53–69, Federal Reserve Bank of St. Louis.

Walsh, Carl. (1986). In defense of base drift. *American Economic Review* September: 692–700.

Yoshida, Tomoo, and Robert Rasche. (1990). The M2 demand in Japan: Shifted and unstable? In *Monetary and Economic Studies*, 9–30. Institute for Monetary and Economic Studies, Bank of Japan, September.

Yue, Piyu, and Robert Fluri. (1991). Divisia monetary services indexes for Switzerland: Are they useful for monetary targeting? *Review* September/October: 19–34, Federal Reserve Bank of St. Louis.

9 Inflation Targeting: A New Framework for Monetary Policy?

Ben Bernanke and Frederic S. Mishkin

The world's central bankers and their staffs meet regularly, in venues from Basle to Washington, to share ideas and discuss common problems. Perhaps these frequent meetings help explain why changes in the tactics and strategy of monetary policymaking—such as the adoption of money growth targets in the 1970s, the intensification of efforts to reduce inflation in the 1980s, and the recent push for increased institutional independence for central banks—tend to occur in many countries more or less simultaneously. Whatever their source, major changes in the theory and practice of central banking are of great importance, for both individual countries and the international economy. In this chapter, we discuss a new strategy for monetary policy known as "inflation targeting," which has sparked much interest and debate among central bankers and monetary economists in recent years. This approach is characterized, as the name suggests, by the announcement of official target ranges for the inflation rate at one or more horizons, and by explicit acknowledgment that low and stable inflation is the overriding goal of monetary policy. Other important features of inflation targeting include increased communication with the public about the plans and objectives of the monetary policymakers, and, in many cases, increased accountability of the central bank for attaining those objectives.

Inflation targeting in various forms has been adopted in recent years by a number of industrialized countries, including Canada, the United Kingdom, New Zealand, Sweden, Australia, Finland, Spain and Israel.[1] Table 9.1 offers some details about the specific plans in each country. There are also important elements of inflation targeting, as we discuss below, in the long-standing and well-regarded monetary policy approaches of Germany and Switzerland. In the United States, inflation targeting has been advocated by some influential policymakers, and Senator Connie Mack (R-Fla.) has introduced a bill that, if passed, would establish price stability as the primary goal of monetary policy [S.R. 1266, 104th Cong. 1st sess.]. Finally, the Maastricht treaty mandates price stability as the primary objective of the European Central Bank, and it seems likely—if European monetary union in fact occurs—that

Table 9.1
Operational Aspects of Inflation Targets

Country (date of adoption)	Target Series Definition	Target Level (percentage annual inflation)	Time Horizon
Australia (1993)	Underlying CPI (excluding fruit and vegetables, petrol, interest costs, public sector prices and other volatile prices)	2–3	Ongoing
Canada (February 1991)	Core CPI (excluding food, energy and first-round effects of indirect taxes)	1–3	18 months
Finland (February 1993)	Underlying CPI (excluding government subsidies, indirect taxes, housing prices and mortgage interest payments)	about 2	Ongoing
Israel (December 1991)	CPI	8–11	1 year
New Zealand (March 1990)	Underlying CPI (excluding changes in indirect taxes or government changes, significant changes in import or export prices, interest costs and natural disasters)	0–2 (until November 1996; 0–3 thereafter)	1 year
Spain (January 1995)	CPI (excluding first-round effects of indirect tax changes)	below 3	Through 1997
Sweden (January 1993)	CPI	2 ± 1	Ongoing
United Kingdom (October 1992)	RPIX (RPI excluding mortgage interest payments)	lower half of 1–4 until spring 1997; 2.5 or less thereafter	Until the end of this Parliament

the ECB would incorporate major elements of the inflation targeting approach in its procedures (Issing, 1996).

We begin our discussion of inflation targeting with some details of how this approach has been implemented in practice. We focus on the practice of inflation targeting, rather than the theory, because we believe that the rhetoric associated with inflation targeting is often misleading. In particular, we will argue that actual experience with this approach shows that inflation targeting does not represent an ironclad policy *rule*, as some writers on the subject and even some advocates of this approach seem to assume. Instead, inflation targeting is better understood as a policy *framework*, whose major advantage is increased transparency and coherence of policy, and in which fairly flexible, even "discretionary" monetary policy actions can be accommodated.[2] We next discuss in more detail why viewing inflation targeting as a framework, rather than a rule, blunts some of the arguments that have been made against it and in general enhances the appeal of this approach. This is not to say that valid questions do not remain about this strategy for monetary policy; in the final portion of the chapter we discuss some important additional issues and draw conclusions about the usefulness of the inflation targeting framework.

9.1   Inflation Targeting in Practice

Although every country that has adopted inflation targeting has customized the approach in various ways, certain empirical generalizations about this strategy can be made.

The hallmark of inflation targeting is the announcement by the government, the central bank, or some combination of the two that in the future the central bank will strive to hold inflation at or near some numerically specified level. As can be seen in table 9.1, inflation targets are more often than not specified as ranges—for example, 1–3 percent—rather than single numbers, and they are typically established for multiple horizons ranging from one to four years. However, there are exceptions to both observations; indeed, Germany, with the longest experience with inflation-focused monetary policy, specifies its implicit inflation target as a point and only for a one-year horizon. Initial announcements of inflation targeting generally allow for a gradual transition from the current level of inflation to a desired steady-state level, usually the level deemed consistent with price stability. "Price stability" never in practice means literally zero inflation, however, but usually something closer to a 2 percent annual rate of price change, for reasons we discuss later.

There is a lively debate over whether targeting should be of the inflation rate per se or of the price level. Of course, a targeted price level need not remain constant indefinitely, but could be allowed to drift upward in a predetermined way over time (Goodhart and Vinals, 1994; Svensson, 1996). The relative disadvantage of targeting the inflation rate is that unanticipated shocks to the price level may be treated as bygones and never offset; as a result, forecasts of the price level at long horizons might have a large variance under inflation targeting, which presumably impedes private-sector planning.[3] On the other hand, strict price-level targeting requires that overshoots or undershoots of the target be fully made up, which reduces the variance of long-run forecasts of prices but could impart significantly more volatility into monetary policy in the short run.[4] In practice, central banks tend to compensate partially for target misses, particularly at shorter horizons.

Associated with the announcement of inflation targets there is usually some statement to the effect that control of inflation is the "primary" or "overriding" goal of monetary policy and that the central bank will be held accountable for meeting the inflation targets. For example, Section 8 of the Reserve Bank of New Zealand Act of 1989 assigns the central bank the statutory responsibility "to formulate and implement monetary policy directed to the economic objective of achieving and maintaining stability in the general level of prices," with no mention of competing goals.

Section 9 of the act requires the Minister of Finance and the Governor of the Reserve Bank to negotiate and make public a Policy Targets Agreement (PTA), setting out specific inflation targets. In other countries, such as Switzerland, Canada and the United Kingdom, the inflation goal is embodied in public statements by the central bank rather than mandated by law.

The rationale for treating inflation as the primary goal of monetary policy is clearly strongest when medium- to long-term horizons are considered, as most economists agree that monetary policy can affect real quantities, such as output and employment, only in the short run. Of course, some economists of new classical or monetarist persuasions might claim that inflation should be the sole concern of monetary policy in the short run as well, arguing that using monetary policy for short-run stabilization of the real economy is undesirable, infeasible, or both. However, in practice no central bank has of yet completely forsworn the use of monetary policy for short-run stabilization, and so the phraseology "primary" or "overriding" must be taken to refer to the longer term.

The degree to which the central bank is held formally accountable for inflation outcomes varies considerably. The New Zealand law links the tenure of the governor of the Reserve Bank to the achieving of the inflation targets, and thus comes closest to providing an explicit "incentive contract," as proposed by Persson and Tabellini (1993) and Walsh (1995).[5] In other countries, no explicit sanctions on the central bank for missing the target are given; presumably, however, missing the target badly would impose implicit institutional or personal costs in terms of lost reputation or prestige. It is rather early in many of the inflation-targeting experiments to judge the extent to which the prospective penalties for missing announced targets will constrain central bank behavior.

Despite the language referring to inflation control as the primary objective of monetary policy, as we have said, inflation-targeting central banks always make room for short-run stabilization objectives, particularly with respect to output and exchange rates.[6] This accommodation of short-run stabilization goals is accomplished through several means. First, the price index on which the official inflation targets are based is often defined to exclude or down-weight the effects of "supply shocks;" for example, the officially targeted price index may exclude some combination of food and energy prices, indirect tax changes, terms-of-trade shocks, and the direct effects of interest rate changes on the index (for example, through imputed rental costs). Second, as already noted, inflation targets are typically specified as a range; the use of ranges generally reflect not only uncertainty about the link between policy levers and inflation outcomes but is also intended to allow the central bank some flexibility in the short run. Third, short-term inflation targets can and have been adjusted to accommodate supply shocks or other exogenous changes in the inflation rate outside the central bank's control. A model here is the Deutsche Bundesbank's practice of stating its short-term (one-year) inflation projection as the level of "unavoidable inflation." In the aftermath of the 1979 oil shock, for example, the Bundesbank announced the "unavoidable" inflation rate to be 4 percent, then moved its target gradually down to 2 percent over a six-year period. In other cases, the central bank or government makes explicit an "escape clause," which permits the inflation target to be suspended or modified in the face of certain adverse economic developments.

In making inflation, a goal variable, the focus of monetary policy, the inflation-targeting strategy in most cases significantly reduces the role of formal intermediate targets, such as the exchange rate or money growth. To the extent that intermediate targets are used, it is emphasized that the inflation goal takes precedence in case of conflict. Unconditional commitment to an intermediate target is of course inconsistent with inflation targeting (except in the unusual case that the intermediate target effectively summarizes all current information about inflation at the forecast horizon). The fact that in most countries the relation between intermediate targets, such as money growth, and the central bank's goal variables has proven to be relatively unreliable—the so-called "velocity instability" problem—is a major motivation for dropping formal intermediate targets and instead attempting to target the goal variable directly.

On the other hand, since targeting inflation directly requires that the central bank form forecasts of the likely path of prices, close attention is typically paid to a variety of indicators that have shown predictive power for inflation in the past. For example, as an aid to inflation forecasting, monetary policymakers in Canada and Sweden make use of a "monetary conditions index," a weighted combination of the exchange rate and the short-term interest rate, in conjunction with other standard indicators such as money and credit aggregates, commodity prices, capacity utilization and wage developments.[7]

In most inflation-targeting regimes, the central bank publishes regular, detailed assessments of the inflation situation, including current forecasts of inflation and discussions of the policy response that is needed to keep inflation on track. A good example is the Bank of England's *Inflation Report*, published quarterly, which contains detailed analyses of factors likely to affect the inflation rate as well as probabilistic forecasts of inflation, assuming no change in interest rates. The central banks of Canada and Sweden release similar documents, and the Reserve Bank of New Zealand is required to issue a policy statement at least every six months. As we discuss further below, the use of such reports reflects a key objective of inflation targeting, which is improved communication with the public about monetary policy, its goals and, in particular, the long-run implications of current policy actions.

The adoption of inflation targeting is often linked with changes in the laws or administrative arrangements associated with the central bank. Typically, reforms are in the direction of increased independence for the central bank, particularly in respect to its choice of instrument settings.[8] This seems to be a logical consequence of making price stability the overriding goal of policy, since the central bank is the best place to make the technical decisions necessary to achieve price stability and to make judgments about whether the pursuit of other objectives is consistent with this goal. Exceptions to this observation are the United Kingdom and, to a lesser extent, Canada, where despite the commitment to inflation targeting, the government, rather than the central bank, retains the final control over monetary policy. However, even in the British case the adoption of inflation targeting seems to have increased the relative influence of the central bank, as the *Inflation Report* and the timely publication of the minutes of the monthly meeting between the Governor and the Chancellor of the Exchequer provide an independent forum for the bank to express its views; in effect, the government must rationalize for the public any deviations of its policies from those recommended by the bank.

Most or all of the characteristics of inflation targeting described in this section apply to countries adopting this approach within the last eight years or so; as noted in the introduction, these include Canada, the United Kingdom, New Zealand, Sweden, Australia, Finland, Spain and Israel. Germany and Switzerland, which have conducted inflation-focused monetary policies since the mid-1970s, are better viewed as "hybrid" cases, which meet some but not all of the above criteria. These two countries differ from the "pure" inflation targeters primarily in their greater focus on money growth as an intermediate target, and indeed, the Bundesbank has emphasized the superiority (in their view) of money targeting as a means of insuring monetary discipline and transparency (for example, Deutsche Bundesbank, 1995, pp. 67–8). In fact, many observers (including ourselves) would argue that the distinction between inflation and money targeting is overstated and that monetary policies in both countries are driven in the medium and long term primarily by inflation goals. For example, the Bundesbank's money growth targets are derived, using the quantity equation, to be consistent with an annual inflation target, given projections of the growth of potential output and of possible changes in the velocity of money. This inflation target, in turn, has been brought down steadily over time and has remained at 2 percent—the level deemed consistent by the Bundesbank with price stability—since 1986. Further, the Bundesbank has shown itself quite willing to miss its money targets when pursuing these targets threatens to conflict with the control of inflation (von Hagen, 1995; Bernanke and Mihov, 1997).

All in all, the philosophy guiding German and Swiss monetary policies seems relatively consistent with the one motivating the self-declared inflation targeters. The main practical difference between the two sets of countries is that the Germans and Swiss believe that the velocity of money has been relatively more stable in their countries, and so they view money-growth targeting as a useful tool for implementing their inflation objectives. It is also true that Germany and Switzerland have been less explicit in stating their inflation targets; neither central bank publishes a regular inflation report per se. But this distinction seems relatively unimportant; inflation developments receive prominent attention in the regular publications of both banks. Moreover, there may be less need for public declarations given the long-standing commitment of the Bundesbank and Swiss National Bank—and the popular support for that commitment—to price stability. The examples of Germany and Switzerland are important because, unlike the other countries mentioned, these two countries have been following their monetary policy strategies fairly consistently for more than two decades, rather than for only a few years; thus, their experiences may provide researchers attempting to assess the value of inflation-focused monetary policy with useful information.

9.2 A Framework, Not a Rule

The motivations for an inflation-targeting approach have been varied. In a number of cases, such as those of the United Kingdom and Sweden, the collapse of an exchange rate peg led the monetary authorities to search for an alternative "nominal anchor" for monetary policy, a way of reassuring the public that monetary policy would remain disciplined. The demise of a fixed-exchange-rate regime similarly motivated the adoption of a money-focused approach by Germany in the mid-1970s. Some countries, such as Canada, came to inflation targeting after unsuccessful attempts to use a money-targeting approach. For example, in the case of Canada, by 1980 inflation was as high as it was in 1975 (10 percent per year) despite adherence to monetary targets that led to lower money growth rates (Howitt, 1993). In other cases, countries that by tight monetary policies had succeeded in reducing their core rate of inflation adopted inflation targeting as an institutional means of locking in their inflation gains.

Developments in macroeconomic theory also played some role in the growing popularity of the inflation targeting approach. These familiar developments included reduced confidence in activist, countercyclical monetary policy; the widespread acceptance of the view that there is no long-run tradeoff between output (or unemployment) and inflation, so that monetary policy affects only prices in the long run; theoretical arguments for the value of precommitment and credibility in monetary policy (Kydland and Prescott, 1977; Calvo, 1978; Barro and Gordon, 1983); and an increasing acceptance of the proposition that low inflation promotes long-run economic growth and efficiency.

Unfortunately, the interpretation of inflation targeting in terms of some long-standing debates in monetary economics has also been the source of confusion. For many years the principal debate about the best approach for monetary policy was framed as an opposition between two polar strategies, termed "rules" and "discretion." Advocates of rules—such as the fixed rule for money growth proposed by Milton Friedman, or a gold standard—argued that "tying the hands" of policymakers will prevent the monetary authorities from implementing counterproductive attempts at short-run stabilization and will thus eliminate the inflationary bias inherent in discretionary monetary policy. Supporters of discretionary policymaking—under which the central bank is left free to "do the right thing" as economic conditions evolve—stress the inability of ironclad rules to deal with unforeseen shocks or changes in the structure of the economy.

For various reasons, including the rhetoric of some of its proponents, inflation targeting is sometimes interpreted as falling on the "rule" side of this traditional dichotomy (for example, Friedman and Kuttner, 1996). We view this characterization of inflation targeting as a mistake; indeed, we would go farther and say that the traditional dichotomy of monetary policy strategies into rules and discretion is itself misleading. In particular, some useful policy strategies are "rule-like," in that by their forward-looking nature they constrain central banks from systematically engaging in policies with undesirable long-run consequences; but which also allow some discretion for dealing with unforeseen or unusual circumstances. These hybrid or intermediate approaches may be said to subject the central bank to "constrained discretion." We argue below that inflation targeting should be viewed in this way, rather than as a rigid policy rule.

If inflation targeting is interpreted as a rule in the classic Friedman sense, then it would have to be conceded that this approach is vulnerable to some important criticisms. First, the idea that monetary policy has (essentially) no legitimate goals besides inflation would find little support among central bankers, the public and most monetary economists. Second, given that central banks do care about output, employment, exchange rates and other variables besides inflation, treating inflation targeting as a literal rule could lead to very poor economic outcomes. As Friedman and Kuttner (1996) emphasize, much in the same way that money-growth targeting in the United States was done in by unpredicted shocks to the velocity of money, so an exclusive emphasis on inflation goals could lead to a highly unstable real economy should there be significant supply shocks, such as large changes in the price of oil.

Finally, critics of inflation targeting *as a rule* might well ask what is gained by the loss of flexibility entailed by precommitting monetary policy in this way. The academic literature on rules argues that tying the hands of policymakers will reduce the inflation bias of discretionary policy and perhaps allow for less costly disinflations, as increased credibility leads inflation expectations to moderate more quickly. However, critics of inflation targeting could point out that, although inflation-targeting countries have generally achieved and maintained low rates of inflation, little evidence supports the view that these reduced rates of inflation have been obtained at a lower sacrifice of output and employment than disinflations pursued under alternative regimes (at least so far). Even the Deutsche Bundesbank and the Swiss National Bank, whose pursuit of low inflation over the last two decades has presumably given the maximum credibility, have been able to achieve inflation reductions only at high costs in lost output and employment (Debelle and Fischer, 1994; Posen, 1995). Nor is there evidence that the introduction of inflation targets materially affects private-sector expectations of inflation, as revealed either by surveys or by the level of long-term nominal interest rates. Inflation expectations have come down, in most cases, only as inflation-targeting central banks have demonstrated that they can deliver low inflation (Posen and Laubach, 1996).

These objections are certainly important, as far as they go. However, again, they derive much of their force from the assumption that inflation targeting is to be viewed as an ironclad rule. As we have said, we believe that interpreting inflation targeting as a type of monetary policy rule is a fundamental mischaracterization of this approach *as it is actually practiced by contemporary central banks.* First, at a technical level, inflation targeting does not qualify as a policy rule in that it does not provide simple and mechanical operational instructions to the central bank. Rather, the inflation targeting approach enjoins the central bank to use its structural and judgmental models of the economy, in conjunction with all relevant information, to determine the policy action most likely to achieve the inflation target, and then to take that action. Unlike simple policy rules, inflation targeting never requires that the central bank ignore information that bears on its achieving its objectives. Second, and more importantly, inflation targeting as it is actually practiced contains a considerable degree of what most economists would define as policy discretion. Within the general constraints imposed by their medium- to long-term inflation targets, central bankers have in practice left themselves considerable scope to respond to current unemployment conditions, exchange rates and other short-run developments.

The 1989 reform of the Reserve Bank of New Zealand, for example, is often held up as an example of the rule-making impulse. It is important to note that New Zealand is the most extreme of all the inflation-targeting countries in its use of formal institutional constraints on policy. Even so, the New Zealand law does provide the central bank some discretion and flexibility; for example, the target inflation series excludes movements in commodity prices; the target may be readjusted if necessary in the judgment of the bank in response to supply or terms-of-trade shocks; the inflation target is specified as a 3 percentage point range rather than as a single number; and there is an explicit escape clause that permits amending the target in the face of unexpected developments. In practice, inflation targeting in New Zealand has been implemented even more flexibly. Inflation was brought down to its current low level only gradually; and when inflation moved briefly above the target range in 1996, the Parliament did not seriously consider its option of replacing the governor of the central bank.

If inflation targeting is not a rule in the way this term is usually understood, then what is it, and what good is it? We believe that it is most fruitful to think of inflation targeting not as a rule, but as a framework for monetary policy within which "constrained discretion" can be exercised. This framework has the potential to serve two important functions: improving communication between policymakers and the public, and providing increased discipline and accountability for monetary policy.

In terms of communication, the announcement of inflation targets clarifies the central bank's intentions for the markets and for the general public, reducing uncertainty about the future course of inflation. (Of course, this assumes that the announcements are believable and believed; more on this later.) Arguably, many of the costs of inflation arise from its uncertainty or variability more than from its level. Uncertain inflation complicates long-term saving and investment decisions, exacerbates relative price volatility, and increases the riskiness of nominal financial and wage contracts. Uncertainty about central bank intentions may also induce volatility in financial markets—a common phenomenon in the United States, where stock market analysts parse every sentence uttered by the Fed chairman in search of hidden meanings. Inflation targets offer transparency of policy; they make explicit the central bank's policy intentions in a way that should improve private-sector planning, enhance the possibility of public debate about the direction of monetary policy, and increase central bank accountability. Transparency has been claimed as a positive feature of other policy strategies, such as money-growth targeting, but we doubt that concepts like the growth rates of particular money aggregates are nearly so understandable to the general public as is the predicted rate of change of consumer prices.

To see the practical advantage of policy transparency, consider the familiar scenario in which an upcoming election or a slow economic recovery induces the government to pressure the central bank to apply some short-run stimulus. In an inflation-targeting regime, the central bank would be able—indeed, would be required—to make explicit that the short-run benefits of this policy (faster real growth) may well be purchased at the price of medium- and long-term inflation. These projections could then be debated by politicians, press and public, but at least the issue of long-run inflation effects would be on the table, serving as an explicit counterweight to the short-run benefits of monetary expansion. Making the linkage of short-term policies and long-term consequences explicit would clarify for the public what monetary policy can and cannot do.

Aggregate supply shocks, such as oil price shocks, present a thornier policy problem. If a severe supply shock hits the economy, keeping medium-term inflation close to the long-run target could well be very costly in terms of lost output. However, in practice, a well-implemented inflation-targeting regime need not strongly constrain the ability of the monetary authorities to respond to a supply shock. Remember, the inflation target itself can be and typically is defined to exclude at least the first-round effects of some important supply shocks, such as changes in the prices of food and energy or in value-added taxes; the use of target ranges for inflation gives additional flexibility. Escape clauses, which permit the central bank to change its medium-term targets in response to major developments, are another possibility. We have seen, for example, that the Bundesbank's one-year inflation targets were often defined by its view of how much inflation was "unavoidable," rather than by its long-run objective of price stability. Thus, intermediate-run inflation targets can be used to define a transition path by which the temporary inflation induced by a supply shock is eliminated gradually over time. Relative to a purely discretionary approach, the inflation-targeting framework should give the central bank a better chance of convincing the public that the consequences of the supply shock are only a one-time rise in the price level, rather than a permanent increase in inflation. A relevant example occurred in Canada in 1991, shortly after their implementation of inflation targeting, when a sharp increase in indirect taxes caused a blip in the price level but had no apparent effect on the underlying inflation rate.

The idea that inflation targeting requires an accounting of the long-run implications of short-run "discretionary" actions is also central to the argument that inflation targeting helps to discipline monetary policy. In practice, exactly who needs disciplining may differ from country to country, depending on politics, institutional arrangements and personalities. In the macroeconomic literature on central bank credibility, it is the central bank that needs discipline, because it is assumed to desire an unemployment rate lower than the natural rate. This desire leads the monetary authority to try to "fool" the public with surprise inflation, inducing producers (who confuse nominal and real price increases) to increase output and employment above the natural rate. If the public has rational expectations, however, it will anticipate the central bank's actions, and producers will not be fooled, so that in equilibrium the economy will suffer higher-than-optimal inflation with no benefits in terms of lower unemployment.[9]

If a story along these lines describes the actual situation in a given economy, then an inflation-targeting framework will not *directly* prevent the counterproductive attempts of the central bank to engage in excessive short-run stimulus. In this respect, inflation targeting is inferior to an ironclad rule, if such could be implemented. However, in contrast to the purely discretionary situation with no explicit targets, under inflation targeting the central bank would be forced to calculate and to publicize the implications of its short-run actions for expected inflation in the long run (and again, these projections would be subject to scrutiny and debate). To the extent that the central bank governors dislike admitting publicly that they are off track with respect to their long-run inflation targets, the existence of this framework would provide an additional incentive for the central bank to limit its short-run opportunism.

Although the theoretical literature typically posits the central bank as the entity who chooses to inflate opportunistically, we suspect that in most cases the executive and legislative branches of the government have the greater incentive to engage in such behavior, often because of approaching elections. Central bankers, in contrast, tend to view themselves as defenders of the currency. This view may be the result of intentional appointments of "tough" central bankers (for reasons described by Rogoff, 1985), or it may just be that self-selection and socialization act to make central bankers relatively hawkish on inflation. But in either case, the existence of longer-term inflation targets can prove a useful device by which the central bank can protect itself politically from overexpansionist pressures. In particular, by making explicit the long-run, as well as the short-run, implications of overexpansionist policies, the central bank may be better able to get the support it needs to resist such policies. Our impression is that the Bank of England, for example, has on occasion used numerical inflation targets in precisely this way.

9.3   Further Issues with Inflation Targeting

If viewed as a framework rather than as a rule, inflation targeting can confer some important advantages. It provides a nominal anchor for policy and the economy. By communicating the central bank's objectives and views, it increases the transparency of monetary policy. It has the potential to provide increased discipline and accountability for policymakers. Importantly, it may be able to achieve all this without entirely giving up the benefits of discretionary policies in the short run. These optimistic conclusions notwithstanding, important questions and controversies remain around inflation targeting, even when interpreted in the way that we prefer. Let us consider a few of these.

9.3.1   Which Inflation Measure? What Target Value?

A critical aspect of the design of an inflation-targeting regime is the definition of the price series to be used in the inflation target. The series needs to be considered accurate, timely and readily understood by the public, but may also need to allow for individual price shocks or one-time shifts that do not affect trend inflation, which is what monetary policy should influence. As table 9.1 indicates, all inflation-targeting countries have chosen some variant of the consumer price index (CPI) as their target series. However, this choice is not typically the "headline" CPI figure, but an index that excludes some components or focuses on "core" inflation; clearly, it is incumbent on the central bank to explain its choice of index and to help the public understand its relation to the headline index.

In all inflation-targeting regimes, the inflation objective has been set at a low number, 4 percent or less. Is this the ideal range for the inflation target? Or would a somewhat higher range for inflation, which might involve lower initial output cost to attain, be acceptable?

Obtaining direct empirical confirmation of a link between inflation and economic performance is very difficult. Inflation is, after all, an endogenous variable; and so we rarely if ever see variation in inflation that is not associated with some third factor, such as supply shocks or political instability, which would plausibly affect other elements of economic performance as well.[10] As a result, economists' views on the subject have been based largely on prior arguments, intuition and indirect evidence. That conceded, it is nevertheless clear that the professional consensus, which at one time did not ascribe substantial costs to moderate inflation, has over the past few decades begun to take the costs of inflation more seriously. For example, Feldstein (1996) has emphasized the importance of inflation-induced inefficiencies, via the tax code, on capital formation. Fischer (1993) and others have provided some evidence that macroeconomic stability, including control of inflation, is an important precondition for economic growth. Shiller's (1996) opinion surveys of public attitudes about inflation, while confirming economists' suspicions that the public is confused about even the definition of inflation, also show that people believe inflation to be highly uneven in its distributional impacts and hence corrosive of the social compact. A strengthening preference for low inflation is quite visible in policy circles, perhaps most strikingly in the tough limits on inflation imposed by the Maastricht treaty on countries that want to join the European currency union.

Given the growing consensus that the long-term goal of monetary policy should be a low inflation rate, there remains the question of how low it should be. It seems clear that an inflation target of zero or near zero is not desirable, for several reasons. First, much recent research suggests that official CPI inflation rates tend to overstate the true rate of inflation, due to various problems such as substitution bias in the fixed-weight index and failure to account adequately for quality change. Studies for the United States have estimated this overstatement of inflation to be in the range of 0.5 to 2.0 percentage points per year.[11] Thus, as a practical matter, even if the central bank chooses to pursue a zero rate of true inflation, the target for the measured inflation rate should be greater than zero.

Putting aside measurement issues, there are other risks of setting the inflation target too low. In a much discussed recent article, Akerlof, Dickens and Perry (1996) point out that if nominal wages are rigid downward (a possibility that they argue is consistent with the evidence), then reductions in real wages can occur only through inflation in the general price level. Very low inflation therefore effectively reduces real-wage flexibility and hence may worsen the allocative efficiency of the labor market; indeed, the authors perform simulations suggesting that inflation rates near zero would permanently increase the natural rate of unemployment.[12] Another danger of setting the inflation target too low is that there is a greater chance that the economy will be tipped into deflation, with the true price level actually falling—as may have happened during the recent recession in Japan. As pointed out in the literature on financial crises, persistent deflation—particularly if unanticipated—can create serious problems for the financial system, interfering with its normal functioning and precipitating an economic contraction (Bernanke and James, 1991; Mishkin, 1991).

These risks suggest that the inflation target, even when corrected for measurement error, should be set above zero, as has been the practice of all inflation-targeting countries to date. Indeed, a potentially important advantage of inflation targeting is that it provides not only a ceiling for the inflation rate, but also a floor. Inflation targeting thus acts to attenuate the effects of negative, as well as positive, shocks to aggregate demand. An interesting historical example is that of Sweden in the 1930s, which adopted a "norm of price stabilization" after leaving the gold standard in 1931. As a result, Sweden did not undergo the devastating deflation experienced by other countries during the Great Depression (Jonung, 1979).

9.3.2 Is Inflation Sufficiently Predictable and Controllable to Be "Targeted"?

It has been noted by several authors that inflation is very difficult to predict accurately, particularly at both very short and very long horizons (Cecchetti, 1995). This lack of predictability poses two important problems for the inflation targeting strategy. The first is strictly operational: given the long lags between monetary policy actions and the inflation response, low predictability suggests that accurate targeting of inflation could be extremely difficult. The second issue has to do with the central bank's credibility: if inflation is largely unpredictable, and hence not finely controllable, then it will be difficult to judge whether the central bank has made its best effort to hit the inflation targets. For example, the central bank could always argue that wide misses were the result of bad luck, not bad faith; since central bank forecasts of inflation contain substantial judgmental components, such claims would be difficult to disprove. This possible escape hatch for the central bank weakens the argument that inflation targeting increases accountability of monetary policy and suggests that building up credibility for its inflation-targeting framework could be a long and arduous process.

While we agree that inflation targeting is less effective, the less predictable or controllable is the inflation rate, several observations should be made. First, statistical measures of predictability are themselves likely to be sensitive to the monetary policy regime in place. Inflation was no doubt difficult to predict during the 1970s, when monetary policymakers tried to deal with oil price shocks and other stagflationary pressures without a coherent, clearly articulated framework. In contrast, the stability of the inflation rate in the United States and other industrialized countries since the mid-1980s, a period during which the maintenance of low and steady inflation has received much greater weight in central bank decision making, suggests that inflation will be easier to predict in the future.

Second, the relative unpredictability of goal variables is not in itself an argument for the use of intermediate targets in the conduct of monetary policy. As Svensson (1997a) points out, from an optimal control perspective, the best possible intermediate target is the current forecast of the goal variable itself—in this context, inflation. Using an intermediate target such as money growth is acceptable in an optimal control framework only if the intermediate target contains all information relevant to forecasting the goal variable; in this extreme case, using the intermediate target is equivalent to targeting the forecast of the goal variable. However, if any variable other than the intermediate target contains marginal information about the future values of the goal variable, then targeting the inflation forecast strictly dominates using any single intermediate target. Thus, from a strictly operational point of view, while it is unfortunate if the goal variable is hard to predict or to control, no improvement is available by using an intermediate target.[13]

When the credibility of the central bank is at issue, the problem of whether to target inflation directly or to rely on an intermediate target becomes more complex. By Svensson's argument, use of the intermediate target must increase the variance of the goal variable, which is a cost of the intermediate targeting approach; the benefit, however, is that by hitting its announced target for the intermediate variable, the central bank can demonstrate the seriousness of its intentions to the public more quickly and reliably (Cukierman, 1995; Laubach, 1996). If credibility building is an important objective of the central bank, and if there exists an intermediate target variable—such as a monetary aggregate—that is well controlled by the central bank, observed and understood by the public and the financial markets, and strongly and reliably related to the ultimate goal variable, then targeting the intermediate variable may be the preferred strategy. All of these are big "ifs," particularly the last one. However, this analysis may help to explain the continued use of money-growth targets by Germany and Switzerland, where financial institutions and hence velocity have evolved rather slowly, while countries such as the United Kingdom, with a history of unstable velocity, have opted for targeting inflation directly.

9.3.3 Is Inflation the Right Goal Variable for Monetary Policy?

The consensus that monetary policy is neutral in the long run restricts the set of feasible long-run goal variables for monetary policy, but inflation is not the only possibility. Notably, a number of economists have proposed that central banks should target the growth rate of nominal GDP rather than inflation (Taylor, 1985; Hall and Mankiw, 1994). Nominal GDP growth, which can be thought of as "velocity-corrected" money growth (that is, if velocity were constant, nominal GDP growth and money growth would be equal, by definition), has the advantage that it does put some weight on output as well as prices. Under a nominal GDP target, a decline in projected real output growth would automatically imply an increase in the central bank's inflation target, which would tend to be stabilizing.[14] Also, Cecchetti (1995) has presented simulations that suggest that policies directed to stabilizing nominal GDP growth may be more likely to produce good economic outcomes, given the difficulty of predicting and controlling inflation.

Nominal GDP targeting is a reasonable alternative to inflation targeting, and one that is generally consistent with the overall strategy for monetary policy discussed in this article. However, we have three reasons for mildly preferring inflation targets to nominal GDP targets. First, information on prices is more timely and frequently received than data on nominal GDP (and could be made even more so), a practical consideration that offsets some of the theoretical appeal of the nominal GDP target. Although collection of data on nominal GDP could also be improved, measurement of nominal GDP involves data on current quantities as well as current prices and thus is probably intrinsically more difficult to accomplish in a timely fashion. Second, given the various escape clauses and provisions for short-run flexibility built into the inflation-targeting approach, we doubt that there is much practical difference in the degree to which inflation targeting and nominal GDP targeting would allow accommodation of short-run stabilization objectives. Finally, and perhaps most important, it seems likely that the concept of inflation is better understood by the public than is the concept of nominal GDP, which could easily be confused with real GDP. If this is so, the objectives of communication and transparency would be better served by the use of an inflation target. As a matter of revealed preference, all central banks that have thus far adopted this general framework have chosen to target inflation rather than nominal GDP.

9.3.4 If It's Not Broke, Why Fix It?

Friedman and Kuttner (1996) decry the tendency of economists to want to impose restrictions and rules on central bank policymaking. They survey the problems with policy rules in the past, notably the failure of money-growth targeting to become a reliable policy framework in the United States, and they correctly point out that U.S. monetary policy has performed quite well in the recent past without the benefit of a formal rule or framework. Why, they ask, should we change something that is working well, especially given our inability to know what types of challenges will confront monetary policy in the future?

We would respond that a major reason for the success of the Volcker-Greenspan Fed is that it has employed a policymaking philosophy, or framework, which is de facto very similar to inflation targeting. In particular, the Fed has expressed a strong policy preference for low, steady inflation, and debates about short-run stabilization policies have prominently featured consideration of the long-term inflation implications of current Fed actions.

To take the next step and to formalize this framework would have several advantages. It would increase the transparency of the Fed's decision-making process, allowing more public debate and discussion of the Fed's strategy and tactics and, perhaps, reducing the financial and economic uncertainty associated with the Fed's current procedures. It would create an institutional commitment to the current approach that would be less dependent on a single individual's philosophy and might thus be expected to survive when, inevitably, new leadership takes over at the Fed. Finally, inflation targeting will be easiest to implement in a situation, like the current one, in which inflation is already low and the basic approach has been made familiar to the public and the markets. By adopting this approach now when it is relatively easy politically, we could ensure that the new procedures will be in place to provide guidance when the next difficult decisions about monetary policy have to be made.

9.4 Conclusion

It is too early to offer a final judgment on whether inflation targeting will prove to be a fad or a trend. However, our preliminary assessment is that this approach—when construed as a framework for making monetary policy, rather than as a rigid rule— has a number of advantages, including more transparent and coherent policymaking, increased accountability, and greater attention to long-run considerations in day-to-day policy debates and decisions.

Acknowledgments

We thank Alan Blinder, Brad De Long, Mervyn King, Don Kohn, Alan Krueger, Bennett McCallum, Michael Peytrignet, Adam Posen, Georg Rich, Julio Rotemberg, Lars Svensson and Timothy Taylor for their helpful comments. Any opinions expressed are those of the authors and not those of Princeton University, Columbia University, the National Bureau of Economic Research, the Federal Reserve Bank of New York, or the Federal Reserve System.

Notes

1. Detailed analyses of experiences with inflation targeting can be found in Goodhart and Vinals (1994), Leiderman and Svensson (1995), Haldane (1995) and McCallum (1996), among others.

2. King (1996) adopts a similar view.

3. Technically, ensuring only that the inflation rate is stationary may leave a unit root in the price level, so that the forecast variance of the price level grows without bound. This problem is analogous to the issue of "base drift" in the literature on money-growth targeting.

4. However, Svensson (1996) gives examples in which price-level targeting actually reduces the volatility of output.

5. Svensson (1997b) relates inflation targeting to the contracting approach.

6. Another short-run objective that is almost always retained by inflation-targeting central banks is the maintenance of financial stability. For example, see Mishkin (1997).

7. Users of the monetary conditions index would probably argue that treating the MCI simply as a forecasting variable is oversimple; they tend to view the MCI more specifically as a measure of how overall monetary conditions are affecting aggregate demand and thus as a potential guide to policy actions. See Freedman (1994) for further discussion.

8. Debelle and Fischer (1994) make the useful distinction between goal independence and instrument independence for the central bank. Goal independence implies the unilateral ability of the central bank to set its inflation targets and other goals, while instrument independence means that, although goals may be set by the government or by the government in consultation with the central bank, the central bank is solely responsible for choosing the instrument settings (for example, the level of short-term interest rates) necessary to achieve those goals. Instrument independence would seem to be the form of independence that maximizes central bank accountability and minimizes opportunistic political interference, while still leaving the ultimate goals of policy to be determined by democratic processes.

9. McCallum (1997) argues that the central bank can simply choose not to behave myopically, and the public's expectations will come to reflect this more farsighted behavior. He also points out, however, that to the extent time-inconsistency is a problem, it will affect the government as well as the central bank; we agree, as we discuss below.

10. Studies that attempt to overcome these problems include Lebow, Roberts and Stockton (1992) and Barro (1995).

11. This bias was the subject of an official report to the Senate Finance Committee, the so-called Boskin report (Boskin et al., 1996). See also Moulton (1996) and Shapiro and Wilcox (1997).

12. The force of this argument should not be overstated. First, the inflation rates which Akerlof, Dickens and Perry (1996) argue would significantly affect the natural rate of unemployment are really quite low, for example, measured rates (as opposed to "true" rates) of inflation of 2 percent per annum or less. Second, their simulation studies do not take into account forces that may work in the opposite direction: for example, Groshen and Schweitzer (1996) point out that high and variable inflation rates may increase the "noise" in relative wages, reducing the efficiency of the process by which workers are allocated across industries and occupations; thus higher inflation can represent sand as well as grease in the wheels of the labor market.

13. In characterizing the forecast of inflation as the intermediate target, Svensson (1997a) is careful to define "forecast" to mean the forecast derived internally by the central bank using its structural model of the economy. An intriguing alternative would be to try to "target" private-sector forecasts of inflation, that is, set short-run policy instruments so that private-sector forecasts of inflation equal the announced target. Unfortunately, as shown by Woodford (1994) and Bernanke and Woodford (1996), such a policy is usually not consistent with the existence of a unique rational expectations equilibrium. However, Bernanke and Woodford also show that, while targeting private-sector forecasts is not a good idea, private-sector forecasts can typically be combined with the central bank's own information to improve the efficiency of its operating procedure. Further, private-sector forecasts that the public observes to be close to the central bank's official targets may help to provide some validation of the bank's internal procedures for forecasting and controlling inflation.

14. Hall and Mankiw (1994) point out, however, that the equal weighting of real output growth and inflation implied by a nominal GDP targeting is not necessarily the optimal one; in general, the relative weight put on the two goal variables should reflect social preferences.

References

Akerlof, George, William Dickens, and George Perry, "The Macroeconomics of Low Inflation," *Brookings Papers on Economic Activity*, 1996, *1*, 1–59.

Barro, Robert, "Inflation and Economic Growth," *Bank of England Quarterly Bulletin*, May 1995, *35*, 166–76.

Barro, Robert, and David Gordon, "Rules, Discretion, and Reputation in a Model of Monetary Policy," *Journal of Monetary Economics*, July 1983, *12*, 101–21.

Bernanke, Ben, and Harold James, "The Gold Standard, Deflation, and Financial Crisis in the Great Depression: An International Comparison." In Hubbard, R. G., ed., *Financial Markets and Financial Crises.* Chicago: University of Chicago Press for NBER, 1991, pp. 33–68.

Bernanke, Ben, and Ilian Mihov, "What Does the Bundesbank Target?," *European Economic Review*, 1997.

Bernanke, Ben, and Michael Woodford, "Inflation Forecasts and Monetary Policy," unpublished paper, Princeton University, September 1996.

Boskin, Michael J., Ellen R. Dulberger, Robert J. Gordon, Zvi Griliches, and Dale Jorgenson, "Toward a More Accurate Measure of the Cost of Living: The Final Report to the Senate Finance Committee from the Advisory Commission to Study the Consumer Price Index," December 4, 1996.

Calvo, Guillermo, "On the Time Consistency of Optimal Policy in a Monetary Economy," *Econometrica*, November 1978, *46*, 1411–28.

Cecchetti, Stephen, "Inflation Indicators and Inflation Policy," *NBER Macroeconomics Annual*, 1995, 189–219.

Cukierman, Alex, "Towards a Systematic Comparison Between Inflation Targets and Money Targets." In Leiderman, L., and L. Svensson, eds., *Inflation Targets.* London: Centre for Economic Policy Research, 1995, pp. 192–209.

Debelle, Guy, and Stanley Fischer, "How Independent Should a Central Bank Be?" In Fuhrer, Jeffrey, ed., *Goals, Guidelines, and Constraints Facing Monetary Policymakers.* Boston: Federal Reserve Bank of Boston, 1994, pp. 195–221.

Deutsche Bundesbank, *The Monetary Policy of the Bundesbank.* Frankfurt am Main: Deutsche Bundesbank, 1995.

Feldstein, Martin, "The Costs and Benefits of Going from Low Inflation to Price Stability." NBER Working Paper No. 5469, February 1996.

Fischer, Stanley, "The Role of Macroeconomic Factors in Growth." NBER Working Paper No. 4565, December 1993.

Freedman, Charles, "The Use of Indicators and of the Monetary Conditions Index in Canada." In Balino, T., and C. Cottarelli, eds., *Frameworks for Monetary Stability: Policy Issues and Country Experiences.* Washington, D.C.: International Monetary Fund, 1994, pp. 458–76.

Friedman, Ben, and Kenneth Kuttner, "A Price Target for U.S. Monetary Policy? Lessons from the Experience with Money Growth Targets," *Brookings Papers on Economic Activity*, 1996, *1*, 77–125.

Goodhart, Charles, and José Vinals, "Strategy and Tactics of Monetary Policy: Examples from Europe and the Antipodes." In Fuhrer, Jeffrey, ed., *Goals, Guidelines, and Constraints Facing Monetary Policymakers.* Boston: Federal Reserve Bank of Boston, 1994, pp. 139–87.

Groshen, Erica, and Mark Schweitzer, "The Effects of Inflation on Wage Adjustments in Firm-Level Data: Grease or Sand?" Staff Report No. 9, Federal Reserve Bank of New York, January 1996.

Haldane, Andrew G., ed., *Targeting Inflation.* London: Bank of England, 1995.

Hall, Robert, and N. Gregory Mankiw, "Nominal Income Targeting." In Mankiw, N. G., ed., *Monetary Policy.* Chicago: University of Chicago Press for NBER, 1994, pp. 71–94.

Howitt, Peter W., "Canada." In Fratianni, Michelle U., and Dominick Salvatore, eds., *Monetary Policy in Developed Economies, Handbook of Comparative Economic Policies.* Vol. 3, Westport: Greenwood Press, 1993, pp. 459–508.

Issing, Otmar, "Monetary Policy Strategies: Theoretical Basis, Empirical Findings, Practical Implementation." In Deutsche Bundesbank, ed., *Monetary Policy Strategies in Europe.* München: Verlag Franz Vahlen, 1996, pp. 197–202.

Jonung, Lars, "Knut Wicksell's Norm of Price Stabilisation and Swedish Monetary Policy in the 1930s," *Journal of Monetary Economics*, October 1979, *5*, 459–96.

King, Mervyn, "Direct Inflation Targets." In Deutsche Bundesbank, ed., *Monetary Policy Strategies in Europe*. München: Verlag Franz Vahlen, 1996, pp. 45–75.

Kydland, Finn, and Edward Prescott, "Rules Rather than Discretion: The Inconsistency of Optimal Plans," *Journal of Political Economy*, June 1977, *88*, 473–92.

Laubach, Thomas, "Signalling with Monetary and Inflation Targets," unpublished paper, Princeton University, August 1996.

Lebow, David, John Roberts, and David Stockton, "Economic Performance Under Price Stability." Working Paper No. 125, Division of Research and Statistics, Federal Reserve Board, 1992.

Leiderman, Leonardo, and Lars E. O. Svensson, eds., *Inflation Targets*. London: Centre for Economic Policy Research, 1995.

McCallum, Bennett, "Inflation Targeting in Canada, New Zealand, Sweden, the United Kingdom, and in General." NBER Working Paper No. 5579, May 1996.

McCallum, Bennett, "Crucial Issues Concerning Central Bank Independence." NBER Working Paper No. 5597; *Journal of Monetary Economics*, forthcoming 1997.

Mishkin, Frederic S., "Asymmetric Information and Financial Crises: A Historical Perspective." In Hubbard, R. Glenn, ed., *Financial Markets and Financial Crises*. Chicago: University of Chicago Press, 1991, pp. 69–108.

Mishkin, Frederic S., "What Monetary Policy Can and Cannot Do." In *Monetary Policy in Transition: Strategies, Instruments and Transmission Mechanisms*. Vienna: Oesterreichische Nationalbank, 1997, pp. 13–32.

Moulton, Brent, "Bias in the Consumer Price Index: What is the Evidence?," *Journal of Economic Perspectives*, Fall 1996, *10*, 159–77.

Persson, Torsten, and Guido Tabellini, "Designing Institutions for Monetary Stability," *Carnegie-Rochester Conference Series on Public Policy*, 1993, *39*, 53–84.

Posen, Adam, "Declarations are Not Enough: Financial Sector Sources of Central Bank Independence," *NBER Macroeconomics Annual*, 1995, 253–74.

Posen, Adam, and Thomas Laubach, "Some Comparative Evidence on the Effectiveness of Inflation Targets," unpublished paper, Federal Reserve Bank of New York, 1996.

Rogoff, Kenneth, "The Optimal Degree of Commitment to an Intermediate Monetary Target," *Quarterly Journal of Economics*, November 1985, *100*, 1169–89.

Shapiro, Matthew, and David Wilcox, "Mismeasurement in the Consumer Price Index: An Evaluation," *NBER Macroeconomics Annual*, 1996, pp. 93–142.

Shiller, Robert, "Why Do People Dislike Inflation?" Cowles Foundation Discussion Paper No. 1115, March 1996.

Svensson, Lars E. O., "Price Level Targeting vs. Inflation Targeting: A Free Lunch?" NBER Working Paper No. 5719, 1996.

Svensson, Lars E. O., "Inflation Forecast Targeting: Implementing and Monitoring Inflation Targets." NBER Working Paper No. 5797; *European Economic Review*, 1997a.

Svensson, Lars E. O., "Optimal Inflation Targets, 'Conservative' Central Banks, and Linear Inflation Contracts." NBER Working Paper No. 5251; *American Economic Review*, 1997b.

Taylor, John, "What Would Nominal GDP Targeting do to the Business Cycle?" In *Carnegie-Rochester Conference Series on Public Policy*. Vol. 22, Amsterdam: North-Holland, 1985, pp. 61–84.

von Hagen, Jurgen, "Inflation and Monetary Targeting in Germany." In Leiderman, L., and L. Svensson, eds., *Inflation Targets*. London: Centre for Economic Policy Research, 1995, pp. 107–21.

Walsh, Carl, "Optimal Contracts for Central Bankers," *American Economic Review*, March 1995, *85*, 150–67.

Woodford, Michael, "Nonstandard Indicators for Monetary Policy: Can Their Usefulness be Judged from Forecasting Regressions?" In Mankiw, N. G., ed., *Monetary Policy*. Chicago: University of Chicago Press for NBER, 1994, pp. 95–116.

10 International Experiences with Different Monetary Policy Regimes

Frederic S. Mishkin

10.1 Introduction

In recent years a growing consensus has emerged for price stability as the overriding, long-run goal of monetary policy. However, despite this consensus, the following question still remains: how should monetary policy be conducted to achieve the price stability goal? To shed light on this question, this chapter examines the experience with different monetary policy regimes currently in use in a number of countries.

A central feature of all of these monetary regimes is the use of a nominal anchor in some form, so first we will examine what role a nominal anchor plays in promoting price stability. Then we will examine four basic types of monetary policy regimes: (1) exchange-rate targeting, (2) monetary targeting, (3) inflation targeting, and (4) monetary policy with an implicit but not an explicit nominal anchor. The basic theme that comes out of this analysis is that the success of different monetary regimes depends on their ability to constrain discretionary policymaking so that long-run price stability is more likely to result.

10.2 The Role of a Nominal Anchor

A nominal anchor is a constraint on the value of domestic money, and in some form it is a necessary element in successful monetary policy regimes. Why is a nominal anchor needed? First, from a purely technical viewpoint, a nominal anchor provides conditions that make the price level uniquely determined, which is obviously necessary for price stability. It helps do this by tying down inflation expectations directly through its constraint on the value of domestic money.

However, a nominal anchor can be thought of more broadly as a constraint on discretionary policy that helps weaken the time-inconsistency problem so that in the long run, price stability is more likely to be achieved. The time-inconsistency problem arises because discretionary policy at each point in time can lead to poor long run outcomes. In the case of monetary policy, expansionary monetary policy will produce higher growth and employment in the short run, and so policymakers have incentives to pursue this policy even though it ends up producing higher inflation, but not higher growth or employment, in the long run. However, it is important to recognize that the time-inconsistency problem may not reside in the central bank because, as McCallum (1995) points out, a central bank can avoid the time-inconsistency problem by simply recognizing the problem that forward-looking expectations in the wage- and price-setting process creates for a strategy of pursuing expansionary monetary policy. The central bank can just decide not to play that game. However, even so, there will still be pressures on the central bank to pursue overly expansionary monetary policy by the politicians. Thus even if the source of time inconsistency is not within central banks, a nominal anchor which limits political pressures to pursue overly expansionary, monetary policies has an important role to play in the achievement of price stability.

10.3   Exchange-Rate Targeting

Targeting the exchange rate is a monetary policy regime with a long history. It can take the form of fixing the value of the domestic currency to a commodity such as gold, the key feature of the gold standard. More recently, fixed exchange-rate regimes have involved fixing the value of the domestic currency to that of a large, low-inflation country. Another alternative is adoption of a crawling target or peg in which a currency is allowed to depreciate at a steady rate so that the inflation rate in the pegging country can be higher than that of the anchor country.

Exchange-rate targeting has several advantages. First, the nominal anchor of an exchange-rate target fixes the inflation rate for internationally traded goods, and thus directly contributes to keeping inflation under control. Second, if the exchange-rate target is credible, it anchors inflation expectations to the inflation rate in the anchor country to whose currency it is pegged. Third, with a strong commitment mechanism, an exchange-rate target provides an automatic rule for the conduct of monetary policy that helps mitigate the time-inconsistency problem. It forces a tightening of monetary policy when there is a tendency for the domestic currency to depreciate or a loosening of policy when there is a tendency for the domestic currency to appreciate, so that discretionary, time-inconsistent, monetary policy is less of an option. Fourth, an exchange-rate target has the advantage of simplicity and clarity, which make it easily understood by the public. A "sound currency" is an easy-to-understand rallying cry for monetary policy. This has been important in France, for example, where an appeal to the "franc fort" is often used to justify tight monetary policy.

Given its advantages, it is not surprising that exchange-rate targeting has been used successfully to control inflation in industrialized countries. Both France and the United Kingdom, for example, successfully used exchange-rate targeting to lower inflation by tying the value of their currencies to the German mark. In 1987, when France first pegged their exchange rate to the mark, its inflation rate was 3%, two percentage points above the German inflation rate. By 1992 its inflation rate had fallen to 2%, a level that can be argued is consistent with price stability, and was even below that in Germany. By 1996, the French and German inflation rates had converged, to a number slightly below 2%. Similarly, after pegging to the German mark in 1990, the United Kingdom was able to lower its inflation rate from 10% to 3% by 1992, when it was forced to abandon the exchange rate mechanism (ERM).

Exchange-rate targeting has also been an effective means of reducing inflation quickly in emerging market countries. An important recent example has been Argentina, which in 1991 established a currency board arrangement, requiring the central bank to exchange US dollars for new pesos at a fixed exchange rate of 1:1. A currency board is just one form of a fixed-exchange rate regime with an important difference. The currency board makes a much stronger and transparent commitment to an exchange-rate target than the typical fixed-fixed exchange rate regime because it requires that the monetary authority stands ready to exchange the domestic currency for foreign currency at the specified fixed exchange rate whenever the public requests it. In order to credibly meet these requests, a currency board typically has more than 100% foreign reserves backing the domestic currency and allows the monetary authorities absolutely no discretion. The early years of Argentina's currency board looked stunningly successful. Inflation which had been running at over a one-thousand percent annual rate in 1989 and 1990 fell to under 5% by the end of 1994, and economic growth was rapid, averaging almost 8% at an annual rate from 1991 to 1994.

Despite the inherent advantages of exchange-rate targeting, it is not without its serious problems, as the international experience demonstrates. There are several serious criticisms of exchange-rate targeting, which have been articulated brilliantly in Obstfeld and Rogoff (1995). First is that, with open capital markets, an exchange-rate target results in the loss of independent monetary policy, since the targeting country loses the ability to use monetary policy to respond to domestic shocks that are independent of those hitting the anchor country. Furthermore, an exchange-rate target means that shocks to the anchor country are directly transmitted to the targeting country because changes in interest rates in the anchor country lead to a corresponding change in interest rates in the targeting country.

A striking example of these problems occurred when Germany reunified in 1990. Concerns about inflationary pressures arising from reunification and the massive fiscal expansion required to rebuild East Germany led to rises in German long-term interest rates until February 1991 and to rises in short-term rates until December 1991. This shock to the anchor country in the exchange rate mechanism (ERM) was transmitted directly to the other countries in the ERM whose currencies were pegged to the mark because their interest rates now rose in tandem with those in Germany. The result was that continuing adherence to the exchange-rate target produced a significant slowing of economic growth and rising unemployment, which is exactly what France experienced when it remained in the ERM and adhered to the exchange-rate peg.

An exchange-rate target has the additional disadvantage that it removes the signal that the foreign exchange market provides about the stance of monetary policy on a daily basis. Under an exchange-rate-target regime, central banks often pursue overly expansionary policies that are not discovered until too late, when a successful speculative attack has gotten underway. The problem of lack of accountability of the central bank under an exchange-rate-target regime is particularly acute in emerging market countries where the balance sheets and actions of the central banks are not as transparent as in developed countries. This can make it harder to ascertain the central bank's policy actions, as occurred in Thailand before the July currency crisis. Although, an exchange-rate peg appears to provide rules for central bank behavior that ameliorate the time-inconsistency problem, it can actually make the time-inconsistency problem more severe because it may make central bank actions less transparent and less accountable. Indeed, an exchange-rate depreciation when the exchange rate is not pegged can provide an early warning signal that monetary policy is overly expansionary, and fear of depreciation can make overly expansionary, time-inconsistent, monetary policy less likely.

A third problem with exchange-rate targets is that they leave countries open to speculative attacks on their currencies. Indeed, one aftermath of German reunification was the foreign exchange crisis of September 1992. As we have seen, the tight monetary policy in Germany resulting from German reunification meant that the countries in the ERM were subjected to a negative demand shock that led to a decline in economic growth and a rise in unemployment. It was certainly feasible for the governments of these countries to keep their exchange rates fixed relative to the mark in these circumstances, but speculators began to question whether these countries' commitment to the exchange rate peg would weaken because these countries would not tolerate the rise in unemployment that would result from keeping interest rates sufficiently high to fend off speculative attacks on their currencies.

At this stage, speculators were in effect presented with one-way bets because the currencies of countries like France, Spain, Sweden, Italy and the United Kingdom could only go in one direction, depreciate against the mark. Selling these currencies thus presented speculators with an attractive profit opportunity with potentially high expected returns, and the result was the speculative attack in September 1992. Only in France was the commitment to the fixed exchange rate strong enough, so that France did not devalue. The governments in the other countries were unwilling to defend their currencies at all costs and so eventually allowed their currencies to fall in value.

The different response of France and the United Kingdom after the September 1992 exchange rate crisis illustrates the potential cost of an exchange-rate target. France, which continued to peg to the mark and thereby was unable to use monetary policy to respond to domestic conditions, found that economic growth remained slow after 1992 and unemployment increased. The United Kingdom, on the other hand, which dropped out of the ERM exchange-rate peg and adopted inflation targeting (discussed later), had much better economic performance: economic growth was higher, the unemployment rate fell, and yet inflation performance was not much worse than France's.

The aftermath of German reunification and the September 1992 exchange rate crisis dramatically illustrate two points: (1) an exchange-rate target does not guarantee that the commitment to the exchange-rate based, monetary policy rule is sufficiently strong to maintain the target, and (2) the cost to economic growth from an exchange-rate regime with its loss of independent monetary policy can be high.

For emerging market countries, it is far less clear that these countries lose much by giving up an independent monetary policy when they target exchange rates. Because many emerging market countries have not developed the political or monetary institutions that result in the ability to use discretionary monetary policy successfully, they may have little to gain from an independent monetary policy, but a lot to lose. Thus, they would be better off by, in effect, adopting the monetary policy of a country like the United States through targeting exchange rates than in pursuing their own independent policy. Indeed, this is one of the reasons that so many emerging market countries have adopted exchange-rate targeting.

Nonetheless, as is emphasized in Mishkin (1998a), there is an additional disadvantage from an exchange-rate target in emerging market countries that suggests that for them this monetary policy regime is highly dangerous. Exchange-rate targeting in emerging market countries is likely to promote financial fragility and possibly a full-fledged financial crisis that can be highly destructive to the economy.

To see why exchange-rate targets in an emerging market country make a financial crisis more likely, we must first understand what a financial crisis is and why it is so damaging to the economy. In recent years, an asymmetric information theory of financial crises has been developed which provides a definition of a financial crisis (Bernanke, 1983; Mishkin, 1991, 1996). A financial crisis is a nonlinear disruption to financial markets in which asymmetric information problems (adverse selection and moral hazard) become much worse, so that financial markets are unable to efficiently channel funds to economic agents who have the most productive investment opportunities. A financial crisis thus prevents the efficient functioning of financial markets, which therefore leads to a sharp contraction in economic activity.

Because of uncertainty about the future value of the domestic currency, many non-financial firms, banks and governments in emerging market countries find it much easier to issue debt if the debt is denominated in foreign currencies. This tendency can be further encouraged by an exchange-rate targeting regime which may encourage domestic firms and financial institutions to issue foreign denominated debt. The substantial issuance of foreign denominated debt was a prominent feature of the institutional structure in the Chilean financial markets before the financial crisis in 1982, in Mexico before its financial crisis in 1994 and in East Asian countries before their recent crisis.

With an exchange-rate target regime, depreciation of the currency when it occurs is a highly nonlinear event because it involves a devaluation. In most developed countries a devaluation has little direct effect on the balance sheets of households, firms and banks because their debts are denominated in domestic currency.[1] This is not true, however, in emerging market countries with their very different institutional structure. With debt contracts denominated in foreign currency as in emerging market countries, when there is a devaluation of the domestic currency, the debt burden of domestic firms increases. On the other hand, since assets are typically denominated in domestic currency, there is no simultaneous increase in the value of firms' assets. The result is that a devaluation leads to a substantial deterioration in balance sheets and a decline in net worth, both for nonfinancial firms and financial firms which now are unable to collect on their loans to nonfinancial firms.

In addition, a devaluation can lead to a dramatic rise in both actual and expected inflation in emerging market countries because their central banks are unlikely to have deep-rooted credibility of inflation fighters. Indeed Mexican inflation surged to 50% in 1995 after the foreign exchange crisis in 1994 and a similar phenomenon has been occurring in Indonesia. The rise in expected inflation then leads to a sharp rise in interest rates, which because of the short duration of debt contracts leads to huge increases in interest payments by firms, thereby weakening firms' cash flow position and further weakening their balance sheets.

The deterioration of balance sheets, by reducing effective collateral, makes lending less attractive and also increases moral hazard incentives for firms to take on greater risk because they have less to lose if the loans go sour. Because lenders are now subject to much higher risks of losses, and because financial intermediaries like banks may be less able to lend because of the deterioration in their balance sheets, there is a decline in investment and economic activity. The damage to balance sheets from devaluation in the aftermath of the foreign exchange crisis was a major source of the contraction of the economies of Chile in 1982, Mexico in 1994 and 1995 and East Asia in 1997–98.

Another potential danger from an exchange-rate target is that by providing a more stable value of the currency, it might lower perceived risk for foreign investors and thus encourage capital inflows. Although these capital inflows might be channeled into productive investments and thus stimulate growth, they might promote excessive lending, manifested by a lending boom, because domestic financial intermediaries such as banks play a key role in intermediating these capital inflows. With inadequate bank supervision, a common problem in emerging market countries, the likely outcome of a lending boom is substantial loan losses and a deterioration of bank balance sheets. Not only will the deterioration in bank balance sheets lead banks to reduce their lending, but it also damages the economy because it makes a currency crisis more likely, which, as we have seen, can trigger a financial crisis. When a country's banking system is in a weakened condition, a successful speculative attack is more likely because the central bank has less of an option to raise interest rates to defend the currency because doing so may cause the banking system to collapse.

The recent events in East Asia and Mexico, in which the weakness of the banking sector and speculative attack on the currency tipped their economies into full-scale financial crises, illustrate how dangerous exchange-rate targeting can be for emerging market countries. Indeed, the fact that an exchange-rate target in these countries leaves them more prone to financial fragility and financial crises, with potentially catastrophic costs to their economies, suggests that exchange-rate targeting in emerging market countries is highly problematic.

Given the above problems with exchange-rate targeting, when might it make sense? In countries whose political and monetary institutions are particularly weak and therefore have been experiencing continued bouts of hyperinflation, exchange-rate targeting may be the only way to break inflationary psychology and stabilize the economy. In this situation, exchange-rate targeting is the stabilization policy of last resort. However, we have seen that in emerging market countries exchange-rate targeting regimes are not always transparent, weakening the commitment mechanism and making them more likely to break down, often with disastrous consequences. This suggests that if exchange-rate targeting is believed to be the only route possible to stabilize the economy, then an emerging market country is probably best served by going all the way and adopting a currency board in which the commitment to the fixed exchange rate is extremely strong and there is total transparency to monetary policy because the actions of the central bank are automatic. However, as is discussed further in Mishkin (1998a), a currency board is still a potentially dangerous monetary policy regime which requires important institutional reforms in order to make it viable.

10.4 Monetary Targeting

In many countries, exchange-rate targeting is not an option because the country (or bloc of countries) is too large or has no obvious country whose currency can serve as the nominal anchor. Exchange-rate targeting is therefore clearly not an option for the United States, Japan or the European Monetary Union. Thus these countries, by default, must look to other monetary policy regimes, one of which is monetary targeting.

A major advantage of monetary targeting over exchange-rate targeting is that it enables a central bank to adjust its monetary policy to cope with domestic considerations. It enables the central bank to choose goals for inflation that may differ from those of other countries and allows some response to output fluctuations. Also, like an exchange-rate target, information on whether the central bank is achieving its target is known almost immediately—announced figures for monetary aggregates are typically reported periodically with very short time-lags, within a couple of weeks. Thus, monetary targets can send almost immediate signals to both the public and markets about the stance of monetary policy and the intentions of the policymakers to keep inflation in check. These signals then can help fix inflation expectations and produce less inflation. Monetary targets also have the advantage of being able to promote almost immediate accountability for monetary policy to keep inflation low and so help constrain the monetary policymaker from falling into the time-inconsistency trap.

All of the above advantages of monetary aggregate targeting depend on there being a strong and reliable relationship between the goal variable (inflation or nominal income) and the targeted aggregate. If there is velocity instability, so that the relationship between the monetary aggregate and the goal variable is weak, then monetary aggregate targeting will not work. The weak relationship implies that hitting the target will not produce the desired outcome on the goal variable and thus the monetary aggregate will no longer provide an adequate signal about the stance of monetary policy. Thus, monetary targeting will not help fix inflation expectations and be a good guide for assessing the accountability of the central bank. The breakdown of the relationship between monetary aggregates and goal variables such as inflation and nominal income certainly seems to have occurred in the United States (Friedman and Kuttner, 1996; Estrella and Mishkin, 1997) and may also be a problem even for countries that have continued to pursue monetary targeting.

This problem with monetary targeting suggests one reason why even the most avid monetary targeters do not rigidly hold to their target ranges, but rather allow undershoots and overshoots for extended periods of time. Moreover, an unreliable relationship between monetary aggregates and goal variables calls into question the ability of monetary targeting to serve as a communications device that both increases the transparency of monetary policy and makes the central bank accountable to the public.

The two countries which have pursued monetary targeting quite seriously are Germany and Switzerland. The success of monetary policy in these two countries in controlling inflation is the reason that monetary targeting still has strong advocates and is part of the official policy strategy for the European Central Bank. (Monetary targeting was less successful in the United States, Canada and the United Kingdom, partially because it was not pursued seriously (Bernanke and Mishkin, 1992) but also because the relationship between monetary aggregates and goal variables such as inflation or nominal income broke down.)

The key fact about monetary targeting regimes in Germany and Switzerland is that the targeting regimes are very far from a Friedman-type monetary targeting rule in which a monetary aggregate is kept on a constant-growth-rate path and is the primary focus of monetary policy. As Otmar Issing, currently the Chief Economist of the Bundesbank has noted, "One of the secrets of success of the German policy of money-growth targeting was that...it often did not feel bound by monetarist orthodoxy as far as its more technical details were concerned" (Issing, 1996, p. 120). Monetary targeting in Germany and Switzerland should instead be seen primarily as a method of communicating the strategy of monetary policy that focuses on long-run considerations and the control of inflation.

The calculation of monetary target ranges is a very public exercise.[2] First and foremost, a numerical inflation goal is prominently featured in the setting of target ranges. Then with estimates of potential output growth and velocity trends, a quantity-equation framework is used to back out the target growth rate for the monetary aggregate. Second, monetary targeting, far from being a rigid policy rule, has been quite flexible in practice. The target ranges for money growth are missed on the order of fifty percent of the time, often because of the Bundesbank's and the Swiss National Bank's concern about other objectives, including output and exchange rates. Furthermore, the Bundesbank has demonstrated its flexibility by allowing its inflation goal to vary over time, raising it when supply shocks occurred and then letting it converge slowly to the long-run inflation goal quite gradually.

Third, the monetary targeting regimes in both Germany and Switzerland have demonstrated a strong commitment to the communication of the strategy to the general public. The money-growth targets are continually used as a framework for explanation of the monetary policy strategy and both the Bundesbank and the Swiss National Bank expend tremendous effort, both in their publications and in frequent speeches by central bank officials, to communicate to the public what the central bank is trying to achieve. Indeed, given that both central banks frequently miss their money-growth targets by significant amounts, their monetary-targeting frameworks are best viewed as a mechanism for transparently communicating how monetary policy is being directed to achieve their inflation goals and as a means for increasing the accountability of the central bank.

Germany's monetary-targeting regime has been quite successful in producing low inflation and its success has been envied by many other countries, explaining why it was chosen as the anchor country for the exchange rate mechanism. An important success story, discussed extensively in Bernanke et al. (1999), occurred in the aftermath of German reunification in 1990. Despite a temporary surge in inflation stemming from the terms of reunification, high wage demands and the fiscal expansion, the Bundesbank was able to keep these one-off effects from becoming embedded in the inflation process, and by 1995, inflation fell back down below the Bundesbank's normative inflation goal of 2%.

One potentially serious criticism of German monetary targeting, however, is that, as demonstrated by Clarida and Gertler (1997), the Bundesbank has reacted asymmetrically to target misses, raising interest rates in response to overshooting of the money-growth target, but choosing not to lower interest rates in response to an undershooting. This suggests that the Bundesbank may not be sufficiently concerned about undershoots of its normative inflation goal. Arguably this might have caused the Bundesbank to be overly tight in its monetary policy stance in the mid 1990s when German inflation fell below the 2% normative goal, which not only led to an unnecessary increase in unemployment in Germany, but also in countries tied to the deutsche mark, such as France.

Monetary targeting has been more problematic in Switzerland than in Germany, suggesting the difficulties of targeting monetary aggregates in a small open economy which also underwent substantial changes in the institutional structure of its money markets. In the face of a 40% trade-weighted appreciation of the Swiss franc from the fall of 1977 to the fall of 1978, the Swiss National Bank decided that the country could not tolerate this high a level of the exchange rate. Thus, in the fall of 1978 the monetary targeting regime was abandoned temporarily, with a shift from a monetary target to an exchange-rate target until the spring of 1979, when monetary targeting was reintroduced although it was not announced. Furthermore, when the return to monetary targeting was formally announced in 1980, the Swiss National Bank deemed it necessary to switch the monetary aggregate targeted from M1 to the monetary base.

The period from 1989 to 1992 was also not a happy one for Swiss monetary targeting because as stated by the Chief Economist of the Swiss National Bank, Georg Rich, "the SNB (Swiss National Bank) failed to maintain price stability after it successfully reduced inflation" (Rich, 1997, p. 115, emphasis in original). The substantial overshoot of inflation from 1989 to 1992, reaching levels above 5%, was due to two factors. The first is that the strength of the Swiss franc from 1985 to 1987 caused the Swiss National Bank to allow the monetary base to grow at a rate greater than the 2% target in 1987 and then raised the money-growth target to 3% for 1988. The second arose from the introduction of a new interbank payment system, the Swiss Interbank Clearing (SIC), and a wide-ranging revision of the commercial banks' liquidity requirements in 1988. The result of the shocks to the exchange rate and the shift in the demand for monetary base arising from the above institutional changes created a serious problem for its targeted aggregate. As the 1988 year unfolded, it became clear that the Swiss National Bank had guessed wrong in predicting the effects of these shocks so that the demand for monetary base fell by more than the predicted amount, resulting in monetary policy that was too easy even though the monetary target was undershot. The result was a subsequent rise in inflation to above the 5% level.

The result of these problems with monetary targeting has resulted in a substantial loosening of the monetary targeting regime in Switzerland. The Swiss National Bank recognized that its money-growth targets were of diminished utility as a means of signaling the direction of monetary policy. As a result, its announcement at the end of 1990 of the medium-term growth path was quite ambiguous because it did not specify a horizon for the target or the starting point of the growth path. Eventually the Bank specified the time horizon of the horizon was a period of three to five years and it was not till the end of 1992 that the Bank specified the basis of the starting point for the expansion path. Finally at the end of 1994, the Bank announced a new medium-term path for money base growth for the period 1995 to 1999, thus retroactively revealing that the horizon of the first path was also five years. Clearly, the Swiss National Bank has moved to a much more flexible framework in which hitting one-year targets for money base growth has been abandoned. Nevertheless, Swiss monetary policy has continued to be successful in controlling inflation, with inflation rates falling back down below the 1% level after the temporary bulge in inflation from 1989 to 1992.

There are two key lessons to our discussion of German and Swiss monetary targeting. First, a targeting regime can restrain inflation in the longer run, even when the regime permits substantial target misses. Thus adherence to a rigid policy rule has not been found to be necessary to obtain good inflation outcomes. Second, the key reason why monetary targeting has been reasonably successful in these two countries, despite frequent target misses, is that the objectives of monetary policy are clearly stated, and both the Bundesbank and the Swiss National Bank actively engage in communicating the strategy of monetary policy to the public, thereby enhancing transparency of monetary policy and accountability of the central bank.

As we will see in the next section, these key elements of a successful targeting regime—flexibility, transparency and accountability—are also important elements in inflation-targeting regimes. Thus, as suggested by Bernanke and Mishkin (1997), German and Swiss monetary policy is actually closer in practice to inflation targeting than it is to Friedman-like monetary targeting, and thus might best be thought of as "hybrid" inflation targeting.

10.5   Inflation Targeting

Given the breakdown of the relationship between monetary aggregates and goal variables such as inflation, many countries have recently adopted inflation targeting as their monetary policy regime. New Zealand was the first country to formally adopt inflation targeting in 1990, with Canada following in 1991, the United Kingdom in 1992, Sweden in 1993, Finland in 1993, Australia in 1994 and Spain in 1994. Israel and Chile have also adopted a form of inflation targeting.

Inflation targeting involves several elements: (1) public announcement of medium-term numerical targets for inflation; (2) an institutional commitment to price stability as the primary, long-run goal of monetary policy and to achievement of the inflation goal; (3) an information-inclusive strategy, with a reduced role for intermediate targets such as money growth; (4) increased transparency of the monetary policy strategy through communication with the public and the markets about the plans and objectives of monetary policymakers; and (5) increased accountability of the central bank for attaining its inflation objectives.

Inflation targeting has several important advantages. In contrast to exchange-rate targeting, but like monetary targeting, inflation targeting enables monetary policy to focus on domestic considerations and to respond to shocks to the domestic economy. Inflation targeting also has the advantage that velocity shocks are largely irrelevant because the monetary policy strategy no longer relies on a stable money–inflation relationship. Indeed, an inflation target allows the monetary authorities to use all available information, and not just one variable, to determine the best settings for monetary policy.

Inflation targeting, like exchange-rate targeting, also has the key advantage that it is readily understood by the public and is thus highly transparent. Monetary targets are less likely to be easily understood by the public than inflation targets, and if the relationship between monetary aggregates and the inflation goal variable is subject to unpredictable shifts, as has occurred in many countries including a long-standing monetary targeter such as Switzerland, then monetary targets lose their transparency because they are no longer able to accurately signal the stance of monetary policy.

Because an explicit numerical inflation target increases the accountability of the central bank, inflation targeting also has the potential to reduce the likelihood that the central bank will fall into the time-inconsistency trap in which it tries to expand output and employment by pursuing overly expansionary monetary policy. But since time-inconsistency is more likely to come from political pressures on the central bank to engage in overly expansionary monetary policy, a key advantage of inflation targeting is that it can help focus the political debate on what a central bank can do in the long run—that is, control inflation—rather than what it cannot do—raise economic growth and the number of jobs permanently through expansionary monetary policy. Thus inflation targeting has the potential to reduce political pressures on the central bank to pursue inflationary monetary policy and thereby reduce the likelihood of time-inconsistent policymaking.

Despite the rhetoric about pursuing "price stability," in practice all the inflation-targeting countries have chosen to target the inflation rate rather than the level of prices per se. In addition, all the inflation targeters have chosen midpoints for their inflation target to be substantially above zero, and above reasonable estimates of possible upward measurement bias in the inflation rates calculated from consumer price indices. For example, currently New Zealand has the lowest midpoint for an inflation target, 1.5%, while Canada and Sweden set the midpoint of their inflation target at 2%; the United Kingdom, Australia and Spain currently have their midpoints at 2.5%, while Israel is at 8.5%. It is important to note that even Germany, considered to be one of the most resolute opponents of inflation in the world, sets its long-run inflation goal at 2% for many years (changed to 1.5 to 2% in December 1996), right in the middle of the pack for inflation targeters.

The decision by inflation targeters (and hybrid targeters like Germany) to choose inflation targets well above zero and not price level targets reflects monetary policy-makers' concerns that too low inflation, or particularly low inflation, can have substantial negative effects on real economic activity. There are particularly valid reasons for fearing deflation, including the possibility that it might promote financial instability and precipitate a severe economic contraction (see Mishkin, 1991, 1996). Indeed, deflation has been associated with deep recessions or even depressions, as in the 1930s, and the recent deflation in Japan has been one factor that has weakened the financial system and the economy. Targeting inflation rates of above zero makes periods of deflation less likely. The evidence on inflation expectations from surveys and interest rate levels (Almeida and Goodhart, 1998; Bernanke et al., 1999) suggest that maintaining a target for inflation above zero (but not too far above) for an extended period does not lead to instability in inflation expectations or to a decline in the central bank's credibility.

Another key feature of inflation-targeting regimes is that they do not ignore traditional stabilization goals. Central bankers responsible in inflation-targeting countries continue to express their concern about fluctuations in output and employment, and the ability to accommodate short-run stabilization goals to some degree is built into all inflation-targeting regimes. All inflation-targeting countries have been willing to take a gradualist approach to disinflation in order to minimize output declines by lowering medium-term inflation targets towards the long-run goal slowly over time.

In addition, many inflation targeters, particularly the Bank of Canada, have emphasized that the floor of the target range should be emphasized every bit as much as the ceiling, thus helping to stabilize the real economy when there are negative aggregate demand shocks. Indeed, inflation targets can increase the flexibility of the central bank to respond to declines in aggregate spending, because declines in aggregate demand that cause the inflation rate to fall below the floor of the target range will automatically stimulate the central bank to loosen monetary policy without fearing that its action will trigger a rise in inflation expectations.

Another element of flexibility in inflation-targeting regimes is that deviations from inflation targets are routinely allowed in response to supply shocks. First, the price index on which the official inflation targets are based is often defined to exclude or moderate the effects of "supply shocks"; for example, the officially targeted price index may exclude some combination of food and energy prices, indirect tax changes, terms-of-trade shocks, and the direct effects of interest rate changes on the index (for example, through imputed rental costs). Second, following (or in anticipation of) a supply shock, such as a rise in the value-added tax, the normal procedure is for the central bank first to deviate from its planned policies as needed and then to explain the reasons for its action to the public. New Zealand, on the other hand, has an explicit escape clause in its targeting regime which the central bank uses to justify such actions, although it has also permitted target deviations on a more ad hoc basis.

Inflation-targeting regimes also put great stress on making policy transparent—policy that is clear, simple, and understandable—and on regular communication with the public. The central banks have frequent communications with the government, some mandated by law and some in response to informal inquiries, and their officials take every opportunity to make public speeches on their monetary policy strategy. These channels are also commonly used in countries that have not adopted inflation targeting, Germany and the United States being prominent examples, but inflation-targeting central banks have taken public outreach a step further: not only have they engaged in extended public information campaigns, even engaging in the distribution of glossy brochures, but they have engaged in publication of *Inflation Report* type documents (originated by the Bank of England).

The publication of *Inflation Reports* is particularly noteworthy because these documents depart from the usual, dull-looking, formal reports of central banks to take on the best elements of textbook writing (fancy graphics, use of boxes) in order to better communicate with the public. An excellent description of the shift in emphasis in these reports is reflected in the following quote from the Bank of Canada.

The new *Monetary Policy Report* will be designed to bring increased transparency and accountability to monetary policy. It will measure our performance in terms of the Bank's targets for controlling inflation and will examine how current economic circumstances and monetary conditions in Canada are likely to affect future inflation (Bank of Canada, 1995, p. 7).

The above channels of communication are used by central banks in inflation-targeting countries to explain the following to the general public, financial market participants and the politicians: (1) the goals and limitations of monetary policy, including the rationale for inflation targets; (2) the numerical values of the inflation targets and how they were determined, (3) how the inflation targets are to be achieved, given current economic conditions; and (4) reasons for any deviations from targets. These communication efforts have improved private-sector planning by reducing uncertainty about monetary policy, interest rates and inflation; they have promoted public debate of monetary policy, in part by educating the public about what a central bank can and cannot achieve; and they have helped clarify the responsibilities of the central bank and of politicians in the conduct of monetary policy.

Another key feature of inflation-targeting regimes is the tendency toward increased accountability of the central bank. Indeed, transparency and communication go hand in hand with increased accountability. The strongest case of accountability of a central bank in an inflation-targeting regime is in New Zealand, where the government has the right to dismiss the Reserve Bank's governor if the inflation targets are breached, even for one quarter. In other inflation-targeting countries, the central bank's accountability is less formalized. Nevertheless, the transparency of policy associated with inflation targeting has tended to make the central bank highly accountable to both the public and the government. Sustained success in the conduct of monetary policy as measured against a pre-announced and well-defined inflation target can be instrumental in building public support for a central bank's independence and for its policies. This building of public support and accountability occurs even in the absence of a rigidly defined and legalistic standard of performance evaluation and punishment.

Two remarkable examples illustrate the benefits of transparency and accountability in the inflation-targeting framework. The first occurred in Canada in 1996, when the president of the Canadian Economic Association made a speech criticizing the Bank of Canada for pursuing monetary policy that he claimed was too contractionary. His speech sparked off a widespread public debate. In countries not pursuing inflation targeting, such debates often degenerate into calls for the immediate expansion of monetary policy with little reference to the long-run consequences of such a policy change. In this case, however, the very existence of inflation targeting channeled the debate into a substantive discussion over what should be the appropriate target for inflation, with both the Bank and its critics obliged to make explicit their assumptions and estimates of the costs and benefits of different levels of inflation. Indeed, the debate and the Bank of Canada's record and responsiveness led to increased support for the Bank of Canada, with the result that criticism of the Bank and its conduct of monetary policy was not a major issue in the 1997 elections as it had been before the 1993 elections.

The second example occurred upon the granting of operational independence to the Bank of England on 6 May 1997. Prior to that date, it was the government, as represented by the Chancellor of the Exchequer (equivalent to the finance minister or the secretary of the treasury), that controlled the decision to set monetary policy instruments, while the Bank of England was relegated to acting as the government's counterinflationary conscience. On May 6, the new Chancellor of the Exchequer, Gordon Brown, announced that the Bank of England would henceforth have the responsibility for setting both the base interest rate and short-term exchange-rate interventions. Two factors were cited by Chancellor Brown that justify the government's decision: first was the Bank's successful performance over time as measured against an announced clear target; second was the increased accountability that an independent central bank is exposed to under an inflation-targeting framework, making the Bank more responsive to political oversight. The granting of operational independence to the Bank of England occurred because it would now be operating under a monetary policy regime that ensures that monetary policy goals cannot diverge from the interests of society for extended periods of time, yet monetary policy can be insulated from short-run political considerations. An important benefit of an inflation-targeting regime is therefore that it makes it more palatable to have an independent central bank which focuses on long-run objectives, but which is consistent with a democratic society because it is accountable.

The performance of inflation-targeting regimes has been quite good. Inflation-targeting countries seem to have significantly reduced both the rate of inflation and inflation expectations beyond that which would likely have occurred in the absence of inflation targets. Furthermore, once inflation is down, it has stayed down; following disinflations, the inflation rate in targeting countries has not bounced back up during subsequent cyclical expansions of the economy.

Also inflation targeting seems to ameliorate the effects of inflationary shocks. For example, shortly after adopting inflation targets in February 1991, the Bank of Canada was faced with a new goods and services tax (GST)—an indirect tax similar to a value-added tax—an adverse supply shock that in earlier periods might have led to a ratcheting up in inflation. Instead the tax increase led to only a one-time increase in the price level; it did not generate second- and third-round rises in wages in prices that would lead to a persistent rise in the inflation rate. Another example is the experience of the United Kingdom and Sweden following their departures from the ERM exchange-rate pegs in 1992. In both cases, devaluation would normally have stimulated inflation because of the direct effects on higher export and import prices and the subsequent effects on wage demands and price-setting behavior. Again it seems reasonable to attribute the lack of inflationary response in these episodes to adoption of inflation targeting, which short-circuited the second- and later-round effects and helped to focus public attention on the temporary nature of the devaluation shocks. Indeed, one reason why inflation targets were adopted in both countries was to achieve exactly this result.

Although inflation targeting does appear to be successful in moderating and controlling inflation, it is not without potential problems. In contrast to exchange-rate and monetary targeting, inflation is not easily controlled by the monetary authorities. This can be a particularly severe problem for an emerging market country that is trying to bring down inflation from a previously high level and so is more likely to experience large inflation forecast errors. This suggests that hard targets from inflation might be worth phasing in only after there has been some successful disinflation. This is exactly the strategy followed by Chile (see Morande and Schmidt-Hebbel, 1997) which adopted a weak form of inflation targeting in September 1990. Initially, inflation targets were announced and interpreted as official inflation projections, rather than as hard targets. However, over time as inflation fell, this procedure was changed and inflation targets came to be viewed by the central bank and the markets as hard targets. Waiting to harden targets until after some success has already been achieved on the inflation front, is also consistent with what inflation-targeting industrialized countries have done: in every case, inflation targeting was not implemented until after substantial disinflation has previously been achieved (see Mishkin and Posen, 1997; Bernanke et al., 1999).

Another potential problem with inflation targeting is that, because of the long lags of monetary policy, inflation outcomes are revealed only after a substantial lag; thus inflation targeting does not provide immediate signals to both the public and the markets about the stance of monetary policy. However, we have seen that exchange-rate targets remove the ability of the foreign exchange market to signal that overly expansionary monetary policies might be in place, while the signals provided by monetary aggregates are unlikely to be very strong because of the instability of the relationship between money and inflation.

It is also important to recognize that the likely effects of inflation targeting on the real side of the economy are more ambiguous. Economic theorizing often suggests that a commitment by a central bank to reduce and control inflation should improve its credibility and thereby reduce both inflation expectations and the output losses associated with disinflation. Experience and econometric evidence (e.g., see Almeida and Goodhart, 1998; Bernanke et al., 1999) does not support this prediction, however. Inflation expectations do not immediately adjust downward following the adoption of inflation targeting. Furthermore, there appears to be little if any reduction in the output loss associated with disinflation, the sacrifice ratio, among countries adopting inflation targeting.

A common concern raised about inflation targeting is that it will lead to low and unstable growth in output and employment. Although inflation reduction is associated with below-normal output during disinflationary phases in inflation-targeting regimes, once low inflation levels have been achieved, output and employment return to levels at least as high as they were previously. A conservative conclusion is that once low inflation is achieved, inflation targeting is not harmful to the real economy. Given the strong economic growth after disinflation was achieved in many countries that have adopted inflation targets, New Zealand being one outstanding example, a case can even be made that inflation targeting promotes real economic growth in addition to controlling inflation.[3]

Some economists, such as Friedman and Kuttner (1996), have criticized inflation targeting because they believe that it imposes a rigid rule on monetary policymakers that does not allow them enough discretion to respond to unforeseen circumstances. This criticism is one that has featured prominently in the rules-versus-discretion debate. For example, policymakers in countries that adopted monetary targeting did not foresee the breakdown of the relationship between these aggregates and goal variables such as nominal spending or inflation. With rigid adherence to a monetary rule, the breakdown in their relationship could have been disastrous. However, the interpretation of inflation targeting as a rule is incorrect and stems from a confusion that has been created by the rules-versus-discretion debate. In my view, the traditional dichotomy between rules and discretion can be highly misleading. Useful policy strategies exist that are "rule-like" in that they involve forward-looking behavior which constrains policymakers from systematically engaging in policies with undesirable long-run consequences, thereby avoiding the time-inconsistency problem. These policies would best be described as "constrained discretion."

Indeed, inflation targeting can be described exactly in this way. As emphasized above, inflation targeting as actually practiced is very far from a rigid rule. First, inflation targeting does not provide simple and mechanical instructions as to how the central bank should conduct monetary policy. Rather, inflation targeting requires that the central bank use all available information to determine what are the appropriate policy actions to achieve the inflation target. Unlike simple policy rules, inflation targeting never requires the central bank to ignore information and focus solely on one key variable. Second, inflation targeting as practiced contains a substantial degree of policy discretion. As we have seen, inflation targets have been modified depending on economic circumstances. Furthermore, central banks under inflation-targeting regimes have left themselves considerable scope to respond to output growth and fluctuations through several devices.

However, despite its flexibility, inflation targeting is not an exercise in policy discretion as subject to the time-inconsistency problem. The strategy of hitting an inflation target, by its very nature, forces policymakers to be forward looking rather than narrowly focused on current economic conditions. Further, through its transparency, an inflation-targeting regime increases the central bank's accountability, which constrains discretion so that the time-inconsistency problem is ameliorated.

10.6 Monetary Policy with an Implicit but Not an Explicit Nominal Anchor

Several countries in recent years, most notably the United States, have achieved excellent macroeconomic performance (including low and stable inflation) without using an explicit nominal anchor such as a target for the exchange rate, a monetary aggregate, or inflation. Although in the US case, no explicit strategy has been articulated, a coherent strategy for the conduct of monetary policy exists nonetheless. This strategy involves an implicit, but not an explicit nominal anchor in the form of an overriding concern by the Federal Reserve to control inflation in the long run. In addition it involves forward-looking behavior in which there is careful monitoring for signs of future inflation, coupled with periodic "preemptive strikes" by monetary policy against the threat of inflation.

The presence of long lags means that monetary policy cannot wait until inflation has already reared its ugly head before responding. If the central bank waited until overt signs of inflation appeared, it would already be too late to maintain stable prices, at least not without a severe tightening of policy: inflation expectations would already be embedded in the wage- and price-setting process, creating an inflation momentum that will be hard to halt. Indeed, inflation becomes much harder to control once it has been allowed to gather momentum because higher inflation expectations become ingrained in various types of contracts and pricing agreements.

In order to prevent inflation from getting started, monetary policy therefore needs to be forward-looking and preemptive: that is, depending on the lags from monetary policy to inflation, monetary policy needs to act well before inflationary pressures appear in the economy. For example, if it takes roughly two years for monetary policy to have a significant impact on inflation, then, even if inflation is quiescent currently and yet, with an unchanged stance of monetary policy, policymakers see inflation rising over the next two years, actions need to be taken today to tighten monetary policy to prevent the inflationary surge.

This preemptive monetary policy strategy is clearly also a feature of inflation-targeting regimes because monetary policy instruments are adjusted to take account of the long lags in their effects in order to hit future inflation targets. However, the policy regime in the United States, which does not have a nominal anchor and so might best be described as a "just do it" policy regime, differs from inflation targeting in that it does not officially have a nominal anchor and is much less transparent in its monetary policy strategy.

The main argument for the "just do it" strategy is simply its demonstrated success. The Federal Reserve has been able to bring down inflation in the United States from double digit levels in 1980 to around the 3% level by the end of 1991; since then, inflation has been stable at about that level or a bit below it. The Fed conducted a successful preemptive strike against inflation from February 1994 until early 1995, when in several steps it raised the federal funds rate from 3% to 6% even though inflation was not increasing during this period. The subsequent lengthy expansion has brought unemployment down below 5%, a level not seen since the 1960s, and despite the business expansion, CPI inflation actually has even fallen to a level below 2%. In addition, the overall growth rate of the US has continued to remain strong. Indeed, the performance of the US economy has become the envy of the industrialized world in the 1990s.

Given the success of the "just do it" strategy, a natural question to ask is why countries such as the United States should consider other monetary policy strategies which would change something that has already worked well, especially given the inability to know what types of challenges will confront monetary policy in the future: In other words, "If it ain't broke, why fix it?" The answer is that the "just do it" strategy has some disadvantages that may cause it to work less well in the future.

An important disadvantage of the "just do it" strategy is a lack of transparency. The constant guessing game about the Fed's intentions created by its close-mouthed approach creates unnecessary volatility in financial markets and arouses uncertainty among producers and the general public about the future course of inflation and output as well. Furthermore, the opacity of its policymaking is hardly conducive to making the Federal Reserve accountable to Congress and the general public, because there are no predetermined criteria for judging its performance. As a result, the central bank is more susceptible to the time-inconsistency problem, whereby it may pursue short-term objectives at the expense of long-term ones.

The lack of an explicit nominal anchor is also a potential problem for the "just do it" strategy: For example, it may be that the Fed risks greater exposure than is necessary to "inflation scares"—the spontaneous increases in inflation fears described by Goodfriend (1993) that can become self-justifying if accommodated by the Fed. In addition, this strategy may make it harder for the Fed to contain the medium-term effects of a supply shock because the absence of a nominal anchor makes inflation expectations more susceptible to rise when this occurs.

Probably the most serious problem with the "just do it" approach is strong dependence on the preferences, skills, and trustworthiness of the individuals in charge of the central bank. In the United States, Federal Reserve Chairman Alan Greenspan and other Federal Reserve officials have emphasized forward-looking policies and inflation control, with great success so far. The Fed's prestige and credibility with the public have risen accordingly. But the Fed's leadership will eventually change, and there is no guarantee that the new team will be committed to the same approach. Nor is there any guarantee that the relatively good working relationship now existing between the Fed and the executive branches will continue. In a different economic or political environment, the Fed might face strong pressure to engage in over expansionary policies, raising the possibility that time-inconsistency may become a more serious problem. In the past, after a successful period of low inflation, the Federal Reserve has reverted to inflationary monetary policy—the 1970s are one example—and without an explicit nominal anchor, this could certainly happen again in the future.

The political problem with the US regime in which there is no explicit nominal anchor is illustrated by events during the spring of 1997. At that time, following several previous reductions of the federal funds rate, the Federal Reserve reversed its policy and hiked the target for the funds rate by 25 basis points (one-quarter of a percentage point). Although that rise was quite modest, particularly given the strong growth of the US economy and the tight labor market at the time, it provoked a storm of criticism, in Congress and elsewhere. Yet at about the same time, increases in interest rates engineered by the Bank of England, an established inflation targeter, were received quite calmly by the British public. Because of inflation targeting, it is plausible that the British public had a better understanding of the long-run objectives being pursued by the monetary authorities, and hence of the reason for their policy action, than the US public. The absence of an explicit nominal anchor and the accompanying transparency may thus make it harder for the Federal Reserve to contain inflation in the future if undesirable shocks begin to propel inflation upward.

10.7   An Overall Assessment of the Different Monetary Regimes

In examining international experiences with different monetary policy regimes, we have looked at four basic types of frameworks: (1) exchange-rate targeting, (2) monetary targeting, (3) inflation targeting, and (4) monetary policy with an implicit but not an explicit nominal anchor. How do these different monetary policy regimes stack up against each other? When might one monetary regime be more effective in producing desirable economic outcomes than another?

Our discussion of exchange-rate targeting suggests that as a strategy for stabilizing the economy and controlling inflation, the disadvantages typically outweigh the advantages, particularly when exchange-rate targets promote financial instability as in emerging market countries. However, if a country does not have political, economic and cultural institutions that allow them to conduct their own monetary policy successfully, then a transparent form of exchange-rate targeting, such as a currency board, might have enough benefits to outweigh the potential costs.[4]

The second monetary policy regime discussed here has worked well in a country like Germany and is a key reason why the Governing Council of the European Central Bank (ECB) announced in October 1998, that a component of its monetary policy strategy is "a prominent role for money with a reference value for the growth of a monetary aggregate." However, our earlier discussion suggests several reasons why monetary targeting by the ECB may not be a very good idea. First, monetary aggregates are not a particularly useful guide for monetary policy unless the relationship between monetary aggregates and inflation is strong and reliable. A stable relationship between money and inflation is, in fact, quite unlikely to exist in the fledgling EMU, since this relationship has not been particularly reliable in the past in most of the constituent countries of the Union, including even Germany (Estrella and Mishkin, 1996). The Bundesbank has not been unaware of the instability of the money–inflation relationship, which helps to explain why it has been willing to tolerate misses of its money-growth targets in half of the years for which the targets have been set. Furthermore, the creation of the European Monetary Union and the European System of Central Banks at the start of Stage Three, together with ongoing financial deregulation and innovation, will cause major change in the operation of the European financial system in coming years. Those changes will affect money and asset demands in unpredictable ways, making it likely that the relationship between monetary aggregates and inflation in the Union as a whole will be even more unstable than it has been in the individual member countries.

The second objection to the adoption of monetary targeting by the European Monetary Union is that monetary targets are likely to prove a less effective vehicle of communication for the EMU than they have for Germany and Switzerland. Despite frequent target misses, both the Bundesbank and the Swiss National Bank are held in such high regard that they lose little by using the announcement of monetary targets as the framework in which they explain their policy strategy, despite the fact that their actual inflation targeting leads them to miss their stated monetary targets so frequently. The European Central Bank, which will be starting from scratch, will not at the outset command the credibility and anti-inflation reputation of the Bundesbank and the Swiss National Bank, which are based primarily on strong political support for low inflation in those two countries and on the demonstrated success of the two central banks in fighting inflation. Missing announced targets for money growth may thus be far more problematic for the European Central Bank than it was for the Bundesbank and the Swiss National Bank, because the public will be less willing to accept the European Central Bank's explanations for these misses and declarations of anti-inflationary determination at face value. Furthermore, in many European countries the public will have no experience with a monetary policy focused on monetary aggregates, and thus may find the targets harder to understand and less relevant to their daily lives than targets for inflation.

Inflation targeting, which is the newest of the monetary regimes studied here, has been gaining popularity in recent years and has several major strengths. It enables monetary policy to focus on domestic considerations as does monetary targeting, but is not subject to velocity shock problems; it is readily understood and highly transparent; it allows flexibility and discretion in the conduct of monetary policy, but because it increases the accountability of the central bank it constrains discretion so that the time-inconsistency problem is ameliorated; and it helps shift the public debate to focus on what monetary policy can do in the long run and thus helps reduce political pressure to engage in time-inconsistent policies. The performance of inflation-targeting countries has been very good up to now, enabling them to do quite well in hitting their targets and maintain low inflation rates, something they have not always been able to do in the past, while it seems to improve the climate for economic growth after the initial disinflation phase is past. However, inflation targeting is no panacea: it does not seem to enable countries to eliminate inflation from their systems without cost, and anti-inflation credibility is not achieved immediately upon the adoption of an inflation target. The evidence seems to suggest that the only way for an inflation-targeting central bank to earn credibility is the hard way: it has to earn it.

In addition to "reference values" for monetary aggregates, the announced strategy of the European Central Bank also includes a numerically explicit inflation goal of a year-on-year increase of below 2%. Because the signals from monetary aggregates are even more likely to be weak when the European Monetary Union comes into existence and a key element of any successful targeting strategy is transparency and effective communication with the public, the European Central Bank is likely to be better served by downgrading the attention to monetary aggregates and putting inflation targets at the forefront instead.

But what about the need of the European Central Bank to inherit the mantle of the Bundesbank, a monetary targeter of long standing? Doesn't this suggest that the European Central Bank should adopt monetary targeting in order to provide continuity with the policies of the Bundesbank, thereby inheriting the Bundesbank's credibility? There are indeed benefits for the European Central Bank to be seen as following in the footsteps of the Bundesbank. However, we have seen that the Bundesbank's policy framework is actually quite close to inflation targeting. Both frameworks have many characteristics in common, including: a strong commitment to price stability; the specification of numerical inflation goals (both in the medium term and the long term); accountability of the central bank for meeting the goals; transparency of policy and effective communication with the public; a forward-looking approach that takes into account the lags inherent in monetary policy; and flexibility to respond to short-run economic developments. In short, in practice an inflation-targeting European Central Bank would function very much like the monetary targeting Bundesbank, and the public could be actively educated to understand this basic continuity. The differences that exist—notably, the deemphasis on money growth as the key piece of information for forecasting inflation—favor the inflation-targeting approach.

The final monetary regime discussed in this chapter is the "just do it" approach followed by the United States in which there is an implicit, but not an explicit nominal anchor. The key argument for this approach is that it has worked in the past and so "if it ain't broke, why fix it?" However, the "just do it" strategy suffers from a lack of transparency and accountability of the central bank, which not only may weaken the support for anti-inflationary monetary policy but also is not fully consistent with democratic principles (see Mishkin, 1999). Also replacement of the "just do it" with an inflation-targeting approach would help to depersonalize US monetary policy, which would strengthen the central bank's commitment to the long-run goal of price stability and make the achievement of low inflation less dependent on the competence or convictions of a few individuals.

It seems likely that US monetary policy performance in the future could be improved by the adoption of inflation targeting. Inflation targeting is not too far from the current policymaking philosophy at the Federal Reserve, which has stressed the importance of price stability as the overriding, long-run goal of monetary policy. Also a move to inflation targeting is consistent with recent steps by the Fed to increase the transparency of monetary policy, such as shortening the time before the minutes of the FOMC meeting are released and the practice of announcing the FOMC's decision about whether to change the target for the federal funds rates immediately after the conclusion of the FOMC meeting. The current conditions for adoption of inflation targeting are propitious: inflation has been low and stable for over five years; the public sees the benefit of a low inflation environment that has helped produce a balanced, long-lived economic expansion; and the success of inflation targeting regimes in other industrialized countries is becoming increasingly apparent. Moving to a more explicit nominal anchor, as with an inflation targeting regime, can help lock in the low and stable inflation rate that the United States is currently experiencing, promoting a more stable and successful monetary policy regime in the future.

10.8   Conclusions

This overview of the international experiences with different monetary policy regimes suggests that transparency and accountability are crucial to constraining discretionary monetary policy so that it produces desirable long-run outcomes. Because the devil is in the details in achieving transparency and accountability, what strategy will work best in a country depends on its political, cultural and economic institutions and its past history. The discussion here of the different international experiences with monetary policy strategies will hopefully help provide guidance for policymakers in particular countries as to which monetary policy strategy is more likely to produce low inflation, a stable economic environment, and a healthy economy.

Notes

Prepared for Sveriges Riksbank-IIES Conference on Monetary Policy Rules, Stockholm, Sweden, June 12–13, 1998. I thank for their helpful comments my discussant, Charles Goodhart, an anonymous referee, Robert King and my co-authors for our book, *Inflation Targeting: Lessons from the International Experience* (Princeton University Press, 1999) on which a substantial part of the discussion in this chapter is based, Ben Bernanke, Thomas Laubach, and Adam Posen. Because of space constraints, many references in this chapter have been deleted, but they can be found in a longer version of this chapter (Mishkin, 1998b). Any views expressed in this chapter are those of the author only and not those of Columbia University or the National Bureau of Economic Research.

1. Indeed, a devaluation in developed countries can actually stimulate economic activity because it makes the country's goods more competitive internationally, thereby increasing its net exports and hence aggregate demand. Indeed, this was exactly the experience of the United Kingdom after the September 1992 foreign-exchange crisis when it was forced to devalue its currency. Its economic performance after the devaluation was substantially better than that of countries which remained in the ERM after 1992.

2. For a more extensive discussion of the procedures used in German monetary targeting, see Bernanke et al. (1999) and the references therein.

3. Some economists have proposed that central banks should target the growth rate of nominal GDP rather than inflation because of concerns that targeting inflation might produce excessive output fluctuations. Because nominal GDP targeting has up to now not been adopted anywhere in the world, I will discuss it only briefly here. Relative to inflation, nominal GDP growth has the advantage that it does put some weight on output as well as prices in the policymaking process. With a nominal GDP target, a decline in projected real output growth would automatically imply an increase in the central bank's inflation target, which would tend to be stabilizing because it would automatically lead to an easier monetary policy.

Nominal GDP targeting is close in spirit to inflation targeting and might provide a reasonable alternative. The most important reason why I believe that inflation targeting has advantages over nominal GDP targeting (other reasons are outlined in Mishkin (1998b)) is that a nominal GDP target forces the central bank or the government to announce a number for potential GDP growth. Such an announcement is highly problematic because estimates of potential GDP growth are far from precise and change over time. Announcing a specific number for potential GDP growth may thus indicate a certainty that policymakers may not have and may also cause the public to mistakenly believe that this estimate is actually a fixed target for potential GDP growth. Announcing a potential GDP growth number is likely to be political dynamite because it opens policymakers to the criticism that they are willing to settle for growth rates that the public many consider to be too low. Indeed, a nominal GDP target may lead to an accusation that the central bank or the targeting regime is anti-growth, when the opposite is true because a low inflation rate is a means to promote a healthy economy with high growth. In addition, if the estimate for potential GDP growth is too high and becomes embedded in the public mind as a target, it can lead to a positive inflation bias. Also, as argued above, inflation targeting as it is actually practiced allows considerable flexibility for policy in the short run. Thus it is doubtful that, in practice, nominal GDP targeting would be more effective than inflation targeting in achieving short-run stabilization, and elements of monetary policy tactics based on nominal GDP targeting could easily be built into an inflation-targeting regime.

4. Note that countries might find it useful to target exchange rates for reasons which have little to do with the conduct of monetary policy, such as encouraging integration of the domestic economy with its neighbors. Clearly this is the rationale for long-standing pegging of the exchange rate to the deutsche mark by countries such as Austria and the Netherlands, and the more recent exchange-rate pegs in the run-up to the European Monetary Union. (However, if economic integration is the goal, it is more likely to be accomplished by currency union rather than an exchange-rate peg.)

References

Almeida, A., Charles, A. E., Goodhart, C. A. E. 1998. Does the adoption of inflation targets affect central bank behaviour? Unpublished paper, London School of Economics, January.

Bank of Canada, 1995. *Monetary Policy Report.*

Bernanke, B. S. 1983. Non-monetary effects of the financial crisis in the propagation of the Great Depression. *American Economic Review* 73, 257–276.

Bernanke, B. S., Laubach, T., Mishkin, F. S., Posen, A. S. 1999. *Inflation Targeting: Lessons from the International Experience*. Princeton University Press, Princeton, NJ.

Bernanke, B. S., Mishkin, F. S. 1992. Central Bank behavior and the strategy of monetary policy: Observations from six industrialized countries. In: Blanchard, O., Fischer, S. (Eds.), *NBER Macroeconomics Annual*. MIT Press, Cambridge, pp. 183–238.

Bernanke, B. S., Mishkin, F. S. 1997. Inflation targeting: a new framework for monetary policy? *Journal of Economic Perspectives* 11 (2) (Spring), 97–116.

Clarida, R., Gertler, M. 1997. How the Bundesbank conducts monetary policy. In: Christina, D., Romer, C. D., Romer, D. H. (Eds.), *Reducing Inflation: Motivation and Strategy*. University of Chicago Press, Chicago, pp. 363–406.

Estrella, A., Mishkin, F. S. 1997. Is there a role for monetary aggregates in the conduct of monetary policy. *Journal of Monetary Economics*, 40 (2) (October), 279–304.

Friedman, B. M., Kuttner, K. 1996. A price target for US monetary policy? Lessons from the experience with money growth targets. *Brookings Papers on Economic Activity* 1, 77–125.

Goodfriend, M. 1993. Interest rate policy and the inflation scare problem: 1979–1992. *Federal Reserve Bank of Richmond Economic Quarterly* 79 (1) (Winter), 1–24.

Issing, O. 1996. Is monetary targeting in Germany still adequate? In: Siebert, H. (Ed.), *Monetary Policy in an Integrated World Economy: Symposium*. Tübingen, Mohr, pp. 117–130.

McCallum, B. T. 1995. Two fallacies concerning central bank independence. *American Economic Review* 85 (2) (May), 207–211.

Mishkin, F. S. 1991. Asymmetric information and financial crises: a historical perspective. In: Hubbard, G. R. (Ed.), *Financial Markets and Financial Crises*. University of Chicago Press, Chicago, pp. 69–108.

Mishkin, F. S. 1996. Understanding financial crises: a developing country perspective. In: Brunod, M., Pleskovic, B. (Eds.), *Annual World Bank Conference on Development Economics*. World Bank, Washington D.C., pp. 29–62.

Mishkin, F. S. 1998a. Exchange-rate pegging in emerging-market countries? *International Finance* 1 (1) (October), 81–101.

Mishkin, F. S. 1998b. International experiences with different monetary policy regimes. Seminar Paper No. 98, Institute for International Economic Studies, Stockholm University.

Mishkin, F. S. 1999. The role of a central bank in a democratic society. In: Mario Blejer, M., Skreb, M. (Eds.), *Major Issues in Central Banking, Monetary Policies, and the Implications for Transition Economies*. Kluwer Academic Publishers: Norwell, Mass., pp. 31–53.

Mishkin, F. S., Posen, A. 1997. Inflation targeting: lessons from four countries. Federal Reserve Bank of New York, *Economic Policy Review* 3 (August), 79–110.

Morande, F., Schmidt-Hebbel, R. 1997. Inflation targets and indexation in Chile. Unpublished paper, Central Bank of Chile, August.

Obstfeld, M., Rogoff, R. 1995. The mirage of fixed exchange rates. *Journal of Economic Perspectives* 9 (4) (Fall), 73–96.

Rich, G. 1997. Monetary targets as a policy rule: lessons from the Swiss experience. *Journal of Monetary Economics* 39 (1) (June), 113–141.

11 Why the Federal Reserve Should Adopt Inflation Targeting

Frederic S. Mishkin

11.1 Introduction

Under Alan Greenspan, the Federal Reserve has achieved extraordinary economic performance: inflation has become low and stable, while over the last twenty years the economy has experienced only two relatively mild recessions in 1990–91 and 2001. Although the Federal Reserve has not articulated an explicit strategy, a coherent strategy for the conduct of monetary policy exists nonetheless. This strategy involves an implicit, but not an explicit nominal anchor in the form of an overriding concern by the Federal Reserve to control inflation in the long run. In addition, it involves forward-looking behaviour in which there is careful monitoring for signs of future inflation, using a wide range of information, coupled with periodic "pre-emptive strikes" by monetary policy against the threat of inflation or deflation.

Because of the long lags from monetary policy to aggregate economic activity and inflation, monetary policy needs to be forward-looking and pre-emptive: that is, depending on the lags from monetary policy to inflation, monetary policy needs to act well before inflationary or deflationary pressures appear in the economy. For example, suppose it takes approximately two years for monetary policy to have a significant impact on inflation. In this case, even if inflation is currently low but policy makers believe inflation will rise over the next two years, they must now tighten monetary policy to prevent the inflationary surge. This is exactly what the Federal Reserve has done. For example, the Federal Reserve raised the federal funds rate from 3% to 6% from February 1994 to February 1995 before a rise in inflation got a toehold. As a result, inflation not only did not rise, but fell slightly. In January 2001, the Federal Reserve reversed course extremely rapidly, cutting the federal funds rate by 100 basis points (1 percentage point) in January even before the business cycle peak in March, and then proceeded to cut the Federal Reserve funds rate by another 350 basis points before the end of November when the NBER declared that a recession had indeed occurred. The recession then turned out to be very mild, especially given the adverse shocks of the September 11 terrorist attacks and the negative impacts of the Enron and other corporate scandals on the credit markets.

The main argument for the Federal Reserve's pre-emptive monetary policy strategy, which I like to call the "just do it" approach, is simply its demonstrated success. In addition, the approach is flexible and appropriately makes use of all available information in setting policy instruments. A natural question to ask then is why the Federal Reserve should consider any other monetary policy strategy. In other words, "If it ain't broke, why fix it?" The answer is that the "just do it" strategy has some disadvantages that may cause it to work less well in the future, particularly when Alan Greenspan steps down from the Federal Reserve, something that will almost surely occur by the time his term expires in two years.

An important disadvantage of the "just do it" strategy is a lack of transparency. The constant guessing game about the Federal Reserve's goals created by its close-mouthed approach creates unnecessary volatility in financial markets and arouses uncertainty among producers and the general public. A case in point is the recent sharp swings in long-term interest rates during the late Spring and Summer of 2003. Because the market was confused about the Federal Reserve's intentions, the ten-year bond rate dropped from a level near 4% at the beginning of May to 3.2% in the middle of June and then rose over 100 basis points to 4.5% by the end of July. The Federal Reserve has been struggling recently with how to communicate its plans with regard to interest-rate policy and how it should structure its formal statement immediately after each FOMC meeting. If the markets had a clearer picture of the Federal Reserve's longer-run objectives, particularly on inflation, then they would focus less on what the Federal Reserve's next policy move would be, making it less likely that Federal Reserve policy moves or changes in its formal statement would lead to whipsawing of the market.

In addition, the opacity of its policy making is hardly conducive to making the Federal Reserve accountable to Congress and the general public: The Federal Reserve cannot be held accountable if there are no predetermined criteria for judging its performance. This lack of accountability is also inconsistent with democratic principles. There are good reasons—notably, insulation from short-term political pressures—for the central bank to have a high degree of independence, as the Federal Reserve currently does, and empirical evidence does generally support central bank independence.[1] Yet the practical economic arguments for central bank independence coexist uneasily with the presumption that government policies should be made democratically, rather than by an elite group.

The lack of an explicit nominal anchor is also a potential problem for the "just do it" strategy. For example, it may be that the Federal Reserve risks greater exposure than is necessary to "inflation scares"—the spontaneous increases in inflation fears described by Goodfriend (1993) that can become self-justifying if accommodated by the Federal Reserve. Indeed, as Goodfriend (2005) points out, even Alan Greenspan faced an inflation scare shortly after becoming the Federal Reserve Chairman.

Probably the most serious problem with the "just do it" approach is that its success is based on highly capable individuals rather than good institutions. In the USA, Federal Reserve Chairman Alan Greenspan and other Federal Reserve officials have emphasized forward-looking policies and inflation control, which have been key elements in their success. The Federal Reserve's prestige and credibility with the public have risen accordingly, with Greenspan having been given the title of "maestro" in the media (Woodward 2000). I have acknowledged elsewhere in Mishkin (2000) that the Federal Reserve currently does not suffer from having a weak nominal anchor, but the strong nominal anchor is embodied in Alan Greenspan. Unfortunately, a nominal anchor based on an individual cannot last forever. Greenspan's tenure at the Federal Reserve will come to an end soon and there might be some doubts that the new Chairman will be committed to the same approach, just as there were some doubts in the markets that Greenspan would be as serious about controlling inflation as his predecessor, Paul Volcker; see Goodfriend (2005). Nor is there any guarantee that the relatively good working relationship now existing between the Federal Reserve and the executive branch, which started with the Clinton administration, will continue. In a different economic or political environment, the Federal Reserve might face strong pressure to engage in over expansionary policies, raising the possibility that the time-inconsistency problem of Kydland and Prescott (1977) and Calvo (1978) may become more serious in the future. In the past, after a successful period of low inflation, the Federal Reserve has reverted to inflationary monetary policy— the 1970s are one example—and without an explicit nominal anchor, this could certainly happen again in the future.

11.2 Why Inflation Targeting?

Inflation targeting has the potential to avoid the above problems in the Federal Reserve's current approach. To be clear, inflation targeting involves the following five elements:

1. Public announcement of forward-looking medium-term numerical targets for inflation

2. An institutional commitment to price stability as the primary, long-run goal of monetary policy and to achievement of the inflation goal

3. An information inclusive strategy

4. Increased transparency of the monetary policy strategy through communication with the public and the markets about the plans and objectives of monetary policy makers

5. Increased accountability of the central bank for attaining its inflation objectives[2]

Inflation targeting has many of the desirable features of the current Federal Reserve approach. It is forward looking, uses all information in deciding on the setting of policy instruments and does focus on achieving long-run price stability. However, it goes beyond the current Federal Reserve approach and this provides several advantages. First, an inflation target is readily understood by the public and is thus highly transparent. Framing the discussion of monetary policy around an inflation goal makes it easier for the Federal Reserve to communicate with the public and the markets. It can help to decrease uncertainty about future monetary policy moves, thereby decreasing market volatility. It can help to focus the political debate on what a central bank can do in the long-run—that is control inflation, rather than on what it cannot do, which is permanently increase economic growth and the number of jobs through expansionary monetary policy. Thus, inflation targeting has the potential to reduce the likelihood that the central bank will fall into the time-consistency trap, trying to expand output and employment in the short-run by pursuing overly expansionary monetary policy. Indeed, inflation targeting has been able to change public debate in countries that have adopted it, with an increased focus on the long-run rather than on the short-run issue of "jobs, jobs, jobs" as in the USA; see Mishkin and Posen (1997) and Bernanke et al. (1999).

Because an explicit numerical inflation target increases the accountability of the central bank, inflation targeting is also more consistent with democratic principles. Sustained success in the conduct of monetary policy as measured against a pre-announced and well-defined inflation target can be instrumental in building public support for a central bank's independence and for its policies. The granting of operational independence to the Bank of England in 1997 illustrates this point. On May 6, 1997, the new Chancellor of the Exchequer, Gordon Brown, announced that the Bank of England would henceforth have the responsibility for setting interest rates, which previously was done by the Chancellor of the Exchequer. In the press conference, Gordon Brown explained that the inflation targeting regime justified the government's decision: the Bank had demonstrated successful performance over time as measured against an announced clear target, and was now more accountable, making it more responsive to political oversight.

11.3 Objections to Inflation Targeting?

Of course not everyone sees inflation targeting positively, as is evidenced by Ben Friedman (2004). There are several important objections to inflation targeting that require a response.

First, inflation targeting might be too inflexible, leading to higher output fluctuations. Ben Friedman has taken this position, especially in Friedman and Kuttner (1996), in which they worry that inflation targeting might be a rigid rule that would fare as badly as Milton Friedman's constant-money-growth-rate rule would have if it had been implemented. As Ben Bernanke and I have argued elsewhere (Bernanke and Mishkin 1997), this is a mischaracterization of inflation targeting which can be quite flexible and is very far from a rigid policy rule. Instead, we have argued that inflation targeting is best described as "constrained discretion."

However, the concern that inflation targeting could lead to increased output fluctuations is one that does have to be taken seriously. If a central bank solely focused on inflation control, something that Mervyn King (1996) has described as being an "inflation nutter," then it could lead to overly high output fluctuations. However, this is not the way inflation targeting is actually practised. I agree strongly with Larry Meyer (2004) that a central bank needs to adhere to a dual mandate of the type in the Federal Reserve Act that indicates that monetary policy objectives include not only price stability but also output stability. Indeed, the literature on optimal monetary policy typically specifies an objective function for monetary policy which puts a negative weight on both output as well as inflation fluctuations—see, for example, the papers in Taylor (1999)—and operating with this type of objective function is consistent with what inflation-targeting central banks have actually done (Bernanke et al. 1999). The result has been that countries that have adopted inflation targeting have not found that output fluctuations have increased.

The argument that inflation targeting might increase output fluctuations can be turned on its head. I would argue that inflation targeting can actually make it easier to reduce output fluctuations and probably has done so. First, the presence of an inflation target which provides an effective nominal anchor enables a central bank to be even more aggressive in the face of negative shocks to the economy because the central bank has less fear that these moves will blow out inflation expectations. A classic example of this happened in Australia in July 1997 when the Reserve Bank of Australia lowered interest rates immediately after the currency crisis in Thailand that brought on the East Asian crisis. Despite the prospects of a substantial depreciation of the Australian dollar, the Reserve Bank believed that the success of their inflation-targeting regime meant that inflation expectations would not rise above their targets with a monetary policy easing and thus they could ease to counter the negative demand shock arising from the deterioration in their terms of trade that was resulting from the East Asian crisis. Second, the emphasis on the floor of the inflation-target range that has become a standard feature of inflation targeting in industrialized countries makes it more likely that central banks will be aggressive in combating negative shocks, so that deflationary spirals are less likely. If the Bank of Japan had an inflation target with the appropriate emphasis on the floor of the target range, then it is very likely that they would have avoided the disastrous policies pursued under the leadership of Masuro Hayami and would have been far more expansionary. Also, they would have been far more likely to avoid the time-inconsistency problem outlined by Eggertsson (2003) in which the Bank of Japan was unable to commit to a long-run policy of expansion, thereby making temporary expansionary policy ineffective.

Critics of inflation targeting, most notably Don Kohn (2004), who is a member of the Board of Governors of the Federal Reserve, have also worried that inflation targeting may be too rigid because inflation-targeting central banks in advanced economies have often adopted a horizon for their inflation targets of two years or so, with the Bank of England being a prominent example. This can give the impression that the horizon for inflation targets is fixed, which could mean that inflation targeting will not be flexible enough. After all, models such as Svensson (1997) and Woodford (2004) tell us that optimal monetary policy will surely adjust the target horizon and path for inflation depending on the nature and persistence of shocks. This criticism is a valid one. The use of a specific horizon such as two years, which is consistent with estimates of policy lags from monetary policy actions to inflation, has not been a problem for inflation targeting in advanced economies like the UK only because inflation has not been subject to big shocks so that it has remained close to the target level. However, as Svensson (1997) demonstrates, if the inflation rate is shocked away from its long-run target, then the target horizon should be longer than the policy horizon. Although this situation has not occurred yet in advanced-economy inflation targeters, a big shock to inflation will come one day. Then for monetary policy to minimize output and inflation fluctuations optimally, the target path for inflation will have to be adjusted as it has been in Brazil recently; see Fraga et al. (2003). This valid criticism of the fixed horizon for inflation targets does not mean that inflation targeting should not be adopted by the Federal Reserve. What it does mean is that an inflation targeting regime in the USA should make it clear, even before it is necessary, that the horizon for inflation targets needs to be flexible and will vary depending on the nature and persistence of shocks.

The second serious objection to inflation targeting is raised in Ben Friedman (2004). He argues that inflation targeting will not lead to transparency because it encourages central banks to avoid discussing reduction of output fluctuations as an objective of monetary policy. I would argue that inflation targeting is not the issue here. Central bankers, whether they inflation target or not, are extremely reluctant to discuss concerns about output fluctuations. Indeed, I like to refer to the fact that central bankers care about output fluctuations but are often reluctant to talk about it as "the dirty little secret of central banking." One remarkable manifestation of this occurred in August of 1994 at the Federal Reserve Bank of Kansas City's Jackson Hole Conference, which is arguably the most prominent central bank conference that occurs on a regular basis. Alan Blinder, then the vice-chairman of the FOMC, had the temerity to mention that a short-run trade-off between output and inflation exists and that therefore monetary policy should be concerned about minimizing output as well as inflation fluctuations. Blinder was then pilloried by many central bankers and in the press, with a *Newsweek* columnist declaring that he was not qualified to be a central banker (Samuelson 1994). From an academic economist's perspective, this was quite amazing since Alan Blinder did not say anything that was inconsistent with what our models tell us. However, it does indicate the discomfort that central bankers as a group have with discussing the role of output fluctuations in the conduct of monetary policy.

Why do central bankers have difficulty with being transparent about their concerns about output fluctuations? I have touched on this issue in an earlier article (Mishkin 2002). Central bankers' interactions with the political process has shown them that, when politicians talk about the need for central banks to reduce output fluctuations, politicians do not focus on the appropriate long-run trade-off between output fluctuations and inflation fluctuations, but rather on the short-run need to create jobs. Central bankers then fear that if they agree that they should try to minimize output fluctuations as well as inflation fluctuations, politicians will use this to pressure the central bank to pursue a short-run strategy of overly expansionary policy that will lead to poor long-run outcomes. In addition, central bankers know that it is extremely difficult to measure potential output and so being forced to focus too much on output fluctuations can lead to serious policy mistakes, as it did during the Arthur Burns' years at the Federal Reserve (Orphanides 2002). The response to these problems is that central bankers engage in a "don't ask, don't tell" strategy which Ben Friedman rightfully criticizes.

I do think that Ben gets it exactly wrong when he criticizes inflation targeting for encouraging "don't ask, don't tell." To the contrary, I believe that inflation targeting can actually help to deal with the problem that Ben raises, making it easier for central bankers to be more transparent about their desire to keep output fluctuations low. Because having an inflation target makes it easier for central banks to focus on the long-run trade-off between output and inflation fluctuations, central bankers will be more comfortable indicating that a dual mandate for monetary policy is completely consistent with pursuit of price stability. Recent speeches which advocated a Federal Reserve announcement of an inflation goal by Federal Reserve governor Bernanke and former governor Meyer at the Federal Reserve Bank of St. Louis conference in October 2003 did exactly this; see Bernanke (2004) and Meyer (2004).

Second, an inflation-targeting central bank should announce that it will not try to hit its inflation target over too short a horizon because this would result in unacceptably high output losses, especially if the economy is hit by shocks that knock it substantially away from its long-run inflation goal. Inflation targeting banks have been moving in this direction: for example, the Reserve Bank of New Zealand has modified its inflation-targeting regime to lengthen the horizon over which it tries to achieve its inflation target; see Sherwin (1999), Drew and Orr (1999) and Reserve

Bank of New Zealand (2000). Inflation-targeting central banks can go even farther in this direction by indicating that they are ready to emulate what the Brazilians have done recently when they were faced with a substantial overshoot of their targets (Fraga et al. 2003). In January 2003, the Banco Central do Brasil announced that it was adjusting its targets upwards for 2003 from 4% to 8.5%. They also explained that reaching to the non-adjusted target of 4% too quickly would entail far too high a loss of output. Specifically, the announcement indicated that an attempt to achieve an inflation rate of 6.5% in 2003 would be expected to entail a decline of 1.6% of GDP, while trying to achieve the previous target of 4% would be expected to lead to an even larger decline of GDP of 7.3%.

By announcing that they would do what the Brazilians have done if a situation arose in which inflation were shocked substantially away from the long-run goal, central bankers can let the dirty little secret out of the closet that they do have an appropriate concern about output fluctuations. Yet, they will still be able to assure the public that they continue to worry about the long run and the importance of achieving price stability. In addition, as I argued above, monetary authorities can further the public's understanding that they have an appropriate concern about reducing output fluctuations by emphasizing that monetary policy needs to be just as vigilant in preventing inflation from falling too low as it is from preventing it from being too high.

11.4   Conclusion: The Federal Reserve Should Adopt Inflation Targeting

The bottom line from my commentary here is that the Federal Reserve should adopt a flexible form of inflation targeting in the near future. Although inflation targeting in the USA would probably have provided small benefits in recent years because of the superb performance of the Federal Reserve under Greenspan and the tremendous credibility that Alan Greenspan has achieved, now is not the time to be complacent. It is time to make sure that the legacy of Greenspan's Federal Reserve of low and stable inflation is maintained. Adopting an inflation target is the best way for the Federal Reserve to do this.

Notes

Any views expressed in this chapter are those of the author only and not those of Columbia University or the National Bureau of Economic Research.

1. For example, see Alesina and Summers (1993), Cukierman (1992), and Fischer (1994). However, there is some question whether causality runs from central bank independence to low inflation, or rather, whether a third factor is involved, such as the general public's preferences for low inflation that create both central bank independence and low inflation (Posen, 1995).

2. Detailed analyses of experiences with inflation targeting can be found in Leiderman and Svensson (1995), Haldane (1995), Mishkin and Posen (1997) and Bernanke et al. (1999).

References

Alesina, Alberto, and Lawrence H. Summers (1993), "Central Bank Independence and Macroeconomic Performance: Some Comparative Evidence," *Journal of Money, Credit, and Banking*, 25(2), May, 151–62.

Bernanke, Ben S. (2004), "Panel Discussion: Inflation Targeting," Federal Reserve Bank of St Louis, *Review*, July/August, 165–168.

Bernanke, Ben S., and Frederic S. Mishkin (1997), "Inflation Targeting: A New Framework for Monetary Policy?" *Journal of Economic Perspectives*, 11(2), Spring, 97–116.

Bernanke, Ben S., Thomas Laubach, Frederic S. Mishkin and Adam S. Posen (1999), *Inflation Targeting: Lessons from the International Experience*. Princeton, NJ: Princeton University Press.

Calvo, Guillermo (1978), "On the Time Consistency of Optimal Policy in a Monetary Economy," *Econometrica*, 46, 1411–28.

Cukierman, Alex (1992), *Central Bank Strategy, Credibility, and Independence: Theory and Evidence*. Cambridge: MIT Press.

Drew, A., and A. Orr (1999), "The Reserve Bank's Role in the Recent Business Cyle: Actions and Evolution," Reserve Bank of New Zealand Bulletin, 62(1).

Eggertsson, Gautti B. (2003), "How to Fight Deflation in a Liquidity Trap: Committing to Being Irresponsible," IMF Working Paper. Washington: International Monetary Fund.

Fischer, Stanley (1994), "Modern Central Banking," in Forrest Capie, Charles A. E. Goodhart, Stanley Fischer and Norbert Schnadt (eds), *The Future of Central Banking: The Tercentenary Symposium of the Bank of England*. Cambridge: Cambridge University Press, 262–308.

Fraga, Arminio, Ilan Goldfajn and Andre Minella (2003), "Inflation Targeting in Emerging Market Economies," in Mark Gertler and Kenneth Rogoff (eds), *NBER Macroeconomics Annual*. Cambridge: MIT Press.

Friedman, Benjamin (2004), "Why the Federal Reserve Should Not Adopt Inflation Targeting," *International Finance*, 7, Spring.

Friedman, Benjamin M., and Kenneth Kuttner (1996), "A Price Target for U.S. Monetary Policy? Lessons from the Experience with Money Growth Targets," *Brookings Papers on Economic Activity*, 1, 77–125.

Goodfriend, Marvin (1993), "Interest Rate Policy and the Inflation Scare Problem: 1979–1992," *Federal Reserve Bank of Richmond Economic Quarterly*, 79(1), Winter, 1–24.

Goodfriend, Marvin (2005), "Inflation Targeting in the United States," in Ben Bernanke and Michael Woodford (eds), *Inflation Targeting*. Chicago: University of Chicago Press for the NBER.

Haldane, Andrew G. (ed.), (1995), *Targeting Inflation*. London: Bank of England.

King, Mervyn (1996), "How Should Central Banks Reduce Inflation?—Conceptual Issues," in *Achieving Price Stability*, Federal Reserve Bank of Kansas City, Kansas City, MO, 53–91.

Kohn, Donald L. (2004), "Panel Discussion: Inflation Targeting," Federal Reserve Bank of St Louis, *Review*, July/August, 179–183.

Kydland, Finn, and Edward Prescott (1977), "Rules Rather than Discretion: The Inconsistency of Optimal Plans," *Journal of Political Economy*, 85(3), June, 473–92.

Leiderman, Leonardo, and Lars E. O. Svensson (1995), *Inflation Targeting*. London: Centre for Economic Policy Research.

Meyer, Laurence H. (2004), "Practical Problems and Obstacles to Inflation Targeting," Federal Reserve Bank of St Louis, *Review*, July/August, 151–160.

Mishkin, Frederic (2000), "What Should Central Banks Do?" Federal Reserve Bank of St. Louis, *Review*, 82(6), November/December, 1–13.

Mishkin, Frederic S. (2002), "The Role of Output Stabilization in the Conduct of Monetary Policy," *International Finance*, 5(2), Summer, 213–27.

Mishkin, Frederic S., and Adam S. Posen (1997), "Inflation Targeting: Lessons from Four Countries," Federal Reserve Bank of New York, *Economic Policy Review*, 3(3), August, 9–110.

Orphanides, Athanasios (2002), "Monetary Policy Rules and the Great Inflation," *American Economic Review*, 92(2), May, 115–20.

Posen, Adam S. (1995), "Declarations Are Not Enough: Financial Sector Sources of Central Bank Independence," in Ben S. Bernanke and Julio J. Rotemberg (eds), *NBER Macroeconomics Annual, 1995*. Cambridge: MIT Press, 253–74.

Reserve Bank of New Zealand (2000), *Monetary Policy Statement*. Wellington, NZ: Reserve Bank of New Zealand, March.

Samuelson, Robert (1994), "Economic Amnesia," *Newsweek*, September 12, 52.

Sherwin, Murray (1999), "Inflation Targeting: 10 Years On," Speech to New Zealand Association of Economists Conference, Rotorua, NZ, 1 July.

Svensson, Lars E. O. (1997), "Inflation Forecast Targeting: Implementing and Monitoring Inflation Targets," *European Economic Review*, 41, 1111–46.

Taylor, John (1999) (ed.), *Monetary Policy Rules*. Chicago: University of Chicago Press for the NBER.

Woodford, Michael (2004), "Inflation Targeting and Optimal Monetary Policy," Federal Reserve Bank of St Louis, *Review*, July/August, 15–41.

Woodward, Bob (2000), *Maestro: Greenspan's Fed and the American Dream*. New York: Simon and Schuster.

Monetary Policy Strategy in Emerging Market and Transition Economies

Introduction to Part III

Before going to the Federal Reserve Bank of New York in September 1994, I had done very little research on emerging market countries, focusing most of my research on the United States. Indeed, although I had traveled extensively, it was almost always to advanced countries. My experience with the developing countries, now referred to as emerging market countries, which were then coming onto the international stage, was extremely limited. This all changed when, shortly after arriving at the New York Fed, the Mexican "tequila" crisis erupted in December 1994. Bill McDonough, the president of the bank, was continually asking me about what was going on in Mexico and I didn't have good answers. In early 1995, I was sent down to the Bank of Mexico to interact with my counterparts there and I came to realize that many of the prevailing assumptions about how the macro economy works were based on the institutional features that apply to advanced economies, but which are not descriptive of conditions in emerging market countries. I began a learning process that has continued ever since and has led me to put a lot of my research efforts into thinking about better policy prescriptions for emerging market countries.

My initial interest in emerging market countries focused on financial crises (for example, Mishkin 1996, 1998a,b,c, 1999a,b,c, 2003; and Hahm and Mishkin 2000), culminating in my recent book, *The Next Great Globalization: How Disadvantaged Nations Can Harness Their Financial Systems to Get Rich* (2006). Given my interest in monetary policy strategy, it was natural that I would broaden my research to think about monetary policy strategies in emerging market and transition countries (which are emerging market countries that were previously under the yoke of communism). These topics are the subject of this part of the book.

For the 1999 Inter-American Seminar on Economics, I was invited to write a paper on monetary policy in Latin America. The ensuing work resulted in chapters 12, 13, and 14. Chapters 13 and 14 were written in 1999 with Miguel Savastano, a Peruvian, who I met when I was conducting an evaluation of research activities in the International Monetary Fund for the executive board of that institution. (The outcome of that evaluation can be found in Giavazzi, Mishkin, and Srinivasan [2000].) These two chapters originally were combined into one paper for the conference, but space limitations in the journal required that the paper be broken into two separate papers. Chapter 13 lays out a general framework to evaluate possible monetary policy strategies for Latin America that may help lock in the gains attained by the region during the 1990s in the fight against inflation, while chapter 14 contains case studies supporting the analysis laid out in the preceding chapter. After writing the papers with Miguel, I wrote a shorter paper with a narrower focus on inflation targeting in emerging market countries, which was presented at the American Economic Association meetings in 2000.

In these three chapters, I argue that much of the debate about the Latin American conduct of monetary policy has been misfocused on whether the nominal exchange rate should be fixed or flexible. Instead, the emphasis should be on whether the monetary policy regime appropriately constrains discretion in monetary policymaking. This alternative focus suggests that there are three basic frameworks that deserve serious discussion to ensure viable and effective long-run strategies for monetary policy in Latin America: 1) a hard exchange-rate peg, 2) monetary targeting, and 3) inflation targeting. These chapters look at the advantages and disadvantages of each of these strategies in light of the recent track record of monetary policy in several Latin American countries for clues as to which of the three strategies might be best suited to the region's economies. The conclusion is that countries that do not appear to have political and other institutional checks to constrain monetary policy may need to resort to hard pegs, including full dollarization, which allow little or no discretion to the monetary authorities. On the other hand, there are many Latin American countries that seem to have the ability to constrain discretion, with Chile being the clearest example, and for these cases inflation targeting is likely to produce a monetary policy that keeps inflation low and yet appropriately copes with domestic and foreign shocks.

Given my interest in emerging market countries, it seemed natural to study inflation targeting in transition countries that have recently emerged from communism. Transition countries are worth studying because of three unique features: 1) these are new democracies, 2) these nations are undergoing radical restructuring, and 3) they are very likely to enter the European Union (EU) and Economic and Monetary Union (EMU) in the near future. I thus wrote chapter 15 with Jiri Jonas, a Czech who knows these countries well. We met while I was evaluating the IMF's research activities, and we presented the paper at an NBER conference in 2003. In this chapter, we look at the inflation targeting experience in the three transition countries that have adopted it: the Czech Republic, Poland, and Hungary. While these countries have often missed inflation targets by a large margin, they nevertheless progressed well with disinflating their economies. A key lesson from the experience of the inflation-targeting transition countries is that economic performance will improve, and support for the central bank will be higher, if the central banks emphasize avoiding undershooting the inflation target as much as they try avoiding overshooting it. Undershooting the inflation target eroded support for the central bank in both the Czech Republic and Poland. Economic performance will be enhanced if inflation-targeting central banks in transition countries do not engage in active manipulation of the exchange rate, which created problems in Hungary. The relationship between the central bank and the government in these countries has been quite difficult, but this conflict can be alleviated by having the government directly involved in setting the inflation target and having the central bank take a more active role in communicating with both the government and the public. In addition, having technocrats appointed as the head of the central bank rather than politicians, as has been common in transition countries, may help depersonalize the conduct of monetary policy and increase support for central bank independence. The chapter also addresses the future perspective of monetary policy in these three transition economies that are slated for EU accession: inflation targeting can remain the main pillar of monetary strategy even after these three countries join the EU and before they join the EMU.

After a decade of experience with inflation targeting, a post-mortem analysis of the experience seemed worth pursuing. Chapter 16 was written with Klaus Schmidt-Hebbel of the Central Bank of Chile and was presented at their annual conference in 2000. This is a wide-ranging chapter that reviews briefly the main design features of eighteen inflation targeting experiences, analyzes statistically if countries under inflation targeting are structurally different from noninflation-targeting industrial countries, and reviews existing evidence about the success of inflation targeting. It then looks at the interaction of inflation targeting design features and the conduct of monetary policy during the transition to low inflation. The chapter ends by discussing two unresolved issues: what the long-run inflation goal should be and the merits of targeting the price level rather than inflation. The chapter's message is that inflation targeting has been quite successful in controlling inflation and improving the economic performance. Yet there is still much to learn about how best to operate inflation-targeting regimes.

The final two chapters of this part of the book look at the perennial debate over whether to fix or float the exchange rate as part of a monetary policy strategy. Chapter 17, written in 1998, suggests that although pegging the exchange rate provides a nominal anchor for emerging market countries that can help them control inflation, there are serious problems with this strategy. First, there are the usual criticisms that exchange-rate pegging entails the loss of an independent monetary policy, exposes the country to the transmission of shocks from the anchor country, increases the likelihood of speculative attacks, and potentially weakens the accountability of policymakers to pursue anti-inflationary policies. However, most damaging to the case for exchange-rate pegging in emerging market countries is that this strategy can increase financial fragility and make the potential for financial crises more likely. Because of the devastating effects on the entire economy that financial crises can leave in their wake, an exchange-rate peg is a very dangerous strategy for controlling inflation in emerging market countries. A strategy with a greater likelihood of success involves granting of independence to the central bank and having it adopt an inflation-targeting regime.

My thinking on the fix-versus-flex debate, however, has evolved over time, particularly because of my interaction with Guillermo Calvo, who has been a close friend for a very long time. (Guillermo, along with Maury Obstfeld, was very active in recruiting me to Columbia more than twenty years ago.) In the economics profession, Guillermo and I have often been viewed as being on the opposite sides of the fix-versus-flex debate: Guillermo has been a hard peg advocate in the past and I have been a strong proponent of flexible exchange rates with inflation targeting. In conversations together, often late at night over a very good bottle of wine, Guillermo and I realized that we have much more in common between our views than first appeared to be the case. We thus started to write chapter 18 in 2002, finished in 2003, which sets out our argument that too much attention in emerging market countries has been focused on the fix-versus-flex debate, a point that Miguel Savastano and I also make in chapter 13. Guillermo and I argue that the standard theory of the exchange-rate regime choice in emerging market countries is missing some key elements because it leaves out the special institutional features of emerging market countries. The chapter next discusses a range of institutional traits that might predispose a country to favor either fixed or floating rates, and then turns to the converse question of whether the choice of exchange-rate regime may favor the development of certain desirable institutional traits. We end up believing that the key to macro-economic success in emerging market countries is not primarily their choice of exchange-rate regime, but rather the health of the individual country's fundamental macroeconomic institutions including the institutions associated with fiscal, financial, and monetary stability. We conclude that less attention should be focused on the general question of whether a floating or fixed exchange rate is preferable, and more on these deeper institutional arrangements. In other words, "It's the Institutions, Stupid." We believe that a focus on institutional reforms rather than on the exchange-rate regime may encourage emerging market countries to be healthier and less prone to the crises that we have seen in recent years.

References

Giavazzi, Francesco, Frederic S. Mishkin, and T. N. Srinivasan. 2000. *External Evaluation of IMF Economic Research Activities: Report by a Group of Independent Experts.* International Monetary Fund: Washington DC.

Hahm, Joon-Ho, and Frederic S. Mishkin. 2000. "The Korean Financial Crisis: An Asymmetric Information Perspective." *Emerging Markets Review*, vol. 1, no. 1 (2000): 21–52.

Mishkin, Frederic S. 1996. "Understanding Financial Crises: A Developing Country Perspective." In Michael Bruno and Boris Pleskovic, eds., *Annual World Bank Conference on Development Economics 1996*. World Bank: Washington DC: 29–62.

Mishkin, Frederic S. 1998a. "The Mexican Financial Crisis of 1994–95." In Scheherazade S. Rehman, ed., *Financial Crisis Management in Regional Blocs*. Kluwer Academic Publishers: Boston: 149–181.

Mishkin, Frederic S. 1998b. "International Capital Movements, Financial Volatility and Financial Instability." *Schriften des Vereins fur Socialpolitik, Band 261, zugleich Beiheft 7, Zeitschrift fur Wirtschafts- und Sozialwissenschaften, Jahrestagung 1997, Finanzmarkete im Spannungsfeld von Globalisierung, Regulierung und Geldpolitik*, Dieter Duwendag, ed. Drucker and Humblot: Berlin: 11–40.

Mishkin, Frederic S. 1999a. "Lessons from the Asian Crisis." *Journal of International Money and Finance* 18, 4 (August): 709–723.

Mishkin, Frederic S. 1999b. "Lessons from the Tequila Crisis." *Journal of Banking and Finance* 23 (1999): 1521–1533.

Mishkin, Frederic S. 1999c. "Global Financial Instability: Framework, Events, Issues." *Journal of Economic Perspectives* (Fall), vol. 13, no. 4: 3–20.

Mishkin, Frederic S. 2003. "Financial Policies and the Prevention of Financial Crises in Emerging Market Countries." In Martin Feldstein, ed., *Economic and Financial Crises in Emerging Market Countries*. Chicago: University of Chicago Press: 93–130.

Mishkin, Frederic S. 2006. *The Next Great Globalization: How Disadvantaged Nations Can Harness Their Financial Systems to Get Rich*. Princeton, N.J.: Princeton University Press.

12 Inflation Targeting in Emerging Market Countries

Frederic S. Mishkin

The unhappy experience of Latin American and East Asian countries with pegged exchange-rate regimes when those countries found themselves in deep financial crises in the 1990's has led emerging-market countries to search for alternative nominal anchors. (I am including transition countries in Eastern Europe and the former Soviet Union in the emerging-market category.) Inflation targeting, a monetary policy strategy which has been successfully used by a number of industrialized countries, has thus become an increasingly attractive alternative and has been adopted by a growing number of emerging-market countries, including Chile, Brazil, the Czech Republic, Poland, and South Africa. In this chapter, I outline what inflation targeting involves for these countries and discuss the advantages and disadvantages of this monetary-policy strategy. The bottom line is that, although inflation targeting is not a panacea and may not be appropriate for many emerging-market countries, it can be a highly useful monetary policy in a number of them.

12.1 What Is Inflation Targeting?

Inflation targeting is a monetary-policy strategy that encompasses five main elements: (i) the public announcement of medium-term numerical targets for inflation; (ii) an institutional commitment to price stability as the primary goal of monetary policy, to which other goals are subordinated; (iii) an information-inclusive strategy in which many variables, and not just monetary aggregates or the exchange rate, are used for deciding the setting of policy instruments; (iv) increased transparency of the monetary-policy strategy through communication with the public and the markets about the plans, objectives, and decisions of the monetary authorities; and (v) increased accountability of the central bank for attaining its inflation objectives. The list should clarify one crucial point about inflation targeting: it entails much more than a public announcement of numerical targets for inflation for the year ahead. This is important in the context of emerging markets countries because many of them routinely reported numerical inflation targets or objectives as part of the government's economic plan for the coming year, and yet their monetary-policy strategy should not be characterized as inflation targeting, which requires the other four elements for it to be sustainable over the medium term.

12.2   Advantages of Inflation Targeting

Inflation targeting has several advantages as a medium-term strategy for monetary policy. In contrast to an exchange-rate peg, inflation targeting enables monetary policy to focus on domestic considerations and to respond to shocks to the domestic economy. In contrast to monetary targeting, another possible monetary policy strategy, inflation targeting has the advantage that a stable relationship between money and inflation is not critical to its success: the strategy does not depend on such a relationship, but instead uses all available information to determine the best settings for the instruments of monetary policy. Inflation targeting also has the key advantage that it is easily understood by the public and is thus highly transparent.

Because an explicit numerical target for inflation increases the accountability of the central bank, inflation targeting also has the potential to reduce the likelihood that the central bank will fall into the time-inconsistency trap. Moreover, since the source of time-inconsistency is often found in (covert or open) political pressures on the central bank to undertake overly expansionary monetary policy, inflation targeting has the advantage of focusing the political debate on what a central bank can do in the long-run (i.e., control inflation) rather than what it cannot do (raise output growth, lower unemployment, and increase external competitiveness) through monetary policy.

For inflation targeting to deliver these outcomes, there must exist a strong institutional commitment to make price stability the primary goal of the central bank. This is particularly important in emerging-market countries which have often had a past history of monetary mismanagement. The institutional commitment involves legislative support for an independent central bank whose charter ought to contain two key features: (i) sufficient insulation of the policy-making board of the central bank from the politicians, with members of the government excluded and the members of the board appointed to long terms and protected from arbitrary dismissal; and (ii) giving the central bank full and exclusive control over the setting of monetary-policy instruments. The institutional commitment to price stability also requires that the central bank be given a mandate to have price stability as its primary goal, making it clear that when there is a conflict with other goals, such as exchange-rate stability or promotion of high employment, price stability must be accorded the higher priority.

Inflation-targeting regimes also put great stress on the need to make monetary policy transparent and to maintain regular channels of communication with the public; in fact, these features have been central to the strategy's success in industrialized countries. As illustrated in Mishkin and Adam Posen (1997) and in Ben Bernanke et al. (1999), inflation-targeting central banks have frequent communications with the government, and their officials take every opportunity to make public speeches on their monetary-policy strategy. Inflation-targeting central banks have taken public outreach a step further: they publish "Inflation Report"-type documents (originated by the Bank of England) to present clearly their views about the past and future performance of inflation and monetary policy.

Another key feature of inflation-targeting regimes is that the transparency of policy associated with inflation targeting has tended to make the central bank highly accountable to the public. Sustained success in the conduct of monetary policy as measured against a preannounced and well-defined inflation target can be instrumental in building public support for an independent central bank, even in the absence of a rigidly defined and legalistic standard of performance evaluation and punishment.

12.3 Disadvantages of Inflation Targeting

Critics of inflation targeting have noted seven major disadvantages of this monetary policy strategy. Four of those disadvantages (that inflation targeting is too rigid, that it allows too much discretion, that it has the potential to increase output instability, and that it will lower economic growth) have been discussed in Mishkin (1999) and in Bernanke et al. (1999) and are in reality not serious objections to a properly designed inflation-targeting strategy, which is best characterized as "constrained discretion." The fifth disadvantage, that inflation targeting can only produce weak central-bank accountability because inflation is hard to control and because there are long lags from the monetary-policy instruments to the inflation outcomes, is an especially serious one for emerging-market countries. The sixth and seventh disadvantages, that inflation targeting cannot prevent fiscal dominance, and that the exchange-rate flexibility required by inflation targeting might cause financial instability, are also very relevant in the emerging-market-country context.

In contrast to exchange rates and monetary aggregates, the inflation rate cannot be easily controlled by the central bank; furthermore, inflation outcomes that incorporate the effects of changes in instruments settings are revealed only after a substantial lag. The difficulty of controlling inflation creates a particularly severe problem for emerging-market countries when inflation is being brought down from relatively high levels. In those circumstances, inflation forecast errors are likely to be large, inflation targets will tend to be missed, and it will be difficult for the central bank to gain credibility from an inflation-targeting strategy, and for the public to ascertain the reasons for the deviations. This suggests that, as noted by Paul Masson et al. (1997), inflation targeting is likely to be a more effective strategy if it is phased in only after there has been some successful disinflation.

One other factor affecting inflation controllability that is especially relevant in the emerging-market context is the (at times large) incidence of government-controlled prices on the index used to compute headline inflation. As a result, inflation targeting may demand a high degree of coordination between monetary and fiscal authorities on the timing and magnitude of future changes in controlled prices or, alternatively, the exclusion of controlled prices from the targeted price index, as in the Czech Republic.

A sixth shortcoming of inflation targeting is that it may not be sufficient to ensure fiscal discipline or to prevent fiscal dominance. Governments can still pursue irresponsible fiscal policy with an inflation-targeting regime in place. In the long run, large fiscal deficits will cause an inflation-targeting regime to break down: the fiscal deficits will eventually have to be monetized or the public debt eroded by a large devaluation, and high inflation will follow. Absence of outright fiscal dominance is therefore a key prerequisite for inflation targeting, and the setting-up of institutions that help keep fiscal policy in check are crucial to the success of the strategy (Masson et al., 1997). Similarly, a sound financial system is another prerequisite for successful inflation targeting because, when financial systems blow up, there is typically a surge in inflation in emerging-market countries. However, as pointed out in Mishkin and Miguel Savastano (2000), a sound financial system and the absence of fiscal dominance are also crucial to the sustainability and success of any other monetary-policy strategy, including a currency board or full dollarization. Indeed, inflation targeting may help constrain fiscal policy to the extent that the government is actively involved in setting the inflation target (including through the coordination of future adjustments to government-controlled prices).

Finally, a high degree of (partial) dollarization may create a potentially serious problem for inflation targeting. In fact, in many emerging-market countries, the balance sheets of firms, households, and banks are substantially dollarized, on both sides, and the bulk of long-term debt is denominated in dollars (Guillermo Calvo, 1999). Because inflation targeting necessarily requires nominal exchange-rate flexibility, exchange-rate fluctuations are unavoidable. However, large and abrupt depreciations may increase the burden of dollar-denominated debt, produce a massive deterioration of balance sheets, and increase the risks of a financial crisis along the lines discussed in Mishkin (1996). This suggests that emerging-market countries cannot afford to ignore the exchange rate when conducting monetary policy under inflation targeting, but the role they ascribe to it should be clearly subordinated to the inflation objective. It also suggests that inflation targeting in partially dollarized economies may not be viable unless there are stringent prudential regulations on (and strict supervision of) financial institutions that ensure that the system is capable of withstanding exchange-rate shocks.

12.4   Lessons from Recent Experience

The earliest example of an emerging-market country's adoption of inflation targeting is Chile, which in 1990, with the inflation rate in excess of 20 percent, first started to announce an inflation objective in September for the 12-month inflation rate ending in December of the following year.[1] As pointed out above, for inflation targeting to be a success, institutions in the country must support independence of the central bank, as well as a strong fiscal position and sound financial system. Before embarking on inflation targeting, Chile passed new central-bank legislation in 1989 (that took effect in 1990), which gave independence to the central bank and mandated price stability as one of its primary objectives.[2] A sound fiscal policy was also in place, with the fiscal balance in surplus in every year from 1991 to 1997. In addition, due largely to the measures taken in the aftermath of its severe banking crisis in the early 1980's, Chile's standards and practices in the areas of banking regulation and supervision were of a quality comparable to those found in industrialized countries.

Chile's central bank was well aware of the difficulty of controlling inflation and precisely hitting the target when inflation was in the double digits, and it dealt with this problem in several ways. First, like the industrialized countries that have adopted inflation targeting (see Bernanke et al., 1999), Chile phased in inflation targeting gradually after initial successes in lowering inflation. When the inflation objective was first announced in September 1990, it was interpreted more as official inflation projections rather than as formal or "hard" targets. Only after the central bank experienced success in both meeting the inflation objectives and lowering inflation, did it begin to emphasize that the inflation objectives should be interpreted as hard targets for which the central bank would be accountable (Felipe Morande and Klaus Schmidt-Hebbel, 1997). Second, Chile's central bank pursued a very gradualist approach to lowering its inflation objectives, starting with targets of over 20 percent for 1991 and lowering them slowly to 3.5 percent by the end of the decade. Third, because of the difficulty of controlling inflation at inflation rates which were still above 10 percent, a realistic range for the inflation outcomes would have been very large. Thus, as part of the process of hardening the inflation targets, Chile's central bank switched from target ranges to point targets with its announcement in September 1994 for the 1995 objective.

The Chilean experience with inflation targeting looks quite successful. Inflation fell from levels above 20 percent, when inflation projections were first introduced, to a level around 3 percent at present. Over the same period, output growth was very high, averaging more than 8 percent per year from 1991 to 1997, a level comparable to those exhibited by the (former) Asian tigers. Only in the last two years has the economy entered a recession with output growth falling to 3.4 percent in 1998 and to a -2.9-percent rate for the first half of 1999. In 1998 the Chilean central bank was reluctant to ease monetary policy and let the exchange rate depreciate in order to cushion the effects of a large, negative terms-of-trade shock. Instead, the Chilean central bank raised interest rates and even narrowed the exchange-rate band. In hindsight, these decisions appear to have been a mistake: the inflation target was undershot, and the economy entered a recession for the first time in more than 15 years. Not surprisingly, the central bank came under increased criticism and in 1999 reversed course, by lowering interest rates and allowing the peso to depreciate.

The Chilean example suggests that inflation targeting can be used as a successful strategy for gradual disinflation in emerging-market countries, even when initial inflation is on the order of 20 percent. It is important to emphasize that the success of inflation targeting cannot be solely attributed to the actions of the Chilean central bank: supportive policies such as absence of large fiscal deficits and rigorous regulation and supervision of the financial sector have been crucial to its success.[3] Another important element of Chile's strategy has been a gradual hardening of the targets over time. However, the experience in Chile of the last two years, as well as that of industrialized countries, indicates that a key requirement for successful inflation-targeting regimes in emerging-market economies is the recognition that undershooting inflation targets is just as costly as overshooting the targets. Support for an independent central bank that is pursuing price stability can erode if the central bank is perceived as focusing solely on lowering inflation to the detriment of other objectives such as minimizing output variability.

In addition, Chile has not yet fully accomplished a full-fledged, inflation-targeting regime. The Chilean central bank has not yet produced an "Inflation Report"-type of document, nor does it publish inflation forecasts; the accountability mechanisms of monetary policy are also weak. Brazil, on the other hand, which adopted inflation targeting in the wake of its currency crisis in early 1999, shows that a full-fledged inflation-targeting regime can be put in place remarkably quickly. Within four months of the announcement by the newly appointed central-bank president that inflation targeting would be adopted, the central bank of Brazil implemented an inflation-targeting regime with all the "bells and whistles" found in inflation targeters in industrialized countries, including an "Inflation Report" with published inflation forecasts. Despite the initial success of Brazilian inflation targeting which has kept inflation below 10 percent despite a substantial exchange-rate depreciation, there are still serious doubts about whether it will be ultimately successful because it is by no means clear whether Brazil can solve its deep-rooted fiscal problems.

As noted, a critical issue for inflation targeting in emerging-market countries is the role of the exchange rate. Emerging-market countries, including those engaging in inflation targeting, have rightfully been reluctant to adopt an attitude of "benign neglect" of exchange-rate movements, partly because of the existence of a sizable stock of foreign currency or a high degree of (partial) dollarization. Nonetheless, emerging-market countries probably have gone too far, for too long, in the direction of limiting exchange-rate flexibility, not only through the explicit use of exchange-rate bands, but also through frequent intervention in the foreign-exchange market. Responding too heavily and too frequently to movements in a "flexible" exchange rate runs the risk of transforming the exchange rate into a nominal anchor for monetary policy that takes precedence over the inflation target, at least in the eyes of the public. One possible way to avoid this problem is for inflation-targeting central banks in emerging-market countries to adopt a transparent policy of smoothing short-run exchange-rate fluctuations that helps mitigate potentially destabilizing effects of abrupt exchange-rate changes while making it clear to the public that they will allow exchange rates to reach their market-determined level over longer horizons.

Notes

I thank Miguel Savastano for helpful comments. The views expressed in this chapter are exclusively those of the author and not those of Columbia University or the National Bureau of Economic Research.

1. See Mishkin and Savastano (2000) for a more detailed discussion of the experience with inflation targeting in Latin America.

2. The legislation also stipulated a central-bank objective to ensure equilibria in domestic and external payments. Partly because of this, Chile maintained an exchange-rate band around a crawling peg during most of the 1990's. Importantly, however, the central bank made it clear that, when there was a potential conflict between the exchange-rate band and the inflation target, the inflation target would take precedence.

3. The Chilean controls on short-term capital flows have often been cited as another important factor behind the relative stability of the Chilean economy and the success of monetary policy, but rigorous prudential supervision was probably more important. For a recent overview of the debate surrounding Chile's capital controls, see Sebastian Edwards (1999).

References

Bernanke, Ben S.; Laubach, Thomas; Mishkin, Frederic S. and Posen, Adam S. *Inflation targeting: Lessons from the international experience.* Princeton, NJ: Princeton University Press, 1999.

Calvo, Guillermo. "Capital Markets and the Exchange Rate." Mimeo, University of Maryland, October 1999.

Edwards, Sebastian. "How Effective are Capital Controls?" *Journal of Economic Perspectives*, Fall 1999, *13*(4), pp. 65–84.

Masson, Paul R.; Savastano, Miguel A. and Sharma, Sunil. "The Scope for Inflation Targeting in Developing Countries." International Monetary Fund (Washington, DC) Working Paper No. 97/130, October 1997.

Mishkin, Frederic S. "Understanding Financial Crises: A Developing Country Perspective," in Michael Bruno and Boris Pleskovic, eds., *Annual World Bank Conference on Development Economics*. Washington, DC: World Bank, 1996, pp. 29–62.

————. "International Experiences with Different Monetary Regimes." *Journal of Monetary Economics*, June 1999, *43*(3), pp. 579–606.

Mishkin, Frederic S. and Posen, Adam S. "Inflation Targeting: Lessons from Four Countries." *Federal Reserve Bank of New York Economic Policy Review*, August 1997, *3*(3), pp. 9–110.

Mishkin, Frederic S. and Savastano, Miguel A. "Monetary Policy Strategies for Latin America." National Bureau of Economic Research (Cambridge, MA) Working Paper No. 7617, March 2000.

Morande, Felipe and Schmidt-Hebbel, Klaus. "Inflation Targets and Indexation in Chile." Mimeo, Central Bank of Chile, Santiago, August 1997.

13 Monetary Policy Strategies for Latin America

Frederic S. Mishkin and Miguel A. Savastano

13.1 Why the Issue Is Not Fixed versus Flexible Exchange Rates

The monetary policy experience of Latin America has not been a happy one. Economies in this region have gone through extreme episodes of monetary instability, swinging from very high inflations, to massive capital flight, to collapses in their financial systems. The unsurprising outcome has been low credibility, slow growth, recurrent recessions and even depressions. However, a new era may be dawning in Latin America. In the past decade or so, most countries in the region have become outward looking, and the public, politicians and policymakers have come to recognize the high costs of protectionism and inflation, producing a growing commitment to open markets and price stability. Evidence of this more favorable environment are the successful inflation stabilization programs adopted by many Latin American countries in the early 1990s, and the historically low rates of inflation attained by the region in recent years, falling from an average of over 400% in 1989 to below 10% by 1999. Where should Latin American countries go from here in designing appropriate long-run strategies for the conduct of their monetary policy?

The central issue in addressing this question is whether the countries of the region have a chance of setting up institutions and mechanisms that will effectively and efficiently constrain the discretion of their monetary authorities. Whether the exchange rate is fixed or flexible (and precisely how flexible) follows from the answer one gives to that question. Thus, we believe that there is a need to refocus the debate away from a discussion of whether the nominal exchange rate should be fixed or flexible. One advantage of the alternative approach that focuses on underlying institutions to appropriately constrain monetary policy discretion rather than on the flexibility of the exchange rate is that it allows one to draw on the experiences of countries outside Latin America to a larger extent than what is possible in the present round of the "Fix versus Flex" debate.[1]

In principle, there are four broad monetary policy strategies that can produce a nominal anchor that credibly constrains the discretion of the central bank over the medium term: "hard" exchange-rate pegs, "soft" exchange-rate pegs, monetary targeting, and inflation targeting.[2] The severe shortcomings of soft pegs (in their multiple manifestations) as a *medium-term* strategy for monetary policy have been amply demonstrated by recent experiences in industrial and emerging market economies (including many from Latin America) and need not be repeated here.[3] This leaves us with three potential medium-term strategies for monetary policy that we evaluate in the following sections. In each section, we look at the advantages and disadvantages of each strategy, and then examine the recent experience of relevant Latin American countries for clues as to which of the three might be best suited for countries in the region.

13.2 Hard Pegs

There are essentially two types of "hard peg" regimes for monetary policy: a currency board and full dollarization. In a currency board, the domestic currency is backed 100% by a foreign currency (say, US dollars) and the note-issuing authority, whether the central bank or the government, fixes a conversion rate to this currency and stands ready to exchange domestically issued notes for the foreign currency on demand. A currency board is a hard peg because the commitment to the fixed exchange rate has a legal (or even constitutional) backing and because monetary policy is, in effect, put on autopilot and completely taken out of the hands of the central bank and the government. Full dollarization involves eliminating altogether the domestic currency and replacing it with a foreign currency (the US dollar). It represents a stronger commitment to monetary stability than a currency board because it makes it much more costly—though still not impossible—for the government to regain control over monetary policy and/or change the parity of the (non-existent) domestic currency.

13.2.1 Advantages of Hard Pegs

The advantages of hard pegs, especially of currency boards, have been discussed extensively in recent years.[4] Put succinctly, hard pegs can deliver everything that fixed-but-adjustable pegs proved incapable of delivering—with or without capital mobility.

First, they provide a nominal anchor that helps keep inflation under control by tying the prices of domestically produced tradable goods to those in the anchor country, attenuating (and eventually breaking) the inertial component of inflation that feeds into wages and prices of nontradable goods, and making inflation expectations converge to those prevailing in the anchor country.

Second, hard pegs reduce and, in the limit, eliminate the currency risk component from domestic interest rates thus lowering the cost of funds for the government and the private sector and improving the outlook for financial deepening, investment, and growth.

Third, hard pegs provide an automatic adjustment mechanism for the money supply that helps mitigate (or plainly eliminates) the time-inconsistency problem of monetary policy. A fall in the demand for domestic assets, including domestic currency notes, produces an automatic outflow of hard currency and a rise in interest rates without creating pressures on the peg, while an increase in the demand for domestic assets has the opposite effects. Discretionary, expansionary and time-inconsistent monetary policy, including to finance the government deficit, is not a policy option.

Finally, hard pegs have the advantage of simplicity and clarity, which make them easily understood by the public. A "sound (foreign) currency" policy is an easy-to-understand rallying cry for monetary stability and, according to some, also for fiscal discipline.

13.2.2   Disadvantages of Hard Pegs

The main disadvantage of a hard peg as a medium term monetary regime is that it leaves (almost) no scope for domestic monetary policy because with open capital markets, a hard peg causes domestic interest rates to be closely linked to those in the anchor country to which it is pegged. The country which chooses a hard peg thus loses the ability to use monetary policy to respond to domestic shocks that are independent of those hitting the anchor country. Furthermore, a hard peg means that shocks to the anchor country are directly transmitted to the pegging country because changes in interest rates in the anchor country lead to a corresponding change in domestic interest rates. As long as domestic prices and wages are "sticky" and markets are incomplete, the loss of an independent monetary policy, which can help the monetary authorities counter the effects of certain of these shocks, can be costly.

This point can be illustrated with the simple model outlined in Svensson (1997), which comprises an aggregate supply curve:

$$\pi_t = \pi_{t-1} + \alpha_1 y_{t-1} + \varepsilon_t \tag{13.1}$$

and an aggregate demand curve:

$$y_t = \beta_1 y_{t-1} - \beta_2 (i_{t-1} - \pi_{t-1}) + \eta_t \tag{13.2}$$

where $\pi_t = p_t - p_{t-1}$ = the inflation rate at time t (with p_t the log of the price level), y_t = the output gap (the log of the actual to potential output), i_t = the nominal interest rate, and ε_t and η_t, i.i.d. aggregate supply and demand shocks, respectively.

In this setup, optimal monetary policy involves setting the interest rate each period to minimize the intertemporal loss function:

$$E_t \sum_{\tau=t}^{\infty} \delta^{\tau-t} L_\tau \tag{13.3}$$

where $\delta < 1$ is the authorities' discount rate and where the period-by-period loss function is

$$L_\tau = (\pi_\tau - \pi^*)^2/2 + \lambda y_\tau^2/2. \tag{13.4}$$

The optimal setting of the interest rate is then a "Taylor rule,"

$$i_t = \pi_t + b_1(\pi_t - \pi^*) + b_2 y_t \tag{13.5}$$

in which the interest rate responds to both the inflation gap, $\pi_t - \pi^*$, and the output gap, y_t.[5]

With a hard peg, the interest rate is in effect set by the anchor country and it will differ from the optimal setting of the interest rate given in Eq. (13.5). The loss from having a hard peg will be small only if the pegging country is so integrated with the anchor country that its inflation and output gaps are highly correlated since in those circumstances setting the interest rate on the basis of the conditions prevailing in the anchor country will also be optimal for the domestic economy. However, this requirement is unlikely to be met in practice, particularly if the anchor country is the United States.[6]

The key message from this analysis is that hard pegs will (almost) always represent a second best solution for most Latin American economies—especially the large ones, so that these countries are better off having some scope for "good" monetary policy than having no monetary policy at all. Of course advocates of hard pegs for Latin America point out that having no monetary policy is better than having "bad"—i.e., discretionary and inflationary—monetary policy. However, although Latin America's dismal monetary history is full of episodes of mismanaged monetary policy, it is not clear why the past should serve as a predictor for the future, especially when one considers the great strides that most countries in the region have made in lowering inflation in recent years.

Another disadvantage of hard pegs is that the central bank, when it exists, loses its ability to act as a lender of last resort. This may turn out not to be a major drawback of those regimes in the short run. As discussed in Mishkin (1999b), central banks of emerging economies typically have very limited scope to act as lenders of last resort, even under flexible rates. The main reason for this is lack of credibility. Central bank lending to the banking system in the wake of a financial crisis is likely to unleash fears of an inflationary explosion and produce a sharp exchange rate depreciation. Given the substantial "liability dollarization" of households, firms and banks in those economies, the depreciation will tend to have a major negative impact on the net worth of the private sector, including banks, which will then amplify asymmetric information problems in financial markets and exacerbate the financial crisis. Over the longer run, however, as central banks demonstrate their commitment to price stability and banking supervision is strengthened, those problems will tend to disappear and the central banks' scope for acting as lenders of last resort will increase. This is something that hard peg regimes can never count on having.

13.2.3   Currency Board versus Full Dollarization

The main disadvantage of a currency board relative to full dollarization is that the former does not eliminate completely the possibility of a devaluation. If investors' sentiment turns against a country with a currency board and speculators launch an attack, they are presented with a one-way bet because the only direction the value of the currency can go is down. The probability of this event is embedded in domestic interest rates, even in "calm" periods, making those rates higher and more volatile than the ones in the anchor country. These problems are mitigated under full dollarization. Since there is no uncertainty about the value of the currency circulating in the country (dollars will always be dollars) the currency risk component of domestic interest rates will necessarily disappear, and interest rates will be lower.

However, this does not mean that under full dollarization domestic interest rates will converge to those prevailing in the US, as has been argued by some—e.g., Schuler (1999). Domestic interest rates will continue to carry a country-risk premium. One important reason for this, but by no means the only one, is that interest rates will continue to reflect a "confiscation risk," at least for a while. Confiscation of assets (denominated in both domestic and foreign currency) has a long tradition in Latin America. In the early 1980s, Bolivia, Mexico and Peru forcedly converted dollar deposits held in domestic banks into domestic currency deposits at below market exchange rates in a desperate—and failed—attempt to arrest capital flight (Savastano, 1992). In the late 1980s, Argentina and Brazil forcedly converted short-term bank deposits into long-term bonds to lower the government's interest bill and pave the way for a rapid disinflation. Ecuador's freeze of bank deposits in March 1999, a year before the abolition of the domestic currency, makes it difficult to argue that the region has abandoned completely those confiscatory practices. The logic here is not just that if it happened (more than) once, it may happen again. Confiscation may be forced upon the authorities.

Consider the following example. Suppose that there is a sudden loss of confidence in a fully dollarized country that leads to a massive withdrawal of bank deposits, a severe squeeze of banks' liquidity and a sharp decline in economic activity. A country fully committed to preserve full dollarization may be willing and able to withstand the outflow and the ensuing economic downturn, but only under some conditions. In particular, if the attack is driven by perceptions, let alone evidence, of fiscal insolvency, confiscation of dollar assets to secure resources for the government and prevent a meltdown of the banking system may become a self-fulfilling prophecy. Of course, this could happen under both types of hard pegs, and in both cases the confiscation of assets would cause the collapse of the regime and have catastrophic consequences for the financial system and the real economy. Under full dollarization, however, the damage is likely to be far more serious because the domestic currency and monetary policy that will have to be created from scratch in the aftermath will have no credibility. A small probability of this catastrophic event occurring sometime in the future is more than sufficient reason to expect a country risk premium in domestic interest rates under full dollarization.

13.2.4 Lessons from Recent Experience

The two prime examples of hard pegs in Latin America are Argentina and Panama. Both hard pegs were created under special, and quite different, historical circumstances. In the case of Argentina, the hard peg of a currency board was the cornerstone of the stabilization program of 1990–1991 that ended the hyperinflation episodes of the 1980s. Up until 1999, Panama was the only fully dollarized country in Latin America, i.e., it was the only country which had decided to adopt the US dollar as the legal tender and to eschew the creation of a central bank, a decision it made in 1904, the year after the country was founded.

The experiences of these two countries suggest a number of conclusions (see Mishkin and Savastano, 2000, for detailed case studies of the two experiences). First, hard pegs do deliver low inflation rates. The first 4 years of Argentina's currency board were highly successful and have become the textbook example of the benefits of a currency board for stopping high inflation (Hanke and Schuler, 1994). Inflation in Argentina fell from an 800% annual rate in 1990, to less than 5% by 1994 and declined even more after the Tequila crisis of 1995. Panama's inflation from 1960 to 1998 averaged 2.8% per year, which is significantly lower than in any other country in Latin America, and is even lower than the 4.6% average over the same period for the United States.

Second, there are two necessary conditions for the success of a hard peg: a solid banking and financial system, and sound and sustainable fiscal policies. The sole adoption of a hard peg does not ensure that these two conditions will be met, at least not rapidly or automatically.

For example, despite its currency board, the weakness of Argentina's banking system almost brought down its (quasi-) currency board during the Tequila crisis of 1995. From December 1994 until March 1995, the prices of Argentine stocks and bonds plummeted, the banking system lost 17% of its total deposits, the central bank lost more than a third of its international reserves ($5.5 billion), the money supply contracted, interest rates shot up—with the interbank rate briefly exceeding 70%, and external credit lines vanished. The Argentine central bank had its lender of last resort role constrained by the Convertibility Law, yet it mitigated the adverse effects of the run on bank deposits by lowering reserve requirements, providing direct credit via rediscounts and swaps, and participating actively in the restructuring, privatization and liquidation of troubled banks. By the end of April, the central bank had managed to provide over $5 billion of liquidity to the banking system, more than a third of it in the form of direct loans, and was able to avert a large scale collapse of the banking system. Despite all these efforts, and substantial assistance from the multilaterals (the IMF, the World Bank and the Interamerican Development Bank) the real economy took a nose dive; the May unemployment rate shot up to 18% and 1995 real GDP fell by more than 3%. It was not until 1996 that the Argentine economy began to recover.

Panama's banking system, on the other hand, has earned a reputation of strength and sophistication. However, although the low inflation environment produced by full dollarization contributed to this outcome, the strength of Panama's banking system cannot be attributed to full dollarization. The take-off of Panama's financial system only began in 1970 with the passage of a banking law—Cabinet Decree 238—that eased licensing and portfolio allocation requirements on foreign banks, strengthened secrecy provisions, and allowed unrestricted movements of capital (Moreno, 1999). The goal of transforming Panama into an offshore banking center was achieved fairly quickly. By 1987, there were more than 120 banks located in the country, the majority foreign-owned, and broad money and private sector credit as a share of GDP had risen by more than 15 percentage points (to 40% and 54%, respectively). Except for a banking crisis in 1988–1989 which occurred as a result of economic sanctions imposed on Panama in 1988, including a freezing of the deposits held in the United States by the Banco Nacional de Panama, the Panamanian banking system has fared well.[7] One result is that private sector borrowers in Panama have access to international financial markets and can borrow at low interest rates. Indeed, Panamanian firms and banks do not face a "sovereign ceiling" and can often borrow at lower rates than the government. However, the small spread between domestic and foreign interest rates is probably more a reflection of Panama's sound and internationally oriented banking system than the result of full dollarization.

On the fiscal requirements, small fiscal deficits were key to the early success of Argentina's currency board but persistent fiscal imbalances in the second half of the 1990s, which averaged 2.7% from 1996 to 1998 despite a pick-up in growth, raised recurrent concerns about the sustainability of the hard peg. The fiscal problems of Panama, on the other hand, have been as entrenched and protracted as those of the typical (non-dollarized) Latin American country. Panama has had fiscal deficits jumping from 2% of GDP in the 1960s to over 7% in the 1970s, and averaging 5% in the 1980s. A reflection of its fiscal profligacy is the fact that Panama has requested

13 IMF programs from 1973 to 1997, more than any country in Latin America during that period. The claim that hard pegs ensure fiscal discipline and prevent fiscal dominance receives little support from these two experiences.

The third conclusion borne out by these experiences is that hard pegs remain subject to speculative attacks and bank runs, as evidenced by the spillovers of the Tequila crisis on Argentina and the runs on Panama's banks in the late 1980s.

The fourth conclusion is that hard pegs are ill-equipped to counter country-specific shocks and so can lead to increased output volatility. Although Panama's real GDP growth has been about one percentage point higher than the average for Latin America from 1960 to 1998, output volatility in Panama has been among the highest in the region (e.g., see Hausmann and Gavin, 1995). The two recessions that Argentina has suffered in less than 5 years—the first after the Tequila crisis which sent the unemployment rate to 18%, and the second accelerated by the Brazilian devaluation in 1999—illustrate even more graphically the consequences for output volatility that a hard peg can bring.

Another problem of hard pegs is that they do not have an easy exit strategy, not even when changes in the country's political and economic institutions make it possible and desirable to have a monetary policy able to focus on domestic considerations. Exiting from a currency board is highly dangerous unless the currency is likely to appreciate, but this is exactly when things are going well and so the political will to exit is likely to be weak, or nonexistent. Exiting from a fully dollarized economy is even more troublesome because the (new) monetary authorities, and the new currency, are likely to encounter a serious problem of lack of credibility.

These shortcomings notwithstanding, we are of the view that hard pegs may be the only sustainable monetary policy strategy for those Latin American countries whose political and economic institutions cannot support an independent central bank focused on preserving price stability. In particular, countries that cannot find ways of locking-in the gains from their recent fight against (high) inflation, or those that have not yet started that fight, may find in hard pegs a reasonable second best strategy for monetary policy.

13.3 Monetary Targeting

A monetary targeting strategy focused on controlling inflation comprises three key elements: (1) reliance on information conveyed by a monetary aggregate to conduct monetary policy, (2) announcement of targets on a monetary aggregate to guide the public's inflation expectations, and (3) some accountability mechanism that precludes large and systematic deviations from the monetary targets. In addition, the strategy presupposes that monetary policy is not dictated by fiscal considerations—i.e., lack of fiscal dominance—and that the exchange rate is "flexible."

13.3.1 Advantages of Monetary Targeting

The two major advantages of monetary targeting over exchange-rate pegs (hard and soft) are that it enables the central bank to choose goals for inflation that may differ from those of other countries, and that it allows some scope for monetary policy to deal with transitory output fluctuations and certain external shocks. Also, like an exchange-rate peg, the strategy is easy to monitor since information on whether the central bank is complying with its target is readily available—actual figures for monetary aggregates are typically reported within a couple of weeks. Thus, comparisons between targeted and actual monetary aggregates might send timely and periodic signals to the public and markets about the stance of monetary policy and the intentions of the authorities to keep inflation in check. In turn, these signals might help consolidate inflation expectations and produce less inflation. Targets on money aggregates might also be conducive to making the central bank accountable for meeting its low inflation objective, helping to mitigate the time-inconsistency problem of monetary policy.

13.3.2 Disadvantages of Monetary Targeting

All the above advantages of monetary targeting depend on a big *if*: there must be a strong and reliable relationship between the goal variable (inflation) and the monetary aggregate chosen as target. If the relationship between the monetary aggregate and the goal variable is or becomes weak, monetary targeting will produce poor outcomes. This is easily seen by adding a money demand equation to the simple model sketched in section 13.2.

$$m_t - p_t = \gamma y_t - \kappa i_t + v_t \tag{13.6}$$

where m_t is the log of money balances and v_t is an error term. To the extent that shocks to the money demand error term are large and unpredictable (or that the parameters of the money demand equation are unstable), the relationship between the monetary aggregate and output and inflation will weaken. In those circumstances, targeting the monetary aggregate will lead to large deviations of the interest rate from the optimal policy as represented by the optimal rule in Eq. (13.5). The result will be larger volatility of output, inflation and interest rates (see Clarida et al., 1999).

As is well-known and amply documented, a weak and unstable relationship between monetary aggregates and the rate of inflation was the main problem with this strategy in industrialized countries.[8] Though the existing evidence is not nearly as conclusive, the problem is likely to be just as bad if not worse for the emerging economies of Latin America. The main reason for this is that in the new environment of low inflation and increasing financial integration, it will be highly unlikely that the relationship between monetary aggregates and inflation in those countries remains, or becomes, stable. A weak and unstable relationship between money and inflation will give rise to situations where hitting the monetary target will not produce the desired inflation outcome, where monetary aggregates will fail to provide reliable signals of the stance of monetary policy, and where there will be no effective anchor for inflation expectations. Furthermore, a weak relationship between the targeted monetary aggregate and inflation will make it difficult for the central bank to be transparent and accountable to the public. Although this does not necessarily imply that monetary policy will be expansionary or irresponsible, it will complicate greatly the central bank's communication with the public and the markets, and impair its credibility.

13.3.3 Lessons from Recent Experience

Despite what is often said, no central bank in Latin America has truly practiced monetary targeting. In their relatively recent experience with low(er) inflation and flexible exchange rates, the monetary policy frameworks of many Latin American central banks have contained the first of the three key elements mentioned earlier— i.e., using the information conveyed by a monetary aggregate to conduct monetary policy—but the other two elements (public announcements of the targets and some type of accountability mechanism) rarely have been present at the same time (see Cottarelli and Giannini, 1997). Regimes where monetary targets are not announced, or are announced but not given a chance to perform as the main nominal anchor, are not monetary targeting regimes. A case in point is Peru, which has been often characterized as having undertaken a "money-based stabilization" (e.g., Calvo and Vegh, 1994, 1999) and relied on a monetary anchor to reduce inflation (Corbo, 1999; Favaro, 1996).[9] Peru's central bank did not pursue a monetary targeting strategy during the 1990s: it did not make its monetary targets public, nor was it accountable for meeting its targets. Instead the central bank used the information contained in a monetary aggregate (specifically, base money) to guide the setting of its policy instruments, a procedure followed in many (non-monetary targeting) industrial countries. Those central banks in Latin America that have been regarded as monetary targeters should instead be seen as having followed a discretionary monetary policy with a focus on price stability. Even if that approach proves to be successful for a period of time as has been the case in Peru, it is a highly dangerous strategy. Two crippling shortcomings of the approach are that it depends too much on the preferences, skills and credibility of the individuals running the central bank, and that it does not lend itself to make monetary policy transparent and accountable.[10]

The instability of the money-inflation relationship has also been very visible in Latin America. For example, Peru's central bank did not make its targets for money base growth public during the 1990s because it was highly aware of the uncertainties surrounding the demand for this aggregate in a dollarized economy (80% of bank deposits and loans in Peru are dollar-denominated). Mexico's central bank also has found the monetary base target it adopted as part of its program with the IMF in the aftermath of the Tequila crisis to be highly problematic. In 1997, the monetary base exceeded its target by 4.1%, yet inflation fell to 15.7%, close to its year-end objective of 15%, while in 1998, inflation exceeded the year-end objective of 12% by almost 7 percentage points, even though base money ended up 1.5% below its forecast. The opposite problem occurred in 1999, when the inflation rate fell below the year-end target (12.3% versus 13%) while base money exceeded its target by more than 21%. Not surprisingly, with this record, the Bank of Mexico under Guillermo Ortiz has backed off from its flirtation with monetary targeting, downplaying publicly the role that money base forecasts play in the setting of monetary policy. Indeed, as we will argue in the next section, the Bank of Mexico has been gradually moving in the direction of inflation targeting.

The recent experiences of Mexico and Peru illustrate the difficulties that the instability of the money-inflation relationship creates for monetary targeting as a strategy for monetary policy in Latin America. This does not mean that monetary aggregates have no role to play in the conduct of monetary policy in the region. The signal-to-noise ratio of monetary aggregates in many countries is likely to be high owing to their history of high inflation and large swings in money growth. However, as inflation falls to single digit levels and remains there, money growth rates are likely to lose informational content and become less useful indicators of monetary policy, as occurred in industrial countries (see Estrella and Mishkin, 1997). As money aggregates become less reliable indicators of future inflation, central banks will be forced to downplay the importance of monetary targets, and search for alternative nominal anchors and communication devices.

In sum, monetary targeting is a strategy for monetary policy that has not been used by Latin American countries in the recent past, and is probably not an advisable medium-term strategy for the future. This is so because the problems that led to the abandonment of this strategy in industrialized countries (Bernanke and Mishkin, 1992) are also likely to arise in Latin America as low inflation becomes a more permanent feature. Indeed, even Germany, the quintessential monetary targeter, encountered problems with the money-inflation relationship which led the Bundesbank to miss the target ranges for its monetary targets on the order of half the time.[11] The secret to the Bundesbank's success was its long-term adherence to a "monetarist" framework to communicate to the public its commitment to price stability, along with the credibility it earned over the years which made its explanations of target misses believable to the public. Germany's relative success with monetary targeting is not a model for Latin America, where central banks need to assert their credibility over the next few years. In fact, the Bundesbank's success may not even be a model for how the European Central Bank should conduct monetary policy (see Bernanke et al., 1999; Mishkin, 1999a).

13.4 Inflation Targeting

Inflation targeting is a monetary policy strategy that involves five main elements: (1) the public announcement of medium-term numerical targets for inflation; (2) an institutional commitment to price stability as the primary goal of monetary policy, to which other goals are subordinated; (3) an information-inclusive strategy in which many variables, and not just monetary aggregates or the exchange rate, are used for deciding the setting of policy instruments; (4) a transparent monetary policy strategy that ascribes a central role to communicating to the public and the markets the plans, objectives, and rationale for the decisions of the central bank; and (5) mechanisms that make the central bank accountable for attaining its inflation objectives. The list should clarify one crucial point about inflation targeting: it entails *much more* than a public announcement of numerical targets for inflation for the year ahead. This is important in the Latin American context, because many countries in the region have routinely reported numerical inflation targets or objectives as part of the government's economic plan for the coming year (see Fry et al., 1999) and yet they *have not* been pursuing an inflation targeting strategy. The monetary policy strategy must contain the other four elements listed above for it to be consistent with inflation targeting and, hence, sustainable over the medium term.

13.4.1 Advantages of Inflation Targeting

Inflation targeting has several advantages over hard pegs and monetary targeting as a medium-term strategy for monetary policy. In contrast to a hard peg, inflation targeting enables monetary policy to focus on domestic considerations and to respond to shocks of both domestic and foreign origin. Inflation targeting also has the advantage that stability in the relationship between money and inflation is not critical to its success because it does not depend on such a relationship. Indeed, an inflation targeting strategy allows the monetary authorities to use all available information, and not just the information contained in one or two variables, to determine the best settings for the instruments of monetary policy. This is also illustrated by the model sketched in section 13.2 (Eqs. (13.1)–(13.5)). If the weight on output fluctuations in the period loss function is zero, i.e., $\lambda = 0$ in Eq. (13.4), then Svensson (1997) has shown that setting the interest rate instrument according to the optimal rule in Eq. (13.5) is equivalent to making the expected value of the inflation rate two periods ahead equal to the inflation target, i.e.,

$$E_t \pi_{t+2} = \pi^*. \tag{13.7}$$

In other words, setting monetary policy so as to attain the inflation target two periods (years) ahead is an optimal policy under these conditions. If $\lambda > 0$, i.e., if policymakers are also concerned about output fluctuations, then the interest rate instrument is also set according to Eq. (13.5), but now optimal policy implies that the approach to the inflation target is more gradual, i.e.,

$$E_t \pi_{t+2} - \pi^* = c(E_t \pi_{t+1} - \pi^*). \tag{13.8}$$

Svensson calls this type of policy reaction "flexible inflation targeting," and the evidence discussed in Bernanke et al. (1999) suggests that it is a realistic approximation of what inflation targeting countries do in practice.

Because an explicit numerical target for inflation increases the accountability of the central bank relative to a discretionary regime, inflation targeting also has the potential to reduce the likelihood that the central bank will fall into the time-inconsistency trap. Moreover, since the source of time-inconsistency is often found in (covert or open) political pressures on the central bank to engage in expansionary monetary policy, inflation targeting has the advantage of focusing the political debate on what a central bank can do on a sustainable basis—i.e., control inflation—rather than on what it cannot do through monetary policy—e.g., raise output growth, lower unemployment, or increase external competitiveness.

For inflation targeting to deliver these outcomes, there must exist a strong institutional commitment to make price stability the primary goal of the central bank. This is particularly important in Latin America, given its history of monetary mismanagement. The institutional commitment involves legislative support for an independent central bank whose charter ought to contain two key features: (1) sufficient insulation of the decision-making board of the central bank from the political process and the politicians—with the members of the board appointed to long terms and protected from arbitrary dismissal; and (2) giving the central bank full and exclusive control over the setting of monetary policy instruments. The institutional commitment to price stability also requires that the central bank be given a mandate to have price stability as its primary goal, making it clear that when there is a (perceived or actual) conflict with other goals, such as exchange rate stability or promotion of high employment, price stability must be accorded the higher priority.

Inflation-targeting regimes also put great stress on the need to make monetary policy transparent and to maintain regular channels of communication with the public; in fact, these features are central to the strategy's success. Inflation-targeting central banks have frequent communications with the government, some mandated by law and some in response to informal inquiries, and their officials take every opportunity to make public speeches on their monetary policy strategy. While these practices are also commonly used in countries that have not adopted inflation targeting (prominent examples being Germany and the United States), inflation-targeting central banks have taken public outreach a step further: not only do they engage in extended public information campaigns, but they publish *Inflation Report*-type documents (originated by the Bank of England) to present their views about the past and *future* performance of inflation and monetary policy. The publication of these documents is noteworthy because they represent a departure from the traditional, more formal reports of central banks and introduce new design elements that help enhance communication with the public.

The rationale for ascribing a central role to communication under inflation targeting is to keep the general public, financial markets and the politicians permanently informed about: (1) the goals and limitations of monetary policy, including the rationale for inflation targets; (2) the numerical values of the inflation targets and how they were determined; (3) how the inflation targets are to be achieved, given current economic conditions—i.e., baseline inflation forecasts; and (4) reasons for any deviations from targets. In countries that have adopted inflation targeting, this emphasis on communication has improved private-sector planning by reducing uncertainty about monetary policy, interest rates and inflation; has promoted public debate of monetary policy, in part by educating the public about what a central bank can and cannot achieve; and has helped clarify the responsibilities of the central bank and of politicians in the conduct of monetary policy (see Bernanke et al., 1999).

Another key feature of inflation-targeting regimes is the tendency toward increased accountability of the central bank. Indeed, transparency and communication go hand in hand with increased accountability. The strongest case of accountability of a central bank in an inflation-targeting regime is that of New Zealand, where the government has the right to dismiss the Reserve Bank's governor if the inflation targets are breached, even for one quarter. In other inflation-targeting countries, the central bank's accountability is less formalized. Nevertheless, the transparency of policy associated with inflation targeting has tended to make the central bank highly accountable to the public and the government. Sustained success in the conduct of monetary policy as measured against a pre-announced and well-defined inflation target can be instrumental in building public support for an independent central bank, even in the absence of a rigid standard of performance evaluation and penalties.

13.4.2 Disadvantages of Inflation Targeting

Critics of inflation targeting have noted at least seven major disadvantages of this monetary policy strategy. Four of those disadvantages—that inflation targeting is too rigid, that it is tantamount to full discretion, that it necessarily increases output instability, and that it hurts economic growth—we believe are misplaced. The fifth disadvantage, that inflation targeting can only produce weak central bank accountability because inflation is hard to control and because there are long lags from the monetary policy instruments to the inflation outcome, is a serious one indeed. This disadvantage is particularly important in the Latin American context because the question of inflation controllability in an environment of low inflation and flexible exchange rates is fairly new for the region and hence central banks cannot draw on minimally robust findings and regularities, and because the accountability and credibility of public institutions, including the central bank, are quite low by international standards. The sixth and seventh disadvantages, that inflation targeting cannot prevent fiscal dominance, and that the exchange rate flexibility required by inflation targeting might cause financial instability, especially when there is partial dollarization, are also very relevant in the Latin American context.

Some economists, most notably Friedman and Kuttner (1996), have criticized inflation targeting because they see it as imposing a rigid rule on the monetary authorities that does not allow them enough discretion to respond to unforeseen circumstances. For example, the central banks of the industrial countries that adopted monetary targeting in the 1970s and 1980s did not foresee the breakdown of the relationship between monetary aggregates and goal variables such as nominal spending or inflation. With rigid adherence to a monetary rule, that breakdown could have had disastrous consequences. But this is not what happened. The point here is that the useful analytical distinction between rules and discretion can be highly misleading when translated into practical policy advice. There exists useful policy strategies that are "rule-like" in that they involve forward-looking behavior that limits policymakers from *systematically* engaging in policies with undesirable long-run consequences. For the case of monetary policy, such policies avoid the time-inconsistency problem and can be suitably described as providing the monetary authorities with "constrained discretion" (see Bernanke and Mishkin, 1997).

Inflation targeting can be described exactly in this way. Inflation targeting, as actually practiced, is far from a rigid rule. Its does not imply simple or mechanical instructions as to how the central bank should conduct monetary policy. Rather, as illustrated in the Eqs. (13.7) and (13.8) above, inflation targeting requires that the central bank uses all the information available at a given point in time to determine what are the appropriate policy actions to achieve its preannounced inflation target. Unlike simple policy rules, inflation targeting mitigates the risk that the central bank ignores important information by focusing exclusively on a reduced set of variables. In fact, it gives the central bank considerable room for choosing what weight to assign to the information its receives, for changing the setting of its policy instruments and, under certain well-defined circumstances, for modifying or even breaching the inflation targets (Bernanke et al., 1999).

Other critics of inflation targeting, (e.g., Calvo 1999; Calvo and Mendoza, 2000) have raised the exact opposite criticism and argue that inflation targeting allows too much discretion to monetary policy making and, thus, is a harbinger for a myriad of undesirable outcomes. As explained in Bernanke et al. (1999), this criticism is also unwarranted. The increased transparency and accountability to which all central banks that adopt inflation targeting become subject substantially constrains their discretion and scope for making systematic policy mistakes. Transparent discussions of the conduct of monetary policy make it very difficult for the central bank to follow an overly expansionary monetary policy without it being noticed, while accountability means that the central bank pays a high price if it engages in discretionary policy that leads to high inflation or to excessive output instability (see below). The incentives and scope for central banks to adopt a purely discretionary monetary policy are thus greatly reduced.

A third criticism of inflation targeting is that by focusing monetary policy on lowering inflation it necessarily exacerbates output instability. The counter to this argument is that inflation targeting does not require an exclusive focus on inflation, but simply makes inflation the primary goal of monetary policy. In fact, experience has shown that inflation targeters do display substantial concern about output fluctuations. For example, all the industrialized countries that follow this strategy have set their inflation targets above zero:[12] at present, New Zealand has the lowest midpoint for an inflation target, 1.5%; Canada and Sweden have set the midpoint of their inflation target at 2%; while the United Kingdom and Australia have them at 2.5%. The decision by inflation targeters to choose inflation targets above zero reflects the monetary authorities' concerns that (de-facto) deflation can have substantial negative effects on real economic activity. More generally, central bankers in inflation-targeting countries continue to express their concern about fluctuations in output and employment, and the ability to accommodate short-run stabilization goals to some degree is built into all inflation-targeting regimes; one manifestation of this is that the behavior of inflation targeters is better captured by Eq. (13.8), than by Eq. (13.7), and have lowered inflation targets quite gradually toward the long-run inflation goal.

Furthermore, many inflation targeters have stressed that the floor of the target range should be considered every bit as binding as the ceiling (which is what Eq. (13.8) suggests should be the optimal policy to follow), thus helping to stabilize the real economy when there are negative shocks to aggregate demand. Inflation targets can in fact increase the central bank's ability to respond to those types of shocks; declines in aggregate demand that may cause the (future) rate of inflation to fall below the floor of the target range will automatically induce the central bank to ease monetary policy without fearing that its action will trigger a rise in inflation expectations. Another element of flexibility in an inflation targeting strategy is that deviations from inflation targets are routinely allowed in response to supply shocks that could have large adverse effects on output. There are two ways in which this is done in practice: excluding certain items from the price index on which the official inflation targets are defined (for example, excluding some combination of food and energy prices from the officially targeted price index); or accommodating the first-round effects on inflation of an observable supply shock (e.g., a rise in the value-added tax or a natural disaster that raises agricultural prices) and then explaining to the public the reasons for the deviations and its implications for the attainment of the inflation target.

A fourth concern about inflation targeting is that it will lead to low growth in output and employment. This is the age-old concern about the output costs of disinflation (from low inflation levels). Although inflation reduction has been associated with below-normal output during disinflationary phases in inflation-targeting regimes, particularly in industrialized countries, evidence shows that once low inflation was achieved, output and employment returned to their pre-disinflation levels. Hence, a conservative conclusion is that inflation targeting is not harmful to the real economy after the disinflation has occurred. Given the strong economic growth experienced by many inflation targeting countries once they attained their medium-term inflation goal, however, a case could be made that inflation targeting in fact fosters output growth in addition to controlling inflation.

The last three disadvantages that have been noted in the current debate—that inflation targeting does little for central bank accountability because inflation is hard to control, that it does not cure or prevent fiscal dominance, and that it might expose the economy to financial instability, especially when there is partial dollarization—deserve, in our view, more serious consideration.

In contrast to exchange rates and monetary aggregates, the inflation rate cannot be easily controlled by the central bank; furthermore, inflation outcomes that incorporate the effects of changes in instruments settings are revealed only after a substantial lag. To address this problem an inflation targeting strategy should place a high value on transparency; periodic releases of the central bank's inflation forecasts and explanations of its policy decisions, for example, become crucial for guiding inflation expectations and building credibility in the regime (see Svensson, 1997). However, the difficulty of controlling inflation creates a particularly severe problem for those countries in Latin America where inflation is being brought down from relatively high levels. In those circumstances, inflation forecast errors are likely to be large, inflation targets will tend to be missed more often, and it will be difficult for the central bank to gain credibility from an inflation targeting strategy, and for the public to ascertain the reasons for the deviations. This suggests that, as noted by Masson et al. (1997), inflation targeting is likely to be a more effective strategy if it is phased in only after there has been some successful disinflation.

Two other factors affecting inflation controllability that are especially relevant in the Latin American context are the (at times large) incidence of government-controlled prices on the index used to compute headline inflation, and the historically high passthrough from exchange rate depreciations. The former suggests that inflation targeting may demand a high degree of coordination between monetary and fiscal authorities on the timing and magnitude of future changes in controlled prices, while the latter suggests that the central banks of the region probably cannot afford an attitude of "benign neglect" towards exchange rate depreciations, at least until low inflation induces a change in the expectations-formation process and in the price-setting practices of households and firms (more on this below).

A sixth shortcoming of inflation targeting is that it may not be sufficient to ensure fiscal discipline or prevent fiscal dominance. Governments can still pursue irresponsible fiscal policy with an inflation-targeting regime in place. In the long run, large fiscal deficits will cause an inflation-targeting regime to break down: the fiscal deficits will eventually have to be monetized or the public debt eroded by a large devaluation, and high inflation will follow. Absence of outright fiscal dominance is a therefore key prerequisite for inflation targeting, and the setting up of institutions that help keep fiscal policy in check are crucial to the success of the strategy (Masson et al., 1997). However, as we have seen, absence of fiscal dominance is also crucial to the success of a full dollarization strategy, and it is not at all clear that full dollarization is more effective than inflation targeting to prevent its occurrence. In fact, inflation targeting may help constrain fiscal policy to the extent that the government is actively involved in setting the inflation target (including through the coordination on future adjustments to government-controlled prices).

Finally, a high degree of (partial) dollarization may create a potentially serious problem for inflation targeting. In fact, in many Latin American countries, the balance sheets of firms, households and banks are substantially dollarized, on both sides, and the bulk of long-term debt is denominated in dollars (Calvo, 1999). Because inflation targeting necessarily requires nominal exchange rate flexibility and because the economies of the region are highly open and dependent on external financing, exchange rate shocks are unavoidable. However, large and abrupt depreciations may increase the burden of dollar-denominated debt, produce a massive deterioration of balance sheets, and increase the risks of a financial crisis along the lines discussed in Mishkin (1996).

The importance of these effects can be appreciated by incorporating an exchange rate term into the aggregate demand and supply Eqs. (13.1) and (13.2) as in Ball (1999).

$$\pi_t = \pi_{t-1} + \alpha_1 y_{t-1} + \alpha_2 e_{t-1} + \varepsilon_t' \tag{13.1'}$$

$$y_t = \beta_1 y_{t-1} - \beta_2 (i_{t-1} - \pi_{t-1}) + \beta_3 (e_{t-1} - e_{t-2}) + \eta_t' \tag{13.2'}$$

with the exchange rate determined by

$$e_t = \phi i_t + u_t \tag{13.9}$$

where e_t is the log of the real exchange rate expressed as a deviation from a "normal" (medium-term) level, u_t is an error term, and ϕ captures the positive relation that exists between interest rates and the value of the currency (e.g., through capital flows and appreciation).

The optimal policy for setting the interest rate in this modified system then becomes:

$$i_t = \pi_t + b_1(\pi - \pi^*) + b_2 y_t + b_3 e_t. \tag{13.5'}$$

This modification of the Taylor rule to take explicit account of the exchange rate in setting the monetary policy instrument is consistent with an inflation-targeting regime. As we have seen before, in the case of $\lambda = 0$, monetary policy tries to achieve the long-run inflation target in two periods, while if $\lambda > 0$, the long-run inflation target is approached more gradually.

The view that in Latin America exchange rate fluctuations are likely to have a bigger affect on aggregate demand and aggregate supply (because the pass-through may be larger) just indicates that the weight on the exchange rate in the modified Taylor-rule, b_3, may be relatively large. However, this is in no way inconsistent with inflation targeting. It just implies that an inflation-targeting regime will care about exchange rate fluctuations, just as it should care about output fluctuations. It also suggests that inflation targeting in partially dollarized economies may not be viable unless there are stringent prudential regulations on, and strict supervision of, financial institutions that ensure that the system is capable of withstanding exchange rate shocks.

13.4.3 Lessons from Recent Experience

Inflation targeting is often in the eyes of the beholder. The monetary policy frameworks of several countries in Latin America—Chile, Colombia, Peru, Mexico and Brazil—contain some of the elements of inflation targeting that we have outlined earlier. However, this does not mean that all these countries should be regarded as following an inflation targeting strategy. (For a more detailed discussion of the inflation targeting experiences in these countries the reader is again referred to Mishkin and Savastano, 2000).

The Chilean experience with inflation targeting is possibly the most important to highlight because Chile was the pioneer in the region with this type of monetary policy strategy. After enacting new central bank legislation in 1989, which gave independence to the monetary authority and mandated price stability as one of its primary objectives, the central bank announced its first inflation objective in September 1990 for the 12-month inflation rate as of December 1991. Since then, the (December to December) inflation objective for the following year has been announced every year in the first 15 days of September. However, because of the uncertainty about inflation control, the inflation objective was initially treated more as an official inflation projection rather than as a formal or "hard" target (Morande and Schmidt-Hebbel, 1997). In fact, Chile's central bank pursued a very gradualist approach to lowering its inflation objectives, starting with targets of over 20% for 1991 and lowering them slowly to below 5%. Over time, the central bank put greater emphasis on the price stability objective and with its success in both disinflating and meeting its inflation objectives, the public began to interpret those objectives as "hard" targets for which the central bank could be made accountable. As part of this process of hardening the targets, in September 1994 the central bank started to announce point targets rather than target ranges for its inflation objective for the following year. However, it was only in 1999 when the central bank explicitly announced a multi-year target for inflation—consisting of a target of 3.5% for the year 2000, and a longer-term target of 2–4% for 2001 onwards.

The Chilean experience with inflation targeting looks quite successful.[13] Inflation has fallen from levels above 20% when inflation projections were first introduced to a level around 3% at present. Over the same period, output growth was very high, almost averaging over 8.5% per year from 1991 to 1997, a level comparable to those exhibited by the (former) Asian tigers. This success suggests that inflation targeting can be used to promote gradual disinflation, even when inflation starts from double digit levels, and that the gradual hardening of targets as inflation falls is an appropriate strategy to deal with the controllability problems when inflation is initially high. Indeed, not only has this strategy been used by Chile, but it is also the strategy that was followed by many of the industrialized countries that adopted inflation targeting, as is documented in Bernanke et al. (1999).

Mexico also appears to be following a gradual approach to implementing inflation targeting. In fact, senior officials of the Bank of Mexico have recently characterized Mexico's monetary policy framework as being in "a transition period towards a clear-cut inflation targeting scheme" (Carstens and Werner, 1999). For a number of years, Mexico has made public an explicit inflation objective at the time the Minister of Finance submitted to Congress the government's economic program for the following year. However, the Bank of Mexico has increasingly placed an emphasis on the inflation goal as the central objective of its monetary policy. In 1999, after annual inflation came in at 12.3%, below the 13% target, the central bank for the first time announced the (10%) inflation target for the year 2000 before the Ministry of Finance submitted to Congress the economic program for the year. Also for the first time, the Bank of Mexico announced a multi-year target for inflation by stating that it intended to lower inflation to "international levels," (i.e., somewhere in the 2–3%

range) by 2003. Starting in April of 2000, the Bank of Mexico has been issuing an *Inflation Report*, which documents what has been happening on the inflation front and how the Bank of Mexico intends to achieve its inflation objective. These developments are likely to contribute to raise the accountability of the Bank of Mexico for complying with its inflation objectives.

In contrast, and despite the central bank's announcement since 1991 of explicit numerical targets for 1-year ahead inflation as part of the government's economic program, Colombia did not make a serious commitment to lowering inflation during the 1990s. Reducing inflation from the 20–25% range was not a priority of monetary policy: Colombia's central bank continued to give priority to other objectives, especially output stability, whenever those goals seemed to be put in jeopardy by the inflation target (see Cardenas and Partow, 1998). Not surprisingly, Colombia's anti-inflation strategy was unsuccessful: average annual inflation in the period 1991–1998 (22.7%) was essentially the same as the average for the 1980s (23.6%), and from 1991 to 1996 the central bank consistently exceeded its always modest inflation targets. The inflation target was met for the first time in 1997—with inflation ending slightly below the 18% target—but the target was breached again in 1998 (16.7% versus 16%). In that year, investors' concerns about Colombia's large fiscal and external deficits (in the order of 4% and 5% of GDP, respectively) and about its political situation led to a string of speculative attacks on the peso. In response, the central bank first raised interest rates to record-high levels and then, in September 1998, depreciated both edges of the exchange rate band by 9%. The response did not arrest the speculative pressures and induced a sharp slowdown in activity. In September 1999, when international reserves reached dangerously low levels, the trading band was eliminated and the peso was allowed to float. The failed defense of the exchange rate band led Colombia to suffer its first recession in seven decades and brought inflation below 10% for the first time since the 1970s, but it was apparent that this was not a desired policy outcome. Nonetheless, as had been done in Brazil a year earlier (see below), the authorities took advantage of the circumstances to reformulate monetary policy. The inflation target for 2000 was set at 10% and, in October 2000, the authorities publicly adopted inflation targeting as their framework for monetary policy by announcing numerical inflation targets for the years 2001 (8%) and 2002 (6%) and taking concrete actions to increase the accountability and transparency of the central bank.

Fiscal discipline and a sound and well-regulated banking system are crucial for the viability and success of inflation targeting, just as they are for the success of hard pegs, and the experience in Chile supports this view. The fiscal balance in Chile ended in surplus every year from 1991 to 1998, and during 1991–1997, the surplus averaged 2.8% of GDP, clear indications that fiscal policy was kept under control. In addition, due largely to the measures taken in the aftermath of the severe banking

crisis of the early 1980s, Chile's standards and practices in the areas of banking regulation and supervision during the 1990s have been of a quality comparable to those
found in industrialized countries and far superior to those found in the rest of Latin
America (with the possible exception of Argentina since 1995). The resulting solidity
of the Chilean financial system has meant that the ability of the central bank to take
steps to defend the currency and the banks has never been in question, which may
have helped Chile experience less pressures on its currency than other countries of
the region at the time of the Tequila crisis (see IMF, 1996). The controls on short-
term capital inflows have also been cited often as another important factor behind
the low vulnerability and relative stability of the Chilean economy in the 1990s.
However, the controls are highly controversial and their contribution is difficult to
ascertain.[14] Our reading of the evidence suggests that, from the perspective of monetary policy and inflation control, strict prudential supervision was probably more
important.

Chile seems to be way ahead of the other countries who have adopted some form
of inflation targeting in Latin America in terms of broad compliance with the basic
requirements. Lack of fiscal discipline is a particularly serious concern in Brazil and
Colombia, whereas weaknesses in the banking system are the big question mark in
Mexico, and, to a lesser extent, Peru. Inflation targeting alone will not solve these
problems; neither will hard pegs. Setting *multi-year* inflation targets in coordination
with the government (including on the issue of government-controlled prices) may
help reduce the risk of fiscal profligacy, but it is not enough. Setting up institutions
that help keep fiscal policy in check and others that promote and enforce sound
banking practices, seem to be the only solutions that may prove lasting and workable
in the region.

The Chilean experience in 1998–1999, when the economy entered a recession (with
output growth falling to 3.4% in 1998 and by an estimated −1.3% in 1999) illustrates
the tricky issues that arise when the exchange rate is an important consideration
in the conduct of monetary policy. As part of its monetary policy regime, from the
mid-1980s until August 1999, Chile had an exchange rate band around a crawling
peg which was (loosely) tied to *lagged* domestic inflation. The central bank stressed
that the purpose of the exchange rate band *was not* inflation control, and this was the
reason why, for most of the period, the rate of crawl was set on a backward-looking
rather than a forward-looking basis. Rather the central bank argued that the purpose
of the exchange rate band was to keep the real exchange rate in a range consistent
with medium- and long-term external equilibrium and, thus, preclude an "excessive"
current account deficit. Over time, the central bank also made it clear through its
actions that the inflation target would take precedence over the exchange rate band
when there was a potential conflict between the two objectives. Thus, for example, in
various instances from 1992 to 1997 when large capital inflows pushed the exchange

rate close to the appreciated edge of the band, the central bank widened the band and even revalued the central parity while keeping the inflation target unchanged, thus signaling to the public that it attached a higher weight to lowering inflation than to resisting a real appreciation that seemed warranted by the "fundamental" determinants of the real exchange rate.

The focus on the exchange rate did help lead to a serious policy mistake in 1998. In the aftermath of the Asian crisis and then the meltdown in Russia, the Chilean central bank was reluctant to ease monetary policy and let the exchange rate depreciate in order to cushion the effects of a substantial negative terms of trade shock. Instead, the central bank raised interest rates sharply and narrowed its exchange rate band. As a result, the inflation target was undershot and the economy entered a recession for the first time under the inflation targeting regime. Not surprisingly given these outcomes, the central bank came under strong criticism.[15] During 1999, the central bank reversed course, eased monetary policy by lowering interest rates, and allowed the peso to depreciate.

The other countries in Latin America that are moving toward inflation targeting also have been reluctant to adopt an attitude of "benign neglect" of exchange rate movements (i.e., a "pure float"). Although some focus on the exchange rate seems broadly appropriate—especially while they were undertaking a disinflation—all of them probably went too far for too long in the direction of limiting exchange rate flexibility—not only through the explicit use of exchange rate bands, employed by all countries, except Peru, for a good part of the 1990s, but also through frequent direct and indirect intervention in the foreign exchange market. The main problem with responding too heavily and too frequently to movements in a "flexible" exchange rate is, of course, that the strategy runs the risk of transforming the exchange rate into a nominal anchor for monetary policy that takes precedence over the inflation target, at least in the eyes of the public. With time, this practice may become observationally equivalent with a strategy of nominal exchange rate targeting.

To mitigate the risk that the exchange rate might replace the inflation target as the economy's main nominal anchor, central banks can increase the transparency of the role of the exchange rate by emphasizing that concerns about exchange rate effects on aggregate demand and supply imply that the setting of interest rates would necessarily reflect exchange rate movements, as is illustrated by Eq. (13.5′). What this means in practice is that the central bank would be smoothing exchange rate fluctuations, but would not involve attempting to prevent the exchange rate from reaching its market-determined level over longer horizons. Exchange rate smoothing via foreign exchange market interventions might be necessary at times to prevent or arrest large and abrupt exchange rate fluctuations that are clearly divorced from fundamentals. However, persistent exchange market interventions, particularly unsterilized ones, are likely to be counterproductive because they are not transparent. Instead, exchange rate smoothing via changes in the interest rate instrument will tend to be more transparent and help signal that the inflation targets, and not the exchange rate remains the primary nominal anchor of the economy.

Central banks should also explain to the public the rationale for exchange rate intervention in a manner analogous to that for interest-rate smoothing, i.e., as a policy aimed not at resisting market-determined movements in an asset price, but at mitigating potentially destabilizing effects of abrupt and sustained changes in that price. More generally, we think it is important that central banks understand that there are no "good floats" or "bad floats," but that there is such a thing as "good" and "bad" monetary policy under flexible exchange rates. Letting the exchange rate become the de-facto nominal anchor of the economy through excessive intervention in a quasi-inflation targeting regime is an example of the latter.

It is also important that central banks in Latin America recognize that, as is the case for most economic relationships, the passthrough from exchange rate changes to prices is likely to be regime-dependent. After a sustained period of low inflation with effective, as opposed to fictional, exchange rate flexibility, the informational content of the exchange rate in the expectations-formation process and price-setting practices of households and firms is likely to fall. Thus, the widespread view that a currently high passthrough from exchange rate changes to prices is a barrier to successful inflation targeting is probably overdone. Indeed, the low pass-through that occurred after the Brazilian devaluation in 1999, which might have been reduced by the adoption of an inflation targeting regime (as well as by the slack in the economy), suggests that a high pass-through is not a permanent feature of Latin American economies.

Another lesson from the Chilean experience is that a key requirement for inflation-targeting regimes in Latin America, as elsewhere, is the recognition that undershooting inflation targets, which occurred recently not only in Chile but also Peru, is just as costly as overshooting the targets. Support for an independent central bank which is pursuing price stability can erode if the central bank is perceived as focusing too narrowly on lowering inflation to the detriment of other objectives, especially output stability. By just as readily admitting their mistakes when an inflation target is undershot as when it is overshot, and continuously refining their technical expertise to minimize the occurrence of such events, central banks may increase support for their independence and for the inflation targeting regime.

Brazil's inflation targeting regime is too recent to evaluate fully, although so far the results have been encouraging, with Brazil able to keep inflation within the target range of 6–10% and 4–8% in 1999 and 2000, respectively. Brazil decided to adopt an inflation-targeting regime shortly after the collapse of the real, when the new governor of the central bank, Arminio Fraga, announced its intention to enact such a framework for monetary policy. On June 21, 1999, the President of Brazil issued a decree instituting an inflation targeting framework for the conduct of monetary policy. The regime contemplated in the decree contains all the key elements of an inflation targeting strategy, namely: (1) the announcement of multi-year inflation targets (with explicit numerical targets for the 12-month rate of inflation in the years 1999, 2000 and 2001, and a commitment to announce the targets for 2002 onwards 2 years in advance); (2) assigning to the National Monetary Council the responsibility for setting the inflation targets and tolerance ranges based on a proposal by the Minister of Finance; (3) giving to the central bank of Brazil full responsibility to implement the policies needed to attain the inflation targets; (4) establishing procedures to increase the central bank's accountability (specifically, if the target range is breached, the central bank president would have to issue an open letter to the Minister of Finance explaining the causes of the deviation, the measures that will be taken to eliminate it, and the time it will take to get inflation back inside the tolerance range); and (5) taking actions to improve the transparency of monetary policy (concretely, the central bank was requested to issue a quarterly *Inflation Report* modeled after that produced by the Bank of England).

The Brazilian framework has all the "bells and whistles" of an inflation targeting regime, and was clearly the first comprehensive attempt to establish a regime of this type in Latin America. What is especially striking about Brazil's move to inflation targeting is how fast it occurred. The first inflation report was issued in July 1999, just a few months after Fraga was confirmed, with the second, right on schedule in September. The reports not only discuss clearly the conditions prevailing in the economy and the prospects for inflation, but also provide the central bank's inflation forecasts under different scenarios—including through the use of "fan charts" depicting the probabilities of different inflation paths. Many central bankers in the Latin American region have been concerned that it might take them a long time to acquire the technical capability to issue an inflation report of this type. Brazil has shown the way, indicating that an inflation targeting regime, with a high degree of transparency and accountability can indeed be implemented quickly.

The other three countries in the region mentioned here have lagged behind in adopting other key elements of inflation targeting. Even, Chile, with the success of its inflation targeting regime in reducing inflation, was slow to adopt a full-fledged inflation targeting regime: it was not until May 2000 that the Chilean central bank began to produce an *Inflation Report*-type of document in which it publishes its baseline inflation forecasts.

13.5 Conclusion

We have taken the view that the real debate over monetary policy regimes in Latin America should not be over whether the exchange rate regime should be fixed or flexible. Instead, the debate should be over what is the best way to constrain discretion over monetary policy in Latin American countries. Like most economists, we come up with the answer that "it depends." In particular, we think that the key to the answer lies on the institutional environment in each country. There are some countries in Latin America which do not appear to have the political and other institutions to constrain monetary policy if it is allowed some discretion. In these countries, there is a strong argument for hard pegs, including full dollarization, which allow little or no discretion to the monetary authorities. On the other hand, there are countries in Latin America that seem to have the ability to constrain discretion, with Chile being the clearest example, and for these cases, we believe that inflation targeting is likely to produce a monetary policy which keeps inflation low and yet appropriately copes with domestic and foreign shocks.

Monetary targeting as a strategy for Latin America is not viable because of the likely instability of the relationship between monetary aggregates and inflation, of which there is ample international evidence. Therefore, it is not surprising that no Latin American country has truly followed a monetary targeting strategy, and those that have tried or have been regarded as trying, have instead conducted a highly discretionary monetary policy which is, of necessity, non-transparent and has the potential of breaking down at any point.

Proponents of different strategies for the conduct of monetary policy often have a tendency to argue that their preferred strategy will be a panacea that will help resolve hard problems such as fiscal dominance. The experience in Latin America suggests that these arguments are quite problematic because a monetary policy strategy, no matter whether it involves a hard peg or an inflation target, will not be successful in maintaining low inflation over the medium term unless government policies create the right institutional environment. Rigorous prudential supervision, which ensures the safety and soundness of the financial system, is crucial to the success of an inflation targeting regime just as it is for hard pegs. Also, sound and sustainable fiscal policy is as essential to the success of inflation targeting regimes as it is to the viability of hard pegs. Large fiscal deficits and the ensuing buildup of government debt will eventually lead to the failure of both types of regime.

The bottom line is that adopting a strategy for monetary policy, whether it be a hard peg or a regime with greater flexibility of exchange rates, like inflation targeting, cannot solve the basic problems that have existed in Latin American economies for a long time. Successful monetary policy in Latin America cannot be done in a vacuum. Design of the basic institutional infrastructure in those economies must be addressed and improved in order to attain and preserve low and stable inflation.

A number of economists (e.g., Eichengreen and Hausmann, 1999) have become convinced that Latin America is subject to some type of "original sin" and thus is unlikely to grow up and develop institutions which would promote good monetary policy. With this view, it seems sensible to effectively close down central banks and adopt a currency board or to go for (unilateral) full dollarization. We are quite skeptical of the "original sin" argument. The recent successes in bringing down inflation in many countries of the region suggests to us that it is possible for Latin America to develop institutions which would allow its central banks to follow a monetary policy focused on keeping inflation low while preserving some scope to mitigate output fluctuations. We are thus not convinced that it is time to give up on the maturation of Latin America, and believe that the move towards inflation targeting that has started in the region will continue and make further inroads in the years ahead.

Acknowledgements

The views expressed in this paper are exclusively those of the authors and not those of Columbia University, the National Bureau of Economic Research or the International Monetary Fund. We thank Sebastian Edwards, Esteban Jadresic, Fernando Losada, Federico Sturzenegger, Lars Svensson, participants in the Macro Lunch at Columbia University, participants at the Interamerican Seminar, and an anonymous referee, for helpful comments and Iván Guerra for helpful research assistance.

Notes

Prepared for the Interamerican Seminar on Economics, Buenos Aires, December 2–4, 1999.

1. For a discussion of two fallacies that arise recurrently in discussions of monetary policy and exchange rate regimes in Latin America, see Mishkin and Savastano (2000).

2. A fifth possible strategy that has been suggested by some as best suited for semi-open economies is nominal income targeting (e.g., Frankel, 1995). A major problem with this strategy, however, is that it has never been tried in practice, either in industrial or emerging economies. This, plus the fact that nominal income targeting could be seen as broadly equivalent to inflation targeting under some reasonable assumptions but with some serious disadvantages (McCallum, 1996; Mishkin, 1999a), leads us to drop it from the set of monetary policy strategies that we consider relevant for Latin American countries.

3. For a review of the main arguments against soft pegs and of the lessons from recent experience, see Obstfeld and Rogoff (1995), Eichengreen and Masson (1998) and Mishkin (1998, 1999a). Note that we are not ruling out the use of exchange-rate pegs, even if not of the hard peg variety, as a tool in the initial phases of a stabilization program. However, the shortcomings of soft pegs indicate that they will be far less useful as a longer-run strategy for monetary policy.

4. See, for example, Hanke and Schuler (1994), Williamson (1995), and Ghosh et al. (1998).

5. As Svensson (1997) indicates, the Taylor rule in Eq. (13.5) above is only optimal if inflation and the output gap are sufficient statistics for the model, i.e., if no other variables enter the aggregate supply and demand functions. If other variables do affect aggregate demand and supply, the optimal rule would need to be modified to have the interest rate respond to these variables as well. Note that in practice, a Taylor rule like Eq. (13.5) would never be followed slavishly in practice because central banks use judgement in setting policy instruments. Thus, a Taylor rule is better thought of providing a useful benchmark for policymakers, but should not be characterized as a rule which solve the time-inconsistency problem. The use of the word "rule" in Taylor rule can therefore be somewhat misleading.

6. Clarida et al. (1998) give a nice illustration of how unlikely this can be by demonstrating that the Taylor rules estimated for countries like Italy, France and the United Kingdom would have led to very different settings of interest rates during the period of the ERM than those generated by Germany.

7. The US economic warfare against Panama sparked a series of bank runs that nearly caused the collapse of the Panamanian payments system (see Garber, 1999). When the standstill ended, after almost 2 years, a number of small banks had disappeared, the money supply had shrunk by 30%, and real output had fallen by 18%. This episode illustrates that a country with a hard peg is not exempt from bank runs and panics, whatever their origin may be. The fact that the United States also had frequent bank panics in the 19th and early 20th century even when it had a hard peg (the gold standard) also illustrates this point—e.g., see Mishkin (1991).

8. See, for instance, Goodhart (1989), Bernanke and Mishkin (1992), and Estrella and Mishkin (1997).

9. See Mishkin and Savastano (2000) for a fuller discussion of the monetary policy strategy of Peru and Mexico during the 1990s.

10. One of us has argued elsewhere that even the discretionary monetary policy regime in the United States, which has been so successful, may not produce desirable outcomes over the long run and needs to be modified, even though the environment for "good" discretion in the United States is far more favorable than in Latin America (see Mishkin, 1999a).

11. Partly because of this, a number of researchers regard Germany's monetary policy as being closer to an inflation targeting regime than to a monetary targeting regime. See, for example, Clarida and Gertler (1998), Bernanke et al. (1999), and Mishkin (1999a).

12. CPI indices typically contain an upward bias in the measurement of true inflation and so it is not surprising that the chosen inflation targets were all above zero. However, the point is that these countries have chosen targets for inflation that exceed zero even after taking account of measurement bias.

13. Corbo (1998) and Landerretche et al. (1999) analyze the factors behind Chile's successful disinflation of the 1990s. For a critical view of the disinflation, see Calvo and Mendoza (1999).

14. For a recent overview of the debate surrounding Chile's capital controls, see Edwards (1999).

15. In contrast, during this same period, Australia eased monetary policy, thereby allowing the currency to depreciate to cushion the effects of its own negative terms of trade shock. This policy met with great success, resulting in an economy that remained strong while the inflation target continued to be met. One reason why Chile's central bank did not react in a similar manner to a comparable shock may have been its (unwarranted) concern that a large peso depreciation would lead to inflation exceeding the target and, hence, erode its credibility.

References

Ball, L., 1999. Policy rules for open economies. In: Taylor, J. B. (Ed.), *Monetary Policy Rules*. University of Chicago Press, Chicago.

Bernanke, B., Mishkin, F., 1992. Central bank behavior and the strategy of monetary policy: observations from six industrialized countries. *NBER Macroeconomics Annual*, 183–228.

Bernanke, B., Mishkin, F., 1997. Inflation targeting: a new framework for monetary policy? *Journal of Economic Perspectives* 11 (2), 97–116, Spring.

Bernanke, B., Laubach, T., Mishkin, F., Posen, A., 1999. *Inflation Targeting: Lessons from the International Experience*. Princeton Univ. Press, Princeton, NJ.

Calvo, G., 1999. "Capital Markets and the Exchange Rate," mimeo, University of Maryland, October.

Calvo, G., Mendoza, E., 1999. Empirical puzzles of Chilean stabilization policy. In: Perry, G., Leipziger, D. (Eds.), *Chile: Recent Policy Lessons and Emerging Challenges*. The World Bank, Washington, DC.

Calvo, G., Mendoza, E., 2000. Capital-market crises and economic collapse in emerging markets: An Informational-Frictions Approach," mimeo, Duke University and University of Maryland, January.

Calvo, G., Vegh, C., 1994. Inflation stabilization and nominal anchors. *Contemporary Economic Policy*, 12.

Calvo, G., Vegh, C., 1999. Inflation stabilization and BOP crises in developing countries. In: Taylor, J., Woodford, M. (Eds.), *Handbook of Macroeconomics*. Elsevier, North Holland.

Cardenas, M., Partow, Z., 1998. "Does Independence Matter? The Case of the Colombian Central Bank," mimeo, Bogota: Fedesarrollo.

Carstens, A., Werner, A., 1999. "Mexico's Monetary Policy Framework under a Floating Exchange Rate Regime," Banco de Mexico Research Paper 9905, May.

Clarida, R., Gertler, M., 1998. How the Bundesbank conducts monetary policy. In: Romer, C., Romer, D. (Eds.), *Reducing Inflation*. The University of Chicago Press for the NBER, Chicago.

Clarida, R., Gali, J., Gertler, M., 1998. Monetary policy rules in practice: some international evidence. *European Economic Review* 42, 1033–1068.

Clarida, R., Gali, J., Gertler, M., 1999. The science of monetary policy: a new keynesian perspective. *Journal of Economic Literature* 37, 1661–1707 (December).

Corbo, V., 1998. Reaching one-digit inflation: the Chilean experience. *Journal of Applied Economics* 1 (1), 123–163.

Corbo, V., 1999. "Monetary Policy in Latin America in the '90s," paper presented at the Third Annual Conference of the Central Bank of Chile, September 20–21, 1999.

Cottarelli, C., Giannini, C., 1997. Credibility Without Rules? Monetary Frameworks in the Post-Bretton Woods Era, IMF Occasional Paper 154, Washington, DC: International Monetary Fund.

Edwards, S., 1999. "How Effective are Controls on Capital Inflows? An Evaluation of Chile's Experience," mimeo, UCLA, June.

Eichengreen, B., Hausmann, R., 1999. "Exchange Rates and Financial Fragility," NBER Working Paper 7448, November.

Eichengreen, B., Masson, P., 1998. Exit Strategies: Policy Options for Countries Seeking Greater Exchange Rate Flexibility, IMF Occasional Paper 168, September.

Estrella, A., Mishkin, F., 1997. Is there a role for monetary aggregates in the conduct of monetary policy? *Journal of Monetary Economics* 40, 279–304.

Favaro, E., 1996. "Peru's Stabilization Under Floating Exchange Rates," mimeo, The World Bank, September.

Frankel, J., 1995. Monetary regime choice for a semi-open country. In: Edwards, S. (Ed.), *Capital Controls, Exchange Rates and Monetary Policy in the World Economy*. Cambridge Univ. Press, New York.

Friedman, B., Kuttner, K., 1996. A price target for U.S. monetary policy? Lessons from the experience with money growth targets. *Brookings Papers on Economic Activity* 1, 77–125.

Fry, M., et al., 1999. "Monetary Policy Frameworks in a Global Context," report prepared for a Central Bank Governors' Symposium at the Bank of England, June 4, 1999, London: Bank of England.

Garber, P., 1999. "Hard-Wiring to the Dollar: From Currency Board to Currency Zone," Global Markets Research, London: Deustche Bank, March.

Ghosh, A., Gulde, A., Wolf, H. "Currency Boards: The Ultimate Fix?" IMF Working Paper 98/8, January.

Goodhart, C., 1989. The conduct of monetary policy. *The Economic Journal* 99, 293–346.

Hanke, S., Schuler, K., 1994. Currency Boards for Developing Countries: A Handbook. ICS Press, San Francisco.

Hausmann, R., Gavin, M., 1995. "Overcoming Volatility in Latin America," Office of the Chief Economist, Washington, D.C.: Inter-American Development Bank, August.

IMF, 1996. International Capital Markets: Developments, Prospects and Key Policy Issues. IMF, Washington, DC, September.

Landerretche, O., Morandé, F., Schmidt-Hebbel, K., 1999. "Inflation Targets and Stabilization in Chile," Central Bank of Chile, Working Paper 55, December.

Masson, P., Savastano, M., Sharma, S. 1997. "The Scope for Inflation Targeting in Developing Countries," IMF Working Paper 97/130, October.

McCallum, B., 1996. "Inflation Targeting in Canada, New Zealand, Sweden, The United Kingdom, and in General," NBER Working Paper 5579, Cambridge, MA, May.

Mishkin, F., 1991. Asymmetric information and financial crises: a historical perspective. In: Hubbard, R. G. (Ed.), *Financial Markets and Financial Crises*. University of Chicago Press, Chicago, pp. 69–108.

Mishkin, F., 1996. Understanding financial crises: a developing country perspective. In: Bruno, M., Pleskovic, B. (Eds.), *Annual World Bank Conference on Development Economics*. World Bank, Washington, DC, pp. 29–62.

Mishkin, F., 1998. The dangers of exchange-rate pegging in emerging markets countries. *International Finance* 1 (1), 81–101.

Mishkin, F., 1999a. International experiences with different monetary regimes. *Journal of Monetary Economics* 43, 579–606.

Mishkin, F., 1999b. Lessons from the Asian crisis. *Journal of International Money and Finance* 18 (4), 709–723, August.

Mishkin, F., Savastano, M., 2000. "Monetary Policy Strategies for Latin America," National Bureau Working Paper No. 7617, March.

Morande, F., Schmidt-Hebbel, K., 1997. "Inflation Targets and Indexation in Chile," mimeo, Central Bank of Chile, August.

Moreno, J., 1999. Lessons from the monetary experience of Panama: a dollar economy with financial integration. *Cato Journal* 18 (3) (Winter).

Obstfeld, M., Rogoff, K., 1995. The mirage of fixed exchange rates. *Journal of Economic Perspectives* 9 (4), Fall.

Savastano, M., 1992. The pattern of currency substitution in Latin America: an overview. Revista de Analisis Economico (special issue), June.

Schuler, K. 1999. "Encouraging Official Dollarization in Emerging Markets," Joint Economic Committee Staff Report, Washington, DC: United States Senate, April.

Svensson, L., 1997. Inflation forecast targeting: implementing and monitoring inflation targets. *European Economic Review* 41, 1111–1146.

Williamson, J., 1995. What Role for Currency Boards? Policy Analyses in International Economics, 40 Institute for International Economics, Washington, DC.

14 Monetary Policy Strategies for Emerging Market Countries: Lessons from Latin America

Frederic S. Mishkin and Miguel A. Savastano

14.1 Introduction

The conduct of monetary policy in emerging market (and transition) countries confronts different challenges from that in industrialized countries. In contrast to the experience in industrialized countries, the past monetary policy experience of many emerging market countries has been dismal, with extreme episodes of monetary instability, swinging from very high inflations, to massive capital flight, to collapses in their financial systems. However, in recent years the prospects for successful monetary policy in emerging market countries have increased, as exemplified by the far lower rates of inflation in the Latin American region, which have fallen from an average of over 400% in 1989 to below 10% at the beginning of the millennium. (See figures 14.1 and 14.2.)

Given the more favorable environment for the conduct of monetary policy in emerging market and transition countries, where should they go from here in designing appropriate long-run strategies for the conduct of their monetary policy? The central issue in addressing this question is whether an emerging market country has a chance of setting up institutions and mechanisms that will effectively and efficiently constrain the discretion of its monetary authorities. In principle, there are three broad monetary policy strategies that can produce a nominal anchor that credibly constrains the discretion of the central bank over the medium term: "hard" exchange-rate pegs, monetary targeting, and inflation targeting.[1]

An earlier paper, Mishkin and Savastano (2001), provides a theoretical framework for discussing the advantages and disadvantages of each of these three strategies. This chapter complements the analysis in that paper by conducting detailed case studies of recent monetary policy experiences in Latin America in order to evaluate how well each strategy has worked in practice. The evidence from these case studies provides useful clues as to which of the three strategies might be best suited to conditions in different emerging market countries.

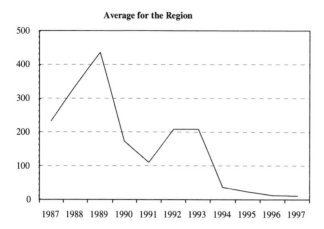

Figure 14.1
Latin America: Inflation in the 1990s. 12-month percentage change in the regional CPI.
Source: IMF, World Economic Outlook.

14.2   Hard Pegs

There are essentially two types of "hard peg" regimes for monetary policy: a currency board and full dollarization. In a currency board, the domestic currency is backed 100% by a foreign currency (say, U.S. dollars) and the note-issuing authority, whether the central bank or the government, fixes a conversion rate to this currency and stands ready to exchange domestically issued notes for the foreign currency on demand. A currency board is a hard peg because the commitment to the fixed exchange rate has a legal (or even constitutional) backing and because monetary policy is, in effect, put on autopilot and completely taken out of the hands of the central bank and the government. Full dollarization involves eliminating altogether the domestic currency and replacing it with a foreign currency (say, the U.S. dollar). It represents a stronger commitment to monetary stability than a currency board because it makes it much more costly—though still not impossible—for the government to regain control over monetary policy and/or change the parity of the (non-existent) domestic currency.

14.2.1   Lessons from the Recent Experience in Latin America
The two prime examples of hard pegs in Latin America are Argentina and Panama. Both hard pegs were created under special, and quite different, historical circumstances. In the case of Argentina, the hard peg was the cornerstone of the stabilization program of 1990–91 that ended the hyperinflation bouts of the 1980s. In the case of Panama, the government's decision to adopt the U.S. dollar as the legal ten-

Argentina, Brazil and Peru

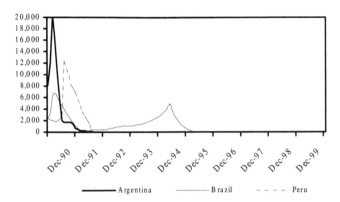

Chile, Colombia and Mexico

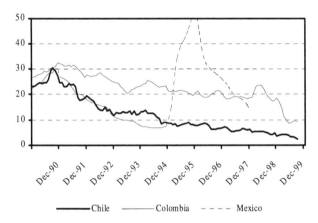

Figure 14.2
Latin America: Inflation 1990–1999. 12-month percentage change in CPI.
Source: IMF, International Financial Statistics.

der and to eschew the creation of a central bank was made in 1904, the year after the country was founded.

Argentina   The extreme inflation of the 1980s wreaked havoc with the Argentine economy. Numerous stabilization plans failed to break the inflationary dynamics and psychology fueled by high fiscal deficits, entrenched indexation practices and ballooning interest payments on government debt. To end this cycle of inflationary surges, Argentina tightened monetary and fiscal policies in early 1990 and then decided to adopt a hard peg with the passage of the Convertibility Law of April 1, 1991. The law transformed the central bank into a quasi-currency board that could only issue domestic currency when it was fully backed by foreign exchange (except for up to 10% of the monetary base which could be backed by dollar-denominated government bonds), could not alter the exchange rate from one new peso to the dollar, and could not provide credit to the government. The law also eliminated all exchange controls, banned automatic indexation clauses and allowed contracts to be expressed and settled in foreign currency (Cavallo, 1993).

The first four years of Argentina's quasi-currency board were highly successful and have become the textbook example of the benefits of a currency board for stopping high inflation (Hanke and Schuler, 1994). Inflation fell from an 800% annual rate in 1990 to less than 5% by the end of 1994, and economic growth was rapid, averaging almost 8% per year from 1991 to 1994 (see figures 14.2 and 14.3). Fiscal deficits were also kept moderate, averaging below 1% of GDP, and the government implemented far-reaching structural reforms, especially in the areas of privatization and trade.

However, in the aftermath of the Mexican crisis of late 1994, a speculative attack against the Argentine currency board quickly turned into a major banking crisis. From December 1994 until March 1995, the prices of Argentine stocks and bonds plummeted, the banking system lost 17% of its total deposits, the central bank lost more than a third of its international reserves ($5.5 billion), the money supply contracted, interest rates shot up—with the interbank rate briefly exceeding 70%, and external credit lines vanished. An interesting feature of this attack is that the run on the banks had two distinct phases: a first phase where the public moved peso deposits from small banks to large banks and switched part of those deposits into dollars, and a second phase, during March 1995, where the run of deposits spread to the dollar segment of the system and affected all financial institutions—including local branches of large foreign banks (IMF, 1996). A run on dollar deposits in large banks (including foreign ones) clearly suggests that the public was not only hedging against a devaluation of the peso but against something worse, such as a confiscation, the imposition of exchange controls or a complete meltdown of the banking system. Whatever the forces at play, the severity of the attack brought home the point that the Argentine currency board was not exempt from a sudden loss of confidence from

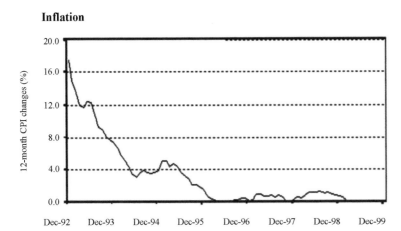

Figure 14.3
Argentina: Inflation and growth, 1993–1999.
Source: Central Bank of Argentina, Ministry of Economy and IFS.

domestic and foreign investors, and that the Argentine banking system was not prepared to cope with those shocks.

The Argentine central bank had its lender of last resort role constrained by the
Convertibility Law, yet it mitigated the adverse effects of the run on bank deposits
by lowering reserve requirements, providing direct credit via rediscounts and swaps,
and participating actively in the restructuring, privatization and liquidation of
troubled banks. By the end of April, the central bank had managed to provide over
$5 billion of liquidity to the banking system, more than a third of it in the form of
direct loans, and was able to avert a large-scale collapse of the banking system. An
often overlooked aspect of the success of the Argentine government in containing the
banking crisis and preserving its quasi-currency board was the substantial assistance
it received from the multilaterals (i.e., the IMF, the World Bank, and the Interamerican Development Bank) who lent Argentina almost $5 billion during 1995. Despite
all these efforts the real economy took a nosedive; the May unemployment rate shot
up to 18% and 1995 real GDP fell by more than 3%. It was not until 1996 that the
economy began to recover.

The overall performance of the Argentine economy from 1996 to 1998 was more
uneven than in the first half of the 1990s. Real output grew at an average rate of 6
percent and inflation fell to practically zero, but, apart from a strengthening of prudential regulations and supervision and a fast process of bank consolidation, the
authorities' drive for undertaking further structural reforms and fiscal adjustment
started to falter. The fiscal deficit, which had reached almost 4% of GDP in 1995,
averaged 2.7% from 1996 to 1998 despite the pick-up in growth; the current account
deficits widened, and all debt indicators deteriorated markedly. Investors' concerns
about these developments surfaced in the Fall of 1998, following the Russian crisis
and the decline in commodity prices. Domestic interest rates and spreads on Argentine bonds, which had been largely unaffected by the Asian crises of 1997, shot up in
September 1998 to levels not seen since the Tequila crisis. Although the spike was
short lived and the Argentine government continued tapping the markets with IMF
support, external financing dried up and real output fell by 3.5 percent in the second
half of the year (see figure 14.3).

The devaluation of the Brazilian real in January 1999 sent Argentina into a full-
blown recession that lasted more than three years. The sudden loss of competitiveness vis-à-vis a major trading partner exacerbated the downturn that had started in
late 1998. Although there was no run on deposits and no loss of reserves until late
2000, interest rates and spreads on Argentine paper rose steadily, bank credit stalled,
and industrial production plummeted. By mid-2001 the unemployment rate reached
18% and the fiscal situation became completely unsustainable, with spreads on government debt in excess of 2,500 basis points, collapsing tax revenues and no available
sources of financing. On December 25, 2001, in the midst of a social and political

crisis that brought down the de la Rua government, Argentina declared default on $150 billion of government debt.

What transpired in Argentina in 2001 is a dramatic example of the perils of fiscal profligacy in a hard peg regime stressed in Mishkin and Savastano (2001). Faced with a weakening fiscal position and with no access to foreign credit, the Argentine government forced the banks to absorb large amounts of government debt (first by removing the central bank governor and appointing one that was willing to lower banks' liquidity requirements, and later by resorting to all forms of "arm twisting"). The ensuing decline in the value of the government debt in banks' balance sheets along with rising bad loans caused by the severity of the recession fueled increasing doubts about the solvency of the banking system. This led to a full scale banking panic in October–November, with the public rushing to withdraw their deposits and interbank interest rates soaring. On December 1, after losing more than $8 billion of deposits, the government imposed wide-ranging controls on banking and foreign exchange transactions, including setting a $1000 monthly limit on deposit withdrawals. Three weeks later the government was pushed out of office.

The government of President Duhalde that took office at the beginning of 2002 finally pulled the plug on the currency board. On January 6, the exchange rate applicable to exports, essential imports and most capital transactions was set at 1.4 pesos/dollar, while a floating exchange was created for all other transactions. Announcements that banks would (eventually) be required to repay their dollar deposit liabilities in full, while bank loan assets of under $100,000 would be converted into pesos (with their consequent lower value) created, overnight, a massive hole on banks' balance sheets. The draconian limits on deposit withdrawals were maintained, thus aggravating the disruption to the payments system and bringing the whole economy to a virtual halt. The precise unfolding of the crisis remained unclear at the time of this writing, but the near term prospects seem unambiguously grim.

Panama   Panama has recently come into the limelight because it was the only fully dollarized country in Latin America until Ecuador abolished its domestic currency in 2000.[2] The inflation performance of Panama illustrates the key advantage of full dollarization: its ability to deliver low inflation. From 1960 to 2000, Panama's inflation rate has averaged 2.8% per year, which is significantly lower than in any other country in Latin America, and is even lower than the 4.6% average over the same period for the United States. Panama's growth performance during the same period was also good, but far less impressive. Since 1960, Panama's real GDP grew at an average of 4.2%—about one percentage point faster than Latin America as a whole (see figure 14.4). However, some studies have shown that output volatility in Panama has been among the highest in the region, and that a main factor behind that volatility has been its exchange-rate regime (e.g., Hausmann and Gavin, 1995, tables 4 and

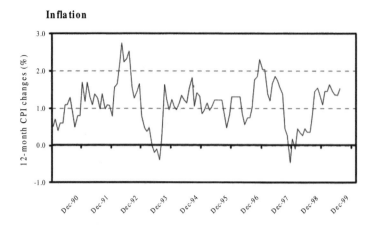

Figure 14.4
Panama: Inflation and growth, 1990–1999.
Source: IFS, ECLAC.

14). These findings seem fully consistent with the earlier noted tradeoff between price stability and output stability that affects countries with no monetary policy.

A hallmark and a key strength of Panama's economy is the soundness and sophistication of its banking system. Although the low inflation environment produced by full dollarization contributed to this outcome, full dollarization does not appear to be the primary source of the well-functioning banking system. The take-off of Panama's financial system only began in 1970 with the passage of a banking law—Cabinet Decree 238—that eased licensing and portfolio allocation requirements on foreign banks, strengthened secrecy provisions, and allowed unrestricted movements of capital (Moreno, 1999). The goal of transforming Panama into an offshore banking center was achieved fairly quickly. By 1987 there were more than 120 banks located in the country, the majority foreign-owned, and broad money and private sector credit as a share of GDP had risen by more than 15 percentage points (to 40% and 54% respectively). Except for a banking crisis in 1988–1989 which occurred as a result of economic sanctions imposed on Panama in 1988, including a freezing of the deposits held in the United States by the Banco Nacional de Panama, the Panamanian banking system has fared well.[3] One result is that private sector borrowers in Panama have access to international financial markets and can borrow at low interest rates. Indeed, Panamanian firms and banks do not face a "sovereign ceiling" and can often borrow at lower rates than the government. However, the small spread between domestic and foreign interest rates is probably more a reflection of Panama's sound and internationally-oriented banking system than the result of full dollarization.

The rest of Panama's economy displays many of the maladies common to Latin America. Until the late 1980s, Panama had a large and inefficient public sector that spent more than 25% of GDP on public sector wages and other current outlays, rigid labor markets that led to high unemployment (of more than 15%), a distorted trade regime that thwarted the development of agriculture and manufacturing, and a weak system of property rights (Loayza and Palacios, 1997). Given these problems, Panama had a lackluster fiscal performance, with fiscal deficits jumping from 2% of GDP in the 1960s to over 7% in the 1970s, and averaging 5% in the 1980s. Like the rest of Latin America, Panama financed its large fiscal deficits mainly with foreign borrowing, and when the debt crisis of the 1980s hit the region, the country was not spared. In fact, partly due to the political upheaval, the resolution of Panama's external debt problems was particularly difficult and protracted. A reflection of this and of its fiscal profligacy is the fact that Panama has needed continued support from the IMF: from 1973 to 1997, Panama requested thirteen IMF programs, the greatest number for any country in Latin America during that period. Although the size of the IMF loans was generally small, and many of the loans were not drawn, the recurrent need to solicit IMF support cast doubts on the claims about self-adjusting properties of Panama's dollarized economy that have become popular in some circles.

14.2.2 Bottom Line
Our review of the advantages and disadvantages of hard pegs and of the experience with those regimes in Argentina and Panama suggests two main conclusions.

The first one is that there are two necessary conditions for the success of a hard peg: a solid banking and financial system, and sound and sustainable fiscal policies. The sole adoption of a hard peg does not ensure that these two conditions will be met, at least not rapidly or automatically. The weakness of Argentina's banking system almost brought down its (quasi-) currency board during the Tequila crisis of 1995, whereas the strength of Panama's banking system—badly shaken by the incidents of the late 1980s—seems to owe at least as much to the policies and regulations that transformed Panama into an offshore financial center for the region than to its hard peg regime. On the fiscal requirements, small fiscal deficits were key to the early success of Argentina's currency board but persistent fiscal imbalances in the second half of the 1990s and early 2000s raised recurrent concerns about the sustainability of the hard peg and eventually led to its demise. Furthermore, the fiscal crisis spilled over into a banking crisis which has been very damaging to the Argentinian economy. The fiscal problems of Panama, on the other hand, have been as entrenched and protracted as those of the typical (non-dollarized) Latin American country. The claim that hard pegs ensure fiscal discipline and prevent fiscal dominance receives little support from these two experiences.

The second conclusion is that hard pegs remain subject to speculative attacks and bank runs, and are ill-equipped to counter country-specific shocks. The spillovers of the Tequila crisis on Argentina, its banking crisis in 2001–2002 and the runs on Panama's banks in the late 1980s provide evidence of the first point. The deepening recession in Argentina after the devaluation of the Brazilian real in 1999 and the high volatility of output in Panama are illustrations of the second.

Another problem of hard pegs is that they do not have an easy exit strategy. Not even when changes in the country's political and economic institutions make it possible and desirable to have a monetary policy able to focus on domestic considerations. Exiting from a currency board is highly dangerous unless the currency is likely to appreciate, but this is exactly when things are going well and so the political will to exit is likely to be weak, or nonexistent. Exiting from a fully dollarized economy is even more troublesome because the (new) monetary authorities, and the new currency, are likely to encounter a serious problem of lack of credibility. The dire situation of Argentina in January 2002 provides the best possible illustration of the enormity of the challenges involved.

Notwithstanding their shortcomings, hard pegs may be the only sustainable monetary policy strategy in the medium term for those emerging market countries whose political and economic institutions cannot support an independent central bank focused on preserving price stability. Countries that cannot find ways of locking-in the gains from their fight against (high) inflation, or those that have not yet started that fight, may find in hard pegs a reasonable second best strategy for monetary policy.

14.3 Monetary Targeting

A monetary targeting strategy focused on controlling inflation comprises three key elements: 1) reliance on information conveyed by a monetary aggregate to conduct monetary policy, 2) announcement of targets on a monetary aggregate to guide the public's inflation expectations, and 3) some accountability mechanism that precludes large and systematic deviations from the monetary targets. In addition, the strategy presupposes that monetary policy is not dictated by fiscal considerations—i.e., lack of fiscal dominance—and that the exchange rate is "flexible."

14.3.1 Lessons from the Recent Experience in Latin America

Despite what is often said, no central bank in Latin America has truly practiced monetary targeting. In their relatively recent experience with low(er) inflation and flexible exchange rates, the monetary policy frameworks of many central banks in Latin America, and in emerging markets in other regions, have contained the first of the three key elements mentioned earlier—i.e., using the information conveyed by a monetary aggregate to conduct monetary policy. However, the other two elements (public announcements of the targets and some type of accountability mechanism) rarely have been present at the same time—see Cottarelli and Giannini (1997).

The commonly held view that Latin American countries have pursued monetary targeting is probably rooted on the observation that most central banks in the region traditionally have used monetary aggregates for the *internal design* of their monetary policy. In fact, they have followed this practice in "good" and "bad" times: in periods of high inflation and complete fiscal dominance and in periods of low inflation and high central bank independence; in periods when the exchange rate was fixed and when it was allowed to float more or less freely; during episodes of stabilization, both failed and successful; and as an integral part of the many IMF programs these countries have had over the years. However, the fact that monetary aggregates have played an important role in monetary policymaking in Latin America does not mean that the central banks of the region have implemented a monetary targeting strategy. Regimes where monetary targets are not announced, or are announced but not given a chance to perform as the main nominal anchor, are not monetary targeting regimes. Instead these regimes are better characterized as ones where central banks make vague references to monetary aggregates, while they retain a high degree of discretion and instrument independence. A discussion of the experience in Mexico and Peru in recent years illustrate this point.

Mexico From late 1987 to 1994 the inflation rate in Mexico fell from a record high 140% to 7% (see figure 14.5). The disinflation program comprised drastic cuts of government spending, a pegged exchange rate, and the periodic announcement of guidelines for public sector prices, the exchange rate and wages (see Aspe, 1993). Starting in November 1991, when inflation was running at 20% in annual terms, Mexico adopted a system of gradually widening exchange rate bands aimed at giving the central bank scope to strike a better balance between the "credibility" and "flexibility" of its monetary regime (Helpman et al., 1994). In effect, however, Mexico's monetary policy in the early 1990s was overburdened by multiple objectives: accumulating

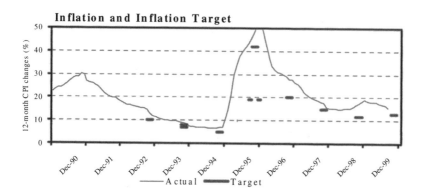

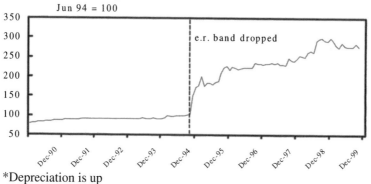

*Depreciation is up

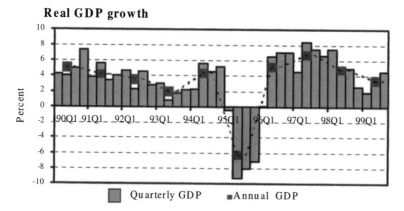

Figure 14.5
Mexico: Inflation, exchange rate and growth, 1990–1999.
Source: Bank of Mexico and INEGI.

international reserves, lowering interest rates, limiting exchange rate volatility, preserving the exchange rate band, and reducing inflation. To achieve these, the central bank conducted monetary policy guided by its internal forecasts of the demand for base money, and relied heavily on sterilized intervention to prevent the massive capital inflows that flooded Mexico in those years from fueling base money growth and inflation. Hence, from 1991 to 1994, excluding the December spikes, Mexico's monetary base hovered around a remarkably narrow range, while the central bank accumulated more than $11 billion of reserves.

In 1994 the conflicting demands placed on monetary policy clashed. The central bank reacted to the long string of adverse shocks hitting Mexico during the year by sticking to its internal forecast for base money and sterilizing the outflows of reserves. Instead of raising interest rates to arrest the reserve losses, the authorities issued $40 billion of dollar-denominated short-term debt (the infamous *Tesobonos*) worsening the system's vulnerability to a speculative attack.[4] The end came on December 20, when the central bank tried to undertake a "controlled" 15% devaluation. The plan did not work, and two days later the peso was allowed to float.

In the ensuing panic Mexico's central bank maintained its adherence to base money targeting. In January 1995 the central bank released to the public, for the first time, its monetary program for the year. The program had an inflation objective of 19%, and projected a 10 billion pesos increase in base money, which was presented as the main nominal anchor of the "new" regime. The program lacked credibility and the free fall of the peso continued until late March, when Mexico secured a $52 billion support package arranged by the U.S. Treasury and the IMF. At that time, the central bank announced a modified monetary program that maintained the projected increase in base money at 10 billion pesos, revised the forecast of inflation to 42%, and, crucially, raised interest sharply and kept them high until May, when the peso showed signs of stabilizing. For the remainder of the year, the central bank seemed to gear its monetary policy to preventing "large" peso depreciations; every fall in the peso of more than 2–3% was followed by a large increase in the interest rates of *Cetes* (Mexico's T-bills), both at the primary auction and in the secondary market (see Edwards and Savastano, 1998). At the end of 1995, the central bank actually complied with its announced target for base money (though with less foreign reserves and more domestic credit than it had projected), but inflation, at 52%, exceeded the program target by 10 percentage points (see figure 14.5).

The confusion about the instruments and targets of Mexico's monetary policy continued for the following two years. The central bank maintained its (new) practice of releasing to the public its (quarterly) monetary program, which contained targets for base money, domestic credit and international reserves at about the same time as the government submitted to Congress a document containing the budget and the broad economic objectives for the following year (including an end-point objective for the rate of inflation). Starting in late 1996, the bank went one step further and released (and posted on its website) its *daily* forecast of the monetary base for the following year. However, it gave no indication of the expected path of inflation over the period covered by the forecast. Moreover, the fact that the nominal exchange rate exhibited remarkable stability from early 1996 to mid 1997 triggered suspicions that the central bank, despite its repeated pronouncements to the contrary, was once again targeting the peso/dollar exchange rate.

Assessing the stance of monetary policy in Mexico during this period, let alone understanding how the central bank conducted monetary policy, was a daunting task for analysts and the general public. Although inflation fell steadily, albeit slowly, throughout 1996–97, the Bank of Mexico had serious trouble communicating its monetary strategy to the public and producing a nominal anchor that would help lower inflation expectations. These problems became particularly acute in 1997 when the monetary base, which had remained fairly close to its preannounced (quarterly) path in 1996, started to show large and sustained deviations from its daily forecasts early in the year. As a result, the Bank of Mexico went to great lengths trying to explain to the public the reduced role that its own forecasts of the monetary base were playing in guiding its monetary policy (see Bank of Mexico, 1998). Even though the monetary base exceeded its target by 4.1%, inflation in 1997 fell to 15.7%, very close to the year-end objective of 15%. The unreliability of the relationship between the monetary base and inflation became apparent again in 1998 when inflation exceeded the year-end objective of 12% by almost 7 percentage points even though base money ended up 1.5% below its forecast. The opposite problem occurred in 1999, when the inflation rate fell below the end-year inflation target (12.3% vs. 13%), while base money exceeded its forecast by more than 21%.

Though it can hardly be argued that the instability of the monetary base-inflation relationship produced terribly bad outcomes since the floating of the peso in late 1994 until 1997, it was fairly apparent that it had left the Bank of Mexico without a useful nominal anchor to guide inflation expectations. Aware of this situation, the central bank gradually backed off from its flirtation with monetary targeting. When Guillermo Ortiz became Governor in 1998, the bank started to downplay publicly the role that base money forecasts play in the setting of monetary policy, even though it has maintained the practice of releasing its year-ahead daily forecast of base money, and has allowed considerably more scope for exchange rate fluctuations. In fact, we will argue in the next section that the Bank of Mexico has been moving gradually in the direction of inflation targeting.

Peru In August 1990, Peru launched an ambitious economic reform program aimed at stopping hyperinflation and dismantling the numerous controls and distortions prevailing in the economy. The central elements of the anti-inflation effort were the adoption of a freely floating and fully convertible exchange rate, the establishment of a cash management committee to handle the finances of the public sector without resorting to central bank credit, the de-facto elimination of interest rate ceilings, and a once-off large adjustment of administered prices—including a 3,000% increase in the price of gasoline—that helped push the inflation rate that month to 400% (Paredes, 1991). The decision to refrain from using the exchange rate as the main nominal anchor of the disinflation was probably the most distinctive feature of Peru's stabilization.

The stabilization program was highly successful (see figures 14.2 and 14.6). In its first phase, from August 1990 to late 1992, annual inflation fell steadily, though gradually, from a high of a 12,000% rate in August 1990 to 57%. Key elements of the program during this phase were the tight control over government spending exercised by the cash management committee, the major reforms of the tax and tariff codes, and a bold program of privatizations. The second phase of the stabilization started in 1993, with the approval of a new charter for the central bank, and lasted until late 1996. The new charter provided a strong institutional foundation for the conduct of an independent monetary policy by making price stability the sole objective of the central bank, by prohibiting the bank from lending to the public sector, from providing any type of subsidized credit or from creating multiple exchange rates, and by making the central bank's Board accountable to Congress in case those directives were breached (de la Rocha, 1998). In addition, in 1994, Peru's central bank started to announce at the beginning of each year a target range for annual inflation at year end (the December to December 12-month inflation rate) which had been agreed on with the Minister of Finance and used in the preparation of the coming year's fiscal budget. These changes helped to consolidate the stabilization. Inflation fell from 56.7% in 1992 to 11.8% in 1996, while output growth averaged 9% from 1993 to 1995. Importantly, the disinflation proceeded at a fairly steady pace and the rate of inflation did not get "stuck" in the 20% range as had happened often in other stabilization programs in the region. In the final phase, from 1997 to the present, inflation has fallen to the single digit level, an outcome Peruvians had not seen for almost thirty years.

At least since 1993, Peru's central bank has used estimates of the demand for base money as its main intermediate target for monetary policy. However, and *most crucially*, Peru's central bank has not made its monetary targets public. Aware of the uncertainties surrounding those forecasts in a dollarized economy (80% of bank deposits and bank loans in Peru are dollar-denominated), the central bank has retained considerable discretion to revise and update its base money demand estimates, and to modify the setting of policy instruments whenever it has deemed necessary (de la Rocha, 1998). By doing so, Peru avoided the type of problems

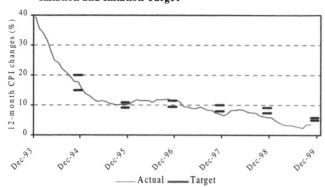

Inflation and Inflation Target

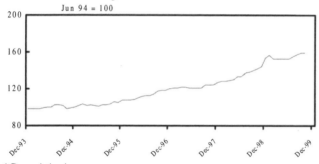

Nominal Exchange Rate

Jun 94 = 100

* Depreciation is up

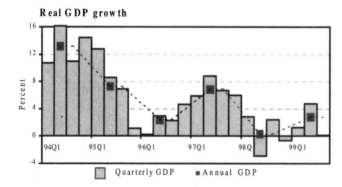

Real GDP growth

Figure 14.6
Peru: Inflation, Exchange rate and growth, 1994–1999.
Source: Central Reserve Bank of Peru and IFS.

encountered by Mexico when it tried to employ base money forecasts as a nominal anchor for inflation expectations.

Even though the Peruvian authorities did not announce targets for monetary aggregates nor any type of money rule as an anchor for inflation expectations at any point during the 1990s, Peru's program has become the prime case of a "money-based stabilization" in the large literature on inflation-stabilization strategies (e.g., Calvo and Vegh, 1994, 1999). The "money-based stabilization" label has been pushed further recently with Corbo (1999), who argues that Peru used a monetary anchor as the central element of its stabilization program—see also Favaro, 1996. These characterizations are misleading: In the 1990s Peru's central bank did not pursue a monetary targeting strategy with a money anchor but instead followed a conventional two-step approach for the *internal* design of its monetary policy, using the growth of base money as one of the elements guiding its decisions on instruments settings. Peru's strategy in the past decade should be seen as one of *discretionary* monetary policy with an increasing focus on price stability, not too different from the approach to monetary policy followed by many non-inflation targeting industrial countries (including the U.S.).

14.3.2   Bottom Line

The recent experiences of Mexico and Peru illustrate the difficulties that the instability of the money-inflation relationship creates for monetary targeting as a strategy for monetary policy in emerging market countries. This does not mean that monetary aggregates have no role to play in the conduct of monetary policy in those countries. In many emerging market economies the signal-to-noise ratio of monetary aggregates may be high, owing to their history of high inflation and large swings in money growth. However, as inflation falls to single digit levels and remains there, money growth rates are likely to lose informational content and become less useful indicators of monetary policy, as occurred in industrial countries (see Estrella and Mishkin, 1997). As money aggregates become less reliable indicators of future inflation, central banks will be well advised to downplay the importance of monetary targets, and search for alternative nominal anchors and communication devices.

Central banks in emerging market economies are oftentimes regarded as monetary targeters (e.g., Fry et al., 1999); almost always that characterization is inappropriate. As in Mexico and Peru, the alleged monetary targeting is typically a disguise for a highly discretionary monetary policy. Even when that approach proves to be successful for a period of time, as has been the case especially in Peru, it is a highly dangerous strategy. Two crippling shortcomings of the approach are that it depends too much on the preferences, skills and credibility of the individuals running the central bank, and that it does not lend itself to make monetary policy transparent and accountable.[5]

In sum, our review of the evidence suggests that monetary targeting is a strategy for monetary policy that has not been used by Latin American countries in the recent past, and is probably not an advisable medium-term strategy for the future. This is so because the problems that led to the abandonment of this strategy in industrialized countries (Bernanke and Mishkin, 1992) are also likely to arise in emerging market countries as low inflation becomes a more permanent feature. Indeed, even Germany, the quintessential monetary targeter, encountered problems with the money-inflation relationship which led the Bundesbank to miss the target ranges for its monetary targets on the order of half the time.[6] The secret to the Bundesbank's success was its long-term adherence to a "monetarist" framework to communicate to the public its commitment to price stability, along with the credibility it earned over the years which made its explanations of target misses believable to the public. Germany's relative success with monetary targeting is not a model for emerging market countries, where central banks need to assert their credibility over the next few years. In fact, the Bundesbank's success may not even be a model for how the European Central Bank should conduct monetary policy.

14.4 Inflation Targeting

Inflation targeting is a monetary policy strategy that involves five main elements: 1) the public announcement of medium-term numerical targets for inflation; 2) an institutional commitment to price stability as the primary goal of monetary policy, to which other goals are subordinated; 3) an information-inclusive strategy in which many variables, and not just monetary aggregates or the exchange rate, are used for deciding the setting of policy instruments; 4) a transparent monetary policy strategy that ascribes a central role to communicating to the public and the markets the plans, objectives, and rationale for the decisions of the central bank; and 5) mechanisms that make the central bank accountable for attaining its inflation objectives. The list should clarify one crucial point about inflation targeting: it entails *much more* than a public announcement of numerical targets for inflation for the year ahead. This is important in the emerging markets context, because many emerging market countries have routinely reported numerical inflation targets or objectives as part of the government's economic plan for the coming year (see Fry, et al., 1999) and yet they *have not* been pursuing an inflation targeting strategy. The monetary policy strategy must contain the other four elements listed above for it to be consistent with inflation targeting and, hence, sustainable over the medium term.

14.4.1 Lessons from the Recent Experience in Latin America

Inflation targeting is often in the eyes of the beholder. The monetary policy frameworks of several countries in Latin America contain some of the elements of inflation targeting that we have outlined. However, this does not mean that those countries should be regarded as having followed an inflation targeting strategy. To understand why we examine the recent experience of five countries: Chile, Colombia, Peru, Mexico and Brazil.[7]

Chile The new central bank legislation of 1989, which took effect in 1990, gave independence to the central bank and mandated price stability as one of its primary objectives. However, the legislation also stipulated objectives of the central bank to ensure equilibria in domestic and external payments. Over time, the central bank of Chile gradually increased the weight it attached to its price stability objective. The first inflation objective under the new legislation was announced in September 1990 for the twelve-month inflation rate in 1991 and has been announced every year since then in the first fifteen days of September for the following year (December to December). However, the inflation objective was initially interpreted by the public more as official inflation projections rather than as formal or "hard" targets (Morandé and Schmidt-Hebbel, 1997). In fact, Chile's central bank pursued a very gradualist approach to lowering its inflation objectives, starting with targets of over 20% for 1991 and lowering them slowly to below 5% (see figure 14.7). Over time, as the central bank experienced success in both disinflating and meeting its inflation objectives, the public began to interpret those objectives as "hard" targets for which the central bank could be made accountable. As part of this process, in September 1994 the central bank started to announce point targets rather than target ranges for its inflation objective for the following year. However, it was only in 1999 that the central bank explicitly announced a multi-year target for inflation—consisting of a target of 3.5% for the year 2000, and a longer-term target of 2 to 4% for 2001 onwards.

The Chilean experience with inflation targeting looks quite successful.[8] Inflation has fallen from levels above 20% when inflation projections were first introduced to a level around 3% at present. Over the same period, output growth has been very high, averaging over 8.5% per year from 1991 to 1997, a level comparable to those exhibited by the (former) Asian tigers. Growth performance faltered in 1998–99; output growth fell to 3.4% in 1998 and the economy experienced a mild recession in 1999 (see figure 14.7). In 1998 the Chilean central bank was reluctant to ease monetary policy and let the exchange rate depreciate in order to cushion the effects of a substantial negative terms of trade shock. Instead, the central bank raised interest rates sharply and even narrowed the exchange rate band. In hindsight, these decisions appear to have been a mistake: the inflation target was undershot and the economy entered a recession for the first time under the inflation targeting regime. Not surprisingly given these outcomes, the central bank came under strong criticism.[9] During 1999 the central bank reversed course, eased monetary policy by lowering

Inflation and Inflation Target

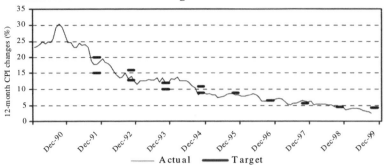

Nominal Exchange Rate
Jun 94 = 100

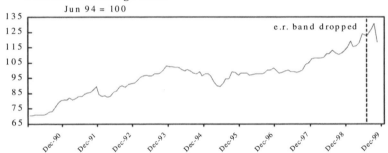

* Depreciation is up

Real GDP growth

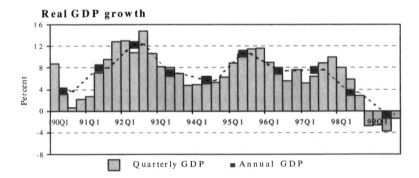

Figure 14.7
Chile: Inflation, exchange rate and growth, 1990–1999.
Source: Central Bank of Chile and IFS.

interest rates, and allowed the peso to depreciate, thus setting the stage for a strong rebound of output growth in 2000.

As part of its monetary policy regime, from the mid-1980s until August 1999, Chile had an exchange rate band around a crawling peg which was (loosely) tied to *lagged* domestic inflation. The central bank stressed that the purpose of the exchange rate band *was not* inflation control, and this was the reason why, for most of the period, the rate of crawl was set on a backward-looking rather than a forward-looking basis. Rather the central bank argued that the purpose of the exchange rate band was to keep the real exchange rate in a range consistent with medium- and long-term external equilibrium and, thus, preclude an "excessive" current account deficit. Over time, the central bank also made it clear through its actions that the inflation target would take precedence over the exchange rate band when there was a potential conflict between the two objectives. Thus, for example, in various instances from 1992 to 1997 when large capital inflows pushed the exchange rate close to the appreciated edge of the band, the central bank widened the band and even revalued the central parity while keeping the inflation target unchanged, thus signaling to the public that it attached a higher weight to lowering inflation than to resisting a real appreciation that seemed warranted by the "fundamental" determinants of the real exchange rate.

A strong fiscal position and a sound financial system are two key features of the Chilean economy that have supported the inflation targeting regime. The fiscal balance ended in surplus every year from 1991 to 1998, and during 1991–97 the surplus averaged 2.8% of GDP, clear indications that fiscal policy was kept under control. In addition, due largely to the measures taken in the aftermath of the severe banking crisis of the early 1980s, Chile's standards and practices in the areas of banking regulation and supervision during the 1990s have been of a quality comparable to those found in industrialized countries and far superior to those found in the rest of Latin America (with the possible exception of Argentina from 1995 to 2000). The resulting solidity of the Chilean financial system has meant that the ability of the central bank to take steps to defend the currency and the banks has never been in question, which may have helped Chile experience less pressures on its currency than other countries of the region at the time of the Tequila crisis (see IMF, 1996). The controls on short-term capital inflows have also been cited often as another important factor behind the low vulnerability and relative stability of the Chilean economy in the 1990s. However, the controls are highly controversial and their contribution is difficult to ascertain.[10] Our reading of the evidence suggests that, from the perspective of monetary policy and inflation control, strict prudential supervision was probably more important.

The Chilean example suggests that inflation targeting can be used as a successful strategy for gradual disinflation, even when inflation starts from levels of around 20%. It is important to emphasize that the success of inflation targeting cannot be solely attributed to the actions of the Chilean central bank: supportive policies such as sustained fiscal surpluses and rigorous regulation and supervision of the financial sector have been crucial to that outcome. Another important element of Chile's strategy has been the gradual hardening of the inflation targets and, most recently, the announcement of multi-year targets. However, it was not until early 2000, when the central bank began publishing an *Inflation Report*-type document that included baseline inflation forecasts, that Chile arguably completed its transition to a full-fledged inflation targeting regime.

Colombia   A decade ago, the prospects for Colombia's monetary policy were quite promising. The country had avoided the populist excesses that had ravaged many of its neighbors, had not been much affected by the debt crisis, and had not suffered a hyperinflation (see Urrutia, 1991). Next to Chile, Colombia was seen by many as the country in the region best positioned for economic take-off. Breaking double-digit inflation, a feature of Colombia's economy since the early 1970s, was considered a key prerequisite for attaining that goal (see Dornbusch and Fischer, 1993). The Colombian authorities seemed up to the challenge. The 1991 constitution—and the supportive legislation passed in 1992—made the central bank independent from the government, made inflation control the overriding objective of monetary policy, prohibited the central bank from financing private sector activities, and placed tight limits on the bank's financing of government deficits (see Steiner, 1995). In addition, since 1991 the central bank started to announce explicit numerical targets for the one-year ahead inflation rate, as part of the authorities' economic program—which continued to be centered around the crawling peg system which had been a hallmark of Colombia's economic policy since the late 1960s (see Williamson, 1996).

The anti-inflation strategy was unsuccessful. Average annual inflation in the period 1991–1998 (22.7%) was essentially the same as the average for the 1980s (23.6%), and from 1991 to 1996 the central bank consistently exceeded its always modest inflation targets (see figure 14.8). The inflation target was met for the first time in 1997—with inflation ending slightly below the 18% target—but the target was breached again in 1998 (16.7% vs. 16%). In that year, investors' concerns about Colombia's large fiscal and external deficits (in the order of 4% and 5% of GDP, respectively) and about its political situation led to a string of speculative attacks on the peso. In response, the central bank first raised interest rates to record-high levels and then, in September 1998, depreciated both edges of the exchange rate band by 9%. The response did not arrest the speculative pressures and induced a sharp slowdown in activity. In 1999 the pressures on the peso continued and Colombia suffered its first recession in seven decades. By mid-year it was apparent that the inflation target of 15% would be undershot by a large margin, but it was also clear that this was not a desired policy outcome. In late September the exchange rate band was aban-

Inflation and Inflation Target

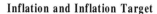
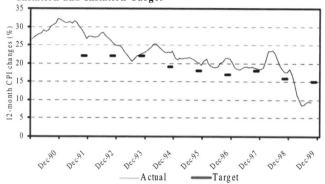

Nominal Exchange Rate

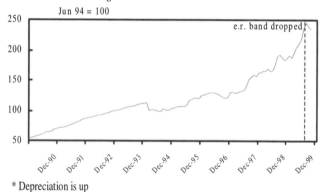

* Depreciation is up

Real GDP growth

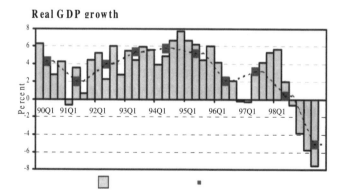

Figure 14.8
Colombia: Inflation, exchange rate and growth, 1990–1999.
Source: DANE, Central Bank of Colombia and IFS.

doned, the peso was allowed to float, and Colombia requested its first IMF program in more than 30 years in an attempt to allay investors' concerns and end the recession.

It is self-evident from Colombia's inflation performances that reducing inflation from the 20–25% range was not a priority of monetary policy for most of the 1990s. Its increased independence notwithstanding, the central bank continued to give priority to other objectives, especially output stability, whenever those goals seemed to be put in jeopardy by the inflation target (see Cardenas and Partow, 1998). The central bank seemed relatively content with its approach to monetary policy; indeed, in 1998, the (former) Vice-Governor of the bank stated boldly that: "the stance of economic policy in Colombia has been defined in the context of a global objective which has been to maintain moderate inflation in the 20–30% range" (Carrasquilla, 1998, p. 87). Interestingly, as had happened in Brazil a few months earlier (see below), the failed defense of the exchange rate band in September 1999 prompted a reformulation of Colombia's monetary regime. As part of the policy response to the currency crisis, the authorities let the peso float and set an inflation target of 10% for 2000 which, in the event, was undershot by about 1%. Later, in October 2000, the Colombian authorities moved further in the direction of inflation targeting by announcing targets for 2001 (8%) and 2002 (6%) and taking concrete actions to increase the accountability and transparency of the central bank.

Peru   As noted in the previous section, Peru's central bank announced an inflation target since 1994 and was quite successful in bringing down inflation. However, from 1997 to 1999, the central bank consistently undershot its inflation targets. In 1997, the target range was 8–10% while the actual end-of-year rate of inflation closed at 6.5%; in 1998 the target range was set at 7.5–9% and actual inflation was 6%; and in 1999 the range was 5–6% and inflation fell to 3.4%. Only in 2000 did the end-year rate of inflation (3.7%) fall within the target range set by central bank at the end of the previous year (3.5%–4%)—see figure 14.6.

In 1998 a series of adverse shocks (i.e., el Niño, low commodity prices, and the Russian crisis) provoked a collapse in exports, a substantial depreciation of the sol, and a sharp slowdown of bank credit. Those events brought the Peruvian economy to the verge of its first recession since 1992. Economic activity remained depressed in 1999–2000 despite an agriculture-led rebound of aggregate output. As a result, monetary policy came under fire from all fronts fueling a debate on whether there is a need for an alternative monetary framework for Peru, including the option of full dollarization. Thus, notwithstanding the successful disinflation, Peru's monetary authorities continued to lack credibility.

Although the central bank announces inflation targets, Peru's monetary policy framework does not contain many crucial features of an inflation targeting regime, such as the publication of *inflation reports* (and, hence, of the central bank's inflation forecasts), mechanisms for making the central bank accountable for attaining its inflation targets, or the announcement of multi-year targets. However, probably the most serious shortcoming of Peru's monetary policy has been its lack of transparency. A main contributing factor has been the profusion of instruments of monetary policy employed by the central bank: intervention in the money market (through the auction of certificates of deposits), intervention in the foreign exchange market (through direct sales and purchases of foreign exchange), and several other secondary instruments such as rediscounts, reserve requirements on the sizable foreign currency deposits and the interest paid on those reserve requirements. The proliferation of signals, compounded by the apparent lack of a coherent framework to communicate and evaluate monetary policy, has made it difficult for the public to decipher the central bank's actions, intentions and priorities, as well as to assess the stance of monetary policy at any given point in time. Instances where these problems have arisen abound, but they have been particularly acute and frequent with regard to two indicators: the observed rate of growth of base money (which on many occasions has been considered excessive and inconsistent with the inflation target—for example during 1995–1996) and the intervention in the foreign exchange market (which is often perceived as interfering excessively with equilibrium short-run movements in the nominal exchange rate—especially with depreciations). Although the latter criticism is probably warranted, Peru's central bank has consistently, and in our view, prudently, refrained from making any type of commitment, explicit or implicit, regarding the (expected or desired) level or path of the nominal exchange rate, and has let the exchange rate depreciate at a faster rate when market pressures have proved persistent—for example, in late 1998 and 1999. This flexibility, added to the desirable features already included in the central bank's charter, bodes well for a smooth transition to a monetary policy regime more consistent with inflation targeting.

One feature of the Peruvian experience that is of great interest is the high degree of dollarization of the economy. As noted before, more than 70% of bank deposits and bank loans in Peru are dollar-denominated; moreover, U.S. dollars circulate freely and are widely accepted as means of payment. As in other countries of the region, Peru's dollarization has its roots in the high inflation of the 1970s and 1980s. The process of remonetization that accompanied the successful stabilization of the early 1990s was driven by repatriation of flight capital of domestic residents and was channeled primarily to the fully convertible dollar deposits offered by the banking system. Thus, also as in other countries—i.e., Argentina, Bolivia, Uruguay—the banking system has remained highly dollarized despite the success in fighting inflation.[11] As noted earlier, partial dollarization has the potential to make an inflation targeting regime, which requires some degree of exchange rate flexibility, vulnerable to financial instability. However, this does not seem to have presented a severe problem in the case of Peru. The country suffered no contagion whatsoever from the Tequila crisis of December 1994 and weathered the crisis nicely, although this outcome was substantially helped by Peru's limited access to short-term capital flows at that time. Similarly during the Russian crisis of 1998, when there was a substantial depreciation, Peru did not experience severe financial instability, although bank credit and economic activity slowed down considerably. The overhaul of banking supervision and prudential regulations undertaken since the mid-1990s are likely to have contributed to this outcome.

Mexico   We noted in section 14.3 that Mexico's attempt at using base money forecasts as a nominal anchor has not been too successful, and that the central bank has started to back off from that practice. In fact, senior central bank officials have recently characterized Mexico's monetary policy framework as being in "a transition period towards a clear-cut inflation targeting scheme" (Carstens and Werner, 1999). We also noted earlier that for a number of years Mexico has made public an explicit inflation objective at the time the Minister of Finance submitted to Congress the government's economic program for the following year. However, Mexico's monetary policy still lacks some important elements of an inflation targeting strategy such as a transparent policy framework, and high accountability for meeting the inflation target. It is true that the Bank of Mexico has increased the emphasis on the inflation goal as the central objective of its monetary policy and that, since 1998, has let the exchange rate fluctuate more freely. But those changes did not go far enough. Mexico's central bank has continued to release its year-ahead forecasts for the daily monetary base, has insisted on explaining its monetary policy actions in terms of its system of daily liquidity management (the "corto" and "largo"), does not produce or release to the public mid-course inflation forecasts and, until recently, maintained the one-year ahead horizon for the inflation target. These practices are not credibility-enhancing and tend to create confusion, especially when there are (downward) pressures on the exchange rate.

It is possible that the Bank of Mexico was waiting for the "right" time to move to a more explicit inflation targeting regime. After all, up until 2000, inflation remained in the (low) double digits, external financing conditions were tight, and the pass-through from exchange rate changes did not seem to have fallen much (see Bank of Mexico, 1998). In addition, the inflation rate in 1998 overshot the announced target by almost 7 percentage points, damaging the Bank of Mexico's anti-inflation credentials. As we have argued, there is a case to be made for central banks to wait until they have acquired some anti-inflation credibility before they "harden" their targets for inflation. From this perspective, 1998 was probably not a good year for the Bank of Mexico to push further in the direction of inflation targeting.

In 1999, however, things started to look different. Annual inflation, at 12.3%, fell below the 13% target, the pass-through from exchange rate changes seemed to abate slightly, and, unlike the other large countries of the region, the economy grew by more than 3% (see figure 14.5). These outcomes helped enhance the credibility of the Bank of Mexico. Appropriately, the central bank stepped up its commitment to inflation targeting. For the first time, the central bank announced the 10% inflation target for the year 2000 before the Ministry of Finance submitted to Congress the economic program for the year. This (subtle) move contributed to raising the accountability of the central bank for complying with its inflation objectives. Also for the first time, the Bank of Mexico announced a multi-year target for inflation by stating that it intends to lower inflation to "international levels," (i.e., somewhere in the 2 to 3% range) by 2003. Starting in April 2000, the Bank of Mexico began issuing an *Inflation Report*. The report explains developments on the inflation front and discusses their relationship with the policy actions taken by the bank, but it does not present the bank's inflation forecasts. Nonetheless, publication of the report was a welcome step that augurs well for a rapid transition to full-fledge inflation targeting. All in all, starting in the late 1990s the Bank of Mexico followed a strategy quite similar to the one followed by the central bank of Chile a few years earlier, i.e., it "hardened" gradually the inflation targets as the bank's credibility increased because of its demonstrated success on the inflation front.

Brazil   The exchange-rate based stabilization under the *Real* plan from 1994 until January 1999 was extremely successful, reducing inflation from 2,500% in December 1993 to less than 2% by December 1998 (see figures 14.2 and 14.9).[12] However, the inability of the Brazilian government to put its fiscal house in order led to a gradual build up of public debt that increased the regime's vulnerability to speculative attacks and, following a costly defense in the fall of 1998, the *real* collapsed in January 1999. In the immediate aftermath of the currency crash, the (de-facto) resignation of two central bank presidents and the lack of a clear strategy for monetary policy made Brazilian prospects look bleak; doomsday predictions—such as: "*one caipirinha will amount to ten tequilas*"[13]—became common in the press and in market commentary. However, soon after his appointment in early February, the new central bank president, Arminio Fraga, took two crucial steps. First, as the British had done in the fall of 1992,[14] he recognized the need to rapidly put in place a nominal anchor and announced that Brazil would be soon adopting an inflation targeting strategy. And second, he decided to increase the interbank interest rate by 600 basis points, to 45%, to arrest the plunge of the *real* and re-establish credibility in monetary policy.

On June 21, 1999 the President of Brazil issued a decree instituting an inflation targeting framework for the conduct of monetary policy. The regime contemplated in the decree contains all the key elements of an inflation targeting strategy, namely:

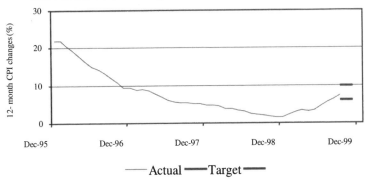

Inflation and Inflation Target

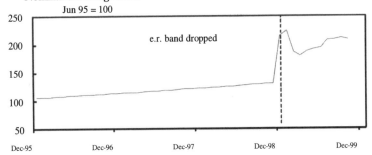

Nominal Exchange Rate

* Depreciation is up

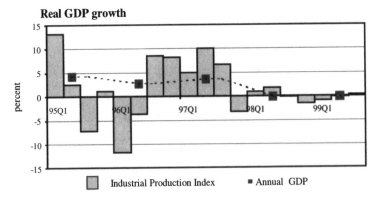

Real GDP growth

Figure 14.9
Brazil: Inflation, exchange rate and growth, 1995–1999.
Source: Central Bank of Brazil IFS.

1) the announcement of multi-year inflation targets (with explicit numerical targets for the 12-month rate of inflation in the years 1999, 2000 and 2001, and a commitment to announce the targets for 2002 onwards two years in advance); 2) assigning to the National Monetary Council the responsibility for setting the inflation targets and tolerance ranges based on a proposal by the Minister of Finance; 3) giving to the central bank of Brazil full responsibility to implement the policies needed to attain the inflation targets; 4) establishing procedures to increase the central bank's accountability (specifically, if the target range is breached, the central bank president would have to issue an open letter to the Minister of Finance explaining the causes of the deviation, the measures that will be taken to eliminate it, and the time it will take to get inflation back inside the tolerance range); and 5) taking actions to improve the transparency of monetary policy (concretely, the central bank was requested to issue a quarterly *Inflation Report* modeled after that produced by the Bank of England).

In terms of its design, the framework set up by Brazil had all the "bells and whistles" of an inflation targeting regime, and it clearly was the most comprehensive attempt to establish a regime of this type in Latin America. What is especially striking about Brazil's move to inflation targeting is how fast it occurred. The first inflation report was issued in July 1999, just a few months after Fraga was confirmed, with the second, right on schedule in September. The reports not only discussed clearly the conditions prevailing in the economy and the prospects for inflation, but also provided the central bank's inflation forecasts under different scenarios—including through the use of "fan charts" depicting the probabilities of different inflation paths. Many central bankers in emerging market countries have been concerned that it might take them a long time to acquire the technical capability to issue an inflation report of this type. Brazil's example suggests that those concerns may be a bit overdone.

The initial inflation targets were set at 8% for 1999, 6% for 2000 and 4% for 2001, with a tolerance range of ±2%. To the surprise of many, the strategy worked well from the start. There was a remarkably small pass-through from the large depreciation of the *real* (which fell by 45% on impact and thereafter stabilized at 30% below its pre-devaluation level) for several months, the output contraction was contained (in fact, annual GDP grew by almost 1 percent in 1999), Brazil was not cut-off from external financing—though there was some "arm twisting" involved—and there were no major bank runs. By March 1999, asset prices had started to recover, the *real* appreciated and the central bank found room to lower interest rates—which it did, quite aggressively (from a high of 45% to below 20% in a seven-month period). Inflation and the exchange rate remained subdued through October, when the monthly inflation rate rose to 1.2%, the largest monthly increase since June 1996, and the exchange rate crossed, briefly, the then "critical" mark of R$2.00 per U.S. dollar (see figure 14.9). In the event, inflation in 1999 reached 8.9%, above the 8% target for the year but well within the 2 percent tolerance range; during 2000 inflation continued falling, and closed the year right at the 6% mid-point target set by the central bank in mid-1999.

Its auspicious beginning notwithstanding, it is still too soon to tell whether Brazil's inflation targeting scheme will be successful. The two big question marks are, first, whether the central bank will be capable of enhancing and asserting its independence from the government and remain committed to controlling inflation, and second, the perennial question in Brazil, whether the government will undertake the steps and reforms needed to put fiscal policy on a sustainable path consistent with low inflation. If Brazil, yet again, cannot meet these challenges, monetary policy will become increasingly overburdened and discretionary, fiscal dominance will reappear, and the inflation targeting regime will blow up. Despite these risks, it is nonetheless useful to identify the factors that may have contributed to Brazil's initial success with inflation targeting. In our view, the three that stand out are the relative strength of Brazil's banking system (which had undergone a major restructuring following the bank crisis of 1994–1996—see Caprio and Klingebiel, 1999), the existence of substantial "slack" in the economy (partly a consequence of the prolonged interest rate defense of the *real* plan), and, especially, the quick measures taken by Governor Fraga to reestablish credibility in monetary policy. Other emerging market countries may want to take note.

14.4.2 Bottom Line

Our review of the conduct and orientation of monetary policy in five Latin American countries in recent years suggests to us that inflation targeting can become a viable medium-term strategy for monetary policy for many emerging market economies. In fact, all the countries reviewed in this section seem to be moving in the direction of a full-fledged inflation targeting regime. In terms of a demonstrated commitment to lowering inflation in line with its target and of the general conduct of monetary policy, Chile is far ahead of the rest of the group. In terms of setting up a framework for monetary policy that contains all the key elements of inflation targeting, Brazil has taken the lead in the region, showing that an inflation-targeting regime can be implemented quite quickly. The other three countries reviewed lag behind in both the commitment to inflation control and adoption of the other key elements of inflation targeting. A key requirement for inflation-targeting regimes in emerging market countries, as elsewhere, is the recognition that undershooting inflation targets, as occurred in Chile and Peru in the late 1990s, is just as costly as overshooting the targets. Support for an independent central bank which is pursuing price stability can erode if the central bank is perceived as focusing too narrowly on lowering inflation to the detriment of other objectives, especially output stability. By just as readily admitting their mistakes when an inflation target is undershot as when it is overshot, and continuously refining their technical expertise to minimize the occurrence of such events, central banks may increase support for their independence and for the inflation targeting regime.

Fiscal discipline and a sound and well-regulated banking system are crucial for the viability and success of inflation targeting, just as they are for the success of hard pegs. Again, Chile seems to be way ahead of the other countries reviewed in terms of broad compliance with these requirements. Lack of fiscal discipline is a particularly serious concern in Brazil and Colombia, whereas weaknesses in the banking system are the big question mark in Mexico, and, to a lesser extent, Peru. Inflation targeting alone will not solve these problems; neither will hard pegs. Setting *multiyear* inflation targets in coordination with the government (including on the issue of government-controlled prices) may help reduce the risk of fiscal profligacy, but it is not a long-term solution. Setting up institutions that help keep fiscal policy in check and others that promote and enforce sound banking practices seem to be the only solutions that may prove lasting and workable for emerging market countries.

Then there is the difficult question of the role of the exchange rate in an inflation targeting strategy for monetary policy in an emerging market country. The five cases reviewed provide only limited guidance for answering this question satisfactorily. The countries' reluctance to adopt an attitude of "benign neglect" of exchange rate movements (i.e., a "pure float") seems broadly appropriate—especially while they were undertaking a disinflation—but all of them probably went too far for too long in the direction of limiting exchange rate flexibility. They did so not only through the explicit use of exchange rate bands, employed by all countries, except Peru, for a good part of the 1990s, but also through frequent direct and indirect intervention in the foreign exchange market. The main problem with responding too heavily and too frequently to movements in a "flexible" exchange rate is, of course, that the strategy runs the risk of transforming the exchange rate into a nominal anchor for monetary policy that takes precedence over the inflation target, at least in the eyes of the public. With time, this practice may become observationally equivalent with a strategy of nominal exchange rate targeting.

To mitigate the risk that the exchange rate might replace the inflation target as the economy's main nominal anchor, central banks in emerging market economies would be well advised to be more transparent regarding the role they ascribe to the exchange rate in their monetary policy framework. For example, they could express a concern for the effects that exchange rate fluctuations may have on aggregate demand and supply and indicate that those concerns would lead the central bank to try to smooth large exchange rate fluctuations, but it would not try to prevent the exchange rate from reaching its market-determined level over longer horizons. Exchange rate smoothing via foreign exchange market interventions might be necessary at times to prevent or arrest large and abrupt exchange rate fluctuations that are clearly divorced from fundamentals. However, systematic exchange market interventions, particularly sterilized ones, are likely to be counterproductive as they would make it very difficult to signal that the inflation targets, rather than the exchange rate, is the primary nominal anchor of the economy.

Central banks should also explain to the public the rationale for exchange rate intervention in a manner analogous to that for interest-rate smoothing, i.e., as a policy aimed not at resisting market-determined movements in an asset price, but at mitigating potentially destabilizing effects of abrupt and sustained changes in that price. More generally, we think it is important that central banks understand that there are no "good floats" or "bad floats," but that there is such a thing as "good" and "bad" monetary policy under flexible exchange rates. Letting the exchange rate become the de-facto nominal anchor of the economy through excessive intervention in a quasi-inflation targeting regime is an example of the latter.

It is also important for central banks to recognize that, as is the case for most economic relationships, the pass-through from exchange rate changes to prices is likely to be regime-dependent. After a sustained period of low inflation with effective, as opposed to fictional, exchange rate flexibility, the informational content of the exchange rate in the expectations-formation process and price-setting practices of households and firms is likely to fall. Thus, the widespread view that a currently high pass-through from exchange rate changes to prices is a barrier to successful inflation targeting is probably exaggerated. Indeed, the low pass-through that occurred after the Brazilian devaluation in 1999, which might have been reduced by the adoption of an inflation targeting regime (as well as by the slack in the economy), suggests that a high pass-through is not a permanent feature of emerging market economies.

A related problem of special relevance for emerging market countries is the extent to which a high degree of dollarization may hinder inflation targeting. To a large extent a transparent and well-designed policy of exchange-rate smoothing combined with strong regulatory and supervision practices in the financial system should mitigate potential inconsistencies. The recent experience of Peru is encouraging in this regard. In fact, the argument can be turned on its head. The high dollarization of bank loans and deposits and the widespread use of U.S. dollars as the unit of account and medium of exchange (though not as legal tender) in countries like Peru, Bolivia and Uruguay is probably irreversible, at least in the medium run. Yet all these countries have retained a domestic currency and have managed to reduce inflation to very low levels.

Even Uruguay, the chronic inflation country *par excellence* has recently brought inflation down to the single digits. Highly dollarized economies are therefore reaping one of the main benefits of full dollarization (low inflation) while preserving some scope to mitigate the effects of other shocks through monetary policy. Because their payments systems and transactions technology are already partially dollarized, it would be relatively easy for these countries to switch unilaterally to full dollarization, if they chose to. Designing a credible strategy that allows them to retain an additional margin of flexibility without impairing their gains on the inflation front, which is what inflation targeting is all about, is probably a more demanding task, but its net benefits over the medium term are also greater, and, we think, worth pursuing.

14.5   Conclusion

The case studies in this chapter suggest that one size does not fit all when it comes to designing monetary policy strategies for emerging market and transition countries. The key to successful monetary policy is the ability to constrain discretion so that monetary policy can focus on the long-run goal of price stability. How best to do this depends on the insitutional environment in each country. There are some emerging market countries which may not have the political and other institutions to constrain monetary policy if it is allowed some discretion. In these countries there is a strong argument for hard pegs, including full dollarization, which allow little or no discretion to the monetary authorities. On the other hand, there are many emerging market countries that seem to have the ability to constrain discretion, with Chile being the clearest example, and for these cases we believe that inflation targeting is likely to produce a monetary policy which keeps inflation low and yet appropriately copes with domestic and foreign shocks. As we have seen, monetary targeting as a strategy for emerging market countries is not viable because of the likely instability of the relationship between monetary aggregates and inflation.

Regardless of which monetary policy strategy is chosen, our case studies suggest that a monetary policy strategy will not be successful in maintaining low inflation over the medium term in emerging market countries unless government policies create the right institutional environment. Rigorous prudential supervision and sound fiscal policy are essential to the success of any monetary policy strategy.

Notes

The views expressed in this chapter are exclusively those of the authors and not those of Columbia University, the National Bureau of Economic Research or the International Monetary Fund.

1. Although a soft peg may be appropriate as a tool in the initial phases of a stabilization program, this strategy is not discussed here, because as has been amply demonstrated by recent experiences in industrial and emerging market economies, it is not an appropriate *medium-term* strategy for monetary policy (see Obstfeld and Rogoff (1995), Eichengreen and Masson (1998) and Mishkin (1998, 1999)).

2. See, for example, Eichengreen and Hausmann (1999), Moreno (1999), and Schuler (1999). Panama has domestic currency coins (balboas) that co-circulate at parity with U.S. dollar coins. The balboas are issued by the Banco Nacional de Panama, a government-owned commercial bank that acts as the financial agent of the government but does not centralize official holdings of reserves nor acts as lender of last resort.

3. The U.S. economic warfare against Panama sparked a series of bank runs that nearly caused the collapse of the Panamanian payments system (see Garber, 1999). When the standstill ended, after almost

two years, a number of small banks had disappeared, the money supply had shrunk by 30%, and real output had fallen by 18%. This episode illustrates that a country with a hard peg is not exempt from bank runs and panics, whatever their origin may be. The fact that the United States also had frequent bank panics in the nineteenth and early twentieth century even when it had a hard peg (the gold standard) also illustrates this point—e.g., see Mishkin (1991).

4. The role of monetary policy in precipitating the Tequila crisis of December 1994 remains a matter of dispute. See, for example, the contrasting views presented in Gil-Diaz and Carstens (1996), Kamin and Rogers (1996), Calvo and Mendoza (1996), and Edwards (1998).

5. One of us has argued elsewhere that even the discretionary monetary policy regime in the United States, which has been so successful, may not produce desirable outcomes over the long run and needs to be modified, even though the environment for "good" discretion in the United States is far more favorable than in emerging market economies (see Mishkin, 1999).

6. Partly because of this a number of researchers regard Germany's monetary policy as being closer to an inflation targeting regime than to a monetary targeting regime. See for example, Clarida and Gertler (1998), Bernanke, et al. (1999) and Mishkin (1999).

7. A questionnaire-based assessment of monetary policy frameworks in emerging economies reported in Masson et al. (1997), identified Chile, Colombia and Mexico as the countries in Latin America that, as of end-1996, appeared to be good candidates for adopting an inflation targeting strategy. Brazil and Peru were not proposed as candidates by the IMF desk officers to whom the questionnaire was sent.

8. Corbo (1998) and Landerretche, et al. (1999) analyze the factors behind Chile's successful disinflation of the 1990s; see also Massad (1998). For a critical view of the disinflation, see Calvo and Mendoza (1999).

9. In contrast, during this same period, Australia eased monetary policy, thereby allowing the currency to depreciate to cushion the effects of its own negative terms of trade shock. This policy met with great success, resulting in an economy that remained strong while the inflation target continued to be met. One reason why Chile's central bank did not react in a similar manner to a comparable shock may have been its (unwarranted) concern that a large peso depreciation would lead to inflation exceeding the target and, hence, erode its credibility.

10. For a recent overview of the debate surrounding Chile's capital controls, see Edwards (1999).

11. See Rodriguez (1993) and Savastano (1996) for evidence on the path of remonetization in these economies.

12. For an overview of the main elements of the *Real* plan and of its initial results see Cardoso (1998), and Lopes (1998).

13. A "caipirinha" is a popular alcoholic drink in Brazil, as is "tequila" in Mexico.

14. See Mishkin and Posen (1997), and Bernanke et al. (1999).

References

Aspe, P., 1993, *Economic Transformation the Mexican Way*, Cambridge, MA: MIT Press.

Bank of Mexico, 1998, *The Mexican Economy 1998*, Mexico City: Bank of Mexico, June.

Bernanke, B. and F. Mishkin, 1992, "Central bank behavior and the strategy of monetary policy: Observations from Six Industrialized Countries," *NBER Macroeconomics Annual*, 1992: 183–228.

Bernanke, B., T. Laubach, F. Mishkin, and A. Posen, 1999, *Inflation Targeting: Lessons from the International Experience*, Princeton, NJ: Princeton University Press.

Calvo, G. and E. Mendoza, 1996, "Mexico's balance-of-payments crisis: A chronicle of a death foretold," *Journal of International Economics*, (special issue), Vol. 41, Nos. 3/4, November.

Calvo, G. and E. Mendoza, 1999, "Empirical Puzzles of Chilean Stabilization Policy," in G. Perry and D. Leipziger (eds), *Chile: Recent Policy Lessons and Emerging Challenges*, Washington, D.C.: The World Bank.

Calvo, G. and C. Vegh, 1994, "Inflation Stabilization and Nominal Anchors," *Contemporary Economic Policy*, Vol. 12.

Calvo, G. and C. Vegh, 1999, "Inflation Stabilization and BOP Crises in Developing Countries," in J. Taylor and M. Woodford (eds), *Handbook of Macroeconomics*, Elsevier: North Holland.

Caprio, G. and D. Klingebiel, 1999, "Episodes of Systemic and Borderline Financial Crises," mimeo, The World Bank, October.

Cardenas, M. and Z. Partow, 1998, "Does Independence Matter? The Case of the Colombian Central Bank," mimeo, Bogota: Fedesarrollo.

Cardoso, E., 1998, "Virtual Deficits and the Patinkin Effect," *IMF Staff Papers*, Vol. 45, December.

Carrasquilla, A., 1998, "Monetary policy transmission: the Colombian case," in *The Transmission of Monetary Policy in Emerging Market Economies*, BIS Policy Papers No. 3, January.

Carstens, A. and A. Werner, 1999, "Mexico's Monetary Policy Framework under a Floating Exchange Rate Regime," Banco de Mexico Research Paper 9905, May.

Cavallo, D., 1993, "The Convertibility Plan," in N. Liviatan (ed.), *Proceedings of a Conference on Currency Substitution and Currency Boards*, Washington, D.C.: The World Bank.

Clarida, R. and M. Gertler, 1998, "How the Bundesbank Conducts Monetary Policy," in C. Romer and D. Romer (eds), *Reducing Inflation*, Chicago: The University of Chicago Press for the NBER.

Corbo, V., 1998, "Reaching one-digit inflation: The Chilean experience," *Journal of Applied Economics*, Vol. 1, No. 1: 123–163.

Corbo, V., 1999, "Monetary Policy in Latin America in the '90s," paper presented at the Third Annual Conference of the Central Bank of Chile, September 20–21, 1999.

Cottarelli, C. and C. Giannini, 1997, *Credibility Without Rules? Monetary Frameworks in the Post-Bretton Woods Era*, IMF Occasional Paper 154, Washington, D.C.: International Monetary Fund.

de la Rocha, J., 1998, "The transmission mechanism of monetary policy in Peru," in *The Transmission of Monetary Policy in Emerging Market Economies*, BIS Policy Papers No. 3, January.

Dornbusch, R. and S. Fischer, 1993, "Moderate Inflation," *The World Bank Economic Review*, Vol. 7, (1): 1–44.

Edwards, S., 1998, "Two Crises: Inflationary Inertia and Credibility," *The Economic Journal*, Vol. 108: 680–702, May.

Edwards, S., 1999, "How Effective are Controls on Capital Inflows? An Evaluation of Chile's Experience," mimeo, UCLA, June.

Edwards, S. and M. Savastano, 1998, "The Morning After: The Mexican Peso in the Aftermath of the 1994 Currency Crisis," NBER Working Paper 6516, April.

Eichengreen, B. and R. Hausmann, 1999, "Exchange Rates and Financial Fragility," NBER Working Paper 7448, November.

Eichengreen, B. and P. Masson, 1998, *Exit Strategies: Policy Options for Countries Seeking Greater Exchange Rate Flexibility*, IMF Occasional Paper 168, September.

Estrella, A. and F. Mishkin, 1997, "Is there a role for monetary aggregates in the conduct of monetary policy?," *Journal of Monetary Economics*, Vol. 40: 279–304.

Favaro, E., 1996, "Peru's Stabilization Under Floating Exchange Rates," mimeo, The World Bank, September.

Fry, M. and others, 1999, "Monetary Policy Frameworks in a Global Context," report prepared for a Central Bank Governors' Symposium at the Bank of England, June 4, 1999, London: Bank of England.

Garber, P., 1999, "Hard-Wiring to the Dollar: From Currency Board to Currency Zone," *Global Markets Research*, London: Deutsche Bank, March.

Gil-Díaz, F. and A. Carstens, 1996, "One Year of Solitude: Some Pilgrim Tales About Mexico's 1994–95 Crisis," *American Economic Review Papers and Proceedings*, May.

Hanke, S. and K. Schuler, 1994, *Currency Boards for Developing Countries: A Handbook*, San Francisco: ICS Press.

Hausmann, R. and M. Gavin, 1995, "Overcoming Volatility in Latin America," Office of the Chief Economist, Washington, D.C.: Inter-American Development Bank, August.

Helpman, E., L. Leiderman and G. Bufman, 1994, "New Breed of Exchange Rate Bands: Chile, Israel and Mexico," *Economic Policy* Vol. 9: 206–306, October.

IMF, 1996, *International Capital Markets: Developments, Prospects and Key Policy Issues*, IMF: Washington, D.C., September.

Kamin, S., P. Turner and J. Vant t' dack, 1998, "The transmission mechanism of monetary policy in emerging economies: an overview," in *The Transmission of Monetary Policy in Emerging Market Economies*, BIS Policy Papers No. 3, January.

Landerretche, O., F. Morandé and K. Schmidt-Hebbel, 1999, "Inflation Targets and Stabilization in Chile," Central Bank of Chile, Working Paper 55, December.

Loayza, N. and L. Palacios, 1997, "Economic Reform and Progress in Latin American and the Caribbean," Policy Research Working Paper 1829, Washington, D.C.: The World Bank, September.

Lopes, F., 1998, "The transmission mechanism of monetary policy in a stabilizing economy: Notes on the case of Brazil," in *The Transmission of Monetary Policy in Emerging Market Economies*, BIS Policy Papers No. 3, January.

Massad, C., 1998, "La Política Monetaria en Chile," *Economía Chilena*, Vol. 1, No. 1.

Masson, P., M. Savastano, and S. Sharma, 1997, "The Scope for Inflation Targeting in Developing Countries," IMF Working Paper 97/130, October.

Mishkin, F., 1991, "Asymmetric Information and Financial Crises: A Historical Perspective," in R. Glenn Hubbard, ed., *Financial Markets and Financial Crises*, Chicago: The University of Chicago Press.

Mishkin, F., 1998, "The Dangers of Exchange-Rate Pegging in Emerging Markets Countries," *International Finance*, Vol. 1, No. 1: 81–101.

Mishkin, F., 1999, "International Experiences with Different Monetary Regimes," *Journal of Monetary Economics*, Vol. 43: 579–606.

Mishkin, F. and A. Posen, 1997, "Inflation Targeting: Lessons from Four Countries," *Federal Reserve Bank of New York Economic Policy Review*, August 1997.

Mishkin, F. and M. Savastano, 2001, "Monetary Policy Strategies for Latin America," *Journal of Development Economics*, Vol. 66: 415–444.

Morandé, F. and K. Schmidt-Hebbel, 1997, "Inflation Targets and Indexation in Chile," mimeo, Central Bank of Chile, August.

Moreno, J., 1999, "Lessons from the Monetary Experience of Panama: A Dollar Economy with Financial Integration," *Cato Journal*, Vol. 18, No. 3 (Winter).

Obstfeld, M. and K. Rogoff, 1995, "The Mirage of Fixed Exchange Rates," *Journal of Economic Perspectives*, Vol. 9, No. 4, Fall.

Paredes, C., 1991, "Epilogue: In the Aftermath of Hyperinflation," in C. Paredes and J. Sachs (eds), *Peru's Path to Recovery*, Washington, D.C.: The Brookings Institution.

Pou, P., 1999, "Más Dolarización para profundizar la Convertibilidad," *El Clarín*, May 26, 1999.

Rodriguez, C., 1993, "Money and Credit under Currency Substitution," *IMF Staff Papers*, Vol. 20: 414–26.

Savastano, M., 1996, "Dollarization in Latin America: Recent Evidence and Policy Issues," in P. Mizen and E. Pentecost (eds), *The Macroeconomics of International Currencies*, Edward Elgar Publishing.

Schuler, K., 1999, "Encouraging Official Dollarization in Emerging Markets," Joint Economic Committee Staff Report, Washington, D.C.: United States Senate, April.

Steiner, R. (ed), 1995, *La Autonomía del Banco Central de la República: Economía Política de la Reforma*, Bogotá: Tercer Mundo Editores.

Urrutia, M., 1991, "On the absence of economic populism in Colombia," in R. Dornbusch and S. Edwards (eds), *The Macroeconomics of Populism in Latin America*, Chicago: The University of Chicago Press for the NBER.

15 Inflation Targeting in Transition Economies: Experience and Prospects

Jiri Jonas and Frederic S. Mishkin

15.1 Introduction

In the second half of the 1990s, several transition countries abandoned fixed ex-change rate regimes and instead introduced inflation targeting as framework for the conduct of monetary policy. In this chapter, we will analyze the experience of three countries that moved to an inflation-targeting regime: the Czech Republic, Hungary, and Poland.

It is worth studying inflation targeting in these transition countries for two reasons. First, the transition countries are becoming an important part of Europe, and design-ing the right monetary policy regime for their transition into successful European economies is valuable in its own right. Second, these countries have three unique fea-tures that make the study of inflation targeting in these countries particularly inter-esting: (a) they are new democracies that are in the process of developing new governmental institutions; (b) their economies are undergoing radical restructuring as part of the transition from socialism to capitalism; and (c) they are very likely to enter the European Union (EU) and Economic and Monetary Union (EMU) in the near future. These three unique features are emphasized in our discussion of their inflation-targeting regimes.

In the next section of the chapter we discuss the reasons why these countries moved to a more flexible exchange rate regime and introduced inflation targeting. In the third section, we examine in more detail the introduction of inflation targeting in the three countries, and in the fourth section, we evaluate the preliminary experi-ence with inflation targeting. In the fifth section, we discuss a number of specific issues for inflation targeting in transition economies: what inflation measure to tar-get, whether to target a point or a range, what should be the time horizon for the in-flation target, who should set the inflation target, what should be the response to faster-than-targeted disinflation, how monetary policy should respond to deviations of inflation from the target, how much the floor of the inflation target should be emphasized relative to the ceiling, and what role the exchange rate should play in an inflation-targeting regime. In the sixth section, we discuss the future prospects of inflation targeting in transition economies in connection with the planned adoption of the euro, focusing on inflation targeting within the fluctuation band of exchange rate mechanism 2 (ERM2) regime and on the potential conflict between the inflation target and the exchange rate target. The final section contains concluding remarks.

15.2   From Peg to Float

In economic history books, the 1990s will be probably remembered as a decade when fixed exchange rate regimes lost much of their attraction as nominal anchors for the conduct of monetary policy. As a result of devastating financial crises, many emerging-market countries were forced to abandon fixed exchange rate regimes and replace them with more flexible exchange rate arrangements. Some countries—albeit a significant minority—even opted to introduce more flexible exchange rate regimes in an orderly way, without being forced to exit the peg as a result of financial crisis or market pressure on their currency.

This trend from more fixed to more flexible exchange rate regimes was also observed in the transition economies of Central and Eastern Europe. In the early years of transition, in the aftermath of price liberalization and exchange rate devaluation, many transition economies have used the exchange rate peg as a nominal anchor to achieve a rapid stabilization of price level. However, as with other emerging-market economies, transition economies too have suffered the standard problem of exchange rate–based stabilization programs: while inflation did decline significantly, it did not decline enough to prevent a large real appreciation that ultimately created a balance-of-payment problem and forced the abandonment of the fixed exchange rate. While some countries opted for a hard version of a fixed exchange rate—a currency board arrangement—others introduced managed float: first the Czech Republic in 1997, then the Slovak Republic and Poland in 1998. Hungary did not move to a fully floating currency regime, but in May 2001 it introduced an exchange rate band, allowing the currency to move up and down within this band by 15 percent.

When abandoning the exchange rate pegs, the authorities of these countries had to decide what nominal anchor to use instead of the fixed exchange rate. While the Slovak Republic did not accompany the move to a floating exchange rate by an explicit introduction of new monetary policy framework, the other three countries opted for inflation targeting. Why did the authorities in these countries opt for inflation targeting, and why did they reject alternative policy frameworks? We can learn why by examining the problems of other monetary policy regimes.

One alternative would be to use monetary aggregates as an intermediate target and nominal anchor. However, targeting monetary aggregates does not have much at-

traction in transition economies.[1] The traditional problem of instability of money demand, and therefore the unstable relationship between the growth of money supply
and inflation, could be a particularly serious obstacle to targeting monetary aggregates in transition economies. Economic transition is characterized by a sequence of
price shocks, including corrections in administered prices and tax reforms, that make
the relationship between money supply and price level very difficult to predict. The
instability of money demand and money-price relationship is further exacerbated by
far-reaching changes in the financial sector, including deep institutional changes, the
emergence of new types of financial assets and players, and so on. Therefore, relying
solely on targeting money supply growth could be a quite ineffective approach to
conducting monetary policy.

Transition economies could have also applied a discretionary, "just-do-it"
approach to monetary policy, as the Federal Reserve in the United States is doing,
in which there is no explicit nominal anchor.[2] Given the difficulty of establishing a
more stable relationship between some intermediate target and price level, some
may think that a less formal approach to monetary policy would be advisable. However, while this approach may work in countries whose central bank has well-
established anti-inflationary credibility, and where inflation is low, it is doubtful that
it would work well in transition economies. Particularly in the Czech Republic where
inflation was relatively high and rising after the fixed exchange rate regime was abandoned, the just-do-it approach to monetary policy was not seen as being potentially
effective in bringing inflation expectations and actual inflation down. Without anti-
inflation credibility, the just-do-it approach would not sufficiently anchor inflation
expectations and persuade economic agents that monetary policy would be actually
conducted to control inflation.

A third option would be to replace a fixed exchange rate regime with a harder variant of exchange rate peg—that is, by introducing a currency board, or even unilaterally euroizing. This option has the advantage that it provides a nominal anchor that
helps keep inflation under control by tying the prices of domestically produced tradable goods to those in the anchor country, and making inflation expectations
converge to those prevailing in the anchor country. In addition, it provides an automatic adjustment mechanism that helps mitigate the time-inconsistency problem of
monetary policy. Hard pegs also have the advantages of simplicity and clarity, which
make them easily understood by the public. However, the hard peg option has the
disadvantage that it leaves little scope for the country to conduct its own monetary
policy in order to react to domestic or foreign shocks.

For transition countries that wanted to retain some control over domestic monetary policy and so opted to keep a flexible exchange rate, the problems with
monetary targeting and the just-do-it approach led them to adopt a fourth option, inflation targeting. Inflation targeting has several advantages over a hard peg,

monetary targeting, and the just-do-it approach. In contrast to a hard peg, inflation targeting enables monetary policy to focus on domestic considerations and to respond to shocks of both domestic and foreign origin. Inflation targeting also has the advantage that stability in the relationship between money and inflation is not critical to its success because it does not depend on such a relationship. Inflation targeting, like a hard peg, also has the key advantage that it is easily understood by the public and thus highly transparent. In contrast, monetary targets, although visible, are less likely to be well understood by the public, especially as the relationship between monetary aggregates and inflation becomes less stable and reliable. Because an explicit numerical target for inflation increases the accountability of the central bank relative to a discretionary regime, inflation targeting also has the potential to reduce the likelihood that the central bank will fall into the time-inconsistency trap. Moreover, since the source of time inconsistency is often found in (covert or open) political pressures on the central bank to engage in expansionary monetary policy, inflation targeting has the advantage of focusing the political debate on what a central bank can do on a sustainable basis—that is, control inflation—rather than on what it cannot do through monetary policy—for example, raise output growth, lower unemployment, or increase external competitiveness.

How well were the transition economies prepared for the introduction of inflation targeting? In the literature, a relatively long list of requirements has been identified that countries should meet if inflation targeting regime is to operate successfully.[3] These requirements include (a) a strong fiscal position, (b) a well-understood transmission mechanism between monetary policy instruments and inflation, (c) a well-developed financial system, (d) central-bank independence and a clear mandate for price stability, (e) a reasonably well-developed ability to forecast inflation, (f) absence of nominal anchors other than inflation, and (g) transparent and accountable monetary policy.

It is not possible to say whether a country meets these requirements or not: it is more a question of the degree to which these preconditions are met. On the whole, it could be argued that the three transition countries that adopted inflation targeting, the Czech Republic, Hungary, and Poland, met these requirements to a sufficient degree to make inflation targeting feasible and useful.[4]

All three countries have an independent central bank with a clear mandate to pursue price stability. In some cases, this independence and price stability mandate has been strengthened just before the introduction of inflation targeting. There has also been significant progress in making monetary policy decisions more transparent and central banks more accountable, although this is still to some extent a work in progress in some countries. Financial markets in the three analyzed economies are relatively well developed, allowing for a reasonably effective transmission mechanism between monetary policy instruments and inflation.

Table 15.1
Inflation-Targeting Countries: General Government Balance (in % of GDP, Excluding Privatization Revenues)

Country	1998	1999	2000	2001
Czech Republic	−2.4	−2.0	−4.2	−5.2
Hungary	−4.8	−3.4	−3.3	−4.7
Poland	−3.2	−3.7	−3.2	−6.0

Source: European Bank for Reconstruction and Development (2002).

With respect to fiscal position, partly as a result of explicit recognition of hidden transformation-related costs, fiscal deficits have widened significantly, particularly in the Czech Republic and Hungary (see table 15.1). However, these deficits have not yet posed a direct problem to inflation targeting in the sense of fiscal dominance of monetary policy, because they have been financed by nonmonetary means at relatively favorable terms.[5] The main reason why large fiscal deficits in accession countries do not trigger adverse market reaction is that they are widely considered to be temporary. In part this reflects the recognition of implicit public-sector liabilities from the past. Moreover, as a result of EU/EMU accession, these countries will adopt an institutional framework (the Stability and Growth Pact, or SGP) that will require them to pursue disciplined fiscal policies. Still, before the constraint of the SGP begins to operate, large fiscal deficits can complicate monetary policy conduct in indirect ways, as we will see in our later discussion of these three countries' experience with inflation targeting.

As for the absence of multiple nominal anchors, this condition is clearly met in the Czech Republic and Poland. These countries have in place a regime of managed floating, and inflation is the only nominal anchor in the economy. In Hungary, the situation is more complicated because of the presence of the exchange rate band. Theoretically, this could be incompatible with the requirement of the single nominal anchor if the band is too narrow. We should note that the existence of the exchange rate fluctuation band is not only an issue of concern to Hungary today; it will be of concern to all transition countries that join the ERM2 system, when they will have to put in place the same fluctuation band. We will discuss the issue of fluctuation band and inflation targeting in the section on monetary policy within the ERM2 system.

Perhaps the most serious objection raised against the adoption of inflation targeting in transition economies is the limited ability to forecast inflation accurately. This is partly the result of the relatively frequent occurrence of shocks to which transition economies are exposed, including price deregulation and catching up with the more advanced economies, and also the result of a relatively large degree of openness of these economies. Actual inflation is relatively unstable relative to the long-term inflation trend (Orlowski 2000). Under such circumstances, there are natural limits to central banks' ability to forecast inflation that cannot be quickly and substantially improved by more sophisticated forecasting models. However, inflation-targeting central banks are nevertheless making progress in improving their inflation-forecasting capacity. One approach is to use alternative and less formal methods of gauging future inflation. For example, in 1999 the Czech National Bank introduced a survey of inflation forecasts by market participants to measure inflation expectations.

15.3   Introduction of Inflation Targeting in Individual Countries

We will now turn in more detail to the introduction of inflation targeting in individual countries. We will briefly examine economic developments preceding the introduction of inflation targeting, and the main operational characteristics of the inflation-targeting regimes in the three countries.

15.3.1   The Czech Republic

The Czech Republic was the first transition economy to introduce an inflation-targeting regime, which it did after abandoning the fixed exchange rate regime following currency turbulence in May 1997.[6]

A fixed exchange rate regime played an important role in the macroeconomic stabilization package introduced in 1991. Several months after liberalization of prices and devaluation of currency in 1991, the rate of inflation came down quickly, although not quite to levels prevailing in advanced economies. Inflation remained stuck at around 10 percent, and wages and other nominal variables soon adjusted to this level. Higher domestic inflation and the fixed nominal exchange rate produced a real appreciation, which was not fully validated by higher productivity growth, and after some time, erosion of competitiveness became a concern. The economy began to overheat, political constraints prevented a sufficiently vigorous and flexible use of fiscal policy to mitigate imbalances in the nonpublic sector, and tightening of monetary policy alone could not cope with these rapidly growing imbalances. The mix of tighter monetary policy and continued loose fiscal policy may have only made things worse: it contributed to higher interest rates, which attracted more short-term foreign capital, further fueling the growth of liquidity, keeping inflation high, and widening the current account deficit.

Ultimately, as the external deficit continued to widen despite the visible deceleration of economic growth later in 1996, the situation became unsustainable. It became increasingly obvious that the policy adjustment that was feasible under the existing political constraints would fall short of what was needed to reverse the unsustainable deterioration of current account position. Uncertainties in financial markets, triggered initially by speculative attacks on the Thai baht, only accelerated the flight of foreign investors from koruna assets, which forced the authorities to stop defending a fixed exchange rate. On May 26, 1997, the government and the Czech National Bank (CNB) decided to allow the koruna to float freely.[7]

Like many other emerging-market countries, the Czech Republic did not exit the peg at a time of strong external position, doing so only when it was forced to do so by market pressure. However, unlike other central banks that were ultimately forced to abandon the defense of a fixed parity, the CNB did not wait too long after the pressure on the koruna intensified. Even though it first tried to fend off the pressure by raising interest rates, it did not waste a large amount of foreign reserves in foreign exchange market intervention. In the week before the decision to float, the CNB's foreign reserves declined by about $2.5 billion, to $10 billion. Given the unsatisfactory experience with interventions as a tool to prevent the exit from a pegged exchange rate regime, this was a correct decision.

Possible inflationary effects of currency depreciation after the exit from the peg, together with the absence of an alternative nominal anchor to guide inflation expectations, created a risk that inflation would increase significantly in the coming months. Therefore, the CNB began to work on a new monetary policy framework, and in the meantime it tried to guide inflation expectations by its public pronouncements. After the koruna (CZK) was allowed to float, the CNB issued a public statement that it expected the average koruna exchange rate to stabilize within months at roughly CZK 17 to 19.50 per 1 deutsche mark (DM) (Czech National Bank 1997). Furthermore, the CNB made it clear that in the future, monetary policy would be unambiguously focused on domestic price-level stability and reduction of potential inflationary effects of the koruna's exchange rate movements (Czech National Bank 1997). The first sentence may seem to have been somewhat at odds with the managed float. The reason for announcing a band in which the CNB expected the CZK/DM exchange rate to settle was to prevent overshooting at a time when there was no other nominal anchor to tie down exchange rate and inflation expectations, and to limit to the extent possible any pass-through of currency depreciation to domestic inflation.

However, the CNB felt that this approach to monetary policy conduct was not satisfactory and could not continue for much longer. Therefore, on December 21, the CNB Bank Board decided that in the future, monetary programs would be formulated on the basis of inflation targeting. The stated purpose of inflation targeting was to provide a nominal anchor in the form of an inflation target, to use monetary policy tools directly to achieve the inflation target, and to regularly inform the public about the conduct of monetary policy.[8]

In deciding what measure of inflation to target, the CNB faced a trade-off between transparency and the ability to control inflation, an issue that we will look at in detail later. The CNB opted for a compromise that it considered most appropriate for an economy in transition. For the purpose of inflation targeting, it introduced a new concept, so-called net inflation. Net inflation measures changes in the consumer price index (CPI), excluding the movement in regulated prices, and is further adjusted for the impact on the remaining items of changes in indirect taxes or subsidy elimination.[9] Unlike many other inflation-targeting countries, the Czech Republic did not exclude from net inflation changes in the prices of energy and agricultural products. Such an exclusion would have narrowed the targeted price index too much and would have made it too detached from the headline inflation. Instead, the CNB subsequently introduced so-called exceptions to deal with this problem (see below).

In choosing whether to target a range or a single numerical value of inflation, the CNB opted for a range. Initially, in 1998 and 1999, it was targeting a band 1 percentage point wide, but from 2000, it widened the band to 2 percentage points. The CNB's decision about the width of the band was guided mainly by its assessment of the accuracy with which it thought it could hit net inflation targets, as well as the past volatility of net inflation.

At the end of 1998, the CNB made some modifications to its inflation-targeting strategy. First, the CNB introduced the "exceptions" that could justify missing an inflation target. Exceptions refer to exceptional and unpredictable factors that cause actual inflation to deviate from the inflation target and for which the CNB cannot bear responsibility. These factors include the following: significant differences between actual and predicted world prices of commodities; significant differences between actual and predicted exchange rate that do not reflect developments of domestic economic fundamentals and monetary policy; significant changes of conditions in agriculture that affect agriculture producer prices; and natural disasters and other extraordinary events that produce demand-led and cost-pushed price shocks (Czech National Bank 1999, 57).

Second, the CNB decided to take a more active role in affecting inflation expectations. It realized that a much more rapid than originally expected decline in inflation in the second half of 1998, together with a large degree of rigidity in nominal variables, could produce undesirable developments in real variables—most importantly, real wages. The CNB therefore initiated an informative meeting with the representatives of trade unions and employees in order to explain what inflation it expected in 1999 and, in this way, to help reduce inflation expectations.[10]

In December 1999, the CNB approved *Long-Term Monetary Strategy*, which specified the long-term inflation target for 2005. The objective was to make the inflation-targeting strategy more forward looking. Importantly, the CNB made an effort to involve the public and the government in discussion of the long-term monetary policy target. No doubt this outreach effort reflected the criticism by some politicians that the process of disinflation was too fast and too costly in 1998 and 1999. The CNB did not wish to announce the quantified long-term target corresponding to price stability and the speed with which this ultimate objective was to be achieved without acquiring the support of the government. The CNB seems to have acknowledged implicitly that the decision on the speed of disinflation is ultimately a political one and that it had to be taken by a body with political mandate.

Another modification of the inflation-targeting framework took place in April 2001. At that time, the CNB decided that the main reasons for favoring net inflation targeting rather than headline inflation targeting had disappeared, and it decided that from 2002 on, it would target headline inflation measured by the CPI.[11] The CNB explained that headline inflation covers more comprehensively price developments in the economy and that it is more relevant for decisions of economic agents. For these reasons, by targeting headline inflation, monetary policy should also be better able to affect inflation expectations. Headline inflation targets for the period 2002–2005 were derived from the trajectory of net inflation specified in the December 1999 *Long-Term Monetary Strategy*. The CNB realized that targeting headline inflation has its risks as well, the most important one being the uncertainty regarding the development of regulated prices and effects of changes in administered prices. For example, the need to achieve a stronger adjustment of fiscal imbalances could require a larger-than-expected increase in administered prices, with consequently larger impact on headline inflation. Another complication could arise from the harmonization of indirect taxes with the EU ahead of the EU entry. But these unexpected effects of changes in regulated prices or administrative measures on headline inflation were included in the exceptions that allowed actual inflation to deviate from the inflation target without necessitating a monetary policy response. After the April 2001 modification, the list of the exceptions included the following:

• Major deviations in world prices of raw materials, energy-producing materials, and other commodities

• Major deviations of the koruna's exchange rate that are not connected with domestic economic fundamentals and domestic monetary policy

• Major changes in the conditions for agricultural production having an impact on agriculture producer prices

• Natural disasters and other extraordinary events having cost and demand impacts on prices

• Changes in regulated prices whose effects on headline inflation would exceed 1–1.5 percentage points

• Step changes in indirect taxes

The CNB has also announced that the list of exceptions could be further widened in the future to include one-time price shocks resulting from the adoption of EU standards.

15.3.2 Poland

After the Czech Republic, Poland was the second transition country to introduce inflation targeting. Its approach to inflation targeting differs in some important aspects from that of the Czech Republic.

As a part of Poland's big-bang approach to macroeconomic stabilization, the zloty was pegged to a basket of currencies in 1990. But inflation did not decline sufficiently rapidly, and a fixed nominal exchange rate resulted in rapid real appreciation and erosion of competitiveness. Therefore, a preannounced crawling peg was introduced in October 1991. Capital account liberalization led in 1994 and 1995 to large capital inflows, which forced the authorities to widen the crawling exchange rate band in May 1995 to ± 7 percent. Upward pressure on the currency continued, and in December 1995 the central rate was revalued by 6.4 percent in order to be aligned with the prevailing market rate. In early 1998, the National Bank of Poland (NBP) began to widen the band again: to ± 10 percent in February 1998, to ± 12.5 percent in October 1998, and finally to ± 15 percent in March 1999. At the same time, the rate of crawl was reduced from an initial 1.8 percent per month in 1991 to 0.3 percent per month. The main reason for the gradual widening of the band was the effort of the NBP to be better able to accommodate large capital inflows.

Poland's transition to an inflation-targeting regime began during 1998. As in Hungary, the introduction of inflation targeting was preceded by the amendment of the Act on the NBP. This Act specified that the primary objective of the NBP is to maintain a stable price level and simultaneously support economic policy of the government, provided that this does not constrain the execution of the primary target. The Act also established the Monetary Policy Council (MPC) of the NBP, which replaced the NBP Management Board as the decision-making body. In April 1998, the MPC updated the *Assumptions of Monetary Policy for 1998*, prepared originally by the NBP Management Board in September 1997, and confirmed that the 1998 NBP inflation target of 9.5 percent remained unchanged.[12] In June 1998, the MPC defined a target for monetary policy in 1999, which was to reduce inflation to 8–8.5 percent, and began to work on *Assumptions of Monetary Policy for 1999*, as well as on *Medium-Term Monetary Policy Strategy for 1999–2003*. These documents were approved in September 1998, and at the same time the NBP officially announced the introduction of inflation targeting. The NBP also announced at that time the medium-term inflation target for 2003: reduction of inflation to less than 4 percent. The NBP also indicated that from that time on, annual inflation targets would be announced in *Assumptions of Monetary Policy*.

It should be noted that at the time of announcement to implement inflation targeting, Poland still maintained an exchange rate band, which at the time of announcement was widened from ± 10 percent to ± 12.5 percent, and later to ± 15 percent.

Only in April 2000 did Poland abandon the exchange rate band and switch to a managed float.

Poland has decided to target the broad CPI. The NBP explained that the CPI has been used extensively in Poland since the beginning of transition, and that it is deeply rooted in public perceptions as the measure of inflation. The CPI provides accurate information about changes in price levels of consumer goods and services. Application of some measure of core inflation would require eliminating from the targeted index some prices of goods and services that strongly affect public perception of inflation developments. However, the NBP has started preparatory work for calculating the core inflation index, and it did not exclude the possibility that it would start targeting core inflation in the future.[13]

Like the Czech Republic, Poland has chosen to target a band rather than a point. Initially, it chose a quite narrow target range, just one-half of a percentage point, which was subsequently widened to 1.2 points. The NBP explains that before the introduction of inflation targeting, monetary targets in Poland were defined as fixed points, and a wider band could possibly signal to the public a weaker commitment to reducing inflation. It could be argued that under such circumstances a fixed point could be better than a narrow band, as both are unlikely to be hit, and the damage of missing a point could be less serious than the damage of missing a band. However, the NBP did not exclude the possibility that it may widen the band in the future.

Unlike the Czech National Bank, the NBP did not explicitly define exceptions that would allow missing the inflation target without requiring the monetary policy response. However, the NBP subsequently analyzed in depth the process of inflation in Poland and the role of monetary and nonmonetary factors (National Bank of Poland 2001, appendix 2). Specifically, the NBP calculates and analyzes different measures of the core inflation. It explains that even though core inflation rates do not replace the headline consumer price index, they provide input for research and analysis and for decisions on monetary policy.

15.3.3 Hungary

The introduction of inflation targeting in the Czech Republic could be characterized as a "big bang" approach. There was a clear break with the past fixed exchange rate regime, and after a few months of technical preparation, a full-fledged inflation-targeting regime was put in place. In contrast, Hungary's introduction of inflation targeting could be characterized as "gradualist," even more so than for Poland.[14]

Like other transition economies, Hungary adopted early in its transition an exchange rate peg of the forint against the basket of currencies. However, the peg was adjusted downward quite often to maintain external competitiveness. The fluctuation band was gradually widened from ± 0.5 percent to ± 2.25 percent, to reduce speculative pressures ahead of the predictable adjustments of the parity. But this mechanism did not prevent large short-term capital inflows in late 1994, and in March 1995, after a devaluation of 8.3 percent, the regime of ad hoc adjustment was replaced with a crawling band. The monthly rate of crawl was initially set at 1.9 percent but was gradually reduced to 0.4 percent after October 1999. This regime succeeded in bringing inflation down from about 30 percent in 1995 to below 10 percent in 1999.

Even at the time when the Czech Republic and Poland were abandoning fixed exchange rate regimes, the Hungarian authorities continued to view this narrow fluctuation band as a useful nominal anchor. The band helped reduce inflation and anchor inflation expectations, while at the same time avoiding excessive real appreciation and erosion of competitiveness. However, like other emerging-market countries with a fixed exchange rate, Hungary too was ultimately forced to deal with the problems caused by large capital inflows. For some time, Hungary was able to avoid pressure on the narrow exchange rate band because of the presence of controls on short-term capital flows. These controls were effective in introducing a wedge between onshore and offshore interest rates, providing some degree of independence to monetary policy. But it was clear that as capital controls were relaxed in line with progression to EU accession a narrow-band regime would become more difficult to sustain.

The problems with the narrow exchange rate band began to intensify in the course of 2000. Inflation, which declined significantly in the period 1995–99, began to creep up again. While this increase in inflation was initially triggered by external shocks, like higher world oil prices, domestic factors began to play a role as well, including the exchange rate regime. The constraints of the narrow band and increasing capital inflows in 2000 began to make it more difficult for the central bank to simultaneously pursue disinflation and nominal exchange rate stability. Early in 2000, the central bank acted to reduce the pressure on the exchange rate band by cutting interest rates, and it also threatened to introduce capital controls. This strategy worked, and the exchange rate depreciated. However, in a situation of strong economic growth, robust domestic demand, and tight labor markets, reducing interest rates did not help much in fighting inflation, which remained relatively high. Periodically, speculative pressures for appreciation and widening of the band appeared, forcing the central bank to cut interest rates and/or intervene in the foreign exchange market. It opted to do mainly the latter, and it sterilized the liquidity created as a result of these interventions.

However, as the sterilization costs were increasing, it was becoming clear that the narrow exchange rate band had outlived its usefulness and that Hungary needed to introduce more exchange rate flexibility if it was to succeed in reducing inflation further.[15] In May 2001, the authorities finally decided to widen the fluctuation band around the forint parity against the euro to ± 15 percent.[16] The crawling regime was maintained, with the rate of crawl reduced to 0.2 percent monthly, and remaining controls on short-term capital flows were phased out. In October 2001, the crawling peg was completely abolished.

While a wider exchange rate band should allow the government to attach more priority to fighting inflation, as we will discuss below, a conflict between the inflation target and exchange rate target could still arise and complicate the conduct of monetary policy. However, the change in the monetary policy regime has been somewhat confused. At the time when the authorities decided to widen the fluctuation band, they did not immediately announce a shift to a new monetary policy regime. Even though the new exchange rate band was too wide to serve as a useful nominal anchor, the authorities were moving to inflation targeting only gradually. But on July 13, 2001, the new Act on the National Bank of Hungary (NBH) was enacted by Parliament, which defined the achievement and maintenance of price stability as the prime objective of the NBH. The Act also sought to reinforce NBH independence, in accordance with the EU requirement.

In its August 2001 Quarterly Inflation report, the NBH explained that for the next couple of years it would be using the inflation-targeting system to achieve a gradual reduction of inflation to a level corresponding to price stability (National Bank of Hungary 2001, 35–36). The NBH objective is to meet the Maastricht criterion on inflation in 2004–2005, so that it can adopt the euro in 2006–2007. Specifically, the NBH states that it will seek to bring inflation down to around 2 percent. In agreement with the government, the NBH set an inflation target of 7 percent for December 2001, 4.5 percent for 2002, and 3.5 percent for 2003 and 2004. In recognition of the fact that the NBH cannot instantly offset unexpected inflationary shocks, it has also established a ± 1 percent tolerance band around the announced disinflation path.

The primary instrument that the NBH uses to attain its inflation targets is changes in its benchmark interest rates. The NBH has particularly emphasized the important role of changes in exchange rate on inflation. It argues that in Hungary, the exchange rate channel is the central bank's fastest and most powerful means of influencing domestic prices. (However, we will see later in section 15.5 that this reasoning may be dangerous.) While the exchange rate will not have the same prominent role as during the narrow-band regime, and the NBH will be less able to control its short-term movements, it will continue to play an important role. The NBH has indicated that it will try to influence the exchange rate in order to achieve the desired inflation outcome. In order to achieve the changes in exchange rate, it will use mainly changes in interest rates, while direct intervention in the foreign exchange market will be used only exceptionally, to deal with emergency situations. The NBH recognizes that in the short term, the actual exchange rate could deviate from an exchange rate path that would be consistent with the disinflation path. All in all, exchange rate movements seem to play a much more important role in Hungary than in other inflation-targeting countries. Such explicit emphasis on the role of exchange rate movements in achieving inflation targets as seen in Hungary is quite unique.

The NBH estimates that it takes up to one and a half years for changes in interest rates to have a full impact on inflation. It argues that if it tried to keep inflation in line with the targeted path over the short-term horizon, the result could be excessive volatility of output (and arguably also excessive instrument volatility). Therefore, it will confine policy responses only to deviation of forecasted inflation from targeted inflation over the horizon of one to one and a half years.

The transparency of this new system should be enhanced by the publication of NBH's inflation projections every quarter for the following six quarters. Moreover, the NBH will also publish the considerations that were behind its monetary policy decisions, and its analysis of the achievement of inflation target. The Quarterly Report on Inflation also contains the projection of inflation using a fan chart.

Unlike the CNB, the NBH began to target headline inflation immediately. But there is no discussion in NBH official documents about the reasons for choosing to target headline inflation rather than adjusted or underlying inflation. The NBH also did not specify any exceptions that would justify a deviation of actual inflation from its inflation target, although there is some discussion in its inflation reports about the possible extent of price deregulation and its effects on headline inflation. When announcing the introduction of inflation targeting, the NBH was also silent about the possible conflict between the exchange rate band and the inflation target.

Overall, the impression is that the NBH has focused less on operational aspects of the inflation-targeting regime than has the CNB or even the NBP. Perhaps this reflects the fact that NBH officials still attach importance to the nominal exchange rate band as an important anchor of the economy. They seem to believe that moving the exchange rate within the band will help them to achieve a long-term inflation target that will allow them to qualify for euro adoption. In a sense, this strategy could be understood: why invest heavily in a detailed design for a policy framework that will be removed in a few years anyway after Hungary adopts the euro? The Czech Republic and Poland introduced inflation targeting much earlier, and they may also be less eager to adopt the euro as soon as possible. This means that inflation targeting could be in place for a longer time and that a well-designed inflation-targeting framework may be more necessary.

15.4 Preliminary Experience with Inflation Targeting

In view of the relatively short period during which inflation targeting has been implemented in the transition economies, it is too early to make a definitive judgment about the experience of the operation of this new policy framework. Nevertheless, some preliminary observations can be made. There are two ways in which we can evaluate the experience with inflation targeting in transition economies.

First, we can look at how successful inflation-targeting central banks were in achieving inflation rates close to their inflation targets. Here the answer is "not all that successful." Initially, the CNB significantly undershot its inflation target several times, while the NBP first overshot it and subsequently undershot it. The NBH hit its targets in 2001 and 2002, but its short experience with inflation targeting does not tell us much yet. But even this short-term experience makes one thing clear: namely, the problems of simultaneously targeting inflation and exchange rate in a world of free capital flows.

Second, we can examine the success of inflation targeting in reducing inflation. Looking only at these countries' success in hitting their inflation targets could be too narrow a perspective for assessing the performance of inflation targeting. All central banks in inflation-targeting transition economies have emphasized that the main purpose of the inflation-targeting framework is to allow these countries to bring inflation down to a level that would qualify them for euro adoption. When we evaluate inflation targeting from this perspective, the preliminary experience with this regime should be judged more positively: all these countries are proceeding well with disinflation, and there is a good chance that in a few years they will be able to reach price stability, as defined for the purpose of euro adoption. However, the process of disinflation is not a smooth one, and there are quite large variations in inflation.

Let us now look in more detail at the record of implementation of inflation targeting in the three analyzed countries. First we will discuss the speed of disinflation implied by announced inflation targets, and then we will examine how successful the inflation-targeting countries were in hitting these targets.

15.4.1 Inflation Targets and the Speed of Disinflation

In many advanced economies that pursue inflation targeting, this regime has been introduced only after price stability has been reached (Bernanke et al. 1999). But this was not the case in the transition economies, where, at the time of introduction of inflation targeting, inflation was still running well above the level considered consistent with price stability. Therefore, the authorities in these countries had to make two decisions: (a) to quantify an inflation target that would be compatible with the long-term objective of price stability, and (b) to decide on the time horizon within which this ultimate objective was to be met—that is, to decide on the speed of disinflation.

There is extensive literature discussing how to quantify price stability. In the literature, we can find several arguments why central banks should not quantify price stability as inflation at zero or near zero (in the range of 0–1 percent). One reason relates to downward nominal wage rigidity. If the inflation rate were to approach zero under the condition of downward wage rigidity, it would be difficult to achieve real wage adjustment in response to changed market conditions, such as a negative demand shock. The result could be higher-than-desirable real wages, higher unemployment, and lower economic growth.[17] A second reason relates to the impossibility of reducing nominal interest rates below zero, which means that if inflation is close to zero, real interest rates cannot be pushed below zero when this might be necessary in order to stimulate economic activity.[18] Furthermore, a zero inflation target may lead to periods of deflation, which could promote financial instability and make it harder to conduct monetary policy because interest rates would no longer provide a useful guide to the stance of monetary policy (Mishkin and Schmidt-Hebbel 2002).

In the literature, one can observe a convergence of views that an inflation rate of 1–3 percent corresponds to price stability (see table 15.2). If we look at how central banks quantify price stability in practice, we see that there is not much difference between the theoretical conclusions and what the central banks actually do. This is the case for all economies—developed, developing, and transition.

However, some have raised the question of whether the specific conditions of transition economies would not justify targeting somewhat higher inflation than in developed economies. High-growth countries typically experience real exchange rate

Table 15.2
Inflation Targets

Country	Targeted inflation (%)	Period
Czech Republic	1–3 (2–4)[a]	2005
Australia	2–3	Average during a business cycle
Brazil[b]	2–6	2001
Chile	2–4	2001
Poland	<4	2003
Hungary	Around	2004–2005
Mexico	3	2003
Izrael	3–4	2001
New Zealand	0–3	From 1996
Canada	1–3	From 1995
Euro area	<2	From 1999
United Kingdom	2.5	From 1996

Source: Schaechder, Stone, and Zelmer (2000); web sites of Banco de México (http://www.banxico .org.mx/), National Bank of Hungary (http://www.mnb.hu/), and European Central Bank (http://www .ecb.int/).
[a] 1–3 percent is for net inflation, 2–4 percent for headline inflation.
[b] For 2002, the target was subsequently set at 2.5–4.5 percent, but as a result of the debt crisis and sharp currency depreciation, inflation in 2002 reached 12.5 percent. In response to higher inflation, the central bank also raised its 2003 and 2004 targets.

appreciation by an amount proportional to the relative difference of traded to non-traded sector productivity growth relative to the rest of the world (the Harrod-Balassa-Samuelson effect). If it is appropriate for these countries to aim at traded goods inflation similar to that of industrialized countries in the long run, then trend real appreciation requires a domestic nontraded goods inflation that is somewhat higher, and so the inflation rate should be slightly higher than would be desirable for average-growth countries. Škreb (1998) notes that in the transition economies it is particularly difficult to measure precisely the improvements in the quality of goods. As a result, actual inflation could be much lower than measured inflation. Because of these measurement problems, as well as other reasons, Škreb argues that in transition economies inflation in the range of 4–5 percent would correspond to price stability.

Other authors argue, however, that during the convergence with the developed economies, transition economies should be expected to experience a rapid growth of labor productivity from implementation of economic reforms, which should produce lower inflation (Deppler 1998). Clinton (2000) argues that rapid productivity growth in transition economies weakens the traditional arguments in favor of a notably higher-than-zero inflation rate. Given the rapid growth of labor productivity, a decline in nominal wages would rarely be needed.[19] Similarly, given the high real return on capital and high trend toward economic growth, it is not very likely that a situation would arise in which a central bank would have to stimulate an economy in recession with the help of negative real interest rates.

What can be said about the speed of disinflation? Theoretically, disinflation could be too quick, resulting in excessively large (although arguably temporary) loss of output and higher unemployment, or it could be too slow; inflation expectations could become more entrenched at a high level, and this would make it more costly to reduce inflation later.[20] Therefore, it could be argued that there exists an optimal speed of disinflation that would minimize the sacrifice ratio (the ratio of loss of output to disinflation).[21] However, the determination of this optimal speed of disinflation is less a matter of exact science and more a matter of judgment.

In the literature, a number of factors have been identified that affect the sacrifice ratio—that is, the output effect of disinflation. These include the structure of the economy, the degree and the means of indexation of wages and other nominal variables, past history of inflation and stabilization, credibility of monetary policy, the degree of openness of the economy, and so on. Furthermore, as has been shown in the case of other countries, change in inflation is positively correlated with the level of economic activity (Stock and Watson 1999). Given the fact that economic reasoning does not provide a hard conclusion about the optimal speed of disinflation, and in view of the important consequences of the decision about the speed of disinflation for the economy and for different population groups, societies pay particular attention to the mechanism through which this decision is reached. By its nature, the

Table 15.3
The Speed of Disinflation

Country	End-1997 inflation	Introduction of inflation targeting	Inflation at that time	Direction of inflation	Ultimate objective	Year to be achieved
Czech Republic	10.0	December 97	10.0	Rising	2–4	2005
Hungary	18.4	August 01	8.7	Falling	Around 2	2004–5
Poland	13.2	June 98	12.2	Falling	<4	2003

Note: All inflation figures refer to CPI.

decision about the speed of disinflation is not a purely technocratic decision that could be put solely in the hands of professional economists or central bankers. Because different speeds of disinflation will have different consequences for different population groups, this decision is by nature a political one, and thus an argument can be made for entrusting it to a political body that has the political legitimacy to make such political choices. This has implications for the debate on the optimal degree of central bank independence that is discussed in section 15.5.

However, for transition countries in Central and Eastern Europe, the desire to adopt the euro at some point in the future is of more practical relevance for monetary policy than the theoretical arguments about the appropriate quantification of price stability and the optimal speed of disinflation. Eventual euro adoption will depend on the ability to meet the Maastricht criteria, including low inflation, and the decision to adopt the euro at a certain date will thus implicitly contain a decision on how quickly and how far disinflation will have to go.

All three countries that we examine will have to adopt the euro at some point after entering the EU, even though they may choose a different speed with which to do so. But notwithstanding this possible different speed, all three countries are committed to a relatively fast disinflation. Table 15.3 summarizes the speed of disinflation implied by the level of inflation at the time of the introduction of inflation targets and by the long-term inflation objective.

As we can see, the ultimate objective is defined in each country in a different way: as a range in the Czech Republic (both upper and lower band are specified); as a maximum ceiling in Poland (only an upper band is specified), and as a "soft" point target in Hungary (no lower and upper bound are specified, but inflation should meet the Maastricht criterion). This also means that one single inflation rate could meet all these constraints at the same time.

Even though the Czech Republic did not reveal a firm intention to choose the fastest possible strategy to adopt the euro, the CNB still opted for a relatively quick disinflation so that it would be able to meet the Maastricht criterion and eventually move quickly to adopt the euro if it chooses to. Figure 15.1 shows the CNB's actual

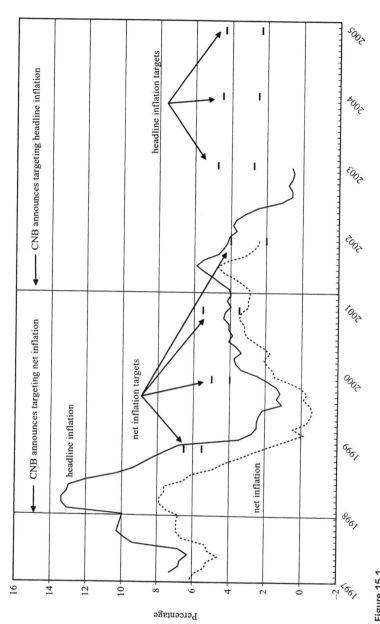

Figure 15.1
Czech Republic, annual inflation and inflation targets, year-over-year.
Source: Czech Statistical Office.

and targeted inflation. When the inflation-targeting framework was adopted in December 1997, inflation was 10 percent, and it continued to rise, to about 13 percent in early 1998 (in CPI terms; net inflation approached 8 percent). The CNB decided that at the end of 1998 net inflation should decline to 5.5–6.5 percent and, at the end of year 2000, to 3.5–5.5 percent. In December 1999, the CNB quantified its long-term objective of price stability: net inflation in the range of 1–3 percent in 2005, which was subsequently complemented by setting the 2005 CPI target in the range of 2–4 percent. Given the inflation target for the year 2000 in the range of 3.5–5.5 percent, this implied an average annual reduction in net inflation by 0.5 percentage points. The CNB explained that this long-term target would basically imply a continuation of the existing pace of disinflation. However, in December 2002, CPI inflation fell to 0.6 percent, which already brought it well below the long-term target range.

In Poland, the NBP first set a short-term inflation target in June 1998 for end-1999 in the range of 8–8.5 percent (see figure 15.2). At the time of the announcement of the inflation target, inflation was above 12 percent and declining. In September 1999, the NBP also announced the medium-term target of CPI inflation of less than 4 percent at the end of 2003. Subsequently, inflation continued to fall faster than expected, and in March 1999, when it fell to around 6 percent, the NBP modified the end-1999 CPI target to 6.6–7.8 percent. In September 1999, in *Monetary Guidelines for the Year 2000*, the NBP set the end-2000 inflation target in the range of 5.4–6.8 percent. However, the process of disinflation in Poland was interrupted, as inflation increased from 5.6 percent in February 1999 to 11.6 percent in July 2000. Therefore, the 2001 inflation target was set higher than in 2000, 6–8 percent, but the targeted inflation range for end-2002 was reduced to 4–6 percent. As inflation at the end of 2001 fell to 3.6 percent, meeting this target would have required another mild pickup in inflation. Instead, inflation in 2002 fell rapidly and in December 2002 reached 0.8 percent, resulting in another significant undershooting of the target. During 2003, inflation in Poland remained below the NBP long-term objective.

Hungary launched official inflation targeting only in mid-2001.[22] At that time, inflation was already declining: from a peak of 10.8 percent in May 2001, it fell to 8.7 percent in August when details of the new inflation-targeting regime were published in the Quarterly Inflation Report (see figure 15.3). For 2001, the inflation target was set in the range of 6–8 percent. For 2002, the inflation target was set at 3.5–5.5 percent, and for 2003 the target was set at 2.5–4.5 percent.[23] The NBH's long-term objective is that Hungary meet the Maastricht criterion on inflation in 2004–2005, which should be possible with inflation even slightly higher than the 2 percent that the NBH seeks to achieve in the long term. Unlike the Czech Republic and Poland, Hungary also specified its long-term inflation target qualitatively, in terms of meeting the Maastricht criterion for inflation, thus underscoring its preference to adopt the

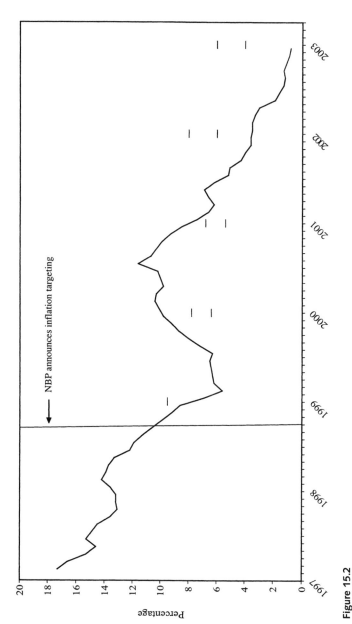

Figure 15.2
Poland, actual inflation and inflation target, year-over-year.
Note: In June 1998, the NBP defined the end-1999 inflation target. However, the NBP officially announced the introduction of inflation targeting only in September.
Source: Central Statistical Office Poland.

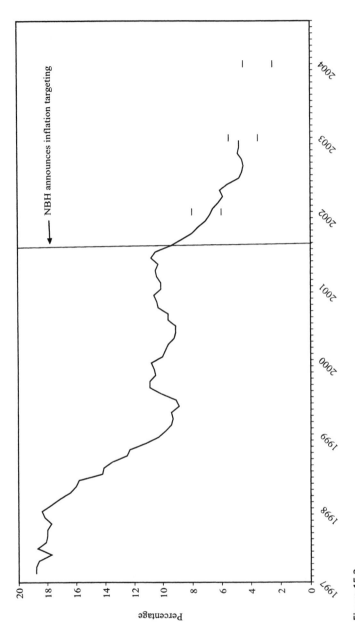

Figure 15.3
Hungary, actual inflation and inflation targets, year-over-year.
Source: Hungarian Central Statistical Office.

Table 15.4
Targeted and Actual Inflation in the Czech Republic and Poland

	Czech Republic (net inflation)		Poland (headline inflation)	
	Target	Actual	Target	Actual
1998	5.5–6.5	1.7	n.a.	8.6
1999	4–5	1.5	6.4–7.8 (8–8.5)[a]	9.8
2000	3.5–5.5	3	5.4–6.8	8.5
2001	2–4	2.4	6–8	3.6
2002	2.75–4.75[b]	0.5	4–6	0.8

Source: Czech National Bank, National Bank of Poland, various documents.
Note: n.a. = not applicable.
[a] Initial target in parentheses.
[b] Headline inflation.

euro sooner rather than later. As inflation in late 2003 approached 6 percent, meeting the long-term inflation target would require bringing inflation below present level, in contrast to the Czech Republic and Poland, where inflation is likely to pick up somewhat from present unsustainable low levels.

15.4.2 Hitting and Missing Inflation Targets

In the previous section, we examined experience with inflation targeting from the perspective of disinflation. In this section, we look at how successful the three countries were in meeting their inflation targets. In this respect, we should keep in mind that countries can be quite successful, in the longer term, in bringing inflation down, but if a successful disinflation is accompanied by a significant instability of inflation (as evidenced by repeated large undershooting or overshooting of inflation targets), this can be costly for the economy as well.

There is not yet much we can read from the history of inflation targeting in Hungary because it is so recent (see figure 15.3). The 2001 target was announced only in August 2001, and it therefore was more of a short-term inflation forecast than an actual inflation target. Therefore, the fact that Hungary met this target and the 2002 target does not tell much about the operation of its inflation-targeting framework. The inflation target for 2002 implied a fairly rapid disinflation, alongside the trend started in mid-2001. In 2001 and 2002, disinflation was helped by the appreciation of the forint. However, since the forint has reached the upper end of the fluctuation band and the government seems to resist the revaluation of parity, there is no room for further nominal appreciation that would assist in further disinflation.

Table 15.4 and figures 15.1 and 15.2, which show the history of inflation targeting in the Czech Republic and Poland, tell a very different story. In the Czech Republic, the CNB significantly undershot its inflation targets, particularly in 1998 and 1999, and less in 2000. Net inflation fell to 1.7 percent at the end of 1998 and to 1.5 percent at the end of 1999, well below the CNB's targets. Only in 2001, in the fourth year of inflation targeting, did the CNB succeed in achieving its inflation target, but it undershot its target again in 2002.

As we can see in figure 15.2, in Poland there was an opposite problem, as the NBP significantly overshot its targets in 1999 and 2000. In the course of 1998, inflation in Poland was falling rapidly, and at the end of the year it fell to 8.6 percent, less than the 9.5 percent projected. A more-rapid-than-expected decline in inflation prompted the NBP to reduce early in 1999 its target for end-1999, from 8–8.5 percent to 6.4– 7.8 percent, a step that in retrospect may seem to have been somewhat premature. If the NBP had maintained its original target, 8–8.5 percent, it would have missed it by only a very small margin. But in the course of 1999, inflation began to increase again, and the 1999 target was missed by a significant margin, as was the 2000 target. Very tight monetary policy and slowing economic activity helped to bring inflation down sharply in 2001, and subsequently the 2001 and 2002 targets were undershot quite sizably.

These repeated large deviations of actual inflation from the inflation target would seem to suggest that inflation targeting was not very successful in the Czech Republic and Poland. But before we make any definitive judgments about the success or failure of inflation targeting in these two countries, it is important to understand the reasons for such significant deviations of actual from targeted inflation. We have to examine more closely both the domestic and the external economic circumstances that prevailed during this period and that affected actual inflation.

At the time when the CNB launched inflation targeting, inflation was rising quite rapidly, but at the same time the economy was already slipping into a prolonged recession. The 1998 and 2000 inflation targets were specified at the time when the CNB (and other public and private forecasters) expected much stronger economic growth than actually materialized.[24] However, with the onset of a major banking crisis in 1997–98, economic activity fell and contributed to a much faster disinflation than was envisaged by the CNB's inflation targets.[25] Moreover, the 1997–98 financial crises and weak global economic activity contributed to falling commodity prices, including energy prices.[26] The CNB calculations suggest that these external factors had a sizeable effect on net inflation: in 1998, these factors reduced net inflation by 2–3 percentage points (Čapek 1999, 9). In the absence of these shocks, net inflation at the end of 1998 would probably have been close to the bottom of the target range. There were also other structural shocks that contributed to lower-than-projected inflation. Among the more important was the continuing unexpected decline in foodstuff prices in 1998 and 1999. Ex post, the decline in foodstuff prices was ascribed to the struggle of the retail distributors for market share in the Czech market. Weak domestic demand, together with strong koruna and strong competitive pressure in the domestic economy resulting from penetration on the Czech market of foreign distributors, continued to keep inflation low even after the effects of external price shocks began to disappear. In addition, the decision not to exclude energy prices and to exclude adjustment of regulated prices from the targeted price index did not achieve its objective of encouraging the government to pursue a "courageous policy of price deregulation," as the CNB initially hoped.

When inflation targeting was introduced, Poland was facing very different economic circumstances from those of the Czech Republic. First, the implications of global developments for domestic inflation were better known to the NBP at that time and could be incorporated into the inflation target. As in the Czech Republic, inflation in Poland declined significantly during 1998 and 1999, but this decline was less dramatic and did not last as long. Already in the second half of 1999, inflation in Poland had begun to exceed by an increasingly wider margin inflation in the Czech Republic. Relatively rapid growth of domestic demand, increase in import prices, and the monopolistic structure of some industries together resulted in the reversal of disinflation in Poland in the course of 1999. Fiscal policy was also much more expansionary than the NBP had expected, and this expansionary stance further fueled domestic demand.

The NBP responded to these developments with a significant tightening of monetary policy, and it continued to keep monetary conditions very tight even when inflation began to fall sharply later in 2000 and in 2001. This (to some excessively) tight monetary policy also brought economic growth nearly to a halt by the end of 2001, and contributed to increased tension between the NBP and the government, which even led by the end of 2001 to threats of reduction of NBP independence. It appears that the NBP tried to use a tight monetary policy stance as an instrument to force the government to strengthen structural fiscal balance, even at the cost of significant undershooting of its inflation target.

Judging by its success in meeting its inflation target, the NBP has not been very successful thus far. In the first two years, inflation targets were overshot, and in the third and fourth years there was significant undershooting. Recent years saw a significant instability of inflation, which fell rapidly from 17.8 percent in the beginning of 1997 to 5.6 percent in February 1999, then rose to 11.6 percent in July 2000, and fell again to 0.8 percent in December 2002. In Poland, external factors may have been of less importance in explaining the failure to meet inflation targets than in the Czech Republic, while the conduct of macroeconomic policy probably mattered more. First, unexpected fiscal expansion, combined with easy monetary policy, contributed to the acceleration of inflation and overshooting of inflation targets; subsequently, sharp tightening of monetary policy, in the absence of further easing of fiscal policy, reduced inflation sharply down and produced a significant undershooting of the target.

15.4.3 Comparison of Inflation and Output Performance of Inflation Targeters with Other Transition Countries

We have seen that hitting inflation targets has not been an easy exercise. However, this may have been unavoidable given the shocks the inflation targeters were subjected to. To assess the success of inflation targeting in transition countries, we have to ask how well the inflation targeters have done relative to the nontargeters.

There are two alternative monetary policy regimes to inflation targeting that transition countries have chosen:

1. Exchange rate peg: a crawling peg for Hungary until August 2001, a standard peg for Latvia (peg to SDR), and a hard peg of the currency board type for Bulgaria, Estonia, and Latvia

2. Float without an inflation target: Slovakia, Slovenia, and Romania[27]

Figures 15.4 and 15.5 compare inflation rates (year over year) in the Czech Republic and Poland with those of the other transition countries. A relevant starting date for comparing the different monetary regimes is December 1998 (marked in the figures), which corresponds to the first date that inflation targets were to be met in the Czech Republic. As we can see in figure 15.4, which has a comparison with the non-inflation-targeting floaters, the Czech Republic and Poland experienced lower levels of inflation for most of the 1999–2002 period than did the non-inflation-targeting floaters. On the other hand, figure 15.5, which has a comparison with the exchange rate peggers, does not display a clear dominance of inflation targeting over pegging. Hungary, with its soft peg, and Bulgaria, with its currency board, have typically had higher inflation rates than the Czech Republic and Poland; but Lithuania, with its currency board, and Latvia, with its standard peg, have experienced lower inflation rates. Estonia has had inflation rates comparable to those in the Czech Republic, but up until the last half of 2002 had lower inflation than Poland.

Clearly a low level of inflation is only one measure of success of monetary regimes—equally important is the variability of inflation and output. Table 15.5 provides the standard deviation of both inflation and output for the period 1999–2002. Here we see that the Czech Republic and Poland are in the middle of the pack on both criteria. The Czech Republic and Poland have higher standard deviations of inflation than the hard-pegging Baltic countries, while they have lower variability than Hungary, a soft pegger, Bulgaria, a hard pegger, and Slovakia and Romania, non-inflation-targeting floaters. Slovenia, a non-inflation-targeting floater, has equal inflation variability to the Czech Republic but has lower variability than Poland.

Although we should not make too much of the data in figures 15.4 and 15.5 and table 15.5 because they cover such a short period and because these countries have been subjected to different shocks, it is worth noting that in terms of inflation con-

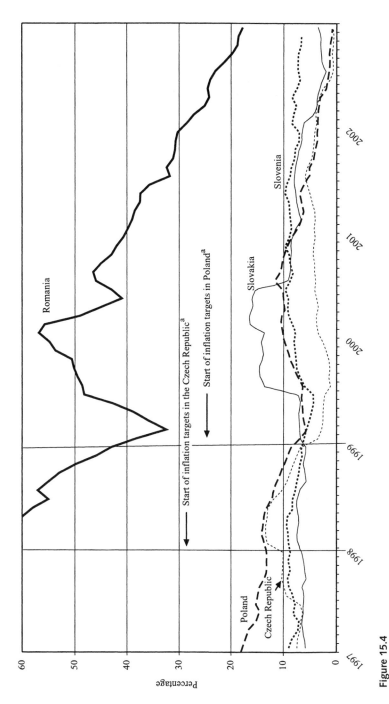

Figure 15.4
Inflation in Czech Republic, Poland, and the non-inflation-targeting floaters, year-over-year.
Note: [a] Indicates the date of the first inflation target.
Source: Czech Statistical Office, Central Statistical Office of Poland, Statistical Office of the Republic of Slovenia, Statistical Office of the Republic of the Slovak Republic, and National Statistical Office of Romania.

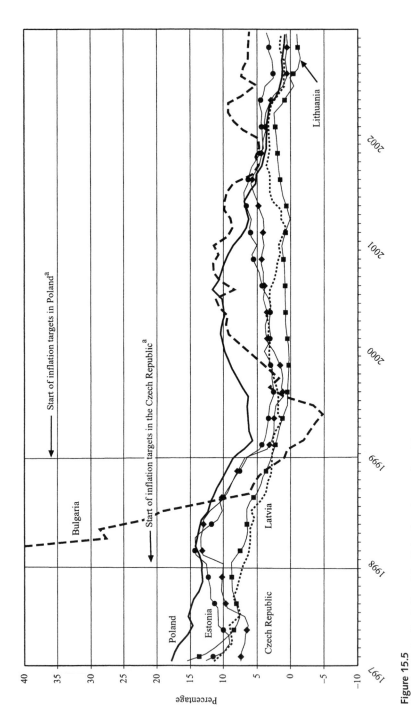

Figure 15.5
Inflation in the Czech Republic, Poland, and countries with peg, year-over-year.
Note: [a] Indicates the date of the first inflation target.
Sources: Czech Statistical Office, Central Statistical Office of Poland, NBP, National Statistical Office of Bulgaria, Statistical Office of Estonia, Statistical Office of the Republic of Slovenia, Statistical Office of the Slovak Republic, Statistics Lithuania, and Central Statistical Bureau of Latvia.

Table 15.5
Inflation and Output Growth Volatility: 1998–2002

Country	Inflation volatility	Output volatility
Czech Republic	3.49	2.00
Poland	3.6	1.82
Hungary	3.08	0.72
Estonia	3.08	3.07
Latvia	1.34	2.52
Lithuania	2.18	3.5
Bulgaria	49.7	3.97
Slovakia	3.88	1.39
Slovenia	1.34	0.82
Romania	18.37	4.83

trol, inflation targeting does not clearly dominate the other monetary policy regimes chosen by transition countries.

We reach a similar conclusion in terms of output variability as seen by the standard deviations of output growth reported in table 15.5.[28] The Czech Republic and Poland have had lower standard deviations than the hard peggers, Bulgaria and the Baltic states, but have had higher standard deviations than Slovakia and Slovenia, non-inflation-targeting floaters. Hungary, a soft pegger for most of the period, had the lowest standard deviation of output growth of all the countries in the table. However, even less should be made of these comparisons, because real shocks have differed dramatically across the transition countries. For example, as we can see in figure 15.6, the Baltic countries, which have a higher proportion of their trade with Russia as a result of their having been part of the former Soviet Union, suffered very dramatic output declines in 1999 in the aftermath of the Russian financial crisis in the fall of 1998. The contraction of the Russian economy at that time had a far smaller impact on transition countries that were less integrated with Russia and whose trade was mostly with Western Europe.

15.5 Lessons and Problems of Inflation Targeting in Transition Economies

Even though the experience of the implementation of inflation targeting in transition economies is relatively short, it has nevertheless brought out several specific issues, which deserve discussion. First, how should the standard operational aspects of inflation targeting be specified—that is, what price index should be targeted? Should the inflation target be a point or a range? And what should the horizon for the target be? Second, given the fact that transition economies began inflation targeting in a

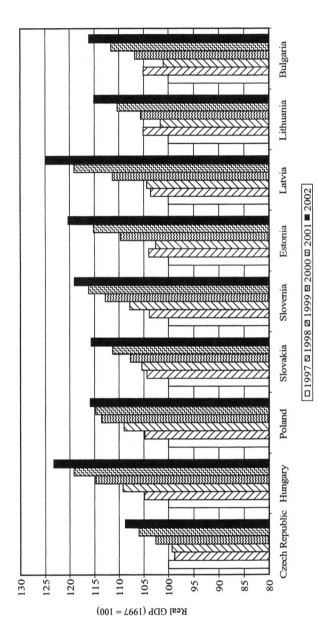

Figure 15.6
Transition economies: Real GDP (1997 = 100).
Sources: Czech Statistical Office, Central Statistical Office of Poland, National Statistical Office of Bulgaria, Statistical Office of Estonia, Statistical Office of the Republic of Slovenia, Statistical Office of the Slovak Republic, Statistics Lithuania, and Central Statistical Bureau of Latvia.

situation of higher inflation than the long-term objective, how should the speed of disinflation be determined, and in a closely related question, how should the government be involved in setting inflation targets? Third, how should monetary policy respond to the deviation of the actual inflation from the targeted disinflation path, and how much should the floor of an inflation target be emphasized relative to the ceiling? Fourth, how should the exchange rate be incorporated into the inflation-targeting framework?

15.5.1   Operational Aspects of Inflation Targeting

What Measure of Inflation to Target?   In deciding what measure of inflation to target, central banks face a trade-off between transparency and the ability to control inflation. The advantage of a broadly defined headline inflation (i.e., the consumer price index) is that it is better understood by the public. However, the problem is that headline movements could reflect factors other than monetary policy measures. A more narrowly defined measure of inflation that excludes possible effects of transitory shocks could be better controlled by a central bank, but at the same time it could be more difficult for the public to assess the conduct of monetary policy on the basis of such measure. Given the emphasis on central banks' accountability and transparency in a regime of inflation targeting, this could potentially be a serious handicap, particularly for a central bank that still has to earn its credibility.

The CNB opted for a compromise that it considered most appropriate for an economy in transition. For the purpose of inflation targeting, it introduced a new concept, so-called net inflation, which excluded regulated prices (see section 15.3.1). Specific conditions of economic transition have played an important role in selecting net inflation as the targeted measure of inflation. Unlike in industrial countries, many prices were still regulated in the Czech Republic in late 1997. The CNB knew that substantial changes in these regulated prices, including rents, would be needed before they reached a market-clearing level. As a result, a given monetary policy stance could produce different future paths of headline inflation, depending on the pace of price deregulation or the size of adjustment of administered prices. At the same time, this approach was supposed to avoid a situation in which the government would be hesitant to pursue a faster adjustment of regulated prices out of concern that the inflationary effects of such policy would force the CNB to tighten monetary policy, with adverse effects on economic growth, thus exacerbating the political cost of deregulation. Indeed, the former acting governor of the CNB, Pavel Kysilka, stated that "by targeting net inflation, we have provided a room to the government to pursue a courageous policy of price deregulation" (Kysilka 1998, 10–12). Obviously, a high share of regulated prices in total CPI does not make it easier for the central bank to deal with this trade-off between transparency and ability to control inflation.[29]

Subsequently, the pace of price deregulation and increase in administered prices was less than the CNB had hoped, and so use of the net inflation construct did not produce the desirable outcome the CNB expected. In addition, the net inflation construct turned out to be more volatile than headline inflation, helping to contribute to larger misses of the target. When it decided to target net inflation, the CNB did not exclude the possibility that in the future it could modify the measure of targeted inflation. The problems with the net inflation measure thus led the CNB to abandon it in April 2001, and it subsequently moved to targeting headline inflation as has been discussed in section 15.3.1.

Target a Point or a Range?   As in other aspects of design of the operational framework, there is a trade-off involved in deciding about the width of the band. A wider band increases the chance that monetary policy will be successful in keeping targeted inflation inside. But a too-large band could reduce the ability of inflation targeting to anchor inflation expectations, and it could be of less help in establishing the anti-inflationary credibility. Some argue that a band that is narrow enough to anchor inflationary expectations is likely to be frequently missed, and that it is preferable to target a point and explain the deviations of actual inflation from that point target (Bernanke et al. 1999; Mishkin 2001).

In a sense, one can argue that a higher degree of uncertainty in projecting inflation and a correspondingly higher probability that even a target range would be missed makes the issue of point versus range less of an issue than in more advanced inflation-targeting economies. By setting a range, the central bank may indicate what is its estimate of uncertainty of reaching the inflation target. This is how the CNB has explained its decision regarding the width of the targeted range. Missing a target range then carries a larger risk of credibility loss than missing a target point. Targeting a reasonably narrow band (that is, narrow enough so that it provides a sufficient nominal anchor) does not make much sense when the probability that it would be missed is not significantly less than the probability of missing a point.

Time Horizon of Inflation Targeting   Monetary policy affects the economy and particularly inflation with long lags. In industrialized countries, lags from monetary policy to inflation are typically estimated to be on the order of two years. Shorter time horizons, such as one year, can be highly problematic. The first problem with too short a horizon is that it can lead to a controllability problem: too-frequent misses of the inflation target, even when monetary policy is being conducted optimally. The second problem is that it can lead to instrument instability, in which policy instruments are moved around too much in order to try to get inflation to hit its targets over the shorter horizon. A third problem is that too short a horizon implies that not enough weight is put on output fluctuations in the central bank's loss function.[30]

The experience with inflation targeting in New Zealand documented in Bernanke et al. (1999) illustrates these problems. In 1995, the Reserve Bank of New Zealand overshot its one-year-horizon inflation target range, making the governor subject to dismissal under the central-banking law. It was recognized in the Reserve Bank that the overshoot was likely to be short-lived and inflation was likely to fall, indicating that monetary policy had not been overly expansionary. Fortunately, this view was accepted outside the Bank, and the governor, Don Brash, whose performance was excellent, retained his job. Attempting to hit the annual target did, however, have the unfortunate consequence of producing excessive swings in the monetary policy instruments, especially the exchange rate. In a small, open economy, like New Zealand, exchange rate movements have a faster impact on inflation than interest rates. Thus, trying to achieve annual inflation targets required heavier reliance on manipulating exchange rates, which led to its having large swings. By trying to hit the short-horizon target, the Reserve Bank also may have induced greater output fluctuations. For example, the Reserve Bank pursued overly tight monetary policy at the end of 1996 with the overnight cash rate going to 10 percent because of fears that inflation would rise above the target range in 1997, and this led to an undesirable decline in output. The Reserve Bank has recognized the problems it had with a too-short target horizon and now emphasizes a horizon of six to eight quarters in their discussions of monetary policy (Sherwin 1999; Drew and Orr 1999). Furthermore, the Policy Target Agreement between the central bank and the government has recently been amended to be more flexible in order to support the longer policy horizon (Reserve Bank of New Zealand 2000).

The solution to avoiding too short a horizon for the inflation target is to set inflation targets for periods two years ahead (or longer). This automatically implies that the central bank will have multiyear inflation targets. The target for the current calendar year will have been set two years previously, while there will also be a target for the following year. With multiyear targets, the target from one year to the next could vary over time. The inflation target would vary in response to shocks to the economy, especially to supply shocks, which might need to be accommodated in order to keep output fluctuations from becoming excessive. Also, putting a weight on output fluctuations in a central bank's objectives, as is sensible, means that the approach of the inflation target to the long-run goal needs to be gradual (Svennson 1997). This also suggests the need for multiyear targets in which the inflation target, even one for two years ahead, may differ from the long-run target if shocks to the economy have driven inflation away from the long-run goal.

Initially, the horizons for inflation targets in the transition countries studied here were short, being on the order of a year, and this may have contributed to the controllability problem and the frequent target misses. Possibly in response to these problems, the CNB was the first to specify a long-term inflation target for a horizon of five years, and the NBH and the NBP have also specified medium-term inflation targets (see table 15.2).

15.5.2   Who Should Set the Inflation Target and Decide the Speed of Disinflation?

In the 1990s, there was a significant shift worldwide toward more independent central banks, partly in response to a better understanding of economic costs of political interference with monetary policy and high inflation. While not all central banks were given complete freedom to set monetary policy targets, most of them gained instrument independence—that is, the freedom to conduct monetary policy without external interference to meet the objective. Among economists, there seems now to be a consensus that central banks should have instrument independence—that is, independence to conduct monetary policy so as to meet the inflation target or other monetary policy objective. There also seems to be a consensus that central banks should not have goal independence—independence to set inflation targets or other monetary policy objectives (Fischer 1994).

From the early stages of economic transition, central banks in all three countries have received a significant degree of de jure independence, not only in the conduct of monetary policy (instrument independence) but also in setting the objectives of monetary policy (goal independence).

In the Czech Republic, the independence of the central bank was anchored in the Constitution, which stated that the government might intervene in the CNB's affairs only for reasons clearly outlined in the Act on CNB. The Act on CNB (No. 6/1993 of Collection of Laws) specified that the primary objective of the CNB is to ensure the stability of the Czech national currency (Article 2) and that the CNB Board should set monetary policy and the instruments for the implementation of these policies (Article 5). Moreover, the Act explicitly states that in providing for its primary objective the CNB shall be independent of any instructions given by the government. The governor, vice-governors, and members of the Board are appointed and recalled by the president (Article 6). The Act was subsequently amended in 2002, and the main objective of the CNB was changed to maintaining price stability, with the standard qualification that without prejudice to its primary objective the CNB shall support economic policies of the government leading to sustainable economic growth. The amended Act also states that "when providing for the primary objective of the CNB and when carrying out their activities, neither the CNB nor the CNB Board shall seek or take instructions from the President of the republics, from Parliament, from the Government, from administrative authorities or from any other body" (Article 9). The appointment of the governor and other CNB officials remains fully the responsibility of the president.

In Hungary, the Act on NBH was passed in October 1991 and reinstated the independence of the NBH. It has been amended several times since. The latest version, from June 2001 (Act LVIII of 2001), states that the primary objective of the NBH shall be to achieve and maintain price stability (Article 3) and that the NBH shall define and implement monetary policy in the interest of maintaining the stability of the national currency (Article 4). Article 6 states that "within the framework provided for by this Act, the NBH shall independently define its monetary policy and the instruments for implementing such policy." Article 38 stipulates that the government may not instruct the NBH in relation to its scope of tasks as set forth in the Act. The president of the NBH is appointed for a period of six years by the president of the Republic at the proposal of the prime minister. The president of the Republic also appoints vice presidents and other members of the Monetary Council.

The legal position of the NBP is similar. The Act on the NBP of August 29, 1997, stipulates that the basic objective of the NBP shall be to maintain price stability, again with the addition that the NBP shall at the same time support government economic policies, insofar as this does not constrain pursuit of the basic objective (Article 3). The president of the NBP shall be appointed by the Sejm, at the request of the president of the Republic, for a period of six years. The vice presidents and other members of the NBP Management Board are appointed by the president of the Republic at the request of the president of the NBP. The nine members of the Monetary Policy Council (MPC) are appointed in equal numbers by the president of the Republics, the Sejm, and the Senate (Article 13). The responsibility of the MPC is to draw annual monetary policy guidelines and submit them to the Sejm for information (Article 12). Article 21 stipulates that in discharging its responsibilities the NBP shall collaborate with the appropriate bodies of the central government in developing and implementing national economic policy and strive to ensure proper performance of monetary policy guidelines. It should submit monetary policy guidelines to the bodies of the central government and report on the performance of monetary policy.

However, de jure independence does not always imply a de facto independence. While the NBP is not explicitly forbidden by the Act on NBP to seek instructions from the government and other bodies in pursuing its responsibilities, de facto, it decides alone on inflation targets. On the other hand, the NBH is de jure independent and forbidden to seek instruction, but in practice, the governor of the NBH seeks government endorsement for the NBH's monetary policy objectives.

The effort to make central banks legally independent reflected the belief of reformist governments and parliaments that politics should not interfere with the conduct of monetary policy. To a large extent, central-bank legislature in these countries was modeled after the German Bundesbank, which itself—for historical reasons—enjoyed a high degree of independence. In the early years of transition, no one really questioned the high degree of central-bank independence in the transition countries, as governments had to deal with the more urgent tasks of liberalization, privatization, and so on. However, the high degree of central-bank independence eventually became a source of tension.

These tensions appeared first in the Czech Republic. As we have discussed, in the early years of inflation targeting the CNB repeatedly undershot its inflation target, while economic growth turned negative. In many countries, this would probably have been sufficient to create tensions between central bank and government. In the Czech Republic, these tensions were further aggravated by political developments. To a large extent as a result of the poor state of the economy in the aftermath of the currency turbulence of 1997, the main pro-reform party split and new elections were called for mid-1998. In the meantime, a caretaker government was formed and the CNB governor became a caretaker prime minister. When a new government was formed after the election, he returned to the CNB. Inevitably, this drew the CNB further into politics, exactly the opposite of what the high degree of de jure independence was supposed to achieve.

The party that lost the election in 1998 criticized the CNB and the governor for mishandling monetary policy, contributing to economic decline, and thus affecting the outcome of the elections. The CNB was considered to be too independent and unwilling to coordinate monetary policy with the economic policy of the government. The speed of disinflation was considered as excessive, hurting economic growth. This criticism eventually resulted in legislative effort to curb the CNB's independence. When the CNB and the new government introduced jointly to Parliament an amendment to the CNB Act to bring it in line with EU standards, members of the party that lost the 1998 election submitted their own amendment that aimed at significantly reducing the CNB's independence. They proposed for Parliament to supervise and approve the operational budget, salaries of Board members to be cut, monetary policy decisions to be made in consultation with the government, and political parties to have more say in appointing the governor and Board members.

This proposal was strongly criticized by domestic and foreign financial analysts, by the International Monetary Fund, and—most importantly—by the EU and European Central Bank. Central-bank independence is a requirement for both EU and EMU membership, and this argument ultimately carried the most weight because of the planned accession of the Czech Republic into the EU/EMU. In the end, the CNB retained its independence, and with the appointment of a new governor in 2000 the relationship with the government improved as well.

Similar tensions between the central bank and the government emerged in Poland during 2000 and 2001. As economic growth began to falter while interest rates remained high, the NBP was blamed by some politicians for having set its monetary policy excessively tight and for contributing to subpar growth performance. Tensions between the government and the NBP accelerated in October 2001, after the new government took office. Contributing to the tensions was the fact that the president of the NBP, Leszek Balcerowicz, was himself a former politician and main author of the cold-turkey stabilization program that was criticized by the center-left politicians who formed the government after the October 2001 elections.

The prime minister and other members of the cabinet have repeatedly attacked the MPC for keeping interest rates too high. The pressure to reduce the NBP's independence rose, and some members of Parliament from the two governing parties drew legal proposals to broaden the NBP's objectives to include economic growth and employment, and to increase the number of members of the MPC. Even though the government did not formally back these proposals, being well aware that this would complicate the EU/EMU accession, it did not mind using them as a tool to put pressure on the NBP to ease monetary policy. Because accession to EU/EMU is an important objective for Poland, it is not likely that these initiatives will succeed.

The Polish experience also illustrates the peril of a central-bank effort to use monetary policy as a tool to force the government to pursue a more disciplined fiscal policy. The NBP tried to use tight monetary policy to pressure the government to improve structural fiscal balance, and kept interest rates very high even as inflation was falling below its target and growth came nearly to a halt. But instead of achieving this objective, the NBP only antagonized the government and put its independence under risk.

Even Hungary was not spared tensions between the central bank and the government. Recently, the government put forward a bill that proposed to set up a Supervisory Committee within the NBH. This committee would comprise delegates of political parties and two persons appointed by the minister of finance. Such a committee already existed in the past but was abolished. The NBH argued that such a step would infringe on NBH's operational independence and would go against the EU requirements on central-bank independence. Members of the government have also pressured the NBH to reduce interest rates in order to support growth. They argued that the NBH should not focus too much on inflation.

In Hungary, the reasons for this pressure on the central bank were mainly political and personal. The new NBH president who was appointed in 2001 was a former minister of finance, and from this position he had been exercising pressure on his predecessor. However, the previous NBH president is in close contact with the present prime minister and has used this relationship to put pressure on his successor. More recently, the conflict between the inflation target and exchange rate target has further increased these tensions.

Why do we see these tensions in all three inflation-targeting countries? There are several reasons. First, at the beginning of transition, central banks were given a large degree of both operational and goal independence. In a situation where inflation is still higher than the long-term objective of price stability, this means that central banks are given the freedom to decide on the speed of disinflation. As central bankers tend to be more ambitious with respect to the speed of disinflation than politicians, this creates the potential for tensions. These tensions tend to come into the open once economic growth falters, particularly if this poor growth performance is perceived as contributing to a loss of popularity of the governing party or parties. In our view, this experience suggests the superiority of closer involvement with political authorities in setting monetary policy objectives. Particularly in the difficult period of economic transition, a goal of independence of central banks may complicate rather than facilitate the conduct of monetary policy.

Second, the fact that politicians became central-bank governors, or that central-bank governors stepped into politics, had the unwanted consequence of drawing central banks more into the political arena. Finally, despite significant progress in economic and political reforms, the rule of law still remains less firmly established even in the most advanced transition economies, making politically motivated attacks on central banks more likely.

Public disputes between the central bank and the government of the kind that we have seen in the Czech Republic, Poland, and Hungary are not desirable. They undermine the credibility of the inflation-targeting framework and could increase the costs of future disinflation. As we have already noted, the decision about the speed of disinflation has a different impact on different groups in the society, and there is thus a strong case for such a decision to be made by a politically responsible body like the government. Clearly, it would better serve the credibility of monetary policy if the speed of disinflation were the result of a joint decision by a central bank and the government, although this is obviously not a practice in all inflation-targeting countries.[31] Such a joint decision would have several advantages. Most important, it would be more credible. When a government decides (perhaps jointly with a central bank) on the speed of disinflation, it is explicitly or implicitly committing itself to policies supporting this disinflation objective. The speed of disinflation (co)decided by government would be seen by markets as a political decision that takes into account possible short-term trade-offs, and it would reduce the probability that policies supporting the achievement of targeted disinflation would be challenged on grounds that they do not reflect the preferences of the society and that they are unduly costly.

Even in situations where the ultimate responsibility for deciding on the speed of disinflation would rest with the government, the central bank could still provide important input into this decision by voicing (possibly publicly) its own views about the desirable speed of disinflation. Of course, there is a risk that the government would choose too slow a disinflation. However, it is not clear whether this would impose higher costs on the economy than a unilateral decision by a central bank to pursue a more rapid disinflation that would subsequently be challenged by the government as being too ambitious. Furthermore, a unilateral decision by the central bank to pursue rapid disinflation is likely to weaken support for the central bank, as has occurred in the Czech Republic and Poland. This increases the risk of loss of independence and interferes with the ability of the central bank to control inflation in a longer-run context.

The question of who should set inflation targets has a specific aspect in transition economies that are expected soon to adopt the euro. One can argue that when the political decision to adopt the euro is made, it effectively specifies both the disinflation path and the ultimate inflation target. The inflation target is determined by the need to meet the Maastricht criterion concerning maximum permissible inflation, and the speed with which this inflation is to be achieved is determined by the timing of the euro adoption. To the extent that there is a firm political commitment to adopt the euro at a certain date, it becomes to a large extent irrelevant whether the inflation target is set by a central bank or a government. The government does not have much room to be more lenient on inflation than the central bank, because of the possibly large economic and mainly political costs of not meeting the Maastricht criteria.

15.5.3   How Should a Bank Respond to Deviations of Inflation from the Target, and How Much Should the Floor of an Inflation Target Be Emphasized Relative to the Ceiling?

The implementation of inflation targeting in the Czech Republic and Poland has brought out an interesting problem that arises in other inflation-targeting economies as well: how should a bank respond to a significant deviation of inflation from the inflation target? If the inflation rate overshoots the ceiling of the target range, then the logic of inflation targeting clearly requires the central bank to bring the inflation rate back into the target range. However, should an inflation-targeting central bank try to lock in a lower-than-targeted inflation once actual inflation falls below the targeted path if inflation is not yet at the long-run goal? Another way of asking this question is to ask whether a central bank should emphasize the floor of the inflation target as much as the ceiling and thus work as hard to avoid undershoots of the target as overshoots.

As we have noted, the CNB significantly undershot its inflation target in 1998 and 1999, and less so in 2000. Similarly, at the end of 2001, inflation in Poland fell well below the NBP end-2001 target. What should central banks do in such situations? Should they be upset at the undershoot and indicate that this was a serious mistake? Alternatively, would it be appropriate for them to lock in the unexpectedly rapid disinflation of the previous two years and focus monetary policy on maintaining price stability from then on?

A case could be made for acting opportunistically and using faster-than-expected disinflation to lock in this windfall benefit of lower inflation (Haldane 1999). This is what Poland has tried to do by adjusting its original end-1999 inflation target after actual inflation early in 1999 began to fall faster than projected. It would seem that when inflation has been reduced to less than the central bank target but still remains above the level of inflation corresponding to price stability, it would make no sense to let inflation go up again only to be forced to reduce it again later. Disinflation, even at a moderate pace, could be costly, and if a country can avoid the need to disinflate in the future, this should spare the economy some loss of output. Whether past faster-than-planned disinflation was a result of luck or mistakenly tight monetary policy may seem not to matter—bygones are bygones, past costs, if any, have been incurred, and let's just avoid any future costs of disinflation.[32]

In practice, central banks have treated the floors of inflation-target ranges in different ways (Clifton 1999). Some treat them as seriously as upper sides of a band and have eased monetary policy to bring inflation back up inside the band (e.g., New Zealand in 1991), while others preferred to consolidate the unexpected rapid disinflation (Israel in 1998).

The recent experience of Poland has shown the risks of trying to lock into inflation that is lower than originally targeted. There are several problems with opportunistic disinflation and with treating the bottom of the band leniently. First, there is a possibility that opportunistic disinflation will not find much sympathy with politicians. Particularly if the disinflation that is faster than originally intended coincides with a significant weakening of economic activity, there will be calls for a relaxation of monetary policy, even if this should mean a return to somewhat higher inflation. The NBP has exacerbated this problem because its inflation target is now stated to be less than 4 percent, suggesting that they are not particularly disturbed by undershooting the inflation target. This may have contributed substantially to the poor relations between the NBP and the government and the decrease in public support for the NBP. The CNB was well aware of the danger from its undershoots of the inflation target and did not even suggest that it could lock in the lower-than-targeted inflation.

Second, if rapid disinflation is a result of temporary external shocks like large declines in the price of commodities, it would be a mistake to assume that monetary policy could lock in such disinflation forever without large future costs. Once these shocks are over, prices of commodities usually do not stay low but rise again as global demand recovers. Monetary policy that would try to prevent an accelerated pace of disinflation in times of declining commodity prices or other positive supply shocks would probably be too expansive. In the same vein, monetary policy would risk being too restrictive if it tried to avoid any acceleration of inflation as positive supply shocks are reversed.[33] Like many other inflation-targeting central banks, the CNB has explicitly recognized that monetary policy should not attempt to offset temporary supply shocks that knock disinflation from its projected path.

Third, an opportunistic approach to disinflation could undermine the credibility of an inflation-targeting framework. By setting medium-term inflation targets, central banks attempt to establish a predictable environment that would allow economic agents to plan for the future. Even though there could and will be deviations from the target, credible inflation targeting would lead the agents to expect that a central bank would do its best to return actual inflation to the targeted path. Attempts at opportunistic disinflation could increase the uncertainty, because they would make monetary policy less predictable. For example, economic agents could expect that central banks would adjust an inflation target upward in case of a negative shock as well.

However, a situation may arise where the path of disinflation has been set incorrectly. For example, competitive pressures in the economy due to liberalization, privatization, and a more open trade would produce a faster disinflation for a given monetary policy stance than originally expected. These favorable supply shocks would be likely to cause inflation to undershoot without leading to a decline in output. In this case, maintaining the original disinflation target would require an overly expansionary monetary policy, and it would seem to be more appropriate to accept in such a case a disinflation that is faster than originally intended. This would also likely be politically feasible because the undershoot of the inflation target would not be accompanied by output losses.

15.5.4   Inflation Targets and the Exchange Rate

In the recent literature on inflation targeting, particularly on inflation targeting in emerging-market countries, increased attention has been paid to the open-economy aspect of inflation targeting (Mishkin 2000; Mishkin and Savastano 2001; Eichengreen 2001). It has been recognized that the large degree of openness of some emerging-market economies, in combination with specific characteristics of their financial systems, creates additional challenges for the implementation of inflation targeting. Exchange rate movements directly affect domestic inflation, both as a result of external shocks and as a result of monetary policy measures. The open-economy aspect of inflation targeting plays a prominent role in inflation-targeting transition economies as well.

In the initial stage of transition, all three inflation-targeting countries analyzed in this chapter used a fixed exchange rate as a nominal anchor to import price stability and bring domestic inflation quickly down. The currency peg-based stabilization was quite effective, because it allowed them to bring down inflation relatively quickly. The initial monetary overhang was eliminated by a one-time increase in price level rather than by a sustained growth in prices, and thus its elimination did not become embedded in inflation expectations.

However, first Poland, then the Czech Republic, and finally Hungary abandoned the currency peg and moved to more flexible exchange rate arrangements. This has fundamentally changed the operation of monetary policy and the operation of the monetary transmission mechanism.

The importance of the exchange rate channel of monetary policy depends directly on the degree of openness of the economy to trade flows and on the degree of integration into international capital markets. The Czech Republic and Hungary are very open economies with respect to trade flows: the share of exports plus imports in gross domestic product (GDP) exceeds 100 percent. Poland is a more closed economy: the share of exports plus imports reaches "only" about 50 percent. Therefore, exchange rate movements in the Czech Republic and Hungary will have a more important effect on domestic prices and inflation, and thus on inflation targeting. At the same time, all three countries are very open to international capital flows, because in preparation for EU membership they have largely completed capital account liberalization.

There are several reasons why exchange rate movements are important for inflation targeting in transition countries (Svensson 2000). First, exchange rate movements provide an additional transmission channel of monetary policy. While in a closed economy aggregate demand and expectation channels dominate, in an open economy the exchange rate channel may be the most important one, particularly in the short run. The exchange rate transmission channel operates both directly and indirectly. Changes in nominal exchange rate directly affect the domestic prices of imported final goods and thus the targeted CPI index.[34] Indirectly, the exchange rate channel operates by affecting domestic demand. Changes in real exchange rate affect domestic and foreign demand for domestic goods, thus enhancing the standard aggregate-demand channel. Second, the exchange rate is one channel through which foreign disturbances could be transmitted into the domestic economy. Third, transition countries also have a particular concern with their exchange rates because they want to become part of the EU and the euro zone. Thus they must eventually fix their exchange rates to the euro as part of their planned entry into the EMU and so naturally care more about the exchange rate at which they will convert their currency into the euro upon accession.

Finally, it should be noted that emerging-market countries and transition economies are usually more vulnerable to large exchange rate movements. The reason is the underdeveloped capital market in domestic currency and the need to borrow in dollars or other foreign currency, except for very short-term borrowing. This results in open foreign exchange positions of banks and/or corporations and thus increased vulnerability of their balance sheets to large exchange rate movements. While large appreciation can make domestic producers uncompetitive (both in foreign and domestic markets), large depreciation could cause substantial damage to firms or banks with large open foreign exchange positions and precipitate a financial crisis of the type described in Mishkin (1996, 1999).

While it is generally recognized that in such open economies as the Czech Republic and Hungary the exchange rate represents both an important channel of monetary transmission and an important channel of transmission of external disturbances, it is less obvious what the implications are for the treatment of the exchange rate in the regime of inflation targeting. We can distinguish two approaches to the exchange rate: an active and a passive approach. In an active approach, the central bank cares about the exchange rate over and above its effects on inflation and actively tries to influence the level of the exchange rate. In a passive approach, a central bank cares about the exchange rate only to the extent that it affects aggregate demand and the inflation rate, and it does not try to directly manipulate the exchange rate, only reacting to changes in exchange rate that would threaten its inflation target.[35]

As we have noted, the Czech Republic and Hungary are particularly open economies, and the exchange rate will therefore have an important effect on inflation and other variables. Poland is less open, and exchange rate movements seem to play a less important role in monetary policy deliberations. It seems that the NBH is pursuing this active approach, to judge from its statements on the role of the exchange rate in affecting inflation outcomes. As Orlowski (2000) argues, in Hungary, the central bank has focused its monetary policy on exchange rate stability, and for this reason changes in the exchange rates have a strong effect on inflation. Such a strong effect was not observed in the Czech Republic and Poland. This may explain the relatively larger emphasis put by the NBH on the exchange rate channel of monetary policy.

The problem is that too much reliance on the exchange rate channel of monetary transmission carries the risk that a central bank would focus excessively on a short-term horizon. In open economies, the exchange rate channel not only is important but operates very fast, because changes in exchange rate directly affect domestic prices of imported final goods, and with longer but still potentially quite short lag prices of domestic goods containing imported inputs. This rapid transmission may induce the inflation-targeting central bank into too much of a focus on a short-term horizon and into an effort to keep actual inflation in line with the inflation target by orchestrating exchange rate changes. However, excessive use of the exchange rate channel could have undesirable consequences. It could cause a problem of instrument instability and result in excessive variability of real exchange rate,—and thus in an increased degree of uncertainty in the economy and higher variability of output.[36] In addition, it runs the risk of transforming the exchange rate into a nominal anchor that takes precedence over the inflation target. For example, as documented in Bernanke et al. (1999), Israel's intermediate target of an exchange rate around a crawling peg did slow the Bank of Israel's effort to win support for disinflation and lowering of the inflation targets in the early years of its inflation-targeting regime. In addition, an active focus on the exchange rate may induce the wrong policy response when a country is faced with real shocks such as a terms-of-trade shock. Two graphic examples of these problems are illustrated by the experiences of New Zealand and Chile in the late 1990s.

The short horizon for the inflation target in New Zealand led the Reserve Bank to focus on the exchange rate as an indicator of the monetary policy stance because of the direct impact of exchange rate movements on inflation. By early 1997, the Reserve Bank institutionalized this focus by adopting as its primary indicator of monetary policy a Monetary Conditions Index (MCI) similar to that developed by the Bank of Canada. The idea behind the MCI, which is a weighted average of the exchange rate and a short-term interest rate, is that both interest rates and exchange rates on average have offsetting impacts on inflation. When the exchange rate falls, this usually leads to higher inflation in the future, and so interest rates need to rise to offset the upward pressure on inflation. However, the offsetting effects of interest rates and exchange rates on inflation depend on the nature of the shocks to the exchange rates. If the exchange rate depreciation comes from portfolio considerations, then it does lead to higher inflation and needs to be offset by an interest rate rise. However, if the reason for the exchange rate depreciation is a real shock, such as a negative terms-of-trade shock, which decreases the demand for a country's exports, then the situation is entirely different. The negative terms-of-trade shock reduces aggregate demand and is thus likely to be deflationary. The correct interest rate response is then a decline in interest rates, not a rise as the MCI suggests.

With the negative terms-of-trade shock in 1997, the adoption of the MCI in 1997 led to exactly the wrong monetary policy response to the East Asian crisis. With depreciation setting in after the crisis began in July 1997 after the devaluation of the Thai baht, the MCI began a sharp decline, indicating that the Reserve Bank needed to raise interest rates, which it did by over 200 basis points. The result was very tight monetary policy, with the overnight cash rate exceeding 9 percent by June of 1998. Because the depreciation was due to a substantial, negative terms-of-trade shock that decreased aggregate demand, the tightening of monetary policy, not surprisingly, led to a severe recession and an undershoot of the inflation target range, with actual deflation occurring in 1999.[37] The Reserve Bank of New Zealand did eventually realize its mistake and reversed course, sharply lowering interest rates beginning in July 1998 after the economy had entered a recession, but by then it was too late. It also recognized the problems with using an MCI as an indicator of monetary policy and abandoned it in 1999. Now the Reserve Bank operates monetary policy in a more conventional way, using the overnight cash rate as its policy instrument, with far less emphasis on the exchange rate in its monetary policy decisions.

Chile's inflation-targeting regime also included a focus on limiting exchange rate fluctuations by having an exchange rate band with a crawling peg that was (loosely) tied to lagged domestic inflation. This focus on the exchange rate induced a serious policy mistake in 1998 because the central bank was afraid it might lose credibility in the face of the financial turmoil if it allowed the exchange rate to depreciate after what had taken place in financial markets after the East Asian crisis and the Russian meltdown. Thus, instead of easing monetary policy in the face of the negative terms-of-trade shock, the central bank raised interest rates sharply and even narrowed its exchange rate band. In hindsight, these decisions were a mistake: the inflation target was undershot and the economy entered a recession for the first time in the 1990s.[38] With this outcome, the central bank came under strong criticism for the first time since it had adopted its inflation-targeting regime in 1990, which weakened support for the independence of the central bank and its inflation-targeting regime. During 1999, the central bank did reverse course, easing monetary policy by lowering interest rates and allowing the peso to decline.

The contrast between the experience of New Zealand and Chile during this period with that of Australia, another small open economy with an inflation-targeting regime, is striking. Prior to adoption of their inflation-targeting regime in 1994, the Reserve Bank of Australia had adopted a policy of allowing the exchange rate to fluctuate without interference, particularly if the source of the exchange rate change was a real shock, like a terms-of-trade shock. Thus, when faced with the devaluation in Thailand in July 1997, the Reserve Bank recognized that it would face a substantial negative terms-of-trade shock because of the large component of its foreign trade conducted with the Asian region and that it should not fight the depreciation of the Australian dollar that would inevitably result (McFarlane 1999; Stevens 1999). Thus, in contrast to New Zealand, it immediately lowered the overnight cash rate by 50 basis points to 5 percent and kept it near this level until the end of 1998, when it was lowered again by another 25 basis points.

Indeed, the adoption of the inflation-targeting regime probably helped the Reserve Bank of Australia to be even more aggressive in its easing in response to the East Asian crisis and helps explain why its response was so rapid. The Reserve Bank was able to make clear that easing was exactly what inflation targeting called for in order to prevent an undershooting of the target, so that the easing was unlikely to have an adverse effect on inflation expectations. The outcome of the Reserve Bank's policy actions was extremely favorable. In contrast to New Zealand and Chile, real output growth remained strong throughout this period. Furthermore, there were no negative consequences for inflation despite the substantial depreciation of the Australian dollar against the U.S. dollar by close to 20 percent: inflation remained under control, actually falling during this period to end up slightly under the target range of 2 to 3 percent.

While it would not be desirable if a central bank tried to actively manipulate the exchange rate, this does not imply that it should not respond to an exchange rate shock. However, whether it should respond and how it should respond depend on the nature of the shock. As illustrated above, the response to a real shock to the exchange rate such as a change in the terms of trade should be entirely different from the reaction to a portfolio shock.

The relevant question concerning the transition economies is this: what types of shock are they likely to face in the period ahead of the EU/EMU membership? And how vulnerable are they to large exchange rate movements? How much should they be concerned about exchange rate movements for other reasons than the risk that the inflation target will not be met?

Besides the standard shocks that all open emerging-market economies could face, transition economies could face specific external shocks related to the euro adoption: specifically, the convergence play. The convergence play refers to capital inflows to accession countries stimulated by the expected behavior of interest rates and exchange rates ahead of the euro adoption. Countries that have joined the EMU in the past have experienced a sizable decline in the currency risk premium of their debt—that is, the premium to compensate the debt holders for the risk that their currency would lose value. The decline in the currency risk premium resulted in lower interest rates on their debt instruments in local currency, and thus a higher price of these instruments. Increased prices allowed holders of these instruments to realize capital gains. Therefore, investors could reasonably expect that transition countries that have joined the EU will soon adopt the euro as well, and from past experience they could expect a reduction in interest rates on debt instruments issued by these countries that would allow them to reap capital gains. In other words, these investors have incentive to play on the convergence of interest rates to euro area level and invest in fixed-income instruments issued by accession countries. The resulting increase in capital inflows and currency appreciation could be viewed as a pure portfolio shock that would require interest rate reduction. But reducing interest rates could conflict with the inflation target, because it could stimulate domestic demand too much and result in faster increase in domestic prices. On the other hand, if monetary policy does not respond, the large capital inflow could lead to the standard problems of excessive currency appreciation, balance-of-payments problems, and reversal of capital flow resulting in currency depreciation and higher inflation.

Complicating the problem even more is the exposure of accession countries to a second shock—in this case a real shock. It has been well documented that as transition economies catch up with the more developed EU countries, they experience rapid productivity growth, which produces real exchange rate appreciation, either by means of nominal appreciation or by means of higher inflation. In this case, the appreciation of the domestic currency should be seen as an equilibrium phenomenon, which is sustainable and does not require a monetary policy response. In sum, in the period ahead of the EU/EMU membership, accession countries could be exposed to two simultaneous external shocks that would tend to produce exchange rate appreciation but that would call for a different policy response. In practice, it could be difficult to disentangle what part of the currency appreciation is the result of the porfolio shock and what part results from the real shock. Balance-of-payments data on the size and composition of capital flows, and data on productivity growth, should provide some indication of the relative importance of these two types of shocks.

The recent experience of the Czech Republic illustrates yet another problem: currency appreciation caused by a large inflow of foreign direct investment (FDI) as a result of the sale of state-owned enterprises to foreign owners. One can argue that currency appreciation resulting from the inflow of FDI is the typical real shock that does not call for a monetary policy response: the currency appreciates, but FDI inflow results in more investment, better management, and ultimately in higher productivity, which validates the appreciation of the currency. This argument has two problems. First, while currency appreciation will always happen when there is a sale of domestic assets to foreigners for foreign currency, it is less sure that the increase in productivity validating the currency appreciation will follow. For example, a large part of recent sales consisted of utilities where the potential for increasing the competitiveness in export markets is limited. Second, there is a time discrepancy between the timing of the currency appreciation (immediate) and the productivity increase (later). And third, expectation of currency appreciation as a result of sales to foreigners of state-owned assets could itself induce investors to take positions in the domestic currency, in order to benefit from the expected appreciation once the privatization payment materializes. This would produce a currency appreciation even before the privatization-related capital inflow materializes.

All this complicates significantly the task of the inflation-targeting central bank. To the extent that currency appreciation reflects an equilibrium phenomenon, appreciation of the real equilibrium exchange rate, there would be little reason for concern. Such appreciation would not threaten economic growth and external equilibrium, and if inflation is still above the long-term target, it should help the central bank to bring inflation down. But how much should a central bank worry if this real appreciation is too fast and too large? It could result in a widening current account deficit and subsequent large exchange rate depreciation, with negative effects on inflation. And it could cause problems in the corporate sector, because adjustment to a fast and large currency appreciation could be more difficult. The standard prescription for a central bank dealing with large capital inflows and currency appreciation is sterilized intervention: buy foreign currency in the foreign exchange market and neutralize monetary effects of this intervention by selling bonds. Eventually, this intervention could be complemented by interest rate cuts, to reduce the incentive for capital inflows.

But this prescription may be of little help in the circumstances like those in the Czech Republic in 2001–2002. Large capital inflows are mainly in the form of FDI, and not attracted by a large interest rate differential. Reducing interest is not going to slow down FDI inflows. These are interest rate insensitive. Sterilized intervention would be possible, but this policy has its own problems. In order to be effective, it would have to be of a very large amount (on the order of several billion dollars) and it may not even be effective at all. Sterilizing such intervention could be quite costly for the central bank.[39]

For these reasons, the CNB has pursued a pragmatic strategy of gradual interest rate reduction, combined with occasional foreign exchange market intervention of limited magnitude. This intervention has been subsequently sterilized. The CNB recognized that in 2001–2002 currency appreciation reflected mainly the effect of the FDI inflow, and that it was therefore a real shock that the monetary policy had no business of neutralizing. However, the speed of the appreciation could be occasionally too fast, and at that point, the CNB felt that it could slow down the pace of appreciation by intervening, so that the corporate sector would have more time to adjust to the trend appreciation. In late 2002, capital inflows related to the convergence play (the portfolio shock) were not a serious issue for the Czech Republic, partly because the convergence play and the compression of yield spreads had already taken place.[40] Otherwise, the situation would have been even more complicated.

Another reason for not having benign neglect of the exchange rate is emphasized in Mishkin (2000) and Mishkin and Savastano (2001). For the reasons discussed earlier, transition countries with a lot of foreign-denominated debt may not be able to afford large depreciations of their currencies, which can destroy balance sheets and trigger a financial crisis. Central banks in these countries may thus have to smooth "excessive" exchange rate fluctuations, but not attempt to keep the exchange rate from reaching its market-determined level over longer horizons. The stated rationale for exchange rate smoothing would be similar to that for interest rate smoothing, which is practiced by most central banks, even those engaged in inflation targeting: the policy is not aimed at resisting market-determined movements in the exchange rate, but at mitigating potentially destabilizing effects of abrupt changes in exchange rates.

The challenges facing the central bank are somewhat different in Hungary. As was noted, Hungary still maintains an exchange rate band of ±15 percent. In the literature on inflation targeting, it is often emphasized that the absence of a second nominal anchor is one of the prerequisites of successful inflation targeting. Pursuing two nominal objectives could result in a situation where one objective will need to be given preference over the second objective, but without clear guidance as to how such conflict would be resolved, this could make monetary policy less transparent.[41] The question arises: to what extent might the existence of the ±15 percent exchange rate band in Hungary be considered as a second nominal anchor whose attainment could eventually conflict with the inflation target? The answer has turned out to be "a lot."

In mid-February 2002, the exchange rate of the forint hovered some 12–13 percent above parity, quickly approaching the upper part of the band. Partly as a result of uncertainty related to parliamentary election, the currency weakened somewhat during the spring and summer, but it began to appreciate again later in 2002. In January 2003, it approached the upper end of the band, and speculation about the revaluation of parity resulted in a sharp acceleration of capital inflow that forced the NBH to respond by cutting interest rates by 2 percentage points and intervening heavily in the foreign exchange market. The NBH is reported to have bought more than 5 billion euros, increasing international reserves by 50 percent and base money by 70 percent.[42] Even though the NBH subsequently began to sterilize this huge injection of liquidity, market participants now assume that maintaining the exchange rate band will have priority over the inflation target and expect inflation in 2003 to exceed the NBH inflation target.[43]

This conflict between the inflation target and exchange rate target need not be a unique problem for Hungary. Other accession countries could face this problem once they become members of the EU and once they decide to join the ERM2 mechanism that requires them to limit exchange rate fluctuation in exactly the same way as Hungary already does today—that is, to peg the currency against the euro and allow maximum ± 15 percent fluctuation around the established parity. Therefore, we now turn to the issue of monetary policy implementation in the period after EU accession and before EMU accession.

15.6 Monetary Policy within the ERM2 System

Participation in the ERM2 mechanism and subsequent adoption of the euro are obligatory for all new EU members (no opt-out clause is available). But the new EU members do not have to join the ERM2 mechanism immediately after the EU entry. Therefore, after joining the EU, the new members will have to decide how quickly to join the ERM2 mechanism and adopt the euro, and whether ERM2 membership would require a modification of the inflation-targeting framework.

How would monetary policy in the accession countries operate under the ERM2 regime, and what would be the main nominal anchor of the economy? Formally, the monetary policy framework after joining the ERM2 mechanism will be similar to the monetary policy framework in Hungary today, where the ± 15 percent fluctuation band is already in place. But there will also be important differences. First, the adoption of the euro will be approaching, which could have important implications for capital flows (convergence play) and fiscal policy implementation (the need to meet fiscal criteria). Second, breaching the target band (its lower side) would have different consequences for Hungary today and for accession countries operating within the ERM2 regime. Third, unlike Hungary's monetary policy today, the monetary policy and exchange rate of an accession country within the ERM2 regime will be of common interest to all EMU members, and the European Central Bank (ECB) could intervene to help the accession country to keep the exchange rate within the band.

The ERM2 fluctuation band will allow rather large exchange rate movements, too large to provide a sufficiently firm nominal anchor. For this reason, the inflation target will likely need to continue to play the role of nominal anchor, as it did in Spain before its entry into EMU (see Bernanke et al. 1999). Successful operation of inflation targeting after ERM2 entry should be facilitated by the fact that the process of disinflation is likely to be largely completed. Low inflation could reduce, though not fully eliminate, the probability that the inflation target would conflict with the commitment to maintaining the currency within the ERM2. Still, the possibility of a conflict between the inflation target and the ERM2 exchange rate band cannot be fully excluded. But it is important to be clear about the nature of this risk and how it could be mitigated.

Within the ERM2 framework, two situations could arise where monetary and other policies may be constrained by the fact that the exchange rate is approaching the lower or upper side of the band. One possibility is that the exchange rate would approach the upper (appreciated) band, as was happening in Hungary. In order to prevent breaching the permitted fluctuation band, interest rates may need to be reduced to moderate the pressure on the currency. But lower interest rates could interfere with the inflation target, because they could stimulate domestic demand more than the central bank considers prudent and could produce higher inflationary pressures. However, a strongly appreciating currency would also simultaneously act as a mechanism to dampen inflationary pressures, so it is not at all obvious that this conflict with the inflation target would actually become serious.[44] If reducing interest rates would not help, and pressures on the currency to appreciate persisted, another option would be to revalue the central parity.[45] This would reduce the burden of monetary policy and at the same time introduce a one-time deflationary shock.

A different conflict between the inflation target and exchange rate band would arise if there was downward pressure on the currency and if the exchange rate threatened to break through the lower (more depreciated) end of the band. Breaching the ERM2 lower target band would force the country to start the ERM2 two-year test again, so it could be potentially costly. Central banks could react to such a situation by tightening monetary policy and raising interest rates. But this response certainly should not conflict with the inflation target. On the contrary, it should be in line with the inflation-targeting policy if the reason for downward pressure was too relaxed a policy. And tighter monetary policy would also help to mitigate inflationary pressures that may arise from currency depreciation. Tighter monetary policy would also be appropriate in the case when the currency depreciates as a result of a negative portfolio shock. Higher interest rates should help arrest capital outflow by making domestic currency assets more attractive. But the situation could be more complicated when the currency depreciates as a result of negative real shock which at the same time reduced aggregate demand for domestic output (domestic or foreign demand). Maintaining the currency within the fluctuation band could require a tighter policy stance than what would be required if monetary policy were guided only by the inflation target. As a result, actual inflation would become lower than the inflation target, and monetary policy would further weaken demand and economic activity that was already affected adversely by the negative real shock. Under normal circumstances, this would not be desirable. But temporary lower economic activity may be a price worth paying in a situation where the alternative would be to violate the Maastricht criterion of two years of successful operation within the ERM2 system, thus delaying euro adoption.

To some extent, fiscal policy could be used to reconcile eventual conflict between the inflation target and the ERM2 band. First, maintaining a fiscal policy stance that would clearly indicate authorities' determination to meet Maastricht criteria of public debt and fiscal deficit would reduce the risk of downward pressure on the currency as a result of a negative portfolio shock. It would also allow the maintenance of lower interest rates than if fiscal policy were more expansionary, and thus reduce short-term capital inflows. Second, a changing fiscal policy stance could be used as a defense against large exchange rate movements threatening to breach the ERM2 band. Fiscal policy could be tightened even more than what is required by Maastricht criteria in case of downward pressure on the currency that would threaten to break the lower side of the band, or—to the extent that meeting Maastricht criteria is not threatened—it could be relaxed in case of upward pressure on the currency. But in this case, using interest rate policy would be clearly preferable as a first line of defense.

The risk of conflict between the inflation target and exchange rate target will depend importantly on market expectations of the conversion rate of the national currency into the euro. If market participants expect that the current market rate will be also the conversion rate, there will be less risk of such conflict, as the behavior of market participants should actually limit the fluctuation of the actual exchange rate. However, widespread market expectation that the future conversion rate will differ significantly from the current exchange rate could result in large and volatile capital flows and swings in actual exchange rate that could severely complicate the simultaneous achievement of the inflation target (sufficiently low inflation to meet the

Table 15.6
Lowest Inflation Rates in EU Countries, 1995–2000

	1995	1996	1997	1998	1999	2000	2001
Country A	0.8	0.6	1.2	0.8	0.5	1.7	1.6
Country B	1.5	1.3	1.3	0.9	0.6	1.9	2.5
Country C	1.7	1.4	1.4	0.9	0.6	2.3	2.5
Average inflation	1.3	1.1	1.3	0.9	0.6	2.0	2.2
Maastrict criterion inflation[a]	2.8	2.6	2.8	2.4	2.1	3.5	3.7

Source: United Nations (2002).
[a] Average inflation in three countries plus 1.5 percentage points. Average inflation rounded up.

Maastricht criterion) and exchange rate target (keeping the currency within the fluc-tuation band).

How should inflation targets be set after the countries have joined the EU and eventually the ERM2 mechanism? The obvious answer is to set the inflation target in such way that it will converge to inflation rate estimated to be consistent with the Maastricht criterion. Table 15.6 shows the annual inflation rate in three current EU members with the lowest inflation rate in the period 1995–2001. If we add to the average of inflation in three EU best performers the 1.5 percentage point margin allowed by the Maastricht Treaty, we receive the maximum permissible inflation in the accession countries that would be applied if they were to adopt the euro in that particular year.

If we take the period 1995–2001 as a benchmark, the inflation rate that the acces-sion countries would have to reach in order to meet the Maastricht criterion was in the range of 2.1 to 3.7 percent. In 1998 and 1999, inflation in the EU countries was particularly low, and it would thus seem that reaching the Maastricht objective would have been particularly challenging for accession countries at that time. How-ever, we should note that to some extent exceptionally low inflation in the EU was a part of the global tendency of falling inflation, which affected the transition econo-mies as well. To the extent that inflation in the EU and in the transition economies waiting to adopt the euro moves jointly in response to common external shocks like falling commodity prices and weak global economic activity, accompanied by large excess production capacity and weak pricing power of producers, lower permissible inflation does not make it necessarily more difficult (i.e., it does not require a tighter monetary policy) to qualify for euro adoption.

We can also see that the range of maximum permissible inflation of 2.1–3.7 percent is broadly in line with the long-term inflation targets in the Czech Republic (2–4 percent), Hungary (around 2 percent), and Poland (less than 4 percent).

15.7 Conclusion

In this chapter, we have discussed the experience with inflation targeting in the three transition economies—the Czech Republic, Hungary, and Poland. We have examined the circumstances leading to the switch from exchange rate pegs to inflation targeting and the modalities of inflation targeting in each of these countries. The short history of inflation targeting in these three countries does not yet allow us to draw any definitive conclusions about the success or failure of this regime. However, we conclude that inflation targeting in transition economies could be implemented reasonably successfully. While the examined countries have often missed inflation targets by a large margin, they nevertheless progressed well with disinflation. Still, increased uncertainty prevailing in transition economies makes it particularly difficult to predict inflation sufficiently far ahead, as required by the forward-looking nature of the inflation-targeting approach. In view of that, and given the possibility that transition countries will be more frequently hit by shocks that could divert inflation from the targeted path, misses of inflation targets are more likely there than in the more advanced economies.

This does not imply that monetary policy targeting other nominal variables like monetary aggregates would make the task of controlling inflation easier. Even though inflation targeting in transition economies is more difficult than in advanced economies, it could still bring significant benefits. It should be clear, though, that too much focus on hitting inflation targets at any price at all times could produce a significant instability of monetary policy instruments, damaging economic performance. The focus of inflation-targeting central banks should be on the medium-term horizon to ensure that disinflation remains on track and that inflation converges to a level deemed consistent with price stability. Alongside this trajectory, there will inevitably be misses, possibly sizable ones. Thus, the onus is on central banks' ability to clearly communicate to the public what the limits and possibilities of inflation targeting in transition economies are, and if it happens, to explain credibly and openly why inflation targets were missed.

A key lesson from the experience of the inflation-targeting transition countries is that economic performance will improve and support for the central bank will be higher if central banks emphasize avoiding undershoots of the inflation target as much as avoiding overshoots. Undershoots of the inflation targets have resulted in serious economic downturns that have eroded support for the central bank in both the Czech Republic and Poland. Also, economic performance will be enhanced if inflation-targeting central banks in transition countries do not engage in active manipulation of the exchange rate. This seems to be less of an issue in the Czech Republic and Poland, but it is still a live issue in Hungary.

A difficult problem for inflation targeting in transition countries is the often stormy relationship between the central bank and the government. This can be alleviated by having a direct government involvement in the setting of the inflation target and a more active role of the central bank in communicating with both the government and the public. In addition, having technocrats rather than politicians appointed as the head of a central bank may help in depersonalizing the conduct of monetary policy and increase support for the independence of the central bank.

We have also addressed the future perspective of monetary policy in the transition economies. We concluded that even after EU accession, inflation targeting can remain the main pillar of monetary strategy in the three examined accession countries during the time before they adopt the euro. Inflation targets would be guided toward meeting the Maastricht criterion for inflation, which would require maintenance of inflation at the level defined in long-term inflation objectives.

In addition, an important advantage of the inflation-targeting regimes in transition countries is that the central banks in the countries practicing inflation targeting have been learning how to set monetary policy instruments to hit their inflation goals. Since these central banks will have a role in setting monetary policy instruments at the ECB when they adopt the euro, the monetary policy experience that they have acquired by operating an inflation-targeting regime will help them play a more active and positive role in deliberations at the ECB.

Notes

The views expressed in this chapter are exclusively those of the authors and not those of the International Monetary Fund, Columbia University, or the National Bureau of Economic Research (NBER). We thank the participants in the Macro Lunch at Columbia University and the NBER Inflation Targeting Conference for their helpful comments.

1. Indeed, it is not at all clear that monetary targeting is a viable strategy, even in industrialized countries, because the relationship between monetary aggregates and goal variables such as inflation and nominal spending is typically quite weak. For example, see Estrella and Mishkin (1997).

2. For a description of the just-do-it approach in the United States, see Bernanke et al. (1999). Some transition economies are pursuing a managed float (Romania, the Slovak Republic, Slovenia) or free float (Albania) without a formal inflation-targeting framework in place, although Albania is now introducing full-fledged inflation targeting. It is interesting to compare the development of inflation in these countries that have similarly flexible exchange rate regimes but no formal inflation-targeting regime in place (see section 15.4.3).

3. See Debelle (1997) and Schaechter, Stone, and Zelmer (2000).

4. For a discussion of whether Hungary is ready for inflation targeting, see Siklos and Ábel (2002).

5. Note that one can argue that a strong fiscal position is a requirement for successful conduct of monetary policy under any policy framework, not just inflation targeting. See Eichengreen (1999) and Mishkin and Savastano (2001).

6. For an early analysis of inflation targeting in the Czech Republic see Hrnčíř and Šmidková (1999) and Mahadeva and Šmidková (2000).

7. For a discussion of the Czech exchange rate crisis see Begg (1998). It is noteworthy that, unlike the case of many other emerging-market countries that were forced to abandon the currency peg, the Czech koruna

depreciated only moderately, and it subsequently strengthened again. One reason for this limited depreciation was the relatively low degree of dollarization and currency mismatches in the Czech economy and thus the limited effect of the exit from the peg on companies' and banks' balance sheets.

8. The path to inflation targeting for the CNB has many similarities to the path followed by the Bank of England and the Riksbank after the collapse of their exchange rate pegs in 1992. See Bernanke et al. (1999).

9. At the end of 1997, the CPI consisted of 754 items, 91 items had regulated price, and net inflation measured the movements of 663 items, which in terms of weights in the consumer basket represented about four-fifths of the total basket.

10. Trade unions agreed that it would not be desirable to aim for higher than zero growth in real wages in 1999. The catch was that trade unions' economic experts projected that inflation in 1999 would reach 10 percent, and trade unions therefore demanded a 10 percent increase in nominal wages, which in their view would be consistent with zero growth in real wages. As inflation in 1999 remained close to 2 percent, 10 percent nominal wage growth resulted in a large increase in real wages. At the end of 1999, when the CNB was again discussing with the representatives of trade unions inflation prospects for 2000, they seemed to have learned from their mistake and expressed more trust in CNB's inflation forecast for 2000.

11. However, already in 2000, when it announced the net inflation target for end-2001, the CNB also began publishing its projection of headline inflation.

12. This should be interpreted more as a forecast than as a full-fledged inflation target.

13. See National Bank of Poland (1998). It is noteworthy that the NBP intends to calculate the core inflation itself. Usually, central banks targeting a measure of underlying inflation do not calculate this index. In order to avoid a conflict of interest, they let other agencies, mainly statistical offices, calculate and publish underlying inflation.

14. Perhaps this is just another example of the gradualist approach of Hungary to economic reforms more generally, unlike the "big bang" or "shock therapy" approach applied in the Czech Republic and Poland.

15. In 2000, inflation ended at 10.1 percent (December to December), much more than the government had projected earlier. In 1999, the government projected that average annual inflation would be 6–7 percent in year 2000. In early 2001, inflation increased further, close to 11 percent. Hungary's ambition to join the EU and adopt the euro as soon as possible would probably contributed to the increasing emphasis on further progress with disinflation that could be accomplished only with a higher degree of nominal exchange rate flexibility, and on the willingness to accept the consequences of a stronger currency for the competitiveness and external balance.

16. Israel also adopted an inflation-targeting regime with a narrow exchange rate band in 1991. Like Hungary, it also found it necessary to widen the exchange rate band, doing so in 1995. Over time, the Israelis have further downplayed the exchange rate in their inflation-targeting regime. For a discussion of Israeli inflation targeting and the role of the exchange rate, see Leiderman and Bufman (2000) and Bernanke et al. (1999).

17. This mechanism is described in Akerlof, Dickens, and Perry (1996), but it is highly controversial because the evidence that low inflation leads to a rise in unemployment is very mixed. In addition, as pointed out in Groshen and Schweitzer (1996, 1999), inflation can not only put "grease" in the labor markets as Akerlof, Dickens, and Perry argue, but also put in "sand" that makes the labor markets less efficient.

18. This argument has been made in Summers (1991).

19. One problem with this argument is that the rapid productivity growth applies economywide, but there could still be firms or industries where productivity growth would be small or negative and where decline in nominal wages would be called for if inflation was close to zero.

20. It could be argued that lower inflation usually means higher output growth, and therefore the sooner lower inflation is reached, the sooner will the economy achieve a higher output growth. But there are also counterarguments. For example, due to a loss of marketable skills, persons that could be seen as temporarily unemployed during the period of rapid disinflation could become permanently unemployed, which results in an additional loss of output.

21. For a discussion of the costs of disinflation see Ball (1994). The author comes to the conclusion that fast disinflation reduces the sacrifice ratio.

22. The NBH was publishing inflation objectives based on government budgetary projections for 1998, 1999, and 2000 (12–13 percent, 9 percent, and 6–7 percent respectively), but these were not formal inflation targets and there was no formal requirement for the NBH to meet them (see Siklos and Ábel 2002).

23. The long-term inflation target and the 2002 target were announced in the August 2001 Inflation Report, while the 2003 target was announced in the press on December 2001, when the government agreed with the NBH's proposal.

24. For example, the May 1998 *World Economic Outlook* projected real GDP growth in 1998 of 2.2 percent. This forecast was quite accurate, but with an opposite sign. Actual growth was −2.2 percent.

25. Of course, the hotly debated question was whether and to what extent the CNB's excessively tight monetary itself contributed to slower-than-projected growth.

26. In U.S. dollar terms, oil prices fell by 31.2 percent, while nonfuel commodity prices fell by 14.7 percent in 1998. See International Monetary Fund (1999). It should be noted that this effect of financial crises contributed to an unexpected fall in inflation worldwide. The May 1997 IMF World Economic Outlook projected that in 1998 consumer prices in advanced economies would increase by 2.5 percent, while the actual increase was only 1.5 percent.

27. The currency regimes of these countries are characterized as managed floats. In June 2001, Romania's currency regime was reclassified from a managed float to a crawling band because the central bank intervenes to prevent currency appreciation.

28. The mixed results reported here on the performance of inflation-targeting regimes relative to other monetary policy regimes is not very surprising. As argued by Calvo and Mishkin (2003), the choice of monetary policy regime is likely to be less important to the macroeconomic performance of emerging-market and transition countries than deeper institutions.

29. The Czech economy is very open, with imports representing about 50 percent of GDP, and changes in import prices of oil and gas have a large impact on domestic prices. However, at the time of the introduction of inflation targeting, the CNB had considered isolating the effects of price deregulation as more important than isolating the effects of terms-of-trade shocks or exchange rate effects.

30. As demonstrated by Svensson (1997), a faster target path of inflation to the long-run inflation goal implies a smaller weight on output variability in the central bank's loss function.

31. Such arrangement need not necessarily imply a formal subordination of the central bank to the government in setting inflation targets. For example, in Australia, the inflation target is set by a central bank alone, and the government subsequently publicly endorses this target.

32. Of course, such an argument could be made only if inflation does not fall below the long-term inflation target corresponding to price stability.

33. If a positive price shock was permanent, perhaps as a result of a sudden increase in productivity, it would be appropriate to accommodate the effect of such shocks on inflation.

34. The CPI includes prices of both domestic and imported goods. Consequently, it represents a combined measure of domestic inflation and imported inflation. Domestic inflation is also affected indirectly by changes in prices of imported goods. Changing the price of imported input used for the production of domestic goods would affect costs and—depending on the extent of the pass-through—domestic prices.

35. Again, we can distinguish a more or less active use of this passive approach, depending on the time horizon during which the central bank would try to meet the inflation target by responding to exogenous exchange rate changes.

36. This risk seems to be well recognized by the NBH. See National Bank of Hungary (2001, 35–36).

37. The terms-of-trade shock, however, was not the only negative shock the New Zealand economy faced during that period. Its farm sector experienced a severe drought, which also hurt the economy. Thus, a mistake in monetary policy was not the only source of the recession. Bad luck played a role too. See Drew and Orr (1999) and Brash (2000).

38. Because, given its location in Latin America, Chile's central bank did have to worry more about loss of credibility and also because Chile encountered a sudden stop of capital inflows at the time, the ability of the Chilean central bank to pursue countercyclical policy was more limited than that of the Australian central bank. However, although lowering interest rates in 1998 may not have been as attractive an option, the sharp rise in the policy interest rate in 1998 was clearly a policy mistake.

39. Of course, with falling interest rate differential, the costs of sterilization decline as well.

40. In fact, at the end of 2002, spreads on domestic-currency sovereign bonds compared to the benchmark German bonds were negative for all maturities. See Ceska Sporitelna/Erste bank (2002). Of course, the question is whether such dramatic compression of yield spreads is sustainable.

41. On the experience with inflation targeting in the presence of nominal exchange rate band in Israel, see Leiderman and Bufman (2000).

42. See JPMorgan (2002).

43. Analysts have interpreted this as evidence that the NBH is determined to maintain the currency band even at the cost of temporary higher inflation. See IMF (2002).

44. The direct effect of the appreciated exchange rate on inflation will be felt sooner than the indirect effect of reduced interest rates on aggregate demand and demand-induced acceleration of inflation.

45. For countries in the ERM2 framework, the ECB would also be expected to help a national central bank sustain the currency inside the fluctuation band, of course, to the extent that this does not interfere with the ECB's price stability objective.

References

Akerlof, George, William Dickens, and George Perry. 1996. The macroeconomics of low inflation. *Brookings Papers on Economic Activity*, Issue no. 1: 1–76. Washington, D.C.: Brookings Institution.

Ball, Lawrence. 1994. What determines the sacrifice ratio? In *Monetary policy*, ed. N. Gregory Mankiw, 155–82. Chicago: University of Chicago Press.

Begg, David. 1998. Pegging out: Lessons from the Czech exchange rate crisis. *Journal of Comparative Economics* 26: 669–90.

Bernanke, B. S., T. Laubach, F. S. Mishkin, and A. S. Posen. 1999. *Inflation targeting: Lessons from the international experience*. Princeton, N.J.: Princeton University Press.

Brash, Donald T. 2000. Inflation targeting in New Zealand, 1988–2000. Speech presented at the Trans-Tasman Business Cycle. 9 February, Melbourne, Australia.

Calvo, Guillermo, and Frederic S. Mishkin. 2003. The mirage of exchange rate regimes for emerging market countries. *Journal of Economic Perspectives* 17 (4): 99–118.

Čapek, Aleš. 1999. Udžet inflaci pod kontrolou bude stále obtížnější. [Keeping inflation under control will be ever more difficult]. *Hospodářské Noviny*, 22 October, 9.

Ceska Sporitelna/Erste Bank. 2002. Macroeconomic and fixed income weekly report. Prague: Ceska Sporitelna/Erste Bank, 16 December.

Clifton, Eric V. 1999. Inflation targeting: What is the meaning of the bottom of the band? *IMF Policy Discussion Paper no. 99/8*. Washington, D.C.: International Monetary Fund.

Clinton, Kevin. 2000. Strategic choices for inflation targeting in the Czech Republic. In *Inflation targeting in transition economies: The case of the Czech Republic*, ed. Warren Coats, 165–84. Prague: Czech National Bank.

Czech National Bank. 1997. Monthly bulletin. Prague: Czech National Bank, May.

———. 1999. Inflation report. Prague: Czech National Bank, January.

Debelle, Guy. 1997. Inflation targeting in practice. *IMF Working Papers no. 97/35*. Washington, D.C.: International Monetary Fund.

Deppler, Michael. 1998. Is reducing inflation costly? In *Moderate inflation: The experience of transition economies*, ed. Carlo Cotarelli and György Szapáry. Washington, D.C.: International Monetary Fund and National Bank of Hungary.

Drew, Aaron, and Adrian Orr. 1999. The Reserve Bank's role in the recent business cycle: Actions and evolution. *Reserve Bank of New Zealand Bulletin* 62 (1).

Eichengreen, Barry. 1999. Solving the currency conundrum. Paper prepared for the Council of Foreign Relations Study Group on Economic and Financial Development. University of California, Berkeley, Department of Economics. Mimeograph.

———. 2001. Can emerging markets float? Should they inflation target? University of California, Berkeley, Department of Economics. Mimeograph.

Estrella, Arturo, and Frederic S. Mishkin. 1997. Is there a role for monetary aggregates in the conduct of monetary policy. *Journal of Monetary Economics* 40 (2): 279–304.

European Bank for Reconstruction and Development. 2002. *Transition report 2002*. London: European Bank for Reconstruction and Development.

Fischer, Stanley. 1994. Modern central banking. In *The future of central banking: The tercentenary symposium of the Bank of England*, ed. Forrest Capie, Charles A. Goodhart, Stanley Fischer, and Norbert Schnadts, 262–308. Cambridge, Cambridge University Press.

Groshen, Erica L., and Mark E. Schweitzer. 1996. The effects of inflation on wage adjustments in firm-level data: Grease or sand? Federal Reserve Bank of New York Staff Report no. 9. New York: Federal Reserve Bank of New York.

Groshen, Erica L., and Mark E. Schweitzer. 1999. Identifying inflation's grease and sand effects in the labor market. In *The costs and benefits of price stability*, ed. Martin Feldstein, 273–308. Chicago: University of Chicago Press.

Haldane, Andrew. 1999. Pursuing price stability: Evidence from the United Kingdom and other inflation-targeters. In *Workshop on inflation targeting*, ed. Andrew P. Fischer, 2–17. Prague: Czech National Bank.

Hrnčíř, M., and K. Šmidková. 1999. The Czech approach to inflation targeting. In *Workshop on Inflation Targeting*, ed. Andrew P. Fischer, 18–38. Prague: Czech National Bank.

International Monetary Fund. 1999. *World economic outlook*. Washington, D.C.: IMF, October.

———. 2002. *Global market monitor*. Washington, D.C.: International Monetary Fund, December 17.

JPMorgan. 2002. *Emerging Europe, Middle East, and Africa weekly*. January 31.

Kysilka, Pavel. 1998. Nezdravý růst dlouho nevydrží. [Unhealthy growth will not be sustainable]. *Ekonom* 4: 10–12.

Leiderman, Leonardo, and Gil Bufman. 2000. Inflation targeting under a crawling band: Lessons from Israel. In *Inflation targeting in practice: Strategic and operational issues and application to emerging market economies*, ed. Mario Blejer, Alain Ize, Alfredo M. Leone, and Sergio Werlang, 70–79. Washington, D.C.: International Monetary Fund.

Macfarlane, Ian J. 1999. Statement to Parliamentary Committee. *Reserve Bank of Australia Bulletin* (January): 16–20.

Mahadeva, Lavan, and K. Šmidková. 2000. Inflation targeting in the Czech Republic. In *Monetary frameworks in a global context*, ed. Lavan Mahadeva and Gabriel Sterne, 273–300. London: Bank of England, Centrum for Central Banking Studies.

Mishkin, F. S. 1996. Understanding financial crises: A developing country perspective. In *Annual World Bank conference on development economics*, ed. Michael Bruno and Boris Pleskovic, 29–62. Washington, D.C.: World Bank.

———. 1999. Lessons from the Asian crisis. *Journal of International Money and Finance* 18 (4): 709–23.

———. 2000. Inflation targeting in emerging market countries. *American Economic Review* 90 (2): 105–9.

———. 2001. Issues in inflation targeting. In *Price stability and the long-run target for monetary policy*, 203–22. Ottawa, Canada: Bank of Canada.

Mishkin, F. S., and M. A. Savastano. 2001. Monetary policy strategies for Latin America. *Journal of Development Economics* 66 (2): 415–44.

Mishkin, F. S., and Klaus Schmidt-Hebel. 2002. One decade of inflation targeting in the world: What do we know and what do we need to know? In *Inflation targeting: Design, performance, challenges*, ed. Norman Loayza and Raimundo Soto, 117–219. Santiago, Chile: Central Bank of Chile.

National Bank of Hungary. 2001. *Quarterly report on inflation*. Budapest: National Bank of Hungary, August.

National Bank of Poland. 1998. *Medium-term strategy of monetary policy*. Warsaw: National Bank of Poland.

———. 2001. Inflation report 2000, appendix 2.

Orlowski, Lucjan T. 2000. Direct inflation targeting in central Europe. *Post-Soviet Geography and Economics* 41 (2): 134–54.

Reserve Bank of New Zealand. 2000. Monetary policy statement. Wellington, New Zealand: Reserve Bank of New Zealand, March.

Schaechter, Andrea, M. R. Stone, and M. Zelmer. 2000. Adopting inflation targeting: Practical issues for emerging market countries. IMF Occasional Paper no. 202. Washington, D.C.: International Monetary Fund.

Sherwin, Murray. 1999. Inflation targeting: 10 years on. Speech to New Zealand Association of Economists conference. 1 July, Rotorua, New Zealand.

Siklos, Pierre L., and István Ábel. 2002. Is Hungary ready for inflation targeting? *Economic Systems* (Netherlands) 26 (4): 309–33.

Škreb, Marko. 1998. A note on inflation. In *Moderate inflation*, ed. Carlo Cotarelli and György Szapari, 179–84. Washington, D.C.: International Monetary Fund.

Stevens, Glenn R. 1999. Six years of inflation targeting. *Reserve Bank of Australia Bulletin* (May): 46–61.

Stock, James H., and Mark W. Watson. 1999. Business cycle fluctuations in U.S. macroeconomic time series. In *Handbook of macroeconomics*, ed. J. B. Taylor and M. Woodford, 3–64. Amsterdam: Elsevier.

Summers, Larry. 1991. Panel discussion: Price stability: How should long-term monetary policy be determined? *Journal of Money, Credit and Banking* 23: 625–31.

Svensson, Lars E. O. 1997. Inflation forecast targeting: Implementing and monitoring inflation targets. *European Economic Review* 41: 1111–46.

———. 2000. Open-economy inflation targeting. *Journal of International Economics* 50: 155–83.

United Nations. 2002. *Economic survey of Europe*, no. 1. New York and Geneva: United Nations.

16 A Decade of Inflation Targeting in the World: What Do We Know and What Do We Need to Know?

Frederic S. Mishkin and Klaus Schmidt-Hebbel

The emergence of inflation targeting over the last ten years represents an exciting development in central banks' approach to the conduct of monetary policy. After initial adoption by New Zealand in 1990, a growing number of central banks in industrial and emerging economies have opted for inflation targeting, and many more are considering future adoption of this new monetary framework.

A full decade of inflation targeting in the world offers lessons on the design and implementation of inflation-targeting regimes, the conduct of monetary policy, and country performance under inflation targeting. In section 1, this chapter briefly reviews the main design features of eighteen inflation targeting experiences, statistically analyzes whether countries under inflation targeting are structurally different from industrialized countries that do not target inflation, and considers the existing evidence on the success of inflation targeting. The interaction of inflation targeting design features and the conduct of monetary policy during the transition to low inflation are tackled in section 2. The chapter then focuses on unresolved issues in the design and implementation of inflation targeting and their relation to the conduct of monetary policy (section 3). Brief conclusions close the chapter.

16.1 What Do We Know about Inflation Targeting after a Decade of World Experience?

To discuss what we know about the inflation-targeting experience, we address three questions: (1) who targets inflation and how? (2) are inflation targeters different? and (3) is inflation targeting a success?

16.1.1 Who Targets Inflation and How?

Inflation targeting started a decade ago, with public announcements of inflation targets in New Zealand and Chile. According to our count, nineteen countries have implemented inflation targeting as of November 2000. They include industrial and emerging economies, transition and steady-state inflation targeters, semi and full-fledged targeters, early and recent starters, and current and former targeters.[1] Figure

Inflation (percent)

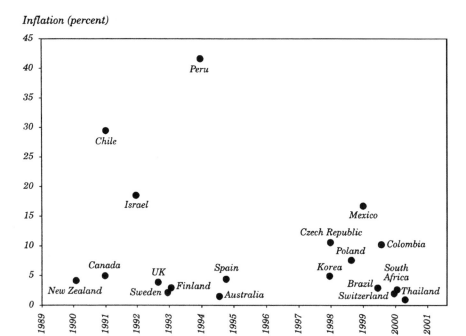

Figure 16.1
Inflation at adoption of inflation targeting in nineteen countries, 1988–2000[a].
Note: [a]Annual inflation rates are those observed one quarter before adopting inflation targeting.
Source: Authors' calculations, based on data from IMF, *International Financial Statistics*, various issues;
country sources; Schaechter, Stone, and other (2000).

16.1 depicts adoption dates and initial inflation rates (at year of adoption) for the nineteen-country sample.[2]

We introduce two country groups as the basis for our empirical analysis conducted in the 1990s, a sample of inflation targeters and a control group of non-targeters (see table 16.1). The first sample, inflation targeters, comprises a heterogeneous group of eighteen industrial and emerging economies: Australia, Brazil, Canada, Chile, Colombia, the Czech Republic, Finland, Israel, Korea, Mexico, New Zealand, Peru, Poland, South Africa, Spain, Sweden, Thailand, and the United Kingdom. (Finland and Spain dropped out of this group when they relinquished monetary policy on adopting the euro in 1999.[3] The second sample is a control group of nine industrial economies that were not inflation targeters during the 1990s: Denmark, France, Germany, Italy, Japan, Norway, Portugal, Switzerland, and the United States. Among these, Germany and Switzerland had explicit monetary targets in place throughout most of the 1990s and could thus be classified as implicit inflation targeters (as argued by Bernanke and others, 1999).[4] Japan and the United States had no explicit

Table 16.1
Inflation Targeters and Nontargeters

Inflation targeters		Nontargeters
Australia	Mexico	Denmark
Brazil	New Zealand	France
Canada	Peru	Germany
Chile	Poland	Italy
Colombia	South Africa	Japan
Czech Republic	Spain	Norway
Finland	Sweden	Portugal
Israel	Thailand	Switzerland
Korea	United Kingdom	United States

targets, and the remaining five European countries targeted their exchange rate to the deutsche mark before adopting the euro in 1999.[5]

Inflation targeters exhibit some commonalities and many differences in the preconditions, target design, and operational features of their inflation-targeting regimes. Four stylized facts emerge from country experiences and features, as summarized in table 16.A1 in the appendix. First, full-fledged inflation targeting is based on five pillars: absence of other nominal anchors, an institutional commitment to price stability, absence of fiscal dominance, policy instrument independence, and policy transparency and accountability. While the second through the fifth of these pillars are necessary for effective conduct of monetary policy under any regime, they are particularly important prerequisites for effective policy under inflation targeting. The success of inflation targeting depends strongly on high market credibility in the central bank's resolve and ability to put into place policies geared at meeting the target, and credibility is fostered by the five institutional pillars.

Second, the adoption of inflation targeting ranges from evolutionary to revolutionary. Many countries adopted inflation targeting without satisfying one or more of the above conditions. For example, Chile and Israel targeted the exchange rate during most of the 1990s (as Israel still does today). The Bank of England started inflation targeting well before attaining instrument independence. Most countries adopted inflation targeting before achieving high levels of policy transparency (including the publication of inflation reports, inflation projections, and monetary policy meeting minutes) and full accountability, and some countries, including Colombia, Israel, Korea, Mexico, Peru, and South Africa, still do not publish inflation forecasts. On the other extreme is Brazil, who adopted full-fledged inflation targeting right from the start.

Country experience suggests that the adoption of inflation targeting in the 1990s represented a monetary policy learning process. There is now a broad consensus about the conditions that should be in place for effective full-fledged inflation targeting. These prerequisites were less obvious in the first half of the 1990s, however, when early inflation targeters perfected their frameworks by learning from their own and the other inflation targeters' cumulative experience.

Third, inflation at the moment of adopting an inflation targeting framework ranges from moderately high to very low. Some countries adopted inflation targeting when their inflation rates were well above steady-state levels, using inflation targeting as the main device to build up credibility, bring down inflation expectations, and pursue a path of convergence to low, stationary inflation. This is the case of early inflation targeters in emerging countries that started at initial inflation rates of 15 to 45 percent (Chile, Israel, Peru) and subsequent emerging countries that adopted inflation targeting when initial inflation was in the range of 7 to 20 percent (the Czech Republic, Colombia, Mexico, Poland). This stands in contrast to all industrialized and some emerging inflation targeters that started at initial inflation close to stationary low levels.

Multi-year transitions toward steady-state inflation pose serious challenges and difficulties to inflation targeting, including the need for announcing annual inflation targets (that are much harder to meet) under conditions of high inflation expectations and limited policy credibility. We discuss the issues related to transition to low inflation in section 16.2.2 below.

Fourth, inflation targeters vary widely with regard to implementation features, including the target price index, target width, target horizon, escape clauses, accountability of target misses, goal independence, and overall transparency and accountability of the conduct of policy. Some of these differences can be attributed to country variation in institutions and history; others reflect the differences between inflation targeting in transition to low inflation versus inflation targeting at low inflationary levels. Additional differences in the design features of inflation targeting stem from divergent views among policymakers and academics about how monetary policy under inflation targeting should be conducted in conditions of low inflation.

16.1.2 Are Inflation Targeters Different?

Are the structural conditions and macroeconomic performance of countries that adopt inflation targeting different from those of industrial countries that do not target inflation? To tackle this question we compare the sample of eighteen inflation targeters to the control group of nine industrialized nontargeters, focusing on the relation between having an inflation-targeting framework in place and exhibiting a set of structural, institutional, and macroeconomic features. The empirical analysis presented here is necessarily preliminary because (as discussed in note 1) it is not always easy to decide whether a country should be classified as engaging in inflation targeting.[6] Furthermore, determining the exact date at which an inflation-targeting regime was adopted is often quite difficult. Officials at many of the central banks we consulted give adoption dates that are earlier than those given by outsiders (see, for example, Bernanke and others, 1999). The uncertainty of dating often follows from the fact that inflation targeting is adopted gradually, making the exact date of adoption difficult to determine.

Our data set consists of annual variables for twenty-seven countries over ten years (1990–99). The focus is on a discrete variable for an inflation-targeting regime, which takes a value of 1 when an inflation-targeting regime is in place or 0 when an alternative monetary regime is in place, together with a set of variables that could be associated with the choice of an inflation-targeting regime.[7] The latter variables include measures of the use of alternative nominal anchors (a measure of exchange rate band width and a monetary target dummy), structural conditions (trade openness), measures of central bank independence (formal independence, instrument independence, and goal independence), and macroeconomic variables (the inflation rate and the fiscal surplus ratio to GDP).

Table 16.2 reports cross-country and panel statistics and correlations for inflation targeting and related variables. The data reflect large variation in all variable catego-

Table 16.2
Descriptive Statistics and Simple Correlations for Cross-Section and Panel Samples, 1990–99[a]

Statistic	IT	Inf	Open	Fiscal	BW	MT	CBFI	CBGI	CBII
Cross-section statistics									
Mean	0.29	0.11	0.50	−0.02	0.56	0.25	0.30	0.30	0.59
Standard deviation	0.46	0.37	0.19	0.04	0.45	0.43	0.46	0.46	0.49
Maximum	1.00	5.55	0.85	0.06	1.00	1.00	1.00	1.00	1.00
Minimum	0.00	0.00	0.03	−0.16	0.00	0.00	0.00	0.00	0.00
Panel statistics									
Mean	1.00	0.97	0.85	0.06	1.00	1.00	1.00	1.00	1.00
Standard deviation	0.00	0.00	0.03	−0.16	0.00	0.00	0.00	0.00	0.00
Maximum	0.30	0.08	0.50	−0.02	0.58	0.26	0.31	0.30	0.61
Minimum	0.46	0.15	0.19	0.04	0.45	0.44	0.46	0.46	0.49
Variable correlations: panel/cross-section									
IT	1.00	−0.11	0.35	0.10	0.24	−0.29	−0.03	−0.07	0.23
Inf	−0.20	1.00	−0.10	−0.17	−0.01	−0.04	−0.10	−0.12	−0.18
Open	0.25	−0.42	1.00	0.16	−0.08	−0.13	−0.11	0.08	−0.03
Fiscal	0.21	−0.22	0.27	1.00	−0.01	0.11	0.12	0.15	0.19
BW	0.02	−0.07	−0.32	0.16	1.00	0.08	−0.01	0.01	0.14
MT	−0.45	0.22	0.07	0.19	0.26	1.00	0.04	0.02	−0.01
CBFI	−0.22	−0.08	−0.09	0.25	−0.22	0.09	1.00	0.68	0.51
CBGI	−0.13	−0.23	−0.01	0.22	−0.35	−0.18	0.79	1.00	0.50
CBII	0.30	−0.15	0.18	0.35	−0.06	−0.03	0.40	0.52	1.00

Source: Authors' calculations.
[a] The panel sample comprises ten years of data (1990–99) for each of the twenty-seven countries identified in the text. Panel sample correlations are reported in the upper-half matrix triangle, while cross-section correlations are reported in the lower-half matrix triangle. Standard errors are 0.06 for the panel sample and 0.19 for the cross section.

ries across countries and over time in our sample of twenty-seven countries. Panel correlations are sometimes very different from cross-country correlations, including cases changing signs. This is likely the result of the noise encountered in annual country data; we therefore focus on cross-country correlations.

Having inflation targeting in place is positively and significantly correlated with no individual variable and negatively and significantly correlated only with monetary growth targets (MT). Inflation targeting is positively and not significantly correlated with trade openness (*Open*), the ratio of the fiscal surplus to GDP (*Fiscal*), the width of the exchange rate band (BW), and instrument independence of the central bank (*CBII*). It is negatively and not significantly correlated with normalized inflation (*Inf*), formal independence of the central bank (*CBFI*), and goal independence of the central bank (*CBGI*).[8]

Next we introduce a multivariate probit model for the likelihood of having an inflation-targeting regime in place, based on the observation of the variables identified above. The model specifies the probability of having an inflation-targeting regime in place $\Pr(IT \mid \ldots)$ as a function of these variables:

$$\Pr(IT \mid \ldots) = \mathrm{f}(Inf, Open, Fiscal, BW, MT, CBFI, CBGI, CBII)$$

Expected coefficient signs are positive for *Fiscal*, BW, and the three measures of central bank independence, negative for MT, and ambiguous for *Inf* and *Open*.

Before turning to the results, we note that caution should be exercised in the causal interpretation of this equation. While certain structural features may be exogenous to the choice of inflation targeting, it is very likely that adoption of inflation targeting requires—and thus contributes to—renouncing the use of other nominal targets, improving macroeconomic performance (such as reducing inflation and improving the fiscal stance), and strengthening central bank independence. Potential reverse causation means that the empirical results should be interpreted carefully.

The full-panel probit regression produced noisy results. We therefore report cross-country results only, based on country decade-averages for each variable, including the dependent variable, that is, the choice of an inflation-targeting regime. We start by discussing the full-sample results in the first column of table 16.3.

Inflation targeting is positively and significantly associated with the level of normalized inflation. This result reflects the fact that inflation targeting has been adopted by countries that, on average, exhibited higher levels of inflation than have industrial nontargeters. Indeed, most emerging countries adopted inflation targeting as a device for bringing inflation down to low, single-digit levels, and most inflation targeters—both emerging and industrial countries—made major progress in reducing inflation either during or shortly before or after adopting inflation targeting (Bernanke and others, 1999; Corbo, Landerretche, and Schmidt-Hebbel, 2002). Countries that trade relatively more (because they are more open or smaller than nontargeters)

Table 16.3
Empirical Results for the Likelihood of Implementing an Inflation-Targeting Regime

Variable	Full sample[a] (27 countries)		Restricted sample 1[b] (24 countries)		Restricted sample 2[c] (24 countries)	
	(1)	(2)	(3)	(4)	(5)	(6)
Cons.	−9.7	−5.8*	−13.4***	−5.7*	−12.5	−4.7**
	(8.2)	(2.2)	(7.5)	(2.0)	(8.2)	(2.1)
Inf	45.2***	33.6*	69.2**	43.7*	69.1**	46.9*
	(25.2)	(12.3)	(28.5)	(13.5)	(27.8)	(15.7)
Open	11.5***	7.6**	11.4**	7.1*	10.5***	5.3***
	(6.7)	(3.0)	(5.0)	(2.7)	(6.0)	(3.1)
Fiscal	−20.4		−49.7		−46.7	
	(45.1)		(45.7)		(46.8)	
BW	0.3		3.4		3.2	
	(3.0)		(3.2)		(3.3)	
MT	−12.9**	−9.3*	−13.4*	−9.6*	−12.5**	−7.9*
	(5.7)	(3.0)	(4.3)	(2.8)	(5.3)	(3.0)
CBFI	2.2		1.3		1.0	
	(1.9)		(1.7)		(2.0)	
CBGI	−14.7*	−9.6*	−11.3*	−9.8*	−10.5*	−8.2*
	(5.4)	(3.2)	(2.6)	(2.8)	(3.8)	(3.1)
CBII	12.0**	8.5*	11.9*	8.4*	11.0**	6.7**
	(6.0)	(2.7)	(4.2)	(2.3)	(5.1)	(2.7)
Wald chi-squared	9.8	10.8	23.0	13.7	18.3	11.9
Pseudo R^2	0.61	0.57	0.63	0.57	0.63	0.58
No. observations	27	27	24	24	24	24

Source: Authors' calculations.
* Statistically significant at the 1 percent level.
** Statistically significant at the 5 percent level.
*** Statistically significant at the 10 percent level.
[a] Probit regressions for 1990–99 cross-country sample. Standard errors for the full and restricted samples are reported in parentheses.
[b] Restricted sample 1 excludes three countries with very high inflation in the early 1990s (Brazil, Peru, and Poland).
[c] Restricted sample 2 excludes three countries that may not be classified as inflation targeters (Colombia, Korea, and Peru).

are significantly more likely to adopt inflation targeting, while most large industrial countries are not inflation targeters.

Inflation targeting is negatively associated with the ratio of fiscal surplus to GDP. This result again follows from having a control group of nontargeters comprised by nine industrial countries that, on average, show a stronger fiscal position than the eighteen inflation targeters. This association does not attain conventional significance levels, however.

Inflation targeting is positively but not significantly associated with the width of the exchange rate band. As expected, inflation targeting is negatively and significantly associated with the adoption of monetary growth targets, reflecting the incompatibility of having explicit monetary and inflation targets in place at the same time.

Finally, the likelihood of having inflation targeting in place is associated positively with the formal independence of the central bank (although its coefficient is not significant at conventional levels) and significantly with instrument independence. However, inflation targeting is negatively and significantly associated with central bank goal independence. The latter result suggests that when central banks have the freedom to determine their target levels, they are more likely to be operating under exchange rate or monetary-growth anchors than under inflation targets. Inflation targeting is thus associated with surrendering goal independence to governments. The second column of table 16.3 reports a regression that drops the less significant variables. All five remaining regressors become more significant.

The preceding results are based on the full sample of twenty-seven countries, which includes three countries with very high inflation rates in the early 1990s, namely Brazil, Peru, and Poland. Dropping the three from the sample yields regression results for a restricted sample (reported in columns 3 and 4 of table 16.3). Coefficient signs, values, and significance levels change little from those reported for the full sample. Thus our results are robust to exclusion of high-inflation outliers. We perform one more robustness test by dropping Colombia, Korea, and Peru from the sample. As discussed in note 5, there are some questions about whether these three countries should be classified as inflation targeters. The regression results for this alternative restricted sample, reported in columns 5 and 6 of table 16.3, also confirm our full-sample results.

16.1.3 Is Inflation Targeting a Success?

Many analysts argue that the structural features and macroeconomic performance of inflation-targeting countries differ in some respects from those of countries that have adopted alternative monetary frameworks.[9] Others find that some industrial countries without formal inflation targets (such as Germany before the euro, Switzerland before 2000, and the United States) pursue a monetary policy that is close to explicit inflation targeting (Mishkin, 1999a). This raises the question of whether inflation targeting is observationally equivalent to alternative monetary frameworks with regard to the conduct of policy and its results. To address this issue, we review the recent empirical literature evaluating a decade of worldwide experience with inflation targeting. Far from attempting a comprehensive evaluation, we identify a few tentative conclusions that provide a partial view of the relative success of inflation targeting.[10]

Central bank independence and inflation targeting are mutually reinforcing. Country experience in the 1990s suggests that extending larger degrees of independence to central banks often supports the adoption of inflation targeting. In some countries inflation targeting was adopted after granting formal and instrument independence to central banks, as was the case in New Zealand and Chile. In other countries, like the United Kingdom, instrument independence came after inflation targeting. Our empirical results confirm the positive association for formal and instrument independence, but not for goal independence.

Communication, transparency, and accountability are improved under inflation targeting. Adoption of inflation targeting has typically been followed (and sometimes preceded) by major improvement in central bank communication with the public and markets and by significant upgrade in monetary policy transparency. Most inflation targeters publish inflation reports, monetary policy statements, the minutes of central bank board meetings, central bank models, and inflation forecasts (see table 16.A1). This major communication effort on the part of central banks is arguably more important under inflation targeting than under alternative monetary regimes, considering the central role played by policy credibility and inflation expectations in attaining inflation targets (Bernanke and others, 1999).

Inflation targeting helps countries reduce inflation below the levels they would have attained in the absence of inflation targeting. However, it does not yield inflation below the levels attained by industrial countries that have adopted other monetary regimes, as shown by Bernanke and others (1999) and our own results above. The adoption of inflation targeting is typically associated with a major upfront investment in inflation reduction (Corbo, Landerretche, and Schmidt-Hebbel, 2002).

Inflation targeting has been tested favorably by adverse shocks. With the exception of the emerging country financial crises of 1997–99, the 1990s were very favorable to the world economy, led by the largest U.S. expansion in the post–World War II era. Many observers therefore argue that inflation targeting is as yet untested, since no major adverse shocks have strained the achievement of low, stable inflation in many inflation targeters. This is incorrect, however. Many inflation targeters are small, open economies that were subject to severe shocks in the aftermath of the 1997 Asian crisis, in contrast to the large industrial nontargeters that were unaffected by these shocks. The combined adverse financial and terms-of-trade shocks suffered by Australia, Chile, Israel, and New Zealand, among other inflation targeters, led to major exchange rate devaluation in these countries and thus significantly tested the attainment of their inflation targets. They weathered this storm successfully, by recording little pass-through from devaluation to inflation. The 1999–2000 oil price shock represented the second test for oil-importing inflation targeters, including the countries mentioned above as well as Brazil, the Czech Republic, and Poland. Significant increases in imported inflation—through both energy prices and exchange rate devaluation—could put these countries' targets in jeopardy. The effects of the oil shock on core inflation appear to have been minor, however, and only temporary and modest increases in headline inflation have been observed.

Inflation targeting has helped reduce sacrifice ratios and output volatility in countries that have adopted inflation targeting, bringing them to levels close to those in industrial nontargeters. Bernanke and others (1999) find that inflation targeting does not make disinflation less costly in industrialized countries, as it does not alter sacrifice ratios and Phillips curves. Corbo, Landerretche, and Schmidt-Hebbel (2002), however, examine new evidence for a larger sample of inflation targeters and nontargeters. They conclude that sacrifice ratios have declined in emerging countries after the adoption of inflation targeting and that output volatility has fallen in both emerging and industrialized economies after adopting inflation targeting, reaching levels that are similar to (and sometimes lower than) those observed in industrial countries that do not target inflation.

Inflation targeting may help bring down and guide inflation expectations and deal better with inflation shocks. According to Almeida and Goodhart (1998) and Bernanke and others (1999), inflation targeting does not reduce inflation expectations quickly, but rather does so gradually over time. Corbo, Landerretche, and Schmidt-Hebbel (2002) report that inflation forecast errors, based on country vector autoregression (VAR) models, fall consistently with the adoption of inflation targeting, approaching the low levels prevalent in nontargeting industrial countries. They also find that inflation persistence declined strongly among targeters in the 1990s, which suggests that inflation targets strengthen forward-looking expectations on inflation and thus weaken the weight of past inflation.

Monetary policy under inflation targeting is flexible inasmuch as it responds symmetrically to inflation shocks and accommodates temporary inflation shocks that do not affect the medium-term attainment of the target. Inflation targeters are not inflation nuts, as King (1996) holds, because they typically react symmetrically to positive and negative shocks, pursue disinflation gradually, and react to temporary output shocks. Cecchetti and Ehrmann (2000) show that output deviations have a positive weight in all objective functions of inflation targeters.

Monetary policy is more clearly focused on inflation under inflation targeting and may be toughened by inflation targeting. Central bank mandates to focus on price stability tend to be strengthened by inflation targeting (Bernanke and others, 1999). Cecchetti and Ehrmann (2000) provide evidence that central banks' aversion to inflation shocks (relative to output shocks) is toughened with the adoption of inflation targeting, a conclusion that is partly confirmed by Corbo, Landerretche, and Schmidt-Hebbel (2002).

We conclude that inflation targeting has proved to be a very successful new monetary framework, both in comparison to inflation targeters' preceding experience and relative to alternative monetary regimes adopted by a control group of highly successful industrial countries that pursued other monetary arrangements in the 1990s.

16.2   Revisiting Operational Design Issues

The previous section outlined some elements of the operational design of inflation-targeting regimes. Four design issues deserve detailed discussion: the interaction of the length of the target horizon, the width of the target range, and the use of escape clauses; inflation targeting during the transition from high to low inflation; the designation of who should set the medium-term inflation target; and the role of the exchange rate and other asset prices. We discuss each of these in turn.

16.2.1   Interaction of the Target Horizon, Width of Target Range, Escape Clauses, and Choice of Core Inflation Targets

A central problem for the design of inflation-targeting regimes is that monetary policy affects the economy and inflation with long lags. For countries that have already achieved low inflation, the lags are estimated to be quite extended, at two years or even longer. Shorter time horizons are quite common in inflation-targeting regimes, however, which frequently specify annual inflation targets.

Using a time horizon that is too short can lead to a controllability problem, particularly when combined with a narrow target range of an inflation. The result may be frequent misses of the inflation target even when monetary policy is being conducted optimally. This occurred in New Zealand in 1995, when the Reserve Bank overshot its inflation target range of 0 to 2 percent by a few tenths of a percentage point in the one year horizon. This overshoot made the governor subject to dismissal under the central banking law, even though it was widely recognized that the overshoot was likely to be short-lived and that inflation would soon fall, as it later did. Although the breach of the inflation target range did not result in a substantial loss of credibility in the New Zealand case, under other circumstances or in an emerging market country, such an event could result in a serious loss of credibility for the central bank.

Combining too short a horizon with a narrow target range can also lead to instrument instability, in which excessive swings in the monetary policy instruments occur when the central bank tries to hit the inflation target. This problem can be especially serious in a small, open economy, where it results in greater reliance on manipulating the exchange rate to achieve the inflation target because exchange rate movements have a faster impact on inflation than do interest rates. The annual target in New Zealand and the 2 percentage point range for the inflation target were important factors in the Reserve Bank emphasis on exchange rates in the conduct of monetary policy. This resulted in overly tight monetary policy at the end of 1996—the overnight cash rate reached 10 percent because of fears that inflation would rise above the target range in 1997. Another consequence of New Zealand's overly tight monetary policy was that it contributed to the recession in 1997 and 1998, which was made worse by the negative terms-of-trade shock resulting from the East Asian crisis. Too short a horizon and too narrow a range can thus induce undesired output fluctuations, as well.

Central banks can take four routes to avoid controllability and instrument instability problems in an inflation-targeting regime. First, they can build in formal escape clauses in their inflation-targeting regime to allow for misses of the inflation target under particular circumstances. Second, they can target core inflation rather than headline inflation. Third, they can widen the range of the inflation target. Fourth, they can set inflation targets for several years ahead.

Only New Zealand has incorporated formal escape clauses into its inflation-targeting regime by allowing for misses of the inflation target range when there are significant changes in the terms of trade, changes in indirect taxes that affect the price level, or supply shocks such as a major livestock epidemic. Note that the New Zealand escape clauses are designed to deal exclusively with supply shocks because they are the only shocks that can be readily identified as being exogenous. Aggregate demand shocks may be exogenous, but they are just as likely to be induced by monetary policy. Allowing central banks to use them to justify misses of an inflation target would likely destroy central bank credibility and undermine the inflation-targeting regime. Thus formal escape clauses, although providing some increased flexibility, are only able to partially cope with the controllability and instrument instability problems from too short a horizon and too narrow a target range.

The second alternative for coping with supply shocks is to target a core inflation measure that excludes items such as food and energy from the price index, as they are especially subject to supply shocks. Using a core inflation measure has the advantage that it involves no discretion after a supply shock occurs. The use of such discretion, as in the case of escape clauses, can lead the public to question the central bank's honest commitment to achieving the inflation targets. Instead, which items are to be excluded from the construction of the inflation measure are decided ex ante. This is probably why targeting core measures of inflation has been used more widely than the specification of escape clauses.

Like escape clauses, however, targeting core inflation measures has the disadvantage of dealing only with instrument instability and controllability problems arising from supply shocks, and not those stemming from aggregate demand shocks. Furthermore, core inflation measures are not as well understood by the public as headline inflation measures, thus making core inflation targets a somewhat weaker communication vehicle than headline inflation targets. Core inflation measures also exclude items that consumers care a lot about, particularly poorer consumers for whom food and energy form a larger share of their budget. If these items are excluded from the targeted inflation measure, the central bank may be subjected to criticisms that it does not care sufficiently about poorer members of society.

The third option, widening the target range, is similarly not, by itself, a solution to controllability and instrument instability problems. Estimates of the irreducible uncertainty around an inflation target with a one-year horizon are on the order of 5 percentage points, although over time, success with inflation targeting might decrease the volatility of inflation expectations and hence inflation.[11] Choosing such a wide range for the inflation target is highly problematic because it will likely confuse the public about the central bank's intentions. The resulting high ceiling for the range is likely to make the commitment to low inflation less clear-cut, thereby reducing the credibility of monetary policy. This type of problem occurred in the United Kingdom in 1995, when inflation exceeded the target midpoint of 2.5 percent by over one percentage point, but without breaching the 4 percent ceiling. This gave the Chancellor of the Exchequer cover to resist the Bank of England's recommendation for tightening of monetary policy (see Bernanke and others, 1999).

Finally, lengthening the target horizon to correspond more closely to the lags in the effect of monetary policy on inflation would seem to be the best solution to the problems of controllability and instrument instability. Given the problems encountered in New Zealand 1997 and 1998, the Reserve Bank of New Zealand now emphasizes a target horizon of six to eight quarters in their discussion of monetary policy (see Sherwin, 1999; Drew and Orr, 1999). Other central banks, including the Bank of Canada and the Bank of England, have for a long time emphasized a target horizon of closer to two years; this has recently become a feature of the Chilean targeting regime, as well (Central Bank of Chile, 2000b).

As Svensson (1997) emphasizes, however, if central banks are concerned about output fluctuations and include a weight on output fluctuations in their loss function, then the inflation forecast should approach the long-run inflation target gradually. This implies that a horizon even longer than the policy lags might be appropriate for the inflation target. Such a long horizon for the inflation target may create problems for an inflation-targeting regime in that the long period before there is verification of hitting the target may weaken credibility, particularly if credibility of the central bank is not high to begin with. One possible way to deal with this is to recognize that the optimal horizon and the target range interact: the target horizon could be kept relatively short, say two years, if the target range is widened. The Reserve Bank of New Zealand, for example, now acknowledges that widening the target range from 2 to 3 percentage points improved the inflation-targeting regime, even though the Bank initially did not support this change. Widening the target range is not without its problems, however, because it can also increase confusion and weaken the credibility of the targeting regime.[12]

Another way to allow for longer horizons is to use multi-year annual targets, such that the path of the inflation target can approach the long-run inflation goal more gradually. Both Brazil and Mexico recently adopted this strategy (Central Bank of

Brazil, 1999; Bank of Mexico, 2000). An alternative approach is for the central bank to continue to announce only one medium-term inflation target while also announcing a long-run target with a specific date as to when it should be achieved. A third alternative for the central bank is to announce only one long-term inflation target and to publish inflation forecasts for future years, thus describing the expected path of inflation toward the long-run target. Chile recently adopted this approach, following other industrial countries (Central Bank of Chile, 2000a).

16.2.2 Inflation Targeting during the Transition from High to Low Inflation

The credibility of the central bank is likely to be low when inflation starts out well above the long-run inflation goal consistent with price stability. In addition, with initially high inflation rates (say, over 10 percent), the monetary authorities cannot easily control inflation. Inflation targeting faces extra challenges to achieve a disinflation from a high inflation rate.

One way to address the complications arising from an initially high inflation rate is to phase in inflation targeting gradually, making it more formal in line with increasing success on the disinflation front, as suggested by Masson, Savastano, and Sharma (1997). This is exactly the strategy that emerging market countries with initially high inflation have pursued (Mishkin, 2000b; Mishkin and Savastano, 2000).[13] For example, when Chile adopted inflation targeting in 1991, inflation exceeded 20 percent, and the inflation target was treated more as an official inflation projection rather than as a formal hard target (Morandé and Schmidt-Hebbel, 1997, 2000; Morandé, in this volume). Over time, the Central Bank put greater emphasis on the price stability objective. The Central Bank's success in both lowering inflation and meeting its inflation objectives eventually led the public to interpret those objectives as hard targets for which the Central Bank could be held accountable. Finally, in May 2000, the Central Bank of Chile began to issue an inflation report, with all the features seen in similar documents in industrialized countries. For example, not only does the *Monetary Policy Report* outline developments on the inflation front and how the Bank intends to achieve its inflation target, but it also includes inflation and output forecasts, along with confidence intervals for these forecasts displayed in the famous fan charts pioneered by the Bank of England.

Mexico has also followed a gradual approach to implementing inflation targeting. Senior officials of the Bank of Mexico recently characterized Mexico's monetary policy framework as being in "a transition period toward a clear-cut inflation targeting scheme" (Carstens and Werner, 1999). The Bank of Mexico has increasingly emphasized the inflation goal as the central objective of its monetary policy. For a number of years, Mexico has made public an explicit inflation objective, which was initially announced when the Minister of Finance submitted to Congress the government's economic program for the following year. In 1999, after annual inflation fell below the 13 percent target to 12.3 percent, the central bank announced the 10 percent inflation target for the year 2000 before the Ministry of Finance submitted the year's economic program to Congress. Starting in April 2000, the Bank of Mexico has issued an *Inflation Report*, which documents what has been happening on the inflation front and how the Bank of Mexico intends to achieve its inflation objectives, but which does not provide inflation and output forecasts. The third *Inflation Report*, published in October 2000, announced multi-year, annual targets that converge to a long-run target of 3 percent by December 2003.

Weak credibility stemming from high initial inflation increases the likelihood that the public and markets will not believe that the central bank is serious about hitting its targets if verification has to wait for more than one year in the future. This problem may make it very difficult for a central bank adopting inflation targeting under circumstances to choose inflation targets with horizons longer than a year. As discussed in the previous subsection, this presents the central bank with a dilemma, because the lags in transferring the effects of monetary policy to inflation are likely to be longer than one year. A solution to this dilemma is to specify a path for the inflation target with multi-year targets, which is what the central banks of Brazil, the Czech Republic, Mexico, and Poland have done since 1998. However, specifying a multi-year path for the annual inflation targets carries its own risk: even though a central bank is making good progress toward its long-run inflation goal, the greater uncertainty of controlling inflation at high rates might still cause inflation to deviate substantially from the multi-year path. This problem helps explain why the Central Bank of Chile chose not to specify multi-year inflation targets when it embarked on its inflation-targeting regime in 1991.

When countries are in the transition from high to low inflation, there appears to be a strong rationale for adopting a wide range for inflation targets to reflect the substantial uncertainty of controlling inflation when it is initially high. However, as discussed above, a wide range for the inflation target can lead to credibility problems, because the government may be willing to advocate that all is well on the inflation front when the inflation rate is substantially above the midpoint of the target range, but is still below the ceiling of the range. A point target makes this behavior on the part of the government less likely. Making sure that the government does not weaken its commitment to lowering inflation is especially important for inflation-targeting regimes when inflation is high because credibility is so much more precarious in these situations. This strengthens the argument for choosing a point target over a target range in an inflation-targeting regime during the transition from high to low inflation. Interestingly, the Central Bank of Chile switched from target ranges to point targets in 1994 in the process of hardening its inflation-targeting regime.

Imperfect credibility during the transition from moderately high to low inflation implies that inflation expectations are more geared to higher past inflation than to the lower official inflation targets. Inflation inertia is thus potentially larger, and rapid disinflation potentially more costly, in the transition to low inflation. Evidence for Chile, based on counterfactual simulations carried out by Corbo, Landerretche, and Schmidt-Hebbel (2002) and Morandé (2002), suggests that a quicker pace of disinflation toward the long-term 2–4 percent target would have involved a larger output sacrifice.

As argued in Mishkin (2000a), focusing on not undershooting the inflation target is likely to improve the performance of inflation-targeting regimes. When inflation approaches levels that are consistent with price stability, a symmetric approach to inflation targeting, which seeks to avoid undershoots just as strongly as overshoots, reduces the likelihood of output declines and deflation. It also indicates that the central bank cares appropriately about output fluctuations and thus helps maintain support for its independence. However, an asymmetric approach to inflation targeting may have some advantages when credibility is weak as a result of relatively high inflation rates, which is often the situation for emerging market countries adopting inflation targeting. Overshooting the target when inflation is still high may create fears that monetary policy is going back to its old, high-inflation ways; they could thus have devastating effects on central bank credibility. Given high inflation, therefore, the central bank may want to be particularly aggressive if it thinks that inflation could possibly overshoot the target. This bias to preventing overshoots of the target necessarily implies that the central bank's preferences would be somewhat asymmetric, with overshoots receiving a greater weight in the loss function than undershoots. For example, the behavior of the Bank of Israel in recent years seems to be consistent with asymmetric preferences of this type.

Asymmetric preferences can be taken too far, however. If the central bank is not sufficiently concerned about undershooting the targets, uncertainty about inflation may increase and thus interfere with private sector planning. Undershooting the target can also lead to sharp declines in aggregate output, which is not only harmful to the economy, but can also lead to decreased public support for the central bank and the inflation-targeting regime. Even if asymmetric preferences make sense at high inflation rates, they are no longer appropriate once the transition from high to low inflation is complete.

16.2.3   Who Should Set the Medium-Term Inflation Target?

Debelle and Fischer (1994) and Fischer (1994) make the useful distinction between goal independence, in which the central bank sets the goals of monetary policy, and instrument independence, in which the central bank controls monetary policy instruments. Instrument independence for central banks is supported by the need to insulate the central bank from short-run political pressures that may lead it to pursue time-inconsistent, expansionary policy that produces bad long-run outcomes. However, the argument that a central bank's long-run preferences should coincide with society's preferences suggests that a central bank should be goal dependent. Having the government decide on the long-run inflation target for the central bank thus receives a lot of support.

Whether the government rather than the central bank should set the medium-term inflation target is a trickier question. If inflation is currently low, the medium-term target is likely to be the same as the long-run target and so there is no conflict between them. This makes it easier to argue that the government should set the medium-term target, as it does in many inflation-targeting regimes. If inflation is currently far from the long-run target, however, the designation of who sets the medium-term target is more complicated. The length of the lags from monetary policy to inflation is a technical issue that the central bank is far more qualified to determine than are politicians. How long it should take for inflation to return to the long-run target necessarily requires judgement about these lags; such decisions should be insulated from short-term political pressure if time-inconsistent policies are to be avoided. This points to having the central bank set the medium-term inflation target, because how quickly it approaches the long-run target reflects the lags of monetary policy effects on inflation.

On the other hand, preferences on the weight given to minimizing output fluctuations relative to inflation fluctuations affect the speed at which inflation should be adjusted toward the long-run goal (Svensson, 1997). Thus if the government's long-run preferences are to be reflected in monetary policy, the government should have a role in setting the medium-term target, because this determines how fast inflation converges to the long-run target.

Clearly, there is a tradeoff with regard to who should set medium-term inflation targets when inflation is far from the long-run goal. The argument for instrument independence suggests that the central bank should set the medium-term target, while the argument for goal dependence indicates that the government should set the medium-term target. For industrial countries, this may not represent much of a dilemma because medium-term targets and long-run targets are likely to be quite close. For countries in the transition from high to low inflation, however, it is far less obvious that the government should determine the medium-term inflation target.

16.2.4 The Role of the Exchange Rate and Other Asset Prices

Movements of the exchange rate are clearly a major concern of central banks in both inflation-targeting and non-inflation-targeting countries. Changes in the exchange rate can have a major impact on inflation, particularly in small, open economies. For example, depreciations lead to a rise in inflation as a result of the pass-through from higher import prices and greater demand for exports, while an appreciation of the domestic currency can make domestic business uncompetitive. A depreciation is often seen as a sign of failure on the part the central bank, as has recently been the case for the European Central Bank, even if this view is an unfair one. In addition, the public and politicians pay close attention to the exchange rate, and this puts pressure on the central bank to alter monetary policy.

Emerging market countries, quite correctly, have an even greater concern about exchange rate movements. Not only can a real appreciation make domestic industries less competitive, but it can lead to large current account deficits which can make the country more vulnerable to currency crisis if capital inflows turn to outflows. Depreciations in emerging market countries are particularly dangerous because they can trigger a financial crisis along the lines suggested in Mishkin (1996b, 1999b). These countries have much of their debt denominated in foreign currency; when the currency depreciates, the debt burden of domestic firms increases. Since assets are typically denominated in domestic currency and so do not increase in value, net worth declines. This deterioration in balance sheets then increases adverse selection and moral hazard problems, which leads to financial instability and a sharp decline in investment and economic activity. This mechanism explains why the currency crises in Mexico in 1994–95 and East Asia in 1997 pushed these countries into full-fledged financial crises, with devastating effects on their economies.

The fact that exchange rate fluctuations are a major concern in so many countries raises the danger that monetary policy may put too much focus on limiting exchange rate movements, even under an inflation-targeting regime. The first problem with a focus on limiting exchange rate movements is that it can transform the exchange rate into a nominal anchor that takes precedence over the inflation target. For example, as part of its inflation-targeting regime, Israel established an intermediate target of a quite narrow exchange rate band around a crawling peg, whose rate of crawl was derived from the inflation target for the coming year. Although the Bank of Israel downplayed the exchange rate target relative to the inflation target over time, the use of a secondary target slowed the Bank's efforts to win support for disinflation and the lowering of the inflation targets (see Bernanke and others, 1999).

The second problem that results from a focus on limiting exchange rate fluctuations is that the impact of changes in exchange rates on inflation and output can differ substantially depending on the nature of the shock that causes the exchange rate movement. Different types of shocks call for different monetary policy responses. If the domestic currency depreciates because of a pure portfolio shock, inflation is likely to rise; the appropriate response to keep inflation under control is for the monetary authorities to tighten monetary policy and raise interest rates. If the depreciation occurs in an emerging market country which has a substantial amount of foreign-denominated debt, tightening monetary policy to prevent a sharp depreciation may be even more necessary to avoid financial instability. On the other hand, if the exchange rate depreciation occurs because of real shocks, the impact is less likely to be inflationary and a different monetary policy response is warranted. Even here, however, the response depends on the nature of the shock. A negative terms-of-trade shock, which lowers the demand for exports, reduces aggregate demand and is thus likely to be deflationary. In this situation, the correct interest rate response is to lower interest rates to counteract the drop in aggregate demand, and not to raise interest rates. If the negative terms-of-trade shock is instead due to a rise in import prices, the result is a negative income effect, which could be offset by lowering interest rates. But there is also a direct inflationary effect, particularly if there is high indexation and pass-through, which might suggest that interest rates should rise to prevent second-round effects.

One graphic example of a focus on limiting exchange rate fluctuations that induced the wrong policy response occurred in New Zealand in 1997 and 1998. As mentioned above, the short horizon for the inflation target in New Zealand led the Reserve Bank to focus on the exchange rate as an indicator of the monetary policy stance because of the direct impact of exchange rate movements on inflation. By early 1997, the Reserve Bank institutionalized this focus by adopting as its primary indicator of monetary policy a Monetary Conditions Index (MCI) similar to that developed by the Bank of Canada. The idea behind the MCI, which is a weighted average of the exchange rate and a short-term interest rate, is that both interest rates and exchange rates on average have offsetting impacts on inflation, on the assumption that portfolio shocks dominate exchange rate movements. The adoption of the MCI in 1997 led to a questionable monetary policy response to the East Asian crisis. When the crisis began in July 1997 after the devaluation of the Thai baht, depreciation set in and the MCI began a sharp decline, indicating that the Reserve Bank needed to raise interest rates, which it did by over 200 basis points. The result was very tight monetary policy, and the overnight cash rate exceeded 9 percent by June of 1998. Because the depreciation was due to a substantial negative terms-of-trade shock that decreased aggregate demand, the tightening of monetary policy, not surprisingly, led to a recession and an undershooting of the inflation target range, with actual deflation occurring in 1999.[14] The Reserve Bank of New Zealand eventually reversed its course: it lowered interest rates sharply beginning in July 1998 after the economy had entered a recession. It also recognized the problems with using an MCI as an indicator of monetary policy and abandoned the measure in 1999. Now the Reserve Bank operates monetary policy more conventionally, using the overnight cash rate as its policy instrument and placing far less emphasis on the exchange rate in its monetary policy decisions.

Another example is the case of Chile in 1998. At that time Chile's inflation-targeting regime included a focus on limiting exchange rate fluctuations by having an exchange rate band with a crawling peg that was loosely tied to lagged domestic inflation. In response to the combined financial and terms-of-trade shock stemming from the Asian crisis, the Central Bank of Chile adopted a stringent monetary policy and a defense of the peso, with a narrowing of the exchange rate band and intervention in the foreign exchange market. When the economy entered into a mild recession in late 1998, the tight monetary policy was reversed, interest rates were lowered, and the peso was allowed to decline. The exchange rate band was abolished in September 1999 and the peso now floats freely.

The experiences of New Zealand and Chile during this period contrast sharply with that of Australia, another small open economy with an inflation-targeting regime. Prior to adopting its inflation-targeting regime in 1994, the Reserve Bank of Australia adopted a policy of allowing the exchange rate to fluctuate without interference, particularly if the source of the exchange rate change was a real shock, such as a terms-of-trade shock. When faced with the devaluation in Thailand in July 1997, the Reserve Bank recognized that it would face a substantial negative terms-of-trade shock because of the large component of its foreign trade conducted with the Asian region and that it should not fight the inevitable depreciation of the Australian dollar.[15] It thus immediately lowered the overnight cash rate by 50 basis points to 5 percent and kept it near this level until the end of 1998, when it was lowered again by another 25 basis points.

The adoption of the inflation-targeting regime probably helped the Reserve Bank of Australia to be even more aggressive in its easing in response to the East Asian crisis, and it helps explain why the response was so rapid. The Reserve Bank was able to make clear that easing was exactly what inflation targeting called for in order to prevent an undershooting of the target, so that the easing was unlikely to have an adverse effect on inflation expectations. The outcome of the Reserve Bank's policy actions was extremely favorable. In contrast to New Zealand and Chile, real output growth remained strong throughout this period. Furthermore, there were no negative consequences for inflation despite the substantial depreciation of the Australian dollar against the U.S. dollar by close to 20 percent: inflation remained under control and actually fell during this period, finishing slightly under the target range of 2 to 3 percent.

Targeting the exchange rate is thus likely to worsen the performance of monetary policy. This does not imply, however, that central banks should pay no attention to the exchange rate. The exchange rate serves as an important transmission mechanism for monetary policy, and its level can have important effects on inflation and aggregate demand, depending on the nature of the shocks. This is particularly true in small, open economies. The control of inflation and aggregate demand therefore requires monitoring exchange rate developments and factoring them into decisions on setting monetary policy instruments. A depreciation of the exchange rate resulting from portfolio shocks requires a tightening of monetary policy to keep inflation from rising. On the other hand, a depreciation from a negative terms-of-trade shock stemming from falling export prices requires a different response, namely, an easing of monetary policy as pursued in Australia in 1997.

Mishkin (2000b) and Mishkin and Savastano (2000) emphasize another reason why central banks should not pursue a benign neglect of exchange rates. As mentioned above, emerging market countries with large foreign-denominated debt may not be able to afford sharp depreciations of their currencies, which can destroy balance sheets and trigger a financial crisis. Central banks in these countries may thus have to smooth excessive exchange rate fluctuations, although without attempting to prevent the exchange rate from reaching its market-determined level over longer horizons. Exchange rate smoothing via foreign exchange market interventions might sometimes be necessary because such interventions can prevent dynamics in the microeconomic structure of this market that may lead to exchange rate fluctuations that are divorced from fundamentals. Continuing exchange market interventions, particularly unsterilized ones, are likely to be counterproductive, however, because they are not transparent. Instead, exchange rate smoothing via changes in the interest rate instrument are more transparent, and they indicate that the nominal anchor—and not the exchange rate—continues to be the inflation target. Central banks can also explain to the public the rationale for exchange rate intervention in a manner analogous to that for interest rate smoothing, that is, as a policy aimed not at resisting market-determined movements in an asset price, but at mitigating potentially destabilizing effects of abrupt and sustained changes in that price.

The conclusion that targeting the exchange rate is likely to worsen the performance of monetary policy also applies to targeting other asset prices. Clearly, setting monetary policy instruments to achieve inflation targets requires factoring in asset price movements. Changes in asset prices such as common stock, housing or long-term bonds have important effects on aggregate demand and inflation, and they thus act as important transmission mechanisms for monetary policy (see Mishkin 1996a). The response to fluctuations in these asset prices cannot be mechanical, however, because optimal monetary policy responds in different ways depending on the nature of the shocks driving these asset prices. Furthermore, because many asset prices matter, targeting just one would be suboptimal.

It is also highly problematic for a central bank to target variables that are hard to control—and asset prices such as housing and stock prices clearly fall into this category. Central banks look foolish if they act to control asset prices and then are unable to do so. Furthermore, when central banks act as if they can control asset prices such as common stocks, the public may begin to fear that central banks are too powerful and thus to question support for central bank independence. Some researchers (such as Cecchetti and others, 2000) suggest that the monetary authorities should act to limit asset price bubbles to preserve financial stability. However, this requires that the monetary authorities identify appropriate asset values. It is, to say the least, highly presumptuous to think that government officials, even if they are central bankers, know better than private markets what the asset prices should be, given that markets have stronger incentives to get things right. Furthermore, as pointed out in Bernanke and Gertler (1999), an inflation-targeting approach that does not target asset prices, but instead makes use of an information-inclusive strategy in setting policy instruments, has the ability to make asset price bubbles less likely, thereby promoting financial stability.

The bottom line is that the optimal conduct of monetary policy requires that many asset prices, whether the exchange rate, stock prices, housing prices, or long-term bond prices, be factored into decisions about the setting of monetary policy instruments. Doing so is completely consistent with inflation targeting, which is an information-inclusive strategy for the conduct of monetary policy. Targeting asset prices, on the other hand, is likely to lead to serious mistakes in monetary policy, and it may weaken not only the commitment to the inflation target as a nominal anchor, but also the support for central bank independence.

16.3 Some Unresolved Issues

Inflation-targeting regimes are continually evolving as experience and new research suggests better ways to conduct monetary policy. Two unresolved issues that are central to inflation-targeting regimes are currently high on the research agenda of monetary economists: the specification of the optimal long-run inflation goal and the merit of targeting the price level rather than inflation.

16.3.1 Long-Run Inflation Goal

A key question for any central bank pursuing an inflation-targeting strategy is what the long-run goal for inflation should be. Much research finds a negative relationship between inflation and economic growth.[16] As pointed out in Bruno and Easterly (1996), however, the evidence for this negative relationship is weak at low inflation rates.

Because the empirical evidence on the direct relationship between inflation and growth is unlikely to help discriminate between different long-run goals that are under 10 percent, another approach to deciding on the appropriate long-run inflation target is to ask the deeper question of what price stability means. Alan Greenspan has provided a widely cited definition of price stability: a rate of inflation that is sufficiently low that households and businesses do not have to take it into account in making everyday decisions. This definition of price stability is a reasonable one, and, operationally, any inflation number between 0 and 3 percent seems to meet this criterion. Some economists, such as Feldstein (1997) and Poole (1999), argue for a long-run inflation goal of 0 percent, which has a psychological appeal. Indeed, one concern is that an inflation goal greater than zero might lead to a decline in central bank credibility and an increase in the instability of inflation expectations, which could, in turn, trigger an upward creep in inflation. However, Bernanke and others (1999) suggest that maintaining an inflation target above zero—but not too far above (less than 3 percent)—for an extended period does not lead to instability in the public's inflation expectations or to a decline in central bank credibility.

One prominent argument against setting the long-run inflation target at zero is that setting inflation at too low a level produces inefficiency and will result in a higher natural rate of unemployment (Akerlof, Dickens, and Perry, 1996). The authors argue that downward rigidity of nominal wages, which they say is consistent with the evidence, indicates that reductions of real wages can occur only through inflation. The implication is that a very low rate of inflation might prevent real wages from adjusting downward in response to declining labor demand in certain industries or regions, thereby leading to increased unemployment and hindering the re-allocation of labor from declining sectors to expanding sectors.

The evidence for the Akerlof-Dickens-Perry mechanism through which low inflation raises the natural rate of unemployment is not at all clear-cut. Carruth and Oswald (1989), Ingrams (1991), McLaughlin (1994), and Yates (1995) all find little evidence for downward nominal rigidities in wages in the United States and the United Kingdom. As pointed out by Groshen and Schweitzer (1996, 1999), inflation can not only "grease" the labor markets and allow downward shifts in real wages in response to a decline in demand along the lines of Akerlof, Dickens, and Perry (1996), but it can also put in "sand" by increasing the noise in relative real wages. This noise reduces the information content of nominal wages and hence the efficiency of the process by which workers are allocated across occupations and industries.

A more persuasive argument for a long-run inflation goal above zero is that the economy is less likely to experience episodes of deflation. Deflation is a key factor promoting episodes of financial instability in industrialized countries (Mishkin, 1991, 1997). Because debt contracts in industrialized countries frequently have long maturities, a deflation leads to an increase in the real indebtedness of firms and households, which in turn leads to a decline in their net worth and a deterioration of their balance sheets. Irving Fisher (1933) named this phenomenon debt deflation (although it might more accurately be referred to as debt inflation in real terms through deflation) and saw it as a major factor promoting the economic downturn of the Great Depression.[17] With decreased net worth, adverse selection and moral hazard problems increase for lenders, who therefore cut back on lending. The decline in net worth also leads to a decline in the amount of collateral a lender can grab if the borrower's investments turn sour, and the reduction in collateral therefore increases the consequences of adverse selection, because loan losses resulting from default are likely to be more severe. In addition, the decline in net worth increases moral hazard incentives for borrowers to take on excessive risk because they now have less to lose if their investments fail. This reasoning indicates that deflation can promote financial instability in industrialized countries through the debt-deflation mechanism. A recent example of this phenomenon is the case of Japan in the last decade (Mishkin, 1998; Bernanke, 1999).

Another reason for choosing an inflation goal that reduces the likelihood of deflation is that deflation may make it more difficult to conduct monetary policy. Frequent periods of deflation resulting from too low a level of the inflation target will cause short-term interest rates to hit a floor of zero during deflations, as occurred during the Great Depression and recently in Japan. Some economists argue that monetary policy becomes ineffective when the interest rate hits a floor of zero.[18] This argument is a fallacy for the reasons outlined in Meltzer (1995) and Mishkin (1996a). Monetary policy works through many other asset prices besides those of short-term debt securities. Even when short-term interest rates hit the floor of zero, monetary policy can still be effective, and indeed was so during the Great Depression (see Romer, 1992).

Nonetheless, monetary policy becomes more difficult during deflationary episodes when interest rates hit a floor of zero because the usual guides to the conduct of monetary policy are no longer relevant. In recent years, much of the research on how central banks should optimally conduct monetary policy focus on so-called Taylor rules, in which the central bank sets the short-term interest rates at a level that depends on both output and inflation gaps. The Taylor (1999) volume is an excellent example of this type of research. Once the interest rate hits a floor of zero, however, this entire class of research on optimal monetary policy rules is no longer useful because manipulating short-term interest rates ceases to be an effective tool of monetary policy. In such a deflationary environment, central banks do have the ability to lift the economy out of recession by pursuing expansionary policy and creating more liquidity, but it becomes much less clear how far they need to go. This rightfully makes central bankers quite uncomfortable. Therefore, an important disadvantage of too low a level of the long-run inflation target is that it makes deflationary environments more likely to occur, leaving central bankers at sea without the usual knowledge to guide them and thus making it harder for them to get monetary policy exactly right.

Another reason why central banks might be better off with a long-run inflation goal above zero is that it is crucial that they not be perceived as being overly obsessed with controlling inflation at the expense of output stability. A central bank is likely to lose the support of the public if it is perceived as being inflation nutters, in Mervyn King's (1996) terminology, and putting no weight on output fluctuations in making its decisions about monetary policy. Too low an inflation target, say, 0 or even 1 percent, may signal to the public that the central bank does not care sufficiently about the public's concerns.

On the other hand, Fischer (1986), Feldstein (1997), and the papers in Feldstein (1999) find that lowering the inflation rate from currently low levels to zero in industrialized countries reduces distortions caused by the interaction of inflation with the tax system. This can produce substantial welfare gains, on the order of 1 percent of GDP.[19] However, these distortions can also be eliminated by changes in the tax code, so they do not provide a clear justification for choosing a zero long-run inflation goal.

Emerging market countries that grow at high levels may be better off having inflation rates that are slightly higher than those in industrialized countries. High-growth countries typically experience real exchange rate appreciation that is proportional to the difference in the productivity growth of the traded and nontraded sectors relative to the rest of the world (the Harrod-Belassa-Samuelson effect). If it is appropriate for these countries to aim for a long-run traded goods inflation similar to that of industrialized countries, then trend real appreciation requires a domestic nontraded goods inflation that is somewhat higher. Hence, the long-run inflation goal in high-growth economies might need to be slightly higher than would be desirable for average-growth countries. This explains why Chile, a high-growth country, has chosen a long-term inflation target range of 2–4 percent per year.

Given these conflicting arguments, the definition of an appropriate long-run goal for inflation is still an open question. As a practical matter, all inflation-targeting countries have chosen long-run inflation goals slightly above zero, with the midpoints of the long-run target ranges lying between 1 and 3 percent. Future research may help central banks decide whether a long-run goal outside this range is appropriate and provide more precision as to what this goal should be.

16.3.2 Price-Level versus Inflation Targets

All countries that currently implement an inflation-targeting regime have chosen to target inflation rather than the price level. However, which of these two targets would result in better economic performance is an open question.

A price-level target has two key advantages relative to an inflation target. First, a price-level target can reduce the uncertainty about what the price level will be over long horizons. With an inflation target, misses of the inflation target are not reversed by the central bank. Consequently, inflation will be a stationary stochastic process, that is, integrated of the order zero, I(0), while the price level will be nonstationary, an I(1) process. The uncertainty regarding the future price level thus grows with the forecast horizon. This uncertainty can make long-run planning difficult and may therefore lead to a decrease in economic efficiency. Although McCallum (1999) argues that the amount of long-run uncertainty about the future price level arising from successful adherence to an inflation target may not be all that large, it still complicates the planning process and may lead to more mistakes in investment decisions.

The second possible advantage of a price-level target is that it produces less output variance than an inflation target in models with a high degree of forward-looking behavior on the part of firms.[20] However, empirical evidence (such as that presented in Fuhrer, 1997) does not clearly support the formation of forward-looking expectations, and models with forward-looking behavior have counterintuitive properties that seem to be inconsistent with inflation dynamics (Estrella and Fuhrer, 1998).

The traditional view, forcefully articulated by Fischer (1994), argues that a price-level target produces more output variability than an inflation target because unanticipated shocks to the price level are not treated as bygones and must be offset.[21] A price-level target requires that overshoots or undershoots of the target must be reversed, which could impart significantly more volatility to monetary policy and, with sticky prices, to the real economy in the short run. Although the models with forward-looking price setting cited above do not find that this feature of a price-level target increases output variability, they do not focus on one particular problem with a price-level target: the fact that a price-level target may lead to more frequent episodes of deflation. As demonstrated in the previous subsection, episodes of deflation present policymakers with two problems, namely, a possible increase in financial instability with potentially high output losses for the economy and an increased likelihood that nominal interest rates hit a floor of zero, which complicates the conduct of monetary policy.

Another problem for a price-level target that has received little attention in the literature is the presence of measurement error in inflation. Most research on measurement error takes the view that it is inflation that is measured with error rather than the price level. This was the approach taken by the Boskin Commission.[22] This implies that the measurement error in the price level is I(1), such that a price-level target results in growing uncertainty about the true price level as the forecast horizon lengthens. Many of the arguments that a price-level target results in lower long-run uncertainty about the true price level may thus be overstated.

Such conflicting arguments indicate that whether price-level rather than inflation targets would produce better outcomes is an open question. Given this uncertainty about the benefits of price-level targeting, it is not surprising that no central bank has decided to target the price level in recent years. However, the arguments made here for preferring an inflation target over a price-level target do not rule out hybrid policies that combine features of an inflation target and a price-level target and so might provide the best of both worlds. For example, an inflation target could be announced with a commitment to some error correction in which target misses would be offset to some extent in the future. Recent research shows that an inflation target with a small amount of error correction can substantially reduce the uncertainty about the price level in the long run, while generating very few episodes of deflation

(Black, Macklem, and Rose, 1997; King, 1999; Batini and Yates, 1999). Furthermore, putting a small weight on the price-level error correction term improves the trade-off between output and inflation fluctuations (see Williams, 1999; Smets, 2000; Gaspar and Smets, 2000; McLean and Pioro, 2000). Evaluating hybrid policies of this type is likely to be a major focus of future research.

One issue that would have to be addressed if such a hybrid policy were adopted is how to explain the mechanism to the public. As emphasized in Bernanke and Mishkin (1997), Mishkin (1999a), and Bernanke and others (1999), a critical factor in the success of inflation targeting is that it provides a vehicle for more effective communication with the public. The public will clearly not understand the technical jargon of error correction models. However, an error correction feature of an inflation-targeting regime could be communicated fairly easily by not only announcing an intermediate-term inflation target, but also indicating that there is a target for the average inflation rate over a longer period, say five years.

Another possible hybrid policy would be to pursue an inflation target under normal conditions, but to provide an escape clause that activates a price-level target only when the unusual condition of deflation sets in, particularly if interest rates near a floor of zero. The inflation target under normal conditions would not require that overshoots of the inflation target be reversed and so would not increase the likelihood of deflation. On the other hand, if deflation sets in, then activating a price-level target to induce expectations of reflation of the economy would not only make it less likely that nominal interest rates would hit a floor of zero, but would also lead to higher inflation expectations. This would lower real interest rates, thereby stimulating the economy, and would help induce a rise in the price level, which would repair balance sheets. Given the success of a price-level target in ameliorating the effects of the Great Depression in Sweden in the 1930s (Berg and Jonung, 1998), price-level targets have recently been proposed to help jumpstart the Japanese economy (Bernanke, 1999; Blinder, 1999; Goodfriend, 1999; Svensson, 2000).

16.4 Conclusions

The emergence of inflation targeting over the last ten years is an exciting development in the central banks' approach to the conduct of monetary policy. The review in this chapter has indicated that inflation targeting has been quite successful in controlling inflation and improving the performance of the economy. However, our discussion of operational design issues for inflation targeting and unresolved issues indicates that there is still much to learn about how best to operate inflation-targeting regimes. We expect that future experience and research will help refine the inflation targeting approach and further improve the process of monetary policymaking.

Appendix A: Summary of Inflation-Targeting Regimes

Table 16.A1
Implementation and Design of Inflation Targeting in Nineteen Countries

Country	Date introduced	Target price index	Target width	Target horizon
Australia	Sept. 1994	Core CPI	2–3%	Over one business cycle
Brazil	Jun. 1999	Headline CPI	1999: 8% (±2%) 2000: 6% (±2%) 2001: 4% (±2%)	1 year
Canada	Feb. 1991	Core CPI (excl. food, energy, and indirect taxes)	1991: 3–5% 1992: 2–4% Jun. 94: 1.5–3.5% 1995–2001: 1–3%	1991: 22 months; since 1992: multi-year
Chile	Jan. 1991	Headline CPI	1991: 15–20% 1992: 13–16% 1993: 10–12% 1994: 9–11% 1995: 8% 1996: 6.5% 1997: 5.5% 1998: 4.5% 1999: 4.3% 2000: 3.5% 2001 onwards: 2–4%	1991–2000: 1 year; 2001 onwards: indefinite
Colombia	Sept. 1999	Headline CPI	1999: 15% 2000: 10% 2001: 8% 2002: 6%	1 year
Czech Republic	Jan. 1998	Core CPI (excl. regulated prices and indirect taxes)	1998: 5.5–6.5% 1999: 4–5% 2000: 3.5–5.5% 2001: 2–4%	1 year
Finland	Feb. 1993 to Jun. 1998	Core CPI (excl. indirect taxes, subsidies, housing prices, and mortgage interest)	Annual average of 2% by 1995	Until 1995: multi-year; since 1996: indefinite

Escape clauses	Accountability of target misses	Entity that sets target	Publications and accountability
None	None	Jointly by government and central bank	Inflation report; inflation projections (2-year point estimate)
None	Issuance of open letter to Minister of Finance explaining target breach and measures taken to bring inflation within the target (and the time required)	Government in consultation with central bank	Inflation report; inflation projections (2-year fan chart); extract of board meetings; models used for inflation outlook
Revision of target path under exceptional circumstances (e.g., major oil price shock, natural disaster)	Public explanation	Jointly by government and central bank	Monetary policy report; inflation projections (1-year point estimate)
None	None	Central bank in consultation with government	Inflation report (2000); minutes of monetary policy meetings; inflation projections (2-year fan chart)
None	None	Jointly by government and central bank	Inflation report
Natural disasters, global raw material price shocks, exchange rate shocks unrelated to domestic economic fundamentals and monetary policy, and agricultural production shocks	None	Central bank	Inflation report (1998); minutes of monetary policy meetings; inflation projections (1-year range)
None	None	Central bank	None

Table 16.A1
(continued)

Country	Date introduced	Target price index	Target width	Target horizon
Israel	Jan. 1992	Headline CPI	1992: 14–15% 1993: 10% 1994: 8% 1995: 8–11% 1996: 8–10% 1997: 7–10% 1998: 7–10% 1999: 4% 2000: 3–4% 2001: 2.5–3.5	1 year
Korea	Jan. 1998	1998: 9% (±1%) 1999: 3% (±1%) 2000: 2.5% (±1%) 2001 onwards: 2.5%	1998–2000: 1 year; 2001 onwards: indefinite	None (before 2000: changes caused by major forces)
Mexico	Jan. 1999	Headline CPI	1999: 13% 2000: <10% 2001: 6.5% 2002: 4.5% 2003: similar to trade partners' inflation (3%)	1998–2002: 1 year; 2002 onwards: indefinite
New Zealand	Mar. 1990	Headline CPI (since 1999, headline CPI excludes interest charges; prior to 1999, targets were defined in terms of headline CPI less interest charges and other first-round-effect prices)	1990: 3–5% 1991: 2.5–4.5% 1992: 1.5–3.5% 1993–1996: 0–2% Since 1997: 0–3%	1990–92: 1 year; 1993–96: multi-year; since 1997: indefinite
Peru	Jan. 1994	Headline CPI	1994: 15–20% 1995: 9–11% 1996: 9.5–11.5% 1997: 8–10% 1998: 7.5–9% 1999: 5–6% 2000: 3.5–4% 2001: 2.5–3.5% 2002: 1.5–2.5% 2003: 1.5–2.5%	1 year

Escape clauses	Accountability of target misses	Entity that sets target	Publications and accountability
None	Public explanation of deviation of inflation forecast from target in excess of 1%	Government in consultation with central bank	Inflation report (1998)
None	Government in consultation with central bank	Inflation report (and submission to Parliament); monthly announcement of monetary policy direction; minutes of monetary policy meetings	
None	None	Central bank	Inflation report (2000)
Unusual events, provided they do not cause general inflationary pressures	Public explanation of target breach and measures taken to bring inflation within the target (and the time required); Minister of Finance may ask for resignation of RBNZ Governor	Jointly by government and central bank	Inflation report (1990); inflation projections
None	None	Central bank in consultation with government	None

Table 16.A1
(continued)

Country	Date introduced	Target price index	Target width	Target horizon
Poland	Oct. 1998	Headline CPI	1998: <9.5% 1999: 6.6–7.8% 2000: 5.4–6.8% 2003: <4%	1998–2000: 1 year; 2000–03: multi-year; 2003 onwards: indefinite
South Africa	Feb. 2000	Core CPI (excl. interest costs)	2003: 3–6%	Multi-year
Spain	Nov. 1994 to Jun. 1998	Headline CPI	Jun. 1996: 3.5–4% 1997: 2.5% 1998: 2%	Until 1996: multi-year; 1997–98: 1 year
Sweden	Jan. 1993	Headline CPI	Since 1995: 2% ($\pm$1%)	Until 1995: multi-year; since 1996: indefinite
Switzerland	Jan. 2000	Headline CPI	<2%	3 years
Thailand	Apr. 2000	Core CPI (excl. raw food and energy prices)	2000: 0–3.5%	Indefinite
United Kingdom	Oct. 1992	RPIX (excl. mortgage interest)	1992–95: 1–4% Since 1996: 2.5%	Until 1995: multi-year; since 1996: indefinite

Source: J. P. Morgan, "Guide to Central Bank Watching;" country sources; central banks' Web pages; Schaechter, Stone, and Zelmer (2000).

Escape clauses	Accountability of target misses	Entity that sets target	Publications and accountability
None	None	Central bank	Inflation report; inflation guidelines; report on monetary policy implementation
Major unforeseen events outside central bank's control	None	Central bank	Inflation report
None	None	Central bank	Inflation report (1995); governor reports regularly to Parliament
None	None	Central bank	Inflation report (1997); minutes of monetary policy meetings; inflation projections (2-year fan chart); submission of monetary policy report to Parliament
Unusual events, provided they do not cause general inflationary pressures	None	Central bank	Inflation report; inflation projections (3 years)
None	Public explanation of target breach and measures taken to bring inflation within the target (and the time required)	Government in consultation with central bank	Inflation report (2000); inflation projections (2-year fan chart); minutes of monetary policy meetings
None	Issuance of open letter to the Minister of Finance explaining target breach and measures taken to bring the inflation within the target (and the time required)	Government	Inflation report; inflation projections (2-year fan chart); models used for inflation outlook

Appendix B: Specification of the Data Set

This appendix defines the variables and outlines the data sources used for the analysis in section 16.1.

IT: a dummy variable for implementing inflation targeting. Specifies a value of 1 (0 otherwise) for a year in which at least six months are covered by a previously announced inflation target. Source: country sources; Schaechter, Stone, and Zelmer (2000).

Inf: CPI inflation, normalized as the percentage variation of the annual average CPI divided by one plus the percentage variation of the average annual CPI. Source: IMF, *International Financial Statistics*, various issues (code 64e).

MT: a dummy variable for pursuing monetary growth targets. Specifies a value of 1 (0 otherwise) for a year in which any month is covered by a previously announced monetary target. Source: country sources; J. P. Morgan, "Guide to Central Bank Watching."

BW: the width of the exchange rate band, normalized as the band width divided by one plus the band width. Source: IMF, "Exchange Arrangements and Exchange Restrictions," various issues.

Fiscal: the ratio of the government surplus to GDP. Source: country sources; IMF, *International Financial Statistics*, various issues (codes 80 and 99b).

Fin: financial depth, measured as the ratio of M2 to GDP. Source: country sources; IMF, *International Financial Statistics*, various issues (codes 80 and 99b).

Open: trade openness, measured as the ratio of the sum of exports and imports to GDP. Source: country sources; IMF, *International Financial Statistics*, various issues (codes 90c, 98c, and 99b).

CBFI: a dummy for formal independence of the central bank. Specifies a value of 1 (0 otherwise) for a year in which any month is covered by central bank formal independence. Formal independence is attained when a central bank is established as a legally independent or autonomous state institution. Source: country sources; J. P. Morgan, "Guide to Central Bank Watching."

CBGI: a dummy for goal independence of the central bank. Specifies a value of 1 (0 otherwise) for a year in which any month is covered by central bank goal independence. Goal independence is attained when the central bank alone determines the levels for its monetary policy targets (that is, the exchange rate, monetary growth, and inflation targets). When target levels are determined separately by the government or congress, jointly by the bank and either government or congress, or by a government representative who casts votes on central bank board decisions, the central bank is considered goal dependent. Source: country sources; J. P. Morgan, "Guide to Central Bank Watching."

CBII: a dummy for instrument independence of the central bank. Specifies a value of 1 (0 otherwise) for a year in which any month is covered by central bank instrument independence. Instrument independence is attained when the central bank freely sets its instrument in its pursuit of monetary policy goals. When central bank policy decisions are either subject to government approval or can be reversed by the government, instrument independence is not in place. Source: country sources; J. P. Morgan, "Guide to Central Bank Watching;" Schaechter, Stone, and Zelmer (2000).

Acknowledgments

We thank Mark Stone for excellent comments, as well as Ben Bernanke and Bennett McCallum for insightful discussion. We are also grateful to Verónica Mies for outstanding research assistance.

Notes

1. Classifying country cases into inflation-targeting and other monetary regimes involves subjective choices for two reasons. First, there is lack of full agreement on the main conditions and features of inflation targeting and how they apply during transition to low inflation—an issue that we discuss below. Second, some countries have simultaneously used inflation targets and other nominal anchors (the exchange rate or a monetary aggregate or both), particularly in their early years of inflation targeting. IMF (2000), Mahadeva and Sterne (2000), and Sterne (2000) discuss and present comprehensive country classifications of monetary regimes. The different classification criteria is reflected in the different country samples of recent cross-country studies of inflation-targeting experiences. See, for example, Bernanke and others (1999); Schaechter, Stone, and Zelmer (2000); Corbo, Landerretche, and Schmidt-Hebbel (in this volume); Corbo and Schmidt-Hebbel (2000).

2. Starting dates are defined by the first month of the first period for which inflation targets have been announced previously. For example, the starting date for Chile is January 1991 (the first month of calendar year 1991, for which the first inflation target was announced in September 1990). The initial inflation level is defined as the year-on-year consumer price index (CPI) inflation rate of the last quarter before the first month of inflation targeting (for example, the fourth quarter of 1990 in the case of Chile).

3. The sample includes eighteen inflation targeters, as opposed to the nineteen listed in figure 16.1, because Switzerland did not adopt inflation targeting until 2000.

4. Germany adopted the euro in early 1999 and Switzerland adopted explicit inflation targeting in 2000.

5. The use of this control group of high-income industrial economies with alternative monetary frameworks in place reflects our objective of linking the adoption of inflation targeting with structural features, as observed in the world sample of eighteen industrial and higher-middle-income countries. Defining a control group of high-performing economies with similar features to those that have adopted inflation targeting makes it statistically more difficult to identify significant determinants of the choice of inflation targeting than if we had chosen a control group including developing countries that do not target inflation.

6. For example, although the central banks of Peru and Colombia announce inflation targets, their monetary policy frameworks do not contain many crucial features of an inflation-targeting regime (Mishkin and Savastano, 2000). Korea is classified as an inflation targeter because it announces an inflation target, yet it appears to have pursued a de facto exchange rate peg in the first two years of its inflation-targeting regime, which is inconsistent with inflation targeting. Dropping these three countries from the sample does not appreciably affect the empirical results.

7. Similar definitions are used for other discrete variables used here (see the appendix for variable definitions and data sources).

8. There are only a few large positive or negative correlations among variables other than inflation targeting. In particular, the three measures of central bank independence are highly and positively correlated with each other.

9. See, for example, Bernanke, and others (1999); Cecchetti and Ehrmann (2000); Schaechter, Stone, and Zelmer (2000); Corbo and Schmidt-Hebbel (2000); Corbo, Landerretche, and Schmidt-Hebbel (2002).

10. Inferences about inflation targeters' success are still highly tentative, in view of the ambiguities surrounding the sample definitions for inflation-targeting countries, the possible systemic equivalence of some features of inflation targeting with those of alternative monetary regimes, the relevant potential and counterfactual selection bias, and mutual causation of inflation-targeting adoption and country performance.

11. See, for example, Haldane and Salmon (1995); Stevens and Debelle (1995).

12. Mishkin (2000c) argues that a point target for inflation may be more desirable than a target range because the edges of the target range can take on a life of their own. Politicians, financial markets, and the public often focus on whether inflation is just outside or inside the edge of a range, rather than on the magnitude of the deviation from the midpoint. As discussed above, the opposite problem occurred in the United Kingdom in 1995, when inflation exceeded the target midpoint by over one percentage point, but without breaching the upper band. Too much focus on the edges of the range can lead the central bank to concentrate on keeping the inflation rate just within the bands rather than on trying to hit the midpoint of the range. It is difficult to imagine a sensible objective function for policymakers that would justify such asymmetric reactions to inflation rates just inside and outside the bands.

13. It has even been a feature of the adoption strategy of industrialized countries that adopted inflation targeting when inflation was at rates of less than 10 percent (Bernanke and others, 1999).

14. The terms-of-trade shock, however, was not the only negative shock the New Zealand economy faced during that period. The farm sector experienced a severe drought that also hurt the economy. Thus a mistake in monetary policy was not the only source of the recession; bad luck played a role too. See Drew and Orr (1999); Brash (2000).

15. See MacFarlane (1999); Stevens (1999).

16. For example, see Kormendi and Meguire (1985); Grier and Tullock (1989); Cozier and Selody (1992); Fischer (1993); Andersen and Gruen (1995); Barro (1995); Andres and Hernando (1999).

17. Technically this debt-deflation mechanism requires that the deflation be unanticipated, that is, it must come as a surprise after the debt contracts have been written. Because in industrialized countries many of these contracts are quite long, a deflation that becomes anticipated after a period of time may still be unanticipated from the point of view of many debt contracts, such that the debt-deflation story still holds. If debt contracts are of very short duration, as is typically the case in emerging market countries, then deflations are less likely to be unanticipated, and so the debt deflation mechanism is inoperative (see Mishkin 1997).

18. Summers (1991) is one prominent example, and officials of the Bank of Japan recently used this argument to indicate that expansionary monetary policy is likely to be ineffective in promoting Japanese recovery.

19. Welfare costs arising from inflation because interest is not paid on high-powered money (the so-called shoe leather costs) are estimated to be an order of magnitude smaller than costs stemming from tax distortions, and they are thus unlikely to be important for deciding the optimal long-run inflation goal. See Lucas (1981, 2000); Fischer (1986); Cooley and Hansen (1989).

20. For example, Svensson (1999); Woodford (1999); Svensson and Woodford (1999); Clarida, Galí, and Gertler (1999); Dittmar and Gavin (2000); Dittmar, Gavin, and Kydland (1999); Vestin (2000).

21. This view is supported by simulations of macroeconometric models with backward-looking expectations, which typically find that a price-level target leads to greater variability of output and inflation than an inflation target. See, for example, Haldane and Salmon (1995).

22. See, for example, Boskin and others (1996); Moulton (1996); Shapiro and Wilcox (1996).

References

Akerlof, G., W. Dickens, and G. Perry. 1996. "The Macroeconomics of Low Inflation." *Brookings Papers on Economic Activity* 1996(1): 1–59.

Andersen, P., and D. Gruen. 1995. "Macroeconomic Policies and Growth." In *Productivity and Growth*, edited by P. Andersen, J. Dwyer, and D. Gruen, 279–319. Sydney: Reserve Bank of Australia.

Andres, J., and I. Hernando. 1999. "Does Inflation Harm Economic Growth? Evidence from the OECD." In *The Costs and Benefits of Price Stability*, edited by M. Feldstein. University of Chicago Press.

Almeida, A., and C. Goodhart. 1998. "Does the Adoption of Inflation Targets Affect Central Bank Behaviour?" *Banca Nazionale del Lavoro Quarterly Review* 51(204), March Supplement: 19–107.

Bank of Mexico. 2000. *Inflation Report, July–September 2000*. Mexico City.

Batini, N., and A. Yates. 1999. "Hybrid Inflation and Price Level Targeting." Bank of England. Mimeographed.

Barro, R. 1995. "Inflation and Economic Growth." Working Paper 5326. Cambridge, Mass.: National Bureau of Economic Research.

Berg, C., and L. Jonung. 1998. "Pioneering Price Level Targeting: the Swedish Experience, 1931–37." Working Paper Series 63. Central Bank of Sweden.

Bernanke, B. S. 1999. "Japanese Monetary Policy: A Case of Self-Induced Paralysis." Princeton University. Mimeographed.

Bernanke, B. S., and M. Gertler. 1999. "Monetary Policy and Asset Price Volatility." In *New Challenges for Monetary Policy*. Federal Reserve Bank of Kansas City.

Bernanke, B. S., and F. S. Mishkin. 1997. "Inflation Targeting: A New Framework for Monetary Policy?" *Journal of Economic Perspectives* 11(2): 97–116.

Bernanke, B. S., T. Laubach, F. S. Mishkin, and A. S. Posen. 1999. *Inflation Targeting: Lessons from the International Experience*. Princeton University Press.

Black, R., T. Macklem, and D. Rose. 1997. "On Policy Rules for Price Stability." In *Price Stability, Inflation Targets and Monetary Policy*, 411–61. Ottawa: Bank of Canada.

Blinder, A. S. 1999. "Monetary Policy at the Zero Lower Bound: Balancing the Risks." Paper presented at the conference on Monetary Policy in a Low Inflation Environment. Federal Reserve Bank of Boston, 18–20 October.

Boskin, M. J., E. R. Dulberger, R. J. Gordon, Z. Griliches, and D. Jorgenson. 1996. "Toward a More Accurate Measure of the Cost of Living." Final Report to the Senate Finance Committee, December.

Brash, D. 2000. "Inflation Targeting in New Zealand, 1988–2000." Speech to the Trans-Tasman Business Cycle. Melbourne, 9 February.

Bruno, M., and W. Easterly. 1996. "Inflation and Growth: In Search of a Stable Relationship." Federal Reserve Bank of St. Louis *Review* 78(3): 139–46.

Carruth, A., and A. Oswald. 1989. *Pay Determination and Industrial Prosperity*. Oxford University Press.

Carstens, A., and A. M. Werner. 1999. "Mexico's Monetary Policy Framework under a Floating Exchange Rate Regime." Research Paper 9905. Mexico City: Bank of Mexico.

Cecchetti, S., and M. Ehrmann. 2000. "Does Inflation Targeting Increase Output Volatility? An International Comparison of Policymakers' Preferences and Outcomes." Working Paper 69. Santiago: Central Bank of Chile.

Cecchetti, S., H. Genberg, J. Lipski, and S. Wadhwani. 2000. "Asset Prices and Central Bank Policy." Geneva Reports on the World Economy 2 (July). International Center for Monetary and Banking Studies and Centre for Economic Policy Research.

Central Bank of Brazil. 1999. *Inflation Report, July 1999* Brasília.

Central Bank of Chile. 2000a. *Monetary Policy of the Central Bank of Chile: Objectives and Transmission* (May). Santiago.

———. 2000b. *Monetary Policy Report* (May). Santiago.

Clarida, R., J. Galí, and M. Gertler. 1999. "The Science of Monetary Policy: A New Keynesian Perspective." *Journal of Economic Literature* 37 (December): 1661–707.

Cooley, T. F., and G. D. Hansen. 1989. "The Inflation Tax in a Real Business Cycle Model." *American Economic Review* 79(4): 733–48.

Corbo, V., and K. Schmidt-Hebbel. 2000. "Inflation Targeting in Latin America." Paper prepared for the Latin American Conference on Financial and Fiscal Policies. Stanford University, November.

Corbo, V., O. Landerretche, and K. Schmidt-Hebbel. 2002. "Does Inflation Targeting Make a Difference?" In *Inflation Targeting*, edited by Norman Loayza and Raimundo Soto, 221–269. Central Bank of Chile.

Cozier, B., and J. Selody. 1992. "Inflation and Macroeconomic Performance: Some Cross-Country Evidence." Working Paper 92-06. Ottawa: Bank of Canada.

Debelle, G., and S. Fischer. 1994. "How Independent Should a Central Bank Be?" In *Goals, Guidelines, and Constraints Facing Monetary Policymakers: Proceedings of a Conference held at North Falmouth.* Federal Reserve Bank of Boston.

Dittmar, R., and W. T. Gavin. 2000. "What Do New-Keynesian Phillips Curves Imply for Price-Level Targeting?" Federal Reserve Bank of St. Louis *Review* 82(2): 21–30.

Dittmar, R., W. T. Gavin, and F. E. Kydland. 1999. "The Inflation-Output Variability Tradeoff and Price Level Targets." Federal Reserve Bank of St. Louis *Review* 81(1): 23–31.

Drew, A., and A. Orr. 1999. "The Reserve Bank's Role in the Recent Business Cycle: Actions and Evolution." *Reserve Bank of New Zealand Bulletin* 62(1).

Estrella, A., and J. Fuhrer. 2002. "Dynamic Inconsistencies: Counterfactual Implications of a Class of Rational Expectations Model." *American Economic Review* 92(4): 1013–1028.

Feldstein, M. 1997. "Capital Income Taxes and the Benefits of Price Stability." Working Paper 6200. Cambridge, Mass., National Bureau of Economic Research.

———, ed. 1999. *The Costs and Benefits of Price Stability*. University of Chicago Press for the National Bureau of Economic Research.

Fischer, S. 1986. *Indexing, Inflation and Economic Policy*. MIT Press.

———. 1993. "The Role of Macroeconomic Factors in Growth." *Journal of Monetary Economics* 32(3): 485–512.

———. 1994. "Modern Central Banking." In *The Future of Central Banking*, edited by F. Capie and others, 262–308. Cambridge University Press.

Fisher, I. 1933. "The Debt-Deflation Theory of Great Depressions." *Econometrica* 1: 337–57.

Fuhrer, J. 1997. "The (Un)Importance of Forward-Looking Behavior in Price Specifications." *Journal of Money, Credit and Banking* 29(3): 338–50.

Gaspar, V., and F. Smets. 2000. "Price Level Stability: Some Issues." *National Institute Economic Review* 2000(174): 68–79.

Goodfriend, M. 2000. "Overcoming the Zero Bound on Interest Rate Policy." *Journal of Money, Credit and Banking* 32 (November, Part 2): 1007–35.

Grier, K., and G. Tullock. 1989. "An Empirical Analysis of Cross-National Economic Growth, 1951–80." *Journal of Monetary Economics* 24(2): 259–76.

Groshen, E. L., and M. E. Schweitzer. 1996. "The Effects of Inflation on Wage Adjustments in Firm-Level Data: Grease or Sand?" Staff Report 9. Federal Reserve Bank of New York.

———. 1999. "Identifying Inflation's Grease and Sand Effects in the Labor Market." In *The Costs and Benefits of Price Stability*, edited by M. Feldstein, 273–308. University of Chicago Press.

Haldane, A. G., and C. K. Salmon. 1995. "Three Issues in Inflation Targets." In *Targeting Inflation*, edited by A. G. Haldane, 170–201. London: Bank of England.

IMF (International Monetary Fund). 2000. *International Financial Statistics*. Washington.

Ingrams, P. 1991. "Ten Years of Manufacturing Wage Settlements." *Oxford Review of Economic Policy* (Spring).

King, M. 1996. "How Should Central Banks Reduce Inflation? Conceptual Issues." In *Achieving Price Stability*, 53–91. Federal Reserve Bank of Kansas City.

———. 1999. "Challenges for Monetary Policy: New and Old." In *New Challenges for Monetary Policy*, 11–57. Federal Reserve Bank of Kansas City.

Kormendi, R. C., and P. G. Meguire. 1985. "Macroeconomic Determinants of Growth: Cross-Country Evidence." *Journal of Monetary Economics* 16(2): 141–63.

Lucas, R. E. 1981. "Discussion of 'Towards an Understanding of the Costs of Inflation: II,' By Stanley Fischer." *Carnegie-Rochester Conference Series on Public Policy* (Autumn): 43–52.

———. 2000. "Inflation and Welfare." *Econometrica* 68(2): 247–74.

MacFarlane, I. J. 1999. "Statement to Parliamentary Committee." *Reserve Bank of Australia Bulletin* (January): 16–20.

Mahadeva, L., and G. Sterne, eds. 2000. *Monetary Policy Frameworks in a Global Context*. London: Bank of England CCBS and Routeledge.

Masson, P., M. Savastano, and S. F. Sharma. 1997. "The Scope for Inflation Targeting in Developing Countries." Working Paper 97/130. Washington: International Monetary Fund (IMF).

McCallum, B. T. 1999. "Issues in the Design of Monetary Policy Rules." In *Handbook of Macroeconomics*, edited by J. B. Taylor and M. Woodford. Amsterdam: North-Holland.

McLaughlin, K. 1994. "Rigid Wages?" *Journal of Monetary Economics* 34(3): 383–414.

McLean, D., and H. Pioro. 2000. "Price Level Targeting—The Role of Credibility." Paper prepared for the conference on Price Stability and the Long-Run Target for Monetary Policy. Bank of Canada, Ottawa, 8–9 June.

Meltzer, A. H. 1995. "Monetary, Credit and Other Transmission Mechanism Processes: A Monetarist Perspective." *Journal of Economic Perspectives* 9: 49–72.

Mishkin, F. S. 1991. "Asymmetric Information and Financial Crises: A Historical Perspective." In *Financial Markets and Financial Crises*, edited by R. G. Hubbard, 69–108. University of Chicago Press.

———. 1996a. "The Channels of Monetary Transmission: Lessons for Monetary Policy." *Banque De France Bulletin Digest* 27: 33–44.

———. 1996b. "Understanding Financial Crises: A Developing Country Perspective." In *Annual World Bank Conference on Development Economics*, edited by M. Bruno and B. Pleskovic. Washington: World Bank.

———. 1997. "The Causes and Propagation of Financial Instability: Lessons for Policymakers." In *Maintaining Financial Stability in a Global Economy*, 55–96. Federal Reserve Bank of Kansas City.

———. 1998. "Promoting Japanese Recovery." In *Towards the Restoration of Sound Banking Systems in Japan: The Global Implications*, edited by K. Ishigaki and H. Hino. Kobe University Press and International Monetary Fund (IMF).

———. 1999a. "International Experiences with Different Monetary Policy Regimes." *Journal of Monetary Economics* 43(3): 579–606.

———. 1999b. "Lessons from the Asian Crisis." *Journal of International Money and Finance* 18(4): 709–23.

———. 2000a. "From Monetary Targeting to Inflation Targeting: Lessons from Industrialized Countries." Paper prepared for the conference on Stabilization and Monetary Policy: The International Experience. Banco de México, Mexico City, 14–15 November.

———. 2000b. "Inflation Targeting in Emerging Market Countries." *American Economic Review* 90 (May, *Papers and Proceedings, 1999*): 105–09.

———. 2000c. "Issues in Inflation Targeting." Paper prepared for the conference on Price Stability and the Long-Run Target for Monetary Policy. Bank of Canada, Ottawa, 8–9 June.

Mishkin, F. S., and M. Savastano. 2001. "Monetary Policy Strategies for Latin America." Working Paper 7617. Cambridge, Mass.: National Bureau of Economic Research. *Journal of Development Economics* 66(2): 415–444.

Morandé, F., and K. Schmidt-Hebbel. 1997. "Inflation Targets and Indexation in Chile." Santiago: Central Bank of Chile. Mimeographed.

———. 2000. "Monetary Policy and Inflation Targeting in Chile." In *Inflation Targeting in Practice: Strategic and Operational Issues and Application to Emerging Market Economies*, edited by Mario I. Blejer and others. Washington: International Monetary Fund (IMF).

Morandé, F. 2002. "A Decade of Inflation Targeting in Chile: Developments, Lessons, and Challenges." In *Inflation Targeting*, edited by Norman Loayza and Raimundo Soto, 583–626. Central Bank of Chile.

Moulton, B. R. 1996. "Bias in the Consumer Price Index: What Is the Evidence?" *Journal of Economic Perspectives* 10(4): 159–77.

Poole, W. 1999. "Is Inflation Too Low?" Federal Reserve Bank of St. Louis *Review* 81(4): 3–10.

Romer, C. 1992. "What Ended the Great Depression?" *Journal of Economic History* 52(4): 757–84.

Schaechter, A., M. R. Stone, and M. Zelmer. 2000. "Practical Issues in the Adoption of Inflation Targeting by Emerging Market Countries." International Monetary Fund (IMF). Mimeographed.

Shapiro, M. D., and D. W. Wilcox. 1996. "Mismeasurement in the Consumer Price Index: An Evaluation." In *NBER Macroeconomics Annual*, edited by B. S. Bernanke and J. J. Rotemberg, 83–154. MIT Press.

Sherwin, M. 1999. "Inflation Targeting: Ten Years On." Speech to the New Zealand Association of Economists Conference, Rotorua, New Zealand, 1 July.

Smets, F. 2000. "What Horizon for Price Stability." Working Paper 24. Frankfurt: European Central Bank.

Sterne, G. 2000. "The Use of Inflation Targets in a Global Context." Bank of England. Mimeographed.

Stevens, G. R. 1999. "Six Years of Inflation Targeting." *Reserve Bank of Australia Bulletin* (May): 46–61.

Stevens, G., and G. Debelle. 1995. "Monetary Policy Goals for Inflation in Australia." In *Targeting Inflation*, edited by A. G. Haldane, 170–201. London: Bank of England.

Summers, L. H. 1991. "How Should Long-Term Monetary Policy Be Determined?" *Journal of Money, Credit and Banking* 23(3): 625–31.

Svensson, L. E. O. 1997. "Inflation Forecast Targeting: Implementing and Monitoring Inflation Targets." *European Economic Review* 41: 1111–46.

———. 1999. "Price-Level Targeting versus Inflation Targeting: A Free Lunch." *Journal of Money, Credit and Banking* 31(3): 277–95.

———. 2000. "The Zero Bound in an Open Economy: A Foolproof Way of Escaping from a Liquidity Trap." Working Paper 7957. Cambridge, Mass.: National Bureau of Economic Research.

Svensson, L. E. O., and M. Woodford. 1999. "Implementing Optimal Monetary Policy through Inflation Forecast Targeting." Stockholm University and IIES. Mimeographed.

Taylor, J., ed. 1999. *Monetary Policy Rules*. University of Chicago Press for the National Bureau of Economic Research.

Vestin, D. 2000. "Price Level Targeting versus Inflation Targeting in a Forward-Looking Model." Stockholm University. Mimeographed.

Williams, J. C. 1999. "Simple Rules for Monetary Policy." Finance and Economics Discussion Series. Board of Governors of the Federal Reserve System.

Woodford, M. 1999. "Inflation Stabilization and Welfare." Princeton University. Mimeographed.

Yates, A. 1995. "On the Design of Inflation Targets." In *Targeting Inflation*, edited by A. G. Haldane. London: Bank of England.

17 The Dangers of Exchange-Rate Pegging in Emerging Market Countries

Frederic S. Mishkin

17.1 Introduction

In recent years, there has been a growing consensus, even in emerging-market countries, that controlling inflation should be the primary or overriding long-term goal of monetary policy. Past experience with high inflation in emerging-market countries has not been a happy one, and there is a growing literature that suggests that high inflation can be an important factor that retards economic growth.[1] Although central bankers, as well as the public, in emerging-market countries now put more emphasis on controlling inflation, there is still the crucial question of how best to do this. To achieve low inflation, one choice that emerging-market countries have often made is to peg their currency to that of a large, low-inflation country, typically the United States.[2] Is this choice a good one?

This chapter examines the question of whether pegging its exchange rate is a good strategy for an emerging-market country. The analysis here suggests that the answer is usually no, except in extreme circumstances where a particularly strong form of exchange-rate pegging might be worth pursuing. Indeed, an important point in the analysis of this chapter is that pegging the exchange rate is a less viable strategy for emerging-market countries than it is for industrialized countries.

After examining rationales for exchange-rate pegging, the chapter discusses criticisms of exchange-rate pegging and why it is so dangerous for emerging-market countries. Because the chapter argues that exchange-rate pegging is highly problematic for emerging-market countries, it goes on to explore what other strategies for inflation control might be reasonable alternatives in these countries.

17.2 Rationales for Exchange-Rate Pegging

Fixing the value of an emerging-market's currency to that of a sounder currency, which is exactly what an exchange-rate peg involves, provides a nominal anchor for the economy that has several important benefits. First, the nominal anchor of an exchange-rate peg fixes the inflation rate for internationally traded goods, and thus directly contributes to keeping inflation under control. Second, if the exchange-rate peg is credible, it anchors inflation expectations in the emerging-market country to the inflation rate in the country to whose currency it is pegged. The lower inflation expectations that then result bring the emerging-market country's inflation rate in line with that of the low-inflation, anchor country relatively quickly.

Another way to think of how the nominal anchor of an exchange-rate peg works to lower inflation expectations and actual inflation is to recognize that, if there are no restrictions on capital movements, a serious commitment to an exchange-rate peg means that the emerging-market country has in effect adopted the monetary policy of the anchor country. As long as the commitment to the peg is credible, the interest rate in the emerging-market country will be equal to that in the anchor country. Expansion of the money supply to obtain lower interest rates in the emerging-market country relative to that of the low-inflation country will result only in a capital outflow and loss of international reserves that will cause a subsequent contraction in the money supply, leaving both the money supply and interest rates at their original levels. Thus, another way of seeing why the nominal anchor of an exchange-rate peg lowers inflation expectations and thus keeps inflation under control in an emerging-market country is that the exchange-rate peg helps the emerging-market country inherit the credibility of the low-inflation, anchor country's monetary policy.

A further benefit of having an exchange-rate peg as a nominal anchor in an emerging-market country is that it helps provide a discipline on policymaking that avoids the so-called time-inconsistency problem described by Kydland and Prescott 1977, Calvo 1978 and Barro and Gordon 1983. The time-inconsistency problem arises because there are incentives for a policymaker to pursue discretionary policy to achieve short-run objectives, such as higher growth and employment, even though the result is a poor long-run outcome—high inflation. The time-inconsistency problem can be avoided if policy is bound by a rule that prevents policymakers from pursuing discretionary policy to achieve short-run objectives. Indeed, this is what an exchange-rate peg can do if the commitment to it is strong enough. In this case, the exchange-rate peg eliminates discretionary monetary policy and implies an automatic policy rule that forces a tightening of monetary policy when there is a tendency for the domestic currency to depreciate or a loosening of policy when there is a tendency for the domestic currency to appreciate.

As McCallum 1995 has pointed out, simply by recognizing the problem that forward-looking expectations in the wage- and price-setting process creates for a strategy of pursuing expansionary monetary policy, central banks can decide not to pursue expansionary policy which leads to inflation. However, even if the central bank recognizes the problem, there will still be political pressure on the central bank to pursue overly expansionary monetary policy that can lead to this outcome, so that the time-inconsistency problem remains. The simplicity and clarity of an exchange-rate peg can help to reduce pressures on the central bank from the political process because the exchange-rate peg is easily understood by the public, providing "maintenance of a sound currency" as an easy-to-understand rallying cry for the central bank. Thus, an exchange-rate peg can help the monetary authorities to resist any political pressures to engage in time-inconsistent policies.

With all the above advantages, it is not surprising that many emerging-market countries have adopted an exchange-rate peg as a strategy for controlling inflation.[3] However, as discussed in sections 17.3 and 17.4, the dangers inherent in pursuing an exchange-rate peg make it an unwise course for most emerging-market countries.

17.3 General Criticisms of Exchange-Rate Pegging

There are several criticisms levelled against exchange-rate pegging in both developed and emerging-market countries.[4] These include the loss of an independent monetary policy, the transmission of shocks from the anchor country, the likelihood of speculative attacks and the potential for weakening the accountability of policymakers to pursue anti-inflationary policies. These criticisms are analysed in this section. However, there is an additional criticism of exchange-rate pegs in emerging-market countries that does not apply to developed countries: the potential for an exchange-rate peg to increase financial fragility and the likelihood of a financial crisis (as discussed in the following section 17.4).

17.3.1 Loss of Independent Monetary Policy

One prominent criticism of adopting an exchange-rate peg to control inflation is that it results in the loss of an independent monetary policy for the pegging country. With open capital markets, interest rates in the country pegging its exchange rate are closely linked to those of the anchor country it is tied to, and its money creation is constrained by money growth in the anchor country. A country that has pegged its currency therefore loses the ability to use monetary policy to respond to domestic shocks that are independent of those hitting the anchor country. For example, if there is a decline in domestic demand specific to the pegging country, perhaps because of a decline in the domestic government's spending or a decline in the demand for exports specific to that country, monetary policy cannot respond by lowering interest rates because these are tied to those of the anchor country. The result is that output and even inflation may fall below desirable levels, with the monetary authorities powerless to stop these movements.

This criticism of exchange-rate pegging may be less relevant for emerging-market countries than for developed countries. Because many emerging-market countries have not developed the political or monetary institutions which result in the ability to use discretionary monetary policy successfully, they may have little to gain from an independent monetary policy but a lot to lose. Therefore, they would be better off by, in effect, adopting the monetary policy of a country such as the United States through exchange-rate pegging than in pursuing their own independent policy.

17.3.2 Transmission of Shocks from the Anchor Country

Another criticism of exchange-rate pegging is that shocks in the anchor country will be more easily transmitted to the pegging country, with possible negative consequences. For example, in 1994 concerns about inflationary pressure in the United States led the Federal Reserve to implement a series of increases in the federal funds rate. Although this policy was appropriate and highly successful for the United States, the consequences for Mexico, which had adopted a peg to the dollar as part of its stabilization strategy, were severe. The doubling in short-term US rates from around 3% to 6% was transmitted immediately to Mexico, which found its short-term rates doubling to around 20%. This rise in rates was damaging to the balance sheets of households, non-financial business and banks, and was a factor in provoking the foreign exchange and financial crisis in Mexico which began in December 1994 (see Mishkin 1996).

17.3.3 Speculative Attacks

A further criticism of exchange-rate pegging is that, as emphasized in Obstfeld and Rogoff 1995, it leaves countries open to speculative attacks on their currencies. As seen in Europe in 1992, Mexico in 1994 and more recently in south-east Asia, it is certainly feasible for governments to maintain exchange-rate pegs by raising interest rates sharply, but they do not always have the will to do so. Defending the exchange rate by raising interest rates can be very costly because it involves having to tolerate the resulting rise in unemployment and damage to the balance sheets of financial institutions. Once speculators begin to question whether the government's commitment to the exchange-rate peg is strong, because of the increased costs of maintaining it, they are in effect presented with a one-way bet, where the value of the currency can only go down. Defence of the currency then requires massive intervention and even higher domestic interest rates.

With all but the strongest commitment to the exchange-rate peg, a government will be forced to devalue its currency. The attempted defence of the currency will not come cheaply because of the losses sustained as a result of the previous exchange-rate intervention. For example, in the September 1992 European crisis, the British, French, Italian, Spanish and Swedish central banks had intervened to the tune of an estimated $100 billion. Press reports estimated that these central banks lost between $4 billion and $6 billion as a result of their exchange-rate intervention in the crisis, a sum in effect paid by taxpayers in these countries. Although the losses suffered by central banks in emerging-market countries after an unsuccessful defence of the currency are harder to estimate, they are likely to be very substantial.

17.3.4 Weakened Accountability

In the United States, the long-term bond market provides signals that make overly expansionary monetary policy less likely. If the Federal Reserve pursues such a policy, or if politicians put a lot of pressure on it to do so, the bond market is likely to undergo an inflation scare of the type described in Goodfriend 1993, in which long-term bond prices sink dramatically and long-term rates spike upwards. Concerns about inflation scares in the long-term bond market help to keep the Federal Reserve from pursuing expansionary policy to meet short-term employment objectives, which reduces the time-inconsistency problem. Thus, the signals from the long-bond market make the Federal Reserve more accountable for keeping inflation under control. Similarly, politicians are more reluctant to criticize the Federal Reserve's anti-inflation actions because of their fears of what the long-bond market's reaction will be. The long-bond market thus not only produces signals which help to diminish the time-inconsistency problem by making the central bank more accountable, but also by reducing political pressure for overly expansionary monetary policy to increase employment in the short-term.

In many countries, particularly emerging-market countries, the long-term bond market is essentially non-existent. In these countries, however, the foreign exchange market can play a similar role to the long-bond market in constraining policy from being too expansionary. In the absence of an exchange-rate peg, daily fluctuations in the exchange rate provide information on the stance of monetary policy, thus making monetary policymakers more accountable. A depreciation of the exchange rate can provide an early warning signal to the public and policymakers that monetary policy is overly expansionary. Furthermore, just as the fear of a visible inflation scare in the bond market that causes bond prices to decline sharply constrains politicians from encouraging overly expansionary monetary policy, fear of immediate exchange rate depreciations can constrain politicians in countries without long-term bond markets from supporting overly expansionary policies.

An important disadvantage of an exchange-rate peg is that it removes the signal that the foreign exchange market provides on a daily basis about the stance of monetary policy. Under a pegged exchange-rate regime, central banks often pursue overly expansionary policies that are not discovered until too late, until after a successful speculative attack has begun. The problem of lack of central bank accountability under a pegged exchange-rate regime is particularly acute in emerging-market countries, where the balance sheets of the central banks are not as transparent as in developed countries, making it harder to ascertain the central bank's policy actions. Although an exchange-rate peg appears to provide rules for central bank behaviour that eliminates the time-inconsistency problem, it can increase the problem by making central bank actions less transparent and less accountable.

17.4 Why Exchange-Rate Pegging Is So Dangerous for Emerging-Market Countries

The potential dangers from an exchange-rate peg described above apply to both developed and emerging-market countries and are indeed serious ones. On these grounds alone, using an exchange-rate peg to control inflation is problematic. However, there is an additional danger that arises for emerging-market countries from an exchange-rate peg—one that does not apply to developed countries: the potential to promote financial fragility and even a fully fledged financial crisis. Indeed, this additional danger is so severe that it argues against an exchange-rate peg except in very rare circumstances.

The credit markets of emerging-market countries have a very different institutional structure than those of developed countries. Industrialized countries typically have long-duration debt, almost all of which is denominated in the domestic currency, and also have a fair degree of credibility that they will not allow inflation to spin out of control. The institutional features of credit markets in emerging-market countries are diametrically opposite. Because of past experience with high and variable inflation rates, these countries have little inflation-fighting credibility and debt contracts are therefore of very short duration and are often denominated in foreign currencies. The structure of debt markets in emerging-market countries means that exchange-rate pegs can make it more likely that they will experience financial crises, with disastrous effects for their economies.

To see why exchange-rate pegs in emerging-market countries make a financial crisis more likely, we must first understand what a financial crisis is and why it is so damaging to the economy. In recent years, an asymmetric information theory of financial crises has been developed which provides a definition of a financial crisis.[5] A financial crisis is a non-linear disruption to financial markets in which asymmetric information problems (adverse selection and moral hazard) become much worse, so that financial markets are unable efficiently to channel funds to the economic agents with the most productive investment opportunities. A financial crisis thus prevents the efficient functioning of financial markets, which therefore leads to a sharp contraction in economic activity.

With a pegged exchange-rate regime, depreciation of the currency is a highly non-linear event because it involves a devaluation. In most developed countries a devaluation has little direct effect on the balance sheets of households, firms and banks because their debts are denominated in domestic currency.[6] This is not true in emerging-market countries, because of their very different institutional structure. In these countries, but not in developed countries, a foreign-exchange crisis can trigger a full-scale financial crisis in which financial markets are no longer able to move funds to those with productive investment opportunities, thereby causing a severe economic contraction.

There are three reasons why exchange-rate pegs make emerging-market countries more prone to financial crises. First, a devaluation under an exchange-rate peg can cause a non-linear deterioration in the balance sheets of non-financial and financial firms that can cause a collapse in the ability of financial markets to move funds to firms with productive investment opportunities. Second, when an exchange-rate peg breaks down, this can lead to a sharp surge in inflation that causes a further weakening of balance sheets, with the negative effects described above. Third, an exchange-rate peg may encourage capital inflows, which lead to a lending boom, bad loans, and a deterioration in banks' balance sheets which interferes with the ability of financial institutions to intermediate funds to those with productive investment opportunities. Each of these factors is examined in more detail below.

With debt contracts denominated in foreign currency, as in emerging-market countries, the debt burden of domestic firms increases when there is a depreciation or devaluation of the domestic currency. On the other hand, because assets are typically denominated in domestic currency, there is no simultaneous increase in the value of firms' assets. The result is that a depreciation or devaluation leads to a deterioration in firms' balance sheets and a decline in net worth, which, in turn, means that effective collateral has shrunk, thereby providing less protection to lenders. Furthermore, the decline in net worth increases moral hazard incentives for firms to take on greater risk because they have less to lose if the loans go sour. Because lenders are now subject to much higher risks of losses, there is a decline in lending and hence a decline in investment and economic activity.

Although depreciation in an emerging-market country under a floating exchange-rate regime does promote financial fragility for the reasons discussed above, it is less likely to cause a fully fledged financial crisis in which financial markets seize up and stop performing their role of moving funds to those with productive investment opportunities. Under a pegged exchange-rate regime, when a successful speculative attack occurs the decline in the value of the domestic currency is usually much larger, more rapid and more unanticipated than when a depreciation occurs under a floating exchange-rate regime. For example, during the Mexican crisis of 1994–95, the value of the peso halved within a few months, and in the recent south-east Asian crisis, the worst-hit country, Indonesia, has seen its currency decline to a quarter of its pre-crisis value, also within a very short period. The damage to balance sheets after these devaluations has thus been extremely severe. In Mexico, there was a several-fold increase in the net debtor position of business enterprises between December 1994 and March 1995, while in Indonesia the four-fold increase in the value of foreign debt arising from the currency collapse has made it very difficult for Indonesian firms with appreciable foreign debt to remain solvent. The results of these collapses in balance sheets were sharp economic contractions. In Mexico, real GDP growth in the second and third quarters of 1995 fell to rates of around -10%, while current forecasts predict similar rates of decline for Indonesia over the coming year.

In addition, the depreciation of the domestic currency can lead to deterioration in banking-sector balance sheets. In emerging-market countries, banks typically have many short-term liabilities denominated in foreign currency which increase sharply in value when a depreciation occurs. However, firms and households are unable to pay off their debts, resulting in loan losses on the assets side of the banks' balance sheets. In the aftermath of the foreign-exchange crises, the share of non-performing loans to total loans in Mexico rose to above 15%, while the proportion has risen to between 15% and 35% in Thailand, Malaysia, South Korea and Indonesia.[7] Once there is a deterioration in bank balance sheets, with the substantial loss of bank capital, banks have two choices: to cut back on lending in order to shrink their asset bases and thereby restore their capital ratios, or to try to raise new capital. However, when banks experience a deterioration in their balance sheets, it is very hard for them to raise new capital at a reasonable cost. The typical response of banks with weakened balance sheets is hence a contraction in their lending, which slows economic activity. In the extreme case in which the deterioration of bank balance sheets leads to a banking crisis which forces many banks to close, thereby directly limiting the ability of the banking sector to make loans, the effect on the economy is even more severe. The non-linear nature of the decline in the value of the domestic currency when an exchange-rate peg collapses means that the possibility of an especially sharp deterioration in bank balance sheets is greater under an exchange-rate peg than a floating exchange-rate regime. Thus the potential for a collapse of the banking system is greater when an emerging-market country adopts an exchange-rate peg.

An additional danger from using an exchange-rate peg to control inflation in emerging-market countries is that a successful speculative attack can lead to a rapid surge in inflation that can be especially damaging to the ability of financial markets to move funds to those with productive investment opportunities. Because many emerging-market countries have previously experienced both high and variable inflation, their central banks are unlikely to have deep-rooted credibility as inflation fighters. A sharp decline in the value of the currency after a speculative attack that leads to immediate upward pressure on prices can therefore lead to a dramatic rise in both actual and expected inflation. Mexican inflation surged to 50% in 1995 after the foreign-exchange crisis of 1994; current forecasts for Indonesia predict that the same will happen there.

The sharp rise in expected inflation after a successful speculative attack against the currency of an emerging-market country leads to particularly sharp rises in interest rates, exacerbating the financial crisis, as has occurred in Mexico and Indonesia.

The interaction of the short duration of debt contracts and the interest-rate rise leads to huge increases in interest payments by firms, thereby weakening their cash-flow positions and their balance sheets. As a result, both lending and economic activity are likely to undergo a sharp decline.

Another potential danger from an exchange-rate peg is that by providing a more stable value of the currency, it might reduce risk for foreign investors and thus encourage capital inflows.[8] Although these inflows might be channelled into productive investments and thus stimulate growth, they might promote excessive lending, manifested by a lending boom, because domestic financial intermediaries such as banks play a key role in intermediating these capital inflows.[9] Indeed, Folkerts-Landau et al. (1995) found that emerging-market countries in the Asia-Pacific region which had large net private capital inflows also experienced large increases in their banking sectors. Furthermore, if the bank supervisory process is weak, as it often is in emerging-market countries, so that the government safety net for banking institutions creates incentives for them to take on risk, there is a greater likelihood that a capital inflow will produce a lending boom. With inadequate bank supervision, the likely outcome of a lending boom is substantial loan losses and a deterioration of bank balance sheets.[10]

The deterioration in bank balance sheets can damage the economy in two ways. First, the deterioration in the balance sheets of banking firms leads them to restrict their lending in order to improve their capital ratios or can even lead to a full-scale banking crisis which forces many banks into insolvency, thereby directly removing the ability of the banking sector to make loans. Second, the deterioration in bank balance sheets can promote a foreign-exchange crisis because it becomes very difficult for the central bank to defend its currency against a speculative attack. Any rise in interest rates to keep the domestic currency from depreciating has the additional effect of weakening the banking system further because the rise in interest rates hurts banks' balance sheets. This negative effect of a rise in interest rates on banks' balance sheets occurs because of their maturity mismatch and their exposure to increased credit risk when the economy deteriorates. Thus, when a speculative attack on the currency occurs in an emerging-market country, the banking system may collapse if the central bank raises interest rates sufficiently to defend the currency. Once investors recognize that a country's weak banking system makes it less likely that the central bank will take the steps required successfully to defend the domestic currency, they have even greater incentives to attack the currency because expected profits from selling it have now risen. The outcome is a successful attack on the currency, and the resulting foreign-exchange crisis causes a collapse of the economy for the reasons already discussed.

The scenarios seen recently in emerging-market countries such as Mexico, Thailand, South Korea, Malaysia and Indonesia illustrate how dangerous exchange-rate

pegs can be. These countries experienced massive capital inflows which were interme-
diated by the banking sector, and the resulting lending booms led to large loan losses
and a deterioration in bank balance sheets, which helped to promote the subsequent
foreign-exchange crises. The collapse of domestic currencies then led to a huge number of insolvencies and sharp rises in inflation and interest rates which caused further
deteriorations in balance sheets. The outcome has been severe depressions in all these
countries, which have engendered substantial social unrest. Their experience suggests
that using an exchange-rate peg to control inflation is highly problematic.

17.5   When Might the Benefits of an Exchange-Rate Peg Outweigh the Costs for an Emerging-Market Country?

So far the discussion on exchange-rate pegging in emerging-market countries has
been sufficiently negative that one might conclude that it should never be adopted
as a strategy to control inflation. However, this view is too strong. Exchange-rate
pegging can be an especially effective means of reducing inflation quickly if there is
a very strong commitment to the exchange-rate peg. In the extreme situation where
there appears to be no alternative way to break inflationary psychology, it is an option that might be considered, although even then it is a dangerous course.

A particularly strong form of commitment mechanism to a pegged exchange rate
is a currency board. A currency board requires that the note-issuing authority,
whether the central bank or the government, announce a fixed exchange rate against
a particular foreign currency and then stand ready to exchange domestic currency for
foreign currency at that rate whenever the public requests it. In order credibly to
meet these requests, a currency board typically has foreign reserves backing more
than 100% of the domestic currency and allows the monetary authorities absolutely
no discretion. In contrast, the typical fixed or pegged exchange-rate regime does allow
the monetary authorities some discretion in their conduct of monetary policy because
they can still adjust interest rates or conduct open-market operations which affect domestic credit. The currency board thus involves a stronger commitment by the central bank to the fixed exchange rate and may therefore be effective in bringing down
inflation quickly and in decreasing the likelihood of a successful speculative attack
against the currency.

An important recent example in which a currency board was implemented to
reduce inflation is Argentina. Because of continuing bouts of hyperinflation and previous past failures of stabilization programmes, the Argentine government felt that
the only way it could break the back of inflation was to adopt a currency board,
which it did in 1991 by passing the Convertibility Law. This law required the central
bank to exchange US dollars for new pesos at a fixed exchange rate of 1 to 1. Argen-

tina's currency board appeared strikingly successful in its early years. Inflation, which had been running at an annual rate of over 1,000% in 1989 and 1990, fell to well under 5% by the end of 1994 and economic growth was rapid, averaging almost 8% per year from 1991 to 1994.

Although the stronger commitment to a fixed exchange rate may mean that a currency board is better equipped than an exchange-rate peg to stave off a speculative attack against the domestic currency, it is not without its problems. In the aftermath of the Mexican peso crisis, concern about the health of the Argentine economy led the public to withdraw their money from the banks (deposits fell by 18%) and to exchange their pesos for dollars, causing a contraction of the Argentine money supply. The result was a sharp contraction in Argentine economic activity with real GDP dropping by over 5% in 1995 and the unemployment rate jumping to above 15%. The economy began to recover only in 1996, with financial assistance from international agencies such as the IMF, the World Bank and the Inter-American Development Bank, which lent Argentina over $5 billion to help shore up its banking system. Because the central bank of Argentina had no control over monetary policy under the currency board system, it was relatively helpless to counteract the contractionary effects of the public's behaviour. Furthermore, because the currency board does not allow the central bank to create money and lend to the banks, it limits the capability of the central bank to act as a lender of last resort, and other means must be used to cope with potential banking crises.

Although a currency board is highly problematic, it may be the only way to break a country's inflationary psychology and alter the political process so that it no longer leads to continuing bouts of high inflation. However, there are two issues that policy-makers must confront in order to make a currency board successful. First there is a need to pay particular attention to preventing excessive risk-taking by the banking sector. As already noted, weakness of the banking sector because of excessive risk-taking is an important factor that can help trigger a speculative attack on the currency. If the currency board does not survive the speculative attack, the resulting financial crisis is likely to be especially severe because a characteristic of debt markets in countries with a currency board is that they have an especially large amount of debt denominated in the foreign currency to which the domestic currency is pegged. Thus a devaluation hits the balance sheets of businesses and banks particularly hard, with even more damaging effects on the economy. Even if the currency board survives the speculative attack, the resulting exchange of the domestic currency for foreign currency leads to a sharp contraction of the money supply, as occurred in Argentina, which also is highly damaging to the economy.

Furthermore, because a currency board limits a central bank's ability to engage in lender-of-last-resort operations, coping with banking crises is very difficult.[11]

Because problems in the banking sector can be so costly to an economy with a currency board, it is especially important that policy-makers keep banks from taking on too much risk which can lead to deterioration in bank balance sheets. Indeed, this has been recognized by policy-makers in Argentina and is an important reason why they have been among the most committed in Latin America to developing a system of bank regulation and supervision that will preserve the health and soundness of the banking sector.[12]

The second issue that policy-makers contemplating institution of a currency board must confront is the need for an exit strategy. The longer a currency board stays in existence, the greater the likelihood that there will occur a sufficiently large shock that leads to its collapse. Furthermore, once inflation is under control, a country with a currency board is subject to three disadvantages: being strongly affected by shocks to the country to whose currency it is pegged; not having its own independent monetary policy; and not having the ability to engage in lender-of-last-resort operations. Thus, even if the currency board is successful, at some point it may outlive its usefulness. The key question for policy-makers is how it can exit from the currency board arrangement.

Clearly, exiting a currency board when the currency is under attack is not an option, because in this situation the collapse of the currency board would lead to a financial crisis and an explosion in inflation. On the other hand, when there is no pressure on the currency, there is no threat to the currency board, and so the usual attitude is "if it ain't broke, don't fix it." Exiting a currency board is thus not a trivial task. It is exactly when things are going well that smooth transition out of the currency board is feasible. On the other hand, this is when the political will to exit from the currency board may be weakest, even if the country would be better served by a different monetary regime.

The discussion in this section provides a qualified answer to the question of when an exchange-rate peg might be a worthwhile option for an emerging-market country. Under extreme circumstances in which past poor inflation performance suggests that there is no other way to alter inflationary psychology, pegging the exchange rate has advantages, although it also presents substantial dangers. However, because the costs of being driven off the exchange-rate peg by a successful speculative attack are so high, if this option is chosen a very strong commitment mechanism to the exchange-rate peg, such as a currency board, is absolutely necessary. Compromises such as an exchange-rate peg with the option for discretionary monetary policy are likely to be doomed to failure and to be severely damaging to the economy. If a currency board is chosen, it is also crucial that policymakers focus on developing a system of bank regulation and supervision that preserves the soundness of the financial system and also prepare for an exit strategy once the currency board has outlived its usefulness.

17.6   Alternative Strategies for Inflation Control

So far this chapter has argued that an exchange-rate peg is a dangerous strategy for inflation control in emerging-market countries. If exchange-rate pegging is not an option, what other strategies can be used by emerging-market countries to control inflation?

A basic strategy for inflation control in emerging-market countries requires two primary components. First, the central bank needs to be given sufficient independence to pursue long-run objectives such as price stability. Politicians in both industrialized and emerging-market countries are likely to be short-sighted because they are driven by the need to win their next election. With their focus on the coming election, they are unlikely to focus on long-term objectives, such as promoting a stable price level. Instead, they will tend to seek short-term objectives, such as low unemployment and low interest rates, even if these objectives may have undesirable long-term consequences. If the central bank is controlled by the government, it is likely to accede to these political demands, resulting in high inflation and low credibility for the central bank. Only with the granting of independence can the central bank be sufficiently insulated from short-term political pressures that it can focus on the long-run goal of inflation control. Recent evidence seems to support the hypothesis that macroeconomic performance is improved when central banks are more independent. When central banks are ranked from least legally independent to most legally independent, the inflation performance is found to be the best for countries with the most independent central banks.[13]

The second component of a successful strategy for inflation control in emerging-market countries is an explicit nominal anchor. As discussed earlier, an explicit nominal anchor helps to establish credibility for monetary policy and to fix inflation expectations, while it also helps to avoid the time-inconsistency problem. It is true that industrialized countries have often been able to conduct successful monetary policy without an explicit nominal anchor, but it is far more crucial to have one in emerging-market countries which have typically had high and variable inflation rates in the past and therefore suffer from a lack of monetary policy credibility.[14]

There are two basic alternatives to an exchange-rate peg for an explicit nominal anchor: monetary targets and inflation targets. Although monetary targets have been used successfully in some countries, particularly Germany, they may not be as effective in the emerging-market country context. Because of velocity shocks, the relationship between monetary aggregates and inflation has not been very tight, even in Germany.[15] Hitting the monetary target will not always produce the desired inflation outcome and may not be a sufficiently good signal about the appropriate stance of monetary policy. Because of instabilities in the money-inflation relationship, no monetary targeter has strictly adhered to its targets: even the Germans miss their monetary target range about half of the time. This is not a serious problem in the German context because of the high credibility of the German central bank, which is able to explain the deviations from the target without losing the public's belief in its commitment to price stability. Because the credibility of central banks in emerging market countries is so much lower than that of the Bundesbank, this strategy is unlikely to be as successful in these countries.

The other alternative nominal anchor for emerging-market countries is an inflation target. Inflation targeting not only involves the public announcement of medium-term numerical targets for inflation, with an institutional commitment by the monetary authorities to achieve these targets, but also includes increased communication with the public and the markets about the plans and objectives of monetary policy-makers and increased accountability of the central bank for obtaining its inflation objectives.[16] As outlined in Bernanke and Mishkin 1997, Mishkin and Posen 1997, Mishkin 1998 and Bernanke, Laubach, Mishkin and Posen 1998 the primary advantage of inflation targeting is its transparency to the public. Like an exchange-rate peg, it is readily understood by the public, but, even more directly than other methods, it makes clear the commitment to price stability. Inflation targeting keeps the goal of price stability in the public's eye, thus making the central bank more accountable for keeping inflation low, which helps to counter the time-inconsistency problem.

In contrast to the exchange-rate target, inflation targets enable monetary policy to focus on domestic considerations and to respond to shocks to the economy. Finally, inflation targets have the advantage that velocity shocks are largely irrelevant because the monetary-policy strategy no longer requires a stable money–inflation relationship. Indeed, an inflation target allows the monetary authorities to use all available information, and not just one variable, to determine the best settings for monetary policy.

One criticism of inflation targets is that, in contrast to exchange rates and monetary aggregates, inflation is not easily controlled by the monetary authorities. This can be a particularly severe problem for an emerging-market country that is trying to bring down inflation from a high level and so is more likely to experience large inflation-forecast errors. This suggests that hard targets for inflation might be worth phasing in only after there has been some successful disinflation. This is exactly the strategy that has been followed by Chile (see Morande and Schmidt-Hebbel 1997), which adopted inflation targeting in September 1990. Initially, inflation targets were announced and interpreted as official inflation projections, rather than as hard targets. However, over time as inflation fell, inflation targets came to be viewed by the central bank and the markets as hard targets. Waiting to harden inflation targets until after some success has already been achieved on the inflation front is also consistent with what inflation-targeting industrialized countries have done; they did not institute inflation targeting until after substantial disinflation had already been achieved.[17]

Another criticism of inflation targets is that a sole focus on inflation may lead to large adverse effects on output. Although this could be a problem if the inflation targeting implied that monetary authorities must try to reduce inflation very rapidly without concern for output fluctuations, this is not the way inflation targeting has been conducted in practice in the industrialized countries. All inflation-targeting central banks have left themselves considerable scope to respond to output growth and fluctuations. When inflation starts at a level that is higher than the long-run inflation goal, inflation targets have been lowered gradually. This feature of inflation targeting is also characteristic of the Chilean case, in which inflation targets were lowered gradually from an annual rate of around 25% when they were instituted in 1991 to around 5% today.

Furthermore, inflation targeting can actually help to minimize output fluctuations. This is because inflation targeting provides not only a ceiling for the inflation rate, but also a floor. Inflation targeting can therefore act to attenuate the effects of negative, as well as positive, shocks to aggregate demand. Indeed, this benefit of inflation targeting has been emphasized by the Canadian monetary authorities.

17.7 Conclusions

Although pegging the exchange rate provides a nominal anchor for emerging-market countries that can help them to control inflation, the analysis in this chapter does not provide support for this strategy for the conduct of monetary policy. First, there are the usual criticisms of exchange-rate pegging; that it entails the loss of an independent monetary policy, exposes the country to the transmission of shocks from the anchor country, increases the likelihood of speculative attacks and potentially weakens the accountability of policymakers to pursue anti-inflationary policies. However, most damaging to the case for exchange-rate pegging in emerging-market countries is that it can increase financial fragility and heighten the potential for financial crises. Because of the devastating effects on the economy that financial crises can bring, an exchange-rate peg is a very dangerous strategy for controlling inflation in emerging-market countries. Instead, this chapter suggests that a strategy with a greater likelihood of success involves the granting of independence to the central bank and the adoption of inflation targeting.

Acknowledgments

I thank Adam Posen, Robert Hodrick, an anonymous referee and participants in the macro lunch at Columbia University for their helpful comments. Any views expressed in this chapter are those of the author only and not those of Columbia University or the National Bureau of Economic Research.

Notes

1. See, for example, Anderson and Gruen 1995, Briault 1995, Bruno 1991, Feldstein 1997, Fischer 1993, 1994 and Sarel 1996.

2. In some cases, this strategy involves pegging the exchange rate at a fixed value to that of the other country so that its inflation rate will eventually gravitate to that of the other country, while in other cases it involves a crawling peg or target in which its currency is allowed to depreciate at a steady rate so that its inflation rate can be slightly higher than that of the other country.

3. Another potential advantage of an exchange-rate peg is that by providing a more stable value of the currency, it might lower risk for foreign investors and thus encourage capital inflows which could stimulate growth. However, as discussed in section 17.4, capital inflows may be highly problematic for an emerging-market country because they may help encourage a lending boom which eventually weakens the banking sector and helps to stimulate a financial crisis.

4. An excellent additional discussion of these criticisms is contained in Obstfeld and Rogoff 1995.

5. See Bernanke 1983, Calomiris and Gorton 1991 and Mishkin 1991, 1994 and 1996.

6. Indeed, a devaluation in developed countries can actually stimulate economic activity because it makes the country's goods more competitive internationally, thereby increasing its net exports and hence aggregate demand. This was the experience of the United Kingdom when it was forced to devalue its currency after the September 1992 foreign-exchange crisis. Its economic performance after the devaluation was substantially better than that of France, which successfully defended its currency in 1992.

7. See Mishkin 1996 and Goldstein 1998.

8. Capital inflows are not only encouraged by exchange-rate pegs but also by convertibility—the right of domestic citizens to convert currencies into one another without restrictions. Capital controls can enable a country to maintain an exchange-rate peg while restricting capital inflows and outflows. It is far beyond this chapter to debate the desirability of capital controls, though it should be noted that there are serious doubts as to whether these can be effective in today's financial environment, with many financial instruments that make it easier to circumvent these controls. Furthermore, capital controls may block entry to funds which will be used for productive investment opportunities. Elsewhere, Mishkin 1997b, I have argued that there is a strong case to improve bank regulation and supervision so that capital inflows are less likely to lead to a lending boom and excessive risk-taking by banking institutions. This may be the more appropriate way to make sure that capital inflows do not lead to excessive risk-taking, rather than restricting convertibility through capital controls.

9. See Calvo, Leiderman and Reinhart 1994.

10. Gavin and Hausman 1996 and Kaminsky and Reinhart 1996 find that lending booms are a predictor of banking crises, yet it is less clear that capital inflows will produce a lending boom which causes a deterioration in bank balance sheets. Kaminsky and Reinhart 1996, for example, find that financial liberalization, rather than balance-of-payments developments, appears to be a more important predictor of banking crises.

11. However, as pointed out in Mishkin 1996, the ability to successfully engage in lender-of-last-resort operations to cope with financial crises is limited in emerging-market countries, even if they do not have a currency board. This is because pumping liquidity into the system is likely to lead to a rise in inflation expectations and a depreciation of the currency, causing a further deterioration in balance sheets, and thus making informational problems worse in financial markets.

12. For a description of the Argentine bank regulatory system, see Banco Central de la Republica Argentina 1997 and Calomiris 1997.

13. See Alesina and Summers 1988, Cukierman 1992 and Fischer 1994 among others. However, there is some question as to whether causality runs from central bank independence to low inflation or whether a third factor is involved, such as the general public's preferences for low inflation, that creates both central bank independence and low inflation (see Posen 1995).

14. Even in industrialized countries, there is a strong case for an explicit nominal anchor such as inflation target (see Mishkin 1997a).

15. See Estrella and Mishkin 1997, for example.

16. Other detailed analyses of experiences with inflation targeting can be found in Goodhart and Vinals 1994, Leiderman and Svensson 1995, Haldane 1995 and McCallum 1996. A variant of inflation targeting is targeting of nominal GDP growth. As discussed in Mishkin 1997a, although nominal GDP-growth targeting is close to inflation targeting, it suffers from distinct disadvantages.

17. Israel is another high-inflation country that, like Chile, has adopted a strategy of inflation targeting only after a successful disinflation. See Bufman, Leiderman and Sokoler 1995 and Bernanke, Laubach, Mishkin and Posen 1998. The example of Chile is used in the text because it is hard to classify Israel as an emerging-market country.

References

Alesina, Alberto, and Lawrence H. Summers (1993), "Central Bank Independence and Macroeconomic Performance: Some Comparative Evidence," *Journal of Money, Credit, and Banking*, 25, 151–62.

Anderson, Palle, and David Gruen (1995), "Macroeconomic Policies and Growth," in Palle Anderson, Jacqui Dwyer and David Gruen, eds, *Productivity and Growth*, 279–319. Sydney: Reserve Bank of Australia.

Banco Central de la Republica Argentina (1997), "Main Features of the Regulatory Framework of the Argentine Financial System" (mimeo, April).

Barro, Robert J., and David B. Gordon (1983), "A Positive Theory of Monetary Policy in a Natural Rate Model," *Journal of Political Economy*, 91, 589–610.

Bernanke, B. S. (1983), "Non-Monetary Effects of the Financial Crisis in the Propagation of the Great Depression," *American Economic Review*, 73, 257–76.

————, and Frederic S. Mishkin (1997), "Inflation Targeting: A New Framework for Monetary Policy?" *Journal of Economic Perspectives*.

Bernanke, Ben S., T. Laubach, F. S. Mishkin and Adam S. Posen (1998), *Inflation Targeting: Lessons from the International Experience*. Princeton: Princeton University Press.

Briault, Clive (1995), "The Costs of Inflation," *Bank of England Quarterly Bulletin*, 35 (February), 33–45.

Bruno, Michael (1991), "High Inflation and the Nominal Anchors of an Open Economy," *Essays in International Finance*, 183 (June). Princeton: Princeton University, International Finance Section.

Bufman, Gil, Leonardo Leiderman and Meir Sokoler (1995), "Israel's Experience with Explicit Inflation Targets: A First Assessment," in Leonardo Leiderman and Lars E. O. Svensson, eds., *Inflation Targets*, 169–91. London: Centre for Economic Policy Research.

Calomiris, C. W. (1997), *The Postmodern Bank Safety Net: Lessons from Developed and Developing Countries*. Washington: AEI Press.

————, and Gorton, G. (1991), "The Origins of Banking Panics: Models, Facts and Bank Regulation," in R. G. Hubbard, ed., *Financial Markets and Financial Crises*, 109–73. Chicago: University of Chicago Press.

Calvo, Guillermo (1978), "On the Time Consistency of Optimal Policy in the Monetary Economy," in *Econometrica*, 46, 1411–28.

Calvo, G. A., L. Leiderman, and C. M. Reinhart (1994), "The Capital Inflows Problem: Concepts and Issues," in *Contemporary Economic Policy*, 12 (July), 54–66.

Cukierman, Alex (1992), *Central Bank Strategy, Credibility, and Independence: Theory and Evidence*. Cambridge, Massachusetts: MIT Press.

Estrella, Arturo, and Frederic S. Mishkin (1997), "Is There a Role for Monetary Aggregates in Conduct of Monetary Policy," *Journal of Monetary Economics*, 7 (October), 279–304.

Feldstein, M. (1997), "The Costs and Benefits of Going from Low Inflation to Price Stability," in C. D. Romer and D. H. Romer, eds, *Reducing Inflation: Motivation and Strategy*, 123–56. Chicago: University of Chicago Press.

Fischer, S. (1993), "The Role of Macroeconomic Factors in Growth," *Journal of Monetary Economics*, 32, 485–512.

———— (1994), "Modern Central Banking," in Forest Capie, Charles Goodhart, Stanley Fischer and Norbert Schnadt, eds, *The Future of Central Banking: The Tercentenary Symposium of the Bank of England*, 262–308. Cambridge, England and New York: Cambridge University Press.

Folkerts-Landau, D., G. J. Schinasi, M. Cassard, V. K. Ng, C. M. Reinhart, and M. G. Spencer (1995), "Effect of Capital Flows on the Domestic Financial Sectors in APEC Developing Countries," in M. S. Khan and C. M. Reinhart, eds, *Capital Flows in the APEC Region*, 31–57. Washington: International Monetary Fund.

Gavin, M., and R. Hausman (1996), "The Roots of Banking Crises: the Macroeconomic Context," in R. Hausman and L. Rojas-Suarez, eds, *Banking Crises in Latin America*, 27–63. Baltimore: Inter-American Development Bank and Johns Hopkins University Press.

Goldstein, Morris (1998), *The Asian Financial Crisis: Causes, Cures, and Sytemic Implications*. Washington: Institute for International Economics.

Goodfriend, Marvin (1993), "Interest Rate Policy and the Inflation Scare Problem: 1979–1992," *Federal Reserve Bank of Richmond Economic Quarterly*, 79(1) (Winter), 1–24.

Goodhart, Charles, and Jose Vinals (1994), "Strategy and Tactics of Monetary Policy: Examples from Europe and the Antipodes" in Jeffrey Fuhrer, ed., *Goals, Guidelines, and Constraints Facing Monetary Policymakers*. Boston: Federal Reserve Bank.

Haldane, Andrew G., ed. (1995), *Targeting Inflation*. London: Bank of England.

Kaminsky, G. L., and C. M. Reinhart (1996), "The Twin Crises: The Causes of Banking and Balance-of-Payments Problems," in Board of Governors of the Federal Reserve System, International Finance Discussion Papers No. 544 (March).

Kydland, Finn E., and Edward C. Prescott (1977), "Rules Rather Than Discretion: The Inconsistency of Optimal Plans," *Journal of Political Economy*, 85, 473–91.

Leiderman, Leonardo, and Lars E. O. Svensson, eds. (1995), *Inflation Targeting*. London: Centre for Economic Policy Research.

McCallum, Bennett T. (1995), "Two Fallacies Concerning Central-Bank Independence," *American Economic Review*, 85 (May), 207–11.

———— (1996), "Inflation Targeting in Canada, New Zealand, Sweden, the United Kingdom, and in General," NBER Working Paper, No. 5597 (May).

Mishkin, F. S. (1991), "Asymmetric Information and Financial Crises: A Historical Perspective," in R. G. Hubbard, ed., *Financial Markets and Financial Crises*, 69–108. Chicago: University of Chicago Press.

———— (1994), "Preventing Financial Crises: An International Perspective," *Manchester School*, 62, 1–40.

———— (1996), "Understanding Financial Crises: A Developing Country Perspective," in Michael Bruno and Boris Pleskovic, eds, *Annual World Bank Conference on Development Economics 1996*, 29–62. Washington: World Bank.

———— (1997a), "Strategies for Controlling Inflation," in Phillip Lowe, ed., *Monetary Policy and Inflation Targeting*, 7–38. Sydney: Reserve Bank of Australia.

———— (1997b), "International Capital Movements, Financial Volatility and Financial Instability," in *Proceedings of the Annual Conference 1997*. German Association of Economic and Social Sciences.

———— (1998), "International Experiences with Different Monetary Policy Regimes," mimeo. for the Riksbank-IIES Conference on Monetary Policy Rules, Stockholm, Sweden, 12–13 June.

————, and A. S. Posen (1997), "Inflation Targeting: Lessons from Four Countries," Federal Reserve Bank of New York, *Economic Policy Review*, 3 (August), 9–110.

Morande, Felipe, and Klaus Schmidt-Hebbel (1997), "Inflation Targets and Indexation in Chile," manuscript, Central Bank of Chile, August.

Obstfeld, Maurice, and Kenneth Rogoff (1995), "The Mirage of Fixed Exchange Rates," *Journal of Economic Perspectives*, 9 (Fall), 73–96.

Posen, Adam S. (1995), "Declarations are Not Enough: Financial Sector Sources of Central Bank Independence," *NBER Macroeconomics Annual 1995*, 253–74.

Sarel, Michael (1996), "Nonlinear Effects of Inflation on Economic Growth," *International Monetary Fund Staff Papers*, 43 (March), 199–215.

18 The Mirage of Exchange-Rate Regimes for Emerging Market Countries

Guillermo A. Calvo and Frederic S. Mishkin

In recent years, a number of emerging market countries have experienced devastating financial crises and macroeconomic turbulence, including Argentina (2001–2002), Turkey (2000–2001), Ecuador (1999), Russia (1998), east Asia (1997), Mexico (1994–1995) and even Chile (1982). In the ensuing postmortems, an active debate has followed over how the choice of exchange rate regime might have contributed to macroeconomic instability—and conversely, how a shift in exchange rate regime might have improved macroeconomic performance. Should an emerging market economy prefer a floating exchange rate, a fixed exchange rate or some blend of the two, like an exchange rate that was usually fixed but might sometimes shift?

Many countries used to choose an intermediate path: that is, an exchange rate that was often stabilized by the central bank, but might sometimes shift, often known as a "soft peg." However, in the aftermath of the macroeconomic crisis across east Asia in 1997–1998, a view emerged that this exchange rate regime was in part responsible for the depth of the macroeconomic crisis. The governments of Thailand, Malaysia, South Korea and other nations in that region had kept exchange rates fixed. There was no explicit institutional guarantee that the exchange rate would remain fixed, but the rates had been stable for long enough that local financial institutions borrowed in dollars abroad and then loaned freely in U.S. dollars to domestic borrowers. But when a surge of foreign investment stopped, the existing exchange rate became unsustainable. For example, when the Thai baht collapsed against the U.S. dollar, Thai borrowers were unable to repay their dollar-denominated loans—and in turn many Thai financial institutions were insolvent. This meltdown of the financial sector led to an enormous economic contraction.

Thus, one often-told lesson of the east Asian experience is that nations must make a bipolar choice: either choose a framework for credibly guaranteeing a fixed exchange rate, known as a "hard peg," or else accept a freely floating exchange rate.[1] Yet neither of these extreme exchange rate regimes has an unblemished record, either.

There are two basic ways a government can offer a credible guarantee of a fixed exchange rate: a currency board and full dollarization. In a currency board, the note-issuing authority, whether the central bank or the government, fixes a conversion rate for this currency vis-à-vis a foreign currency (say, U.S. dollars) and provides full convertibility because it stands ready to exchange domestically issued notes for the foreign currency on demand and has enough international reserves to do so. Full dollarization involves eliminating the domestic currency altogether and replacing it with a foreign currency like the U.S. dollar, which is why it is referred to as "dollarization," although it could instead involve the use of another currency, like the euro. This commitment is even stronger than a currency board because it makes it much more difficult—though not impossible—for the government to regain control of monetary policy and/or set a new parity for the (nonexistent) domestic currency.

Argentina, for example, chose the currency board approach for ensuring a fixed exchange rate. Indeed, Argentina even recognized that full backing of the monetary base may not be enough, because that would leave the banking system without a lender of last resort or a situation where the government might need additional credit, so the Argentines also paid for contingent credit lines. From a legal perspective, the central bank of Argentina was highly independent. But in 2001, large budget deficits (including contingent government obligations, like supporting state-owned banks) forced the Argentine government to look for a new source of funds. After Domingo Cavallo became Minister of the Economy in April 2001, the supposedly independent central bank president, Pedro Pou, was forced to resign. Soon after, Argentina's prudential and regulatory regime for its financial sector, which had been one of the best in the emerging market world, was weakened. Banks were encouraged and coerced into purchasing Argentine government bonds to fund the fiscal debt. An attempt was made to reactivate the economy via expansive monetary policy. With the value of these bonds declining as the likelihood of default on this debt increased, banks' net worth plummeted. The likely insolvency of the banks then led to a classic run on the banks and a full-scale banking crisis by the end of 2001. Because most debt instruments in Argentina were denominated in U.S. dollars, the depreciation of the Argentinean currency made it impossible for borrowers to earn enough Argentinean currency to repay their dollar-denominated loans. The Argentine financial sector melted down, and the economy, as well. Argentina's experiment with its currency board ended up in disaster.

The remaining option of freely floating exchange rates is also problematic. Without further elaboration, "floating exchange rate" means really nothing other than that the regime will allow for *some* exchange rate flexibility. It rules out a fixed exchange rate regime, but nothing else. A country that allows a floating exchange rate may pursue a number of very different monetary policy strategies: for example, targeting the money supply, targeting the inflation rate or a discretionary approach in which the nominal anchor is implicit but not explicit (the "just do it" approach, described in Mishkin, 1999b, 2000, and Bernanke, Laubach, Mishkin and Posen, 1999). But regardless of the choice of monetary regime, in many emerging market economies, exports, imports and international capital flows are a relatively large share of the economy, so large swings in the exchange rate can cause very substantial swings in the real economy. Even a central bank that would prefer to let the exchange rate float must be aware that if the country's banks have made loans in U.S. dollars, then a depreciation of the currency versus the dollar can greatly injure the financial system. Under these circumstances, the monetary authority is likely to display "fear of floating" (Calvo and Reinhart, 2002), defined as a reluctance to allow totally free fluctuations in the nominal or real exchange rate, which Mussa (1986) showed are very closely linked.

Thus, the literature on exchange rate regimes seems to have backed itself into a corner where none of the available options is without problems. In this chapter, we argue that much of the debate on choosing an exchange rate regime misses the boat. We will begin by discussing the standard theory of choice between exchange rate regimes, and then explore the weaknesses in this theory, especially when it is applied to emerging market economies. We discuss a range of institutional traits that might predispose a country to favor either fixed or floating rates and then turn to the converse question of whether the choice of exchange rate regime may favor the development of certain desirable institutional traits. Overall, we believe that the key to macroeconomic success in emerging market countries is not primarily their choice of exchange rate regime, but rather the health of the countries' fundamental macroeconomic institutions, including the institutions associated with fiscal stability, financial stability and monetary stability. In general, we believe that less attention should be focused on the general question of whether a floating or a fixed exchange rate is preferable and more on these deeper institutional arrangements.

18.1 The Standard Theory of Choosing an Exchange Rate Regime

Much of the analysis of choosing an exchange rate regime has taken place using the theory of optimal exchange rate regimes—and its close relative, the theory of optimal currency areas—which owes much to Mundell (1961) and Poole (1970). Models of choosing an exchange rate regime typically evaluate such regimes by how effective they are in reducing the variance of domestic output in an economy with sticky prices.

If an economy faces primarily nominal shocks—that is, shocks that arise from money supply or demand—then a regime of fixed exchange rates looks attractive. If a monetary shock causes inflation, it will also tend to depreciate a floating exchange rate and thus transmit a nominal shock into a real one. In this setting, the fixed exchange rate provides a mechanism to accommodate a change in the money demand or supply with less output volatility.

On the other hand, if the shocks are real—like a shock to productivity, or to the terms of trade (that is, if the relationship between export prices and import prices shifts due to movements in demand or supply)—then exchange rate flexibility of some sort becomes appealing. In this case, the economy needs to respond to a change in relative equilibrium prices, like the relative price of tradables with respect to nontradables. A shift in the nominal exchange rate offers a speedy way of implementing such a change and, thus, ameliorating the impact of these shocks on output and employment (De Grauwe, 1997). On the other hand, if a downturn is driven by real factors in an economy with a fixed exchange rate, the demand for domestic money falls and the central bank is forced to absorb excess money supply in exchange for foreign currency. The result is that (under perfect capital mobility) the decrease in the demand for domestic money leads to an automatic outflow of hard currency and a rise in interest rates. In this case, the hard peg contributes to increasing the depth of the downturn.

This standard model of choosing an exchange rate regime offers some useful insights. However, it ultimately fails to address a challenge issued by Mundell himself in his original 1961 paper, and many of the underpinnings of the model do not apply especially well to emerging market economies.

18.1.1 The Mundell Challenge

In Robert Mundell's (1961) original paper on optimum currency areas, he pointed out that this theory implies that the optimality of fixed exchange rates *within* a given country cannot be taken for granted. Why should Texas and New York in the United States, or Tucuman and Buenos Aires in Argentina, share the same currency? These regions are hit by different real shocks and would, according to the standard theory, benefit by the extra degree of freedom provided by having their own currencies and allow them to float against each other. We will call this deep observation the "Mundell challenge."

The usual response to the Mundell challenge is that a country has internal mechanisms that can substitute for regional exchange rate variability, including labor mobility between regions and compensatory fiscal transfers from the central government. However, these arguments are only partially persuasive. Fiscal transfers, in contrast to currency devaluation, do not change relative prices. Moreover, labor mobility is a poor substitute for exchange rate flexibility. Imagine the social costs of having to ship people from Texas to New York, when a simple movement in the exchange rate would have restored equilibrium.

Indeed, the Mundell challenge cuts even more deeply. After all, why should exchange rate flexibility be limited to large regions like New York or Texas? Why not have differing exchange rates between cities or neighborhoods? Indeed, why not move to a world of complete contingent contracts, with no money at all, and thus in effect have a different flexible exchange rate for every transaction? Of course, no one has pushed the theory to this implausible extreme. However, *not* pushing the theory in this way implies acknowledging the existence of other factors that are key and, actually, that dominate the factors emphasized by the theory of exchange rate regimes.

An important set of such factors relate to the observation that modern economies have not yet been able to function without some kind of money. The fundamental functions of money are to reduce transactions costs and to address liquidity concerns, functions that are especially valuable in a world with seriously incomplete state-contingent markets. A common currency is a useful coordinating mechanism within a national economy, even if it can sometimes go awry. Similarly, a fixed exchange rate may be a useful mechanism for an economy, even if that country faces differential real shocks, because the gains from reducing transactions costs and providing liquidity are great enough. Thus, in choosing an exchange rate regime, it is not enough to analyze the nature of the shocks. The potential benefits from fixed exchange rates must be taken into accounts, too.

18.1.2   The Realities of Emerging Market Economies

The standard framework for choosing an exchange rate regime is based on a number of implicit assumptions that do not apply well to many emerging economies. The standard theory presumes an ability to set up institutions that will assure a fixed exchange rate, but after the experience of Argentina, this assumption of an institutional guarantee seems improbable. The standard theory assumes that a time-consistent choice is made on the exchange rate regime, when in many countries the exchange rate regime may frequently shift. In the standard model of exchange rate choices, the focus is on adjustments in goods and labor markets and the financial sector is thoroughly ignored. However, no recent macroeconomic crisis in an emerging market has been free from financial turmoil of one form or another. Finally, as mentioned a moment ago, the standard exchange rate model pays no attention to transaction costs and liquidity considerations, which are essential to explain why money should exist in the first place. This issue is especially severe for emerging market economies, where the lack of contingent contracts is more severe than in advanced economies.

To illustrate the shortcomings of the standard model of choosing an exchange rate regime for emerging markets, and also to highlight some of the main issues in making such a choice, it is useful to identify several institutional features that are common in emerging market economies: weak fiscal, financial and monetary institutions; currency substitution and liability dollarization; and vulnerability to sudden stops of outside capital flows.

Weak fiscal, financial and monetary institutions make emerging market countries highly vulnerable to high inflation and currency crises. A key lesson from the "unpleasant monetarist arithmetic" discussed in Sargent and Wallace (1981) and the recent literature on fiscal theories of the price level (Woodford, 1994, 1995) is that irresponsible fiscal policy puts pressure on the monetary authorities to monetize the debt, thereby producing rapid money growth, high inflation and downward pressure on the exchange rate. Similarly, poor regulation and supervision of the financial system can result in large losses in bank balance sheets that make it impossible for the monetary authorities to raise interest rates in a way that holds down inflation or to prop up the exchange rate because doing so would likely lead to a collapse of the financial system (Mishkin, 2003). Also, a frail banking system can produce fiscal instability, and hence high inflation and devaluations, because the need for a bailout can imply a huge unfunded government liability (Burnside, Eichenbaum and Rebelo, 2001). Weak monetary institutions in which there is little commitment to the goal of price stability or the independence of the central bank mean that the monetary authorities will not have the support or the tools to keep inflation under control or to prevent large depreciations of the currency. Thus, in an economy where the government may run up enormous fiscal deficits, banks are poorly regulated and the central bank may recklessly expand the money supply, the real value of money cannot be taken for granted.

Firms and individuals in emerging market countries react to the threat that their money may dramatically change in value—either through inflation or the exchange rate—by turning to *currency substitution*, where they use a foreign currency for many transactions (Calvo and Végh, 1996). Currency substitution is likely to be due not only to past inflationary experience resulting from weak monetary, fiscal and financial institutions, but also to the fact that a currency like the U.S. dollar is a key unit of account for international transactions. This phenomenon induces the monetary authority to allow banks to offer foreign exchange deposits—that is, a firm in Argentina can deposit U.S. dollars directly in an Argentine bank without converting to local currency.[2]

Foreign exchange deposits induce banks—partly for regulatory reasons that prevent banks from taking exchange rate risk—to offer loans denominated in foreign currency, usually U.S. dollars, leading to what is called *liability dollarization*. Liability dollarization leads to an entirely different impact of a sharp currency devaluation in an emerging market (Mishkin, 1996; Calvo, 2001). In emerging market countries, a sharp real currency depreciation creates a situation where those who have borrowed in U.S. dollars are unable to repay. The money they are earning is in local currency, but their debts are in U.S. dollars. Thus, the net worth of corporations and individuals falls, especially those whose earnings are primarily in local currency. The result is many bankruptcies and loan defaults, a sharp decline in lending and

Table 18.1
The Incidence of Sudden Stops, 1992–2001

	Emerging markets		Developed economies	
Event type	Number of episodes	Percentage of total	Number of episodes	Percentage of total
Devaluations associated with sudden stop	12	63	4	17
Of which: First sudden stop, then devaluation	8	42	2	9
First devaluation, then sudden stop	4	21	2	9
Devaluations not associated with sudden stop	7	37	19	83

Notes: A sudden stop is defined as a reversal in capital inflows that i) exceeds the mean minus two standard deviations of the annual change in capital inflows observed since 1990, and ii) is associated with a decline in output. The exercise also considers rises in the real exchange rate that i) exceed the mean plus two standard deviations of the annual change in the real exchange rate observed since 1990, and ii) are greater than 20 percent. The sample consists of 15 emerging economies and 17 developed countries. See Calvo, Izquierdo, and Mejía (2003) for further details and some sensitivity analysis.

an economic contraction. Liability dollarization may become a major problem for countries where the level of dollar borrowing has been especially high and where the economy is relatively closed so that most parties earn only in local currency, as has recently been the case in several emerging market countries (Calvo, Izquierdo and Talvi, 2002). However, not all emerging market countries suffer from liability dollarization in a serious way; for example, Chile and South Africa, which have stronger monetary, fiscal and financial institutions, are commonly cited exceptions (Eichengreen, Hausmann and Panizza, 2002).

Vulnerability to large negative changes in capital inflows, which often have a largely unanticipated component (Calvo and Reinhart, 2000), also contributes to susceptibility to currency and financial crises. Table 18.1 shows the incidence of these *sudden stops* over the last decade. Table 18.1 shows that this phenomenon is mostly confined to emerging market countries and is more likely to be associated with large currency devaluations in these countries, probably because of their weak fiscal and financial institutions. (The precise definition of a "sudden stop" and "large" devaluations are found in the note to the table.) In addition, preliminary evidence suggests that there is a high degree of bunching of sudden stops across emerging market countries. This bunching is especially evident after the Russian 1998 crisis and also after the recent Wall Street scandals that included Enron and other firms. This pattern leads us to conjecture that, to a large extent, sudden stops have been a result of factors somewhat external to emerging market countries as a group.[3]

The links from weak institutions and sudden stops to currency substitution and liability dollarization—and then the links from liability dollarization to collapsed balance sheets and economic downturn—naturally differ from country to country.[4] But currency depreciations and sudden stops bring about large changes in relative prices and have a deep impact on income distribution and wealth (Calvo, Izquierdo and

Talvi, 2002). In addition, the sudden stop is typically associated with a sharp fall in growth rates, if not outright collapse in output and employment. A floating exchange rate is clearly the wrong prescription for this situation, since it allows the sharp depreciation that cripples balance sheets and the financial sector. But under the dual stresses of weak institutions and sudden stops, it is not clear that a fixed exchange rate is sustainable, either. Rather than focusing on the choice of exchange rate regime, the appropriate answer to this situation would seem to be an improvement in fiscal, financial and monetary institutions. Such an improvement would limit the amount of currency substitution and liability dollarization and also make the economy more resilient in reacting to sudden stops when they occur. In more graphic terms: "It's the institutions, stupid."

18.2 Choosing between Exchange Rate Regimes

No exchange rate regime can prevent macroeconomic turbulence. But the choice of exchange rate regime can be better- or worse-suited to the economic institutions and characteristics of an economy. In the discussion that follows, we will focus primarily on the overall choice between fixed and floating exchange rates. However, it is worth remembering that exchange rate regimes come in a wide variety of arrangements: currency boards, dollarization, soft pegs, crawling bands, free floating and many others. Moreover, a floating exchange rate regime can be accompanied by a number of different domestically oriented monetary policies (inflation targeting, monetary targeting or a "just do it" discretionary approach).

18.2.1 The Ability to Have Domestic Monetary Policy
The strongest argument in favor of a floating exchange rate regime is that it retains the flexibility to use monetary policy to focus on domestic considerations. In contrast, a hard exchange rate peg leaves very narrow scope for domestic monetary policy, because the interest rate is determined by monetary policy in the anchor country to which the emerging market country has pegged. However, in emerging market economies, this argument is more relevant in some institutional contexts than in others.

One difficulty that emerging market economies face is that their capital markets are geared to interest rates set in major financial centers. Frankel, Schmukler and Serven (2002) show, for example, that in Latin America, all interest rates reflect changes in U.S. interest rates and, furthermore, that countries that do not peg to the dollar see their interest rates change by a larger factor than those that do. In addition, emerging market economies may be hit as a group with financial contagion, as noted earlier, which will affect their interest rates. The central bank in an emerging market country thus faces real practical difficulties.

Moreover, although a floating exchange rate raises the theoretical possibility for domestic monetary authorities to pursue countercyclical monetary policy, the central bank may not possess this capability in practice. If the monetary authorities have little credibility in terms of their commitment to price stability, then monetary policy may be ineffective. For a central bank without inflation-fighting credibility, an expansionary monetary policy will only lead to an immediate jump in interest rates and/or the price level.

Building credible monetary institutions is a difficult task. It requires a public and institutional commitment to price stability. Some of this commitment can be expressed through laws and rules that assure the central bank will be allowed to set the monetary policy instruments without interference from the government, that the members of the monetary policy board must be insulated from the political process and that the central bank is prohibited from funding government deficits. There is a large literature on the forms that central bank independence can take (for example, Cukierman, 1992), but what is written down in the law may be less important than the political culture and history of the country. The contrast between Argentina and Canada is instructive here. Legally, the central bank of Canada does not look particularly independent. In the event of a disagreement between the Bank of Canada and the government, the minister of finance can issue a directive that the bank must follow. However because the directive must be specific and in writing and because the Bank of Canada is a trusted public institution, a government override of the bank is likely to cost the ruling party heavily in the polls. Thus, in practice, the Bank of Canada is highly independent. In contrast, the central bank of Argentina was highly independent from a legal perspective. However, this did not stop the Argentine government from forcing the resignation of the highly respected president of the central bank and replacing him with a president who would do the government's bidding. It is unimaginable in countries like Canada, the United States or in Europe that the public would tolerate the removal of the head of the central bank in such a manner, and, indeed, we do not know of any case of this happening in recent history.[5]

Many emerging market countries, like Argentina, have had a history of poor support for the price stability goal, and laws supporting central bank independence in these countries are easily overturned. It is therefore important for such countries to develop genuine public and political support for central bank independence as well as legal independence in order to have the ability to conduct domestic monetary policy successfully.

If an emerging market country is able to develop fiscal, financial and monetary institutions that provide credibility for society's pursuit of price stability, then monetary policy can be used to stabilize the economy. However, not all emerging market countries are up to this task, and so they may decide to choose a hard exchange rate peg instead. (However, the absence of strong institutions may make it difficult for them to sustain the hard peg.)

This interdependence between institutions and exchange rate regimes helps to explain the general empirical finding that whether a country has a fixed or flexible exchange rate tells us little about whether it has higher economic growth or smaller output fluctuations. Indeed, when you look more closely at which emerging market countries have successful macroeconomic performance, the exchange rate regime appears to be far less important than deeper institutional features of the economy relating to fiscal stability, financial stability and the credibility of monetary institutions that promote price stability.[6] However, there is some evidence that floating exchange rate regimes can help countries cope with terms-of-trade shocks and might promote economic growth (Broda, 2001; Levy-Yeyati and Sturzenegger, 2003).

18.2.2   Reducing Inflation

Just as the main advantage of a floating exchange rate may be that it allows the monetary authorities some discretion and flexibility to use monetary policy to cope with shocks to the domestic economy, the main weakness of a floating exchange rate may be that it allows too much discretion to monetary policy and so may not provide a sufficient nominal anchor (for example, Calvo, 2001; Calvo and Mendoza, 2000).

Of course, many emerging market countries have been able to keep inflation under control with flexible exchange rate regimes, which is why the evidence on whether fixed versus floating exchange rate regimes are associated with lower inflation rates on average is not clear-cut (for example, Edwards and Magendzo, 2001; Reinhart and Rogoff, 2002). But a central bank can only work to reduce inflation if it is supported by the public and the political process. In some countries, giving the central bank an explicit focus on inflation targeting can help focus the public debate so that it supports a monetary policy focus on long-run goals such as price stability (Bernanke, Laubach, Mishkin and Posen, 1999). However, these benefits require excellent communication skills on the part of the central bank in what can be a swirling political environment in emerging market countries.

18.2.3   A Misaligned Exchange Rate?

One danger of a hard exchange rate peg is the risk of being locked into a misaligned exchange rate, which can be defined as a sizable difference between its actual level and the one to which "fundamentals" would dictate. This possibility supports the case for flexible exchange rates, but again, the situation is more complex than it may at first seem.

Even in a country with a fixed nominal exchange rate, it is possible to use taxes and subsidies on imports and exports to alter the effective real exchange rate. For example, a uniform tax on imports accompanied by a uniform subsidy on exports of the same size is equivalent to a *real* currency depreciation—even though the nominal exchange rate stays unchanged. Moreover, a tax-and-subsidy-induced fiscal devaluation has one built-in advantage over nominal denomination. The fiscal devaluation has an upper bound, determined by the fact that beyond a certain point, tax evasion becomes rampant. Nominal devaluation, on the other hand, has no upper bound and can lead to high inflation.

But fiscal devaluation may be difficult to implement in a timely and effective manner without well-run fiscal institutions. For example, politicians may be quick to impose a tax on imports out of protectionist sentiment, happy to use a fiscal devaluation as an excuse, but then slow to remove that import tax later when the reason for the devaluation has evaporated.

18.2.4 Expanding the Gains from Trade

A hard exchange rate peg will tend to promote openness to trade and economic integration (Frankel and Rose, 2002; Rose, 2000). For example, an exchange rate fixed to the U.S. dollar will likely promote trade with the United States and other countries tied to the U.S. dollar. Fixed exchange rates or even a common regional currency as in the European monetary union may help regional economic integration (this point is also discussed further below in connection with the effect of exchange rate regimes on institutions). Thus, countries that are seeking to expand trade would naturally place a higher value on some form of a fixed exchange rate with a trading partner.

Along with gains from trade, an economy that is more open to trade may also be less susceptible to sudden stops. An expansion of trade means that a greater share of businesses are involved in the tradable sector. Because the goods they produce are traded internationally, they are more likely to be priced in foreign currency, which means that their balance sheets are less exposed to negative consequences from a devaluation of the currency when their debts are denominated in foreign currency. Then, a devaluation that raises the value of their debt in terms of domestic currency is also likely to raise the value of their assets as well, thus insulating their balance sheets from the devaluation.[7] Moreover, the more open is the economy, the smaller will be the required real currency depreciation following a sudden stop (Calvo, Izquierdo and Talvi, 2002).

18.2.5 Reducing the Risk Premium in Interest Rates

Advocates of hard exchange rate pegs suggest that it can reduce the currency risk component in domestic interest rates, thus lowering the borrowing costs for both the government and the private sector and improving the outlook for financial deepening, investment and growth. Some, such as Schuler (1999), have even gone so far as to suggest that dollarization will allow domestic interest rates in emerging market countries to converge to those in the United States.

However, the risk of government default and the related risk of confiscation of private assets denominated in both domestic and foreign currency are more likely to be the source of high interest rates in emerging market countries than is currency risk. The experience of Ecuador serves to illustrate this point. The spread between Ecuador's sovereign bonds and U.S. Treasury bonds remained at high levels in the first half of 2000, even though the government had already dollarized in January of the same year. Spreads came down considerably only after the government reached an agreement with its creditors in August 2000 that resulted in a substantial debt reduction of 40 percent. Sound fiscal policies that make government defaults extremely unlikely are thus essential to getting interest rates to approach those in advanced countries. Indeed, Chile, with its flexible exchange rate regime, has been able to achieve lower interest rates on its sovereign debt than Panama, which is dollarized (Edwards, 2001).

18.2.6   Flexibility in Wages and Prices

It is possible that emerging market economies, with their large informal sectors, have greater price and wage flexibility than developed economies. An economy with highly flexible wages and prices has less need of a flexible exchange rate.

To some extent, the degree of flexibility in wages and prices is controlled by government regulation. For example, public sector wages are often a component of the economy that is quite inflexible. However, it may be politically palatable to index public sector wages to their comparable private sector wages and thus create greater flexibility. In general, an emerging market economy with a greater degree of flexibility in wages and prices will benefit less from the additional flexibility of a floating exchange rate.

18.2.7   Widespread Loans in a Foreign Currency

Liability dollarization makes a policy of freely floating exchange rates more difficult to sustain. When the monetary authority knows that a currency devaluation can lead to extreme stress on the financial sector, it cannot turn a blind eye to exchange rate fluctuations (Mishkin and Savastano, 2001). A large devaluation when there is extensive liability dollarization raises the value of the foreign-denominated debt, deals a heavy blow to balance sheets and therefore can lead to a full-fledged financial crisis (Mishkin, 1996).[8]

The extent of liability dollarization is partly affected by government financial regulatory policy. For example, banking regulations can help to ensure that financial institutions match up any foreign-denominated liabilities with foreign-denominated assets and thus reduce currency risk. But even when the banks have equal foreign-denominated (dollar) assets and liabilities, if banks' dollar assets are loans to companies in dollars who themselves are unhedged, then banks are effectively unhedged against currency devaluations because the dollar loans become nonperforming when the devaluation occurs; for discussion of how this problem occurred in Mexico, see Mishkin (1996) and Garber (1999). Thus, limiting currency mismatches may require additional government policies to limit liability dollarization or at least reduce the incentives for it to occur. If a country wishes to choose a floating exchange regime, it would be wise to implement financial regulatory policies to discourage currency mismatches and liability dollarization.[9] For example, both Chile and Argentina experienced a sudden stop after the 1998 Russian crisis, but the impact on the Chilean economy was relatively small because Chile's stronger fiscal, financial and monetary institutions have resulted in much less liability dollarization.

18.2.8 International Reserves

A hard peg exchange rate system, like a currency board, may require a substantial war chest of international reserves. It may seem that a floating exchange rate system could avoid the cost of these reserves, but this conclusion would be too simple.

Many large emerging market economies like Mexico, Chile and Brazil, which have a floating exchange rate and have announced a domestic monetary policy aimed at targeting inflation, also have large international reserves. Indeed, they occasionally hold international reserves in excess of monetary base. Because of these large reserves, it could be said that such countries "float with a large life jacket." Why do large reserves appear to be necessary even with floating exchange rates? One explanation is that international reserves provide collateral for public bonds issued in connection with open market operations. Another explanation is that even a nation with a floating exchange rate must be concerned about the possibility of a run on its currency. Finally, policymakers in emerging market economies are very sensitive to the exchange rate because many such economies often exhibit a high pass-through coefficient; that is, devaluation often leads to inflation (González, 2000; Hausmann, Panizza and Stein, 2001).

Thus, nations with a domestically oriented monetary policy and floating exchange rates also have good reasons to carry high reserves, and it does not appear that they typically have much smaller reserves than nations with fixed exchange rates.

18.2.9 Lender of Last Resort

A hard exchange rate peg is sometimes said to be at a disadvantage relative to a floating exchange rate regime because it cannot accommodate a money-printing lender of last resort. While this argument would seem to weaken the case for fixed exchange rates, the scope for a lender of last resort for emerging market countries with floating rates is oversold (Calvo, 2001; Mishkin, 1999a, 2001).

In advanced economies, the monetary authority can issue liquidity to bail out the banking system, but this extra liquidity is expected to be soaked up by open market operations in the near future, so that bank bailouts can stabilize the banking system with little if any inflationary consequence. In contrast, in emerging market countries, central bank lending to the banking system in the wake of a financial crisis—characterized by a sudden stop in capital inflows—is likely to unleash fears of an inflationary explosion and produce a sharp exchange rate depreciation. If there is substantial liability dollarization, the depreciation will then have a major negative impact on private sector balance sheets, which will then promote even more financial instability.

This discussion reemphasizes an earlier lesson. If monetary institutions are well developed and the central bank has sufficient credibility, only then can the central bank act as a lender of last resort. Alternatively, a government can secure contingent credit lines (like the central bank of Argentina did during the so-called Convertibility Program), but these credit lines can be very expensive and may not be sufficient when a crisis hits.

18.2.10   Shifts from Fixed to Floating Regimes

Even if a country might be better served in the long run by adopting a floating exchange rate regime, the timing of the shift from a peg can have serious economic consequences. The costs of shifting from a fixed exchange rate regime to a floating regime under conditions of economic stress, like a sudden stop, are especially striking. As discussed earlier, a move from a fixed to a floating exchange rate regime in the midst of a sudden stop is likely to exacerbate the crisis. The initial devaluation that raises the value of foreign-denominated debt can cause widespread destruction of corporation and household balance sheets, which sends the economy into a devastating downward spiral. Recent papers by Caballero and Krishnamurthy (2003) and Jeanne (2002) also suggest that de-dollarization (the reestablishment of a domestic currency) may require a major overhaul of the domestic financial sector. Development of the necessary institutions to support a successful domestically oriented monetary policy takes time.

18.3   Can Exchange Rate Regimes Improve Economic Institutions?

The discussion in the preceding section focuses on what institutional traits or policy concerns should cause a country to prefer fixed or floating exchange rates. But the possibility of reverse causation also deserves consideration. Perhaps the choice of exchange rate regime should not be analyzed as a response to existing institutional traits, but instead as a potential cause of preferred institutional outcomes. Research on theories of institutional development in emerging market countries is in its early stages, but is developing rapidly (for example, see La Porta, Lopez-de-Silanes, Shleifer and Vishny, 1998; Shleifer and Vishny, 1999; Boone, Breach, Friedman and Johnson, 2000). Several intriguing hypotheses about how exchange rate regimes may improve institutions have been proposed.

Advocates of hard exchange rate pegs argue that they improve fiscal institutions and trigger sounder budgetary management, because if the central bank is focused on a fixed exchange rate, then the government no longer has access to the money printing press to finance its spending (for example, Hanke and Schuler, 1994). As the recent example of Argentina suggests, where the fiscal tensions between the provinces and the central government were not solved by the currency board, hard pegs may be less effective at constraining fiscal policy than was previously believed. Hard pegs may even weaken incentives for governments to put their fiscal house in order, because the hard peg may make it easier for governments to borrow foreign funds, thus allowing them to delay necessary reforms to fix fiscal imbalances. For example, Panama (which has been dollarized for close to 100 years) has had poor fiscal performance, with fiscal deficits over 7 percent in the 1970s and averaging 5 percent in the 1980s—it is just in recent years that the fiscal position has improved to the point that the fiscal surplus averaged 1.4 percent during the 1990s. On the other hand, it is not clear that in floating exchange rate systems, the conduct of monetary policy has any particular impact in promoting fiscal responsibility. However, one might argue that a floating exchange rate, particularly if it involves the government in setting an inflation target, has the potential to promote government transparency and fiscal responsibility.

Advocates of hard pegs also suggest that dollarization promotes a healthier financial system because it avoids currency mismatches and deepens the financial system, making it less prone to crisis (for example, Hausmann, 1999). However, there is little evidence to support this view (Eichengreen, 2002). On the other hand, a hard exchange rate peg in the form of a currency board might encourage unhedged dollar (foreign-denominated) liabilities that nonfinancial and financial firms might be willing to undertake, thus making the financial system more vulnerable in case the system has to be abandoned, as illustrated by Argentina in 2002. The hard peg might also encourage the issuance of dollar liabilities because financial firms would believe that the government would feel responsible for any devaluation and would, thus, be more likely to offer a bailout (McKinnon and Pill, 1999; Broda and Levy-Yeyati, 2000). However, the evidence that floating rate regimes lead to less liability dollarization is quite weak (Honing, 2003). After all, on its face, a floating exchange rate would seem to encourage holding some assets in several different currencies as a form of diversification. For example, Peru, with its floating exchange rate regime, has a tremendous amount of liability dollarization, while Brazil, when it had a quasi-fixed exchange regime rate in the period of 1994 to 1999, did not.

Can the choice of exchange rate regime help improve monetary institutions that enable the monetary authorities to build credibility? If a fixed exchange rate regime is constructed with a full array of supporting institutions, then it would seem to offer at least a gain in credibility—although after the collapse of Argentina's fixed rate system, such credibility will always remain incomplete. Moreover, a floating exchange rate can be a mechanism for monetary credibility as well, Tornell and Velasco (2000) argue, because the foreign exchange market will anticipate the effects of policy inconsistency by devaluing the exchange rate, providing a clear signal that something is rotten. Moreover, the signal itself could help establish some discipline in government's quarters and possibly lead to a timely rectification of policy inconsistencies (Mishkin, 1998).

Although at the outset, the credibility of the monetary authorities might be weak and the public support for central bank independence may not be all that strong, adoption of inflation targeting might help the central bank to work to produce "constrained discretion" (Bernanke and Mishkin, 1997) in which transparent discussion of the conduct of monetary policy and accountability of the central bank for achieving its inflation target might make it more difficult for the central bank to follow overly expansionary monetary policy. In addition, over time it may help obtain credibility for the central bank as it did in Chile, and it may also increase support for the central bank independence. Indeed, Mishkin and Posen (1997) and Bernanke, Laubach, Mishkin and Posen (1999) suggest that the support for central bank independence in the United Kingdom was a direct result of the inflation targeting regime. However, although inflation targeting might help with central bank credibility and support for central bank independence to some extent, a fair degree of support for good monetary institutions already needs to be present if inflation targeting is to have a chance of success.

There is some evidence that hard exchange rate pegs, particularly those in currency unions, do encourage openness to trade and integration with the countries to which the currency is pegged (Frankel and Rose, 2002; Rose, 2000). As we mentioned earlier, trade openness can reduce the vulnerability of emerging markets to financial crises, while economic integration with an anchor country reduces the cost of the loss of domestic monetary policy with a hard peg.

The possible connections between exchange rate regimes and the improvement of economic institutions is a potentially important topic for future research.

18.4   The Choice of Exchange Rate Regimes in Context

When choosing between exchange rate regimes, one size does not fit all (or always). This argues against international financial institutions like the International Monetary Fund, the World Bank and other development banks having a strong bias toward one type of exchange rate regime. Instead, an informed choice of exchange rate regime requires a deep understanding of a country's economy, institutions and political culture.

Indeed, we believe that the choice of exchange rate regime is likely to be of second order importance to the development of good fiscal, financial and monetary institutions in producing macroeconomic success in emerging market countries. Rather than treating the exchange rate regime as a primary choice, we would encourage a greater focus on institutional reforms like improved bank and financial sector regulation, fiscal restraint, building consensus for a sustainable and predictable monetary policy and increasing openness to trade. A focus on institutional reforms rather than on the exchange rate regime may encourage emerging market countries to be healthier and less prone to crises than we have seen in recent years.

Acknowledgments

We are grateful to Luis Fernando Mejía for excellent research assistance and to Jose De Gregorio, Linda Goldberg, the editors of this journal (especially Timothy Taylor) and participants in the Macro Lunch at Columbia University for helpful comments. The views expressed in this chapter are exclusively those of the authors and not those of the Inter-American Development Bank, the University of Maryland, Columbia University, or the National Bureau of Economic Research.

Notes

1. For a discussion of why soft pegs have fallen out of favor and the rise of the bipolar view, see Obstfeld and Rogoff (1995), Eichengreen and Masson (1998) and Fischer (2001) in *Journal of Economic Perspectives*.

2. In this fashion, a sudden switch away from domestic and into foreign money need not result in a bank run, since in the presence of foreign exchange deposits, such a portfolio shift could be implemented by simply changing the denomination of bank deposits. Otherwise, deposits would be drawn down to purchase foreign exchange, resulting in a bank run.

3. In this symposium, Kaminsky and Reinhardt discuss how the process of contagion occurs.

4. Among the factors that differ across countries, we would mention the problem of tax evasion. As a result of tax evasion, the tax base of many emerging market economies is very small, the informal sector large and, thus, any adjustment to shocks causes major distortion in the formal part of the economy, leading to capital flight. Effects could be large if resulting externalities give rise to multiple equilibria (Calvo, 2002).

5. The stability of the central bank in advanced countries may be partly explained by the size of the shocks, rather than by some advantage in the political culture. After all, except for the Great Depression, advanced countries have not been hit by equally large shocks as in Argentina and other emerging market economies.

6. Indeed, Tommasi (2002) has argued that even deeper institutions, relating to politico-institutional rules as reflected in the constitution, electoral rules and informal practices of the polity, are crucial to the development and sustainability of strong fiscal, financial and monetary institutions. Also, Acemoglu, Johnson, Robinson and Thaircharoen (2003) provide evidence that deeper, fundamental institutions are more crucial to lowering economic volatility and raising growth than are specific macroeconomic policies.

7. If traded goods are not denominated in the same foreign currency as the debt, then this insulation may be incomplete unless the currency used for denominating debt moves very closely with the currency used for denominating traded goods.

8. Furthermore, it may induce the government to provide subsidized hedging instruments, which could substantially increase fiscal imbalance (this was the case in Brazil after the 1999 large devaluation of the *real*), impairing credibility.

9. However, the possible costs of pursuing such a policy also have to be taken into account. The literature on liability dollarization is still in its infancy, and, thus, it is hard to tell whether these costs are significant (Eichengreen, Hausmann and Panizza, 2002; Jeanne, 2002).

References

Acemoglu, Daron, Simon Johnson, James A. Robinson and Yunyong Thaicharoen. 2003. "Institutional Causes, Macroeconomic Symptoms: Volatility, Crises and Growth." *Journal of Monetary Economics*. 50:1, pp. 49–123.

Bernanke, Ben S. and Frederic S. Mishkin. 1997. "Inflation Targeting: A New Framework for Monetary Policy?" *Journal of Economic Perspectives*. 11:2, pp. 97–116.

Bernanke, Ben S., Thomas Laubach, Frederic S. Mishkin and Adam Posen. 1999. *Inflation Targeting: Lessons from the International Experience*. Princeton: Princeton University Press.

Boone, Peter, Alasdair Breach, Eric Friedman and Simon Johnson. 2000. "Corporate Governance and the Asian Crisis." *Journal of Financial Economics*. 58:1–2, pp. 141–86.

Broda, Christian. 2001. "Coping with Terms-of-Trade Shocks: Pegs versus Floats." *American Economic Review*. 91:2, pp. 376–80.

Broda, Christian and Eduardo Levy-Yeyati. 2000. "Safety Nets and Endogenous Financial Dollarization." Mimeo, Universidad Torcuato Di Tella.

Burnside, Craig, Martin Eichenbaum and Sergio Rebelo. 2001. "Prospective Deficits and the Asian Currency Crisis." *Journal of Political Economy*. 109:6, pp. 1155–197.

Caballero, Ricardo J. and Arvind Krishnamurthy. 2003. "Excessive Dollar Debt: Financial Development and Underinsurance." *Journal of Finance*. 58:2, pp. 867–94.

Calvo, Guillermo A. 2001. "Capital Markets and the Exchange Rate: With Special Reference to the Dollarization Debate in Latin America." *Journal of Money, Credit, and Banking*. 33:2, pp. 312–34.

Calvo, Guillermo A. 2002. "Explaining Sudden Stop, Growth Collapse and BOP Crisis: The Case of Distortionary Output Taxes." Mundell-Fleming Lecture, 3rd IMF Annual Research Conference, Washington, D.C., November 7.

Calvo, Guillermo A. and Enrique G. Mendoza. 2000. "Capital-Market Crises and Economic Collapse in Emerging Markets: An Informational-Frictions Approach." *American Economic Review*. 90:2, pp. 59–64.

Calvo, Guillermo A. and Carmen M. Reinhart. 2000. "When Capital Flows Come to a Sudden Stop: Consequences and Policy," in *Reforming the International Monetary and Financial System*. Peter B. Kenen and Alexander K. Swoboda, eds. Washington, D.C.: IMF, chapter 5.

Calvo, Guillermo A. and Carmen M. Reinhart. 2002. "Fear of Floating." *Quarterly Journal of Economics*. 117:2, pp. 379–408.

Calvo, Guillermo A. and Carlos A. Végh. 1996. "From Currency Substitution to Dollarization and Beyond: Analytical and Policy Issues," in *Money, Exchange Rates, and Output*. Guillermo A. Calvo, ed. Cambridge, Mass.: MIT Press, pp. 153–75.

Calvo, Guillermo A., Alejandro Izquierdo and Luis-Fernando Mejía. 2003. "On the Empirics of Sudden Stops." IADB working paper.

Calvo, Guillermo A., Alejandro Izquierdo and Ernesto Talvi. 2002. "Sudden Stops, the Real Exchange Rate and Fiscal Sustainability: Argentina's Lessons." IADB Working Paper No. 469; Available at http://www.iadb.org/res/publications/pubfiles/pubWP-469.pdf.

Cukierman, Alex. 1992. *Central Bank Strategy, Credibility and Independence: Theory and Evidence*. Cambridge, Mass.: MIT Press.

De Grauwe, Paul. 1997. *The Economics of Monetary Integration, 3rd Edition*. London: Oxford University Press.

Edwards, Sebastian. 2001. "Dollarization: Myths and Realities." *Journal of Policy Modeling*. 23:3, pp. 249–65.

Edwards, Sebastian and I. Igal Magendzo. 2001. "Dollarization, Inflation and Growth." NBER Working Paper No. 8671.

Eichengreen, Barry. 2002. "When to Dollarize." *Journal of Money, Credit and Banking*. 34:1, pp. 1–24.

Eichengreen, Barry and Paul Masson. 1998. "Exit Strategies: Policy Options for Countries Seeking Greater Exchange Rate Flexibility." IMF Occasional Paper No. 168.

Eichengreen, Barry, Ricardo Hausmann and Ugo Panizza. 2002. "Original Sin: The Pain, the Mystery, and the Road to Redemption." Presented at the conference *Currency and Maturity Matchmaking: Redeeming Debt from Original Sin*, IADB, Washington, D.C., November 21–22.

Fischer, Stanley. 2001. "Distinguished Lecture on Economics in Government—Exchange Rate Regimes: Is the Bipolar View Correct?" *Journal of Economic Perspectives*. 15:2, pp. 3–24.

Frankel, Jeffrey A. and Andrew K. Rose. 2002. "An Estimate of the Effect of Common Currencies on Trade and Income." *Quarterly Journal of Economics*. 117:2, pp. 437–66.

Frankel, Jeffrey A., Sergio L. Schmukler and Luis Serven. 2002. "Global Transmission of Interest Rates: Monetary Independence and Currency Regime." NBER Working Paper No. 8828.

Garber, Peter. 1999. "Hard-Wiring to the Dollar: From Currency Board to Currency Zone," in *Global Markets Research*. London: Deutsche Bank.

González, José A. 2000. "Exchange Rate Pass-Through and Partial Dollarization: Is There a Link?" CREDPR Working Paper No. 81, Stanford University.

Hanke, Steven and Kurt Schuler. 1994. *Currency Boards for Developing Countries: A Handbook*. San Francisco: ICS Press.

Hausmann, Ricardo. 1999. "Should There be 5 Currencies or 105?" *Foreign Policy*. Fall, 116, pp. 65–79.

Hausmann, Ricardo, Ugo Panizza and Ernesto Stein. 2001. "Why Do Countries Float the Way They Float?" *Journal of Development Economics*. 66:2, pp. 387–414.

Honig, Adam. 2003. "Dollarization, Exchange Rate Regimes and Government Myopia." Mimeo, Columbia University, March.

Jeanne, Olivier. 2002. "Why Do Emerging Economies Borrow in Foreign Currency?" Presented at the conference *Currency and Maturity Matchmaking: Redeeming Debt from Original Sin*. IADB, Washington, D.C., November 21–22.

La Porta, Rafael, Florencio Lopez-de-Silanes, Andrei Shleifer and Robert W. Vishny. 1998. "Law and Finance." *Journal of Political Economy*. 106:6, pp. 1113–155.

Levy-Yeyati, Eduardo and Federico Sturzenegger. 2003. "To Float or Fix: Evidence on the Impact of Exchange Rate Regimes on Growth." *American Economic Review*.

McKinnon, Ronald and Huw Pill. 1999. "Exchange Rate Regimes for Emerging Markets: Moral Hazard and International Overborrowing." *Oxford Review of Economic Policy*. 15:3, pp. 19–38.

Mishkin, Frederic S. 1991. "Asymmetric Information and Financial Crises: A Historical Perspective," in *Financial Markets and Financial Crises*. R. Glenn Hubbard, ed. Chicago: University of Chicago Press, pp. 69–108.

Mishkin, Frederic S. 1996. "Understanding Financial Crises: A Developing Country Perspective." *Annual World Bank Conference on Development Economics*. pp. 29–62.

Mishkin, Frederic S. 1998. "The Dangers of Exchange Rate Pegging in Emerging-Market Countries." *International Finance*. 1:1, pp. 81–101.

Mishkin, Frederic S. 1999a. "Lessons from the Asian Crisis." *Journal of International Money and Finance*. 18:4, pp. 709–23.

Mishkin, Frederic S. 1999b. "International Experiences with Different Monetary Policy Regimes." *Journal of Monetary Economics*. 43:3, pp. 579–606.

Mishkin, Frederic S. 2000. "What Should Central Banks Do?" *Federal Reserve Bank of St. Louis Review*. 82:6, pp. 1–13.

Mishkin, Frederic S. 2001. "The International Lender of Last Resort: What are the Issues?" in *The World's New Financial Landscape: Challenges for Economic Policy*. Horst Siebert, ed. Berling: Springer-Verlag, pp. 291–312.

Mishkin, Frederic S. 2003. "Financial Policies and the Prevention of Financial Crises in Emerging Market Countries," in *Economic and Financial Crises in Emerging Market Countries*. Martin Feldstein, ed. Chicago: University of Chicago Press, pp. 93–130.

Mishkin, Frederic S. and Adam Posen. 1997. "Inflation Targeting: Lessons from Four Countries." *Economic Policy Review*. August, 3:3, pp. 9–110.

Mishkin, Frederic S. and Miguel Savastano. 2001. "Monetary Policy Strategies for Latin America." *Journal of Development Economics*. 66:2, pp. 415–44.

Mundell, Robert A. 1961. "A Theory of Optimum Currency Areas." *American Economic Review*. 51:3, pp. 657–65.

Mussa, Michael. 1986. "Nominal Exchange Rate Regimes and the Behavior of Real Exchange Rates: Evidence and Implications." *Carnegie-Rochester Conference Series on Public Policy*. 25, pp. 117–213.

Obstfeld, Maurice and Kenneth Rogoff. 1995. "The Mirage of Fixed Exchange Rates." *Journal of Economic Perspectives*. 9:4, pp. 73–96.

Poole, William. 1970. "Optimal Choice of Monetary Policy Instruments in a Simple Stochastic Macro Model." *Quarterly Journal of Economics*. 84:2, pp. 197–216.

Reinhart, Carmen M. and Kenneth S. Rogoff. 2002. "The Modern History of Exchange Rate Arrangements: A Reinterpretation." NBER Working Paper No. 8963, June.

Rose, Andrew K. 2000. "One Money, One Market: Estimating the Effect of Common Currencies on Trade." *Economic Policy*. April, 15, pp. 7–46.

Sargent, Thomas and Neil Wallace. 1981. "Some Unpleasant Monetarist Arithmetic." *Federal Reserve Bank of Minneapolis Quarterly Review*. Fall, 5:3, pp. 1–17.

Schuler, Kurt. 1999. "Encouraging Official Dollarization in Emerging Markets." Joint Economic Committee Staff Report. Washington, D.C.: United States Senate.

Shleifer, Andrei and Robert Vishny. 1999. *The Grabbing Hand: Government Pathologies and Their Cures*. Cambridge, Mass.: Harvard University Press.

Tommasi, Mariano. 2002. "Crisis, Political Institutions, and Policy Reform: It is not the Policy, it is the Polity, Stupid." Mimeo, University of San Andres; forthcoming in *Annual World Bank Conference on Development Economics*.

Tornell, Aaron and Andrés Velasco. 2000. "Fixed versus Flexible Exchange Rates: Which Provides More Fiscal Discipline?" *Journal of Monetary Economics*. 45:2, pp. 399–436.

Woodford, Michael. 1994. "Monetary Policy and Price Level Determinacy in a Cash-in-Advance Economy." *Economic Theory*. 4:3, pp. 345–80.

Woodford, Michael. 1995. "Price Level Determinacy without Control of a Monetary Aggregate." *Carnegie-Rochester Conference Series on Public Policy*. 43:3, pp. 1–46.

IV   What Have We Learned?

Introduction to Part IV

Now it is time to extract the lessons from all the chapters in this book and put the material into a wider perspective with a final chapter outlining my current views on monetary policy strategy. Besides being distilled from the research discussed in this book, these views are also shaped by my practical experience in making monetary policy. This chapter, which I have tried to make as nontechnical as possible, can serve as a primer for how contemporary monetary policy strategy should be conducted, albeit written from my particular viewpoint. This chapter, however, will not be my last word on this subject because I and the economics profession will continue to learn from history and question, re-evaluate, and refine our understanding of monetary policy strategy.

19 Everything You Wanted to Know about Monetary Policy Strategy, but Were Afraid to Ask

Frederic S. Mishkin

There have been major advances in economic research on monetary policy over the past thirty years outlined in the previous chapters. What we have learned during this period has helped countries improve their economic performance substantially in recent years. Inflation throughout the world has fallen to levels that would have been unimaginable thirty years ago when I first became an economist; not only has the volatility of inflation declined sharply, but fluctuations in output and employment have declined as well. In this chapter I outline what this collective body of economic research tells us about how monetary policy should be conducted in nine key areas: 1) the importance of price stability and a nominal anchor to successful monetary policy, 2) fiscal and financial preconditions for achieving price stability, 3) central bank independence as an additional precondition, 4) central bank accountability, 5) the rationale for inflation targeting, 6) flexibility of inflation targeting, 7) the optimal inflation target, 8) central bank transparency and communications, and 9) the role of asset prices in monetary policy.

19.1 The Importance of Price Stability and a Nominal Anchor to Successful Monetary Policy

As discussed at the outset of this book, the recognition that price stability and a nominal anchor are important to the successful conduct of monetary policy has stemmed from three intellectual developments in economics: 1) the recognition that expansionary monetary policy cannot raise output and employment, except in the short run; 2) the realization that inflation is costly; and 3) the discovery of the time-inconsistency problem. These developments in economic science have led to the recognition that, first, price stability should be the overriding long-run goal of monetary policy and, second, that an explicit nominal anchor should be adopted to achieve the best economic outcomes.

19.1.1 Expansionary Monetary Policy Cannot Raise Output and Employment, Except in the Short Run

Until the 1970s, many economists thought there was a long-run trade-off between inflation and employment so that lower unemployment in the long run could be achieved by expansionary monetary policy that would result in higher inflation. Research in the late 1960s and 1970s indicated this reasoning was incorrect. Famous papers by Edmund Phelps and Milton Friedman demonstrated that in the long run, the economy would gravitate to some natural rate of unemployment no matter what the inflation rate was.[1] Attempts to lower unemployment below the natural rate would result only in higher inflation. The so-called rational expectations revolution in the 1970s, driven by pathbreaking papers by Robert Lucas, Thomas Sargent, and Neil Wallace, made it clear that the public's and the market's expectations about monetary policy have important effects on almost every sector of the economy.[2] This body of research demonstrated that not only is there no long-run trade-off between employment and inflation, but attempting to lower unemployment below the natural rate through expansionary monetary policy would probably not work, except in the very short run (for example, over a few quarters), to lower unemployment because inflation expectations would adjust upward rapidly and would quickly lead to higher inflation with little improvement in unemployment.

19.1.2 The High Cost of Inflation

Over the past three decades, economists and policymakers have become increasingly aware of the social and economic costs of inflation. The high inflation environment of the 1970s and 1980s made the costs of inflation more apparent to academics, policymakers, and the general public, a recognition which led to a growing consensus that price stability—a low, stable, and predictable inflation rate—provides lasting benefits to the economy. Price stability prevents overinvestment in the financial sector, which in a high-inflation environment expands profitability for middlemen to help individuals and businesses escape some of the costs of inflation. Price stability lowers the uncertainty about relative prices and the future price level, making it easier for firms and individuals to make appropriate decisions, thereby also increasing economic efficiency. Price stability lowers the distortions from the interaction of the tax system and inflation. Inflation also increases poverty because it hurts most the poorest members of society who do not have access to types of financial instruments that would enable them to protect themselves against inflation.

All these benefits of price stability suggest that low and stable inflation can increase the level of resources productively employed in the economy, and can even help increase the rate of economic growth. Over time, the consensus has moved toward the idea that inflation is detrimental to economic growth, particularly when inflation is at high levels.

19.1.3   The Time-Inconsistency Problem

Another important development in the science of monetary policy that emanated from the rational expectations revolutions was the discovery of the importance of the *time-inconsistency problem* in papers by Finn Kydland and Edward Prescott, Guillermo Calvo, and Robert Barro and David Gordon.[3] The time-inconsistency problem is something that we deal with continually in everyday life. We often have a plan that we know will produce a good outcome in the long run, but when tomorrow comes, we just can't help ourselves and we renege on the plan because doing so has short-run gains. This occurs when we make a New Year's resolution to go on a diet, but soon thereafter, we can't resist having one more bite of that piece of cake—and then another bite, and then another bite—and the weight begins to pile back on. We find ourselves unable to *consistently* follow a good plan over *time*; the good plan is said to be *time-inconsistent* and so will soon be abandoned. In other words, it is easier to make short-run compromises than undertake the harder work that results in more permanent long-run gains.

Monetary policymakers also face the time-inconsistency problem. They are always tempted to pursue a discretionary monetary policy to boost economic output and employment in the short run above the level that is consistent with stable inflation with more expansionary policy than firms or people initially expect. The best strategy, however, is *not* to pursue discretionary, expansionary policy because decisions about wages and prices reflect workers' and firms' expectations about policy; when they see a central bank pursuing expansionary policy, workers and firms will raise their expectations about inflation, and push wages and prices up—this is rational behavior in their own self-interest. Yet the overall rise in wages and prices will lead to higher inflation, but will not result in higher output on average.

A central bank will have better inflation performance in the long run if it understands (and makes clear to the public) that it should not have an objective of raising output or employment above what is consistent with stable inflation and will not try to surprise people with an unexpected, discretionary, expansionary policy.[4] Instead, it will commit to keeping inflation under control. However, even if a central bank recognizes that discretionary policy will lead to a poor outcome—high inflation with no gains in output—and so renounces it, the time-inconsistency problem is likely to arise nonetheless from political pressure. To many observers, politicians in a democratic society are shortsighted because they are driven by the need to win their next election. With this as their primary goal, they are unlikely to focus on long-run objectives, such as promoting a stable price level. Instead, they will seek short-run solutions to problems like high unemployment or interest rates by calling on the central bank to lower interest rates and employment with overly expansionary monetary policy.

19.1.4 Price Stability Should Be the Overriding, Long-Run Goal of Monetary Policy

The inability of monetary policy to boost employment in the long run, the high costs of inflation, and the time-inconsistency problem lead to the conclusion that the overriding, long-run goal of monetary policy should be price stability.

The goal of price stability immediately follows from the benefits of stable and low inflation, which promotes higher economic output. Furthermore, an institutional commitment to price stability is one way to lessen the time-inconsistency of monetary policy, and a price stability goal will not lead to lower employment in the long run. An institutional commitment to the price stability goal provides a counterbalance to the time-inconsistency problem because it makes it clear that the central bank must focus on the long run and thus resist the temptation to pursue short-run expansionary policies that are inconsistent with the long-run, price stability goal. An institutional commitment to price stability can also encourage the government to be more fiscally responsible and thus promote one of the preconditions discussed below for good monetary policy. When a government has committed to price stability it is more difficult for it to run large budget deficits. Politicians may be more likely to recognize that eventually they will have to pay for current deficit spending by raising taxes and will not be able to resort to the so-called inflation tax, the issuing or printing of money to pay for goods and services that leads to more inflation and is thus inconsistent with the price stability goal.

But does accepting a price stability goal mean that a central bank should ignore concerns about output and employment fluctuations? The answer is clearly no because monetary policy should be directed at lowering both inflation *and* output/employment fluctuations. Indeed, defining the monetary policy objectives in this way is standard in the academic literature. (Note that because output and employment usually move together, I use the terms output and employment interchangeably. However, there are cases in which output and employment do not move together, especially when there are productivity shocks as have recently occurred in many countries where positive productivity shocks have resulted in high output growth while employment has been stagnant.) The additional aim of lowering employment fluctuations explains why central banks should not try to attain price stability *in the short run* because this would mean that monetary policy then would be directed at minimizing inflation fluctuations and this could lead to excessive employment fluctuations. However, because price stability helps to promote economic growth and because expansionary monetary policy that produces inflation cannot increase employment and can only hurt workers in the long run, price stability should be the overriding goal of monetary policy *in the long run*, but not in the short run.

In some countries, the United States for example, legislation asks the central bank to achieve two objectives: price stability and maximum employment—and is thus known as a *dual mandate*. Other countries, Sweden, the United Kingdom, and the eurozone, for example, have a *hierarchical mandate*, in which the goal of price stability is placed first, but then allows that as long as price stability is achieved, other goals such as high employment can be pursued. As long as price stability is a long-run goal, but not a short-run goal, monetary policy can focus on reducing employment fluctuations by allowing inflation to deviate from the long-run goal for short time periods and therefore can operate under a dual mandate. However, if a dual mandate leads a central bank to pursue short-run expansionary policies that increase output and employment without worrying about the long-run consequences for inflation, the time-inconsistency problem may recur. Concerns that a dual mandate might lead to overly expansionary policy is a key reason why many countries have favored hierarchical mandates in which the pursuit of price stability takes precedence. Yet, hierarchical mandates can also be a problem if these lead to the central bank focusing solely on inflation control, even in the short run, and undertaking policies that lead to large employment fluctuations. The bottom line is that either type of mandate is appropriate as long as it operates to make price stability the primary goal *in the long run*, but not the short run.

19.1.5 A Nominal Anchor Should Be Adopted

Although an institutional commitment to price stability helps solve time-inconsistency and fiscal policy problems, it does not go far enough because the concept of price stability is not clearly defined. Typical definitions of price stability have many elements in common with the informal definition of pornography—you know it when you see it. Describing the theory of price stability as imposing constraints on fiscal policy and on discretionary monetary policy to avoid inflation might thus end up being quite weak in practice because not everyone will agree on what price stability means, providing both monetary policymakers and politicians a loophole to avoid making tough decisions on keeping inflation under control. A solution to this problem is to adopt a nominal anchor that ties down exactly what the commitment to price stability means.

A clue about how to deal with the time-inconsistency problem comes from how-to books on parenting. Parents know that giving in to a child to keep him or her from acting up will produce a very spoiled child. Nevertheless, when a child throws a tantrum, many parents give in because they can't stand the crying. Because parents don't stick to their do-not-give-in plan, children expect that they will get what they want if they behave badly, and so will throw tantrums over and over again. Parenting books suggest a solution to the time-inconsistency problem (although they don't call it that) by telling parents they should set behavior rules for their children and stick to them.[5]

A nominal anchor is like a behavior rule. Just as child-rearing rules help parents resist the discretionary temptation of giving in to a screaming toddler, a nominal anchor can help prevent the time-inconsistency problem in monetary policy by providing an imposed constraint on discretionary policy. Discipline works in both situations.

19.2   Fiscal and Financial Preconditions for Achieving Price Stability

Monetary policy is not conducted in a vacuum. There are two basic preconditions for monetary policy's ability to promote price stability and adopt a credible nominal anchor: 1) responsible fiscal policy, and 2) financial policies that promote the safety and soundness of the financial system. We shall see that if a government has unsound fiscal and financial policies, monetary policy will be unable to keep inflation under control. This is why responsible fiscal policies, sound financial policies, and an independent central bank are preconditions for successful monetary policy.

19.2.1   Responsible Fiscal Policy

Because the government has to pay its bills, just as we private individuals do, it has a budget constraint. When we spend more than we earn, we have to finance the excess spending by borrowing. If we cannot borrow, then our only option is to cut back our spending. When a government spends more than its revenues by running a budget deficit, it borrows the needed funds by issuing government debt. Unlike us, however, if the government cannot borrow, it has another option to finance a deficit: it can issue (print) money to pay for its excess spending. When budget deficits get too large, a government may not be able to borrow sufficient funds to cover the deficit. It is then likely to resort to issuing money directly or pressure the monetary authorities to purchase government bonds (called *monetizing the debt*), which results in the same thing—an expansion of the money supply. The upshot is that when government budget deficits get too large, expansionary monetary policy and high inflation will occur and the monetary authorities will not be able to pursue price stability.

19.2.2   Sound Financial Policies that Promote the Safety and Soundness of the Financial System

Similarly, poor regulation and supervision of the financial system can result in large losses on bank balance sheets. This situation makes it impossible for the monetary authorities to raise interest rates to control inflation because doing so might well lead to the financial system's crash. A collapse in the banking system will inevitably lead to large government bailouts to get the banks back on a sound footing, and this will lead to large budget deficits. These big deficits may also lead to a large expansion of the money supply, which will produce high inflation. Sound financial policies are thus also essential for attaining price stability.

19.3   Central Bank Independence as an Additional Precondition

In democratic societies there is always some discomfort in giving nonelected officials the authority to conduct policy that is important to almost every citizen. Adoption of a credible nominal anchor and achieving price stability, however, require another precondition for successful monetary policy: central bank independence to set its policy instruments.

19.3.1   Goal Independence?

Although there is a strong rationale for the price stability goal and adoption of a nominal anchor, who should set the goals for monetary policy? Should the central bank independently announce its commitment to the price stability goal and what nominal anchor it is choosing, or would it be better to have this commitment be mandated by the government?

Here the distinction between goal independence and instrument independence is quite useful. *Goal independence* is the ability of the central bank to set its own goals for monetary policy, say a goal of a 2 percent inflation rate two years in the future. *Instrument independence* is the central bank's ability to independently set monetary policy instruments, for example, the level of the interest rate, to achieve its goals. The fundamental democratic principle that the public must be able to exercise control over government actions strongly suggests that the goals of monetary policy should be set by the elected government. In other words, a central bank should not be goal-independent. The corollary of this view is that the institutional commitment to price stability should come from the government in the form of an explicit, legislated mandate for the central bank to pursue price stability as its overriding, long-run goal.

Not only is a legislated mandate and goal dependence of the central bank consistent with basic principles of democracy, but it has the further advantage of making time-inconsistency less likely, while making sound fiscal policy that promotes good monetary policy more likely. As we discussed, the source of the time-inconsistency problem is more likely to be embedded in the political process than it is in the central bank. Once politicians commit to the price stability goal by passing central bank legislation with a price stability mandate, it becomes harder for politicians to pressure the central bank to pursue short-run expansionary policies that are inconsistent with this mandate. Furthermore, a government commitment to price stability is also a commitment not to pursue irresponsible fiscal policy that might lead to higher inflation.

An alternative way to solve time-inconsistency problems is to grant both goal and instrument independence to a central bank and then appoint a central banker who focuses more on controlling inflation and less on reducing employment fluctuations than the average citizen would like. (In the academic literature, this type of central banker is referred to as "conservative.") The result will be low inflation, but possibly at the cost of higher output variability than the public desires. There are two problems with this solution. First, having "conservative" central bankers impose different preferences than the public's on the conduct of monetary policy is inherently undemocratic. Basic democratic principles hold that policymaking should be aligned with the preferences of the larger society. Second, in the long run a central bank cannot operate without the public's support. If the central bank is seen to be pursuing goals that are not what the public wants, support for central bank independence is likely to erode. Thus the appointment of conservative central bankers may not make for stability in the long run and will not provide a permanent solution to the time-inconsistency problem.

The reasoning outlined above suggests that the central bank should be goal-dependent. In other words, the government should set the long-run goal for monetary policy, say at a 2 percent level for the inflation rate. This reasoning applies to a parliamentary system, but is far less clear for a congressional system as in the United States. As pointed out in Bernanke, Laubach, Mishkin, and Posen (1999), it is more complicated to have a government set the goals for monetary policy in a congressional system because there is a distinct separation between the executive branch and the legislative branch. In a congressional system it is not as clear who in the government should set monetary policy goals, and so it might be harder to establish strict goal dependence for the central bank. Even in a parliamentary system, where there is less of a distinction between the executive branch and the legislative branch, there is still an issue of whether it should be government ministers or the legislature who should set the long-run goal. Nonetheless, even when the central bank is goal-dependent, the central bank should not be cut out of the decision-making process. Because the central bank has both prestige and expertise in the conduct of monetary policy, governments almost always will be better served by setting the objectives for monetary policy in consultation with the central bank.

Although there is a stronger case for the government setting the goal for monetary policy in the long run, it is more controversial whether it should set inflation targets in the short run or intermediate run. First, there is the concern that having the government set the short or medium-term inflation target could lead to it being changed every month or every quarter, and this could easily lead to a serious time-inconsistency problem in which short-run objectives would dominate. In practice, however, this problem does not appear to be severe because in many countries in which the government sets the annual inflation target, the target is rarely changed once price stability is achieved. Even though in theory governments could manipulate an annual inflation target to pursue short-run objectives, the transparency of the goal-setting decision tends to lead to a long-run approach in setting the inflation target even when it is done on an annual basis.

If inflation is currently far from the long-run target, who sets the medium-term target is more complicated. The length of the lags from monetary policy to inflation is a technical issue that the central bank is far more qualified to determine than politicians. Thus, how long it should take for inflation to return to the long-run target necessarily requires judgment about these lags that should be insulated from short-term political pressure if time-inconsistent policies are to be avoided. This argues for the central bank setting the medium-term inflation target because how quickly it approaches the long-run target reflects the lags of monetary policy effects on inflation. On the other hand, there is an argument for the government having a role in setting the medium-term target in this situation because, as Svensson (1997) has shown, preferences on the weight given to minimizing output fluctuations relative to inflation fluctuations affect the speed at which inflation should be adjusted toward the long-run goal. Therefore, for the government's preferences to be reflected in monetary policy, the government would need to have some role in setting the medium-term target.

Whether the central bank or the government should set medium-term inflation targets is therefore an open question. This may not be much of a dilemma most of the time, especially in advanced countries with parliamentary systems, because medium-term targets and long-run targets are likely to be quite close. But this will not always be the case. However, emerging market countries tend to be subjected to larger shocks and thus often have more variable inflation, which could lead to larger deviations of inflation from the long-run target. Thus, who should set the medium-term inflation target in these countries is even less clear.

19.3.2 Instrument Independence

Although the arguments above suggest that central banks should be goal-dependent, there is a strong case that central banks should be instrument-independent, that is, they should be allowed to set the policy interest rate without government interference. We have seen that the time-inconsistency problem almost surely emanates from the political process. Making central banks independent can help insulate them from political pressures to pursue short-run objectives of lower unemployment that will only lead to higher inflation in the long run and no improvement in employment. Instrument independence means that the central bank is better able to avoid the time-inconsistency problem.

The fact that monetary policy needs to be forward-looking to account for the long lags in monetary policy's effect upon inflation provides another rationale for instrument independence. This independence insulates the central bank from the myopia that frequently arises from politicians' concerns about getting elected in the near future. Instrument independence thus makes it more likely that the central bank will be forward-looking and adequately allow for the long lags from monetary policy actions to achieve inflation targets when setting their policy instruments.

Recent evidence seems to support the conjecture that macroeconomic performance is improved when central banks are more independent and shielded from the political process. When central banks in advanced countries are ranked from least legally independent to most legally independent, the inflation performance is found to be the best for countries with the most independent central banks.[6]

Both economic theory and the better outcomes for countries that have more independent central banks have led to a remarkable trend toward increasing central bank independence throughout the world. Before the 1990s very few central banks were highly independent, most notably the Bundesbank, the Swiss National Bank, and, to a somewhat lesser extent, the Federal Reserve. Now almost all central banks in advanced countries and many in emerging market countries have central banks with a level of independence on par with the pre-2000 Bundesbank and the Swiss National Bank. In the 1990s, greater independence was granted to central banks in such diverse countries as New Zealand, the United Kingdom, South Korea, and those in the Eurozone.

19.4   Central Bank Accountability

A basic democratic principle of democracy is that the public should have the right to control the government's actions. In a democracy, the public must have the capability to punish incompetent policymakers in order to control their actions. If policymakers cannot be removed from office or punished in some other way, this basic principle of democracy is violated. In a democracy, government policymakers need to be held accountable to the public.

A second reason why the accountability of policymakers is important is that it promotes government efficiency. Being subject to sanctions makes it more likely that incompetent policymakers will be replaced by competent policymakers and creates better incentives for policymakers to do their jobs well. Knowing that they are subject to punishment when performance is poor, policymakers will strive to get policy right. If policymakers are able to avoid accountability, then their incentives to do a good job drop appreciably, making poor policy outcomes more likely.

19.4.1 Where Should the Political Debate about Monetary Policy Take Place?

The need for central bank accountability suggests that monetary policy decisions should be subjected to active public debate. But where should this debate take place? Should it take place in a country's legislative branch, its parliament or congress? Should the executive branch, that is, government ministers, get actively involved in the monetary policy debate?

If the credibility of the central bank's pursuit of price stability is weakened, inflation expectations will rise, leading to increased inflationary pressure as a result of demands by workers and businesses to raise their wages and prices. In this situation, the central bank may be confronted with a difficult dilemma: if it does nothing, the nominal anchor will be weakened and inflation will rise; if it tightens monetary policy to restore the nominal anchor's credibility, it may end up tightening too much and cause damage to the economy. A loss of central bank credibility can thus lead to worse monetary policy performance.

The loss of central bank credibility indicates that there can be a cost from politicians' criticisms of the central bank's conduct of monetary policy. Political debate that criticizes only policy actions, particularly when the central bank raises interest rates, but does not criticize the central bank for lowering rates when it might produce too much inflation, can be counterproductive because it weakens the nominal anchor and produces worse economic outcomes. Political debate that focuses on whether a central bank is taking or has taken the appropriate measures to achieve price stability is, in contrast, likely to strengthen the nominal anchor.

Although there can be costs from political debate about the central bank, there are also major benefits. Political debate is central to the workings of democracy and the central bank should not be excluded from this public debate. Criticisms of the central bank both by the politicians and the markets are what make the central bank accountable and give it the incentive to do its job well. Open monitoring and debate about the central bank also can enhance the central bank's ability to learn from its mistakes. Whatever the form of the political debate, the gains from holding a central bank politically accountable indicate that active political debate about monetary policy is vital to a well-functioning democratic system.

The above reasoning argues strongly for having active political debate and scrutiny of monetary policy in a country's legislative branch. It also suggests that debate about the performance of the central bank, particularly after outcomes are known, has great value in enhancing central bank accountability. Debate and criticism of the central bank from the executive branch is far more problematic, however. Because the executive branch has greater influence over legislation that affects the powers and resources of the central bank, government ministers, particularly the prime minister (president) or minister of finance (treasury secretary), have substantial power to punish or reward the central bank. When a government minister criticizes central bank actions, and in particular criticizes monetary policymakers when they raise interest rates, central bank credibility is likely to be weakened. The result could actually be the opposite of what the government minister wants, because to restore credibility to the nominal anchor and keep inflation expectations from rising, the central bank is even more likely to raise interest rates further, which could lead to a contraction in economic output and employment.

Recognizing the danger of having government ministers criticize monetary policy has led some governments to renounce criticizing the central bank, with positive results. The recent example of the relationship between the executive branch and the Federal Reserve in the United States is quite illustrative of the benefits of not having the political debate about monetary policy occur through comments by government officials. Early in Bill Clinton's first presidential term, Robert Rubin, who later became the Treasury secretary, but who worked in the White House heading the National Economic Council, convinced President Clinton that it would be a mistake for the president (or Rubin for that matter) to criticize the Federal Reserve's interest rate increases in early 1994. Doing so would only lead to weakening the Fed's credibility, an upward surge in inflation expectations, a subsequent rise in long-term interest rates, and thus a sharp fall in long-term bond prices.[7] Following this advice, the Clinton administration did not comment on Federal Reserve policy actions throughout its two terms in office. Not criticizing the Fed for raising rates enabled it to earn credibility as a serious inflation fighter, thus promoting more stable inflation expectations. This enhanced credibility enabled the Fed to refrain from tightening monetary policy in the latter part of the 1990s without worrying about escalating inflation expectations, which helped sustain strong economic growth. Furthermore, the high credibility the Fed earned over the 1990s enabled it to aggressively lower interest rates preemptively in the face of negative shocks, even before the 2001–2002 recession began, without worrying that this would lower its inflation-fighting credibility. Given the Fed's quick reaction, the 2001–2002 recession ended up being quite mild. The Clinton administration's policy, which has been continued by the Bush II administration, is viewed as a tremendous success. It not only helped the Fed produce both low and less volatile inflation, but also helped output and employment fluctuations remain fairly stable.

19.5   The Rationale for Inflation Targeting

Although economists and policymakers have now concluded that it makes sense to adopt a nominal anchor, there remains the question which one should be chosen. There are four basic types of nominal anchors for countries that have an independent monetary policy: 1) exchange-rate targets (pegs), 2) monetary targets, 3) inflation targets, and 4) implicit but not explicit. Which of these four categories of nominal anchor should a monetary authority choose to use?

19.5.1 Exchange-Rate Targets (Pegs)

Targeting the exchange rate is a monetary policy strategy with a long history. Exchange-rate targeting regimes involve fixing (pegging) the value of the domestic currency to that of a large, low-inflation (anchor) country like the United States or Germany. An exchange-rate peg directly fixes the prices for internationally traded goods to that of the anchor country and thereby anchors inflation expectations.

As long as the central banks' commitment to an exchange-rate peg is strong, it provides an automatic rule for the conduct of monetary policy that helps avoid the time-inconsistency problem. An exchange-rate peg, however, has serious drawbacks. With capital mobility, the pegging country can no longer pursue an independent policy and loses the ability to use monetary policy to respond to domestic shocks that differ from those hitting the anchor country. In addition, an exchange-rate peg leaves countries open to speculative attacks against the domestic currency, and in emerging market countries, which have debt denominated in foreign currencies, the subsequent depreciation of the domestic currency can lead to the destruction of firms' balance sheets and severe financial crises because the depreciation leads to an increase in firms' liabilities in terms of domestic currency.

Although there are situations in which an exchange-rate peg is desirable, either because a country seeks more integration with its neighbors by fixing the value of its domestic currency to the neighbor's currency, or because it does not have the institutional framework to successfully run its own monetary policy, the desire of many nations to pursue their own domestic monetary policy and avoid the dangers from pegged exchange-rate regimes have led many countries to choose a flexible exchange-rate regime. A flexible exchange-rate regime leaves open what type of nominal anchor the country will choose and so does not imply any particular monetary policy strategy: a strategy requires a choice of another nominal anchor, whether it be a monetary target, an inflation target, or an implicit, but not explicit, nominal target.

19.5.2 Monetary Targeting

Monetary targets were once the nominal anchor of choice for countries that decided to pursue having their own independent monetary policy focused on domestic considerations. A monetary target, however, will have trouble serving as a strong nominal anchor when the relationship between a monetary aggregate and inflation is unstable. This relationship is likely to become even more unstable when there has been a financial liberalization or technological innovations that make it more difficult to define what actually constitutes the domestic money supply. Indeed, this is exactly what happened in the countries that adopted monetary targeting, and the resulting instability of the money-inflation relationship meant that monetary targeting often did not help the monetary authorities control inflation. As mentioned in chapter 1, Gerald Bouey, the governor of the Bank of Canada, colorfully described his central bank's experience with monetary targeting by saying, "We didn't abandon monetary aggregates; they abandoned us."

Note that Germany (and to a lesser extent Switzerland) had substantial success with monetary targeting, but it is important to recognize that the Bundesbank and the Swiss National Bank were not bound by monetarist orthodoxy. The policy each practiced was very far from the monetarist monetary targeting rule advocated by Milton Friedman in which a monetary aggregate was kept on a constant-growth-rate path and was the primary focus of monetary policy. Instead, monetary targeting in Germany and Switzerland was much closer to inflation targeting than they were to a monetarist conception of monetary targeting.

19.5.3   Inflation Targeting

The disappointments with monetary targeting, particularly in Canada and the United Kingdom, led to a search for a better nominal anchor and resulted in the development of inflation targeting in the 1990s. Inflation targeting evolved from monetary targeting by adopting its most successful elements: an institutional commitment to price stability as the primary long-run goal of monetary policy and to achieving the goal inflation rate; increased transparency through public communication about the objectives of monetary policy and the plans for policy actions to achieve these objectives; and increased central bank independence and accountability for achieving its inflation objectives. Inflation targeting, however, differs from monetary targeting in two key dimensions. First, rather than announce a monetary aggregates target, the central bank publicly announces a medium-term numerical target for a future inflation rate. Second, the monetary authority makes use of an information-inclusive strategy, with a reduced role for intermediate targets such as money growth, to forecast future inflation and output in deciding how to set its policy instruments.

Inflation targeting superseded monetary targeting because of several advantages. First, inflation targeting does not rely on a stable money-inflation relationship and so significant shocks to velocity (the ratio of nominal income to the money supply) that distort this relationship are largely irrelevant to monetary policy performance. Second, inflation targeting, which is inherently forward-looking, uses more information, and not one primary variable, to determine the best settings for policy, thereby giving it the potential to produce better policy outcomes. For example, in the case of an energy-supply shock like a sharp rise in the price of oil, strict monetary targeting would overlook important implications that the oil price change would have for forecasts of inflation and future output, while inflation targeting would incorporate this information. Third, an inflation target is readily understood by the public because changes in prices are of immediate and direct concern, while monetary aggregates are farther removed from peoples' everyday experience. (What percentage of a population would know the difference between measures of monetary aggregates like M0, M1, or M2?) Inflation targets, therefore, are better at increasing the transparency of monetary policy because these make the objectives of the monetary authorities clearer. This does not mean that monetary targets could not serve as a useful communication device and increase the central bank's accountability in controlling inflation, as happened in Germany and Switzerland, but once the relationship between monetary aggregates and inflation breaks down—as it has repeatedly—monetary targets lose a substantial degree of transparency because the central bank now must provide complicated discussions of why it is appropriate to deviate from the original monetary target. Fourth, inflation targets increase a central bank's accountability because the performance of the central bank can now be measured against a clearly defined target. Monetary targets work less well in this regard because of the unstable money-inflation relationship that makes it harder to impose accountability because the central bank will necessarily miss its monetary targets frequently, as occurred for the Bundesbank, which missed its target ranges more than half of the time.

An explicit numerical inflation target increases the accountability of the central bank to control inflation. Therefore, inflation targeting also has the potential to reduce the likelihood that a central bank will suffer from the time-inconsistency problem in which it reneges on the optimal plan and instead tries to expand output and employment by pursuing overly expansionary monetary policy. But since time-inconsistency is more likely to come from political pressures on the central bank to engage in overly expansionary monetary policy, a key advantage of inflation targeting is that it is better able to focus the political debate on what a central bank can do in the long-run—control inflation—rather than what it cannot do—permanently raise economic growth and the number of jobs through expansionary monetary policy. Thus, inflation targeting appears to reduce political pressures on the central bank to pursue inflationary monetary policy and thereby reduces the likelihood of time-inconsistent policymaking.

19.5.4 Monetary Policy with an Implicit but Not Explicit Nominal Anchor

A third approach to conducting monetary policy is the one that was used by the Federal Reserve under Alan Greenspan. The Greenspan Fed had an implicit, not explicit, nominal anchor that reflected the Federal Reserve's overriding concern to control inflation in the long run with forward-looking, preemptive strikes against bursts of inflation or deflation. The Greenspan Fed's strategy was enormously successful. With the help of the previous chairman, Paul Volcker, who helped break the back of rampant inflation in the early 1980s, under Greenspan the Fed was able to bring inflation in the United States to around 2 percent, which is similar to what inflation-targeting central banks have achieved. Preemptive strikes against inflation, particularly increasing the federal funds rate from 3 percent in February 1994 to 6 percent in early 1995, helped keep inflation stable. This policy also helped to produce the longest business-cycle expansion in American history, dated from 1991 to 2001. The Fed then engaged in a preemptive strike against a weakening economy and deflation starting in January 2001, with the result that the 2001–2002 recession was quite mild and inflation remained stable. These preemptive strikes against both inflation and weakness in the economy enabled the United States to have relatively steady growth with continuing low inflation for a remarkable fifteen-year period.

There are several disadvantages, however, of an implicit anchor based on an individual's authority as in the United States during the Greenspan era. The most serious disadvantage of the use of an implicit, but not explicit, nominal anchor is its strong dependence on the preferences, skills, and trustworthiness of the individuals in charge of the central bank. Under Alan Greenspan, the Fed has emphasized forward-looking policies and inflation control, with great success, and this strategy is continuing under Ben Bernanke. The Fed's leadership will, however, periodically change, and we are not guaranteed to get chairmen of the caliber of Alan Greenspan or Ben Bernanke who will also be strongly committed to inflation control. In the past, after a successful period of low inflation, the Federal Reserve has reverted to inflationary monetary policy—the 1970s are one example—and without an explicit nominal anchor like an inflation target, this could happen again.

Another disadvantage of an implicit nominal anchor is its lack of transparency. It leads to a constant guessing game about a central bank's goals, which creates unnecessary volatility in financial markets and arouses uncertainty among businesses and the general public. This was illustrated by the recent sharp swings in long-term U.S. interest rates during the late spring and summer of 2003. Because the market was confused about the Fed's mixed signals on the risk of deflation and what actions it might take, the ten-year bond rate first dropped from a level near 4 percent at the beginning of May to 3.2 percent in the middle of June, and then rose more than 100 basis points to 4.5 percent by the end of July. If the markets have a clearer picture of the Fed's longer-run objectives, particularly on inflation, then they would focus less on what the Fed's next policy move may be, making it less likely that Fed statements or policy moves would lead to volatile whipsawing of the market.

Furthermore, the opacity of a central bank without an explicit nominal anchor makes it harder to hold a central bank accountable to the public: a central bank cannot be held accountable if there is no predetermined criteria for judging its performance. Low accountability also may make the central bank more susceptible to the time-inconsistency problem, whereby political pressure might induce it to pursue short-term objectives at the expense of long-term ones.

An additional problem with a central bank not having an explicit nominal anchor is that it, and particularly its leader, is more likely to find its credibility being challenged, leading to what Marvin Goodfriend has called an "inflation scare"—a spontaneous increase in inflation fears that is reflected in a sharp rise in long-term interest rates.[8] When Greenspan first took over as Fed chairman, for example, an inflation scare ensued with a sharp upward spike in long bond rates because the markets had doubts that Greenspan, who had strong ties with the Republican leadership, would be able to resist political pressures and be as serious about controlling inflation as his predecessor, Paul Volcker. It was only after continual emphasis and success on controlling inflation that the Greenspan Fed was able to avoid inflation scares.

Another disadvantage of using an implicit but not explicit nominal anchor is that it is somewhat inconsistent with democratic principles. As we have seen, central bank independence is critical to producing low inflation outcomes, yet the practical economic arguments for central bank independence coexist uneasily with the presumption that government policies should be made democratically, rather than by an elite group.

In contrast, use of an inflation target as a nominal anchor makes the institutional framework for monetary policy more consistent with democratic principles and avoids some of the above problems. Use of an inflation target promotes the accountability of the central bank to elected officials and to the public.

19.5.5 Economic Performance under Inflation Targeting

Given its advantages, it is not surprising that the performance of inflation targeting has performed well in controlling inflation. Countries emphasizing this policy have significantly reduced both the rate of inflation (figure 19.1) and inflation expectations beyond what would likely have occurred in the absence of inflation targets. Furthermore, once lowered, inflation in these countries has stayed down and inflation volatility has declined (figure 19.2); following disinflations, the inflation rate in targeting countries has not bounced back up during cyclical economic expansions as it has in the past.

One concern voiced about inflation targeting is that a sole focus on an inflation goal may lead to monetary policy that is too tight when inflation is above target; thus, a singular focus on this target may lead to larger output and employment fluctuations. Yet in practice, exactly the opposite has happened (figure 19.3). (However, the drop in output volatility has occurred in many countries that have not adopted inflation targeting and so it is not absolutely clear that it is due to better performance of monetary policy. Instead it might be the result of smaller shocks to the economy in

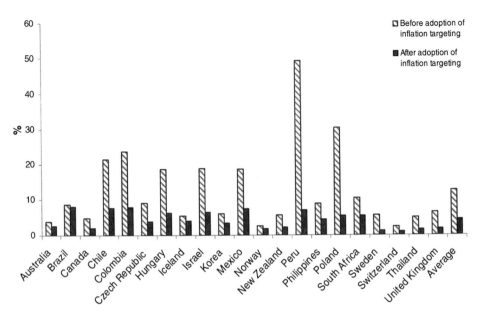

Figure 19.1
Average level of inflation, before and after adoption of inflation targeting.
Source: Data are from 1989, Q1 to 2004, Q4 from IMF *International Financial Statistics.* Adoption dates
of inflation targeting are from Frederic S. Mishkin and Klaus Schmidt-Hebbel, 2002, "A Decade of Inflation Targeting in the World: What Do We Know and What Do We Need to Know?" in Norman Loayza
and Raimundo Soto, eds., *Inflation Targeting: Design, Performance, Challenges*, Santiago: Central Bank of
Chile, 171–219.

recent years. This is a very active area of research). To see how inflation targeting
could lead to lower, rather than higher, output volatility, we need to understand
that there are two factors that are the key determinants of inflation: (1) inflation
expectations and (2) the amount of slack in the economy, described by the so-called
output gap—the difference between actual output and potential output (the output
that the economy would achieve with flexible wages and prices).[9] An inflation target
helps stabilize inflation expectations around the target, telling us that deviations from
the inflation goal will be highly correlated with output gaps. Thus, stabilizing inflation also helps to stabilize output gaps and can help stabilize fluctuations of output
around potential output.

To see how this would work, consider a negative-demand shock, such as a decline
in consumer confidence, which causes a cut in spending, which then leads to a
decline in output relative to its potential. The result is that future inflation will fall
below the inflation target and the central bank will pursue expansionary policy to
prevent an undershooting of the target. The expansionary policy will then result in
an increase in demand that raises output back up to potential output to keep infla-

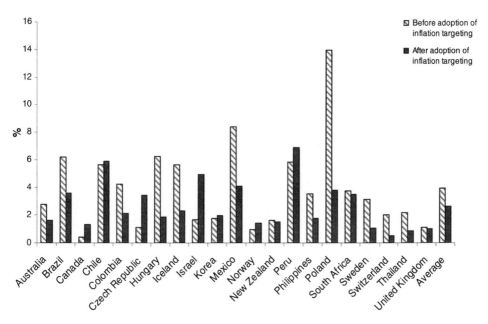

Figure 19.2
Volatility of inflation (standard deviation) before and after adoption of inflation targeting.
Source: Same as figure 19.2.

tion close to the target. Indeed, because an inflation target helps anchor expectations, the central bank will be willing to be more aggressive in pursuing expansionary policy because it does not have to worry that this expansionary policy will lead to an inflation scare with an escalation of inflation expectations.

Inflation targeting has not only produced good inflation outcomes, but has also been associated with declines in output fluctuations. The better performance on output fluctuations from inflation-targeting regimes has surprised many initial skeptics because an increased focus on controlling inflation, everything else equal, should lead to larger, not smaller, output fluctuations. However, if inflation targeting produces a stronger nominal anchor, which is a key to successful economic performance, then inflation targeting can lead not only to a decline in inflation but also output volatility.

19.6   Flexibility of Inflation Targeting

Although inflation targeting has many advantages, it has to be designed well to produce the best outcomes possible. What is best practice for inflation-targeting regimes? First, we look at what degree of flexibility needs to be built into the inflation-targeting regime.

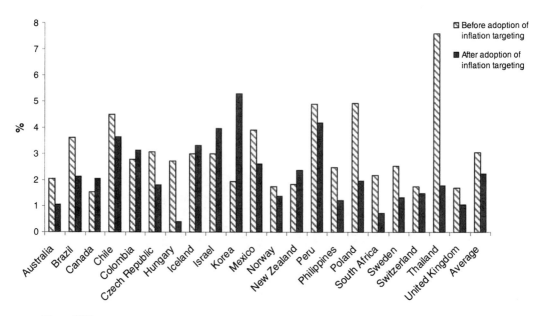

Figure 19.3
Volatility of output (standard deviation) before and after adoption of inflation targeting.
Source: Same as figure 19.1.

Price stability is a means to the end-objective of fostering a healthy economy, and should not be treated as an end in itself. Thus, central bankers should not be obsessed with controlling inflation and become what Bank of England Governor Mervyn King has characterized as "inflation nutters."[10] The public cares about output as well as inflation fluctuations; the objectives for a central bank in the context of a long-run strategy therefore should include not only minimizing inflation fluctuations around the target rate, but also minimizing output fluctuations around potential output (called *output gaps*). As was mentioned before, objective functions with these characteristics now have become standard in the monetary economics literature.

Although, in the face of demand shocks reducing inflation fluctuations helps reduce output fluctuations around potential output, one type of shock could lead to an increase in output fluctuations if there is too much focus on hitting an exact inflation target. A negative supply shock, say a large increase in energy prices, can raise inflation at the same time that output falls below its potential (a negative output gap).[11] Indeed, oil price shocks often lead to a temporary rise in inflation, with a negative impact on output and output gaps. In this situation, if a central bank tightens to return inflation to the target level immediately, output would fall further and this could lead to increased cyclical fluctuations. Because central banks should care about output gap fluctuations, the possibility of supply shocks indicates that inflation targeting should not always try to bring inflation down quickly to the target level. Rather, inflation targeting needs to be quite flexible, and in the face of supply shocks should not try to hit the target immediately, but instead should shoot for having inflation gradually come back down to the inflation target. Lars Svensson has characterized this approach to conducting monetary policy as "flexible inflation targeting."[12] Indeed, his research, and that of others, particularly Michael Woodford, shows that the horizon over which inflation should be brought back down to the long-run inflation goal should vary over time depending on how far current inflation is from the long-run goal and what kind of shocks have hit the economy.[13]

The reasoning proferred above suggests that inflation targeting should not involve a sole focus on inflation or a simple rule that indicates policy rates should be moved in a particular direction, depending on the state of the economy. Instead, an inflation-targeting regime should display substantial concern about output fluctuations and pursue flexible inflation targeting with varying horizons for how long it will take for inflation to be brought back down to the target level. Central bankers in inflation-targeting countries do indeed express concerns about fluctuations in output and employment when discussing how they are conducting monetary policy and have been willing to minimize output declines by gradually lowering medium-term inflation targets toward the long-run goal when they are hit by negative supply shocks. In addition, because financial instability can have such a large negative impact on output fluctuations, concerns about financial instability also provide a justification for changing the horizon for how long it should take to bring inflation back down to its target. Building flexibility into inflation targeting has been critical to its success in not only lowering inflation volatility, but also reducing output fluctuations. (Indeed, flexible inflation targeting is consistent with the highly successful policy actions taken by the Greenspan Fed, and only differs from the Greenspan approach in its greater commitment to transparency by publicly committing to an explicit target.)

Flexible inflation targeting should be seen as a way of pursuing an objective of minimizing inflation and output gap fluctuations, but with an emphasis on couching policy in terms of the inflationary path because, as we will see, measures of output gaps are notoriously unreliable.

19.7   Central Bank Transparency and Communication

Inflation-targeting regimes put great stress on making policy transparent and on communicating regularly with the public. Inflation-targeting central banks frequently communicate with the government's legislative branch, some of which is mandated by law and some in response to formal inquiries. In addition to this, central bank officials take every opportunity to make public speeches on their monetary policy strategy. While these techniques are also commonly used in countries that have not adopted inflation targeting, central banks that do pursue inflation targeting have taken public outreach a step further: not only do they engage in extended public information campaigns, even distributing glossy brochures, but they also publish a document known by its generic name *Inflation Reports*, after the original document published by the Bank of England.

The publication of these documents is particularly noteworthy, because these depart from the usual dull-looking, formal reports of central banks and use fancy graphics, boxes, and other eye-catching design elements to engage the public's interest and to improve communication.

All these channels of communication, especially the *Inflation Reports*, are used by central banks in inflation-targeting countries to explain the following concepts to the general public, financial market participants, and politicians: 1) the goals and limitations of monetary policy, including the rationale for inflation targets; 2) the numerical values of the inflation targets and how these were determined; 3) how the inflation targets are to be achieved; and 4) the reasons for any deviations from targets. Another important purpose of *Inflation Reports* is to provide the central bank's forecasts of future inflation. These communications have improved private sector planning by reducing uncertainty about monetary policy, interest rates, and inflation; they have promoted public debate of monetary policy, in part by educating the public about what a central bank can and cannot achieve; and they have helped clarify the responsibilities of the central bank and politicians in the conduct of monetary policy.

The greater transparency and improved communication of central banks that have adopted inflation targeting is one of the major strengths of this monetary policy framework. Not only does it help decrease uncertainty, with the benefits described earlier, but it also goes hand in hand with increased accountability. More accountability creates better incentives for central bankers to do their jobs well, but also makes the independence of the central bank more compatible with basic democratic principles.

19.7.1 How Should the Central Bank Discuss Its Objectives for Monetary Policy?

As we have seen, central bank objectives should include both lowering inflation *and* minimizing employment/output fluctuations. However, many central banks are extremely reluctant to discuss concerns about output fluctuations even though their actions show they do care about these fluctuations. This lack of transparency about overall objectives is what I called the "the dirty little secret" of central banking in chapter 5.

Central bankers fear that if they are explicit about the need to minimize output fluctuations as well as inflation fluctuations, politicians will use this admission to pressure the central bank into pursuing a short-run strategy of overly expansionary policy that will lead to poor long-run outcomes. Furthermore, a focus on output gaps could lead to policy mistakes similar to those that occurred in the United States in the 1970s (discussed later in this chapter). The response to these problems is that central bankers engage in a don't-ask-don't-tell policy about their overall strategy.

However, the unwillingness of central banks to talk about their concerns with reducing output fluctuations creates two very serious problems. First, is that a don't-ask-don't-tell strategy is dishonest. Doing one thing but saying another is the height of nontransparency, and by not admitting that they care about output fluctuations, central bankers can erode confidence in other more transparent elements of their policy that are clearly beneficial. Second, if central bankers do not discuss their concerns about output fluctuations, they may end up being characterized as "inflation nutters," and this can cause an erosion of support for a central bank's policies and independence because this set of preferences is inconsistent with the public's concerns.

The case for increasing a central bank's transparency with regard to its concerns about output fluctuations are quite strong. But how can central banks do this? One answer is that a central bank can make it absolutely clear that it takes output fluctuations into account when it targets inflation. This is exactly what the Norges Bank did with the following statement at the beginning of its *Inflation Report*: "Norges Bank operates a flexible inflation targeting regime, so that weight is given to both variability in inflation and variability in output and employment." The Norges Bank thus makes it absolutely clear that its objectives include not only reducing inflation fluctuations but also output (employment) fluctuations, and that inflation targeting is a way of doing this.

The second way of making it clear that one of the central bank's objectives is reducing output fluctuations is announcing that it will not attempt to hit its inflation target over too short a horizon because this would result in unacceptably high output losses, especially when the economy gets hit by shocks that knock it substantially away from its long-run inflation goal. Furthermore, the central bank can clarify that the horizon for the inflation target will vary, depending on the nature of the shocks to the economy. Again, the Norges Bank did exactly this with the following statement that appears after the sentence quoted above: "Monetary policy influences the economy with long and variable lags. Norges Bank sets the interest rate with a view of stabilizing inflation at the target within a reasonable time horizon, normally 1–3 years. The relevant horizon will depend on disturbances to which the economy is exposed and how they will affect the path for inflation and the real economy in the period ahead."

Monetary authorities can further the public's understanding that central bankers care about reducing output fluctuations in the long run by emphasizing that monetary policy needs to be just as vigilant in preventing inflation from falling too low as it is from preventing it from being too high. They can do this (and some central banks have) by explaining that an explicit inflation target may help the monetary authorities stabilize the economy because they can be more aggressive in easing monetary policy in the face of negative demand shocks to the economy without being concerned that this will cause a blowout in inflation expectations. However, to communicate this strategy clearly, the explanation of a monetary-policy easing in the face of negative demand shocks needs to indicate that this action is consistent with the preservation of price stability.

In addition, central banks can clarify that they care about reducing output fluctuations by indicating that when the economy is very far below any reasonable measure of potential output, that is, the output gap is definitely negative, they will take expansionary actions to stimulate economic recovery. In this case, measurement error of potential output is likely to be swamped by the size of the output gap; it is far clearer that expansionary policy is appropriate and that inflation is unlikely to rise from such actions. In this situation, the case for taking action to close the output gap is much stronger and does not threaten the central bank's credibility in its pursuit of price stability.

19.7.2   Should Central Banks Announce an Output (Employment) Target?

Given that central banks should make clear that they do have an objective of reducing output fluctuations, why shouldn't they announce an output (employment) target as well as an inflation target? After all, announcing an output or employment target seems like a natural way to express concerns about output or employment fluctuations. This obvious answer is not the right one, however, because potential output and the associated natural rate of employment (or unemployment) are so hard to measure. This is why the section above advocates that central banks express their concerns about output/employment fluctuations by describing how the targeted path of inflation is modified to help minimize these fluctuations.

One measurement problem for potential output occurs because the monetary policy authorities have to estimate it with real-time data, that is, data that is available at the time they set the policy instrument. GDP data frequently is revised substantially and this is one reason why output gaps are mismeasured in real time.[14] Even more important: it is notoriously hard to know what potential GDP and its growth rate actually are without the benefit of hindsight. In the United States it was not until the 1980s that policymakers recognized that potential GDP growth had slowed markedly after 1973, while it wasn't until the late 1990s that policymakers recognized the technology-driven acceleration in potential GDP growth. Errors in measuring output gaps have been very large.

An even more severe measurement problem occurs because economists are not even sure what the concept of potential output means. Some economists argue that conventionally measured potential GDP based on a trend, the most common method, differs substantially from more theoretically grounded measures based on the output level that would prevail in the absence of nominal price stickiness.

The fact that it is so hard to measure potential output or even know how to define it theoretically, indicates that announcing an output target would lead to worse policy outcomes. This is illustrated by the experience of the United States in the 1970s where, as already mentioned, the Federal Reserve had a hard time measuring potential output. Under the Federal Reserve chairman Arthur Burns, the Fed put a lot of weight on hitting an output target. Unfortunately, the Fed had such inaccurate estimates of potential output that it thought there was a lot of slack in the economy when there wasn't. The result was that it did not tighten monetary policy sufficiently during that period even when inflation was rising to double-digit levels. The result was what has been referred to as the "Great Stagflation" in which inflation rose to very high levels and yet employment fluctuations continued to be very high. Research has shown that the reason for the Federal Reserve's poor performance during the 1970s was *not* that it was unconcerned with inflation, but rather that it focused too much on targeting output.

It is true that there are measurement problems with inflation as well as with output gaps, but both the conceptual and real-time measurement problems for inflation are of a far smaller magnitude. Also, although there is some question about what should be the optimal level of the inflation target in the long run, the choice of a number anywhere between 1 and 3 percent does not seem to matter very much. However, a 0.5 percentage point difference in what potential output should be makes a huge difference to the welfare of individuals in the society. This is why it is better to embed concerns about employment fluctuations in an inflation-targeting framework, rather than pursuing an explicit output target. Indeed, as I have argued earlier, a focus on inflation control using a flexible inflation-targeting framework is likely to produce better outcomes not only for inflation but also for output fluctuations.

Announcing an employment target may be even more problematic than announcing an output target because unforeseen shocks to productivity can alter the relationship between the natural rates of output and employment. In many countries we have seen unexpected increases in productivity in recent years so that very rapid output growth has not been accompanied by employment growth. Because predicting productivity shocks has been very difficult in recent years, forecasting the natural rate of employment may be even harder than forecasting the natural rate of output. For this reason, central banks often are even more reluctant to discuss employment targets than output targets.

Announcement of an output or employment target might also increase the tendency for politicians to pressure the central bank to pursue expansionary policies that could exacerbate the time-inconsistency problem and weaken the nominal anchor. The result would not only be inflation subject to higher levels and volatility, but also greater output fluctuations.

19.7.3 Should Central Banks Publish Inflation Forecasts?

Almost all inflation-targeting central banks publish their forecasts of economic variables such as output, unemployment, and inflation. The medium-term target is future inflation, so the medium-term target is actually the inflation forecast. (This is why inflation targeting is sometimes referred to as "inflation forecast targeting.") Since inflation forecasts are key to conducting monetary policy in an inflation-targeting regime, transparency requires that the central bank's inflation forecast be public knowledge. There are a number of advantages from forecasts that are announced and published. First, publication of forecasts can help the public and the markets understand central bank actions, thus making it easier for them to assess whether the central bank is serious about achieving its inflation goal and is setting the policy instruments appropriately. Publishing forecasts is thus crucial to making the central bank accountable. Second, published forecasts enable the markets to understand how the central bank is setting its policy instruments and so help reduce uncertainty. Third, publication of forecasts enables the public to evaluate the quality of central bank forecasts, which will enhance central bank credibility if these forecasts are viewed as constructed using best practice. Fourth, published forecasts increase the incentives for the central bank to produce good forecasts because a poor forecasting record would be embarrassing and lead to reduced credibility.

The publication of inflation forecasts might require several steps. First, a monetary policy committee might have to learn how to agree on a forecast (and the path of policy interest rates that the forecast will be based on, an issue discussed later) and the degree of uncertainty in the forecasts. Once it has accomplished this, it can then publish this information in a so-called *fan chart* (because the resulting graph looks like a fan) in which shaded areas indicate the probability of the forecasted variable being within a particular shaded area and so provide information about the most likely forecast and the uncertainty around that forecast.

An argument against a central bank publishing its forecasts has been made by Stephen Morris and Hyun Song Shin.[15] Market participants may have information that the central bank does not have or they may have useful and different ways to interpret some of the same information. If market participants put a high value on central bank forecasts, they may modify their forecasts to be more like the central bank forecasts; the private forecasts therefore would not reflect the full amount of information that these individual firms have. Thus, there is a possibility that the private sector will end up with less information about the economy and their decisions will then be worse. The Morris-Shin argument, however, depends on market participants having their own sources of information that are quite accurate relative to the information in central bank forecasts. This is unlikely to be true, particularly for inflation forecasts that depend on projections of central bank policies that are clearly better known by the central bank, and so there is still a very strong case for central banks to publish their forecasts.[16]

19.7.4 On What Interest Rate Path Should the Central Bank Condition Its Forecasts?

Given that publishing forecasts is highly beneficial, there is still the question of what the policy interest rate path forecast should be conditioned on. There are three choices: 1) a constant interest rate path, 2) market forecasts of the future policy rates, or 3) a central bank projection of the policy interest rate path.

A constant interest rate path would almost surely never be optimal because future projected changes in interest rates will be necessary to keep inflation on the appropriate target path. The second choice is also problematic for several reasons. Using market forecasts for the interest rate path may give the impression that the central bank's decisions are driven by the analysts in the financial sector. This may weaken confidence in the central bank's capabilities for making independent decisions and could create concerns that the central bank is captive to participants in the financial market. In addition, if the central bank does just what the market expects it to do there is a circularity if the central bank sets its policy rate on the basis of market forecasts when the market forecasts are just guesses of what the central bank will be doing. In this case, there is nothing that pins down the system, and inflation outcomes could be indeterminate.[17] Of course, the central bank may not intend to follow the market's expectations, but if this is the case, the central bank is not being very transparent when it bases its forecasts of the economy on market expectations of its actions. An additional, but more minor, problem of conditioning on market forecasts of policy rates is that these forecasts require making assessments of the risk (term) premiums embedded in interest rates. There is not complete agreement on the best way to do this and this is an active area of economic research. Market participants may not be completely happy with the way the central bank chooses to extract market forecasts of the policy path from interest rates and this could create some doubts about the quality of the central bank forecasts.

Theory therefore tells us that the only appropriate and logically consistent choice is the third one, the central bank's projection of the policy interest rate path used to build its published inflation forecasts. An inflation forecast is meaningless without specifying what policy it is conditioned on, and this is why Lars Svensson has made a strong case that a central bank should publish its projection of the policy rate path used in producing its forecast, which will almost surely be time-varying.[18] In addition, information about the central bank's view on the policy rate's future path would help the market understand and better assess the central bank's approach to monetary policy. Admittedly many central banks, including the European Central

Bank and the Bank of England, base their inflation forecasts not on the interest rate path that they deem appropriate to deliver price stability, but rather on the path implicit in the market yield curve. By so doing they avoid having to fully reveal what they project the future path of the policy interest rate to be. Yet, whenever such a path implies an inflation forecast that deviates from the bank's target, the monetary policy committee will follow a different path. But precise knowledge of such a path is what would be valuable information for the market.

Although the argument for announcing the projection of the policy path is theoretically sound, announcing the policy path does create some problems. Charles Goodhart, a former member of the Monetary Policy Committee of the Bank of England, argues that announcing the policy projection will complicate the decision-making process of the committee that makes monetary policy decisions.[19] The current procedure of most central banks is to make decisions about only the current setting of the policy rate. Goodhart argues that "a great advantage of restricting the choice of what to do now, this month, is that it makes the decision relatively simple, even stark."[20] If a policy projection with time-varying rates is announced, this requires that the monetary policy committee come to an agreement on this policy path. Although Lars Svensson argues that this could be done by a "simple" voting procedure, this procedure is far from simple and is unlikely to work. Forcing committee members to make a decision about the future path of rates and not just the rate today may so complicate matters that the decision-making process could be severely impaired. Although committee members might have some idea of a future direction for policy rates, they are likely to have trouble thinking about a precise policy rate path rather than just the setting of the rate today. Furthermore, getting committee members to agree on a future path of the policy rate might be very difficult and the decision could end up being very contentious.

The second problem with announcing a projection of the policy rate path is that it might complicate communication with the public. Although economists understand that any central bank's policy path projection is inherently conditional because changes in the state of the economy will require a change in the policy path, the public is far less likely to understand this distinction. Indeed, there is a danger that the public and the markets will come to expect that decisions about policy rates will have been made before the next monetary policy committee meeting. When new information comes in and the central bank changes the policy rate from its projected path, the public may see this adjustment as a reneging on its announced policy or an indication that the central bank's previous policy settings were a mistake. Thus, even when the central bank is conducting its policy in an optimal manner, deviations from its projected policy path may be viewed by the public as a central bank failure and could hurt the central bank's credibility. In addition, the deviations of the policy rate from its projected path might be seen as flip-flops by the central bank. As we often see in political campaigns, when candidates change positions even if the shifts reflect changes in circumstances and thus reflect sound judgment, they are vulnerable to attacks that they do not have the leadership qualities of steadiness and consistency. Wouldn't central banks be subject to the same criticism when changing circumstances would force them to change the policy rate from its previously projected path? The result might be a weakening of support for the central bank and its independence, although this has not as yet been a problem in New Zealand, where the central bank does announce its projected policy rate path.

Although there are strong arguments for a central bank to publish its projections of the policy path, the problems with doing this suggest that how it should best be done is very controversial. There are three possible choices that are examined: 1) only the most likely (or mean) policy path could be published,[21] 2) the most likely policy path could be published along with a fan chart showing how much uncertainty there is about the policy path, and 3) a fan chart of the policy path could be published without identifying the most likely path. Currently very few central banks publish their projections of their policy path. The Reserve Bank of New Zealand, however, uses the first procedure in which only the most likely policy path is published, while the Norges Bank uses the second procedure and publishes a fan chart that includes the most likely policy path.

As already pointed out, there are serious problems with the first procedure, particularly for central banks in which the decision about setting policy rates is done by a committee rather than an individual. Decisions about setting policy rates at the Reserve Bank of New Zealand are made solely by the governor, so the complications with having a committee decide the policy projection are not present. Thus, the fact that the Reserve Bank of New Zealand has been able to publish only the most likely policy path does not tell us whether this would work well in most other central banks that have committees decide on policy. Just publishing the most likely policy path also leaves the central bank vulnerable to criticisms that it is not doing what it said it would do when it deviates from the projected path.

The second choice used by the Norges Bank has more to recommend it because it does indicate that the policy projection is highly uncertain. The fan chart will make it clear to market participants that when a central bank deviates from the most likely projection, this does not mean that it has flip-flopped. Rather it makes it easier for the central bank to explain to the public that the economy did not evolve quite as the bank thought was most likely, but this should not be a surprise because there is a lot of uncertainty about future forecasts of the economy. Furthermore, it may be easier for a committee to agree on a most likely policy path because even if some members disagree with the published assessment of the exact most likely path, they may be willing to agree to the fan chart with this path because their assessment of the most likely path may fall within the range of paths indicated by the fan chart.

The only problem with this procedure is that the public and the media may focus too much on the most likely path in the fan chart, and this could lead to some of the problems mentioned above.

The reasoning above suggests that the third option of publishing just the fan chart but not publishing the most likely path may be the best one. The fan chart is consistent with full transparency because it shows the direction the central bank expects for the policy path but can also indicate the degree of uncertainty the central bank has about the economy's future evolution and hence the course of the policy path. Also, publication of the fan chart (and of the data needed to construct it) would enable market participants to derive the most likely policy path, so this information would not be hidden. However, by not publishing the most likely policy path, the central bank could emphasize and make it much clearer to the public that it has not made a commitment to achieving the most likely policy path and that the most likely policy path is not that special because there would almost surely not be a spike in the probability distribution for that particular path. Therefore, not publishing the most likely policy path is actually more transparent, as long as the data for construction of the fan chart is made publicly available.

An additional advantage of not publishing the most likely policy path is that members of the central bank's policy committee who disagreed with the implied most likely policy path might be more comfortable about agreeing to the fan chart that omits depicting the most likely path because they could state that their alternate view is still well within the range of paths indicated by the fan chart. There is a precedent for publishing only fan charts without the most likely policy path: in its *Inflation Report* the Bank of England does not publish the most likely path of the variables for which it provides forecasts, but instead publishes only fan charts. (The Bank of England, however, does not publish information on its projection of the policy path, but rather conditions its forecasts on the market forecasts of policy rates.) The Bank of England refrains from publishing the most likely paths of variables it forecasts because it wants to make clear to the markets that its forecasts are uncertain.

19.7.5 Should Central Banks Announce Their Objective Function for Monetary Policy?

For the public and the markets to fully understand what a central bank is doing they need to understand the central bank's objectives. Because inflation-targeting central banks should and do care about output fluctuations as well as inflation fluctuations, Lars Svensson has argued that announcing an inflation target is not enough: full transparency requires that the central bank reveal its objective function, that is, what is the relative weight that they put on reducing output fluctuations relative to reducing inflation fluctuations.[22] Yet this is harder to implement in practice than in theory.

The first problem with announcing an objective function is that it might be quite hard for members of a monetary policy committee to specify an objective function. Members of monetary policy boards don't think in terms of objective functions and would have a very hard time describing what theirs is. Monetary policy committee members could be confronted with hypothetical choices about acceptable paths of inflation and output gaps and then their choices would reveal how much they care about output, versus inflation, fluctuations. While committee members do this when confronted with a real-world situation, my experience with seeing how policy boards work suggests that members would find this difficult to do when the choices are hypothetical. Hypothetical scenarios do not always focus the mind.

A second problem, raised by Charles Goodhart, is that it would be difficult for a committee to agree on its objective function. As mentioned, committee members might have trouble defining their own objective function. Another issue is that the composition of the committee changes frequently and existing members may change their views on objectives, depending on circumstances, meaning that they would frequently revisit the decision on the committee's objective function. Deciding on the committee's objective function would thus substantially increase the complexity of the decision process, might be quite contentious, and could weaken the quality of monetary policy decisions.

A third problem is that it is far from clear who should decide on the objective function. If the members of the monetary policy board do so, isn't this a violation of the democratic principle that the objectives of bureaucracies be set by the political process? An alternative would be for the government to do so. But if we think that it would be hard enough for a monetary policy committee to do this, it would be even more difficult for politicians to decide on the objective function.

Even if it were easy for the monetary policy committee or the government to come to a decision on the objective function, would it be easy to communicate it to the public? If economists and members of a monetary policy committee have trouble quantifying their objective function, is it likely that the public would understand what the central bank was talking about when it announced its objective function? Announcement of the objective function would likely only complicate the communication process with the public.

Announcing the central bank's objective function can add a further complication to the communication process that might have even more severe consequences for the central bank to do its job well. The beauty of inflation-targeting regimes is that by focusing on one clear target—inflation—communication is fairly straightforward. On the other hand, by announcing the objective function, the central bank may lead the public to believe that the central bank will target on output as well as on inflation. Discussing output as well as inflation objectives can confuse the public and make it more likely that the citizenry will see the central bank's mission as eliminating short-run output fluctuations, and thus worsening the time-inconsistency problem.

One possible negative outcome from perceptions that there is an output target is that workers and firms will raise wages and prices because they know that the monetary authorities are likely to accommodate these rises by pursuing expansionary policy to prevent output gaps from developing. The result is that a self-fulfilling prophecy can occur in which wages and prices rise, then monetary policy accommodates this rise, and this leads to further rises in wages and prices, and so on, thus leading to a new equilibrium with higher inflation without a reduction in output fluctuations. Discussing monetary policy objectives in terms of output fluctuations can thus lead to a loss of inflation-fighting credibility for the central bank, with the result that the inflation-output fluctuation trade-off worsens.

Announcing the objective function also requires the central bank to publish its estimates of the current and future output gaps and hence its estimate of potential output and its growth rate. The announcement of potential output estimates, and particularly its growth rate, may increase the probability that the public sees these predictions as a target for monetary policy and thus may induce politicians to pressure the central bank to eliminate output gaps and pursue high growth in the short run—with negative consequences. This problem is likely to be even more damaging because, as we have seen, potential output and thus output gaps are very hard to measure. Furthermore, some economists argue that measures of output gaps do not provide much information about the true slack in the economy and they find that other alternative measures have substantially different movements and timing than output gaps.

The bottom line is that revealing its objective function to the public is not a useful way to make the monetary policy process more coherent, transparent, or accountable, and not surprisingly, no central bank has revealed its objective function to the public.[23] Furthermore, the discussion here suggests that even if the central bank does not announce its objective function, announcing current and future potential output and output gap estimates still has the potential to worsen monetary policy performance. Thus, the discussion also argues against the publication of central bank estimates and forecasts of the potential output and output gap, as is done, for example, by the Norges Bank.[24]

19.7.6   Should Central Banks Publish Their Minutes?

The benefits of transparency suggest that central banks should provide a substantial amount of information about how monetary policy decisions are made. Central bank minutes, the summary of the deliberations about monetary policy by the members of the policy board, provide an important vehicle for doing exactly that, and there is thus a strong argument for these records to be released in a timely manner. Most central banks do indeed publish minutes within a couple weeks of their policy decisions.

However, could transparency be pushed even further by having the arguments expressed in policy board meetings attributed to the individual board members who make them? This increase in transparency is likely to be counterproductive. An example of the dangers of pushing transparency further in this direction is provided by the experience of the Federal Reserve, which publishes transcripts of its FOMC (the policy board) meetings five years after the meeting. (The publication of these transcripts is unique to the Fed and it occurred because Arthur Burns, the chairman of the Federal Reseve, decided to put in a taping system without the knowledge of his fellow board members. When this was publicly revealed during Alan Greenspan's tenure as Fed chairman, the U.S. Congress insisted that the transcripts be published and the Fed did not feel it could resist the congressional request.) Participants in the FOMC who saw how the FOMC operated both before and after it was announced that the transcripts would be released have indicated that policy discussions became much more formal and less interactive once FOMC members were aware that their statements would be attributed to them. This experience suggests that attributing arguments to particular members would lead to less effective policy board meetings because it would reduce free discussion and exchange of ideas.

Although there are strong reasons not to publish the arguments of individual members in policy board meetings, individual board members should have some accountability for their actions. The ideal solution seems to be that their votes on policy decisions should be recorded as is done in Sweden, the United Kingdom, or the United States.

19.8   The Optimal Inflation Target

We have seen already that good economic performance requires that an inflation-targeting regime have a flexible design. In addition, there are questions about how the target itself should be chosen to generate the best economic performance. There are three issues that must be dealt with in designing the optimal inflation target: 1) what price measure should be used in the inflation target, 2) what is the optimal level of the inflation target, and 3) should the target be in terms of the price level or in terms of inflation?

19.8.1   What Price Measure Should Be Used in the Inflation Target?

Economic theory shows that an inflation target measure that puts more weight on prices that move sluggishly (referred to as *sticky prices*) will do better at reducing employment and output fluctuations.[25] If there is a high weight put on more flexible prices, monetary policy is likely to overreact to short-term fluctuations in these prices, leading to excessive fluctuations in employment and output.

One important element of the consumer price index (CPI) in many countries is mortgage interest payments that are calculated as the price of owner-occupied housing multiplied by the mortgage rate. Including mortgage interest payments in the CPI means that a volatile asset price, that of residential housing, has a major effect on CPI inflation measures. Using an inflation target based on such a CPI measure therefore leads to targeting on an inflation measure that does not put enough weight on sticky prices and this can result in excessive output fluctuations.

In addition, since the mortgage rate in most countries is an interest rate that is not adjusted for inflation (a *nominal* rate rather than a *real* rate), a CPI that includes mortgage interest payments will overstate inflation when nominal rates are rising because expectations of inflation are rising. This can mean that when the central bank is raising interest rates to contain inflation, the inflation measure will be biased upward, which could induce even tighter monetary policy. The resulting over-tightening would lead to an unnecessary output decline.

Targeting an inflation measure that includes mortgage interest payments is highly problematic and this is an important reason why inflation indices used to guide monetary policy in the United States, the United Kingdom, and the Eurozone exclude mortgage interest payments. Indeed, the view that the measure of inflation used for the target should put more weight on sticky prices suggests that monetary policy should target a core inflation measure that removes volatile prices from the price index. This is why many central banks use core inflation measures to guide monetary policy that exclude volatile price items like food and energy from the price index and are more driven by developments in wages. However, no specific core measure will always be appropriate because what are considered sticky price items can change over time.

19.8.2   What Is the Optimal Level of the Inflation Target?

A key question for any central bank using an inflation-targeting strategy is what the long-run inflation target should be. To decide on the appropriate long-run inflation target, we need to answer the deeper question of what does price stability mean. Alan Greenspan has provided a widely cited definition of price stability as a rate of inflation that is sufficiently low so households and businesses do not have to account for it in everyday decisions. This definition of price stability is a reasonable one, and operationally any inflation number between 0 and 3 percent seems to meet this criterion. Some economists, Martin Feldstein and William Poole being prominent examples, have argued for a long-run inflation goal of 0 percent, which has the psychological appeal of the "magic number" of zero. Indeed, one concern is that an inflation goal greater than zero might lead to a decline in central bank credibility and to instability in inflation expectations, which could lead to an upward creep in inflation. However, the experience with inflation targeting suggests that maintaining a target for inflation above zero, but not too far above (less than 3 percent), for an extended period, does not lead to instability in the public's inflation expectations or to a decline in central bank credibility.

One prominent argument against setting the long-run inflation target at zero has been raised in an important paper by George Akerlof, William Dickens, and George Perry,[26] who contend that setting inflation at too low a level produces inefficiency and will increase the natural rate of unemployment. They reason that downward nominal wage rigidity, which they argue is consistent with the empirical evidence, indicates that reductions of real wages can occur only through inflation. The implication is that a very low rate of inflation might prevent real wages from adjusting downward in response to declining labor demand in certain industries or regions, thereby leading to increased unemployment and hindering the reallocation of labor from declining sectors to expanding sectors.

The evidence for the Akerlof-Dickens-Perry mechanism through which low inflation raises the natural rate of unemployment is not at all clear-cut. Furthermore, Akerlof, Dickens, and Perry tell only one side of the story. Inflation not only can "grease" the labor market and allow downward shifts in real wages in response to a decline in demand along the lines of Akerlof, Dickens, and Perry, but can also put friction in the system ("sand") by increasing the noise in relative real wages.[27] This noise reduces the information content of nominal wages and hence the efficiency of the process by which workers are allocated across occupations and industries. Thus, the Akerlof-Dickens-Perry argument is not persuasive for setting the long-run goal for inflation above zero.

A more convincing argument against an inflation goal of zero is that it makes it more likely that the economy will experience episodes of deflation: with a mean of zero, half the time inflation would have to be negative (deflation). Deflation can be highly dangerous because debt contracts in advanced countries frequently have long maturities, so that a deflation, even if anticipated in the short run, leads to an increase in the real indebtedness of firms and households.[28] Deflation can thus lead to what the famous economist Irving Fisher called *debt-deflation*, in which deflation leads to a deterioration of firms' and households' balance sheets, which leads to financial instability.[29] Indeed, this debt-deflation phenomenon is one reason why the Japanese economy has performed so poorly until very recently (although the unwillingness of the government to fix the banking sector was a more important factor). Deflation, even if fully anticipated, also causes a problem for monetary policy because it can lead to a situation in which interest rates hit a floor of zero, the so-called *zero lower bound*, and cannot be lowered any further to stimulate the economy. The conventional monetary policy tool of lowering interest rates to stimulate the economy is no longer an option, making it much more difficult for the monetary authorities to extricate an economy from a deflationary trap.

The dangers of deflation imply that undershooting a zero inflation target (that is, a deflation) is potentially more costly than overshooting a zero target by the same amount. The logic of this argument suggests that setting an inflation target a little above zero is worthwhile because it provides some insurance against episodes of deflation.

Another reason why central banks would be better off with a long-run inflation goal above zero is that it is crucial that they not be perceived as being overly obsessed with controlling inflation at the expense of output stability. If the monetary authorities are perceived as "inflation nutters," to use Mervyn King's terminology, and put no weight on output fluctuations in making their decisions about monetary policy, the central bank is likely to lose public support. Too low an inflation target, say zero or even 1 percent, may signal that the central bank does not care sufficiently about the concerns of real people.

The arguments here suggest that too low an inflation target, below 1 percent, may worsen economic outcomes, while an inflation target above 3 percent is inconsistent with what most people would consider to be price stability. This is why we see that countries choose inflation targets between 1 and 3 percent. Empirical research does not find that it matters much to economic performance whether the inflation target is 1.5, 2, or 2.5 percent. Any number between 1 and 3 percent seems to lead to similar outcomes.

19.8.3   Point Target or Target Range?

Once the optimal level of inflation to shoot for is chosen, there is still a question as to whether the target would be better described as a point target, say 2 percent, or a range (band), say 1 to 3 percent.

The advantages of a target range is that it provides more explicit flexibility to the targeting regime and conveys to the public the important message that there is uncertainty in the inflation process, so the central bank's ability to control inflation will necessarily be imperfect.

However, the use of a range can have a major drawback: it can take on a life of its own. With target ranges in place, politicians, financial markets, and the public might focus on whether inflation is just outside or inside the edge of a range rather than on the magnitude of the deviation from the midpoint. The opposite problem occurred in the United Kingdom in 1995 when inflation exceeded the target midpoint by more than one percentage point, but did not breach the upper band. The fact that inflation was still within the target range gave the Chancellor of the Exchequer cover to resist demands by the Bank of England to tighten monetary policy. The problem with focusing too much on the edges of the range is that his emphasis can lead the central bank to concentrate too much on keeping the inflation rate just within the bands rather than trying to hit the midpoint of the range, and this can result in wider fluctuations of inflation.

This drawback is easily dealt with if the central bank emphasizes the midpoint of its inflation target in its communication, while providing a tolerance range as the Bank of England currently does. In this formulation it is clear that the central bank is not focusing on the edges of the band. Indeed, my recent research demonstrates that having an inflation target specified as a point with a tolerance range around it is an excellent way to mitigate the time-inconsistency problem and provide the appropriate incentives for monetary policy.[30]

19.8.4 Should the Target Be in Terms of Price Level or in Terms of Inflation?

Currently, all countries who have adopted inflation targeting have chosen to target the inflation rate rather than the price level. With an inflation target, misses of the inflation target are not reversed by the central bank so that bygones are bygones. A price-level target can allow for positive inflation because it specifies that the target is moving along a steadily rising path of the price level. However, in contrast to an inflation target, if inflation ends up being above the specified growth rate of the price-level target, inflation will need to be temporarily below this growth rate to return the price level to the target path (as illustrated in figure 19.4). Which of these two targets would result in better economic performance is still an open question. Indeed, it is the subject of active research in the economics profession.

There are two key advantages of a price-level target relative to an inflation target. The first is that a price-level target can reduce the uncertainty about where the price level will be over a long horizon. With an inflation target, as noted, misses of the target are not reversed by the central bank so that bygones are bygones. The result is that the uncertainty of where the price level will be in the future grows as we go further out into the future. This uncertainty can make long-run planning difficult and may therefore lead to a decrease in economic efficiency.

The second advantage of a price-level target is that, as Michael Woodford describes, it is "history dependent."[31] When a negative shock hits the economy so that output falls and lowers inflation below the targeted price-level growth rate, a price-level target implies that inflation will have to be above that growth rate for some time. The higher expected inflation rate that results then implies that the real interest rate (the interest rate adjusted for expected inflation) will decline even without central bank actions; monetary policy automatically becomes more expansionary, which counters the negative shock to output. This desirable feature of a price-level target can therefore produce less output variance than an inflation target.

The history dependence of a price-level target can be particularly stabilizing for the economy when deflation sets in, as it did in Japan in the late 1990s and early 2000s,

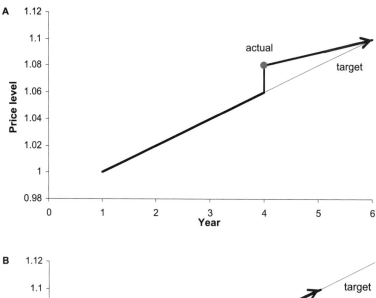

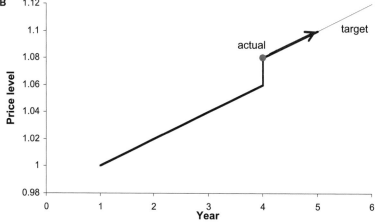

Figure 19.4
Price-level versus inflation targeting.
Panel A. Price-level targeting. Suppose the desired inflation rate is 2 percent so the price-level target is ris-
ing at 2 percent every year and inflation has also been rising at 2 percent every year from year 1 to year 3.
Then the inflation rate jumps to 4 percent in year 4. With a price-level target the overshoot of inflation
requires the central bank to move the price level back to the target path, which means that for a time the
central bank will shoot for an inflation rate below 2 percent.
Panel B. Inflation-level targeting. Suppose the inflation target is 2 percent so the price-level target is rising
at 2 percent every year and inflation has also been rising at 2 percent every year from year 1 to year 3.
Then the inflation rate jumps to 4 percent in year 4. With an inflation target, the price-level path that is
targeted is raised to accommodate the increased price level (bygones are bygones), so the central bank still
tries to achieve an inflation rate of 2 percent.

leading to the *zero-lower-bound problem* in which nominal interest rates cannot go below zero, making the conventional tool of lowering nominal interest rates to stimulate the economy no longer an option for the central bank. As pointed out by Gautti Eggertsson and Michael Woodford, an inflation target can still leave the economy in a *deflationary trap*, in which a large deflationary shock that leads to persistent deflation leads to high real interest rates because nominal interest rates encounter the zero lower bound and cannot fall below zero.[32] The history dependence of a price-level target helps undo this problem because the deflation that sends the price level below its target leads to expectations of even higher inflation, which lowers real interest rates, thereby stimulating the economy and helping the economy escape from the deflationary trap.

The history dependence of a price-level target also can reduce inflation variability over an inflation target, though at first, this may seem surprising. For example, when there is a cost-push shock, such as an increase in oil prices, the amount of the inflation increase that the central bank must accept not to have a large decline in output is lower because businesses expect the general increase in the price level to be undone and so will raise prices by less than they otherwise would, thereby helping to contain inflation. Also, when the central bank makes a mistake in estimating the level of potential output, fluctuations in inflation are likely to be lower. Say the central bank overestimates productivity growth and potential output, as the Federal Reserve did in the 1970s, and this leads to overly expansionary monetary policy and inflation. With a price-level target, businesses will again not raise prices by as much as they otherwise would because they expect the increase in the price level to be undone.[33]

There are, however, disadvantages to a price-level target. The traditional view, forcefully articulated by Stanley Fischer, argues that in non-forward-looking models a price-level target could produce more output variability because overshoots or undershoots of the target must be reversed. This could impart significantly more volatility to monetary policy and, with sticky prices, to the real economy in the short run.[34] A second problem is that a price-level target may lead to more frequent episodes of deflation because an overshoot of the target would require that inflation be unusually low for some time. If the price-level target did lead to episodes of deflation, then the problems of financial instability and having the interest rate hit the zero lower bound could be harmful to the economy. A price-level target might also be more difficult to communicate than an inflation target because the fact that the optimal inflation rate is almost surely positive requires that the price-level target rise over time. Thus, the central bank would have to explain that the price-level target is a moving target, which is somewhat more complicated than explaining that the central bank has a constant inflation target, say at 2 percent.

The disadvantages outlined above, particularly the dangers of more frequent deflationary episodes under a price-level target and possible difficulties of communication, probably explain why no central bank has decided to target the price level in recent years.

However, the arguments for preferring an inflation target over a price-level target suggest that hybrid policies, which combine features of an inflation and a price-level target, would be highly desirable. A hybrid policy would involve an inflation target, but one in which target misses will be offset to some extent in the future. Research at the Bank of England and the Bank of Canada shows that an inflation target with a small amount of offsetting for target misses can substantially reduce the uncertainty about the price level in the long run, but still generate very few episodes of deflation.[35] A hybrid policy would thus in effect state that when inflation has been below the target for a substantial period, the monetary authorities would have a bias for inflation to be slightly higher than the target for a brief period. Similarly, if inflation has been persistently above the target, the central bank would have a bias for inflation to be slightly lower than the target. One way to implement a hybrid policy would be to have an inflation target defined as an average over several years (rather than year-by-year, as is typical in most inflation-targeting regimes), which would induce some offset of annual misses of the target.

19.9   The Role of Asset Prices in Monetary Policy

Changes in asset prices like those on common stock, housing, and long-term bond or exchange rate fluctuations have important effects on output and inflation. Asset price movements are important transmission mechanisms for monetary policy because they affect households' and firms' balance sheets and in turn affect spending, which feeds into changes in both output and inflation. Asset prices thus have a major impact on economic forecasts, which are crucial to central bank decisions about setting their policy instruments. Therefore, setting monetary policy instruments to achieve inflation targets requires factoring in asset price movements. For example, a substantial rise in housing prices, which adds to household wealth, would lead to increased spending, higher output, and thus an eventual rise in inflation. An inflation-targeting central bank would therefore need to respond to the rise in housing prices by raising interest rates to keep the economy from overheating and inflation from rising above the inflation target.

The issue about how central bankers should respond to asset price movements is not whether they should respond at all, but whether they should respond over and above the response called for by the flexible inflation-targeting framework described above. Specifically there is an issue of whether the monetary authorities should try to prick, or at least slow down, asset price bubbles, because subsequent collapses of these asset prices might be highly damaging to the economy, as they were in Japan in the 1990s. Some economists argue that central banks should respond sometimes to asset price changes in order to stop bubbles from getting too far out of hand. For example, research by Stephen Cecchetti, Hans Genberg, Jonathan Lipski, and Sushil Wadhwani finds that outcomes are better when the central bank conducts policy to prick asset price bubbles.[36] However, they assume that the central bank knows the bubble is in progress. This assumption is highly dubious because it is hard to believe that the central bank has this kind of informational advantage over private markets. Indeed, the view that government officials know better than the markets has been proved wrong over and over.

A separate focus on asset prices over and above their impact on employment and inflation that central banks should care about can lead to worse policy outcomes. First, the optimal response to a change in asset prices very much depends on the source of the shock to these prices and the duration of the shock. An excellent example of the pitfall of overly focusing on asset prices was the tightening of monetary policy in Chile and New Zealand in response to the downward pressure on their currencies' exchange rate in the aftermath of the East Asian and Russian crises in 1997 and 1998. Given that the shock to the exchange rate was due to a negative terms of trade shock, which would cause the economy to slow down, a better response would have been an easing of policy rather than a tightening. Indeed, the Reserve Bank of Australia responded in the opposite direction to the central banks of New Zealand and Chile and eased monetary policy after the collapse of the Thai baht in July 1997 because it was focused on inflation control and not the exchange rate. The excellent performance of the Australian economy relative to New Zealand's and Chile's during this period illustrates the benefit of focusing on the main objective of the central bank rather than on an asset price.

A second problem with the central bank focusing too much on asset prices is that it raises the possibility that the central bank will be made to look foolish. The linkage between monetary policy and stock prices, for example, although an important part of the transmission mechanism, is nevertheless a weak one. Most fluctuations in stock prices occur for reasons unrelated to monetary policy and either reflect real fundamentals or animal spirits. The loose link between monetary policy and stock prices therefore means that the central bank's ability to control stock prices is very limited. Thus, if the central bank indicates that it wants stock prices to change in a particular direction, it is likely to find that stock prices may move in the opposite direction, making the central bank look inept. Recall that when Alan Greenspan made his speech in 1996 suggesting that the stock market might be exhibiting "irrational exuberance," the Dow Jones average was around 6,500. This didn't stop the market from rising, with the Dow subsequently climbing to above 11,000.

A third problem with focusing on asset prices is that it may weaken support for a central bank because it may appear that it is trying to control too many elements of the economy. Part of the recent successes of central banks throughout the world has been that they have narrowed their policy focus and have more actively communicated what they can and cannot do. Specifically, central banks have argued they are less capable of managing short-run business-cycle fluctuation and should therefore focus more on price stability as their primary goal. A key element of the Bundesbank's successful monetary-targeting regime was that it did not focus on short-run output fluctuations in setting its monetary policy instruments. This communication strategy for the Bundesbank was very effective, and this element was adopted as a key element in inflation targeting. By narrowing their focus in recent years, central banks have been able to increase public support for their independence. Extending their focus to asset prices has the potential to weaken public support for central banks and may even cause the public to worry that the central bank is too powerful, having undue influence over all aspects of the economy.

A fourth problem with too great a focus on asset prices is that it may create a form of moral hazard. Knowing that the central bank is likely to prop up asset prices if they crash, the markets are then more likely to bid up prices. This may help facilitate excessive asset valuations and encourage a bubble that might burst later, something that the central bank would rather avoid.

A fifth problem is that a focus on asset prices might lead the public to think the central bank has objectives beyond its concerns about inflation and output fluctuations. Indeed, it may lead market participants to suspect that the central bank has an additional target of asset prices. This can substantially complicate the central bank's communication about what its inflation-targeting regime means and why it is setting policy instruments the way it is.

The arguments against overly focusing on asset prices do not deal with one particular concern about asset price movements. Asset price crashes sometimes lead to severe episodes of financial instability, with Japan being the most recent notable example. If this happens, monetary policy may become less effective in bringing the economy back to health. There are several responses to this concern about the impact of asset prices on financial instability.

First, the bursting of asset price bubbles often do not lead to financial instability.[37] The recent bursting of the American stock market bubble is one example. The stock market crash in 2000–2001 did not do substantial damage to the balance sheets of financial institutions, which were quite healthy before the crash. As a result the stock market crash was followed by a very mild recession, despite some very negative shocks to the U.S. economy: the September 11, 2001, terrorist attack on the World Trade Center, which harmed both consumer and business confidence, and the corporate accounting scandals at Enron and other American companies, which caused doubts about the quality of information in financial markets and thus had a very negative impact on credit spreads.

Second, many have learned the wrong lesson from the Japanese experience. The problem in Japan was not so much the bursting of the bubble, but rather the policies that followed.[38] The bubble burst in 1989, but the economy did not substantially weaken until several years afterwards. The problem in Japan was the government's unwillingness to fix the problems in the banking sector, so they continued to get worse well after the bubble had burst. In addition, the Bank of Japan did not ease monetary policy sufficiently in the aftermath of the crisis, as many critics of Japanese monetary policy have pointed out. Indeed, it was not until 1998 that the Japanese economy entered its deflationary period.

The first lesson from Japan is that a central bank does not make a serious mistake in failing to stop a bubble, but rather in not responding fast enough after a bubble bursts. If the Bank of Japan had responded rapidly after the asset price crash and recognized that monetary policy had to be much easier because the decline in asset prices was substantially weakening demand in the economy, then deflation would never have set in. If deflation had not gotten started, Japan would not have experienced the debt-deflation that further weakened the balance sheets of the financial sector along the lines outlined earlier.

The second lesson from Japan is that after a bubble bursts, if it harms the balance sheets of the financial sector, the government needs to take immediate steps to restore the health of the financial system. The procrastination on the part of the Japanese government in dealing with the problems in the banking sector is a key reason why the Japanese economy did so poorly for ten years after the crash.

These two lessons suggest how a central bank should deal with possible bubbles in asset markets. Instead of having to preemptively deal with the bubble, which as argued above is almost impossible to do, a central bank can make sure that financial instability is not a serious problem by being ready to react quickly to an asset collapse if it occurs. One way a central bank can ensure it is ready to react quickly is to conduct simulations assessing how it should respond to an asset price collapse. This approach is similar to the training exercise and war games that militaries conduct to prepare their troops for combat. They train them to respond to different scenarios so they can react quickly and with confidence. Indeed, these central bank simulations can be thought of as stress tests similar to the ones that commercial financial institutions and banking supervisors conduct all the time. They see how financial institutions will be affected by particular scenarios and then propose plans for how to ensure the banks can withstand the negative impacts. By conducting similar exercises, the central bank can minimize the negative impacts of a collapse of an asset price bubble without having to predict that a bubble is taking place or that it will burst in the near future.

Another way that a central bank can respond to possible bubbles is through *Financial Stability Reports* (originated by the Bank of England, but now published by other central banks), if it has them. In these reports, the central bank can evaluate whether rises in asset prices might be leading to excessive risk-taking on the part of financial institutions. If this is what appears to be happening, the central bank can put pressure on the prudential regulators and supervisors of these institutions to rein in excessive risk-taking by financial institutions.

19.10   Conclusions

We have learned much about how to conduct monetary policy in recent years and central banks have been converging to best practices, many of which are described in this book. The results have been gratifying, with improved performance on both the inflation and output fronts. There are, however, still many unanswered questions about how monetary policy should be conducted, and there are areas of monetary policy for which consensus on what is best practice has not yet developed. Active debates are ongoing on how transparent central banks should be, what the optimal long-run level of inflation should be, whether central banks should target the price level or inflation, how central banks should respond to sharp fluctuations in asset prices, and what the impact globalization will have on monetary policy effectiveness will be.[39] As history shows, new challenges will arise for monetary policymakers that economists have not yet thought about. The good news for monetary policy researchers like myself is that much further work will need to be done to ensure progress in our understanding of monetary policy will continue. This future research hopefully will help monetary policy strategy evolve in a direction that continues to improve monetary policy performance.

Notes

I want to thank Ben Bernanke, Francesco Giavazzi, Torsten Persson, Lars Svensson, and Michael Woodford for their helpful comments on this chapter.

1. Phelps (1967) and Friedman (1968).

2. Lucas (1972, 1973, 1976) and Sargent and Wallace (1975).

3. Lucas (1972), Kydland and Prescott (1977), Calvo (1978), and Barro and Gordon (1983).

4. When a central bank does not pursue an objective of raising output or employment above what is consistent with stable inflation, there will be no *inflation bias* (average inflation above the optimal long-run level). In a model with a forward-looking, New Keynesian, Phillips curve, however, there will still be a problem of *stabilization bias* (too much focus on reducing output fluctuations relative to inflation fluctuations) and a lack of *history dependence* (response to initial conditions that would produce better outcomes). See Woodford (2003).

5. The example here has an element of paternalism because the parent knows what is good for the child even if the child doesn't. The time-inconsistency problem still exists even if the child does know what is best for her, but the parents' and the child's objectives differ. In this case, discretion still leads to bad outcomes because it results in tantrums that are painful for both child and parent.

6. See the surveys in Forder (2000) and Cukierman (2006).

7. See Woodward (2000) for a lively discussion of this episode.

8. Goodfriend (1993).

9. Two other important factors are import prices, which are determined by world market prices and exchange rates, and supply shocks such as the price of oil. However, the central bank has no control over

world market or oil prices and so adding these factors into the analysis does not change the basic conclusion here.

10. King (1999).

11. Note that not all supply shocks lead to a trade-off between inflation and output fluctuations. A negative supply shock could lead to a decline in potential output along with higher inflation; then lowering inflation and allowing actual output to decline is the right thing for the central bank to do.

12. Svensson (1997).

13. Woodford (2003).

14. Orphanides (1998, 2002).

15. Morris and Shin (2005).

16. Svensson (2005) and Woodford (2005).

17. See Bernanke and Woodford (1997).

18. Svensson (2002).

19. Goodhart (2001).

20. Goodhart (2001), page 173.

21. Most central banks talk about the most likely path (mode) of their forecasts, but there are strong theoretical arguments for central banks to talk more about the mean path because it takes into account that the risks to the forecast may be biased more in one direction than another. In most cases, however, the mean and the mode will be quite close to each other.

22. Svensson (2002).

23. Michael Woodford (1999) provides an additional argument against announcement of the central bank's objective function positing that this announcement does not make it possible for markets to predict what a central bank will do or how it justifies its decisions. The central bank should not follow a procedure of determining the different paths of the economy through simulations of its models and then pick the one that maximizes the objective function at each of its monetary policy meetings. This procedure leads to the time-inconsistency problem because the same objective function would not lead to a choice of the same path chosen at the previous meeting even if there is no new information.

24. Because estimates of output gap measures are one important input into central bank forecasts of inflation, there is an argument to provide some information about them to the public, but which emphasizes how uncertain these measures are. I do not believe that fan charts are a good way to do this because I do not believe that they sufficiently describe that we are not even sure conceptually how to measure potential output and output gaps. On the other hand, publication of several different conceptual ways of measuring output gaps might provide more information about them and might indicate how uncertain these measures are. This is a subject for further research.

25. Goodfriend and King (1997) and Woodford (2003).

26. Akerlof, Dickens, and Perry (1996).

27. Groshen and Schweitzer (1999).

28. If a deflation is anticipated, it would have less negative consequences for debtors versus creditors, which creates the debt-deflation problem described by Fisher (1933). The fact that the deflation is anticipated does not completely rule out some negative impacts on balance sheets because if the debt is sufficiently long-lived, there still is some redistribution from debtors to creditors.

29. Fisher (1933).

30. Mishkin and Westelius (2006).

31. Woodford (2003).

32. Eggertsson and Woodford (2003).

33. Gorodnichenko and Shapiro (2006) make this argument and show how it also works to stabilize inflation when the central bank underestimates productivity growth.

34. Fischer (1994).

35. See King (1999) and Black, Macklem, and Rose (1998).

36. Cecchetti, Genberg, Lipski, and Wadhwani (2000). See Bernanke and Gertler (2001) for a critique of this work.

37. Mishkin and White (2003).

38. Posen (2003).

39. For an interesting first take on the impact of globalization on monetary policy see Rogoff (forthcoming).

References

Akerlof, George, William Dickens, and George Perry. 1996. "The Macroeconomics of Low Inflation." *Brookings Papers on Economic Activity* 1: 1–59.

Barro, Robert J., and David B. Gordon. 1983. "A Positive Theory of Monetary Policy in a Natural Rate Model." *Journal of Political Economy* 91 (4): 589–610.

Bernanke, Ben S., and Mark Gertler. 2001. "How Should Central Bankers Respond to Asset Prices?" *American Economic Review Papers and Proceedings* 91 (May): 248–252.

Bernanke, Ben S., Thomas Laubach, Frederic S. Mishkin, and Adam S. Posen. 1999. *Inflation Targeting: Lessons from the International Experience.* Princeton, N.J.: Princeton University Press.

Bernanke, Ben S., and Michael Woodford. 1997. "Inflation Forecasts and Monetary Policy." *Journal of Money, Credit and Banking* 29: 653–685.

Black, Richard, Tiff Macklem, and David Rose. 1998. "On Policy Rules for Price Stability." *Price Stability, Inflation Targets and Monetary Policy.* Proceedings of a Conference held by Bank of Canada, May 1997. Ottawa, Canada: 411–461.

Cecchetti, S., H. Genberg, J. Lipski, and S. Wadhwani. 2000. "Asset Prices and Central Bank Policy." *Geneva Reports on the World Economy*, no. 2. International Center for Monetary and Banking Studies and Centre for Economic Policy Research, July.

Cukierman, Alex. 2006. "Central Bank Independence and Monetary Policymaking Institutions: Past Present and Future." Central Bank of Chile Working Papers No. 360 (April).

Eggertsson, Gautti B., and Michael Woodford. 2003. "The Zero Bound on Interest Rates and Optimal Monetary Policy." *Brookings Papers on Economic Activity* 1: 139–211.

Fischer, Stanley. 1994. "Modern Central Banking." In Forest Capie, Charles Goodhart, Stanley Fischer, and Norbert Schnadt. *The Future of Central Banking.* Cambridge, U.K.: Cambridge University Press. 262–308.

Fisher, Irving. 1933. "The Debt-Deflation Theory of Great Depressions." *Econometrica* 1: 337–357.

Forder, James. 2000. "Central Bank Independence and Credibility: Is There a Shred of Evidence?: Review." *International Finance* 3 (1, April): 167–185.

Friedman, Milton. 1968. "The Role of Monetary Policy." *American Economic Review* 58 (March): 1–17.

Goodfriend, Marvin. 1993. "Interest Rate Policy and the Inflation Scare Problem: 1979–1992." *Federal Reserve Bank of Richmond Economic Quarterly* 79 (1, Winter): 1–24.

Goodfriend, Marvin, and Robert G. King. 1997. "The New Neoclassical Synthesis and the Role of Monetary Policy." NBER *Macroeconomics Annual*: 231–283.

Goodhart, Charles A. E. 2001. "Monetary Transmission Lags and the Formulation of the Policy Decision on Interest Rates." Federal Reserve Bank of St. Louis *Review* (July/August): 165–181.

Gorodnichenko, Yuriy, and Matthew D. Shapiro. 2006. "Monetary Policy When Potential Output is Uncertain: Understanding the Growth Gamble of the 1990s." NBER Working Paper No. 12268 (June).

Groshen, Erica L., and Mark E. Schweitzer. 1999. "Identifying Inflation's Grease and Sand Effects in the Labor Market." In Martin Feldstein, ed., *The Costs and Benefits of Price Stability.* Chicago: University of Chicago Press. 273–308.

King, Mervyn. 1999. "Challenges for Monetary Policy: New and Old." In *New Challenges for Monetary Policy.* Kansas City, Mo.: Federal Reserve Bank of Kansas City. 11–57.

Kydland, Finn, and Edward Prescott. 1977. "Rules Rather Than Discretion: The Inconsistency of Optimal Plans." *Journal of Political Economy* 85 (3, June): 473–492.

Lucas, Robert E., Jr. 1972. "Expectations and the Neutrality of Money." *Journal of Economic Theory* 4: 103–124.

Lucas, Robert E., Jr. 1973. "Some International Evidence on Output-Inflation Tradeoffs." *American Economic Review* 63: 326–334.

Lucas, Robert E., Jr. 1976. "Econometric Policy Evaluation: A Critique." In *The Phillips Curve and Labor Markets.* K. Brunner and A. Meltzer, eds. Carnegie-Rochester Conference Series on Public Policy 1: 19–46.

Mishkin, Frederic S., and Niklas J. Westelius. 2006. "Inflation Band Targeting and Optimal Inflation Contracts." Columbia University mimeo.

Mishkin, Frederic S., and Eugene White. 2003. "U.S. Stock Market Crashes and Their Aftermath: Implications for Monetary Policy." In William B. Hunter, George G. Kaufman, and Michael Pormerleano, eds., *Asset Price Bubbles: The Implications for Monetary, Regulatory and International Policies.* Cambridge, Mass.: The MIT Press. 53–79.

Morris, Stephen, and Hyung Song Shin. 2005. "Central Bank Transparency and the Signal Value of Prices." *Brookings Papers on Economic Activity* 2: 1–66.

Orphanides, Athanasios. 1998. "Monetary Policy Evaluation with Noisy Information." Federal Reserve Board FEDS Paper No. 98-50 (October).

Orphanides, Athanasios. 2001. "Monetary Policy Rules Based on Real-Time Data." *American Economic Review* 91 (4, September): 964–985.

Orphanides, Athanasios. 2002. "Monetary Policy Rules and the Great Inflation." *American Economic Review* 92 (2, May): 115–120.

Phelps, Edmund. 1967. "Phillips Curves, Expectations and Optimal Unemployment Over Time." *Economica* 34 (August): 254–281.

Posen, Adam S. 2003. "It Takes More than a Bubble to Become Japan." Institute for International Economics Working Paper No. 03-9 (October).

Rogoff, Kenneth. Forthcoming. "Implications of Globalization on Monetary Policy." In *The New Economic Geography: Effects and Policy Implications.* Kansas City, Mo.: Federal Reserve Bank of Kansas City.

Sargent, Thomas J., and Neil Wallace. 1975. "Rational Expectations, the Optimal Monetary Instrument and the Optimal Money Supply Rule." *Journal of Political Economy* 83: 241–254.

Svensson, Lars E. O. 1997. "Inflation Forecast Targeting: Implementing and Monitoring Inflation Targets." *European Economic Review* 41: 1111–1146.

Svensson, Lars E. O. 2002. "Monetary Policy and Real Stabilization." In *Rethinking Stabilization Policy.* Kansas City, Mo.: Federal Reserve Bank of Kansas City. 261–312.

Svensson, Lars E. O. 2005. "Social Value of Public Information: Morris and Shin (2002) is Actually Pro Transparency Not Con." NBER Working Paper No. 11537 (August).

Woodford, Michael. 1999. "Commentary: How Should Monetary Policy Be Conducted in an Era of Price Stability?" In *New Challenges for Monetary Policy.* Kansas City, Mo.: Federal Reserve Bank of Kansas City.

Woodford, Michael. 2003. *Interest and Prices: Foundations of a Theory of Monetary Policy.* Princeton, N.J.: Princeton University Press.

Woodford, Michael. 2005. "Central Bank Communication and Policy Effectiveness." NBER Working Paper No. 11898 (December).

Woodward, Bob. 2000. *Maestro: Greenspan's Fed and the American Dream.* New York: Simon and Schuster.

Sources

2. Mishkin, Frederic S., "What Should Central Banks Do?" Federal Reserve Bank of St. Louis *Review* 82, no. 6 (November/December 2000): 1–13. Reprinted with permission from Federal Reserve Bank of St. Louis. © 2000

3. Mishkin, Frederic S., "The Transmission Mechanism and the Role of Asset Prices in Monetary Policy," *Aspects of the Transmission Mechanism of Monetary Policy, Focus on Austria 3–4/2001* (2001): 58–71. Reprinted with permission from Osterreichische Nationalbank: Vienna. © 2001

4. Mishkin, Frederic S., "The Role of Output Stabilization in the Conduct of Monetary Policy," *International Finance 5*, no. 2 (Summer 2002): 213–227. Reprinted with permission from Blackwell. © 2002

5. Mishkin, Frederic S., "Can Central Bank Transparency Go Too Far?" *The Future of Inflation Targeting* (2004): 48–65. Reprinted with permission from Reserve Bank of Australia: Sydney. © 2004

6. Arturo, Estrella, and Frederic S. Mishkin, "Is There a Role for Monetary Aggregates in the Conduct of Monetary Policy," *Journal of Monetary Economics* 40, no. 2, (October 1997): 279–304. Reprinted with permission from Elsevier. © 1997

7. Arturo, Estrella, and Frederic S. Mishkin, "Rethinking the Role of NAIRU in Monetary Policy: Implications of Model Formulation and Uncertainty," *Monetary Policy Rules* (1999): 405–430. Reprinted with permission from University of Chicago Press for the NBER. © 1999

8. Bernanke, Ben S., and Frederic S. Mishkin, "Central Bank Behavior and the Strategy of Monetary Policy: Observations from Six Industrialized Countries," *NBER Macroeconomics Annual* (1992): 183–228. Reprinted with permission from MIT Press. © 1992

9. Bernanke, Ben S., and Frederic S. Mishkin, "Inflation Targeting: A New Framework for Monetary Policy?" *Journal of Economic Perspectives* 11, no. 2 (Spring 1997): 97–116. Reprinted with permission from American Economic Association. © 1997

10. Mishkin, Frederic S., "International Experiences with Different Monetary Policy Regimes," *Journal of Monetary Economics* 43, no. 3 (June 1999): 579–606. Reprinted with permission from Elsevier. © 1999

11. Mishkin, Frederic S., "Why the Fed Should Adopt Inflation Targeting," *International Finance* 7, no. 1 (2004): 117–127. Reprinted with permission from Blackwell. © 2004

12. Mishkin, Frederic S., "Inflation Targeting in Emerging Market Countries," *American Economic Review* 90, no. 2 (May 2000): 105–109. Reprinted with permission from American Economic Association. © 2000

13. Mishkin, Frederic S., and Miguel Savastano, "Monetary Policy Strategies for Latin America," *Journal of Development Economics* 66, no. 2 (December 2001): 415–444. Reprinted with permission from Elsevier. © 2001

14. Mishkin, Frederic S., and Miguel Savastano, "Monetary Policy Strategies for Emerging Market Countries: Lessons from Latin America," *Comparative Economic Studies* 44, no. 2 (Summer 2002): 45–83. © 2002

15. Jonas, Jiri, and Frederic S. Mishkin, "Inflation Targeting in Transition Countries: Experience and Prospects," *The Inflation-Targeting Debate* (2005): 353–413. Reprinted with permission from University of Chicago Press. © 2005

16. Mishkin, Frederic S., and Klaus Schmidt-Hebbel, "One Decade of Inflation Targeting in the World: What Do We Know and What Do We Need to Know?" *Inflation Targeting: Design, Performance, Challenges* (2002): 171–219. Reprinted with permission from Central Bank of Chile: Santiago. © 2002

17. Mishkin, Frederic S., "The Dangers of Exchange Rate Pegging in Emerging-Market Countries," *International Finance* 1, no. 1 (October 1998): 81–101. Reprinted with permission from Blackwell. © 1998

18. Calvo, Guillermo, and Frederic S. Mishkin, "The Mirage of Exchange Rate Regimes for Emerging Market Countries," *Journal of Economic Perspectives* 17, no. 4 (Fall 2003): 99–118. Reprinted with permission from American Economic Association. © 2003

Index